MOVEMENTS IN MODERN ART

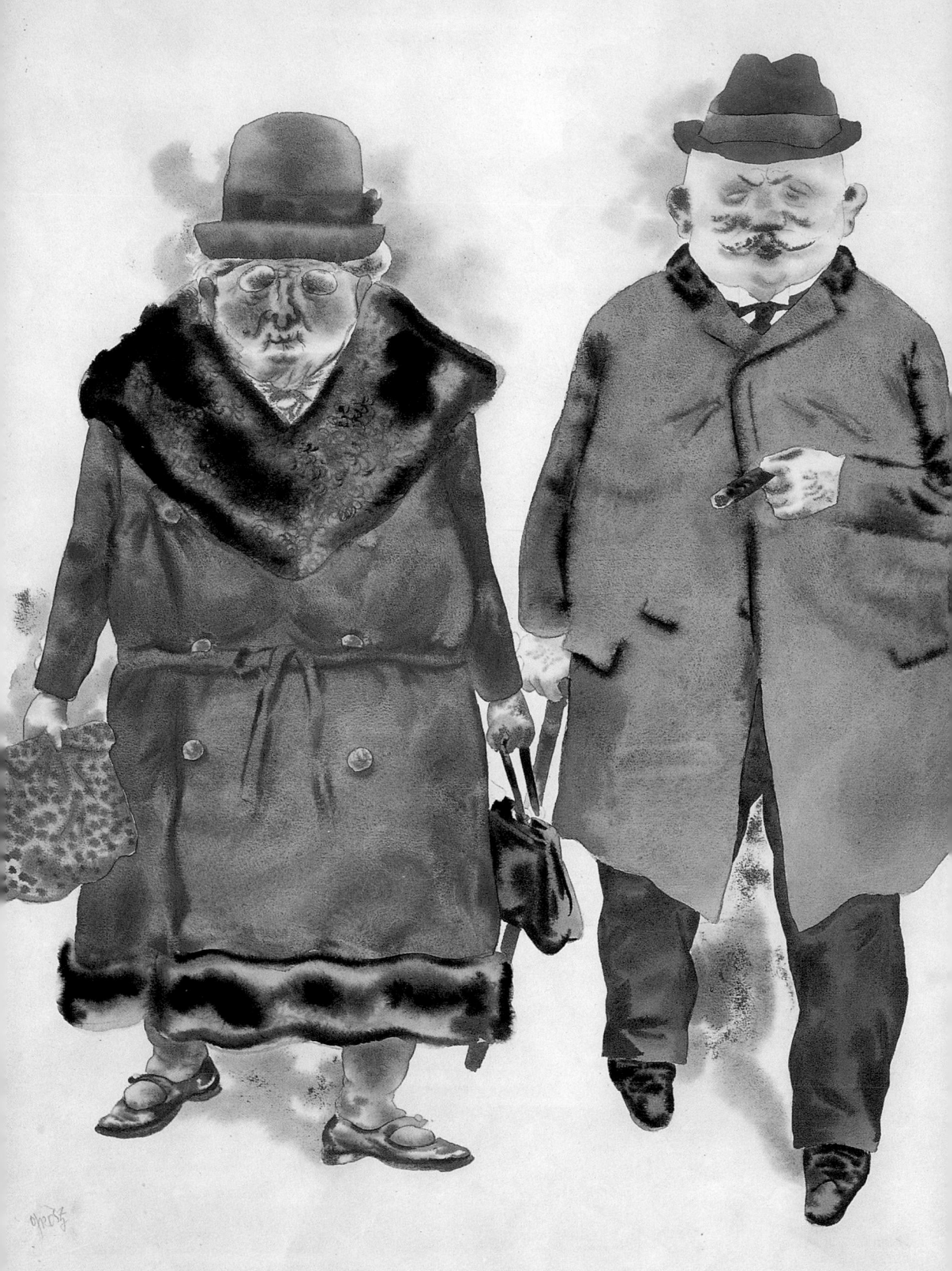

MOVEMENTS IN MODERN ART

REALISM

JAMES MALPAS

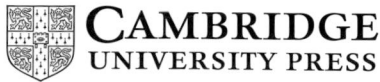

CAMBRIDGE
UNIVERSITY PRESS

PUBLISHED BY THE PRESS SYNDICATE OF THE
UNIVERSITY OF CAMBRIDGE
The Pitt Building, Trumpington Street, Cambridge CB2 1RP,
United Kingdom

CAMBRIDGE UNIVERSITY PRESS
The Edinburgh Building, Cambridge CB2 2RU, United Kingdom
40 West 20th Street, New York, NY 10011-4211, USA
10 Stamford Road, Oakleigh, Melbourne, 3166, Australia

First published by Tate Gallery Publishing Ltd, London 1997

Cover designed by Slatter-Anderson, London
Book designed by Isambard Thomas
Typeset in Monotype Centaur and
Adobe Franklin Gothin

Printed in Hong Kong by South Sea International Press Ltd

Library of Congress Cataloguing-in-Publication Data has been applied for

A catalogue record for this book is available from the British Library

Measurements are given in centimetres, height before width,
followed by inches in brackets

Cover:
Stanley Spencer, *The Resurrection, Cookham* 1924–7
(fig.12)

Frontispiece:
Georg Grosz, *A Married Couple* 1930
(fig.21)

ISBN 0 521 62757 5

Contents

Introduction 6

I
The Beginnings of Realism 9

2
Realist Painting in England 1900–1940 16

3
Realism Between the Wars 26

4
European and British Realism after 1945 50

5
American Pop Art and Realist Painting since 1955 62

6
Superrealism, Photorealism and Realism in the 1980s 69

7
American and British Realism Post-Pop 72

Conclusion 75

Select Bibliography 77

Index 78

INTRODUCTION

Realism is in danger of becoming, to use Henry James's phrase, a 'baggy monster', spilling out into virtually every art movement and group since it came of age in the declarations and work of the Realist painter Gustave Courbet in France from the 1840s, and in the contemporaneous commitment of the Pre-Raphaelite Brotherhood in England to a return to nature. After all, no artist refers to their work as unreal, or anti-real. Indeed, even the most extreme abstract art has consistently been claimed by its practitioners as a form of realism: in 1920 the Russian Constructivist, Naum Gabo, published his *Realistic Manifesto*; in the early 1960s the New Realist group in France comfortably accommodated Yves Klein, known for his monochrome canvases. These artists stood the term realism on its head to make it mean an art which opposed the imitation of reality in order to establish itself as a new reality in its own right. This definition is a crucial cutting-off point for this book; for a work of art to be included here it has to have some perceptible root in the considerations, both of subject matter and technique, of the nineteenth-century exponents of Realism.

There are also areas of painting where realist subject matter is married to an Expressionist use of paint, loaded with emotional charge, as in much of the Kitchen Sink school in the Britain in the 1950s (John Bratby for example) and in the very painterly work of the British artists Frank Auerbach and Leon Kossoff, where realism seems to be abandoned rather than enhanced. (By contrast, Lucian Freud never goes into the same arena of gestural commitment in his brushwork, maintaining something of a Ruskinian humility before the subject.) If one included such expressionistic gestural painters, one would also need to refer to Meidner, Soutine and de Kooning's majestic *Women* series, as well as earlier German Expressionism as a whole, which would widen the frame of reference so much as to make the term 'realist' almost meaningless in a book of this length.

It is impossible to ignore the relationship of photography to the realist tradition in painting and of course to modern art in general. Photography both provoked painters to become *less* realistic, to distance themselves from this rival, and gave them the means to become *more* realistic. In the latter case, their often unacknowledged use of the 'foe-to-graphic' art (Edwin Landseer's pun) shows how sensitive they were to accusations of plagiarism. However, photography, though an *eminence grise* of realism, needs far more extensive treatment than the scope of this book will allow; and there are many easily available histories of the subject (see Further Reading).

As a quality, realism is positive, denoting toughness, down to earth attitudes to life or death and a practical outlook on the way things should be managed. It also presupposes the need for management of, or at least of some measure of control by man over, the environment or his fellow human beings. The need for realism, in both life and art, may be the result of a sense that fantasy, imagination, speculation have all run away with human attention and that things as they are have been shunted into the area labelled 'ordinary, everyday, uninteresting'.

In relation to art, realism has the great advantage of ubiquitous subject matter. Anything that actually happens or exists is seen as worthy material. However, it is at the level of interpretation of those events and things that the interesting difficulties in defining realism appear.

In their response to things and events in the world, realists aim at a level of objectivity that 'romantics' abhor. Yet what is the nature of this objectivity? That proposed by Courbet in about 1849 is different from that simultaneously embraced by the Pre-Raphaelites, yet both could be accommodated under the realist umbrella.

Paradox underlies the approach of nearly all artists claiming to be 'realists' and this applies particularly to those in the twentieth century. Unlike Courbet, these artists do not usually establish a proselytising Realist stance, with defined aims. They are often individuals, defining themselves against the so-called progressive or avant-garde trends of the day, or indeed, simply ignoring them. The concept of an avant-garde, popularised by the critic Julius Meier-Graefe around 1910 to account for the successive waves of 'isms' in European art from the early nineteenth century, is in danger of skewing any assessment of art into the 'cutting edge' versus the 'has-beens'. Certainly, except for brief periods, the realist tendency has been relegated to the also-ran category throughout the twentieth century, by the cognoscenti, the major collectors, and often the avant-garde artists themselves.

Realism in the twentieth century, then, exhibits a protean stylistic and ideological approach. It can range from the passionate and quirky individualism of a Stanley Spencer to, contemporaneously, the most demoralised institutionalism of an 'apparatchik' painter like Alexander

Gerasimov in the Stalinist USSR, where it appears under the guise of 'socialist realism'. Any attempt to provide a cogent definition, as one can in the case of a relatively team-based, well-knit 'ism' such as Surrealism, will be thwarted at the start. For the most part, realism in the twentieth century is not 'Realism', that's to say, something consciously signed up for, via a manifesto, to show a party allegiance.

From its roots in the nineteenth century, Realism encompasses a bewildering range of styles: we now see Courbet and the Pre-Raphaelites equally as Realist painters, but their stylistic hallmarks and paint-handling are significantly different. And, whereas a Surrealist, having 'joined up', made more or less conscious efforts to ensure a correct Surrealist component in his work, no such compunction weighed on so-called 'realists', except in

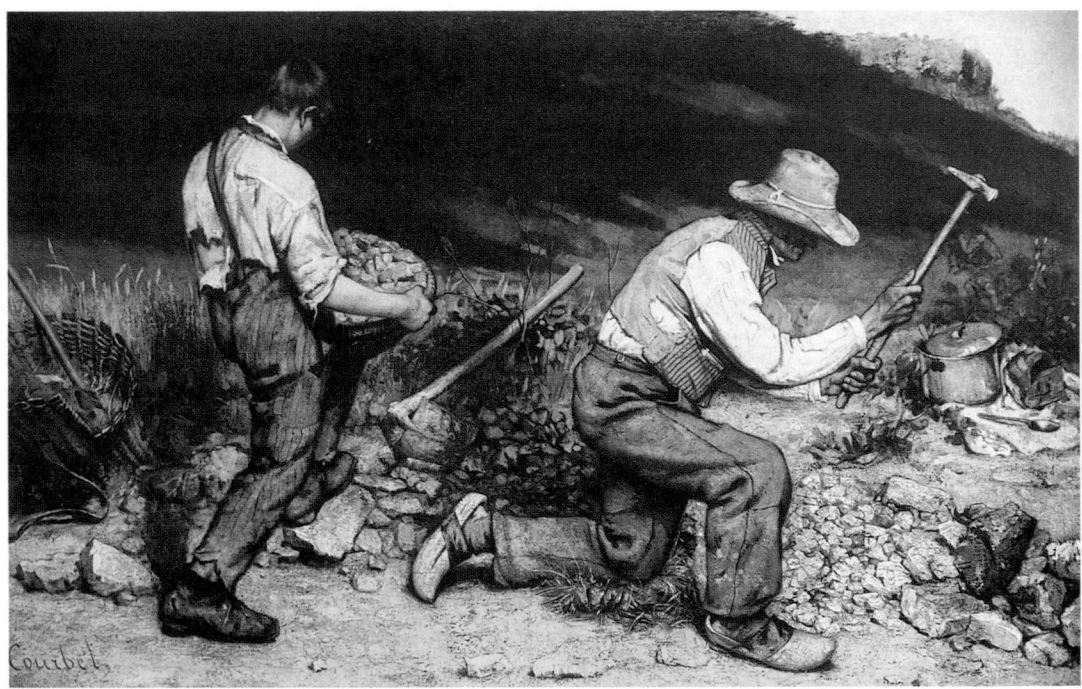

totalitarian states. For the realist, the saleability of a work might motivate the artist as much as any ideology. Realism in the twentieth century can thus be seen in terms of highly individual figures appearing almost at random. And yet there were periods when the tide of realism was flowing high, notably after the cataclysm of the 1914–18 Great War (see chapter 2) and to some extent after the Second World War.

Many interesting questions arise when considering realism in later twentieth-century art. How 'realist' is Pop Art? On one level its adherence to the trivial, the everyday, the trashy and throw-away is counter to Courbet's notion of contemporary heroism (let alone Pre-Raphaelite moralising). Yet at the same time this aspect corresponds to the realist idea that art can encompass the most humble and everyday subject matter, and Pop's heroes were often working class, like Courbet's.

I

1
Gustave Courbet

The Stonebreakers
1850
Oil on canvas
165 × 238
(65 × 93¾)
Stadtmuseum, Dresden
(destroyed 1945)

THE BEGINNINGS OF REALISM

It would be impossible to present the themes, concerns and works of realism in the twentieth century without some consideration of 'Realism', the art movement that developed from the prevailing Romanticism of the 1830s in France and which, by the mid-century, had gained adherents in England as well. In 1798 the arch-romantic philosopher-poet Friedrich von Hardenberg (known as Novalis) had begun his book of aphorisms: 'We seek above all the Absolute, and always find only things'. That 'only' is the quintessence of Romantic disappointment with the merely material. If one reverses the dictum, however, so that 'things' become the goal of the search, something of the Realist approach can be seen. Certainly, Courbet, the painter- spokesman for Realism, was determined that 'things as they are' should be the subject of painting.

At the time – the 1840s – they weren't. A few artists, such as Valenciennes, had unselfconsciously produced sketches (still marvels of freshness today) that had challenged the academic standards of 'composition' and 'finish'; but these were 'mere' sketches. Courbet was determined that the rules and regulations of the ateliers and the Academy, which had become so much more strict since J.-L. David's virtual dictatorship on behalf of Neoclassicism at the time of the French Revolution, should be set aside. Gustave Courbet proposed that instead of a history subject, or the moral, sentiment or 'story' of the painting dictating how it should look, as was nineteenth-century academic practice, the painter should let things and their appearance stand for themselves. This is what Courbet did in *Burial at Ornans* (fig.2), which shocked conservative critics at the Salon of 1851 and baffled even the liberal-minded. They did not understand what the 'subject' was; was it the hole in the ground? How could that be a serious subject for a huge painting intended for the Salon, the prestigious annual show? Was Courbet simply laughing at them? (Certainly, we shall see a satiric or at least ironic edge as a major feature of realism in the twentieth century.) And the people! What a strange bunch of village misfits! Yet they were not caricatures in the way Daumier would

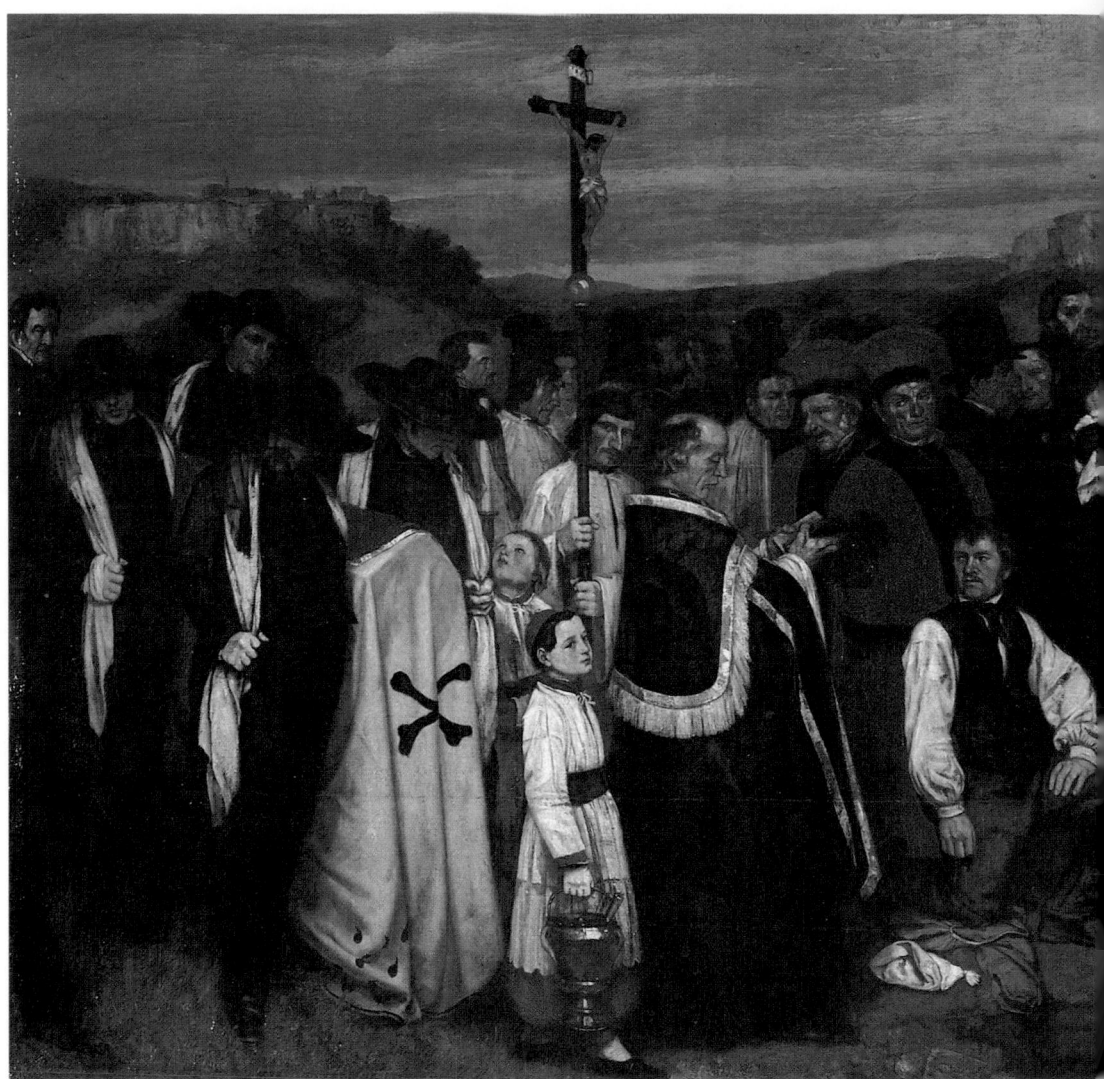

have portrayed them. The red-nosed priest is shown indubitably to exist, by virtue of the very care that Courbet has taken to record his idiosyncrasies. The effect was startling: the clumsy procession shows none of the professional grace of learned poses, derived from tradition, that the gallery-goers would have expected.

Realism here lies as much as anywhere in the dovetailed awkwardness of the figures as they plod across the picture-space, the very subtle rhythm of

2
Gustave Courbet

Burial at Ornans
1849–50

Oil on canvas
314 × 665
(123½ × 261¼)
Musée d'Orsay

design that Courbet uses to link up the trudging group. This rhythm does all it can not to attract attention to itself, whereas the average Salon piece would ostentatiously display the artist's skill at manipulating stock figures into a traditional academic format, so as to prove that the work had been done according to the rules.

This was the challenge Courbet threw at his contemporaries: that rules were to be provisional and not permanent fixtures. This was the first sign of a

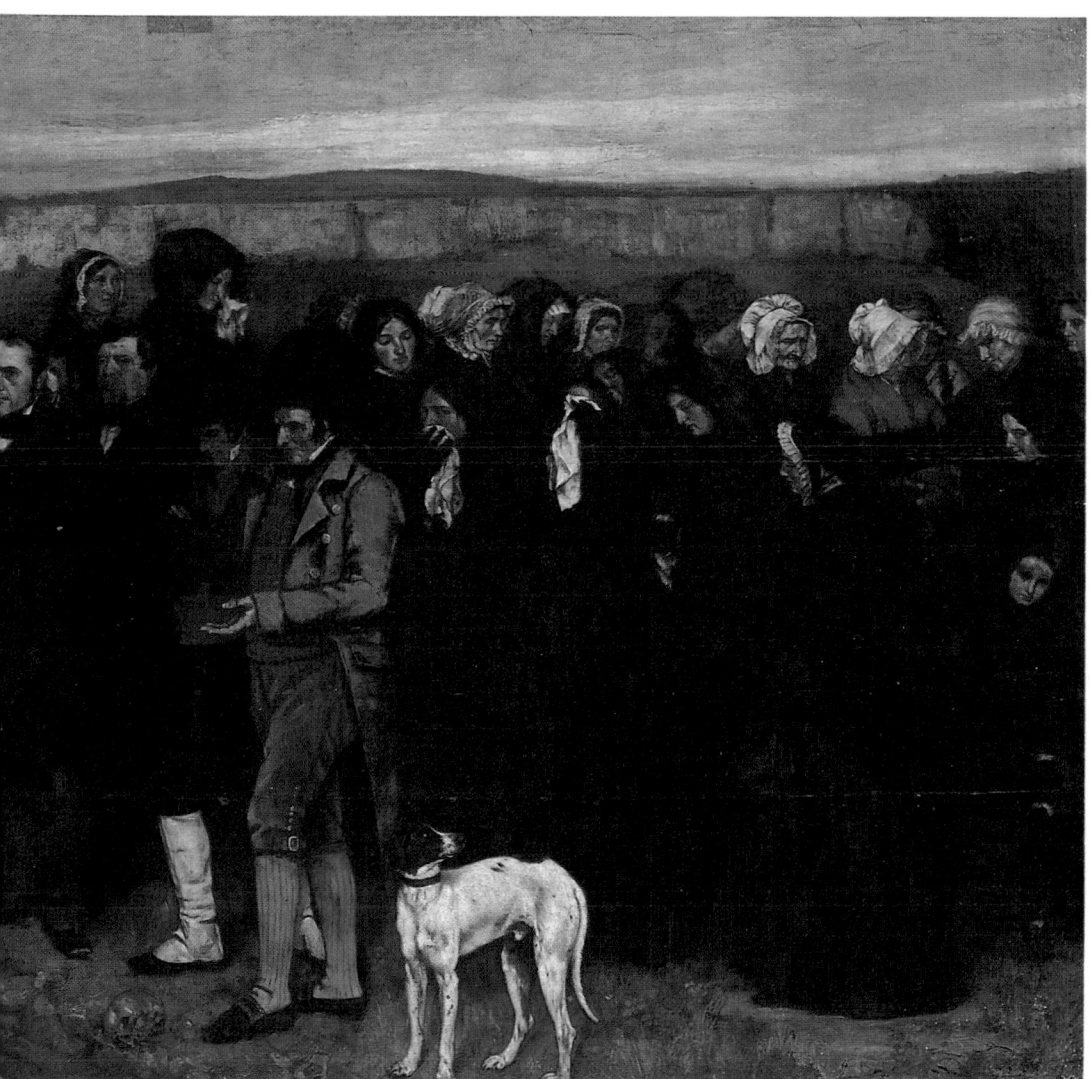

pluralism in painting – whereby the appropriate technique, and style even, was more important than the academic hierarchy of subject. In France, at any rate, this would lead to the concept of a modern, avant-garde development from Courbet (and even Delacroix as far as colour was concerned) through to Seurat and beyond. In short, the avant-garde was that band of artists for whom how a painting was done became increasingly more important than the ostensible subject. By the First World War, the development of abstract, non-

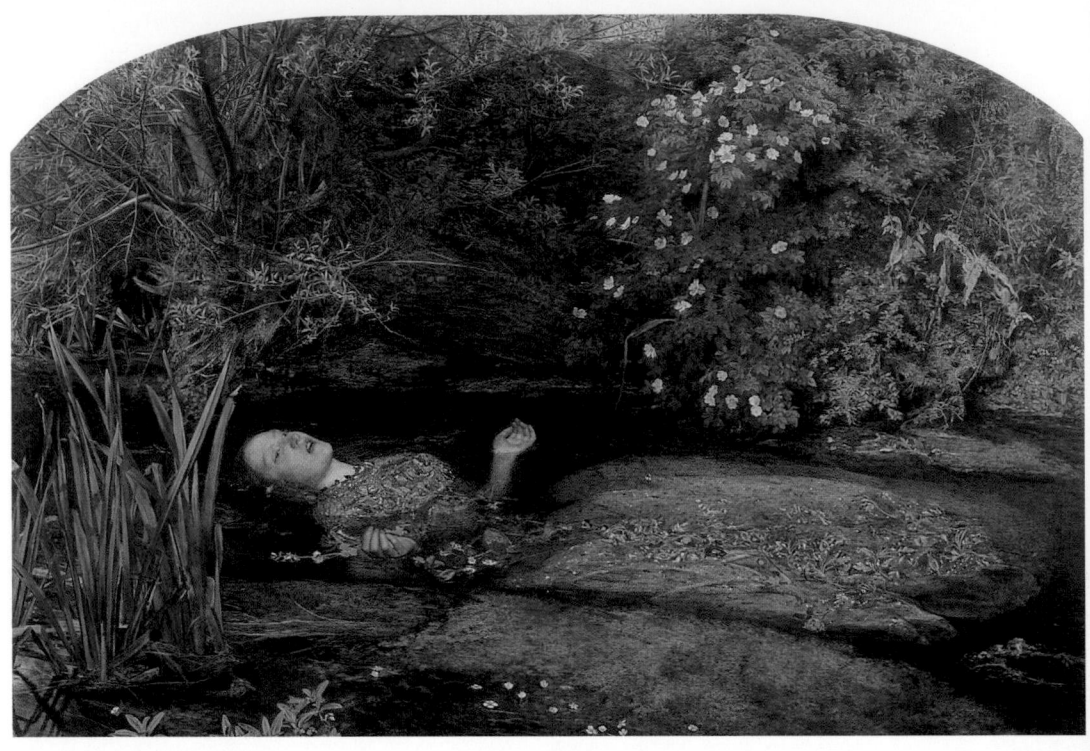

representational painting, would mean that the 'how' of the painting *was* the subject.

Meanwhile, painters adopted and adapted the themes and theories that Courbet proposed throughout a tumultuous career. This ended in despondency and illness in exile in Switzerland in the 1870s and death in 1877. It should also be remembered that not all his work was as pictorially challenging as the *Burial at Ornans* and he could churn out effectively conservative landscapes full of 'nature-philosophy' feeling for bourgeois German clients. But around Courbet's banner in the early 1850s swarmed artists as diverse as the peasant-painter Jean-François Millet, and the brilliant and vituperative cartoonist and illustrator Honoré Daumier, as well as a number of minor figures who had produced one or two Realist works, but found the negative publicity or the close contact with their subjects too gruelling and so moved into more lucrative and easy-going avenues. One might cite Jean-Pierre Antigna, whose *Fire* was shown at the same Salon as the *Burial at Ornans*: a peasant family is shocked by the outbreak of fire in their small cottage. The pose of the mother and child seems to be a cunning adaptation of Delacroix's *Medea* (1838), a classically based, High Art subject here transformed to suggest similar courage and fortitude in the lower orders. It was an appropriate theme during the short-lived Second Republic of 1848–52.

In England at the same time but from a very different direction came another impulse towards realism in painting. Again, the academic was the butt

3
John Everett Millais

Ophelia 1851–2

Oil on canvas
76.2 × 111.8
(30 × 44)
Tate Gallery

4
Robert Martineau

The Last Day in the Old Home 1862

Oil on canvas
107.3 × 144.8
(42¼ × 57)
Tate Gallery

of the attack by various young turks who (rightly) saw that the formulaic conventionalities hung at the Royal Academy every year were stultifying. However, social concerns of the kind revealed in Courbet's depictions of real people hardly impinged on John Everett Millais (though his image of a fireman rescuing children of 1853 makes an interesting comparison with the *Antigna*), William Holman Hunt and Dante Gabriel Rossetti, the ringleaders of the Pre-Raphaelites. The name itself shows just how disaffected with contemporary art they were. Their realism consisted partly in their doctrine of painting every element in a picture meticulously from life. In doing this they sometimes achieved an illusionism which is almost hallucinatory. Luckily, the subjects themselves were often hallucinatory as well, as in the case of Millais' popular painting of mad Ophelia (1853) for example. *Ophelia* is typical of the largely historical and literary subject matter of the Pre-Raphaelites which ranged from the Bible, Dante and Shakespeare through to Romantic poetry, particularly that of Tennyson who, though contemporaneous, wrote in a pseudo-medieval style. In painting such subjects Pre-Raphaelite realism also consisted in reconstructing the scene with as much historical and psychological accuracy as possible. There are a few Pre-Raphaelite modern life paintings, for example Holman Hunt's topical blow against masculine sexual hypocrisy *The Awakening Conscience*, also of 1853, where the detail is used to construct a moral allegory, and Rossetti's significantly unfinished *Found*, where the evil of prostitution is likewise the subject.

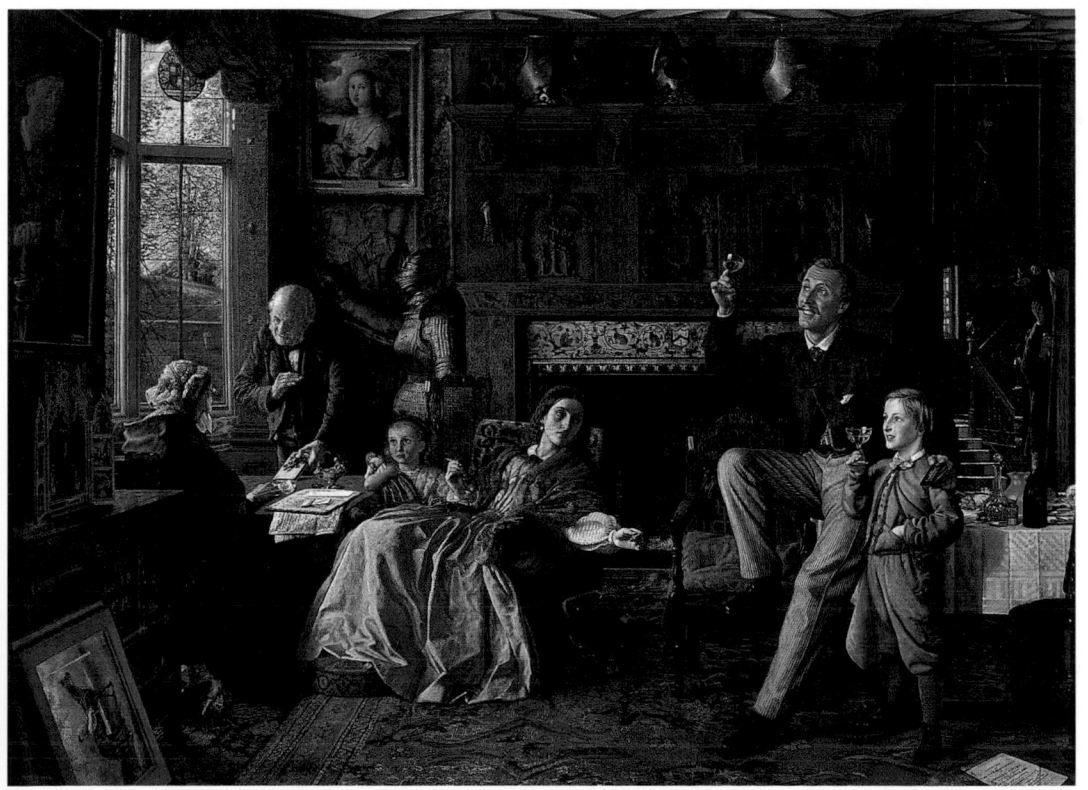

Bright colours, detailed still-life and the use of new chemical and aniline colours from Germany marked off these young artists from the generality at the Royal Academy. By 1860 however, many of the latter were following suit, and though they could not match the perfervid imagination of the original Pre-Raphaelites, they managed to produce works as equally loaded with material detail (easy enough with Victorian furnishings of the time). R.B. Martineau's *The Last Day in the Old Home*, a product of ten years' work, is a good example. Again, the strength of detail is used to point to the moral and adorn the tale.

A rather different form of social realism appeared in England during the 1870s. Its chief exponents were Luke Fildes, Hubert von Herkomer and Frank Holl and it can be related to Millet's 1848–53 depictions of peasants in

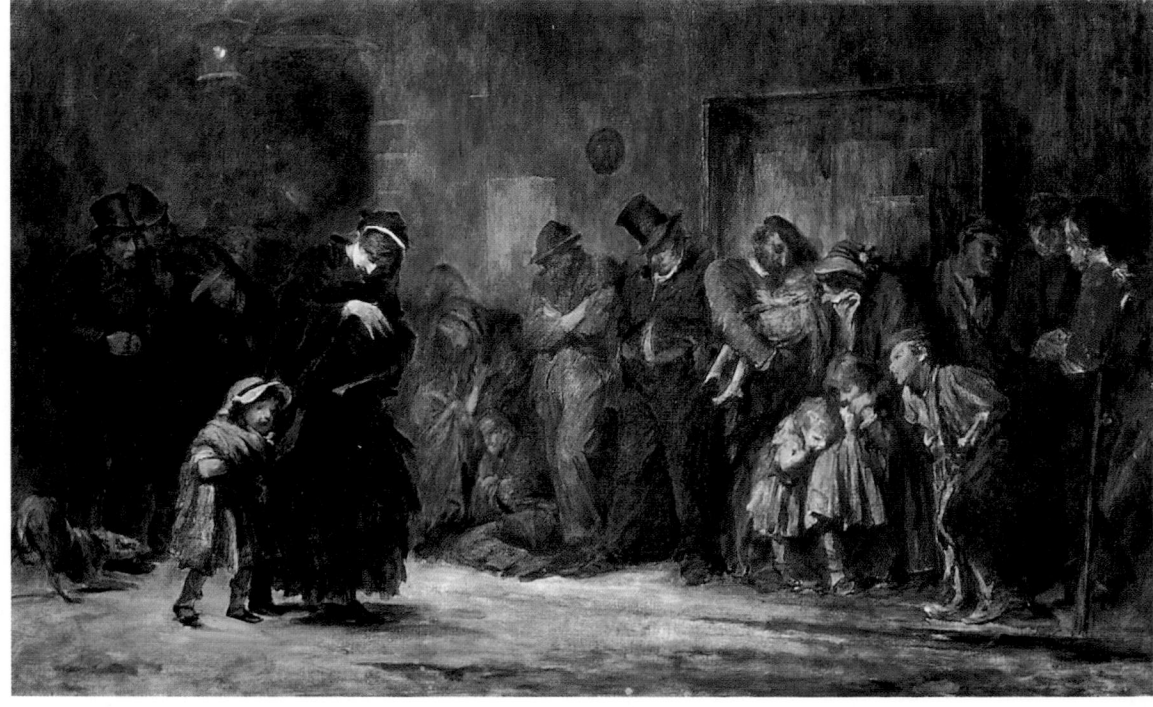

the fields of France or Courbet's *The Stonebreakers*, of which he declared: 'I have invented nothing. I saw the wretched people in this picture every day as I went on my walks'. A celebrated example of the British realism of the 1870s is Luke Fildes's very popular Royal Academy exhibit *Applicants for Admission to a Casual Ward* of 1874 (of which the illustrated version is a replica from after 1908), which has all the descriptive pull of a Dickens narrative as it presents the parlous state of the urban poor in the city snow. It looks melodramatic set against the Courbet *Burial*, but in comparison with other Academy works of the time it is rough and blunt in its sympathies.

Another English realist style popular in the 1880s particularly, derived from topographical painting. Atkinson Grimshaw's moody, atmospheric nocturnal scenes, with tonal subtleties and flickering chiaroscuro that seem to owe as much to photography as to painting are good representatives of this trend. Close to these, though more concerned with social subjects and the figure, is the elegant artist James Tissot, who called himself a 'realist'. Certainly, he takes a cool gaze at the folk in their finery who are generally at leisure in his opulent work.

His generally upper-middle class subject-matter (the exception is soldiery, but then their tunics are so bright and cheery) could be contrasted with the products of Jules Bastien-Lepage's English followers, from the mid-1880s onwards. This French artist (1848–1884) specialised in chic peasant children posing artlessly close up to the picture plane – photography was very much an influence. In 1882 he visited London and thereafter a clique adopted his

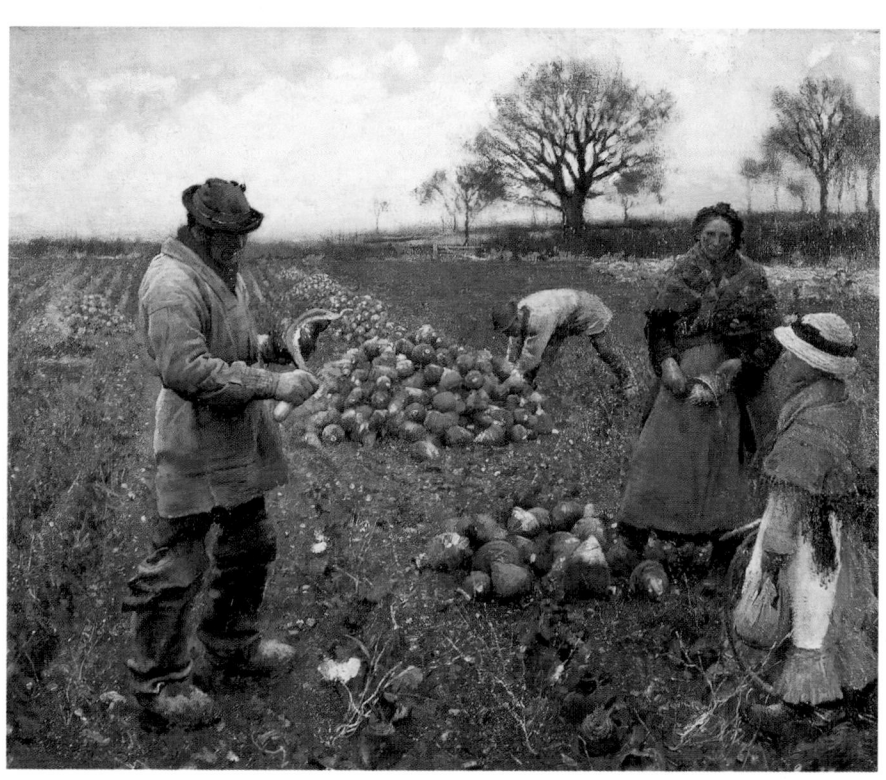

5
Luke Fildes

Applicants for Admission to a Casual Ward after 1908

Oil on canvas
57.1×94
(22½×37)
Tate Gallery

6
George Clausen

Winter Work 1883–4

Oil on canvas
77.5×92.1
(30½×36¼)
Tate Gallery

block-like use of paint, with the use of square-tipped brushes, the neutral grey-blue palette and the winsome models that make Murillo's peasant children look louche by comparison. George Clausen is an important follower of Bastien-Lepage and there is a trace of social comment in his *Winter Work* of 1883–4 as the warm gallery-goer is confronted with the mangold-grubbing field workers with frozen fingers.

2

7
Walter Richard Sickert
*La Hollandaise c.*1906
Oil on canvas
51.1 × 40.6
(20¼ × 16)
Tate Gallery

REALIST PAINTING IN ENGLAND 1900–1940

In the years before and during the First World War realism in England has to be seen in the context of a belated catching up with the continental avant-garde. The zeal and polemical energy of the Vorticist movement reached an apogee of non-representational painting around 1914, with Edward Wadsworth, Frederick Etchells and William Roberts joining Wyndham Lewis and others in what Alan Bennett calls the 'jagged school' of English painting. Ironically, the style is best exemplified by Bomberg's massive *In The Hold*; he wasn't officially in the movement.

Less extreme was the art associated with Roger Fry and the Bloomsbury circle. Fry's two Post-Impressionist exhibitions of 1910 and 1912 certainly surprised – and in the case of conservatives, dismayed – the viewers, leading Virginia Woolf to note portentously later, 'On or about December 1910 human nature changed'. Sir Philip Burne-Jones, the famous Pre-Raphaelite's painter son, fulminated against Cézanne, declaring him 'mad', and such a response was typical of academicians as a whole.

However, a third area of the avant-garde, the Camden Town Group, had been assiduously applying Post-Impressionist techniques for several years, but to realist subjects. This development was given a fresh and dynamic twist by Walter Sickert in the new, grainy subject-matter that erupted around 1907. His *Camden Town Murder* series has a bleak tawdriness about it that is completely unidealistic.

He claimed that newspaper reports of gruesome murders of prostitutes had prompted the title, and this attraction to reportage would always haunt

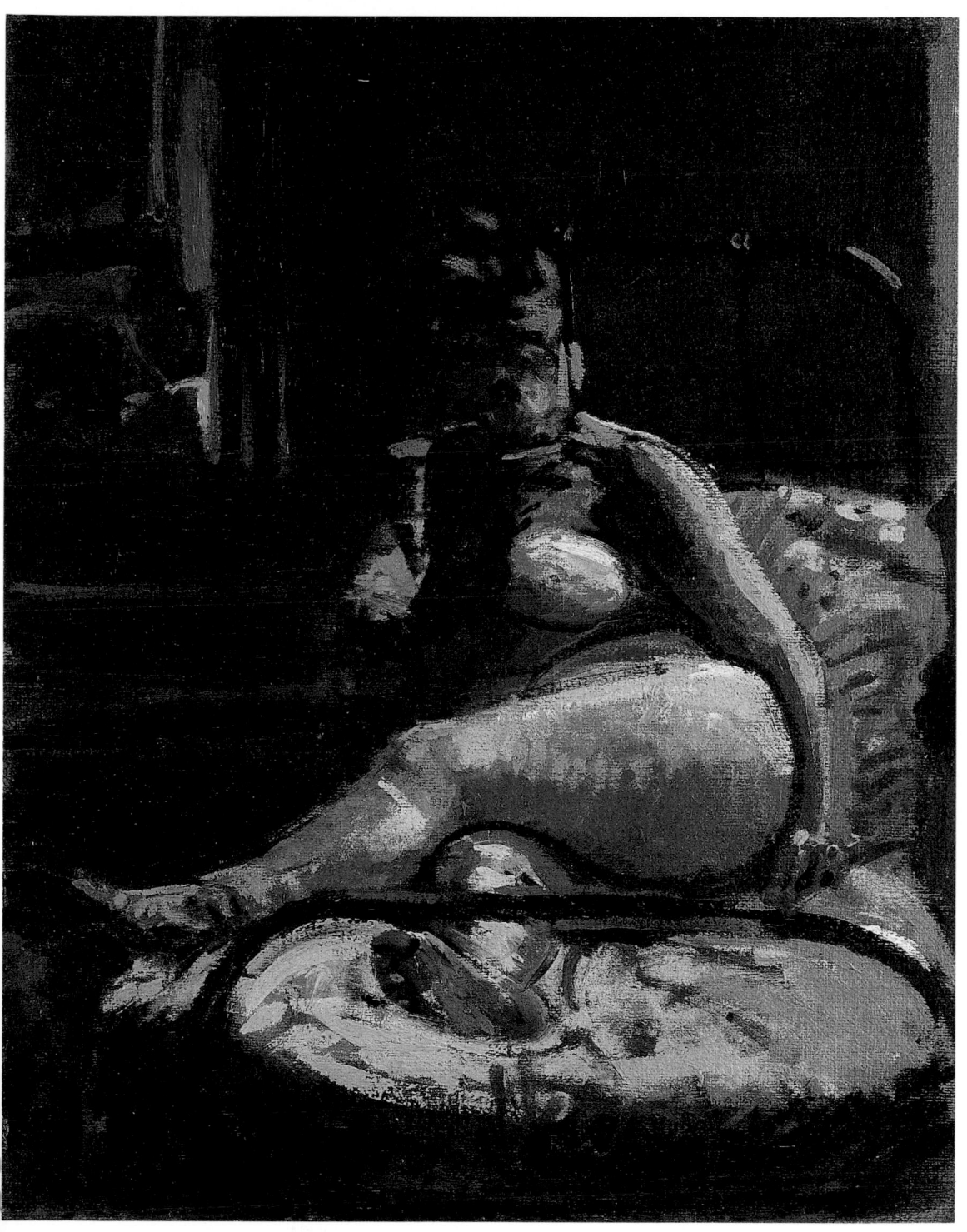

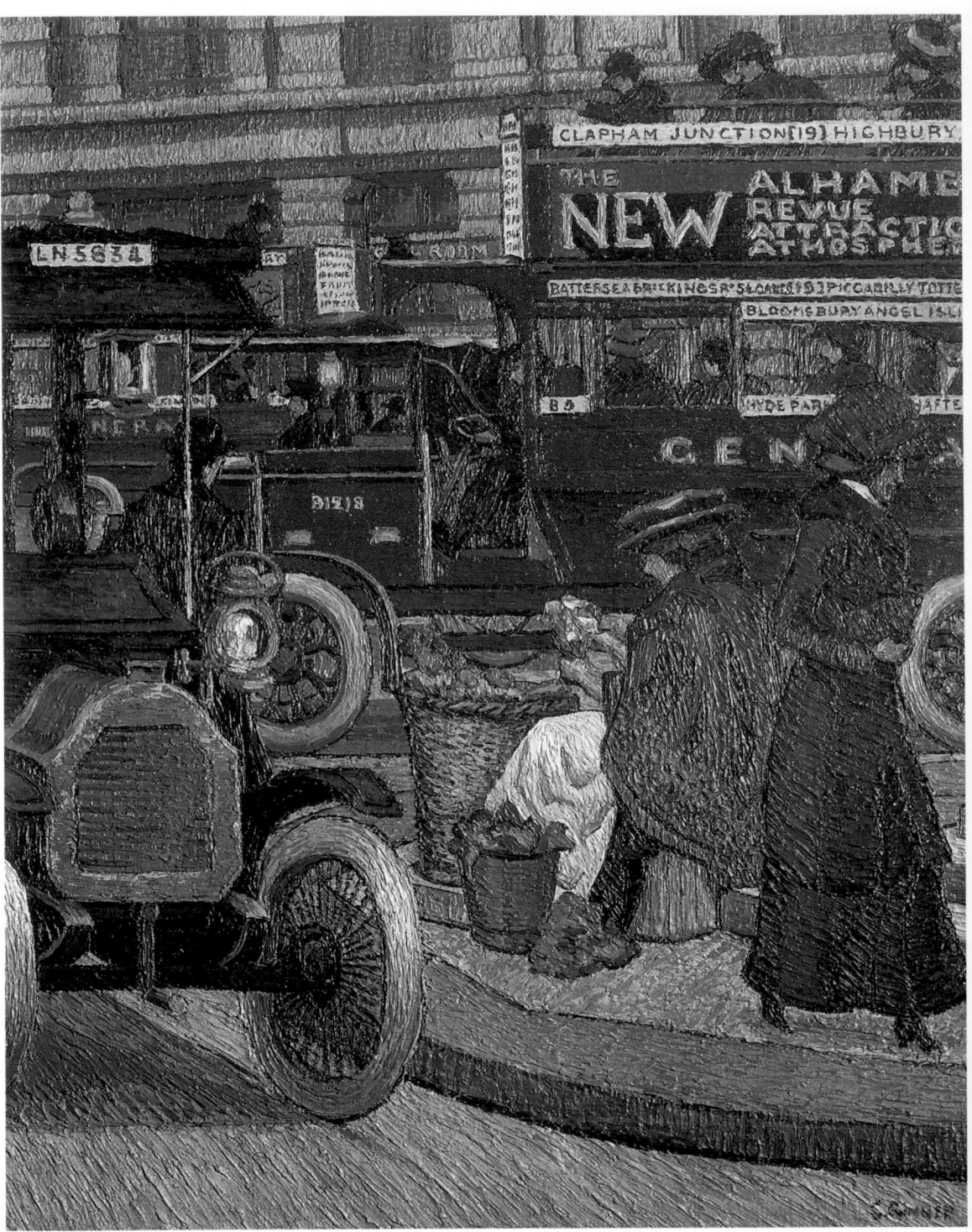

Sickert. Certainly the cadaver-like appearance of the flaccid models on rented beds deviated wildly from the decorous poses of drawing-school life models. Such works derive in part from Cézanne's gruesome portrayals of sex-murders, probably inspired by Emile Zola. Sickert's flat, attenuated brushstrokes, as if he too were stabbing at the figure, and the bald, often muddy colouring, would have seemed repellent even to those used to the cursory brushwork of the other Camden Town artists like Charles Ginner, Harold Gilman and Spencer Gore.

This is a case of realistic subject-matter being treated in an unconventional painterly manner, and it would characterise much of what passed for realism in England between the wars. Sickert's flat, almost distemper-like blocks of paint adapt imagery culled from newspapers, whether of Amelia Earhart's arrival in rainy Britain after a record-breaking air flight, or a snap-shot portrayal of a uniformed Edward, Prince of Wales, striding from a car. There is still much critical division as to the merits of such work, but it is remarkable how Sickert kept on experimenting with such approaches until the end of his long life.

8
Charles Ginner

Picadilly Circus 1912

Oil on canvas
81.3 × 66
(32 x26)
Tate Gallery

9
Walter Richard Sickert

Miss Earhart's Arrival
1932

Oil on canvas
71.7 × 183.2
(28 × 72¼)
Tate Gallery

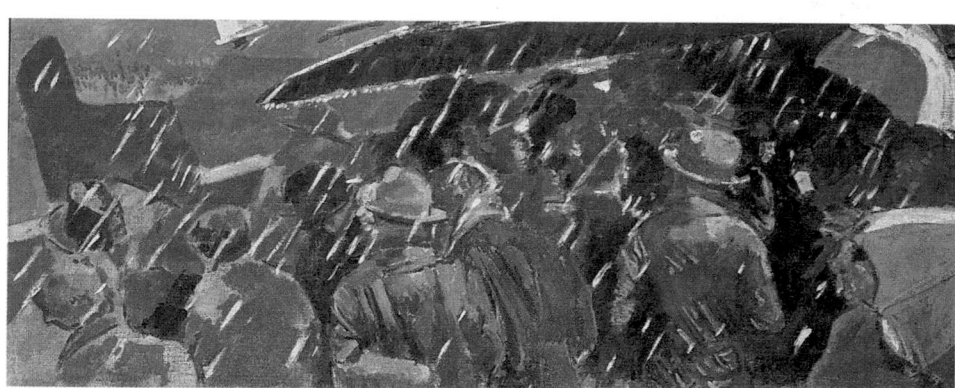

Apart from two images in early 1914 Sickert was not directly involved in depicting the Great War. The profound change that came over war-weary Britain by 1916, when conscription was established, made the dynamic and generally optimistic energy of the Vorticists seem jejune, if not downright tasteless. What energy there was became converted to the mission of showing the civilians just how appalling the conditions were at the Front, just ninety miles from London. As Paul Nash wrote: 'It is unspeakable, godless, hopeless. I am no longer an artist interested and curious, I am a messenger who will bring back word from the men who are fighting to those who want the war to go on forever. Feeble, inarticulate, will be my message, but it will have a bitter truth.' In fact, by 1918, Nash's work was anything but 'feeble' or 'inarticulate', especially in the way it envisaged the destruction of the natural order.

Officially, there was no call to do other than record the scenes met with, though there was a certain amount of censorship. William Orpen was occasionally criticised for the sunny landscapes he depicted, the only dead being German. His employers at the War Office wanted something more arresting. Ironically, when they got it in the increasingly dour imagery of Christopher Nevinson they were equally dissatisfied. The bleak swampish battlefields on which dead British lie, which Nevinson was producing by 1917, such as the sardonically titled *Paths of Glory*, were censored by the authorities as bad for morale. By contrast, his lithographs of aerial combat, clean and thrilling, found great favour. This determination of many artist-participants to show the civilians 'just what it was like' did produce an astonishing work in Sargent's *Gassed* of 1918, in which the irony of the bright summer sunlight of the last few weeks of the war, unseen by the frieze of blinded 'Tommies' in mud- and blood stained khaki, is inescapable.

Even Wyndham Lewis found his abstract energies displaced by the contingencies of war. His most famous full-size painting on the theme is *A Battery Shelled* of 1919, in which some supercilious officers, one smoking a pipe, observe the ant-like soldiers scurrying about as enemy shells land among their guns. The smoke looks like ribbons of twisted metal. It can be contrasted with the more tangibly smoke-like substance the Turkish shells are producing amidst the Irish troops encamped in the Judaean hills depicted by Henry

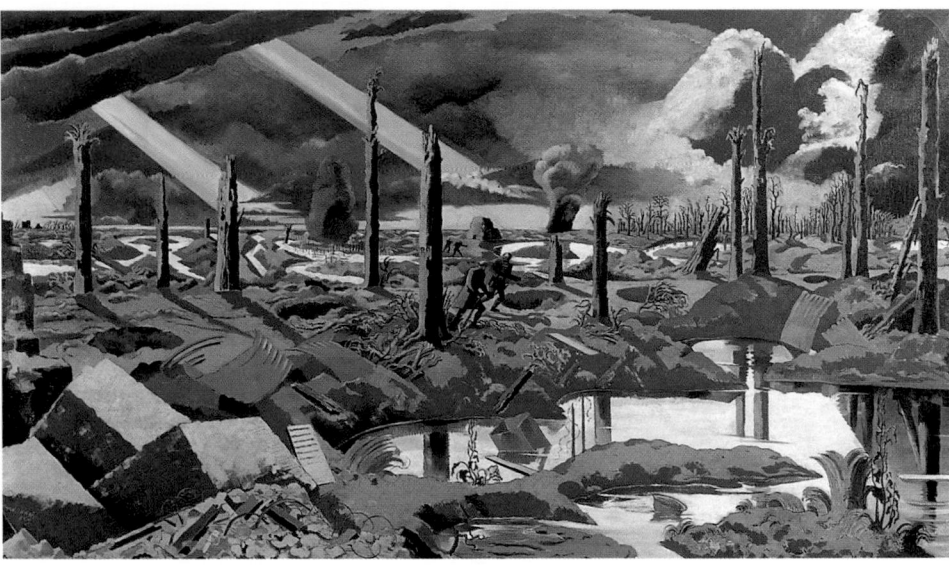

10
Paul Nash
The Menin Road 1919
Oil on canvas
182.8 × 317.5
(72 × 125)
Imperial War Museum,
London

11
John Singer Sargent
Gassed 1918
Oil on canvas
228.6 × 609.6
(90 × 240)
Imperial War Museum,
London

Lamb, generally better known as portraitist of a limp and effete-looking Lytton Strachey, noted essayist and pacifist. The realism of Lamb's war-picture is tempered by the fact that it was incomplete at war's end and the 'Irish' were in fact models found in Camden in 1918–19. This artist and his fellow Slade school contemporary, Stanley Spencer, had both been impressed by the Italian early Renaissance artists from Giotto and his pupils through to Massacio, Masolino and Fra Angelico in the fifteenth century. Their clarity of line, the subordination of anatomical or perspective accuracy to emotional charge, allowed Spencer and Lamb to escape from the rigours of the Slade's academic teaching.

Spencer's realism is a vivid hybrid, combining this early Renaissance manner with echoes of William Blake and Samuel Palmer, where medieval overtones persist in form and colour. Its power first makes itself felt in the haunting 1914 work, *The Centurion's Servant*, with its awkward positioning of the body on the bed, perhaps reminiscent of Sickert's Camden Town nudes, and the stricken expression on the face. Is it a reworking of Holman Hunt's *The Awakening Conscience*? Certainly Spencer seems to be trying to depict an inner state of struggle that goes far beyond the melodramatic or theatrical. Spencer's involvement in the war, on the home front and then in Macedonia, was less traumatic for him than for many others, though not without its alarms and excursions. In fact, he seems to have been brought out of himself, made to interact with humanity, which liberated his pictorial vision. By the time he produced *Arrival of the Travoys*, his great, immediate record of his time as a medical orderly in Macedonia, the constraint visible in his early work had gone. As is common among the artists influenced by the early Renaissance, he takes a high viewpoint, and this foreshortens the arriving ambulances wildly; but the gestures of the orderlies and the amiable gaucheness of the mules (which *are* pink in Macedonia) show a flair for realistic observation. The same spirit later infused his panels for the Sandham Memorial Chapel at Burghclere, completed in 1932, where his humorous recollection of army

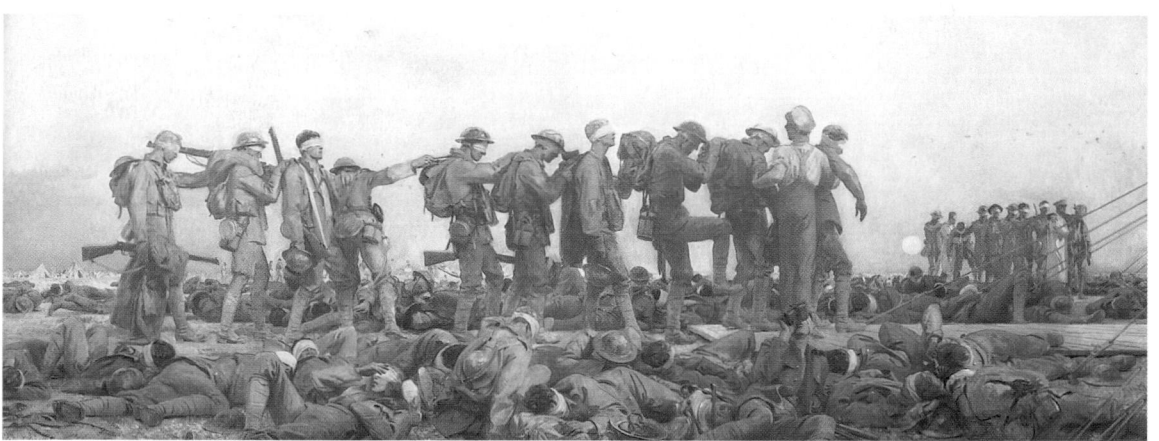

camp-duty portrays a scampish Spencer, like a scruffy schoolboy, stabbing litter with a bayonet. He was once on a charge for 'picking up litter in an unmilitary manner'. Local colour is represented by English summer flowers depicted with the intensity of Samuel Palmer and, out in Macedonia, the native tortoises shuffling about.

Spencer's grandiose *The Resurrection, Cookham* (1924–7) is a fine example of his ability to combine natural and illusionistic elements to produce something rich and strange. The artist appears several times in the work, as does his wife. Other Cookham notables are shrewdly and humorously portrayed emerging from their lopsided graves in the village churchyard. A more universalist theme is stressed by the black people also emerging at the centre of the work. As in medieval or early Renaissance religious works, sequential events are depicted happening simultaneously.

Spencer's sense of realism was rooted in the religious significance he felt was inherent in ordinary activity. William Blake believed 'everything that lives is Holy!' and something of this view can be seen in Spencer's *Resurrection*, best described by the term 'magic realism'. No doubt the Renaissance basis of his art, rather than the emotional uncertainties at the root of, for example, German Expressionism accounts for this.

In the Second World War, Spencer produced an emphatic and energised series of canvases showing the war-driven ship-building on the Clyde. Again, his fundamental interest in humanity enabled him to mix and merge with the workforce and, as his diaries show, he found himself moved and fascinated by this very different world. The works themselves are occasionally prey to fervid distortions, not helped by the strange format he was working with, but the

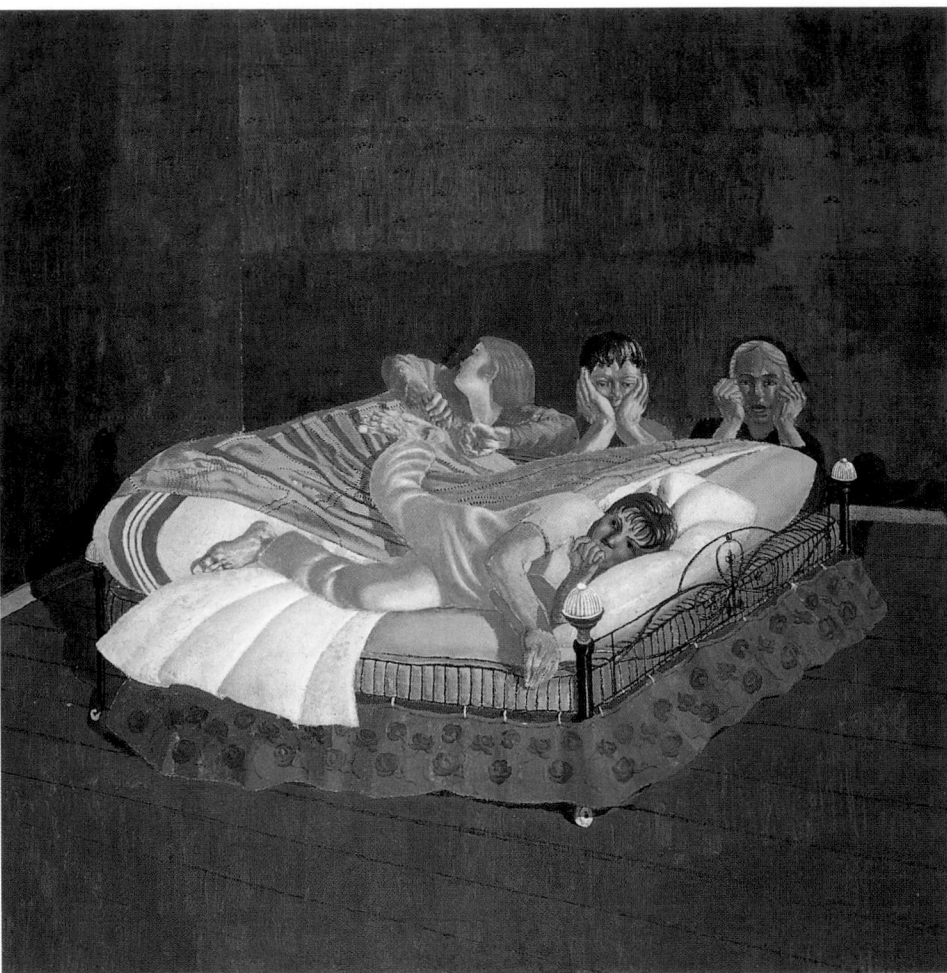

12
Stanley Spencer
The Centurion's Servant
1914
Oil on canvas
114.3 × 114.3
(45 × 45)
Tate Gallery

13
Stanley Spencer
The Resurrection,
Cookham 1924–7
Oil on canvas
274.3 × 548.6
(108 × 216)
Tate Gallery

extraordinarily sacerdotal effect – as if Giotto spent the 1940s in a shipyard – gives the realism Spencer deploys a memorable resonance.

Much British art in the 1920s was vitiated by trying to ape Matisse's Fauve work of around 1905–8. Such pastiches corrupt the work of Mark Gertler, while the vivid Fauve palette produces some oddities in the work of Matthew Smith. With hindsight, it can be suggested that Roger Fry and Clive Bell's hijacking of the aesthetic bandwagon in British art around 1910 (an activity so scathingly attacked by Wyndham Lewis) with 'significant form' as their catchword, was as much an aberration from British concerns with detail, decoration and surface pattern, as French Romanticism went against the grain of that nation's fascination with logic. From that viewpoint, the return to favour in the 1960s of the Pre-Raphaelites and other Victorian artists was a foregone conclusion, despite the Bloomsbury group's condemnation that had them swept out of the galleries for fifty years.

The Anglo-Saxon world (the United States even more than Britain) is fascinated by things, not ideas. A painting is a gadget, just as a story is; both have to be 'well-made', regardless of any philosophy they may contain. But where Roger Fry wanted the significance of the form to count, the British preferred to stay with the forms themselves. Perhaps that is why British sculpture is so powerful and why a painter like Ben Nicholson is most admired for his sculptural white reliefs. Certainly, realism has never been demoted to the second rank in Britain this century in the way it has on the Continent and abstract art has never gained such a hold. However, the

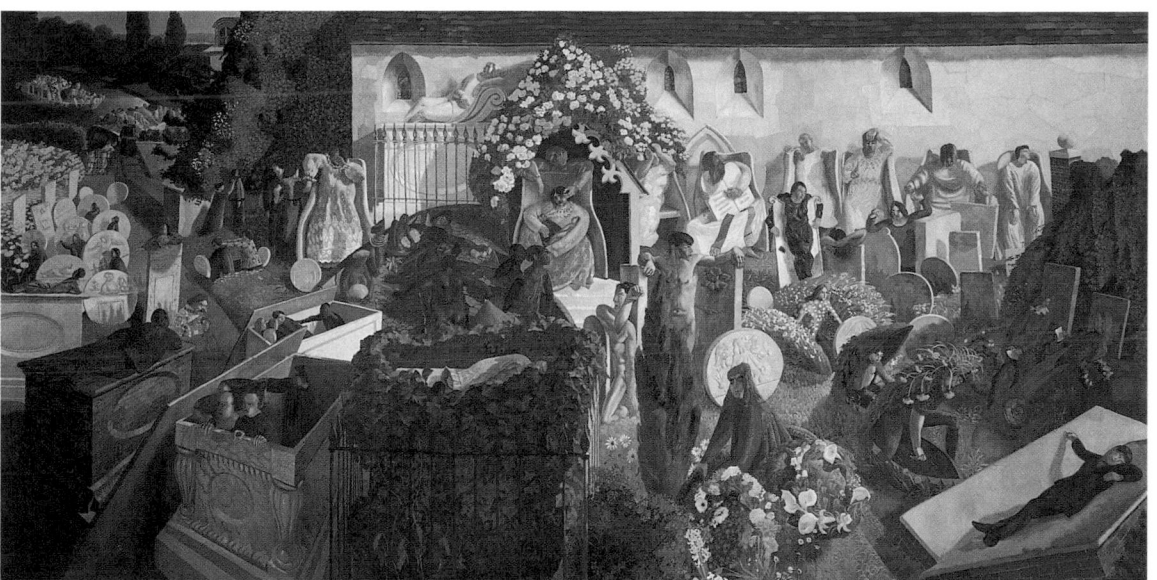

'realists' tended to be individuals and even eccentrics, at least until the period of Pop Art. The figure of Edward Burra is a fascinating example of someone who pre-empted Pop in some ways, lived through it, and emerged as though nothing had happened.

Ironically, Burra was one of the most cosmopolitan young British artists of the 1920s, travelling to the South of France, where Cocteau's charmed life appealed to the dramatic flair of the young Englishman, as did the raffish life in downtown Marseille and Toulon. America, and jazz (as experienced in Harlem in the late 1920s) toughened up his style. Laconic, drawling humour and sharp, snarly observation of the low-life around him give an atmosphere akin to an exotic Georg Grosz (see p.32). Burra was never bitter, however; instead, a cartoon-book brashness and wide-eyed amazement predominates, a quality he was to recapture in the late 1960s when his work took on a hippy-like abandonment. Accusations that his work is simply eclectic, shallow illustration can be countered by his grim and mordant paintings of the late

1930s. In England during the war, he produced sardonic grotesqueries depicting soldiers stationed in the Kentish town of Rye where he lived at the time. Humanoids, rather than humans, they relate to the demonic figures Wyndham Lewis produced in the 1920s. Gentler veins of narrative landscape emerge after the war in Burra's radiant watercolours, though the sardonic edge is never far away: in *Lake District* of 1970 the view is obscured by the traffic thundering past.

Burra is an elusive artist to assess in terms of realism, as are Grosz and the angrier Weimar German artists. Emotional values are of central importance to all of them, but such values have their own reality as equally as the apparently rational ones of *Valori Plastici* (see p.40) and its neo-classicism. Stanley Spencer's great achievement in his greatest works was to 'square the circle' so that the emotional and the rational cohabit.

After the First World War the Vorticist William Roberts turned to

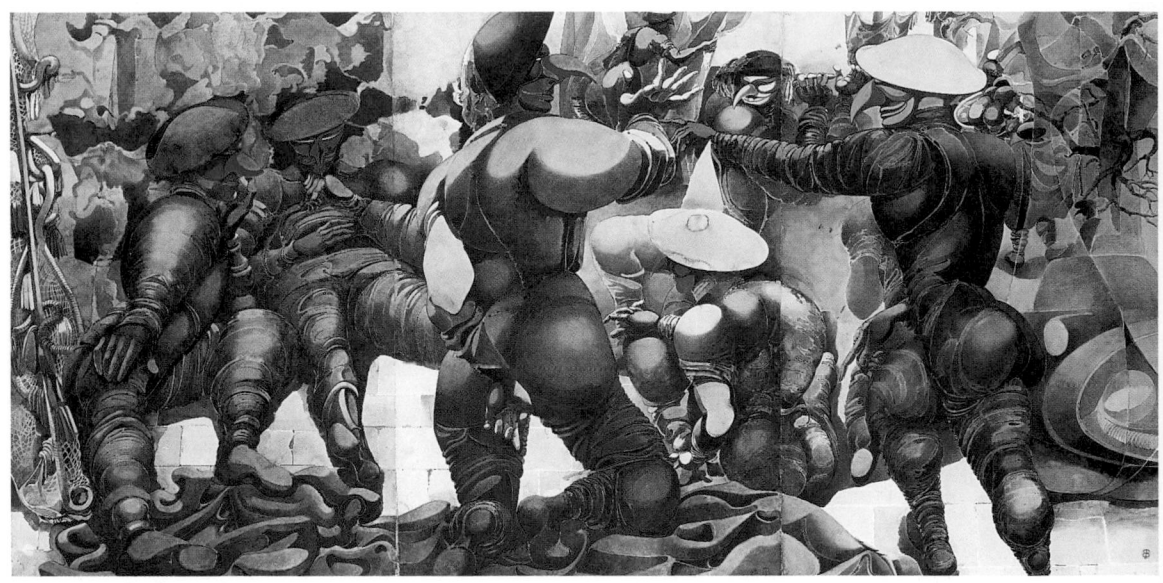

realism, as did so many of the pre-war avant-garde. In *Self-Portrait Wearing a Cap* Roberts depicts himself in a shirt, wearing braces, tie and flat cap. He thus identified himself as a working man, a persona he projected in later self-portraits of the 1950s and 1960s.

In the early 1930s there was a resurgence of avant-garde activity in British art. Two groups strongly concerned with abstraction emerged, the Seven and Five Abstract Group and Unit One, both with links to the Paris based Abstraction-Création group. The influence of Surrealism was also strong, reaching a climax in the International Surrealist Exhibition in London in 1936. Towards the end of the 1930s something of a reaction seems to have taken place and was most visible in the group of artists known as the Euston Road School, from the school of art of that name founded in London in 1937 by Victor Pasmore, Claude Rogers and William Coldstream. Influenced in their political and social attitudes by the harsh economic climate of the 1930s these artists adopted realism in the hope of bringing art to a wider audience than was reached by the avant-garde. They laid particular emphasis on painting from observation, and in subject matter they favoured scenes of everyday London life, and the nude, in much the same way as had Sickert and the Camden Town painters earlier in the century.

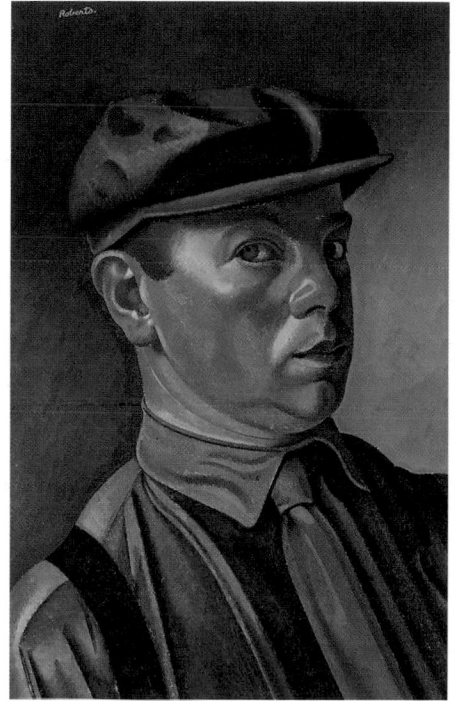

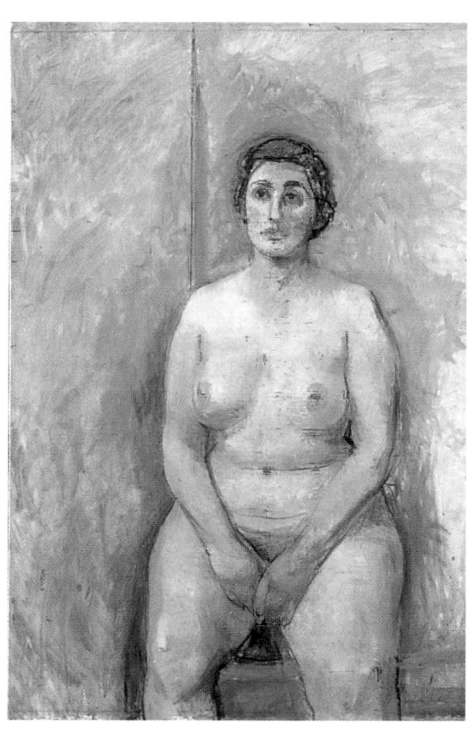

14 *left*
Edward Burra

Soldiers at Rye 1941

Gouache, watercolour
and ink wash on paper
102.2 × 207
(40½ × 81½)
Tate Gallery

15
William Roberts

*Self-Portrait Wearing
a Cap* 1931

Oil on canvas
55.9 × 35.9
(22 × 14¼)
Tate Gallery

16 *far right*
William Coldstream

Seated Nude 1951–2

Oil on canvas
106.7 × 70.7
(42 × 28)
Tate Gallery

3

REALISM BETWEEN THE WARS

The exhaustion of the combatant nations in the Great War and the moral and financial bankruptcy that threatened them after the November 1918 Armistice combined to make the world of the 1920s an unfruitful place for many of the Utopian, transformational aims and goals with which art – particularly non-representational art – had been preoccupied before 1914. Instead, there was a gathering together of depleted forces and a 'call to order'. This phrase, the title of a book published by Jean Cocteau in 1926, became the catchphrase of the decade, even if order was hard to locate, or, as in Italy from 1922 , Russia from 1924 and Germany from 1933, to separate from a state-sponsored rule of terror. In comparison with the late nineteenth century, a new diversity of what was thought to constitute realism appears, a mirror to the fracturing social and political structure at this time.

In particular, realism between the wars needs to be seen in the context of the alternative definition of realism put forward by the avant-garde (see introduction). For example, while the artists who were grouped together in 1920s Germany under the banner of the New Objectivity (Neue Sachlichkeit) are evidently more traditional, more realist, than the non-representational artists of the Bauhaus such as Paul Klee and Wassily Kandinsky, at the same time the latter would argue that mechanically produced, geometrically based two-dimensional and non-illusionistic works are more realistic in themselves and in relation to modern society than the academic illusionism that was still at the core of figurative art. This new concept of reality in art was even more fervently pursued in post-

17
Kasimir Malevich
Peasant Woman 1925

Oil on canvas
53 × 53 (21 × 21)
State Russian Museum,
St Petersburg

Revolutionary Russia by the Suprematists and Constructivists, though it was to fall foul of the political authorities by 1922.

RUSSIA

In about 1915–16, the Russian painter Kasimir Malevich titled one of his Suprematist abstract works *Peasant Woman*, her red dress signified by the red square that dominated the canvas. This cocks a snook at the literal-minded, but whoever said that that state of mind was a realist one? Clearly Malevich took the opposite view and this may largely explain why he stayed on in Russia to fight his corner against the encroachments of state-administered Socialist Realism. As for many of his like-minded contemporaries, it was to be a lonely struggle, involving exile from positions of power and authority (which he had held at the time of the Revolution). Nevertheless, visual evidence of his combining of illusionistic realism with the avant-garde variety of his Suprematist works is to be found in such late works as his portrait of his wife of 1933. Her gnarled worker's hands, in sharply observed textural three dimensionality, contrast vividly with the bright, flattened areas of colour that denote the dress and collar she wears. It is a marvellous, coded criticism of the bludgeoning political-aesthetic policy pursued by Stalin and his cultural henchman Zhdanov.

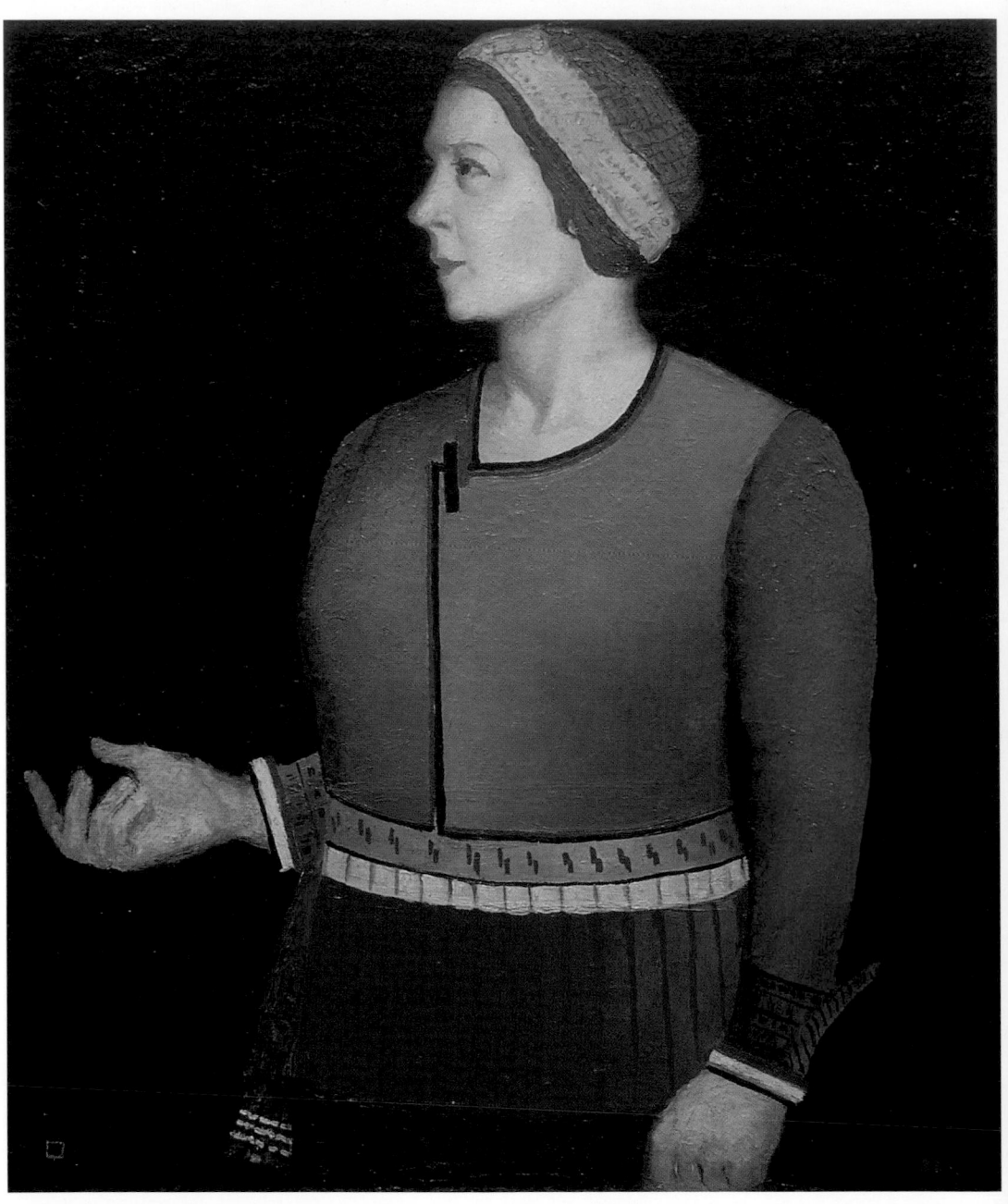

They proposed that only obvious transcriptions of the life of the people should be provided by artists, as anything else would not be understood. The word used to condemn intellectual or conceptually based art was 'formalist'. Even social realism in a Russian variant of French late nineteenth-century practice was not sufficient; it smacked too much of liberal individualism. Instead, a new cultural ethos of collective, group activity, geared to the glorification of the great Soviet state, was to be pursued, heroicising (rather than idealising – an important distinction between Communist State art and its non-identical Fascist twin) workers, peasants and the Motherland. The only individual as such was the father of the people himself, but none of the paintings of Stalin reveal more than an apparatchik, a supreme party factotum, an emblem of state. No psychology is allowed to intrude, hardly surprisingly, since artists whose portraits displeased the great aesthetician were liable for Siberia, or even in one case, shooting.

In this context, the subtlety of Malevich's handling of paint and image in the portrait of his wife is masterly, though largely wasted on the purblind authorities. Far more than any of the pasty, poster-like portraits of Stalin by academic creatures of the state arts apparatus, Malevich's work commits two crimes, not against art, but the aesthetics of the Soviet totalitarian state: the flat areas of paint denoting cloth are definitely 'formalist', that is, can be read as paint before being read as the material they are supposed to denote, and the individual psychology of the sitter is also conveyed. Other Russian artists achieved this latter feature, but never attempted the former as well. Perhaps Malevich's lonely position deserves the name of 'anti-socialist realism'?

Certainly, Malevich and a number of followers had seen their Suprematist ideas and works as examples of a new realism for the modern age, an art appropriate to the new Utopias devised by avant-garde artists in the wake of the political revolution (and which they had been thinking about for many years before). The schism in Russian art came between those who felt that such realism in art was sufficient in itself, and those who took the view that art should be subservient to the needs and goals of the Revolution. It is no surprise that as the Bolshevik position strengthened, it opted for the latter approach. Numerous artists went along with it. Others, like Naum Gabo and Kandinsky, fled. Perhaps the outstanding symbol of the short-lived combination of avant-garde 'realist' art and the real world is the agitprop train, bearing graphic propaganda through the countryside in an attempt to educate barely literate peasantry. It is perhaps a parallel to the 'dazzle-painting' camouflage on First World War ships by Edward Wadsworth, designed to protect Atlantic convoys against submarine attack. Paradoxically, in each case, abstract art is more useful than 'realistic' illusionism would be.

18
Kasimir Malevich

Portrait of the Artist's Wife 1933

Oil on canvas
67.5 × 56 (26½ × 22)
State Russian Museum,
St Petersburg

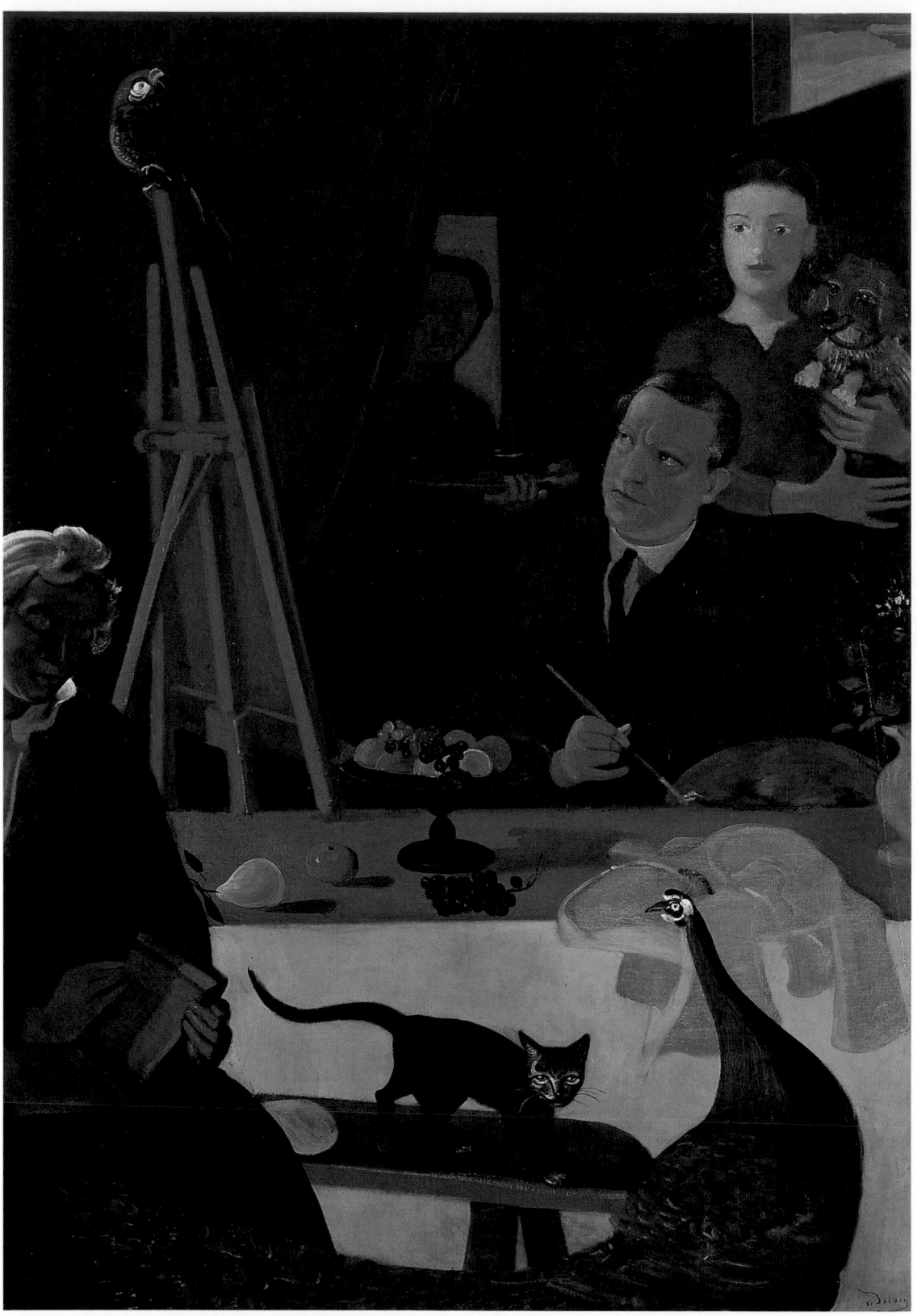

FRANCE

Meanwhile, in France the 'call to order' was manifest right across the spectrum of the pre-war avant-garde: Picasso entered his neo-classical phase, Matisse painted odalisques in seclusion in the south of France. But a return to realism was most apparent and most focused in the work and thought of André Derain, a leading member of the avant-garde Fauve group before the war. Derain became a central and influential figure in the current of theory and practice of painting in France between the wars which is sometimes referred to as *traditionisme*. Derain believed that art was timeless and that its function was to reveal meaning through elements of the real world that had,

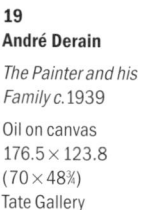
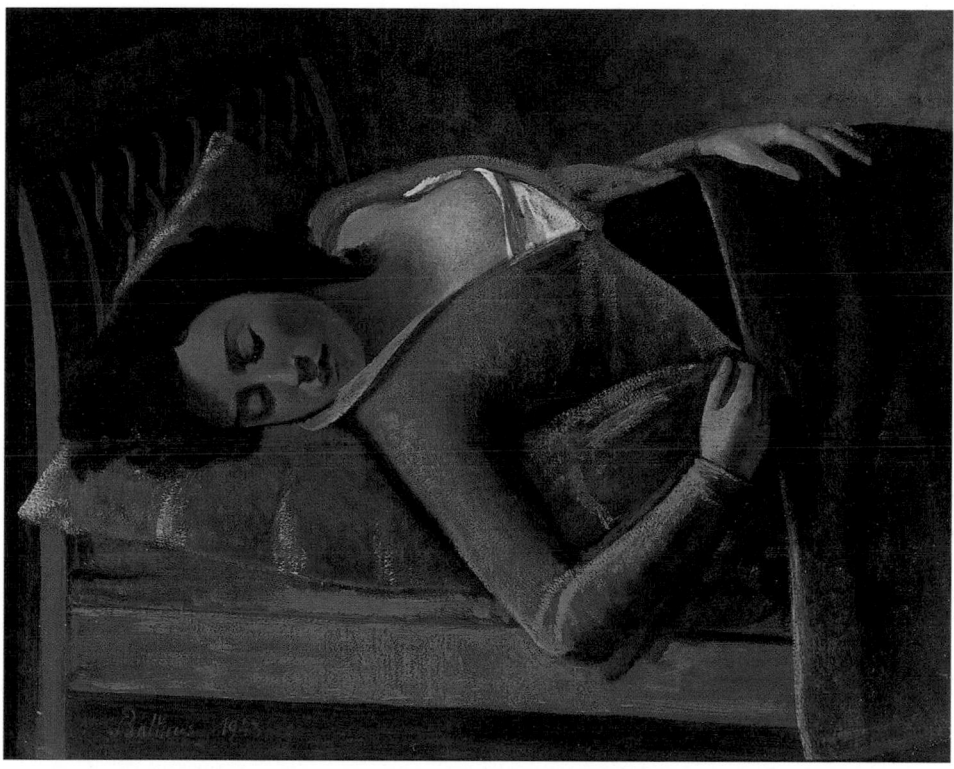

or could be given by the painter, a symbolic significance. *The Painter and his Family* is an allegory of the life of the artist which pays an almost direct homage to Courbet's own celebrated painting of his studio. Derain particularly admired seventeeth-century painting and this work has echoes of religious pictures of that period. The artist is at his easel surrounded by his family, one of whom brings refreshments. His wife, his muse, reads — a reference to the artist's literary interests, an integral part of his art.

In Paris in 1934 the first solo exhibition took place of one of the most remarkable of all twentieth-century realist painters, Balthus Klossowski de Rola, known simply as Balthus. Courbet is probably Balthus's single most important point of reference in the art of the past, although, like Derain, he looks also to the seventeenth century and beyond that to the early

Renaissance and the frescoes of Piero della Francesca. From the 1970s to the present his principal theme has been a haunting vision of the life of young women. Based on sketches from life his paintings are then painstakingly composed, often taking on an almost visionary quality while nevertheless remaining firmly rooted in the visible world.

NEUE SACHLICHKEIT: REALIST PAINTING IN THE WEIMAR REPUBLIC

In Germany the Neue Sachlichkeit or New Objectivity was a remarkably self-conscious stylistic development, responding to the collapse of Expressionism's subjective pathos and emotionalism in the wake of defeat in the First World War. There was a need for the ordinary to be reinstated. As Wieland Schmied, an authority on the subject, put it:

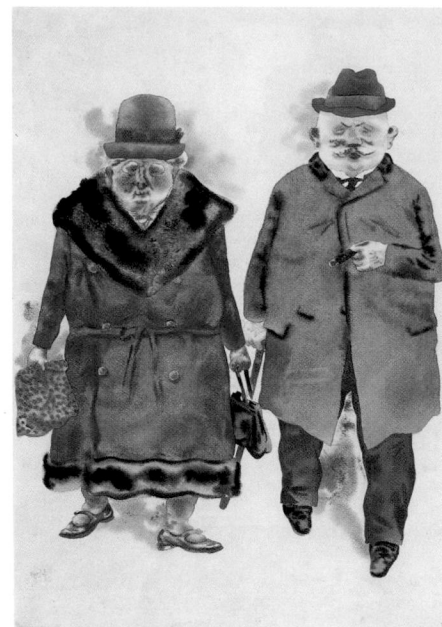

21
Georg Grosz
A Married Couple 1930
Watercolour on paper
66 × 47.3
(26 × 18¾)
Tate Gallery

22
Georg Scholz
Small Town by Day: The Butcher 1922–3
Watercolour and pencil on paper
31 × 24
(12¼ × 9½)
Staatlichen Kunsthalle Karlsruhe

> The important thing was to focus one's gaze upon the here-and-now, upon the view out of the window, upon everyday life taking place in front of one's house, upon the alleyways and gutters, upon the factory floor and the shipyard, upon the scene in the operating theatre and the brothel – even if it should sometimes fall upon someone's allotment, or on a level-crossing keeper's hut, or on happiness in the corner.

This view was endemic throughout Europe in the early 1920s, but despite the general chaos of the Weimar Republic, it found almost its first organised artistic expression in Germany. Only the Italian magazine *Valori Plastici* signalled an earlier emergence of it. As early as 1922 a survey by the Berlin art magazine *Das Kunstblatt* enquired 'Is there a new Naturalism?'. The critic Franz Roh, in his 1925 book *Post-Expressionism, Magic Realism*, answered yes. The latter term fitted a number of fantastic and illusionistic works, sometimes labelled 'poor man's Surrealism'.

In 1923, the director of the Karlsruhe Kunsthalle, G.F. Hartlaub, sent a circular to likely parties informing them of an exhibition of contemporary German art he wished to put on. In the event, it was delayed until 1925, but its title, Neue Sachlichkeit, then put this term on the cultural map. Another term bandied about was 'verism', relating to the 'truth to appearances' which was now to be encouraged and which Expressionism had avoided.

Many German artists charted courses between various positions in the

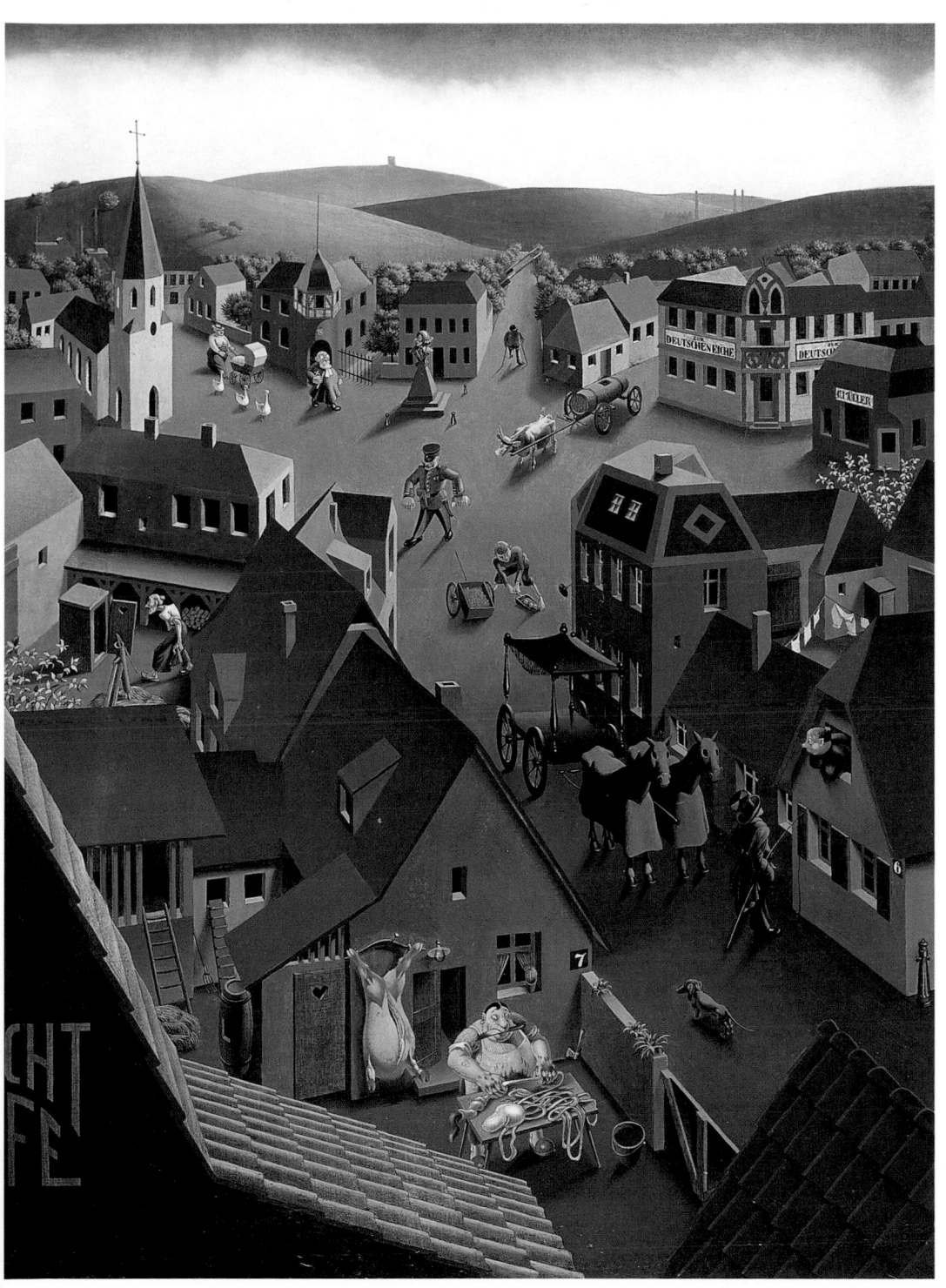

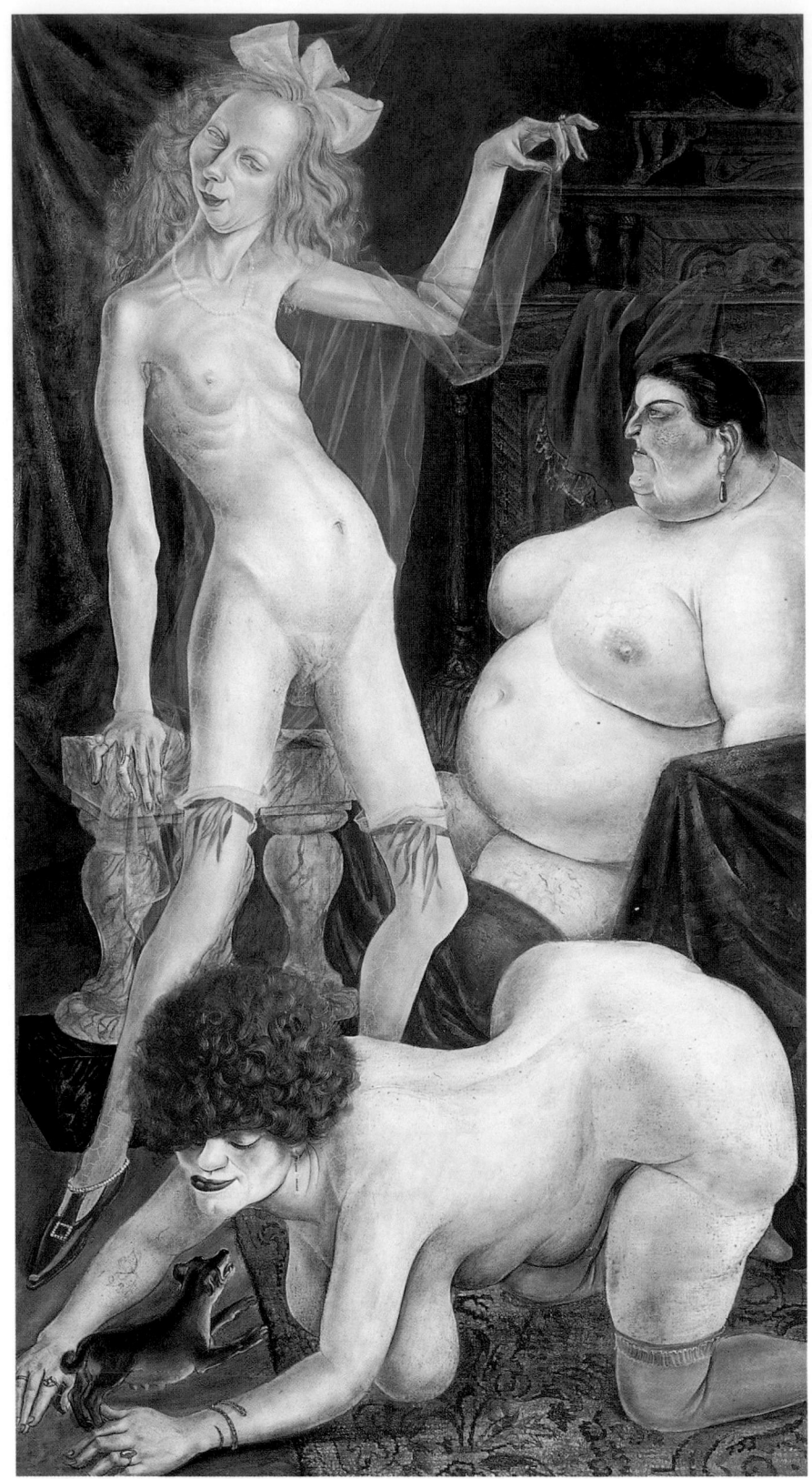

23
Otto Dix

Three Women 1926

Oil on canvas
181×105.5
($71\frac{1}{8} \times 41\frac{1}{2}$)
Galerie der Stadt
Stuttgart

early, chaotic post-war years: in the late 1920s, once-angry Dadaists like Georg Grosz and Otto Dix often mellowed their vision to mere sardonic reflections on street-life and social turpitude. *A Married Couple* of 1930, a watercolour by Grosz of an elderly couple shuffling along, has overtones of sympathy but also a suggestion of mockery for their smug, blinkered self-absorbtion. The void around them suggests they are oblivious of their surroundings. The old man is probably dreaming of his carpet slippers and a stein of beer, while his wife probably has the ironing to get on with. In his oil paintings Grosz's response to such 'kleinbuerger' (petit-bourgeois) was a ferocious mixture of pity and contempt (his real hatred he kept for army officers, bureaucrats and profiteers); this sketch has the artist's claws sheathed, for the time being. However, these folk of the 'Mittelstand', the 'middling sort', were to be among Hitler's most fervent early supporters.

Georg Scholz was another artist who mellowed in the 1920s; his *Small Town by Day: the Butcher*, of 1922–3, is at first sight enchanting, comparable in its toy-town festive appearance to Spencer's *The Lovers*, where the dustbin men are seen stomping up the Cookham garden paths. Here, similar domesticity is recorded, though a curious sense of unease, even menace, hangs over the view from the rooftops. The striding policeman in his crisp uniform seems too keen on the job and the somnambulistic-looking butcher (who could be the son of Grosz's old man) looks as though he'd not be too fussed at what – or who – he cuts up. The small cart in the middle of the picture belonging to the barefoot boy seems to be borrowed from de Chirico's *Mystery and Melancholy of a Street* (1914) as does the spectral atmosphere around the horse-drawn hearse and the sinister undertaker asking directions of a plump, if nervous Hausfrau: de Chirico's 'metaphysical' paintings, with their downbeat sense of alienation and anguish, had a great impact on the German art scene immediately after the Great War.

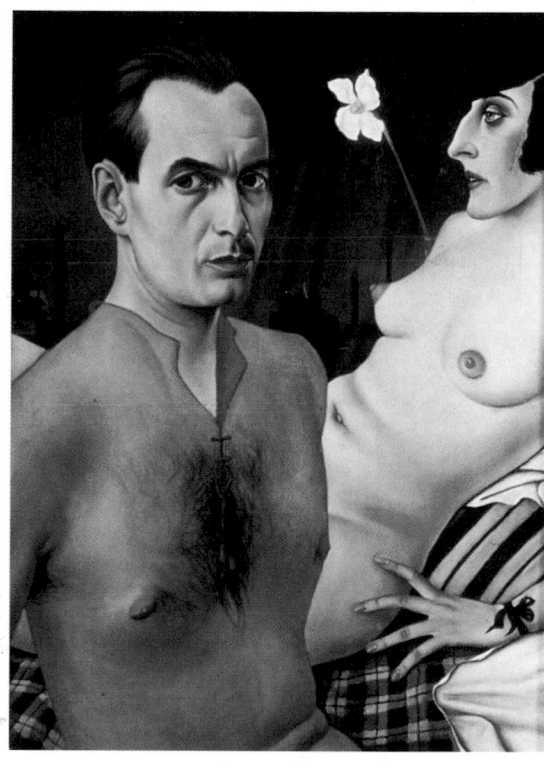

24
Christian Schad
Self-Portrait 1927
Oil on canvas
76 × 71
(30 × 28)
Private Collection

The peculiar proclivities of Berlin's nightlife, made familiar to the Anglo-Saxon world by Isherwood's novels (and, much later, over-smoothly by the film 'Cabaret') were captured by Otto Dix's unflattering records of 'working women' such as *Three Women* of 1926, which derives its angular style from Renaissance German artists like Grünewald and Cranach. Rudolf Schlichter, a shoe fetishist, specialised in women wearing tight-fitting boots with high

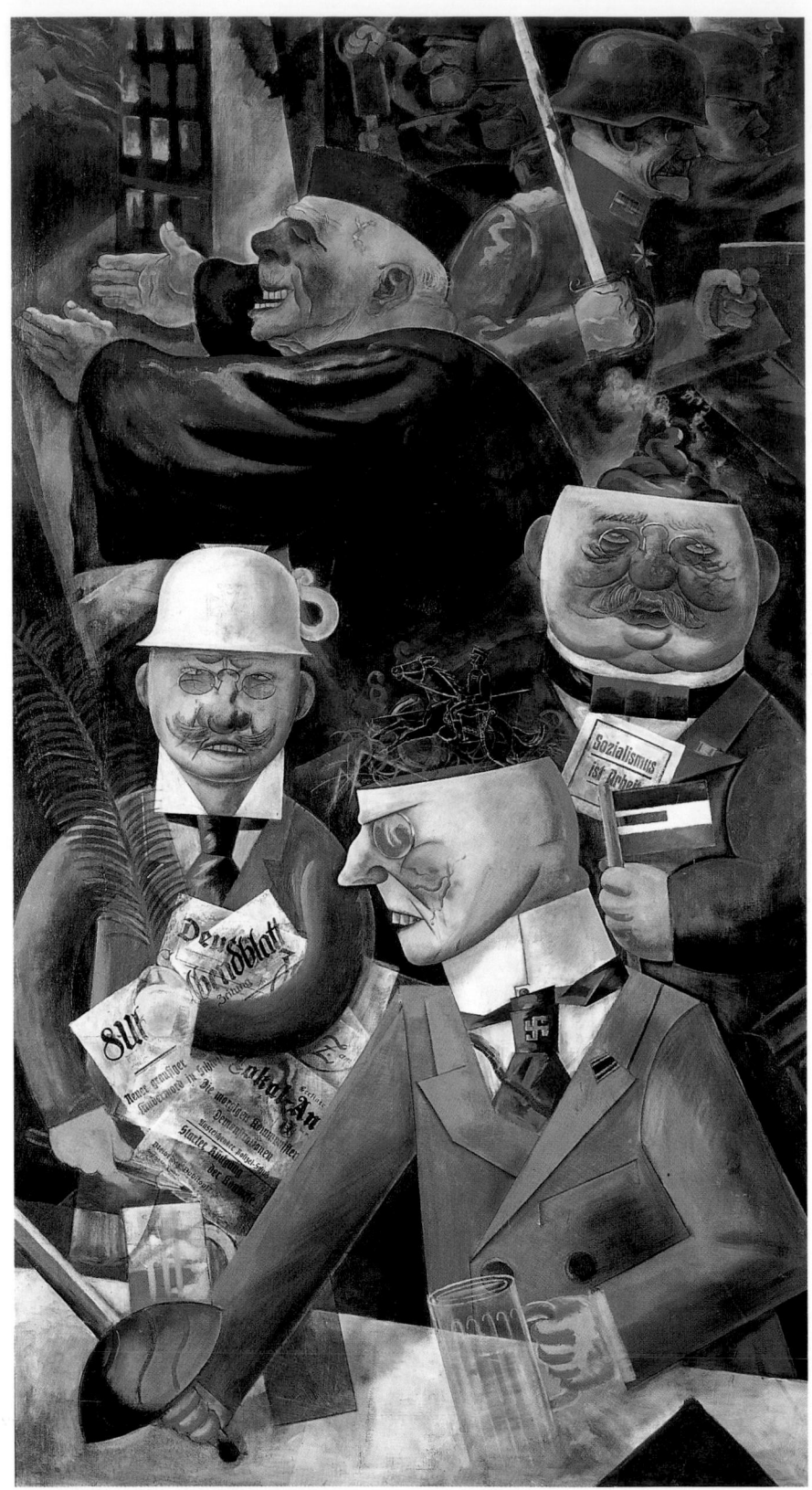

25
George Grosz

Pillars of the Community
1926

Oil on canvas
200 × 108
(78⅜ × 42½)
Staatliche Museen zu
Berlin – Preussischer
Kulturbesitz
Nationalgalerie

heels, surrounded by simian-looking clients, as in *Meeting of Fetishists and Maniacal Flagellants* of *c.*1921.

This painting has the sharp social satire of the 1920s. The work of Christian Schad takes a cooler view at the end of the decade with the scarred woman in *Self-Portrait* of 1928. The artist's translucent shirt, useless as a practical garment, reinforces both the nakedness of the angular model (a vivid antithesis to Wesselmann's pneumatic 1960s creature in fig.52) and his own nervous vulnerability. The stylish cropping of the image is a design feature which derives from his lucrative career as book-cover designer.

For Grosz and other haters of authority, the Weimar Republic's failure lay in its connivance with the entrenched positions of the judiciary, the army and the clergy. Indeed, there was no real enthusiasm for the Republic anywhere in a humiliated nation that had been an empire for fifty years and had no previous experience of democratic rule. Biding their time until a favourable moment, the old triumvirate depicted so viciously in Grosz's *Pillars of the Community* of 1926 were at best 'provisional republicans', whose real enthusiasm was reserved for political extremism. They probably did not mourn when the Depression from 1930 and the increasing powerlessness of the government in the face of mass unemployment (six million by 1932) swept the Weimar Republic away. The urban themes of Grosz and Dix were pursued by others. Grosz's fellow 'Objectivist' Gustav Wunderwald described being, in Berlin, 'attracted by the most dreary things, which prey on my mind ... with their interesting soberness and wretchedness' and his *Corner* (fig.26) of 1928 is a powerful expression of this response. Others, like Conrad Felixmueller in Dresden found a muted Romanticism in the daily life of the city, as in *Lovers from Dresden*; again the affinities with Spencer's Cookham humility are striking in the clumsy but heartfelt gesture of the couple and the references to the 'old masters' of the German Renaissance, much admired by Felixmueller:

> It has become increasingly clear to me that the only necessary goal is to depict the direct, simple life which one has lived oneself — in the manner in which it was cultivated by the Old Masters.

This could be true of Grosz's old couple as well, who are modern urban descendants of Bruegel's peasants.

Perhaps the most striking realist picture of the period as far as portrayal of a group is concerned is Otto Griebel's *The Internationale* of 1928–30, in which a solid phalanx of representatives from all branches of industry are chanting the song in an airless space. They don't look optimistic, but there is a certain grim force in their features and stance. It is the artist's refusal to heroicise the figures, however, that makes them so different from the Socialist Realism developing in the USSR at this time.

A very different realism was sought by Alexander Kanoldt, in Munich. Known now for the claustrophobic still lifes that reveal an obsession with order, he perhaps felt the weight of history: his father had been one of the last important Nazarenes, that academic-romantic group so influential in nineteenth-century Germany and on the English Pre-Raphaelites. His own training had taken him through Fauve colour and Cubist formalist disintegrations, to brief membership of the Blue Rider group around Franz Marc and Wassily Kandinsky from whom he broke away in 1911 when he was unable to accept abstraction. Then there is Franz Radziwill, one of the most magical of the Magic Realists: disasters are imminent behind supernaturally lit skies in the bleakly panoramic views Radziwill painstakingly produces, his hallmark being aircraft that swoop like predatory birds (he wanted to be an aircraft designer). In his work, humanity is a numbed victim of approaching cataclysmic forces or, like Grosz's old couple, oblivious to what is signified by the world around. The detail of his paintings and the old-fashioned use of glazes in his technique enhances the doom-laden atmosphere.

The Nazi attitude towards the New Objectivity was dismissive; they preferred the neo-romantic certainties of propagandist 'falsism' to what Frick, Minister of the Interior, attacked in October 1933 as 'the spirit of

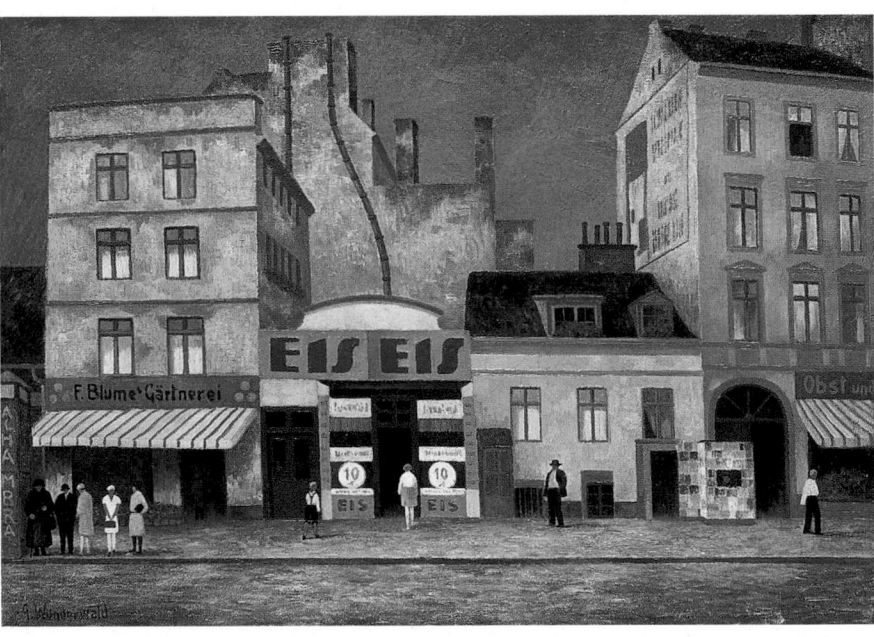

26
Gustav Wunderwald

Corner 1928

Oil on canvas
60.5 × 85.5
(23¾ × 33¾)
Staatliche Museen zu
Berlin – Preussischer
Kulturbesitz
Nationalgalerie

27 *right*
Franz Radziwill

Karl Buchstätter's Fatal Dive 1928

Oil on board
90 × 95
(35½ × 37½)
Museum Folkwang,
Essen

28 *below right*
Otto Griebel

The Internationale
1928–30

Oil on canvas
127 × 186
(50 × 73¼)
Deutsches Historiches
Museum, Berlin

subversion ... those ice-cold, completely un-German constructions'. Hitler, in 1935, condemned the word 'objectivity' itself, though strangely, in connection with 'Dadaist-Cubist and Futurist experience'. Certainly, most of the practitioners of New Objectivity were eased out of official positions by 1935, only those able to exploit such titles as *German Soil* in their works continuing to be tolerated by the regime. Even the tolerated Kanoldt would have his works removed from show in the wake of the 'Degenerate Art' campaign of 1937–8; perhaps because of his historical link to the Blue Rider, *bête noir* for the Nazis, and also because of his rearguard defence of persecuted colleagues. When even Radziwill was expelled from the Nazi party in 1938 Michalski commented: 'Hitler's party unerringly rid itself of its last artist of any importance'.

In many ways, Neue Sachlichkeit aesthetics represented a retreat from the

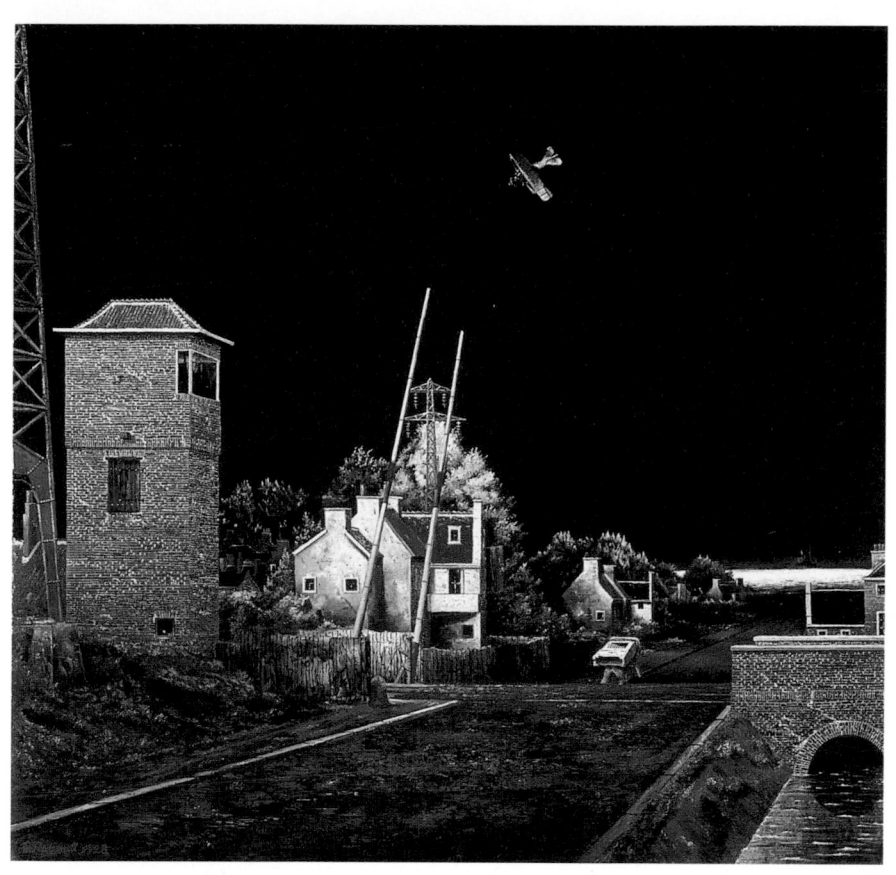

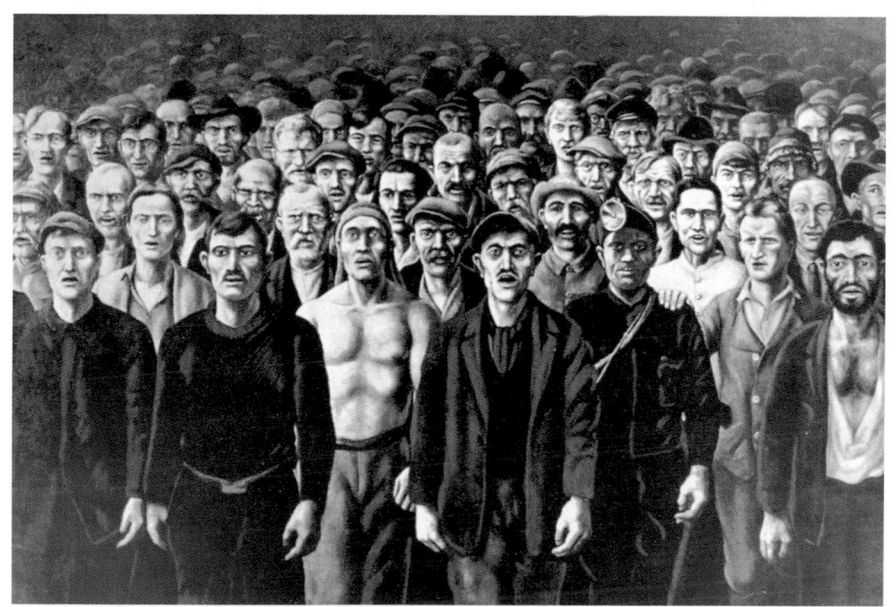

modern world, its machinery and the dispossession of the human that was associated with it. Only in America, at least until 1929, did humanity seem in charge of its destiny. In Europe the First World War had shown the pitiless power of the machine gun and heavy artillery and in the aftermath of the conflict this new relationship of machinery and war seared deeply into the European mind, particularly in defeated Germany. Only totalitarian attitudes seemed able to overcome the prevailing lethargy; in 1930 the critic Wilhelm Michel, a supporter of the New Objectivity, explained its ideological weakness thus:

> From an objective point of view, we have been besieged with too much that is new. Our powers of comprehension have been unable to keep pace with it … We stand, not in front of machines but rather in front of machine-culture, exactly as if before a war … without the secure sense of our humanity, forced to make a virtue out of the 'experience' and the observation of details, since we cannot continue to exist as whole … human beings in the face of the reality rising up all around us.

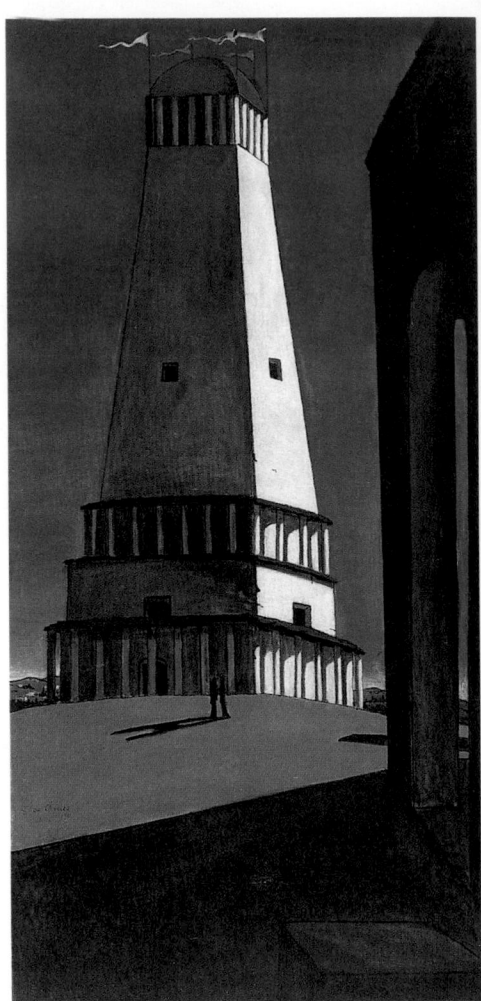

Fernand Léger apart, it would take the rise of Pop Art and its embracing of the 'brave new world' of consumerism in the late 1950s and 1960s to enable man to co-exist with the machine in anything like an equable relationship.

ITALY

Carlo Carrà met Giorgio de Chirico in military life in Ferrara in 1916. They evolved a style, of much influence on Surrealism after the war, which they termed Pittura Metafisica. It evoked the angst of their barracks captivity and sense of powerlessness. They sought certitude – and found it in the Renaissance geometries of the old masters. The result was a determination to recall the calm grandeur of classical art and reinvent it for the post-war world. Their message found acceptance among a number of young Italian artists, with Felice Casorati, Giorgio Morandi (a specialist in still life) and Ubaldo Oppi being the most significant as far as realism is concerned. Another important artist, whose work remained more gestural than these, was Mario Sironi. Loosely gathered around the magazines *Valori Plastici* (*Plastic Values*) and *Novecento* (*Twentieth Century*) they wished fundamentally to reverse the Futurist experiment and embrace the past – what Marinetti, the Futurist leader, had contemptuously described as 'Passeism'. Nevertheless, the cold marmoreal finish to the flesh

29
Giorgio de Chirico

The Nostalgia of the Infinite? 1913–14, dated on work 1911

Oil on canvas
135.2 × 64.8
(53¼ × 25½)
The Museum of Modern Art, New York

30
Giorgio Morandi

Still Life 1946

Oil on canvas
37.5 × 45.7
(14¾ × 18)
Tate Gallery

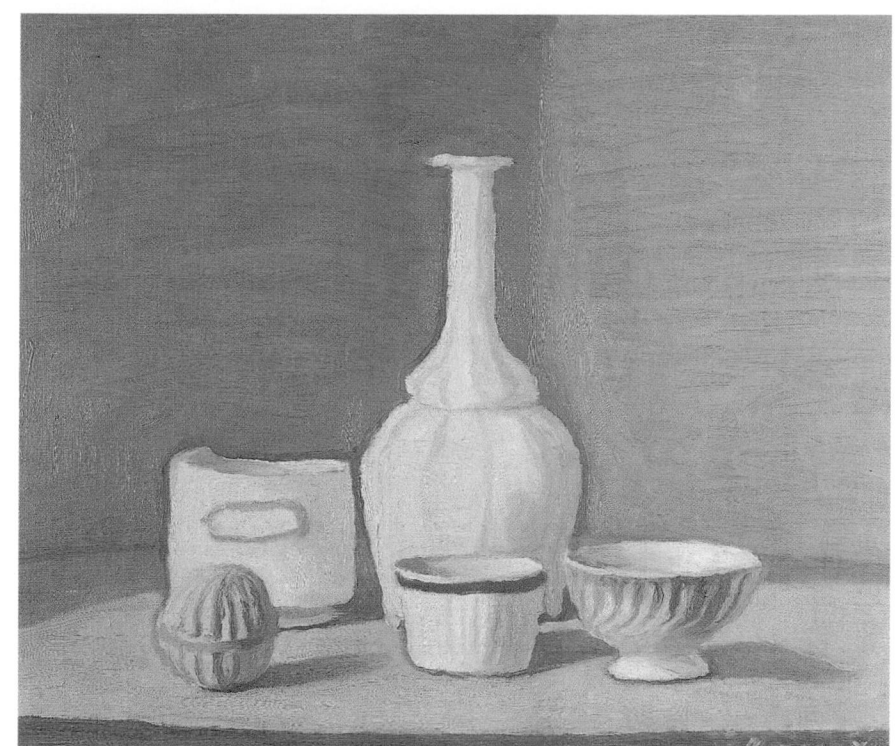

31
Mario Sironi

*Mountains c.*1928

Oil on canvas
81.9 × 107.9
(32¼ × 42½)
Tate Gallery

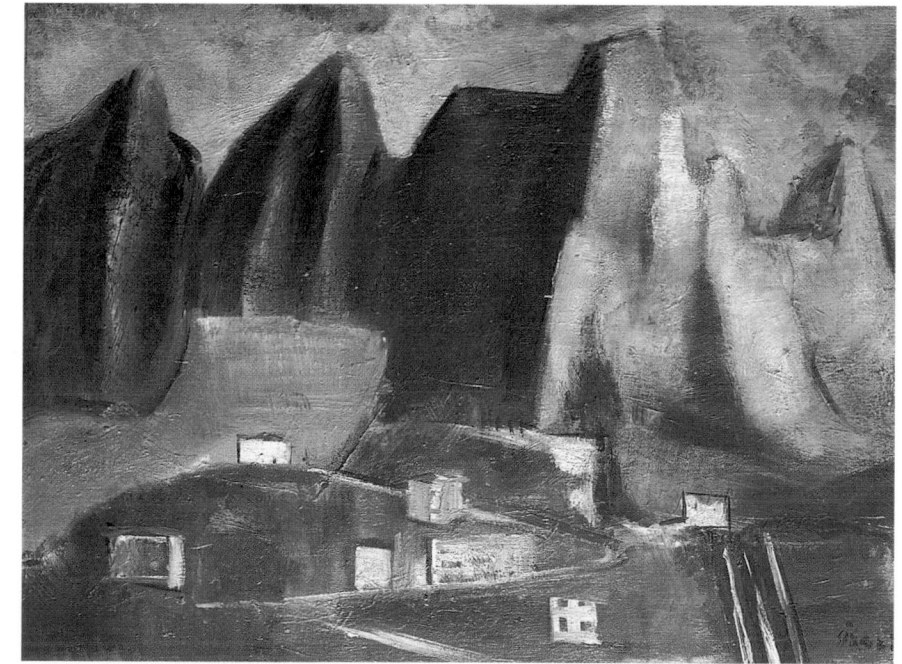

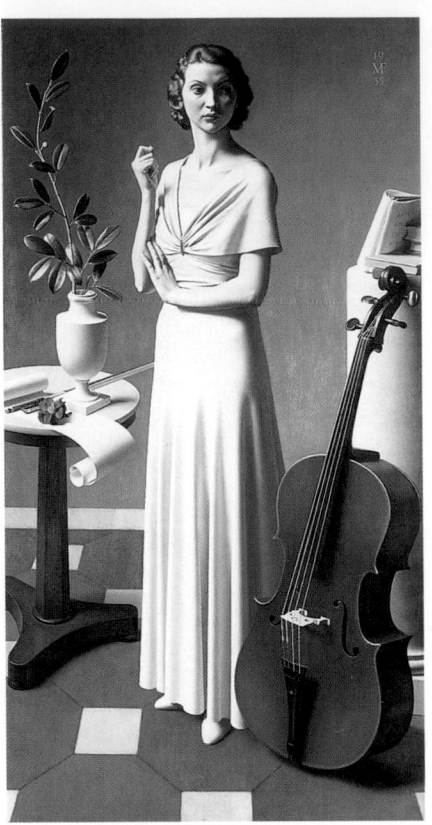

textures and the chilly decor that Casorati in particular utilised, have a machine-tooled element not to be found in Italian painting of the past.

Throughout the 1920s, as Mussolini consolidated power, there was a jostling for influence around the Duce, who had a general interest in art but no desire to meddle. Consequently, considerable freedom of style was afforded Italian artists into the 1930s, when he came increasingly under the influence of Hitler, to his and Italy's detriment. The fanatical quality of national aggrandisement noticeable in German 'Statist' art is largely absent from Italian realist painting, and in this it is closer to the work of a British artist such as Meredith Frampton in the detached and emotionally neutral temperature it prefers. Frampton's *Portrait of a Young Woman* of 1935 might be interchangeable with a Casorati society portrait. Perhaps the lesson here is that it is as false to associate scrupulous illusionistic realism in the 1930s with totalitarianism alone as it is to associate neo-classical architecture in public buildings exclusively with Fascism.

The cold fixity of this Italian imagery was challenged both by abstract art and by the impassioned figurative style of the left-wing artist Renato Guttuso, whose *The Escape from Etna* of 1940 allegorised the foreseeable disaster for Fascist Italy.

32
Meredith Frampton

Portrait of a Young Woman 1935

Oil on canvas
205.7 × 107.9
(81 × 42½)
Tate Gallery

33
Adolf Wissel

Kalenberg Farmer's Family 1939

Oil on canvas
150 × 200
(59 × 78¾)
Oberfinanzdirektion,
Munich

PAINTING IN THE THIRD REICH

Under Nazi rule there seemed to be two avenues open to artists looking for subjects that would be approved by the regime. The first, realist only in its illusionist technique, was that of superficial classicism, exemplified in the bombastic posturing of muscle-men allegorising the forces of the new state in the sculpture of Arno Brekker. Even Hitler was allegorised as a knight in armour in H. Lanzinger's *The Flag Bearer*; more usually, he was portrayed full-length in contemporary military uniform as Führer – although he took very seriously his self-appointed role as leader of the nation in aesthetic matters too. Heroic Realism, as the posturing classicistic work of artists such as Brekker might be termed, could occasionally masquerade in contemporary dress as well, usually for propaganda-poster-like effects as in H.O. Hoyer's *SA Man Rescuing Wounded Comrade in the Street* of 1933.

Art was to pervade every area of national life, demanded the Führer, and the *Great German Art* exhibitions held in Munich even during the later war years were intended to promote this aim. Children's colouring books (there was one called *Soldiers,* for example) were paralleled by academic works called *German Youth.* As well as such promotions of martial spirit, there was endless reiteration of the glories of the good, rural, peasant life, the 'Blood and Soil' connection perhaps not at first having the sinister connotations of self-sacrifice it would later assume. Many city dwellers found this idealisation dull; even the 'characterful' portrayals of *Peasant from Samerberg* or Andri's *Mother and Child* were hardly found more inspiring.

Since National Socialism forbade criticism of the regime and any

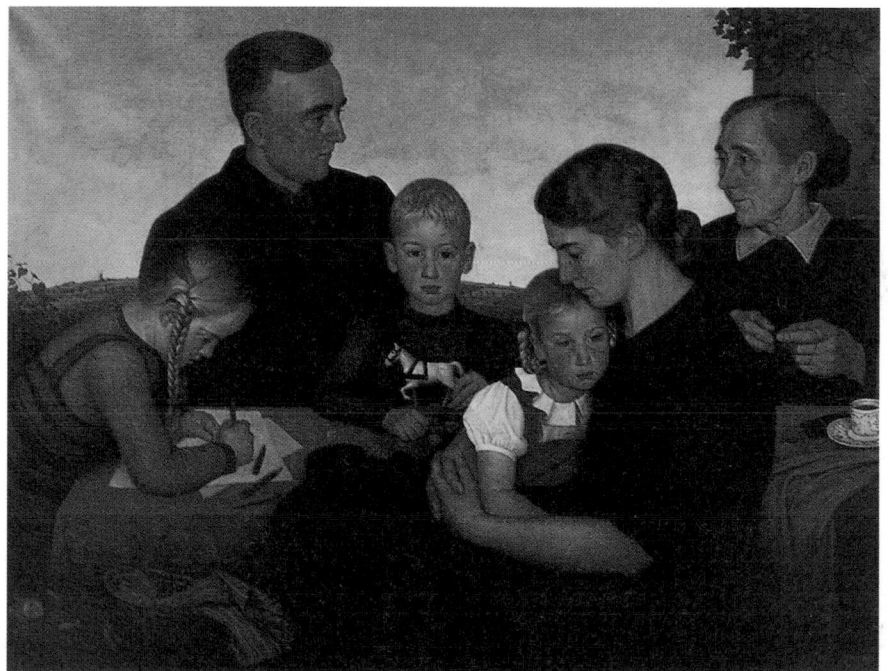

pluralism in the arts, a monolithic uniformity was inevitable. Exhibitions were 'harvests of the artistic will' and artists were seen as aesthetic soldiers. 'Art is a mighty and fanatical mission', declared Hitler, while Goering hoped for an art 'that the ordinary man could understand' (he was busy salting the rest away in Salzburg mines). The ghosts of Cranach, Altdorfer, Dürer and Holbein are evoked in the static linearity and solidly impacted facial features that characterise a supposed return to 'national' roots in painting. One or two works do seem to transcend the narrow party line however, and something of early German Romantic intensity still lingers in Adolf Wissel's *Kalenberg Farmer's Family* of 1939. It lacks dynamism, or even very much interest, but it has a static piety and poise that recalls August Sander's Weimar photographs and Nazarene simplicity. Its technique is faultless and considerably more skilful in its use of glazes than comparable Soviet painting of the same period.

As the war progressed from bad to worse after 1942, German National Socialist realism had to come to terms with defeat. Paintings became more and more exhortatory and fanciful, as with *Hitler at the Front* by E. Scheiber of 1942–3. The Führer seems to enjoy being the centre of devotion of a packed group of soldiers, who would seem to be myopic, so close do they crowd him. This contrasts with the intensely photographic feeling of Paul Mathias Padua's *The Tenth of May 1940*, in which a camera angle on huddled troops paddling across a river on the first morning of the invasion of France is edited so that the captain strikes a pose not far removed from the overstrained gestures of Brekker's Nazi sculpture, only here we are closer to the pages of *Signal*, the Nazi war photography magazine. Yet sections of the picture transcend mere Nazi propaganda. It does have a psychological

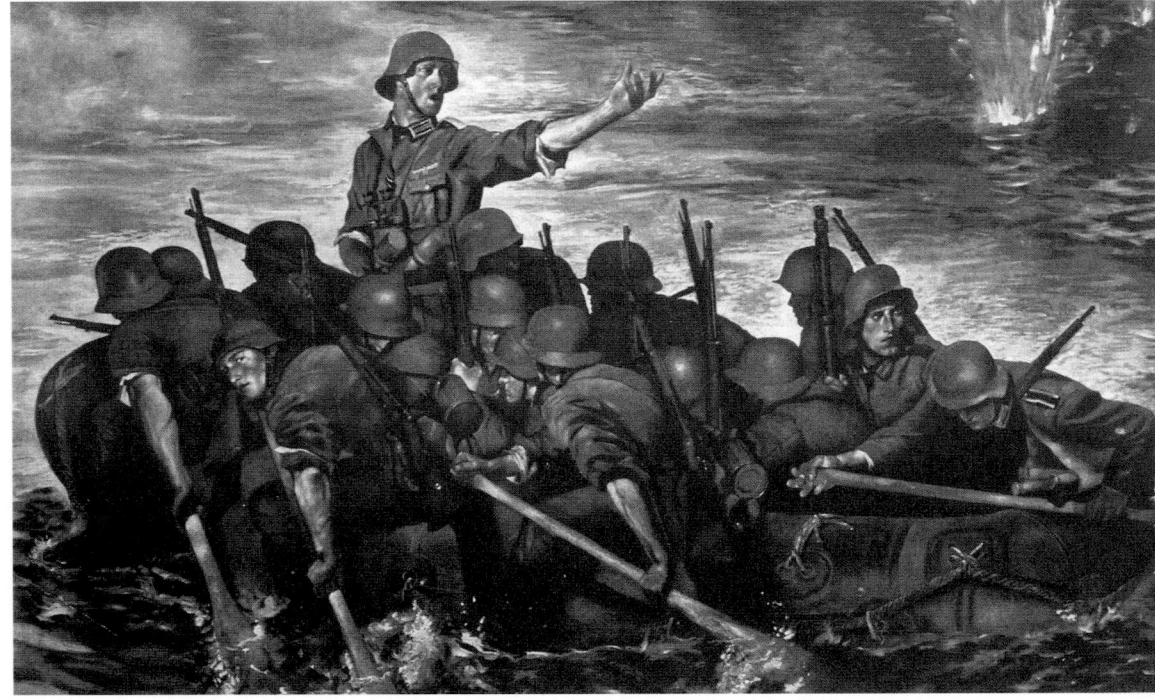

realism about it – after all, heroism is possible – conveyed by the unease of several soldiers under enemy gunfire. The extraordinary glance of one of them, as if into camera, challenges the viewer's security even though the look is curiously difficult to read. On the whole, however, the imagery of Nazi realism remained shallow, like the cultural life of the country, though this is true of most art produced during modern wartime. The state censored the too painful truth (as had occurred in Britain in World War One with Nevinson's war paintings); it might be claimed that after truth, the second casualty in war is realism.

Although much of the work was destroyed in wartime air raids, and the survivors have rarely surfaced from the museum basements, in the late 1970s the legacy of the Third Reich's art produced some uneasy echoes in the imagery of Anselm Kiefer and Jörg Immendorf. Their realism can be related to that of the 'tendentious' group of Neue Sachlichkeit painters. In the case of Immendorf his work is characterised by distortions which can be spatial, caricatural or reminiscent of comic books, as in the *Cafe Deutschland* cycle he began in 1977. Something of the kaleidoscopic, committed quality of Gunter Grass's novels seems reflected in the magical realism he employs, in which traditional materials are used to portray characters from German history. The symbols are easy enough to read in his work – the German eagle for instance – and the aim is legibility for the political intent of the work, which suggests a revved-up Socialist Realism. It is given a sense of relating to a tradition, however, by a range of references to classic German Expressionist painters like Max Beckmann and Ernst Ludwig Kirchner and so escapes the trap of literalness the Soviet painters were caught in.

More haunting and impressive in their reference back to troubled times are Kiefer's depth-concealing presentations of landscapes or interiors, both appearing equally empty. The pigment is heavy, often loaded with straw, as if to reinforce the reference to nature, and a profound sense of place imbues all his mature work. The interiors, however, are nearer in spirit to the sites of psychic devastation in Francis Bacon than to the 'Blood and Soil' mythology of the Nazis. Yet the latter is what Kiefer often comments on, weaving together guilt, renewal, death, transcendence and the dead weight of history and fact in works both earthbound and suggestive.

AMERICA

America's involvement in the First World War seems to have brought about a revulsion from Europe and European affairs in the two decades that followed. In art this resulted in a strong emphasis on American subject matter and a strong tilt towards forms of realism, away from the experimental avant-gardism that, as in Europe, had exerted its sway in the pre-war years. Of course, avant-garde forms persisted and some notable artists such as Charles Demuth and Charles Sheeler, the so-called Precisionists, combined realist subject matter with a clear-cut geometric style.

One of the most characteristic phenomena of between-the-wars American art was Regionalism. Supported by the critic Thomas Craven, Regionalism nevertheless had no specific style; it was an art that grew from national or local experience, was opposed to dependency on European influence and called for the emergence of an American art. Its leading figures were Thomas Hart Benton, John Steuart Currey and Grant Wood, whose *American Gothic* (fig.35), with its high focus realism and intensity of feeling, is one of the most celebrated of all American paintings.

But perhaps the dominant genius of realist painting in America between the wars was Edward Hopper. As Matthew Baigell (*American Painting*, 1971) has pointed out, Hopper's style is highly traditional but his subject matter is absolutely contemporary. Crucially, however, his subject matter is domestic

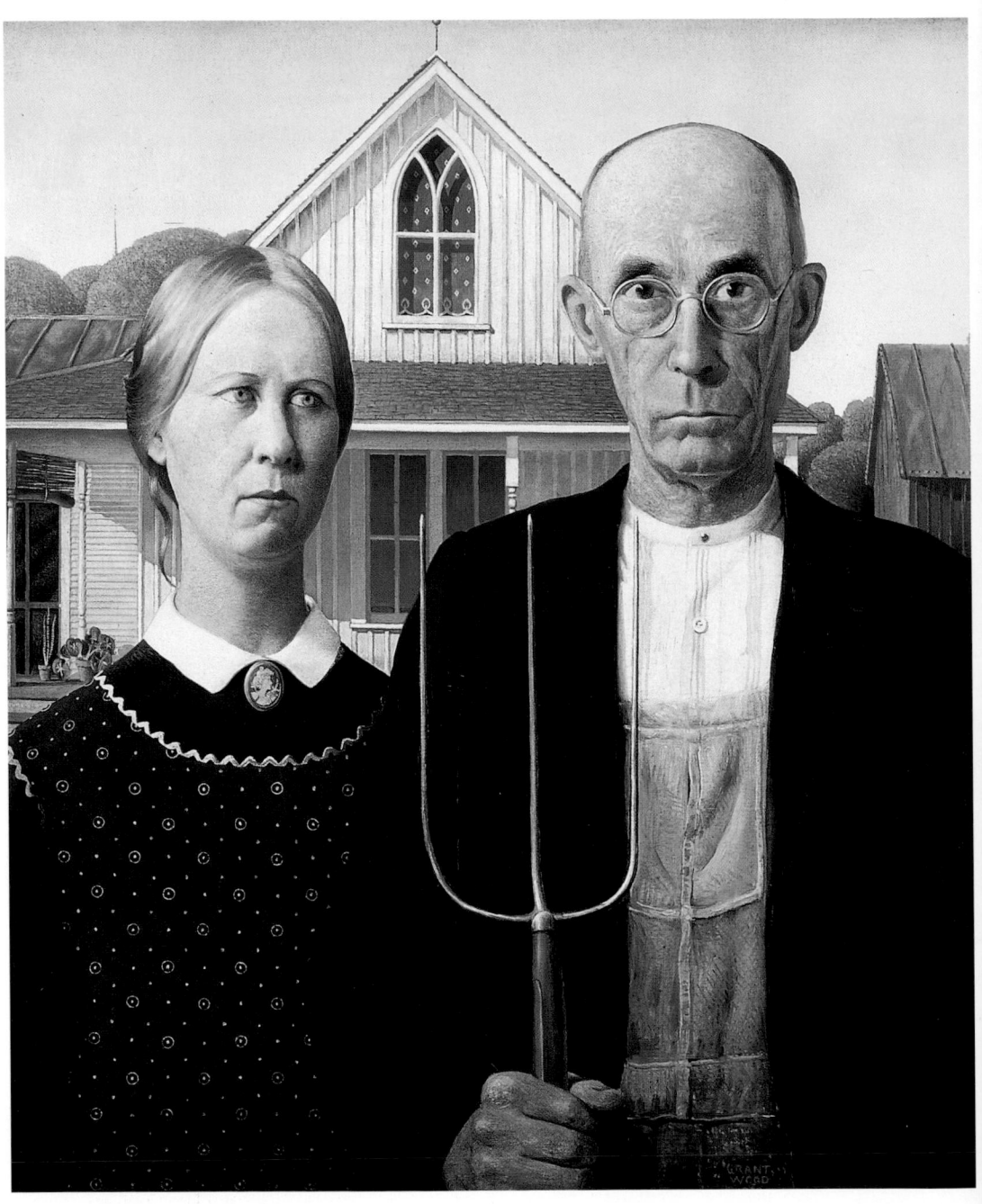

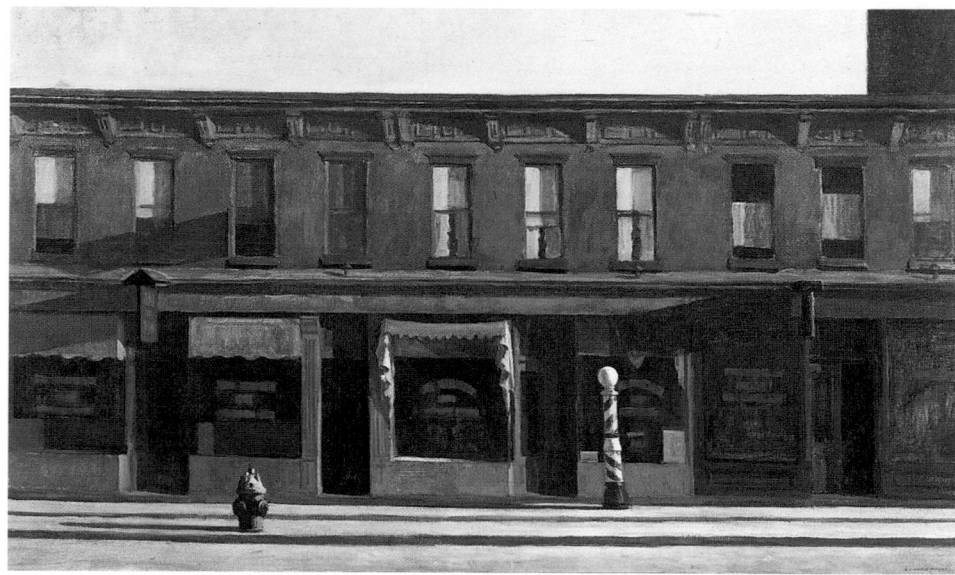

35
Grant Wood

American Gothic 1930

Oil on board
74.3 × 62.4
(29¼ × 24½)
The Art Institute of
Chicago and VAGA New
York, Friends of
American Art Collection

36
Edward Hopper

Early Sunday Morning
1930

Oil on canvas
88.9 × 152.4
(35 × 60)
Collection of Whitney
Museum of American
Art. Purchase, with
funds from Gertrude
Vanderbilt Whitney

and psychological rather than being drawn from the modern industrial scene or modern artefacts. Hopper himself stated that his aim was to make 'the most exact transcription possible of my most intimate impressions of nature'. For Hopper this 'nature' was what he, writing of another artist but equally well describing his own art, described as 'all the sweltering, tawdry life of the American small town, and behind all, the sad desolation of our suburban landscapes'.

THE REALISM OF THE MEXICAN MURALISTS

The Mexican Muralists constitute one of the most intriguing phenomena in twentieth-century painting. In many ways, not least politically, the circumstances of the creation of the industrial murals by Diego Rivera in the early 1930s typify the great dilemma for artists in this period: should ideology be allowed to dictate subject-matter and style, or should the artist trust to his individualism and what might be termed his talent, to comment on or illustrate the ideology? This was a battle lost by the 'individualist' artists both in Germany and Russia at this time, although a few, like Malevich (see p.27), managed to put up a wily, despairing defence for a while.

   With Rivera and his followers, the equation is somewhat different. This is partly because Mexico shared the somewhat febrile politics of South America rather than aspiring to the monolithic states of Hitler and Stalin, and also because Rivera produced art in more than one country at just the time when Stalin had advocated the 'socialism in one country' that led to Socialist Realism's sway in Soviet Russia.

   It is still remarkable that American capitalists should have been content to employ not merely a radical but a Marxist painter to provide large-scale decorations, in the midst of a hitherto unparalleled economic slump. The whole question of automated mass-production was causing widespread concern among American unions at the time, but they were cowed by strong-arm management tactics, made possible by the economic uncertainties produced by the October 1929 stock market crash.

It is against this background that the Detroit Institute of Arts frescoes depicting the Ford plant at River Rouge, Detroit, painted by Rivera in 1932–3, take on a particular significance. They epitomise the stresses and strains that beset the socially aware artist (as compared to an artist like Matisse, for example). The work consists of twenty-seven panels painted in true fresco, a medium of the Renaissance, which gives an aura of authority to the designs, as well as a mellow matt finish that enhances the cool, distant approach Rivera

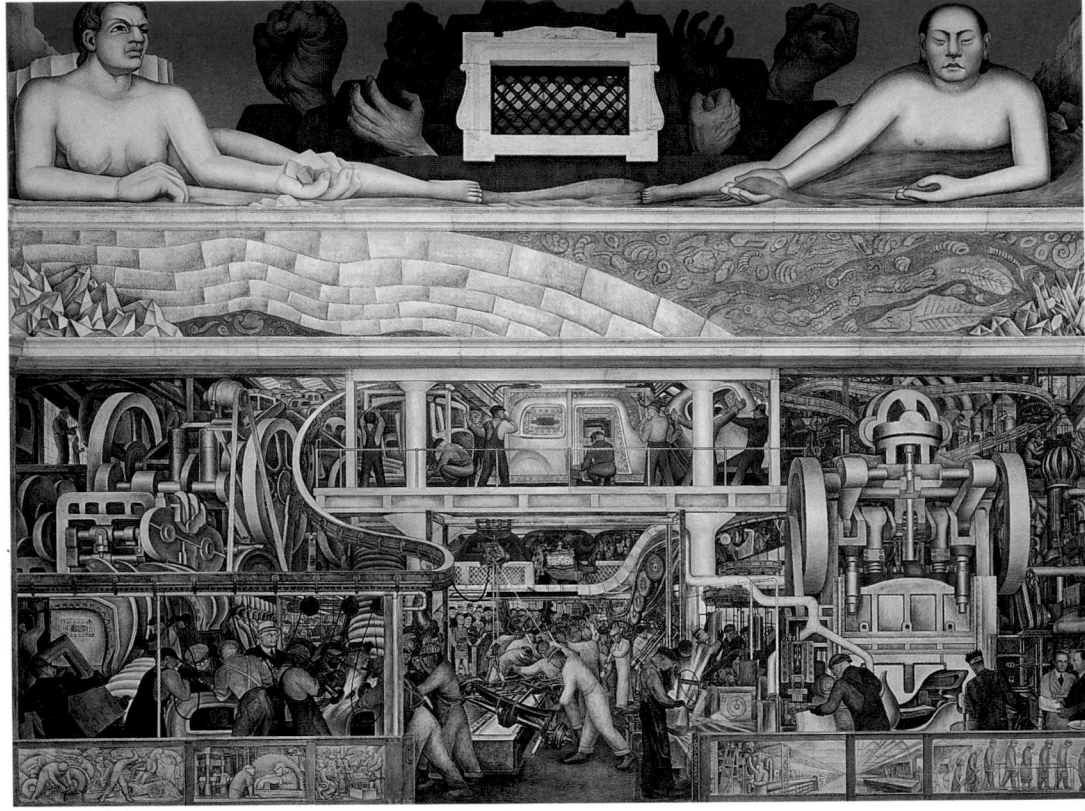

appears to take towards the mechanical processes celebrated in the murals. Indeed, in many images there are atavistic, non-modern elements that are drawn from Rivera's particular national and ancient cultural background. The crouching nude figures, some dark, some pale – but even these with facial characteristics of southern Americans – loom over the scurrying activities of modern workers like ancient deities. This may be part of Rivera's perception, from his Marxist position, that contemporary industry was a destructive juggernaut comparable to the bloodthirsty gods of human sacrifice of pre-European South American culture. In this light, the works may be seen as warnings to the workers and adjurations to the management. In this it is reminiscent of the naïve plot and moral of Fritz Lang's megalomaniacal fantasy movie *Metropolis* of 1926, which also reflects concerns about the dehumanising of workforces by factory methods.

It seems clear that Rivera's mature art was shaped by worries about the elitism that avant-gardism appeared to spawn. In Paris as a young Cubist painter connected with Juan Gris, he became disenchanted with the diminishing audience of 'superior persons' that Cubism spoke to. Like Léger, he saw the role of art as to educate the public into new ways of seeing the modern world. This as it might be called 'sense of function' for painting drove him away from easel painting, whose scope for proselytising about 'life and labour and the times' was limited to galleries and private homes, towards a view of 'art as a weapon', a phrase also used by Picasso. Perhaps this idea of painting as a form of attack was why the Marxist Rivera decided to paint works for capitalists like the Rockefellers within their strongholds, rather than simply preaching to the converted. It was a risky business, as Rivera discovered when the Rockefellers obliterated his mural *Man at the Crossroads* because it depicted Lenin. Were the Rockefellers surprised by Lenin's appearance in it? Nevertheless, Rivera did take his work into the enemy camp, as with the mural he did for the luncheon club of the San Francisco Stock Exchange. Rivera's attitude in this case contrasts interestingly with the very different response of the Abstract Expressionist Mark Rothko in the 1950s when he discovered that the space he was making murals for was to become the Four Seasons restaurant. He withdrew his paintings, stating that he did not want his works to be displayed where rich people were gorging themselves. An incident that underlines the ironies of Rivera's position was the purchase in 1931, also by a Rockefeller, of Rivera's sketchbook containing impressions of the 1928 May Day processions in Moscow.

Yet it can also be argued that realism is tempered and reduced in a work 'that depicted clean and well fed workers in apparent harmony with management as well as with the latest technology, producing cars they could scarcely afford, in a plant where production was down to a fifth of pre-1929 levels' (Wood 1993) and where a short while before Rivera's arrival a 3,000-strong Communist-inspired hunger march had resulted in three shot dead and many wounded at the factory gates. The same argument can be used against the squeaky-clean view of Russian worker relations promulgated by Soviet State Realism at the same time, when, as we now know, Collectivism was producing famine and mass starvation in vast areas of the country. In fact, the works of Gerasimov and Rivera alike depict a wished-for state, rather than an actuality: this is a Utopian realism. Nevertheless, these works are not caricatures. Rivera's have the advantage of a freedom of individual response denied to his Russian contemporaries and they are enriched too by their deep-rooted cultural allusions to his Indian heritage. The Russians can look no further back than to various aspects of nineteenth-century bourgeois realism, which they can tentatively annexe. Perhaps it can even be argued that the allegorical figures representing birth and the races of the Americas, that hold working humanity in thrall in the Detroit murals, are as 'classic' in a South American way as the less visually convincing ploys of Nazi 'classicistic' works were intended to be under Hitler.

37
Diego Rivera
Detroit Industry 1932–3
Fresco
257.8 × 213.4
(101½ × 84¾)
The Detroit Institute of
Arts. Gift of Edsel B. Ford

4

EUROPEAN AND BRITISH REALISM AFTER 1945

Much European art after 1945 was nurtured by the philosophy of existentialism, particularly in France. Existentialism's influence saw painters and writers asserting the responsibility of individuals for their actions and finding a close relationship between this position and the making of art. Only by realising their freedom and therefore their responsibility could a person's life become 'authentic', as opposed to being hostage to a totalitarian force. The Nazi defendants' cry at Nuremberg that 'Hitler was their conscience' was the excuse for the abdication of personal responsibility that had led to the evils of the Nazi regime. Bearing witness to these evils was never going to be easy. Antonin Artaud, Henri Michaux, Bram van Velde, Giacometti and Francis Bacon are leading examples of those artists who, immediately after the war, refused to leave Europe's conscience alone, gnawing at it like a terrier at a bone. This confrontation was their form of realism, although in strictly pictorial terms it approached Expressionism. At the other end of the pendulum swing of the post-war years (until 1956 or so) was a response which in Britain became known as Neo-Romanticism. This was less realistic than escapist, perhaps looking to the past and drawing on William Blake and Samuel Palmer, the dreamier Pre-Raphaelites and the tradition of manual graphic arts like wood-cutting and engraving. The Neo-Romantics sought to hearken back to a more innocent, unshattered time, which, of course, had never existed. John Piper, Graham Sutherland and Paul Nash were the godfathers of this movement and John Minton, John Craxton and Keith Vaughan among its leading figures. Like their nineteenth-century Romantic

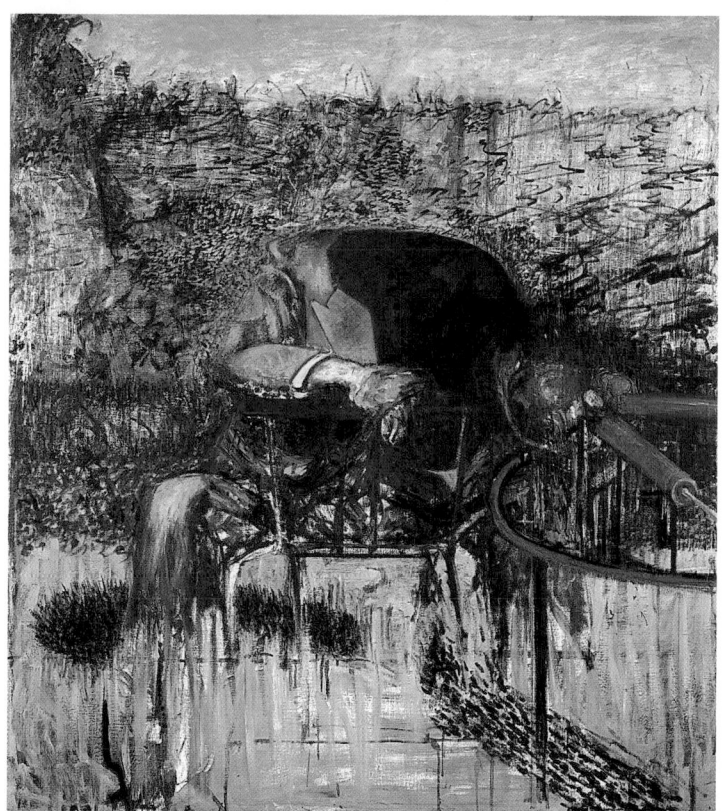

38
Francis Bacon

Figure in a Landscape
1945

Oil on canvas
144.8 × 128.3
(57 × 50½)
Tate Gallery

39
Renato Guttuso

The Discussion
1959–60

Tempera, oil and various
media on canvas
220 × 248
(86½ × 97½)
Tate Gallery

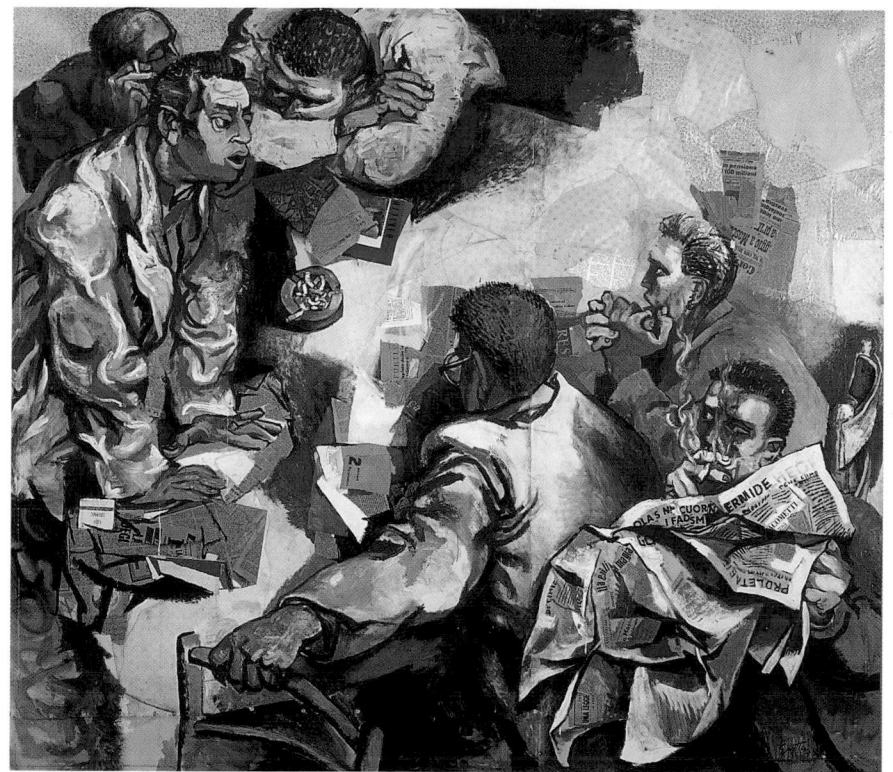

forerunners, they elaborated a stylised, organic shape-shifting, using the 'wiry line' that Blake had praised as the medium of 'energy' which was 'eternal delight'. But throughout, the natural world was a springboard into a poetic fantasy world, rather than an anchorage in the here and now.

A form of realism closer to the tradition of Courbet appeared in Italy in the work of the doctrinaire Communist Renato Guttuso. His crowds of Italian workers and families have a pungent presence and his approach recalls the Italian realist cinema of those years, from Rossi's *Roma, citta aperta* through to Visconti's *Rocco and his Brothers*. As will be shown, Lucian Freud developed into the leading British exponent of a realist style at this time.

POP ART IN BRITAIN

By the late 1950s, with consumer culture spreading from America to Western Europe — and to Britain in particular — there was a challenge to the artistic status quo which involved an unprecedented involvement of the art world with popular culture. Material prosperity for a majority of the middle class in Britain, many of whom found themselves with spare money to spend for the first time in their life, led to rapid social change: holidays abroad, the spread of ownership of cars and other 'consumer durables' like televisions and washing machines.

Whereas gadgetry had long been a feature of American daily life, the sheer novelty of such things in most British households gave rise to comment, notably in Richard Hamilton's small but effective collage *Just what is it that makes today's homes so different, so appealing?*, with its title

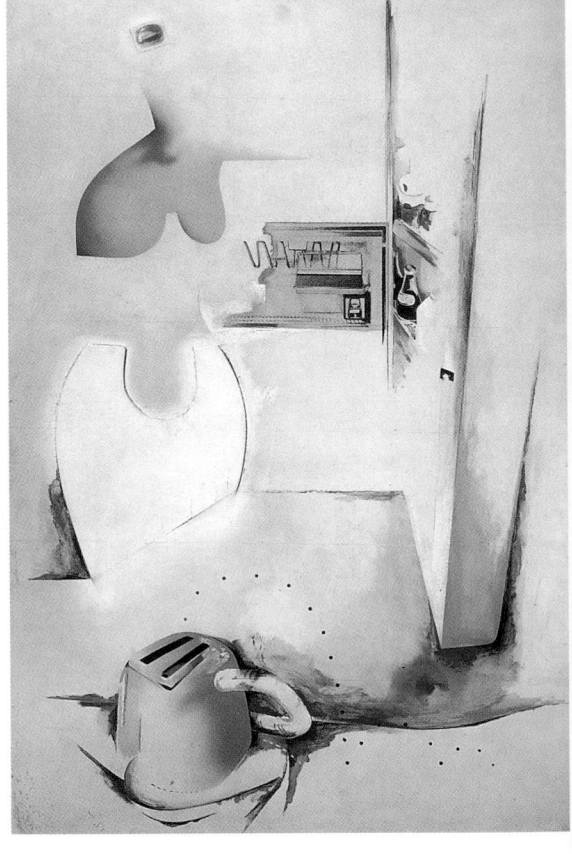

sounding like the burble of an advertising salesman on television. Hamilton's *$he* makes a similar point. Hamilton was one of the new wave of British artists who created the exhibition *This is Tomorrow* of 1956 at the Whitechapel Art Gallery, a launch pad for their concept of an art based on advertising and other aspects of popular culture and the contemporary urban environment. The term Pop had been coined to describe popular culture itself, being applied to art that was not only based on pop sources but sought to share the characteristics of pop that he and his friends admired. These characteristics included, in a famous list compiled by Hamilton, 'Popular, Transient, Expendable', as well as 'Witty, Sexy, Glamorous'. To many people at the time such qualities, and popular culture itself, seemed despicable, and utterly alien to art. But in choosing such subject matter the Pop artists were harking back to the approach of Courbet and the nineteenth-century Realists and their British followers such as Sickert who remained much admired in some quarters, especially for his late works based on newspaper photographs. Hamilton's approach mixed a scholarly oil painting method as currently taught in British art schools (he would later teach in one himself) with the collage and photo-montage techniques associated with Dada and Surrealist practice before the Second World War and promulgated in Britain by the exiled Kurt Schwitters and, in the late 1940s, Eduardo Paolozzi. Pop art was a manifestation of social, political and aesthetic revolt whose literary equivalent was the phenomenon of the 'angry young men' led by the playwright John Osborne. Combined with this revolt was nevertheless a desire to make the most of the new affluence. The appearance of Pop Art

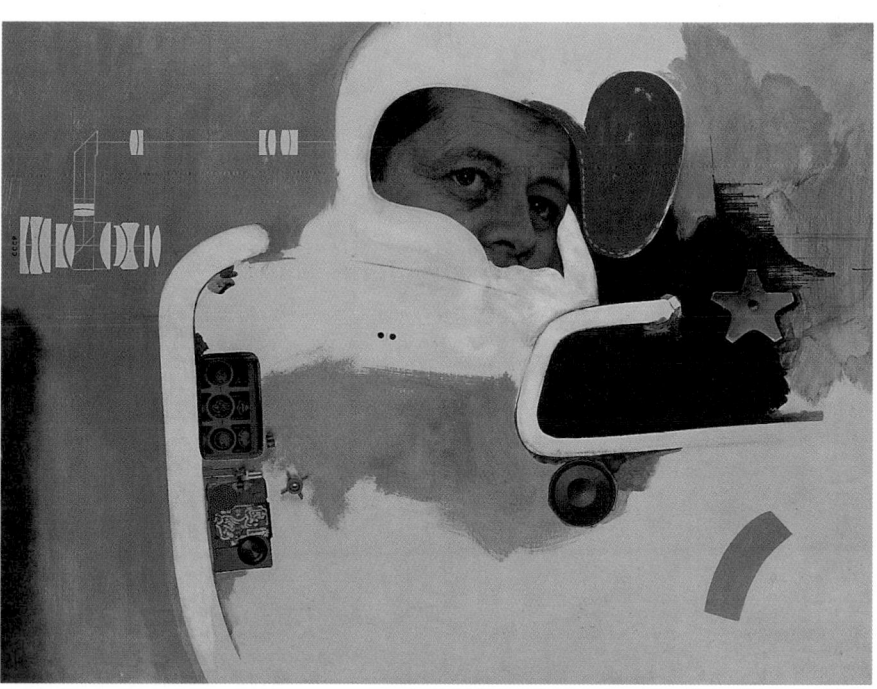

40
Richard Hamilton

$he 1959–61

Oil, cellulose paint and collage on wood
121.9 × 81.3
(48 × 32)
Tate Gallery

41
Richard Hamilton

Towards a Definitive Statement on the Coming Trends in Men's Wear and Accessories (a) Together Let us Explore the Stars 1962

Oil, cellulose paint and collage on wood
61 × 81.3
(24 × 32)
Tate Gallery

coincided with the development of the distinctive youth culture so brilliantly described in Colin MacInnes's novel *Absolute Beginners* of 1958. A separate lifestyle for the young (pop music, coffee bars and scooters at least in the big cities) gave rise to the media concept of the 'generation gap'. Something like full employment meant that the gulf was between the ages of man, not those with jobs and those without.

From this heady period emerged work such as Richard Hamilton's *Towards a Definitive Statement on the Coming Trends in Menswear and Accessories*, its jokey, jaunty manner relaying the fact that 'sex appeal' has become a major feature in such artwork, paralleling the increasing role of sex in advertising, especially in the USA. Peter Blake has been the most consistently realist of the British Pop painters, from his work of the late 1950s to date. In the mid-1970s he even co-founded a group called the Ruralists which sought to restore

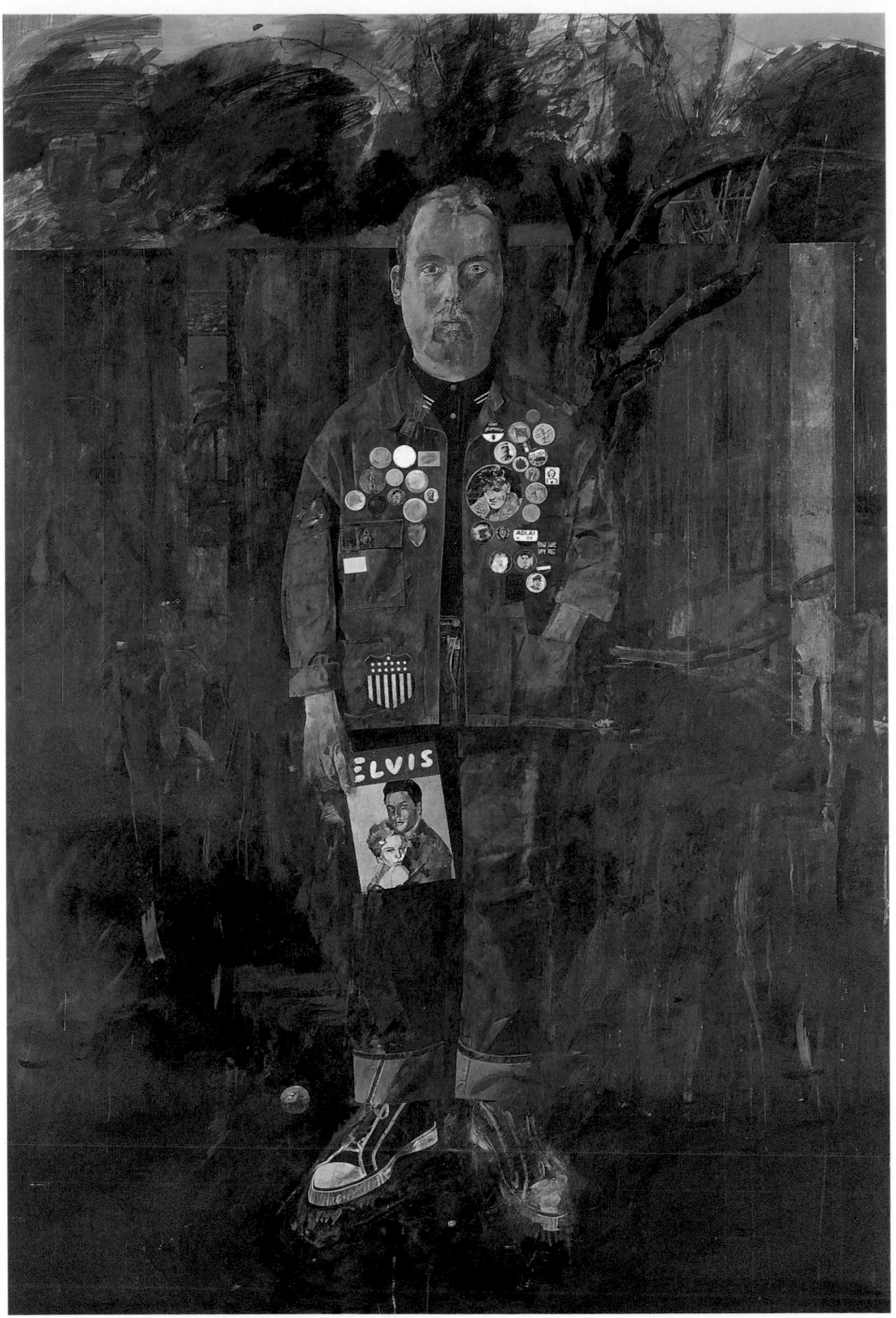

both the spirit and the approach to painting of the Pre-Raphaelites. His *Self-Portrait with Badges* of 1961 blends popular culture (denims and pop music badges) with a style that bows to the Euston Road school. The most prominent badge in this painting refers to Elvis Presley and the work has a comic strip tongue-in-cheek quirkiness as though this pudgy gentleman in denim might transform himself into the superhero singer, who was in fact at the time transforming himself into a pudgy southern gentleman. This poignancy, a certain 'softness', is a special characteristic of Blake's that makes him humanly accessible in a way that American Pop rarely is. His painting methods are manual and homely; the objects he uses are garnered from toyshops, sweetshops and trawls through junkshops that specialise in the relics of childhood.

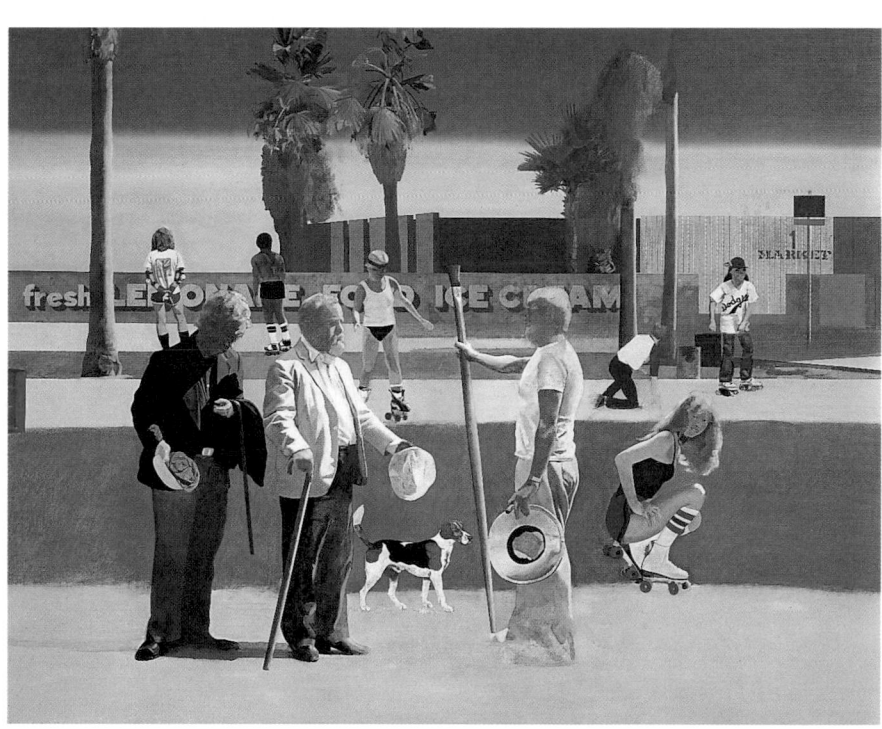

42
Peter Blake

Self-Portrait with Badges 1961

Oil on board
174.3 × 121.9
(68¾ × 48)
Tate Gallery

43
Peter Blake

'The Meeting' or 'Have a Nice Day, Mr Hockney' 1981–3

Oil on canvas
99.2 × 124.4
(39 × 49)
Tate Gallery

Blakes's consciousness of the nineteenth-century roots of his work emerges in his art-historical conundrum, *'The Meeting' or 'Have a Nice Day, Mr Hockney'* of 1981–3. This is a camp reworking, under brilliant Californian sun, of Courbet's 1854 portrayal of his meeting with his patron under the southern French sun. The poses in Blake's picture are parodistically close to the original, with Harry Geldzahler, Hockney's leading patron at the time, adopting the slightly hangdog, welcoming gesture of Bruyas in Courbet's image. It is an affectionate parody, however, in its cataloguing of the attractions of California for both artists: the sun, the lightly clad rollerskaters in the background, the typically Blakeian crouching girl in the foreground, who stares out at the viewer, as if at a camera. Her grin reinforces this impression and perhaps underscores the role of photography in the work of both Blake and Hockney. An easily overlooked surreal touch is the staff the painter is holding: actually a six and a half foot paintbrush.

David Hockney has always resisted being associated with the label Pop Art but his work of the early 1960s does seem inextricably entangled with the phenomenon that was British Pop. His work of that time can however, be called realist only in its subject matter, Hockney's own life and interests as an art student from a northern working-class background discovering himself in London. His style was broad-brushed, graffiti-like, influenced by both Dubuffet and Francis Bacon. But from the mid-1960s, Hockney began to make paintings based on a combination of drawings from life and photographs, either found or, increasingly, taken by himself. Over the next decade he produced a succession of magisterial canvases that must be seen as one of the most significant contributions made anywhere to the continuation of the realist tradition in the late twentieth century.

A Bigger Splash, one of a celebrated group of paintings inspired by California swimming pools, marks the inauguration of this phase of Hockney's career in 1967 and it reached a climax in the late 1960s and early 1970s in his extraordinary series of large double portraits of which *Mr and Mrs Clark and Percy* is probably the best known. The evident realism of these paintings which has brought them such a wide audience is to some extent deceptive. Hockney ruthlessly eliminates superfluous detail and both these

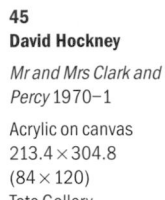

45
David Hockney
Mr and Mrs Clark and Percy 1970–1
Acrylic on canvas
213.4 × 304.8
(84 × 120)
Tate Gallery

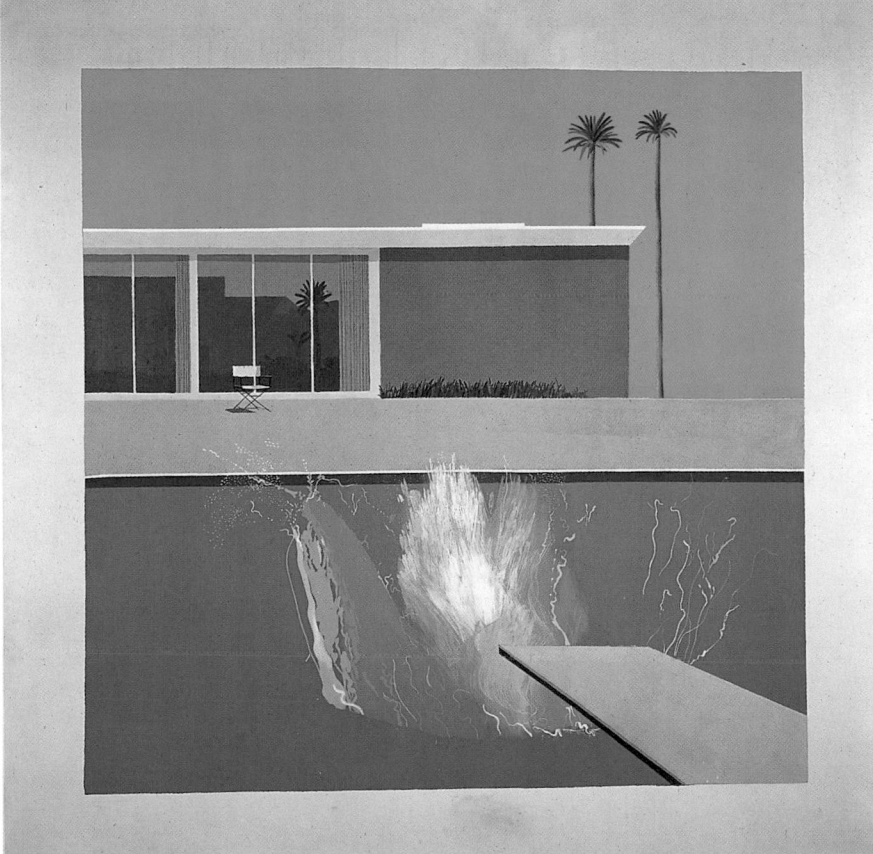

44
David Hockney
A Bigger Splash 1967
Acrylic on canvas
242.6 × 243.8
(95½ × 96)
Tate Gallery

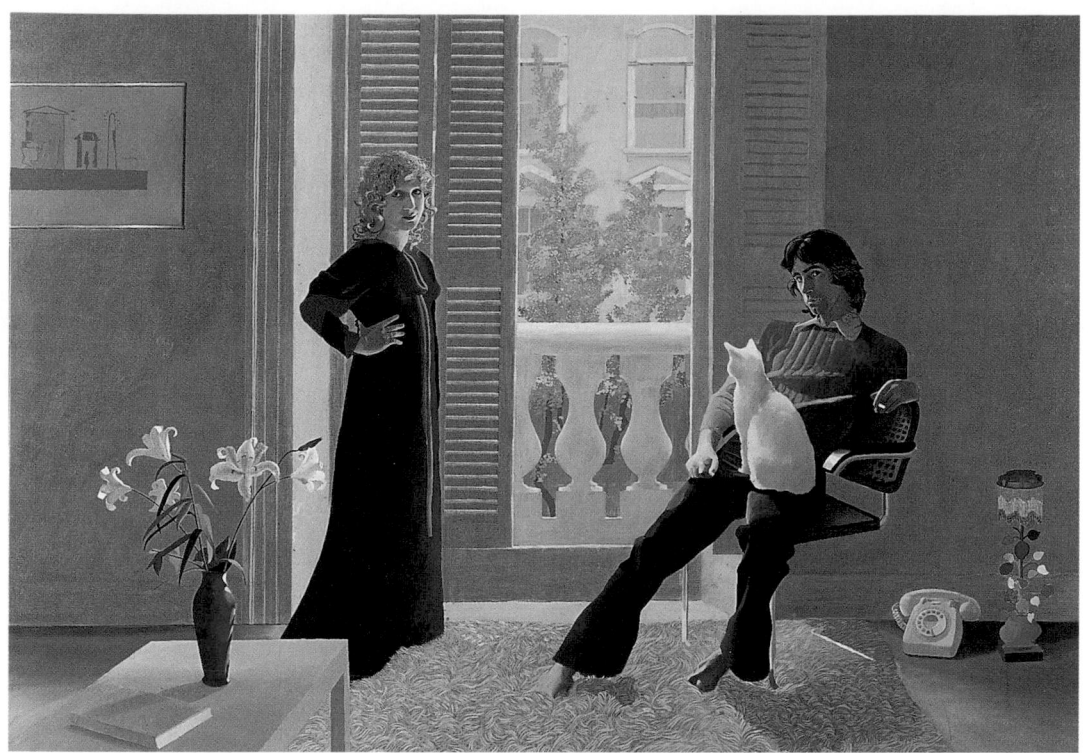

paintings have a rigorous linear geometry underlying their composition. *A Bigger Splash* has a wide white border around the main image, whose function is to destroy the spectator's reading of the image as an illusion. This modernist gesture was not repeated but Hockney's realism always pays knowing tribute to the traditions of modern as well as pre-modern art.

REALIST PAINTING IN BRITAIN SINCE 1945

Whereas Pop Art was seduced by the glossy surfaces of magazine advertising and the novelty of domestic colour photography, other realist artists in Britain during this period rejected the flashy and ephemeral elements that made Pop so irritating to the art establishment. A remarkable survivor from an earlier generation was William Roberts, erstwhile member of the avant-garde Vorticist group, formed in London at the outbreak of the First World War, and since the 1920s, depicter of (generally) lighter moments in urban life. His early abstract style gave way to a rather mechanistic figuration which in the post-war years smoothed its surfaces and became ever more tightly structured and controlled. In *Trooping the Colour* (1958–9) the interplay of colours and lines and the placement of the black and red outcrops of the Horse Guards against the orangey background elicits very much the same response that the event itself might: awe at the precision of the organisation, questions about the real nature of the people in the serried ranks (and looking quite toy-like here) and a sense of the geometry and abstraction latent within the event itself. The portrait of the Queen is sufficiently exact to maintain the sense of reality. It is an astonishing work insofar as it suggests links between Vorticism and Pop Art rarely found elsewhere.

Pure realism continued to surface in the work of Stanley Spencer after the Second World War. In his late self-portrait, done in the year of his death, 1959, a moving sense of mortality pervades the work. The thinness of the paint suggests the urgency of the task but perhaps also reflects a determination, as with many artists at the end of long careers, to pare away anything extraneous and unnecessary. The painting seems to go beyond appearances to reveal the artist's inner life; it has an extraordinary combination of pride and humility.

Many of Lucian Freud's figurative paintings seem to strive for a similar amalgam of seer and modest witness, a combination which gives him a penetrative acuity of vision few twentieth-century artists can rival. This is

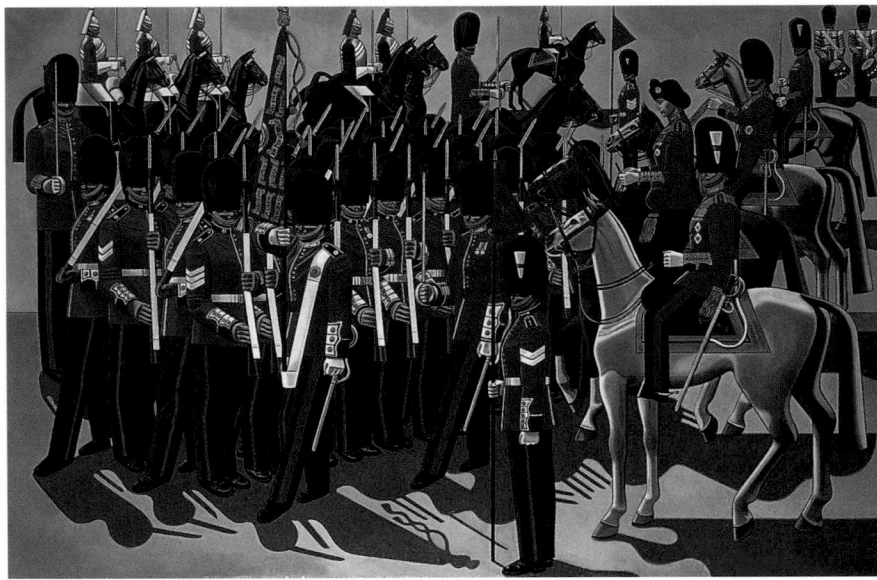

46
William Roberts

Trooping the Colour
1958–9

Oil on canvas
182.9 × 274.3
(72 × 108)
Tate Gallery

47
Stanley Spencer

Self-Portrait 1959

Oil on canvas
50.8 × 40.6
(20 × 16;)
Tate Gallery

combined, however, with an equally powerful quality of detachment. The result is a tension that emerges between the scalpel-like probing of the surface of the bodies presented and a painterliness that leaves out no unbecoming tone, tint or residue, yet never imposes on the figures a meltdown of their humanity as can occur in Francis Bacon's pursuit of 'brutality of fact'. In Freud's portraits of Leigh Bowery in the 1990s, the majestic bulk of the standing figure has a nobility both because of and despite the ravages that the artist perceived and recorded – Bowery died soon after. The spirit of Stanley Spencer's late work infuses that of Freud in recent years, where the realism is manifest in the physical presence of the paint itself rather than as previously through the nature of the poses, for example, *Girl with a White Dog* of 1950–1 where a studio pose endeavours to be natural. Twenty years later, *Naked Portrait*, where the brushes and palette knife replace the redundant hound, has a straightforwardness that is like a blast of fresh air. There is a rawness in the

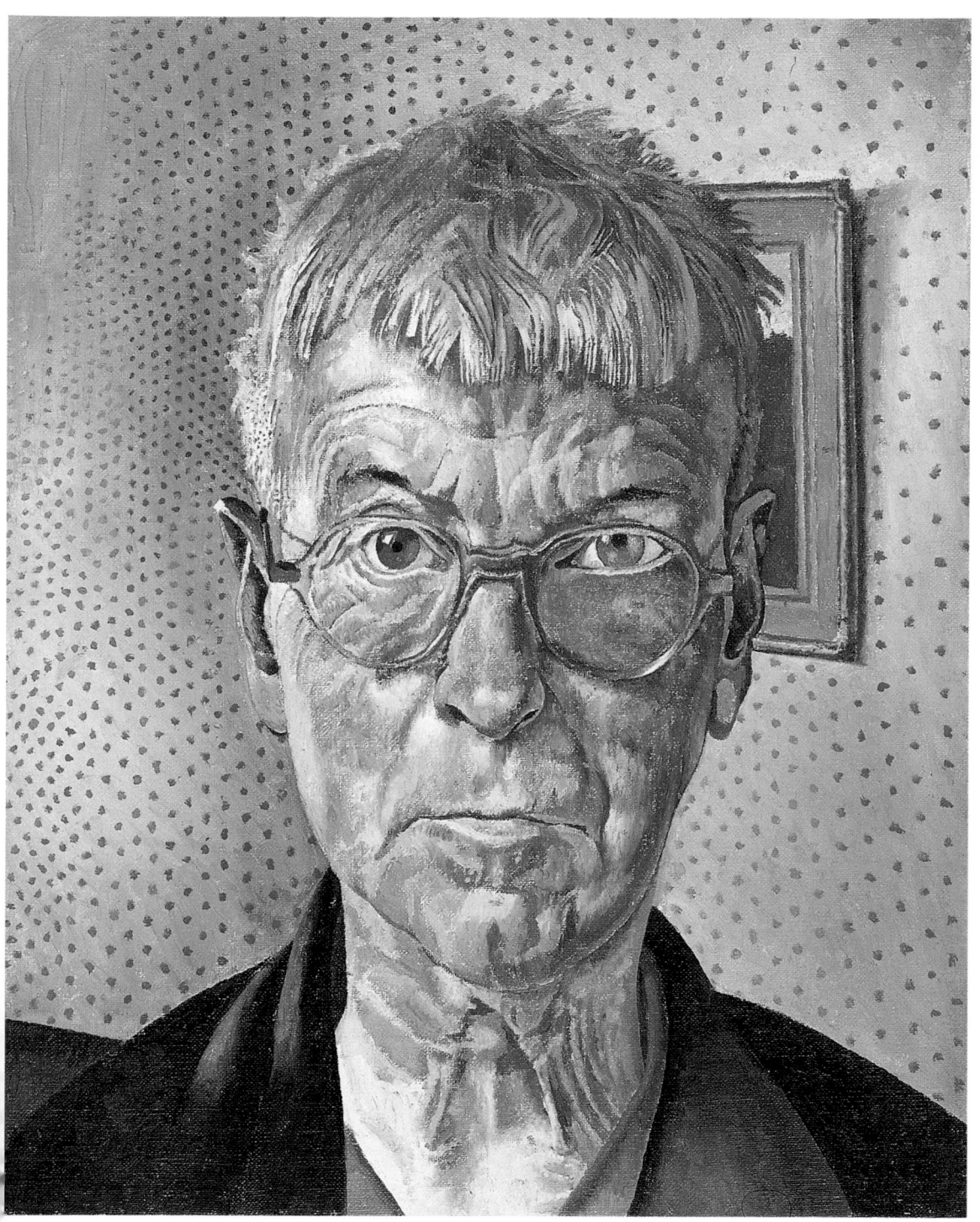

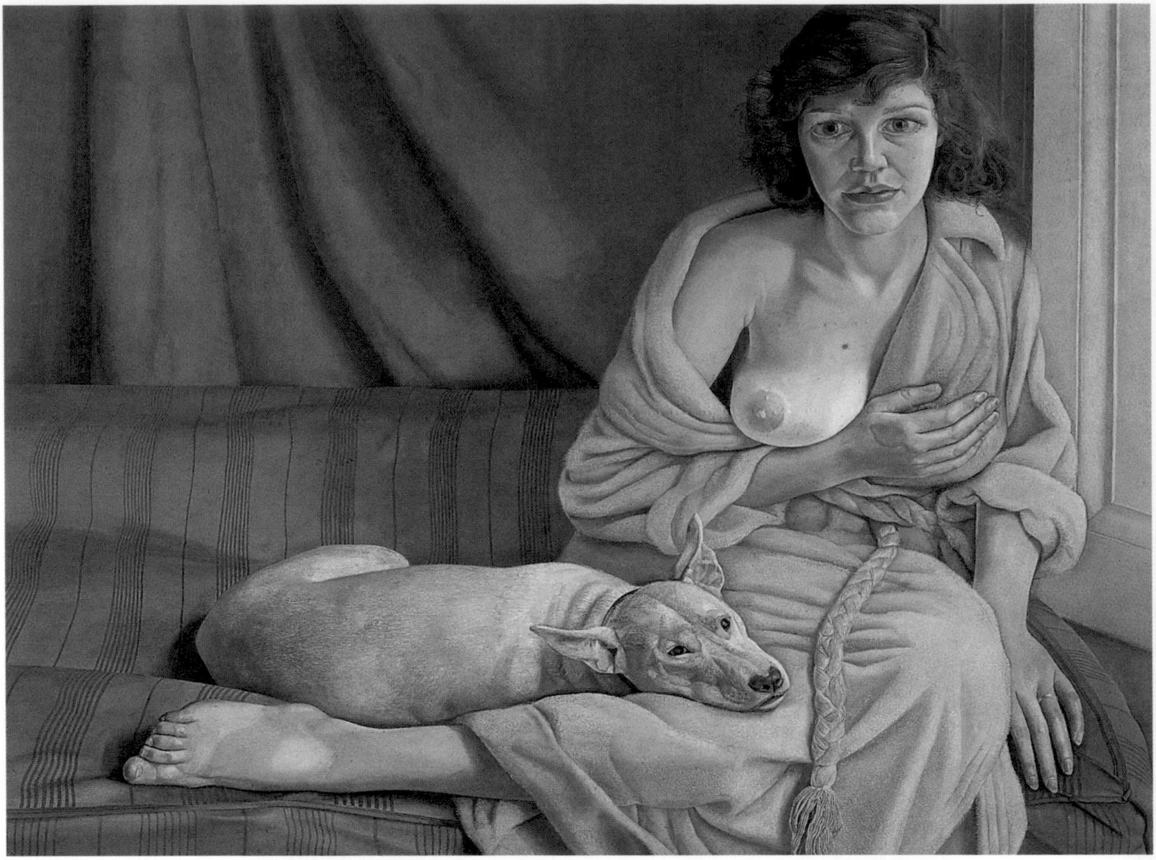

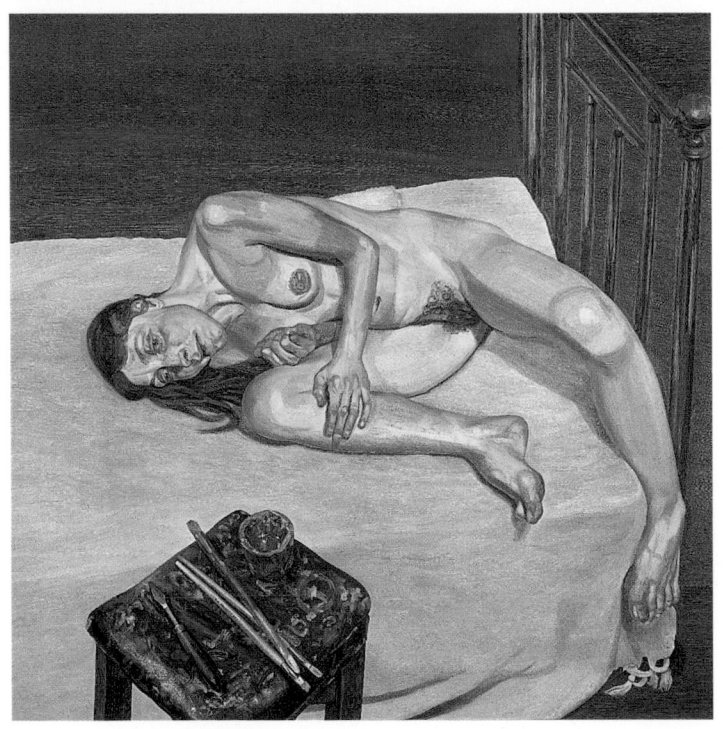

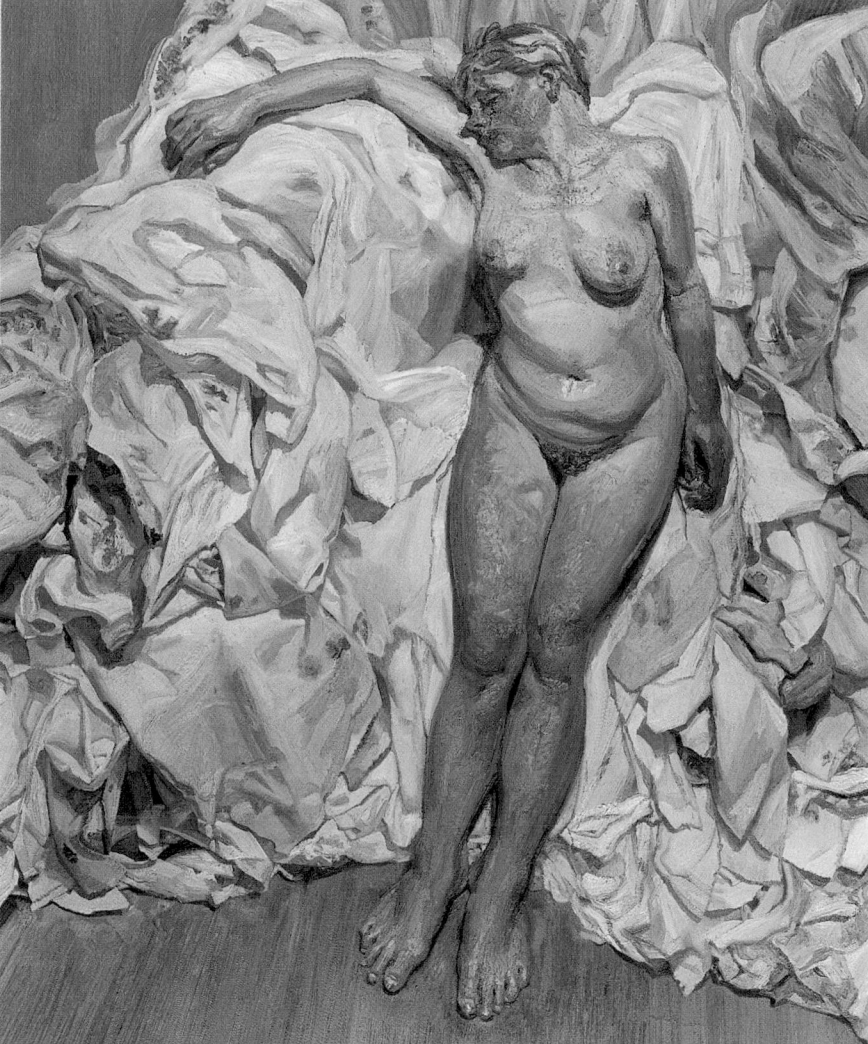

image that derives from the clumsy, explicit nature of the pose, which has a brutalised element to it, as though the brushes and knife have been, or are about to be, weapons. Shakespeare's famous phrase from *King Lear*, 'Thou art nothing but such a bare fork'd animal', comes to mind , although in relation to Freud the line would have to be delivered with a cold impassivity bordering on that of the speaking clock, rather than in the tone of passionate avowal commonly given to it.

The monolithic quality of Lucian Freud's recent work – uncompromising as an iceberg – is perhaps its most striking and impressive feature. *Standing by the Rags* of 1988–9 has a warmer tone than in his earlier work to the sagging flesh of the standing woman whose right arm drapes painfully over the piled white cloths, but such mellowing doesn't go very far. The tension of her feet gripping the floorboards in this awkward pose is tangible but, as so often in Freud's work, no eye contact is established and so what the model might be feeling, if she is feeling anything (apart from pins and needles), remains unspecified.

5

AMERICAN POP ART AND REALIST PAINTING SINCE 1955

On the whole, Pop Art in America was a more impersonal phenomenon
than the British version. It tended to present reality in such a way that the
object as depicted in the work of art retained an exceptionally close
relationship to the original, as though a very brightly coloured shadow
had been invented.

The reality these artists portrayed was presented to them by the
expanding economy of the United States, its rising standard of living and
super-abundance (for the middle class) of food, goods, entertainment and
time for leisure. In contrast to the academic artists of the time or the artists of
the modernist 'High Art' avant-garde represented by Abstract Expressionism,
the youngsters who followed the Pop route had been trained in commercial
art schools (as Andy Warhol was in Pittsburgh for example). They were also
'realistic' enough to see painting as, first and foremost, a way of earning a
living, and only after that as a form of philosophy. This set them apart
from Rothko, Still, Motherwell, Newman and the coterie around the
influential modernist critics Greenberg and Rosenberg, who seem to have
been surprised, then shocked, then outraged that this new figurative art had
jumped back through the window after the door had been shut on it. By the
end of the 1950s, galleries like Leo Castelli were interested in the new matter-
of-fact style, but critical acclaim was often withheld. 'Welcome figuration,
say goodbye to art', propounded the Abstract Expressionist pundits.

The weapons the American Pop artists could use were their links to the
mass media, both as source material and means of publicity, the accessibility

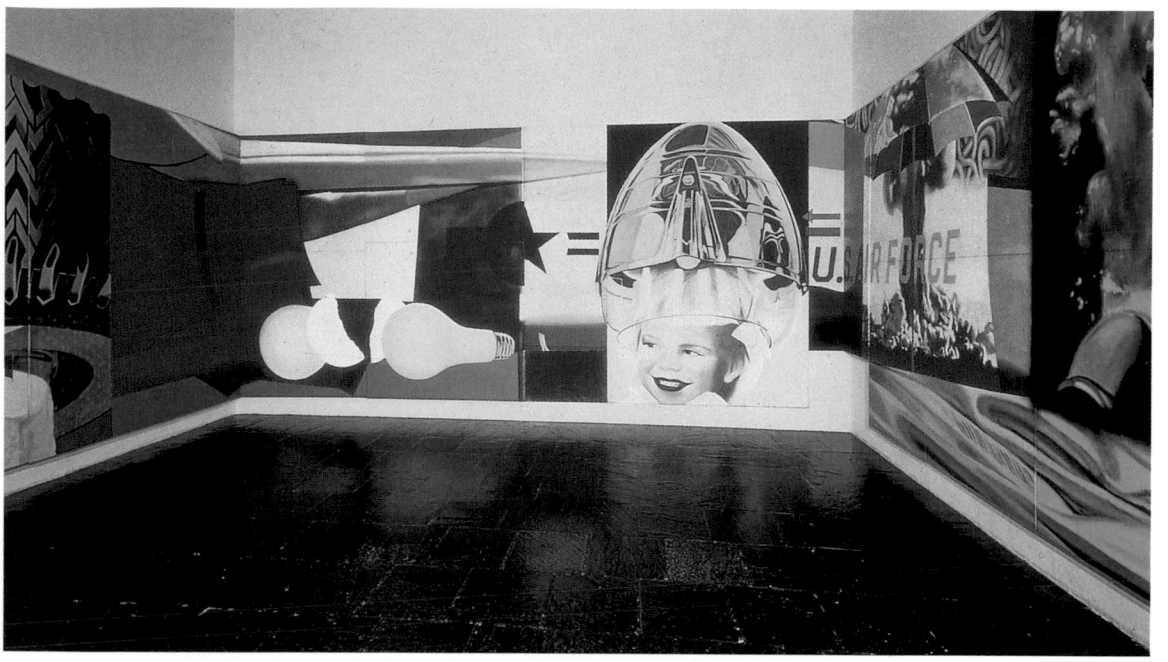

of the imagery they used and the sense of fun their response to the everyday world around them engendered, as opposed to the (often unwittingly) po-faced attitude of the abstractionist 'thinkers'. Television was an undoubted ally, as had been recognised in Britain too. As Gore Vidal has noted, things are rarely as bad as they might be on television, nor are they as good: it levels everything out. Together with Marshall McLuhan's famous dictum of 1964, 'the medium is the message', this fits in with Pop's ethos very well. There is nothing transcendent about Pop, in the way that, say, Mark Rothko intended his work to be. It disclaims individuality and, as did so many of Andy Warhol's less-is-more statements, this fitted in with the easy-come, easy-go state of mind advocated by Pop and exemplified in Warhol's statement 'In the future everyone will be famous for fifteen minutes'. And when Warhol said that art was ' just a guy's name', he added that he was as interested in the art of business as he was in the business of art.

Undoubtedly much of this casualness was a pose designed by the Pop artists to annoy the modernist art critics who had such extraordinary influence in the contemporaneous New York art world. They succeeded brilliantly. Tom Wesselmann, James Rosenquist and Warhol himself had all been commercial artists and this enabled them to treat 'fine' art with a certain insouciance. Rosenquist had thought his painting of billboards enjoyable enough to warrant translation into 'fine' art form. In this way he took his commercial accomplishments, such as being able to control illusionism sufficiently well that spaghetti painted from three feet away and on a giant

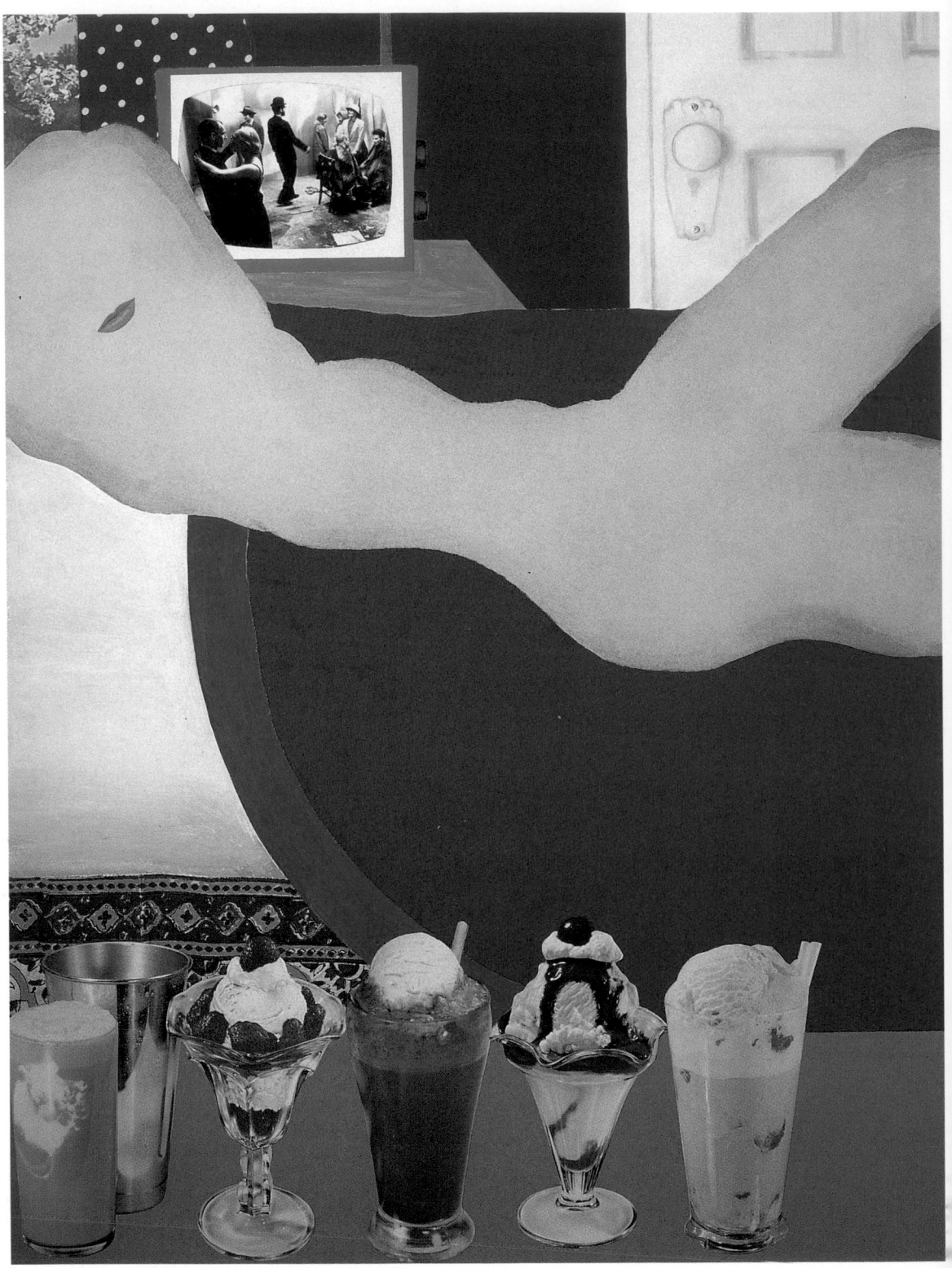

scale would look in focus and in scale when seen from three hundred feet, into the art gallery world.

The salient feature of James Rosenquist's work was his awareness of social stress and strain in the American Dream after the assassination of President Kennedy. What is remarkable is that the flippancy and deliberate short-termism of Pop could, in Rosenquist's hands, transform itself into an icon of the age, a summation of its forces, hopes and fears. This was his *F-111* of 1965. Grandiose though it might be with its four panels, and the eponymous aircraft portrayed as larger than life-size, the work is an astonishing *tour de force*, produced at a time when Pop's enemies were trying to consign Pop Art to the art-historical dustbin. It has a sense of completeness, undisrupted by extraneous elements. The vivid colours cohabit with the echoing shapes: the umbrella and the nuclear explosion, the hairdrier cone over the girl's head, which echoes the nose cone of the aircraft. The result is Pop turned stream-of-consciousness. Rosenquist himself said he wanted to 'accumulate experience' as though the painting might discharge to the viewer a consummate sense of the mid-1960s.

Whereas Rosenquist's exuberant works grew in scale and vivid coloration through the 1960s, this was not the case with Tom Wesselmann, who maintained much closer links with the advertising images he so often plundered and then transmuted in his work. Found objects are sometimes inserted into his paintings, like *trompe l'œil* intrusions from the outside world. They perform the same function as collage did in Picasso's Cubist work of the 'synthetic' period, but Wesselmann's objects are new and shiny, standing for the consumer society. His ironic referencing of tradition is evident in the title *Still Life* given to many works. *Still Life no.12*, for example, has a coke bottle in shallow relief set among illustrations of food from glossy magazines and, like a clue to the source of much Pop imagery, a cut-out of a camera. Names and labels are important to Wesselmann, as to Warhol, but whereas the deliberately clumsy screen-printing of Warhol blunts the impact of the labelling, Wesselmann often gives it a sharp-focused prominence that brings a whole new meaning to 'product placement'. By contrast, the increasingly vague, if pneumatic, forms of his *Great American Nudes* lose all but salient distinguishing features: *Great American Nude no.27*, for example, is reduced to a scrupulously detailed set of lipsticked lips. Otherwise, she is a parody of a Matisse cut-out.

Andy Warhol is one stage away from this approach to reality, drawing attention to the means of making the signs, rather than skilfully disguising them as Wesselmann and Rosenquist tended to do. The crucial phase of Warhol's own run-in with 'reality' characteristically began with money. He attempted to display real dollar bills on a gallery wall but was informed that this was a federal offence, so he produced some clumsily screen-printed versions instead. In fact, the message, that art equals money in the New York gallery world – doesn't seem to have been impaired by this infringement. The world of consumerism, and above all celebrity, seemed to offer Warhol a parallel 'reality' far more glamorous than the one he was lumbered with as the child of Ruthenian emigrants to the States. His whole life turned into the

52
Tom Wesselmann
The Great American Nude no.27 1962
Enamel, casein and collage
121.9 × 91.4 (48 × 36)
The Mayor Gallery, London

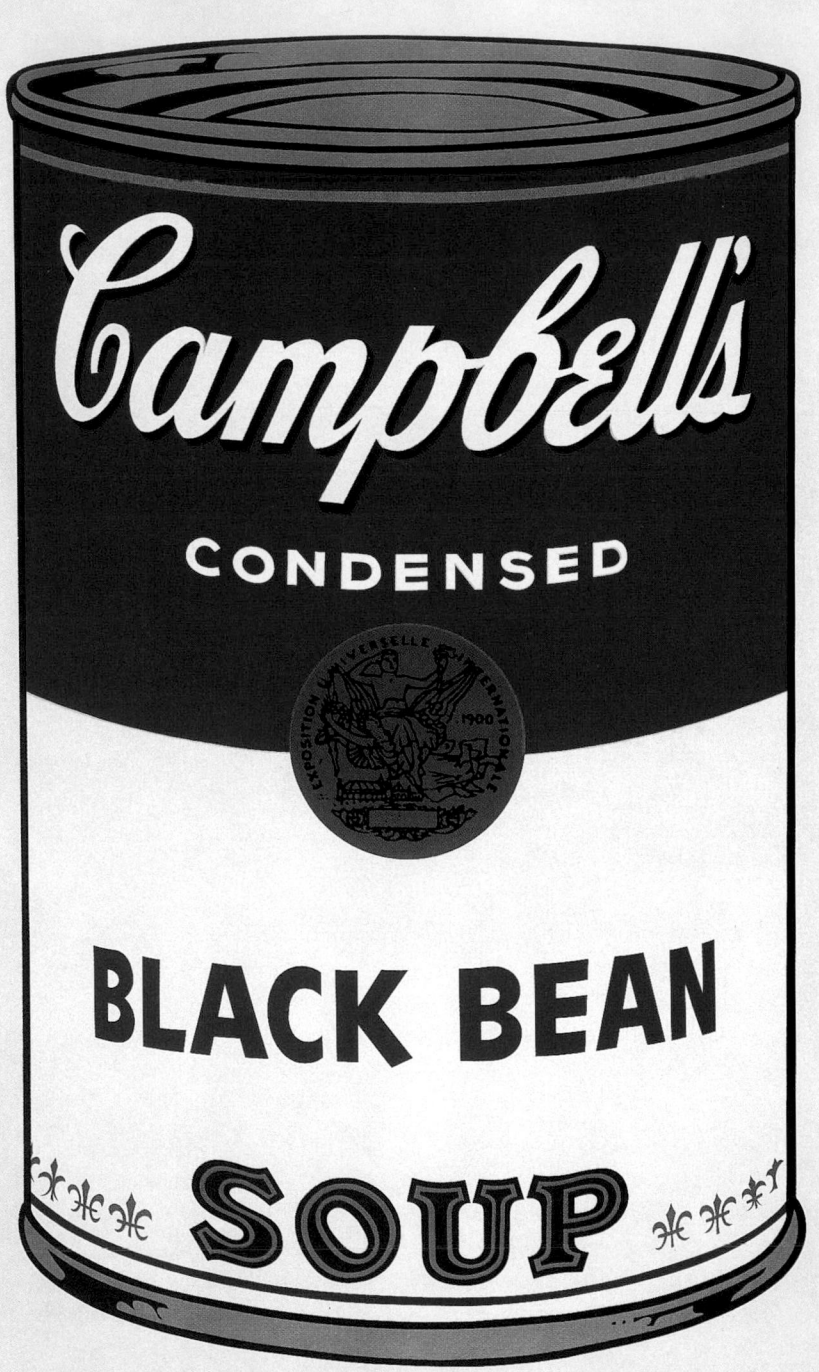

53
Andy Warhol
Black Bean (from Soup Can Series I) 1968
Screenprint on paper
88.9 × 58.7
(35 × 23)
Tate Gallery

54
Andy Warhol
Marilyn Diptych 1962
Acrylic on canvas
205.4 × 144.8
(81 × 57)
Tate Gallery

odyssey of an outsider trying to become an insider. In the end, thanks to American society's exuberant mobility, he succeeded beyond his dreams and seemed to become more of an insider than most. By combining his art and his life, he created – at least while the magic held in his lifetime – the sense that the peculiar reality he proposed would indeed supplant the everyday one. A few shrewd psychological tenets helped him (though it was nothing as cogent as a 'philosophy'), mainly concerned with the nature of boredom thresholds and the diminishing returns achieved by the images of horror portrayed in the press and on television. The *Disaster* series of paintings of car accidents is a case in point, later followed by the *Riots* and, most famously, the *Electric Chairs*, in which a grainy photograph of the machine is awash with a single

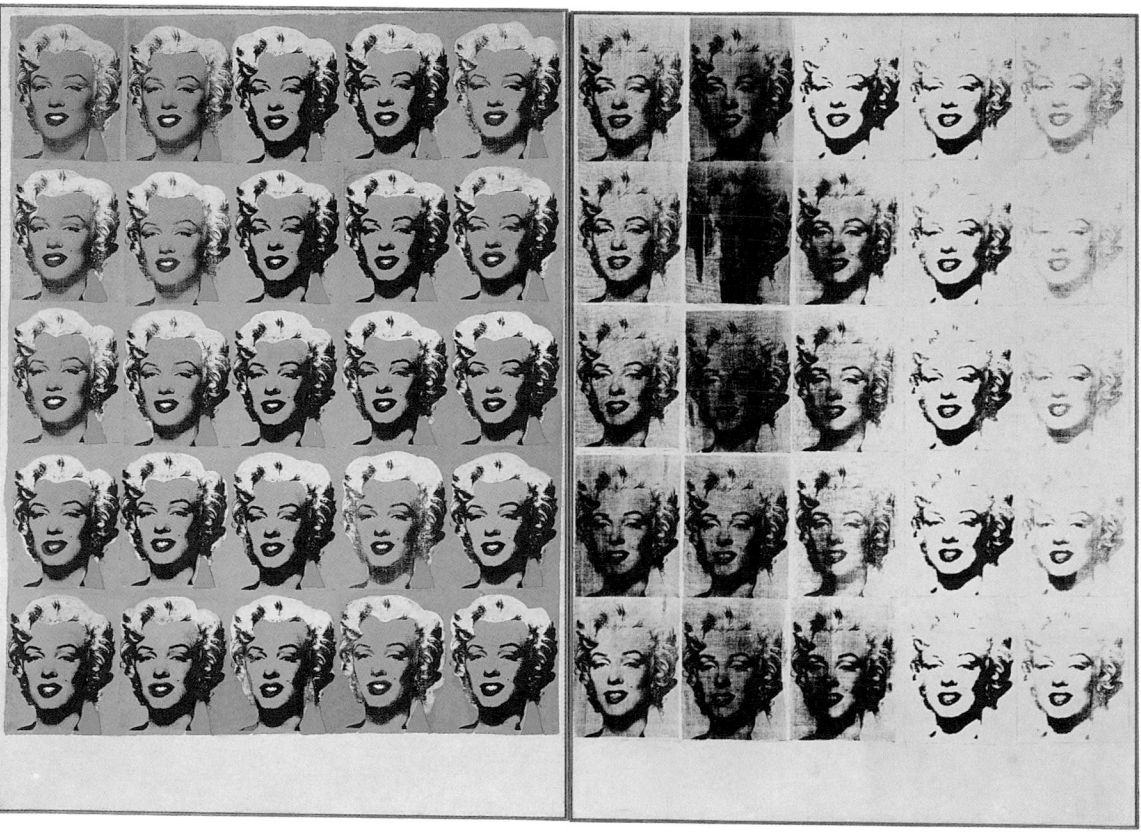

colour, different in each painting in the series. Warhol imagined that people would choose the colour that would 'go with the drapes'. One could also construct a critique of reality through the repetition undergone in Warhol's paintings of his chosen icons, whether soup cans or Marilyn Monroes. He suggests their equivalence as manufactured objects – in the case of Monroe a product of the Hollywood star machine. Monroe's tragedy was that, unlike the soup, she knew she was being manufactured, but there was no escape. Warhol's fascination with this alternative reality is manifest in his remark, 'I love Hollywood … Everybody's plastic … I want to be plastic'. He also wanted to be a machine – they are manufactured too. The converse of this was that Warhol was obsessed by fame, and especially people who were famous for just being famous. When Warhol moved his peculiarly literal approach to reality beyond painting into film and literature, problems arose. A home movie of 'a whole day in Edie's life' (she was an assistant at the Factory, his studio, where he manufactured his works) or an eight hour sequence focusing on the top of the Empire State Building (*Empire*, 1964), are so stultifyingly dull that they have become cult movies, which is polite avant-garde-speak for the fact that no-one wants to see them. His aim was, indeed, to avoid being 'artistic' or to 'direct' the movies in any way: 'I never liked the idea of picking out certain scenes ... and putting them together, because it ends up being different from what really happened – it's just not like life, it seems so corny'. But in fact his movies are not like life, nor are his paintings, created though they are by screen printing from photo-mechanically made screens using photographic images. Perhaps the painted or silk-screened boxes of Brillo pads and Kelloggs corn flakes, three dimensional objects, come closest to a transcription of reality in Warhol's work. But they aren't 'real' either as Warhol himself knew: 'Everything is sort of artificial. I don't know where the artificial stops and the real starts'.

6

SUPERREALISM, PHOTOREALISM AND REALISM IN THE 1980s

What is known as Superrealism or Photorealism is a specifically American and generally urban phenomenon that was the result of a collision between Pop Art's cult of the iconic object – modern, manufactured and, where possible, new and shiny – and photography's equable response to those objects, under a contrived and static light. This sleek, sometimes slick art was also termed New Realism at the time, to differentiate it from the grainy, socially inclined realism of the 1930s (see p.46). By the late 1960s, artists like Richard Estes, Chuck Close, Audrey Flack, Frank Gertsch (who specialised in portraiture) and Charles Bell (who concentrated on still lifes) were making an impact in the New York shows with their still lifes, and irritating the old guard of Abstract Expressionism very greatly. Social commitment was scarcely present in their work; indeed, emotion was expunged, abandoned in favour of a technical virtuosity and dispassion before the object that gives the works a curious 'teflon factor': the eye slips off them, leaving the spectator to clutch at the lifebelt of admiration for technique.

The alternative label of Photorealism is perhaps a more accurate title for a style heavily dependent on new techniques in magazine photography which maximised the sheen and allure demanded by the advertising industry. New techniques, ironically, gave advertisers a mechanical way of achieving on their hoardings what in the early sixties they had employed future Pop artists like Wesselmann and Rosenquist to produce; namely, total identification with the 'product', an illusionism that would beguile consumers into thinking it was already part of 'their' world.

A super-smooth quality dominates the work of the artists named above, giving to the urban landscapes and to the uncanny immobility of the chromed, streamlined vehicles they depict, be they motor-homes or Harley Davidson motorcycles, an often chilly effect. These icons of the later twentieth century, signifying escape and leisure, are here without a price tag, but are betrayed by the stillness of their surroundings. No photorealist work gives the impression of a breeze blowing, which may be why Richard Estes's New York streets are litter-free and anything but 'mean', and not, as he modestly puts it, because 'I can't really get it to look right. It's really a technical deficiency on my part. I really try to make things look dirty, but it's interesting

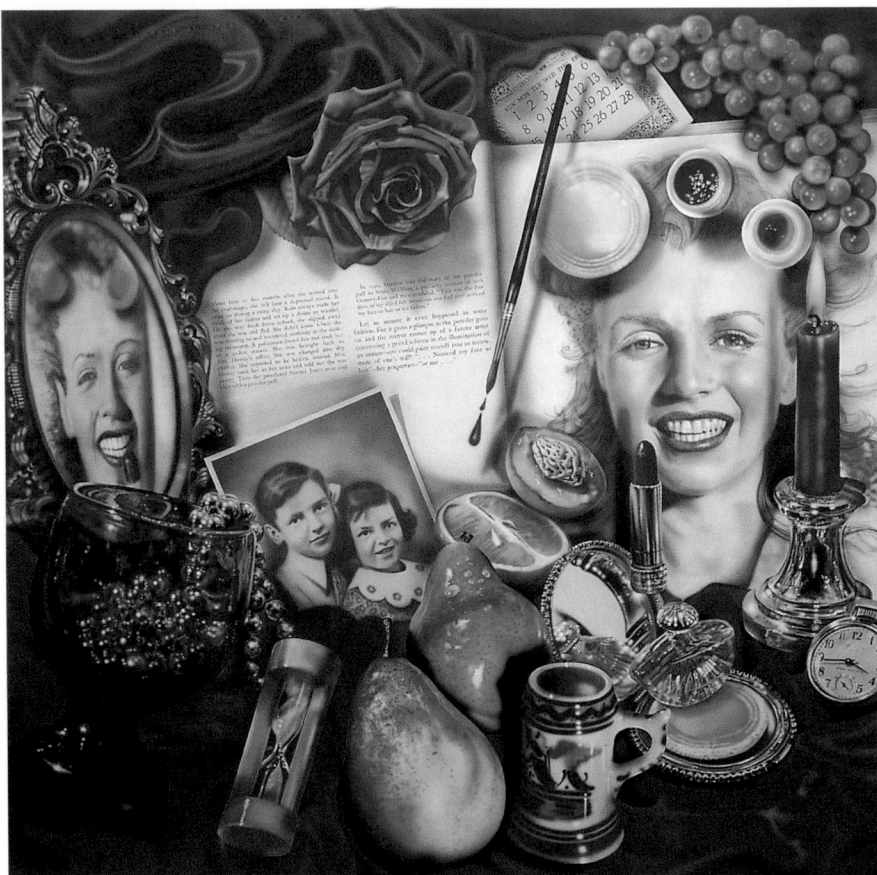

55
Audrey Flack

Marilyn 1977

Oil over acrylic on canvas
243.8 × 243.8
(96 × 96)
Collection of the University of Arizona Museum of Art

56
Richard Estes

Movies 1981

Screenprint
50.2 x 69.9
(19¾ x 27½)
Parasol Press

because even in a photograph it doesn't look as dirty as it really is'. But perhaps the real significance of this fascinating remark is that it reveals the extent to which even Photorealism is a long way from reality itself.

Does the fact that it has no 'message' — not even one as relatively mindless as that of Pop Art, mean that Photorealism enshrines mediocrity, as some critics maintain, despite — or because of — its popularity with the public? It lacks the 'fun' element of Pop Art. There is none of the 'sexiness' otherwise endemic in this period. This is perhaps its most remarkable feature. This blank neutrality makes it seem more attuned to the 1990s than the 1960s, except that its proponents lack the ironising distance from the subject itself, as well as the challenging conceptual aspect that has emerged in recent 'realism' such as that of the British artist Mark Wallinger. Estes's *Welcome to 42nd Street Victory Theater* in the Detroit Institute of Art is an example: instead of glamour there is glare – which kills off any theatricality. Estes has said: 'I've always considered light to be the real subject of painting' and speaks of giving the 'illusion of light'. This probably accounts for the slipperiness of the objects in his paintings, particularly so in his fascination with mirrored, reflective surfaces such as the one-way glass modishly employed in modern office structures; 'insiders' can see those outside, but not the reverse. As the spectators' eye bounces off the preternaturally gleaming surfaces they are left feeling more like outsiders than ever.

The Photorealists felt that the art establishment side-stepped them. Estes complained: 'The battle for Realist art was not won; it was not even seriously fought'. On the other hand he considered that this allowed the artists concerned 'more of a chance to be themselves'. They believed in the recording of order and form in the exterior world rather than recording any

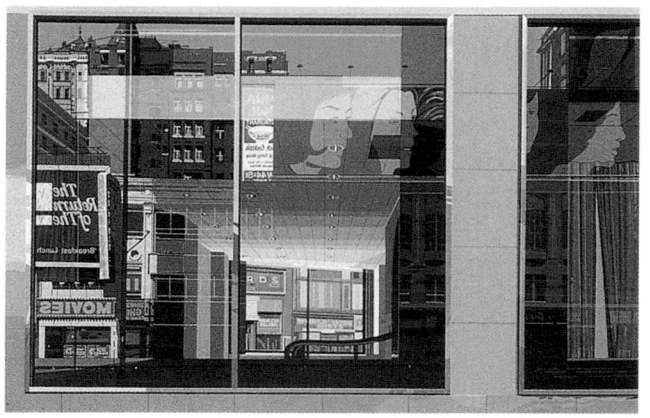

expression of emotion towards that world. Their aim in this was to create 'a sense of completeness that life itself doesn't have. Order. You take the elements of reality, but you eliminate the chaos'. Yet the establishment of such 'order' may be a dubious, even deadening thing. This detachment would seem to be taken even further in Estes's declaration that: 'I don't enjoy looking at the things I paint, so why should you enjoy it . . . I think I would tear down most of the places I paint'. This is very different from the embattled viewpoint of Neue Sachlichkeit artists such as Otto Dix and Georg Grosz in Weimar Germany.

Something needs to be said about the relationship of Photorealist painting and photography. In photography, the placing of lines and the spaces they enclose are 'givens', instantaneously captured in the photograph. The artist, on the other hand, maintains a choice. Photography is ultimately out of the practitioner's control; Photorealist painting never is. Estes comments darkly: 'unfortunately, it has been too easy for anybody to take a photograph, trace it and make a lousy painting'. Photorealism is perhaps the one realist style that unashamedly admits its direct worship of the veristic old masters, and Vermeer in particular, in praise of whom only Dalí was more hyperbolic. It is also more open in admitting its dependence on the camera, an essential tool even though its results had to be somehow transcended. This openness contrasts with the attitude of, for example, the precisionist painter Charles Sheeler in the 1930s, who denied using photography to structure his painting, even though he had a separate career as a photographer.

57
Robert Longo
National Trust 1981

Cast aluminium,
charcoal and graphite
160 × 594.3
(63 × 234)
Walker Art Center,
Minneapolis

AMERICAN AND BRITISH REALISM POST-POP

In their attitudes to authority and received ideas about history, the German artists discussed in chapter 3 have affinities with two American artists of the 1980s, Robert Longo and Eric Fischl. Longo, in particular, breaks out of conventional strictures of realism while at the same time doing scrupulously modelled and measured work that seems to depend on stills from grainy black-and-white movies. The sprawled figures in *National Trust* (1981) look as if they have been gunned down, linked by the anonymous authority of the aluminium stylised office block that may have been the origin of this denouement.

58
Eric Fischl
Bad Boy 1981

Oil on canvas
167.6 × 243.8
(66 × 96)
Mary Boone Gallery,
New York

This work is concerned with a loss of individual identity that results from corporate culture ruling peoples' lives from a distance. This 'global' influence is also the mainspring of Fischl's tense examinations of responsibility, expressed in a legible, but questioning visual language. Sexuality is the arena he often chooses, as in *Sleepwalker* (1979), where a naked boy in a private garden swimming pool is masturbating, seen by Fischl as a gesture of self-awareness, much as the adolescents in Frank Wedekind's play *Spring Awakening* experienced it eighty years before. Sometimes the scene is more problematic, as in *Bad Boy*. Again the viewer is made voyeur and the scene is set as a play, where a youth confronts a naked woman lying provocatively on a bed, while, shielding it with his body, he is stealing – or at any rate, taking – money from a purse. The filtered rays of light through the drawn blinds make interpretation much harder but adds to the sultry intimacy of the scene; a bowl of fruit and lush bananas nestling

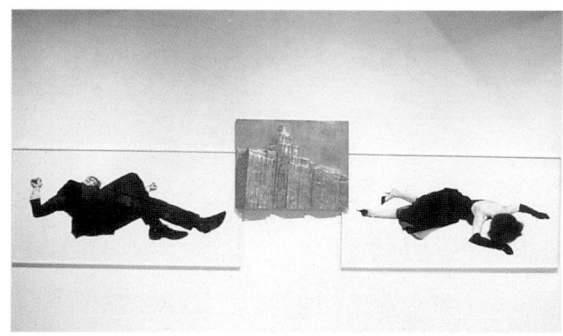

up to the boy irradiate colour but have all the connotations of the forbidden.

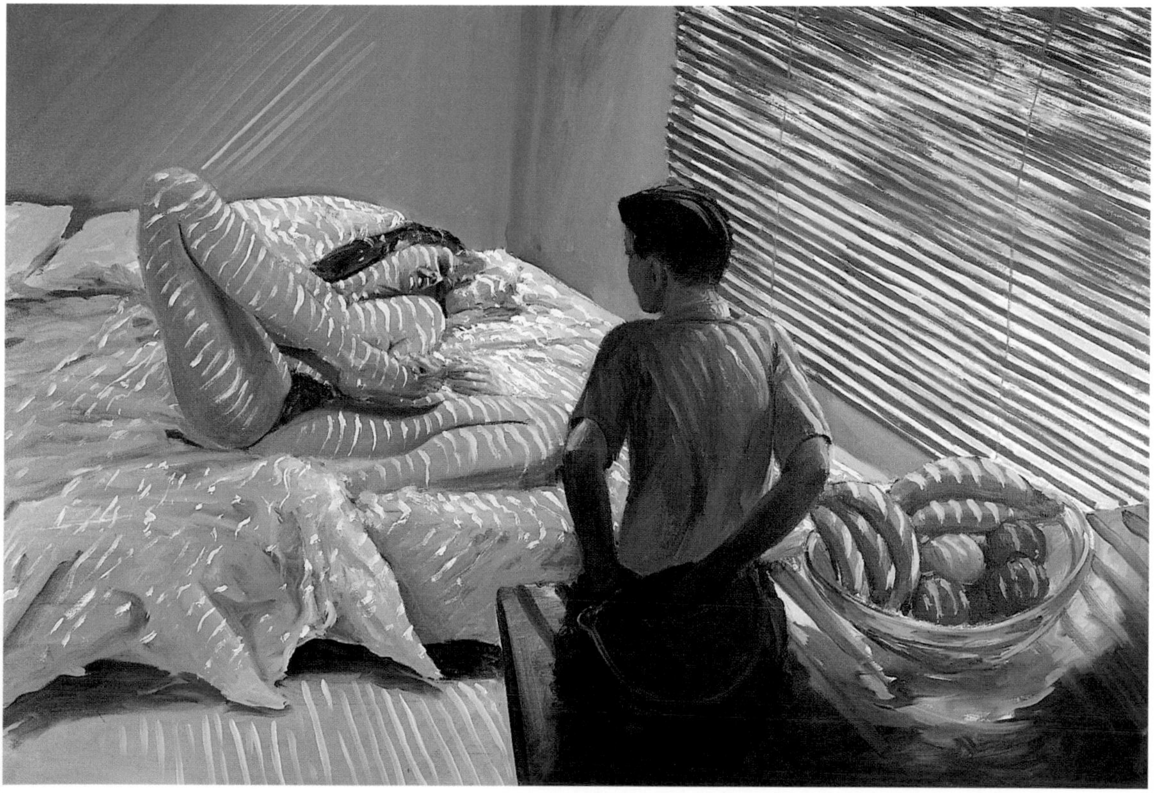

In Britain in the 1980s, the figurative current was flowing quite strongly, especially from Scotland. John Keane is one of the most painterly of the new generation of figurative artists and his response to the Gulf War, for which he was the British official war artist, was trenchant and expansive by turns, making use of close connections between social comment and realism, as in his painting of the model of Mickey Mouse in downtown Kuwait City. Subsequently, Peter Howson recorded his experiences in the more muddled world of the Bosnian battlegrounds in 1993–4. His pastels are dispassionate likenesses of, for example, refugees or soldiers on the roads, while the oil paintings derived from them amplify the recollected emotion and make emblems from the casualties, as in *Dog*, depicting a hung animal, huge in the foreground like an icon, rigor mortis in stiffened paint. This scene is transformed through gesticulatory use of paint, and the sheer size and scale of the design. But the hanging was witnessed and the sources from which Howson's images spring are certainly real.

The Saatchi Gallery display *Young British Artists III* in 1994 contained paintings that suggested a Lucian Freud observed through convex mirrors:

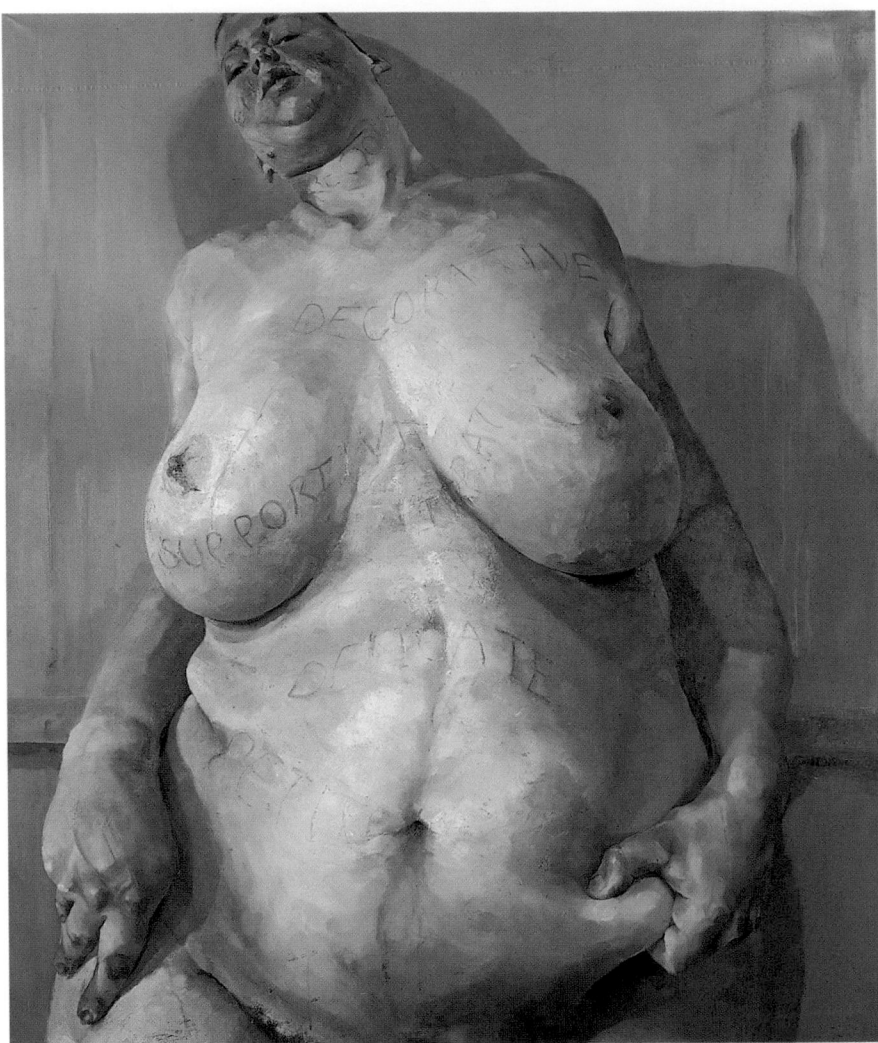

59
Jenny Saville
Branded 1992
Oil on canvas
213.4 × 182.9
(84 × 72)
Saatchi Collection,
London

carefully contrived distortions ballooned parts of the torsos. Another device used by Jenny Saville is to inscribe words onto the flesh of the sitter with the pointed handle of the brush, creating an effect more like graffitti than a tattoo. This technique seems strangely mutilatory and suggests that mere painting of the bodily surface no longer suffices (as it does for Freud). This may be more a sign of a young artist's frustrations with the expressive limits of painting than an advance into new regions of realism.

Conclusion

As this brief, by no means conclusive survey suggests, Realism, in the painterly tradition stemming from nineteenth-century British and French art, has all too often been seen as the Cinderella of twentieth-century art, overawed by the glamour of the avant-garde, that concept which gained such power about the year 1910 and held sway until post-modernism's pluralism suggested there might be other, more balanced arrangements of artistic forces.

The description of the work of the Neue Sachlichkeit sub-group, the Magical Realists, as 'poor man's Surrealism' (see p.32) is a case in point, where comparison with an avant-garde proved detrimental. All too often, realism has been its own worst enemy, hoist by its own petard during the ideological decades from the 1920s to the 1950s in particular, as it was co-opted by totalitarian regimes of Left and Right. And yet in America during the Cold War the CIA supported Abstract Expressionism as the 'art of freedom' and the American way, against Soviet Socialist Realism, but because of Abstract Expressionism's claim to intrinsic lofty spiritual and aesthetic ideals it has never been held to blame for such politicking.

The case of Diego Rivera (see p.49) illuminates the would-be realist's problems, faced with what W.B. Yeats, as exasperated theatre director, once termed the 'pragmatical pig of a world'. Yet for all the accusations of selling out or fellow-travelling that were levelled at naïve or wilful painters in the service of various regimes, there were also those who 'told the Truth to Power', including Rivera himself. The darkly brooding presences of Anselm Kiefer's mythopoeic reconstructions of German history in the series of paintings titled *Germania*, and Gerhard Richter's elision of news photographs and oil painting call into question ways of seeing and how we, as viewers, respond to previously received information in a new guise.

At its best then, realist art is deeply psychological, probing and penetrating the surface of life. The facets which are revealed are as varied as the outlooks of the artists themselves, but only carry conviction when based on the artist's own experience rather than some party line. This is why the ideological art of the totalitarian regimes strikes such a false note, however scrupulous it is to surface appearances. Photorealism suffers from much the same problem; caught up by the sheer thrill of exercising skills of representation, artists like Flack and Estes seem essentially uninterested in any personal presence in their work. It could be done by machines. Perhaps Andy Warhol should have tried being a photorealist for more than fifteen minutes.

This element of the personal in the realist vision subverts the tendency of art historians to present, often for the sake of convenience, realism's practitioners as (admittedly loose-limbed and shambling) groups of artists: rather, on closer inspection, they are seen to be an atomised set of loners, coralled into groups by the collectivising trends of much of this century. Perhaps it can be argued that the more vivid the realist language of the painter, the more individual and the more isolated he or she will appear.

The revival of figurative imagery and of painting itself in the 1980s paralleled the development of a 'cutting edge' agitprop art, whose creators believed that art could influence the external world (after the loss of nerve which followed the Vietnam War). The social person began to count for something again – and the way the individual is manipulated in the West by the forces of government and capital was cannily analysed and exposed in works using photographic, collage and mass-media techniques by Victor Burgin, Barbara Kruger and Jenny Holzer, to name but three. Holzer's sloganeering style and content (for example, 'Protect Me From What I Want' and 'Abuse of Power Comes as No Surprise') puts into words the traumas alluded to and borne witness to by an image like Howson's hung dog (see p.74). Faced with such developments, the notion of 'avant-garde' or 'non-progressive' as labels to be slung round the necks of artists seems at best irrelevant, at worst malign.

Realism may well emerge as a key choice among attitudes and stances available to artists at the start of the new millennium thanks to the previously mentioned pluralism encouraged by the rise of the post-modern viewpoint; one suspects realism flourishes most when the outlook is one of carefully balanced scepticism and activism, in other words, when there's the ability to laugh at something and take it seriously at the same time, however sardonic that laughter.

SELECT BIBLIOGRAPHY

Adam, Peter, *The Arts of the Third Reich*, London 1992.

Cardinal, Robert, *The Landscape Vision of Paul Nash*, London 1989.

Clark, Tim, *The Image of the People*, London 1973.

Clark, Tim, *The Absolute Bourgeois*, London 1973.

Cork, Richard, *A Bitter Truth: Avant-garde Art and the Great War*, London 1994.

Fer, Briony, Batchelor, David and Wood, Paul, *Realism, Rationalism, Surrealism: Art Between the Wars*, New Haven 1993.

Fineberg, Jonathan, *Strategies of Being: Art since 1940*, London 1995.

Harrison, Charles, *Modernism in English Art 1900–1939*, London 1993.

Heller, Robert, *Peter Howson*, Edinburgh 1993.

Kent, Sarah, *Shark-Infested Waters*, London 1995.

Kranzfelder, Ivo, *Edward Hopper*, Cologne 1995.

Maas, Jeremy, *Victorian Painters*, London 1988.

Michalski, Sergiusz, *New Objectivity: Painting, Graphic Art and Photography in Weimar Germany 1919–1933*, Cologne 1993.

Osterwald, Tilman, *Pop Art*, Cologne 1993.

Picon, Gaeton, *Surrealists and Surrealism*, London 1983.

Popple, Kenneth, *Stanley Spencer*, London 1996

Schrader, Bärbel and Schebera, Jürgen, *The 'Golden Twenties': Art and Literature in the Weimar Republic*, New Haven and London 1990.

Stangos, Nikos, *Pictures by David Hockney*, London 1976.

Willett, John, *The New Sobriety: Art and Politics in the Weimar Republic 1917–33*, London 1978.

Wortley, Laura, *A Garden of Bright Images: British Impressionism*, London 1988.

EXHIBITION CATALOGUES

A Paradise Lost: British Neo-Romanticism 1935–55, Barbican Art Gallery, London 1987.

The Last Romantics: The Romantic Tradition in British Art: Burne-Jones to Stanley Spencer, Barbican Art Gallery, London 1989.

Italian Art of the Twentieth Century, Royal Academy, London 1989.

German Art of the Twentieth Century, Royal Academy, London 1985.

American Art of the Twentieth Century, Royal Academy, London 1993.

British Art of the Twentieth Century, Royal Academy, London 1986.

Neue Sachlichkeit and German Realism of the Twenties, Hayward Gallery, London 1978.

On Classic Ground: Picasso, Léger, de Chirico and the New Classicism 1910–1930, Tate Gallery, London 1990.

Frances Morris, *Paris Post War: Art and Existentialism 1945–55*, Tate Gallery, London 1993.

Leslie Parris (ed.), *The Pre-Raphaelites*, Tate Gallery, London 1984.

Frank Whitford et al., *Otto Dix*, Tate Gallery, London 1992.

PHOTOGRAPHIC CREDITS

COPYRIGHT CREDITS

INDEX

Abstract Expressionism 62, 69, 75

Abstraction-Création group 24

Altdorfer, Albrecht 43

Andri *Mother and Child* 43

angry young men 53

Antigna, Jean-Pierre *Fire* 12, 13

apparatchiks 7–8, 29

Artaud, Antonin 50

Auerbach, Frank 6

avant-garde 7, 26, 45

Bacon, Francis 45, 50, 56, 58; *Figure in a Landscape* fig.38

Balthus (Balthus Klossowski de Rola) 31–2; *Sleeping Girl* fig.20

Bastien-Lepage, Jules 15

Bauhaus 26

Beckmann, Max 45

Bell, Charles 69

Bell, Clive 22

Benton, Thomas Hart 45

Blake, Peter 53, 55; 'The Meeting' or 'Have a Nice Day, Mr Hockney' 55–6, fig.43; *Self-Portrait with Badges* 55, fig.42

Blake, William 20, 21, 50, 52

Bloomsbury group 16, 22–3

Blue Rider 38

Bomberg, David *In The Hold* 16

Bowery, Leigh 58

Bratby, John 6

Brekker, Arno 42, 44

Britain 6–7, 12–15, 16–25, 50, 52–3, 55–8, 61, 73–4

Bruegel, Pieter 37

Burgin, Victor 78

Burne-Jones, Sir Philip 16

Burra, Edward 23–4; *Lake District* 24; *Soldiers at Rye* fig.14

call to order 26, 31

Camden Town Group 16, 19, 20, 25

Carrà, Carlo 40

Casorati, Felice 40, 42

Cézanne, Paul 16, 19

Clausen, George 15; *Winter Work* 15, fig.6

Close, Chuck 69

Cocteau, Jean 23; *Call to Order* 26

Cold War 75

Coldstream, William 24; *Seated Nude* fig.19

collage 53, 77

Constructivism 6, 27

Courbet, Gustave 6, 7, 8, 9–14, 31, 52, 53, 55; *Burial at Ornans* 9–12, 14, fig.2; *The Stonebreakers* 14, fig.1

Cranach, Lucas 37, 43

Craven, Thomas 45

Craxton, John 50

Cubism 49, 65

Currey, John Steuart 45

Dadaism 35

Dalí, Salvador 71

Daumier, Honoré 10

David, Jacques-Louis 9

de Chirico, Giorgio 35, 40; *Mystery and Melancholy of a Street* 35; *The Nostalgia of the Infinite?* fig.29

de Kooning, Willem *Women* series 7

Delacroix, Eugène 11; *Medea* 12

Demuth, Charles 45

Derain, André 31; *The Painter and his Family* 31, fig.19

Dix, Otto 35, 37, 71; *Three Women* 35, 37, fig.23

Dubuffet, Jean 56

Dürer, Albrecht 43

Estes, Richard 69–71, 77; *Movies* fig.56; *Welcome to 42nd Street Victory Theater* 71

Etchells, Frederick 16

Euston Road school 24–5, 55

existentialism 50

Expressionism 6–7, 22, 32, 45, 50

Fauvism 22, 31

Felixmueller, Conrad; *Lovers from Dresden* 37

Fildes, Luke 14; *Applicants for Admission to a Casual Ward* 14, fig.5

film 52, 68

Fischl, Eric 72; *Bad Boy* 72–3, fig.58; *Sleepwalker* 72

Flack, Audrey 69, 77; *Marilyn* fig.55

Fra Angelico 20

Frampton, Meredith 42;

Portrait of a Young Woman 42, fig.32

France 7–12, 31–2, 50

Freud, Lucian 6–7, 52, 58, 74; *Girl with a White Dog* 58, fig.48; *Naked Portrait* 58, 61, fig.49; *Standing by the Rags* 61, fig.50

Frick 38

Fry, Roger 16, 22–3

Futurism 40

Gabo, Naum 29; *Realistic Manifesto* 6

Gerasimov, Alexander 7–8, 49

Germany 26, 75–6; German Expressionism 7, 22, 32, 45; Third Reich 38, 42–5, 50; Weimar Republic 24, 32, 35, 37–8, 40, 45

Gertler, Mark 22

Gertsch, Frank 69

Giacometti, Alberto 50

Gilman, Harold 19

Ginner, Charles 19; *Piccadilly Circus* fig.8

Giotto de Bondone 20, 22

Goering, Hermann 43

Gore, Spencer 19

Grass, Günter 45

Greenberg, Clement 62

Griebel, Otto *The Internationale* 37, fig.28

Grimshaw, Atkinson 14–15

Gris, Juan 49

Grosz, Georg 23, 24, 35, 37, 71; *A Married Couple* 35, 37, fig.21; *Pillars of the Community* 37, fig.25

Grünewald, Matthias 37

Guttuso, Renato 52; *The Discussion* fig.39; *The Escape from Etna* 42

Hamilton, Richard 52–3; *She* 52, fig.40; *Just what is it that makes today's homes so different, so appealing?* 52; *Towards a Definitive Statement on the Coming Trends in Menswear and Accessories* 53, fig.41

Hardenberg, Friedrich von (Novalis) 9

Hartlaub, G.F. 32

Herkomer, Hubert von 14

Heroic Realism 42–3

Hitler, Adolf 35, 38, 42–4, 50

Hockney, David 55–6; *A Bigger Splash* 56–7, fig.44; *Mr and Mrs Clark and Percy* 56,

fig.45

Holbein, Hans 43

Holl, Frank 14

Holzer, Jenny 78

Hopper, Edward 46–7; *Early Sunday Morning* 47, fig.36

Howson, Peter 73–4, 78; *Dog* 74

Hoyer, H.O. *SA Man Rescuing Wounded Comrade in the Street* 43

Hunt, William Holman 13; *The Awakening Conscience* 13, 21

Immendorf, Jörg 44–5; *Cafe Deutschland* cycle 45

Isherwood, Christopher 35

Italy 26, 40, 42, 52

Kandinsky, Wassily 26, 29, 38

Kanoldt, Alexander 37–8

Keane, John 73

Kiefer, Anselm 44–5; *Germania* series 75

Kirchner, Ernst Ludwig 45

Kitchen Sink school 6

Klee, Paul 26

Klein, Yves 6

Kossoff, Leon 6

Kruger, Barbara 78

Kunstblatt, Das magazine 32

Lamb, Henry 20

Landseer, Edwin 7

Lang, Fritz *Metropolis* 48

Lanzinger, H. *The Flag Bearer* 42

Léger, Fernand 40, 49

Lewis, Wyndham 16, 22, 24; *A Battery Shell* 20

Longo, Robert 72; *National Trust* 72, fig.57

MacInnes, Colin *Absolute Beginners* 53

McLuhan, Marshall 63

Magic Realism 38, 75

Malevich, Kasimir 47; *Portrait of the Artist's Wife* 27, 29, fig.18; *Peasant Woman* 27, fig.17

Marc, Franz 38

Marinetti, Tommaso Filippo Emilio 40

Martineau, Robert B. *The Last Day in the Old Home* 14, fig.4

Masolino 20

Massacio 20
Matisse, Henri 22, 31, 48
Meidner, Ludwig 7
Meier-Graefe, Julius 7
metaphysical painting
   see Pittura Metafisica
Mexican Muralists 47–9
Michalski 38
Michaux, Henri 50
Michel, Wilhelm 40
Millais, John Everett 13, 14;
   Ophelia 13, fig.3
Minton, John 50
Morandi, Giorgio 40;
   Still Life fig.30
Motherwell, Robert 62
Mussolini, Benito 42

Nash, Paul 19, 50; The Menin
   Road fig.10
Nazarenes 37, 43
Neo-Romanticism 50, 52
Neoclassicism 9
Nevinson, Christopher
   19–20, 44; Paths of Glory 20
New Objectivity (Neue
   Sachlichkeit) 26, 32, 35,
   37–8, 40, 45, 71, 75
New Realism 6, 69
Newman, Barnett 62
Nicholson, Ben 23
Novalis 9
Novecento magazine 40

Objectivism 37
Oppi, Ubaldo 40
Orpen, William 19
Osborne, John 53

Padua, Paul Mathias The Tenth
   of May 1940 44; fig.34
Palmer, Samuel 20, 21, 50
Paolozzi, Eduardo 53
Pasmore, Victor 24
photo-montage 53
photography 7, 55, 71, 76, 77
Photorealism 69–71, 77
Picasso, Pablo 31, 49, 65
Piero della Francesca 32
Piper, John 50
Pittura Metafisica 35, 40, 42
Pop Art 8, 23, 40, 52–3, 55–7,
   58, 62–3, 65, 67–8, 69
Post-Impressionism 16
Pre-Raphaelite Brotherhood
   6, 8, 13–14, 23, 37, 50, 55
Precisionism 45, 71

Radziwill, Franz 38; Karl
   Buchstätter's Fatal Dive fig.27
Regionalism 45

Richter, Gerhard 75–6
Rivera, Diego 47–9, 75;
   Detroit Institute of Art
   frescoes 48, 49, fig.37;
   Man at the Crossroads 49;
   San Francisco Stock
   Exchange club mural 49
Roberts, William 16, 24, 57;
   Self-Portrait Wearing a Cap
   24, fig.15; Trooping the Colour
   57–8, fig.46
Rogers, Claude 24
Roh, Franz Post-Expressionism,
   Magic Realism 32
Romanticism 9, 13
Rosenberg, Harold 62
Rosenquist, James 63, 65, 69;
   F-111 65, fig.51
Rossetti, Dante Gabriel 13;
   Found 13
Rossi 52
Rothko, Mark 62, 63
Ruralists 53, 55
Russia 6, 7–8, 26, 27, 29, 49,
   75

Sander, August 43
Sargent, John Singer Gassed
   20, fig.11
Saville, Jenny Branded 74,
   fig.59
Schad, Christian 37;
   Self-Portrait 37; fig.24
Scheiber, E. Hitler at the Front
   44
Schlichter, Rudolph 37;
   Meeting of Fetishists and
   Maniacal Flagellants 37
Schmied, Wieland 32
Scholz, Georg 35; Small Town
   by Day: the Butcher 35, fig.22
Schwitters, Kurt 53
Second Republic 12
Seurat, Georges 11
Seven and Five Abstract
   Group 24
Sheeler, Charles 45, 71
Sickert, Walter Richard
   16, 19, 20, 25, 53;
   Camden Town Murder 16, 19;
   La Hollandaise fig.7; Miss
   Earhart's Arrival 19, fig.9
Signal magazine 44
Sironi, Mario 40; Mountains
   fig.31
Smith, Matthew 22
Socialist Realism 8, 27, 29, 37,
   44, 45, 47, 49, 75
Soutine, Chaim 7
Spencer, Stanley 7, 20–2, 24,
   37, 58; Arrival of Travoys 21;
   The Centurion's Servant 20–1,

fig.12; Clyde ship-building
   series 22; The Lovers 35;
   The Resurrection, Cookham
   21–2, fig.13; Sandham
   Memorial Chapel,
   Burghclere 21; Self-Portrait
   58, fig.47
Stalin, Joseph 27, 29
Still, Clyfford 62
Superrealism 69–1
Suprematism 27, 29
Surrealism 8, 24, 40
Sutherland, Graham 50

television 63
Tennyson, Alfred, 1st Baron
   13
Third Reich 38, 42–5, 50
Tissot, James 15
traditionisme 31

Unit One 24
United States 40, 45–7, 62–3,
   65, 67–8, 69–73, 75

Valenciennes, Henri de 9
Valori Plastici magazine 24, 32,
   40
Vaughan, Keith 50
Velde, Bram van 50
Vermeer, Jan 71
Vidal, Gore 63
Visconti, Count Luchino 52
Vorticism 16, 19, 24, 57–8

Wadsworth, Edward 16, 29
Wallinger, Mark 71
war artists 19–21, 44, 73–4
Warhol, Andy 62, 63, 65,
   67–8, 77; Disaster series
   67; Electric Chairs series 67;
   films 68; Marilyn Diptych
   67, fig.54; Riots series 67;
   Soup Can series 67, fig.66
Wedekind, Frank 72
Weimar Republic 24, 32, 35,
   37–8, 40
Wesselmann, Tom 63, 65, 69;
   The Great American Nude
   series 65, fig.52; Still Life
   series 65
Wissel, Adolf; Kalenberg
   Farmer's Family 43, fig.33
Wood, Grant; American Gothic
   45–6, fig.35
Woolf, Virginia 16
World War I 8, 11, 16, 19–21,
   26, 45
World War II 8, 22

Wunderwald, Gustav 37;
   Corner 37, fig.26

Zhdanov 27, 29
Zola, Emile 19

CONTENTS

List of Contributors   v

Preface   vii

Acknowledgements   viii

Editors' Introduction   1
Jim Stewart and Jim McGoldrick

ACTIVITIES   5

SECTION I – PERSPECTIVES ON HRD

1 **The HRM–HRD Nexus**   9
    Jim McGoldrick and Jim Stewart

2 **Managerial Stances: Perspectives on Manager Development**   28
    Colin Fisher

3 **Inter-cultural Perspectives on HRD**   47
    Valerie Stead and Monica Lee

4 **International HRD**   71
    Paul Iles

ACTIVITIES   98

SECTION II – HRD STRATEGIES

5 **The Strategy–HRD Connection**   101
    John Fredericks and Jim Stewart

6 **The Provision of Learning Support for Non-Employees**   120
    John Walton

7 **New Forms of Work Organisation and HRD**   138
    Michael Kelleher

8   **Managing Diversity and HRD**   158
    Elisabeth M. Wilson

9   **Power and Influence and the HRD Function**   180
    Rita Johnston

    ACTIVITIES   195

SECTION III – HRD PRACTICE

10 **The Trainer as Change Agent: Issues for Practice**   199
    Bob Hamlin and Goronwy Davies

11 **Influence, Communication and Neuro-Linguistic
    Programming in Practice**   220
    Ursula Lyon

12 **Action Learning as a Cross-Cultural Tool**   240
    Monica Lee

13 **The Role of the Action Learning Set**   261
    Sue Williams

14 **Research Methods and HRD**   280
    Goronwy Davies

    ACTIVITIES   302

    Editors' Conclusion: The Future of HRD?   303
    Jim Stewart and Jim McGoldrick

    ACTIVITIES   307

    Index   308

LIST OF CONTRIBUTORS

JOINT EDITORS

Jim Stewart — Reader in HRD and Course Leader MSc HRD, Nottingham Business School

Jim McGoldrick — Professor of HRM and Vice Principal, University of Abertay Dundee, and formerly Professor of Human Resource Development, Nottingham Business School

CONTRIBUTORS

Goronwy Davies — Principal Lecturer, Wolverhampton Business School

Colin Fisher — Principal Lecturer, Nottingham Business School

John Fredericks — Senior Lecturer, Nottingham Business School

Bob Hamlin — Divisional Manager, Management Development Division, and Course Leader MSc HRD, Wolverhampton Business School

Paul Iles — Littlewoods Professor of HRD and Head of The Liverpool Centre for HRD, Liverpool Business School

Rita Johnston — Director, MEd Training and Development, The University of Sheffield

Michael Kelleher — Research Fellow, Gwent Tertiary College

Monica Lee — Director, HRD Pathway Unit, Lancaster University

Ursula Lyon — Senior Lecturer, HRM, Nottingham Business School

Valerie Stead — Teaching Fellow, HRD Pathway Unit, Lancaster University

John Walton — Principal Lecturer and Course Leader, MA Human Resource Strategies, London Guildhall University and Chair, University Forum for HRD

Sue Williams — Senior Lecturer, Wolverhampton Business School

Elisabeth Wilson — Senior Lecturer, Liverpool Business School

PREFACE

This book has a number of origins. We joined the staff of Nottingham Business School within six months of each other, one as an Organisational Behaviour and Human Resource Development specialist within the Department of Human Resource Management, and one to establish and lead the same Department as its first Head. We found a common interest in the subjects of learning, development and HRD. We also found a common view that HRD is generally, and unhelpfully, treated as unproblematic and a subject which is not considered with the seriousness it deserves within academia. It may be the case, as Karen Legge (1995, *Human Resource Management: Rhetorics and Realities*) argues, that HRM has been more about academic careers than the practice of organising and managing, and that may or may not be a 'good thing'. The same could certainly not be said of HRD, which academics, and those engaged in organising and managing alike, too easily assume to be a simplistic and technical activity. Thus the idea of a book such as this arose out of our decision and intent to support the establishment of HRD as a field of organisational and managerial behaviour worthy of academic study and enquiry.

Jim Stewart had initiated development of a Masters level programme at Wolverhampton Business School prior to joining Nottingham Business School. That development continued and came under the umbrella of what is now termed The University Forum For HRD. The Forum, a collaborative network of universities, has supported the establishment of Masters programmes in HRD throughout the UK. This includes the Masters programme we initiated within the Nottingham Business School. We were however both dissatisfied with the lack of a substantial text which gave serious consideration to defining and analysing the range and scope of what constitutes HRD. We discovered that this dissatisfaction was widely shared within the University Forum for HRD and within our wider academic and professional networks. Thus a second origin of the book is a desire to support the study of HRD at Masters level. Masters students, though, are not the only 'reflective practitioners' working in HRD, and in managing, and so the book was and is intended to inform a wider readership than Masters programmes in HRD audiences alone.

These origins did not, and could not, crystalise into a solid project without one further event. The event in question demonstrates the significance of serendipity in human affairs. A chance meeting with Penelope Woolf of Pitman Publishing allowed the thoughts outlined above to be brought into the conversation. This meeting led to the usual processes which, with a fair wind and a little luck, end in publication. This book therefore is intended to help establish HRD as an academic subject. Our motivation is not career advancement, or at least not entirely (although one of us has enjoyed the benefit of 'promotion' since we began the project). It is primarily a shared belief that the subject is important for furthering understanding of and informing the practices of organising and managing. We have support for that belief within our own universities, within the University Forum for HRD, from our contributors and, eventually we hope, from our readers.

ACKNOWLEDGEMENTS

We would like to thank a number of people, both collectively and individually. Our contributors deserve our joint thanks for offering their work to the project and for diligence and professionalism in meeting deadlines. So too do Doreen Cox, Sheila Popple, Sheilah Tinkory and Liza Pybus at Nottingham Business School for a combination of secretarial support, information technology expertise and detective skills. We would also wish to thank the publishing and editorial team at Pitman, especially Penelope Woolf and Lisa Howard for their support and hard work in bringing the book to publication and for giving meaning to the phrase 'an iron fist in a velvet glove'. Jim Stewart would like to publicly thank Pat Stewart for her continuing patience and support. Jim McGoldrick would similarly like to thank Diane, especially for the Saturdays spent teaching him how to save files properly.

Jim Stewart, Nottingham Business School
Jim McGoldrick, University of Abertay Dundee
January 1996

Editors' Introduction

Jim Stewart and Jim McGoldrick

This volume, for many readers, will be ground breaking. It sketches out perhaps for the first time in print the range and the scope of *human resource development*, HRD, as a new field of studies and scholarship as well as a field of practice. In this introduction to the book we set out something of our own philosophy of HRD, the ideas behind the selection of the topics and our rationale for their ordering and presentation in the book. We also set out some thoughts on the audience at which the book is aimed and how the book might be best used.

PHILOSOPHY OF HRD

This book is about human resource development. In common with a number of related terms, for example HRM, empowerment and the learning organisation, HRD is a relatively new concept which has yet to become fully established and accepted, either within professional practice or as a focus of academic enquiry (see McGoldrick and Stewart, this volume). However, the growth of academic programmes incorporating the term in named awards at masters level is one of many reasons for a more rigorous analysis of the meaning and practice of HRD. Hence the publication of this book.

What, though, is HRD? The previous paragraph would suggest that this question is not yet amenable to a definitive answer, and we believe that to be the case. We also recognise that it would be barely credible to edit a book with HRD in the title without holding and offering some view on what constitutes HRD. Therefore, with the double caveat of it being both personal and tentative, the following paragraphs set out our 'philosophy' of HRD.

Human resource development encompasses activities and processes which are *intended* to have impact on organisational and individual learning. The term assumes that organisations can be constructively conceived of as learning entities, and that the learning processes of both organisations and individuals are capable of influence and direction through deliberate and planned interventions. Thus, HRD is constituted by planned interventions in organisational and individual learning processes.

The nature of interventions which constitute HRD can and does vary. There are commonly used terms to label and categorise different types of methods which can be utilised within interventions. Three of these are education, training and development. Specific methods and activities will, in most cases, be capable of allocation to one of these categories. However, the application and use of a particular method will not of itself constitute HRD. The level at which the method is applied, that is the extent to which it is intended to have impact on organisational as well as individual learning, will be a key determinant. Other determinants can also be suggested and characterised as a set of key dimensions. Figure 1 below sets out some of these dimensions. Those on the left of the scale are suggested as being characteristic of HRD as opposed to non-HRD interventions.

```
Strategic      ————————  Operational
Organisation   ————————  Individual
Long term      ————————  Short term
Cultural       ————————  Structural
Organic        ————————  Packaged
Change         ————————  Maintenance
```

Figure 1 Dimensions of HRD

A further dimension from Fig. 1 is, in our view, particularly significant. Human resource development is constituted by interventions which are intended to *change* organisational behaviour. Many education, training and development activities have the intention of maintaining the status quo, and of enabling 'more of the same'. For us, HRD implies a deliberate purpose of changing the behaviour of organisations or, at least, improving the capability for change. Thus, the defining feature of HRD is the extent to which interventions in the learning process are intended to bring about organisation change.

We close this discussion by acknowledging that our view of HRD is not necessarily shared in full by all of the contributors to this book. However, as we identify in the concluding chapter, the reader will find a high degree of coherence in the individual treatments of HRD and related issues.

THE SCOPE OF HRD

The scope of HRD, in our perspective, is broad. It is intimately bound up with strategy and practice and with the functional world of training and development. Of course, as we have indicated above it is fundamentally about change. It covers the whole organisation and addresses the whole person. It embraces a wide range of literature: from corporate strategy to personnel management and from organisational analysis to the psychology and sociology of workplace behaviour. It also addresses a wide range of themes and issues; from managerial consciousness to the role of the action learning set and from the design of work organisation to the development needs of the non-employee. It also identifies and re-examines specific 'tools' of HRD intervention and introduces, in the case of neuro-linguistic programming, a highly specialist set of techniques to a wider audience. However, one of our explicit aims with the book was to step outside the cultural domain of training and development theory and practice in the UK. Thus the book also engages issues of cultural diversity and cross-cultural analysis with a perspective on the international dimensions of HRD.

We have deliberately selected topics and perspectives which are fresh and challenging and have consciously avoided any fixed or single paradigm. We have also adopted a sort of epistemological pluralism. Some of the chapters of the book are predominantly conceptual in their orientation, aiming to examine the ideas sets that are feeding the development of HRD. Others follow a more familiar pattern of reporting original and current research, whilst others draw quite consciously on data derived from consultancy interventions and experience. At the end of the book we look at the research agenda that might come out of this collection, and again we see that agenda as being diverse.

THE ORGANISATION OF THE BOOK

The book is divided into three sections with a concluding brief chapter. The first section contains four chapters which indicate some of the range of different *perspectives on HRD*. These perspectives are both intercultural and international as well as being interdisciplinary and novel; for example Colin Fisher's contribution addresses questions of managerial competencies by use of a series of metaphors. Our own contribution links HRD to the growing literature and theoretical debates on the nature and meaning of HRM. The second section of the book focuses on *HRD strategies*. There are five chapters in this section which examines the different domains of strategy. HRD is seen as being clearly linked to the business strategy of organisations both at the corporate level and at the level of practice. The issue of cultural diversity reappears in this section as part of the strategic challenge for managers in relation to HRD. Similarly, this also addresses issues of work organisation and new patterns of work, and of the development of *non*-employees. Enabling change in organisations also raises questions of power and influence and these are raised in the final chapter of this section, Rita Johnston's contribution. The theme of change agency is developed further in the final section which looks at *HRD practice*. This section, also of five chapters, looks at different kinds of interventions. Again the cross-cultural aspects of HRD feature prominently, as does the use of action learning approaches to self- and organisation development. This section closes with Goronwy Davies' chapter on research methods and HRD interventions which, whilst it links into some of our final reflections on possible research directions for HRD, could equally have fitted into either of the other two sections.

USING THIS BOOK

We have tried to design this book so that it is not simply a 'how to' type of handbook (for which of course there is a valid place in the world of HRD). We have also tried to avoid an overly theoretical book which is dry as dust and just as irritating. Nor have we demanded that every chapter has a prescriptive set of exercises or a mandatory case study. In fact we hope the book embodies the best of all these approaches. In individual chapters the authors themselves have, where appropriate, made suggestions as to how the reader might pause to reflect on what they have just read. Some chapters have 'real' case studies, included because the authors are presenting some of their own original and current work.

However, whilst we acknowledge that some readers, because of particular personal interests in a subject, might not start with this introduction and work through to the conclusion, we do nonetheless feel that there is a balance between the narrative of the book and the structure. Therefore at the end of each major section we have identified a number of activities for the reader. These need not be restricted to use on any academic course, although we have aimed the book at the advanced 'student' of HRD, whether they are on a 'course' or in a different kind of learning environment. The activities are designed to help readers to use the book to make better sense of what HRD means to them in the different situations in which they find themselves. In that respect then, the activities we include, in addition to the specific cases and exercises for specific chapters, are designed first to assist in simple comprehension of what might well be new language and concepts and, second, to develop the analysis of HRD through those concepts.

We have had a fascinating time working through the contributions and putting this volume together. We hope that you share our enjoyment and that we truly and genuinely share in a common learning process.

ACTIVITIES FOR INTRODUCTION

1 (a) Formulate your personal definition of HRD.

   (b) Compare your definition with that given in the introduction. Make a note of the similarities and differences.

   (c) Discuss the results with colleagues. Attempt to arrive at a consensus view on what constitutes HRD.

2 (a) Examine Fig. 1 and provide definitions for each of the extremes of each of the dimensions.

   (b) Construct some means of assessing any intervention against the dimensions, e.g. a rating scale.

   (c) Consider the extent to which you agree that assessing interventions against the dimensions would be an appropriate way of determining HRD.

   (d) Discuss the results with colleagues and re-examine your definition of HRD in the light of this activity.

3 (a) Select and describe a recent intervention you were involved in designing and implementing.

   (b) Assess this intervention against the dimensions given in Fig. 1.

   (c) Determine the extent to which your intervention constitutes HRD against the dimensions.

   (d) Consider ways in which the methods/activities in your intervention could have been utilised differently to meet the HRD criteria of the dimensions in Fig. 1.

Section I

PERSPECTIVES ON HRD

1

THE HRM–HRD NEXUS

Jim McGoldrick and Jim Stewart

2

MANAGERIAL STANCES:
PERSPECTIVES ON MANAGER DEVELOPMENT

Colin Fisher

3

INTER-CULTURAL PERSPECTIVES ON HRD

Valerie Stead and Monica Lee

4

INTERNATIONAL HRD

Paul Iles

1

The HRM–HRD Nexus

Jim McGoldrick and Jim Stewart

INTRODUCTION

The aim of this chapter is to develop an analysis of the relationship between human resource management, HRM, and human resource development, HRD. It is almost axiomatic that our argument contends that neither is a sub-set of the other but rather that each has its distinctive, albeit problematical, space in the analysis of the human aspects of contemporary organisations. Further, it is our argument that viewing HRM and HRD as separate yet complementary processes is vital.

At one level the distinction allows us to develop an analysis which transcends the functional domains of both personnel management and training and development, and yet to acknowledge that – for many observers, writers and practitioners – both HRM and HRD are part of the 'people' function of business organisations. Therefore the conceptual issues which dominate this chapter are vital in clarifying the distinction, both in the argument we develop here and in the book as a whole, between 'strategy' and 'practice' and between 'function' and 'process'. To reveal our position straight away, we see HRM and HRD as embodying all of these dimensions but without privileging any one dimension. For us the 'nexus' in our title expresses itself in the domain of practice, but, as we will go on to argue, that is neither simple nor reductionist.

THE 'SPACE' FOR HRM AND HRD

Part of the argument we seek to make here is that to enhance the quality of debate about HRM and HRD requires some ground clearing. Our starting point is that there are no universally accepted definitive statements of the meaning either of HRM or of HRD, although there is some sense of 'solidification' of meaning emerging in the literature of each. Each of the terms now enjoys a wide currency in the worlds of both practitioners and academics (if that in itself is not an artificial distinction). But there is still, we feel, a need to develop a conceptual analysis that takes us beyond variations on the themes of 'old wine/new wine/old bottles/new bottles/ new labels'. Shortly, we shall vigorously address the novelty claims made on behalf of each and critically appraise their intellectual status. In a sense we are groping towards a framework for 'theorising' on the nature of HRM and HRD rather than planting our flag in the camp of one or other of the contending parties. Whilst we feel that the relationship of HRM with the changing role and function of personnel is important, as is that of the under-pressure training function threatened with 'out-sourcing' in relation to HRD, we nonetheless wish to stand back a little from the sound and fury of debate. The key questions we seek to address concern the conceptual bases of each and the ways in which these are articulated theoretically and empirically in the reality of organisational life.

We begin this task by examining the distinctive features seen both in HRM and HRD but, to be unequivocal from the start, whilst we see the nexus as having its expression through practice, we see the conceptual bonding as lying in the holistic embrace of *strategy*. Elsewhere in this volume Fredericks and Stewart (Chapter 5) develop their own conceptual model of the relationship between strategy and HRD in the wider context of organisational analysis. Not surprisingly we share their broad perspective on strategy as being multifaceted and processual rather than linear and structural, but we will come back to these points later. However, there is a clear cross-over between our chapter and theirs.

THE MEANING OF 'STRATEGY'

For this chapter we have developed a framework for analysing the strategic nature of HRM and HRD. However, we do not want to lose sight of alternative ways of encapsulating strategic HRM and HRD in a more linear form. Figure 1.1 indicates the place of HRM and HRD within a representation of business functional strategies. Like our own framework later on, this begins with vision and mission and ends with practice. This approach tends to identify the more directly functional aspects both of strategy in general and of HRM and HRD in particular.

From this model it can be seen, as we have argued in our introduction to this volume, that the implication for HRM and HRD strategy is that it is likely to be seen not only as a linear process but also as one which unduly emphasises the functional at the expense of the processual aspects of strategy making which is developed below and also features in the analysis of strategy elsewhere in this volume (see Fredericks and Stewart, Chapter 5).

THE NATURE AND MEANING OF HRM

It is, perhaps, some evidence of the maturity of HRM that it is no longer regarded as being particularly controversial in its own right. The academic space for HRM is now well established, with a growing number of academic departments within universities, a range of dedicated journals for both academics and practitioners and a growing number of specialised HRM programmes on offer. The literature surrounding HRM, if taken as a measure of the seriousness with which the subject is regarded, is impressive. It is the subject of large number of textbooks, most of which outline the recent history of the debates on the status and position of HRM (Storey, 1992; Beaumont, 1993; Goss, 1994; Beardwell and Holden, 1994; Bratton and Gold, 1994; Sisson, 1994; and Hendry, 1995).

From our perspective there are a number of themes in the so-called HRM 'debates' that inform our argument. First, there is the argument that HRM is broadly focused on

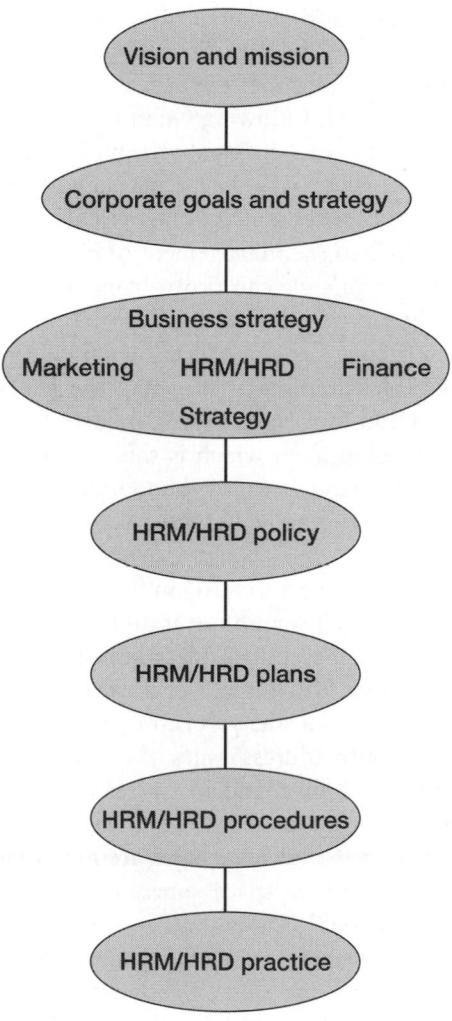

Fig. 1.1

managing people but emphasises *policy, procedure and process*. This position can be seen to fall generally into the personnel management, 'functional' dimension of HRM. Secondly, there is a view best expressed by Poole (1990) that HRM is both *holistic* and *strategic* but is linked to *company performance as well as individual and societal needs*. Thirdly, this theme of 'strategic' is taken further in another strand of HRM, but is linked much more explicitly to competitive forces by Miller (1987) who sees HRM as involving all decisions and actions on the management of people which create and sustain *competitive advantage*; notwithstanding that the ideas of competitive advantage are themselves particularly associated with a whole other literature and set of debates in the realm of corporate strategy (Porter, 1985; Johnson and Scholes, 1989; Hamel and Prahalad, 1994). It can be seen that HRM inhabits a domain that is essentially strategic in its orientation yet must address the mundane and the routine. The tensions and ambiguity of this are very much a part of the sub-text of this chapter. HRM, then, is both strategic and practical and is simultaneously processual and functional. Its relationship with personnel can be seen as one of functional integration with the roles and activities of line managers in organisations which are increasingly decentralised and 'empowering'. In that sense, HRM, following Guest (1987) and Storey (1989) is obviously concerned with a wide agenda – vision, strategy, integration, quality, flexibility, attitudes and values – much of which will also be shared with HRD. Our argument here is that there is a real need for a conceptual and theoretical framework that makes sense of the place of HRM and HRD in the management of business organisations.

In developing such a framework we can profit from the experience and insights of others. Much of the early literature of HRM has focused on the impact in the areas of personnel and industrial relations (see the collection edited by Storey, 1989) although there have been other notable attempts at mapping the developments of HRM [see Salaman (1991) and Blyton and Turnbull (1992)]. Indeed the idea of a 'map' is important to the argument we develop here, which is that, if viewed in the terms we have already set out, HRM is simultaneously strategic and practical, and processual and functional. Noon's (1992) essay is particularly useful in that it argues strongly that HRM has to be taken seriously theoretically even though it is not to be taken as 'theory' in itself. His idea of the 'map' helps with respect to HRD in that reference points and boundaries are now available. This also resonates with the argument we develop later in this chapter with respect to the analysis of culture in organisations. Similarly, Keenoy and Anthony's (1992) arguments that HRM might be portrayed as some kind of post-modernist metaphor are picked up in our analysis through the consideration of HRM and culture. A more serious attempt to address issues of concern to both HRM and HRD in a post-modernist framework can be found in Carter and Jackson's (1993) work on expectancy theory and motivation.

In terms of empirical research the HRM debates are much more tentative. Studies by Storey (1992) indicate that there is a 'space' emerging for HRM although Beaumont (1993) and the Workplace Industrial Relations Survey (see Millward *et al.*, 1992), notwithstanding the high media profile given to some of its findings, are more sceptical. Certainly research in the area of employee involvement (Marchington *et al.*, 1992) and the growing literature on empowerment (Lashley and McGoldrick, 1994) indicate a shift, in the agenda at least, away from traditional industrial relations concerns. Similarly, whilst the recent book by Starkey and McKinlay (1993) was very much framed around *strategic* HRM, it could be argued very persuasively that their study of Ford owed much less to the HRM debates than to an analysis of business strategy *per se* and the intense interest generated by Japanese approaches to manufacturing and the so-called 'Japanisation' debates.

THE NATURE AND MEANING OF HRD

The level of debate within the UK on the nature and meaning of HRD does not compare in volume with that given to HRM. There has been some limited argument in the professional literature though most recent books on the subject emerging from academia seem to assume the meaning of HRD as accepted, if not given (for example see Megginson *et al.*, 1993). However, the current lack of public debate does not mean that diverse views do not exist, indeed one of the purposes of this book is to stimulate such a debate. As Stewart (1992) has argued elsewhere, there is a real need for a more systematic examination of HRD. The views we present here seek to advance both the argument of this chapter and contribute to the future debate.

If the roots of HRD are taken to derive from the literature and practice of organisational development, OD, as well as from training and development education and practice *per se*, then it is clear that it has as long and distinguished a history as the study of personnel management. The argument that HRD encompasses OD is in line with the work of Rothwell and Kazanas (1989) and is implicit in the findings of the American Society of Training and Development's research into HRD practice (McLagan and Suhadolnik, 1989). Thus both conceptual and empirical work in the USA supports the view of HRD as being concerned with organisational as well as individual learning.

This is an important argument for two reasons. First, it suggests that HRD, in common with HRM, is strategic and processual as well as being practical and functional. What might be termed traditional training and development focuses attention on the latter; that is on activities which are the concern of professional practitioners and which reflect immediate and operational needs. Incorporation of OD within HRD, though, suggests concern with organisational renewal and growth through processes which engage all organisation members and are managed, well or badly, by those same members. Thus HRD constitutes activities which can be represented as interventions in *organisational* learning as well as individual learning (Stewart, 1992). Secondly, OD represents a particular approach to organising and managing. This approach is characterised by an emphasis on humanistic values (Stewart, 1994) which can be contrasted with the economic rationalism of scientific management. Anthony (1994, p. 19) describes the contrast as follows: 'In this way a tradition of "soft" management theory and advice came to oppose the "hard" theory that had preceded it'. While having some resonance with the characterisation of 'soft' and 'hard' HRM, this distinction is similarly less to do with valuing individuals over organisational success than with the means of their achievement. Thus, as we argue later, HRD logically implies concern with notions such as leadership, culture and commitment. Equally the practice of HRD is inextricably linked to that of HRM through the strategic implications each has for long-term survival.

From our review of the literature and research on HRM and HRD it is clear that the argument we present concerning the nexus is both timely and important.

HRM AND HRD: A FRAMEWORK FOR ANALYSIS

The problem which we now have to confront for both HRM and HRD is that, having established their academic status, it is now incumbent upon us to look at the articulation between the functional and analytical framework for HRM and for HRD in the context of organisational change based on our experience as researchers and teachers, consultants and writers over a number of years. The HRM framework for analysis was developed by McGoldrick (1992)[*].

There are two distinct dimensions of the framework. At one level it tries to identify the

---

[*] Some of the original elements of the model were developed with M.D. Gibson, University of Central Lancashire, in the design of a strategic HRM input to the MBA programme in 1988.

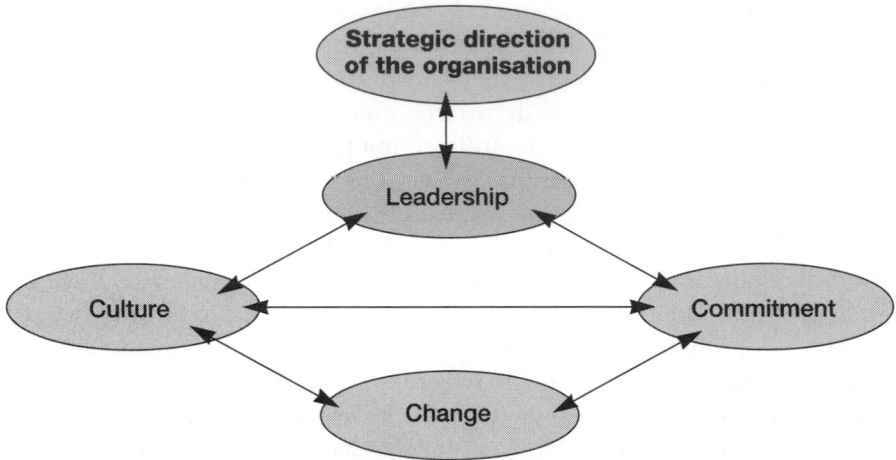

Fig. 1.2   HRM and change: an analytical framework

key HRM elements linking the strategic direction of the organisation to managerial practice. In this case the managers in mind are line managers not functional managers in personnel, training or employee relations. The second dimension then aims to link, via a matrix see Fig. 1.3, p. 25), the key variables to related functional elements. Thus the framework, as shown in Fig. 1.2 above, establishes a connection between the strategic direction of the organisation and the processes of organisational change linked to managerial practice. This connection, for us, is mediated by three key variables: *leadership, culture*, and *commitment*.

Each of these three categories of our framework is analysed in depth below. But it is worth commenting that, in taking the argument through these categories, we have already indicated our view of the limitations of the idea of a linear approach to strategy, as shown earlier in Fig. 1.1. Such an approach, whilst it might also serve to establish the connection between the strategic direction of the organisation and real behaviour and practice, would tend to follow a line of analysis linking an HRM/HRD strategy to policy statements, to procedure statements, to practice with an emphasis on 'plans'; for example a manpower plan or a training plan. Whilst this resonates with the emphasis attached by Sisson (1994) to HRM, it tends to inhibit the analysis of other categories of behaviour and action beyond policy and procedure. It is to those other categories of leadership, culture and commitment that our argument now turns.

Leadership and HRM

At a simple level we can take Michael Armstrong's (1990) statement that 'leadership is getting things done through people . . .' (p. 83) and is a central feature of achieving success. Armstrong's views are supported by some very practical comments and guidelines. However, for us the idea of leadership is a bit more problematic.

The idea of leadership as a key variable in the HRM/HRD nexus is a fairly new one. Just as the mid 1980s saw the emergence of a body of literature, research and academic programmes in HRM and the development of a strategically focused perspective on HRD in the 1990s, so leadership theory also underwent something of a transformation.

Leadership studies of course are not new, with writing on the relationship between 'leading' and 'managing' being well documented in the literature of organisational behaviour (for a summary of these see Adler, 1992; Shafritz and Ott, 1992; Mullins, 1993). In part the attention that has been given to leadership reflects the rhetorical changes in the language of organisational writing. Put simplistically, the focus has moved from administration, to management, to leadership.

In a very useful contribution to the literature on leadership, Alan Bryman (1986) has both mapped the development of writing on leadership and linked it with the development of organisational analysis. To be sure no respectable textbook in organisational behaviour could be complete without a chapter which would review the different approaches to leadership. Bryman's (1986) analysis is both more rigorous and more critical than most treatments of leadership. He argues that, as a subject, leadership goes beyond the now conventional continuum of *trait – style – contingency* that most writers focus on and takes us into the wider organisational issues. He develops his ideas in his later (1992) work. In this Bryman addresses what he calls the emergence of 'transformational leadership' which, like much of the writing on 'strong cultures' and 'employee commitment', developed during the 1980s. This concern with transformation and change is where Bryman's work on leadership intersects with our analysis of the emergence of HRM and HRD.

The *new leadership* paradigm emerged during the 1980s partly, as Bryman (1992, p. 21) argues, out of the 'pessimism' of much of the research on leadership. Whilst Bryman builds his argument around the idea of charismatic leadership – which he traces back to Weber's original writings, but notes the particular emphasis on its applications of ideas of charisma in religious and political leadership – the key conceptual point he makes is that leadership is *socially constructed* partly through the exchange between leaders and led and the matching of expectations. The idea of social construction is important not only for what he calls 'transactional' leadership (1992, p. 95) but also for 'transformational' leadership.

The essence of transformational leadership for Bryman is that it invokes a 'higher purpose' beyond contractual obligation or mere compliance through remuneration. As he notes:

> *'the transforming leader seeks to engage the follower as a whole person, and not simply as an individual with a restricted range of basic needs. Transforming leadership addresses the higher order needs of followers and looks to the full range of motives that make them. Both leaders and followers are changed in pursuit of goals which express aspirations in which they can identify themselves.'*
> (1992, p. 95)

Transformational leadership, then, is characterised by charisma, inspiration and intellectual stimulation. This is strongly evident from recent American literature which takes the conceptual basis of the new leadership in different directions.

Richardson and Thayer (1993) focus heavily on an interpretation of charisma in a way which the sceptical European can find difficult to accept. They divide it into 'easy to learn steps' to transformational and inspirational leadership. By contrast Sims and Lorenzi (1992) develop a more social–psychological approach through their notion of *social learning and cognition* which is ultimately concerned with what they call self-managed leadership. Thus they argue a variation on the themes of high involvement and empowerment which are discussed below. But interestingly their approach, like Bryman's, sees leadership as essentially a social construct.

HRM, HRD and the 'new leadership'

At one level the literature and influence of *transformational leadership* can be seen as very limited. Bryman (1992, p. 174–175) nonetheless argues that it has set an 'agenda' of some kind. The new leadership puts 'vision' at the top of that agenda and restates the ideas of values and purpose as central features of the cultural dimensions of organisational life. It also raises questions of communication, trust and integrity and ethical dimensions, and it also promotes more of a role for subordinates than previous views of leadership. It can also be argued that there might not be much that is 'new' in the new leadership or certainly that there is not enough evidence from qualitative research and case work to show that it is truly transformational. However, to take a simpler notion of the leadership from Sims, Fineman and Gabriel (1993) namely that leadership is 'a process of helping others to do things in a direction which serves the aims of the organisation' (p. 105) then leadership is central to the everyday reality of HRM and HRD. Their emphasis on the everyday life of organisations is disarmingly more complex. They argue that the essence of leadership is the management of meaning through the language of leadership and its symbols. We will return to that later when we look at the cultural aspects of organisations.

The agenda which emerges from the analysis of leadership is of direct relevance to HRM and HRD. Trust and integrity, as well as being central to the ideas of transformational leadership, also lie at the heart of the employment relationship in which the psychological contract, even though it is typically expressed through an economic transaction, is absolutely central to the themes and concerns we have developed in this chapter. Communication is the essential lubricant of all organisational life, yet there are enduring problems both of meaning and of style in the process of communication. Empowerment purports not only to rewrite the terms of the psychological contract but at a more mundane level focuses our attention on the structure and shape of the organisation, and on patterns of work and flexibility. The underlying development agenda in all of this is huge but is largely understated – it is a long way from the world of training plans and budgets yet is endemic to that world as well.

Leadership and culture

The relationship between leadership and culture is often focused around the idea of the visionary leader framing a corporate mission. The popularisation of this view is often associated with the impact of Peters and Waterman's (1982) book *In Search of Excellence* which arguably placed the rhetoric of 'culture' into the everyday vocabulary of managers, academics and other commentators (Bryman, 1989, p. 38). The emphasis in much writing on leadership and culture is given to Peters and Waterman's notion of 'strong cultures' – whilst seeming to offer a recipe for 'excellence' this has in fact posed an interesting and subtle agenda for HRM and HRD. On the one hand HRM, as an approach to managing people, embodies the internal contradiction of a focus on the hard dimensions of economic resources, numbers planning, information systems and staffing levels (especially when undertaken as part of an exercise in downsizing and organisational restructuring) with an equal emphasis on the softer aspects of business in the idea of 'treating people as people'. This of course brings out our earlier comment concerning culture and commitment as a means of understanding, at a conceptual level at least, the contradictory pressures involved in managing people. The agenda that this has created for HRM and HRD is a concern for managing *through* people. The most obvious and visible evidence for this would be the preoccupation in downsizing companies with introducing culture change programmes and, as we shall discuss further shortly, a boom in the cottage industry of culture change consulting.

However, it is also important to note that the leadership, culture and change bandwagon does have implications beyond the stereotyping of organisational cultures. An underlying concern in the so-called new leadership paradigm is the focus on mutuality and consent rather than formal authority. This also implies that leadership in practice is a process and activity distributed more widely within organisations and that it is also a developmental process. This latter point is strongly reinforced by Salaman (1995) who argues that the very nature of management itself is the management of the learning process. Whilst Sims and Lorenzi (1992) crucially define leadership as a social learning process, they do not take up the language of 'the learning organisation' but their agenda for the future 'shape' of organisations (p. 290) has profound implications for both HRM and HRD.

The study of culture

It is difficult to know quite where to begin to locate an analysis of 'culture' within the HRM–HRD nexus. Conceptually, the notion of cultures is one of the great human constructs that enables people to make sense of the world we live in now and in the future from an understanding of the past. In that sense the sociological traditions of analysing culture clearly 'fit' the analysis of organisations, given that organisations or corporations are themselves human constructs which, at one level, represent a simple, transient, pattern of human relationships and behaviour – even if we actually perceive these as complex and enduring.

For our argument culture is essentially about meanings and about learning. It is also the most profound aspect of organisational life, yet much of the writing on corporate and organisational culture has been criticised for a lack of depth and rigour (Thompson and McHugh, 1990; Watson, 1987, 1994), but the classic anthropological writing on culture by Clyde Kluckhohn (1951, 1969) could apply to any modern organisation. In his language, culture is a 'design for living'; for him culture is linked to the whole human environment; it is both structured and 'regular enough to be analysed', yet it is also dynamic and variable because it is also something which is learned (1969, pp. 43, 44). In his approach the anthropological metaphor of culture is that of a map, an abstract representation, which allows us with varying degrees of accuracy to 'situate' events, behaviour and relationships. For Kluckhohn culture is both universal and omnipresent yet expresses itself through what he calls 'traits' and 'items' or 'specialities'. For Leslie A. Whyte (1949) the universality of culture is expressed through symbols which allow the imposition of meaning onto things. For Anthony Giddens (1989) another cultural universal is, of course, language. In the world of corporate organisation, language and symbols dominate the processes of interaction and give meaning to appropriate forms of behaviour. The simple definition of culture coined by a McKinsey consultant and noted by Deal and Kennedy (1982, p. 4) as 'the way we do things round here' actually has pretty deep roots in cultural anthropology.

A slightly different orientation to culture can be found in the work of Norbert Elias (1978) whose lifetime project was to explain the 'civilising process'. This can also serve to help us understand the behavioural aspects of culture. Whilst he paints a huge canvas, some of the finer details can provide neat insights into the world of organisations. Like Giddens, Elias particularly focuses on language and meaning. Through words cultures are expressed and developed, and can be 'polished' in speech and writing. So ideas like those of culture and civilisation in Elias's work '. . . became fashionable words, concepts current in the everyday speech of a particular society' which shows that '. . . they met not merely individual but collective needs for expression. The collective history has crystallised in them and resonates in them' (1978, p. 7). This might express the point in more flowery language than is typically found in writing on corporate culture, but it also represents one of the truths of corporate culture namely that the medium is also part of the message. Whilst Elias, like Giddens and the other authors we have noted in this section, was looking at a wider notion of culture, his ideas can be stretched to embrace the more mundane and historically focused modes of discourse of organisations.

In the literature of organisational culture the anthropological roots of cultural analysis are generally well understood if not always acknowledged, especially with respect to the processes of 'cultural transmission' where the actions of heroes, the creation of myths, legends and rituals are major features of the cultural narrative (Deal and Kennedy, 1982). More recently other writers (Hunt, 1986, and Brown, 1995) have argued the 'space' for organisational culture as field of study in its own right. In Brown's (1995) work he takes a position with which we sympathise, namely, a fairly tight business focus linking the analysis of cultural aspects of organisations with the ideas of strategy and performance. In this comprehensive work Brown pulls together the broad range of writing on culture and change, drawing extensively on an impressive range of case studies. His analysis is thorough and his assessment of the claims made about culture is convincing – and has the benefit of being so through detailed study. Like other critics, notably Thompson and McHugh (1990) and Watson (1994) the main criticism concerns the depth of the research base upon which dimensions of organisations are made. There is no shortage of intellectual resource in analysing culture, for example Deal and Kennedy's (1982) view of strong cultures as being concerned with dominant value systems and superordinate goals could have come straight from Talcott Parsons. What might be at work here is the lag effect between an interesting and suggestive set of ideas and debates (if not fads and fashions) and a substantial body of evidence to support or not the claims that may be made on their behalf.

HRM, HRD *and culture*

The place of culture is central to the development of HRM and HRD. For some critics the renewed interest in culture following the demise of 'excellence' (but before the rise of 'chaos' and 'turbulence') is important in that, given that culture mediates all change processes, it makes the case for an approach to analysing culture which does not confuse style with substance all the more important. To borrow and invert Brown's notion of strategy as a cultural artefact (1995, p. 250) if culture is taken to be an organisational artefact or tool then it is actually a threat to the effective management of people. It should be acknowledged that whilst culture can be seen as a mechanistic way of addressing the communication of values, mission and purpose and is part of the battle for hearts and minds of organisation members, it is nonetheless also about the social construction of meaning. Thus culture is not a unitary concept but is in fact pluralistic and diverse. That issue of diversity also forms a central plank in the wider argument in this volume (see particularly Chapters 3 and 8 below). Culture then can be seen as part of a universe of ideas but tends to be addressed and lived at a micro level. A good way of checking this might be to undertake a rough and ready 'culture audit' of members of your own organisation with an important distinction being drawn between the organisation as a whole and what we refer to as 'your bit' of the organisation. Our expectation is that, perhaps unsurprisingly, people will feel more comfortable in 'their bit'. Their interpretation of the mission statement, their ability to relate closely to shared values and meanings with colleagues who make up the 'us' that we work with every day as opposed to the 'them' elsewhere in the organisation is more likely to express itself on their home turf.

The underlying cultural pluralism implied here is strongly emphasised by other writers. Ralph Stacey (1993) encourages organisations to take risks with cultural diversity to stimulate growth. Even if strong cultures can be seen to exist, for Stacey they are more likely to stultify individual contribution and cut people off from the here and now. For Stacey of course the nature of organisations is characterised by bounded instability or 'chaos' For him the real risk for organisations seeking to manage cultural meanings is that they confuse 'visions' with 'illusions' (1993, p. 40)

We certainly share Stacey's reservations about any claims that can be made about the idea of strong cultures. We feel that the notion of strong culture is itself a gross oversimplification. To be sure there are questions of the degree to which people will adhere to values and beliefs. The flaw is to assume, as Deal and Kennedy appear to, that there are in fact superordinate goals that people 'buy into'. The web of values and beliefs that exists in an organisation is much more intricate. Statements of core values will owe more to position, authority and power than to shared values and meanings. Subordinates may mouth the words of the mission statement and undergo training in, say, total customer care without really changing their attitudes or behaviour. Similarly, the interpretation of cultural plurality and diversity as 'deviant sub-culture' also wrongly, we feel, implies that there is a singular position from which to deviate.

HRM and HRD interventions in culture

Having argued that culture is central to understanding both HRM and HRD the key question becomes that of engagement with culture. Thompson and McHugh (1990) described culture as having a 'seductive appeal' to HRM, with its 'soft' focus and mediation of the individual and the organisation in a quite different way from traditional industrial relations and personnel management. In this sense the engagement is both functional and processual. HRM and HRD functions within organisations will both reflect and reinforce the cultural systems at work because they are part of the cultural apparatus of the organisation. Yet the concern with how people are managed and developed is much more processual than functional.

This contradiction, of course, is not new. It has dominated the whole area of OD and figures in the growing interest in learning arrangements and ideas such as the 'learning organisation'. The latter is an example of a growing number of prescriptions for utilising HRM/HRD to create, or perhaps, more accurately, to re-create, new forms of organisation culture. Such prescriptions are 'cultural' in the sense of claiming to influence and change established cultures, and in the sense of arguing the case for direct intervention in and through existing cultures in order to effect change. Other examples of HRM/HRD interventions might include total quality management, TQM, customer service ethos, and team-based working arrangements. However, these kinds of intervention can and do founder on the organisational confusions over structure versus culture and function versus process.

Commitment

It could be argued that the third dimension of our framework for analysing HRM and HRD is a sub-set of the other two. We are comfortable with that, but at this stage we would retain it in our model. In a sense, by 'commitment' we can paraphrase Martin and Nicholls' (1987) definition as a willingness on the part of individuals to contribute much more to the organisation than their formal contractual obligation. It links individual performance and involvement with their work to some major conceptual dimensions of workplace behaviour, like motivation and orientations to work (Watson, 1987). There is neither the time nor space here to go into these issues but clearly there are linkages into aspects of behaviour and organisational experience. At the heart of any notion of commitment there is an idea of involvement. So for us the idea of commitment provides a useful intersection between the emotional, psychological, social, cultural, economic and political pathways of the organisation. But equally, we do not expect the idea of commitment to bear all of the conceptual weight of these organisational pathways, merely to provide some signposts.

In part commitment can be seen to be about 'giving more', whether this be effort or moral support. Etzioni (1961) provided an excellent framework for understanding what he called *compliance* which was able to match both the idea of forms of *power* with types of *involvement*. Yet much contemporary writing in this area seems to ignore this work. It is true that Etzioni's ideas are influential in some writing on empowerment but his ideas about the different forms of compliance which can be provided by members of organisations has implications for the management and development of people. If people's engagement or involvement is purely calculative or monetary then HRM and HRD policy and practice needs to be highly focused, say, on reward systems or on technical training. Similarly, if the form of involvement on the part of the individual member of the organisation is a moral one based on shared sentiments and beliefs, then the HRM and HRD implications are more likely to dwell in the cultural and processual domain linking values with commitment. It is interesting to note that the problem with moral involvement is arguably just as difficult to deal with for a 'volunteer' as for an employee. Typically the commitment of the non-employee is taken for granted whilst training and development for their functional skills are often neglected (see, for example, Walton's contribution to this volume). For the employee, moral involvement is mediated, if not obscured, by the employment contract and commitment is often assumed not to exist outside the cash nexus.

Of course what writers like Martin and Nicholls were arguing is that emotional and cultural dimensions of work are the domain of commitment. Key measures are loyalty, pride, belonging; where employees in particular are involved and informed; where members of the organisation share success as well as values and identify with the mission and goals of the organisation. As with our earlier comments with respect to culture, it is difficult to find any evidence beyond anecdotes. To be sure there is some robust research in specific aspects of involvement, for example Marchington's (1992) work which we discuss later, but there is little clear evidence available to support any 'commitment' thesis.

Emotional involvement

We have already noted some comments on Etzioni's ideas on moral involvement and this leads us more directly into the realm of emotion and feeling. There is now a growing literature and research base on emotional involvement with work (Fineman, 1993) which links the private self to the meaning systems of organisations. New research aims to get below the 'facade of rationality of organisational goals, purposes, tasks and objectives' (Fineman, 1993, p. 1). This literature exposes more clearly the idea that organisations should be seen not so much as rational structures bonded by systems of rules but rather as non-rational emotional entities with a concern for the place of feelings. In corporate life there are other conceptions of feelings of commitment. For example Sims *et al.* (1993, p. 245) characterise the ever-smiling waitress and the cool professionalism of the air hostess as actually displaying regimes of emotional control which displace genuine emotions or feelings of warmth or support with manufactured representations of those feelings. It could be argued that such behaviour and engagement with the organisation, as indicated in the examples they cite, are likely to be reinforced with competency-based development programmes and vocational qualifications which emphasise behaviour and outcomes but do not articulate the thoughts and feelings which lie behind the behavioural competence.

In a fascinating twist to the analysis of power relations in organisations, Helena Flam (1993) focuses primarily on the emotion of fear and its potential effect on, for example, risk taking in decision making which is taken to characterise dynamic and innovative organisations. The contradictions here operate at two levels. At the level of the organisation people may be encouraged to be innovative and to take risks, but as Flam points out, 'fear compels an individual to construct a cost-and-benefit analysis demonstrating why the spontaneously desired action should not be pursued.' (p. 59). Thus rather than extend and expand choices, the effect of fear is to 'narrow the range of subjectively available options'. Thus for Flam rational concepts such as 'choice' and 'interests' have what she calls an 'emotional foundation and feeling prompted bias' (p. 59). At the level of managerial behaviour there is a contradiction between feeling and expression. Managers display enthusiasm for their work and for the organisation, but in the reality of contingent and uncertain circumstances feel endemic anxiety (1993, p. 71). This is likely to be compounded for them when they have to seek simultaneously to engender commitment and loyalty in their subordinates. Yet in a common sense way emotions such as fear, anxiety are part of most organisations. Think of any organisation experiencing a restructuring or downsizing and it is not difficult to interpret the rational adjustment to market circumstances as in fact a terror-inducing shock. In recent years a concern with job stress and mental health at work has highlighted aspects of the emotional dimensions of organisations (Cooper and Robertson, 1991). There has also been an interest in new areas of enquiry and activity such as neuro-linguistic programming as a useful additional 'tool' for improving communication and personal influencing which start from an operating premise that organisations should be concerned with the whole person (see Lyon, in this volume).

Clearly as this area of research gets more prominence the implications for HRM and HRD will clarify but as things stand at the moment, apart from some highly specialised consultants, the ability of most HRM and HRD practitioners to cope with the emotional aspects of work is highly limited both conceptually and practically (Stewart, 1989).

Employee involvement

Perhaps the area of commitment which has traditionally been most widely written about is employee involvement, EI. It features prominently in the traditional personnel and industrial relations aspects of HRM, but, having said that, it is also the most lively area of debate and research. The underlying concern in the more recent research is with the shift in employee relations away from a collective approach to a more individualistic approach. As we noted earlier this is also seen as reflecting the emergence of HRM as one of what Marchington (1992, p. 270) calls the 'competing paradigms' of employee involvement and participation with the HRM concern for commitment differentiating EI from other paradigms (control, co-operation, satisfaction). For him HRM is about the 'management of resourceful humans' (p. 11) and it differs from other approaches to managing people precisely because it links business objectives with training and development as a means of progressing from mere compliance to outright commitment to both the job and the organisation.

The main focus of Marchingtons's work is on developing a framework to make sense of EI both conceptually and empirically. His idea of an escalator of involvement from one-way information passing to genuine sharing in decision making (p. 24) is useful here but so also is his idea of the EI 'mix'; that is, different combinations of EI techniques will often operate in organisations in different combinations and contexts.

Echoes of Marchington's framework for making sense of the wide range of initiatives and policies which make up EI also appear to have influenced official thinking in the UK. A recent publication from the Employment Department (1994) clearly indicates strong interest on the part of the Government in the area of EI as a possible source of competitive advantage. This is evident from the very strong endorsement for EI in a number of key areas where it is argued that EI has the potential to have a major impact upon performance. These areas are: improved productivity; quality improvement and enhancement; a more co-operative atmosphere in the workplace which is linked to the decline of collective industrial action; lower staff turnover and reduced absenteeism; and finally, the report adopts the language of competitive advantage to argue a general case for the added value that could be derived from utilising the skills, knowledge and abilities of all employees (1994, pp. 3, 4).

The precise form of EI is not stipulated or prescribed. As the report states: 'The Government believes that employee involvement produces the best results when it is flexible and tailored to the needs and culture of each organisation' (1994, p. 2). Whilst the report goes on to differentiate this approach from anything that may be seen as being imposed on the UK by the European Commission, it also matches well with the findings of the major research study of employee involvement undertaken by Marchington *et al.* (1992). This research and Marchington's other work (1992), suggest that the idea of an escalator which we noted above is also accepted by the Employment Department, in that the structure of their report follows Marchington's framework very closely. Thus involvement is seen as progressing from information sharing and consultation, quality circles and teamworking, through to financial participation such as share schemes to a strong emphasis on performance management, appraisal and individual development programmes (p. 30). Not surprisingly there is strong endorsement for official initiatives such as Investors in People and vocational qualification programmes.

In much of this discussion of EI the HRD theme has been expressed at the level of training support. Whether this is the major company customer care initiative or culture change programme, the key fact from Marchington's work is that in EI there is an extended role for HRD as trainer and as facilitator. Similarly the integrated HRM issues link together job and organisational flexibility with the approach to recruitment and selection to achieve the best fit for HRM and business strategies.

EMPOWERMENT

Parallel to the growing literature on EI there has been a mini explosion of writing about empowerment. Taken simply, empowerment can be seen as an extension of EI in which organisations consciously and actively encourage employers to take more responsibility and accountability for their own and the organisation's performance, to take initiative and decisions close to where the decisions are needed and, crucially, to have the resources to do so.

Empowerment addresses many of the themes already developed in this chapter. It is explicitly focused on winning commitment, but it also intersects with our discussion of emotional involvement, employee involvement and with organisation redesign and restructuring. Empowerment, at least rhetorically, sits alongside the notion of leaner and flatter organisations. Indeed as Lashley and McGoldrick (1994) argue, one of the 'limits' of empowerment is a lack of conceptual rigour in the different ways in which the term is actually used. Their argument focuses on employment in the domain of employment strategy. Thus it links together the everyday management of people with the bigger issues of culture and structure and wider business strategy. Empowerment, like other forms of EI, is essentially about organisational choices. However, the parties involved in making the choices extend beyond management alone. To be sure, key decisions in organisations are the essence of what management does, as Watson (1987) argues. Management is all about balancing control imperatives with the need to win and sustain some kind of commitment to the organisation. But for empowerment to have any real force it has also to embrace the conscious choice and involvement of employees. In one sense empowerment may well be the locus of the transition from transactional leadership to transformational leadership and a genuine move in the direction of self-management. In another conception it may simply be part of a myriad of task-based forms of participation. It all depends on just how much power is in empowerment

The problem with empowerment, as with other fashionable ideas such as 'excellence', 'strong culture', 'TQM' 'creating commitment' and the like, is that interesting and exciting ideas take a longer time than some commentators would appreciate to penetrate people's consciousnesses and move beyond the rhetoric to really influencing behaviour and practice. Just as we noted with some of the critics of writing on corporate culture, there needs to be strong empirical evidence as well.

The HRM and HRD implications for empowerment depend to a large extent on managerial and employee support, expectations and practice. It may be that empowerment is destined to end up filed under fads and fashion. Equally it may genuinely represent the means of transforming the nature and quality of workplace relationships. The jury is still weighing the evidence. There are some signposts for an optimistic assessment. The growing literature will eventually strengthen the conceptual and theoretical boundaries thus informing practice more effectively. Anecdotal evidence offers some nice insights. For example, Land Rover, which can be seen as a good example of competitive success in UK manufacturing, partly attributes that success to radical improvements in working relationships. Whilst we would hesitate to say that this was because of empowerment, a senior executive of the company has observed that the company does in fact practice empowerment but does not preach it – at least not in the language of the literature of the subject. For them empowerment, like quality work processes, is part of the overall philosophy of the 'learning business' and is not seen as the latest big idea which enables the company to avoid the shopfloor and managerial cynicism.

CONCLUSIONS: THE HRM–HRD MATRIX

From our discussion so far we have begun to map out the territory where HRM and HRD have a strategic 'fit' in the development of organisations. This, of course, was one of our starting points in the review of the literature of HRM. It is also interesting to note the broad conceptual similarities with Collin's (1994) work which sees HRM as a tapestry. To reinforce our earlier points, we do not see HRM/HRD interventions as a linear process but as an integrated process linking together different combinations of organisational variables such as communications and involvement; structure shape and empowerment; resourcing strategies and flexibility; organisation development strategies; employment strategies and conflict. The strategic fit of all these factors can be seen as a matrix, as shown in Fig. 1.3.

The HRM–HRD matrix indicates where the 'nexus' of our title come together. It brings both the explicit and the implicit themes of the chapter into a multi-dimensional framework. It links the bigger argument we have made about leadership, culture and commitment, framed by our concern with strategy and practice in the context of change, with more focused issues. The matrix also allows what we characterised earlier as some

Managing change in organisations

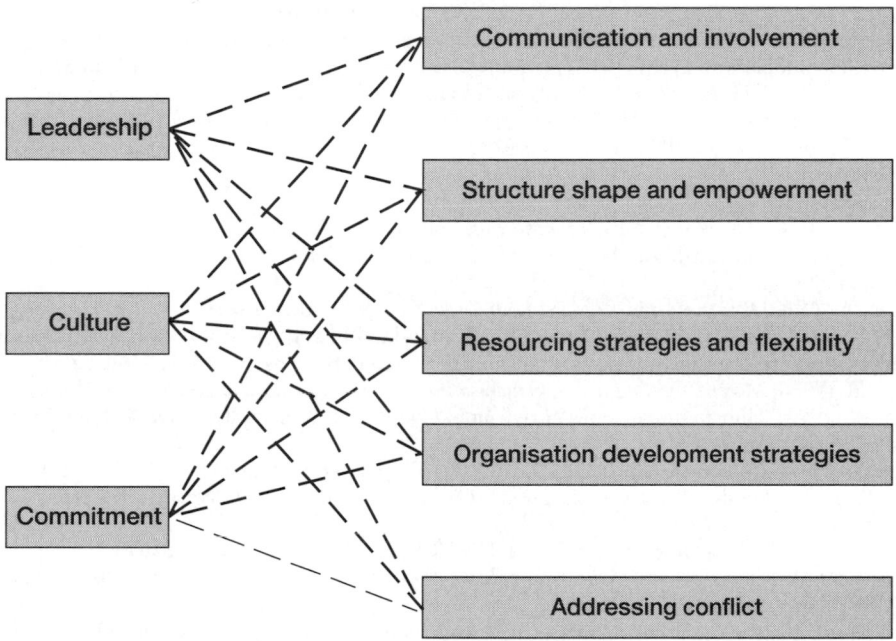

Fig. 1.3   An HRM/HRD matrix

of the tensions and ambiguities of HRM and HRD to be addressed, if not resolved. So the simultaneous properties of strategy and practice, and function and process can sit reasonably comfortably within the matrix.

We have to be clear at this point that we use the matrix as a conceptual framework and not as a model of HRM and HRD. We have found it a useful tool and in particular it helps establish clearly the linkages between the different dimensions of managing and developing people. In this chapter we have indicated the relative weight that we attach to some factors in the matrix (leadership, culture and commitment). We expect that readers may well see their own configuration of concepts and variables and utilise the framework to reposition elements to suit their own interests and problems. That is both right and proper. The matrix is not a prescription. For any framework to be useful it has to be both fluid and dynamic.

To conclude, then, we feel that we have achieved what we set out to do in this chapter. We have argued our case for HRM and HRD to be seen and analysed in relation to one another, rather than as competing approaches to managing and developing people. Equally, we do not see them as a unitary concept. Each has its own conceptual foundation, literature and traditions. But it is interesting to note that, in the UK at least, there has been a convergence within personnel and training professionals into a unified institute. We can also cite our own collaboration as further evidence of complementary approaches. Finally, we also feel that we have made a substantial contribution to the debates on HRM and HRD and have enhanced the process of theorising without falling into the trap of looking for a general theory of HRM and HRD.

References

Adler, N.J. (1992) *International Dimensions of Organisational Behaviour*, Boston Mass, Wadsworth.

Anthony, P.D. (1994) *Managing Culture*, Buckingham, Open University Press.

Armstrong, M. (1990) *A Handbook of Human Resource Management*, London, Kogan Page.

Beardwell, I. and Holden, L. eds (1994) *HRM: A Contemporary Perspective*, London, Pitman.

Beaumont, P.B. (1993) *Human Resource Management: Key Concepts and Skills*, London, Sage.

Blyton, P. and Turnbull, P. eds (1992) *Reassessing Human Resource Management*, London, Sage.

Bratton, J. and Gold, J. (1994) *Human Resource Management: Theory and Practice*, Basingstoke, Macmillan.

Brown, A. (1995) *Organisational Culture*, London, Pitman.

Bryman, A. (1986) *Leadership and Organisations*, London, Routledge.

Bryman, A. (1989) 'Leadership and Culture in Organisations', in *Public Management and Money*, vol. 19, no. 3, pp. 35–41.

Bryman, A. (1992) *Charisma and Leadership in Organisations*, London, Sage.

Carter, P. and Jackson, N. (1993) 'Modernism, Postmodernism and Motivation, or Why Expectations Theory failed, to come up to expectation', in Hassard and Parker eds, pp. 83–100, *op. cit.*

Clegg, S.R. (1990) *Modern Organisations: Organisations Studies in the Post-modern World*, London, Sage.

Collin, A. (1994) 'Human Resource Management in Context', in Beardwell and Holden, pp. 28–67, *op. cit.*

Cooper, C.L. and Robertson, A.J. (1991) *Work Psychology*, London, Pitman.

Deal, T. and Kennedy, A (1982) *Corporate Cultures: the Rites and Rituals of Corporate Life*, Harmondsworth, Penguin.

Elias, N. (1978) *The Civilising Process: Vol. 1 The History of Manners*, Oxford, Blackwell.

Employment Department (1994) *The Competitive Edge: Employee Involvement in Britain*, London, HMSO.

Etzioni, A. (1961) *A Comparative Analysis of Complex Organisations*, New York, Free Press.

Fineman, S. ed. (1993) *Emotion in Organisations*, London, Sage.

Flam, H. (1993) 'Fear, Loyalty and Greedy Organisation', in Fineman ed., pp. 58–93, *op. cit.*

Garrahan, P. and Stewart, P. (1992) *The Nissan Enigma: Flexibility at Work in a Local Economy*, London, Mansell.

Giddens, A. (1989) *Sociology*, Cambridge, Polity Press.

Goss, D. (1994) *Principles of Human Resource Management*, London, Routledge.

Guest, D. (1987) 'Human Resource Management and Industrial Relations' in *Journal of Management Studies*, vol. 24, no. 5.

Hamel, G. and Prahalad, C.K. (1994) *Competing For The Future*, Cambridge Mass., Harvard Business School Press.

Handy, C. (1994) *The Empty Raincoat: Making Sense of the Future*, London, Hutchinson.

Harrison, R. (1992) *Employee Development*, London, IPM.

Hassard, J. and Parker, M. eds (1993) *Post-modernism and Organisations*, London, Sage.

Hendry, C. (1995) *Human Resource Management: A Strategic Approach to Employment*, London, Butterworth-Heinemann.

Höpfl, H. and Linstead, S. (1993) 'Passion and Performance: Suffering and the carrying of organisational roles', in Fineman ed., pp. 94–117, *op. cit.*

Huczyknski, A. and Buchanan, D. (1992) *The Organisational Behaviour: An Introductory Text*, London, Prentice Hall.

Hunt, J.W. (1986) *Managing People at Work: A Managers Guide to Behaviour in Organisations*, London, McGraw-Hill.

Johnson, G. and Scholes, K. (1989) *Exploring Corporate Strategy: Text and Cases*, London, Prentice Hall.

Keenoy, T. and Anthony, P. (1992) 'HRM: Metaphor, meaning and morality' in Blyton and Turnbull eds, pp. 233–55, *op. cit.*

Kluckhohn, C. (1949) 'The Concept of Culture', reproduced in Coser, L. and Rosenberg, B. eds (1976) *Sociological Theory: a book of readings*, (Fourth edition), London, Collier-Macmillan.

Lashley, C. and McGoldrick, J. (1994)'The Limits of Empowerment', *Empowerment in Organisations*, vol. 2, no. 3, pp. 25–38.

McGoldrick, J. (1992) 'Human Resource Management and the End of History?', *Inaugural Professorial Lecture*, The Nottingham Trent University.

McLagan, R.A. and Suhadolnik, D. (1989) *Models for HRD Practice*, Alexandra Va., ASTD.

Marchington, M. (1992) *Managing the Team: A Guide to Successful Employee Involvement*, Oxford, Blackwell.

Marchington, M.P., Goodman, J., Wilkinson, A. and Ackers, P. (1992) *New Developments in Employee Involvement*, Employment Department Research Series, No. 2, Sheffield, HMSO.

Martin, P. and Nicholls, J. (1987) *Creating a Committed Workforce*, London, IPM Publications.

Miller, P. (1987) 'Strategic Industrial Relations and Human Resource Management – Distinction, Definition and Recognition, *Journal of Management Studies*, vol. 24, no. 4.

Millward, N. *et al.* (1992) *Workplace Industrial Relations in Transition: the ED/ESRC/PSI/ACAS Surveys*, Aldershot, Dartmouth.

Mintzberg, H. and Quinn, J.B. (1992) *The Strategy Process: Concepts and Contexts*, London, Prentice Hall Int.

Megginson, D., Joy-Matthews, J. and Banfield, P. (1993) *Human Resource Development*, London, Kogan Page.

Mullins, L.J. (1993) *Management and Organisational Behaviour*, London, Pitman.

Noon, M. (1992) 'HRM: A Map, Model or Theory', in Blyton and Turnbull eds, pp. 16–32, *op. cit.*

Oxtoby, B. and Coster, P. (1992) 'HRD A Sticky Label', *Training and Development*, vol. 10, no. 4.

Peters, T. and Waterman, R. (1982) *In Search of Excellence*, New York, Harper and Row.

Poole, M. (1990) 'Editorial Comment', *International Journal of Human Resource Management*, vol. 1, no. 1, pp. 3–10.

Porter, M. (1985) *Competitive Advantage*, New York, Free Press.

Richardson, R.J. and Thayer, S.K. (1993) *The Charisma Factor: How to Develop Your Natural Leadership Ability*, Englewood Cliffs NJ, Prentice Hall Int.

Rothwell, W. and Kazanas, H.C. (1989) *Strategic Human Resource Development*, New York, Prentice Hall.

Salaman, G. ed. (1991) *Human Resource Strategies*, London, Sage.

Salaman, G. (1995) *Managing*, Buckingham, Open University Press.

Shafritz, J.M. and Ott, J.S. (1992) *Classics of Organisation Theory*, Third edition, Pacific Grove CA, Brooks/Cole Publishing.

Sims, D., Fineman, S. and Gabriel, Y. (1993) *Organising and Organisations: An Introduction*, London, Sage.

Sims, H.P. and Lorenzi, P. (1992) *The New Leadership Paradigm: Social Learning and Cognition in Organisations*, London, Sage.

Sisson, K. (1994) *Personnel Management*, Second edition, Oxford, Blackwell.

Stacey, R.D. (1992) *Managing Chaos: Dynamic Business Strategies in an Unpredictable World*, London, Kogan Page.

Stacey, R.D. (1993) *Strategic Management and Organisation Dynamics*, London, Pitman.

Starkey, K. and McKinlay, A. (1993) *Strategy and the Human Resource: Ford on the Search for Competitive Advantage*, Oxford, Blackwell.

Stewart, J. (1989) 'Managing Emotions – how good are you?', *Training and Development*, ITD, vol. 17, no. 12.

Stewart, J. (1992) 'Towards a Model of HRD', *Training and Development,* vol. 10, no. 10.

Stewart, J. (1994) *OD: History, Perspectives and Relevance to NHS Organisations*, Bristol, NHS Training Directorate.

Storey, J. ed. (1989) *New Perspectives in Human Resource Management*, London, Routledge.

Storey, J. (1992) *New Developments in the Management of Human Resources*, Oxford, Blackwell.

Thompson, P. (1993) 'Post-modernism: Fatal Distraction', in Hassard and Parker eds, pp. 183–203, *op. cit.*

Thompson, P. and McHugh, D. (1990) *Work Organisations: a critical introduction*, London, MacMillan.

Truelove, S. ed. (1992) *Handbook of Training and Development*, Oxford, Blackwell.

Truelove, S. (1992) 'Developing Employees', *ibid.*, pp. 273–86.

Watson, T.J. (1987) *Management, Organisation and Employment Strategy: New Directions in Theory and Practice*, London, Routledge.

Watson, T.J. (1994) *In Search of Management: Culture, Chaos and Control in Management Work*, London, Routledge.

Whyte, L.A. (1949) 'The origin and basis of human behaviour', an extract from 'The science of culture' reproduced in Coser, L. and Rosenberg, B. eds (1976) *Sociological Theory: a book of readings* (Fourth edition), London, Collier-McMillan.

2

Managerial Stances:
Perspectives on Manager Development

Colin Fisher

PROLOGUE

Competence is the central concern of much of the current debate about manager development. But competencies are outcomes, which contribute towards the meeting of functional objectives (Mansfield, 1993), and they are incomplete without consideration of the manager's assumptions about the nature and impact of managerial action. Imagine, by way of explanation, a manager who is competent at making recommendations for improvements in work methods and the quality of products or services. The significance of that competence in practice cannot be assessed until a number of contextual aspects are considered. This could include such questions as whether the manager's proposal for change is sincere and transparent, or whether it is a ploy – an attempt, for example to head off another, and less favoured, proposal. The recommendation might be coloured by the manager's views on the nature of change in organisations and on the relative roles of top-down and bottom-up initiatives for change. The recommendation could be a cynical necessity aimed at attaining the right assessment in a performance related pay scheme; it might be an isolated and well considered proposal or it might be a poorly considered trifle amongst a plethora of ideas. The manager's recommendation for change might indeed be seen, by him/her and by others, as all of these things at once. This category of concerns, with managers' working assumptions about their jobs, which is not explicitly included within the standards/competency approach's concerns with the job/role environment (Stewart and Hamlin, 1992, p. 30), is the subject of this chapter.

Manager development therefore ought to be concerned with these assumptions as well as with the competencies. Indeed this cannot be avoided because a manager's reaction to manager development may be affected by these assumptions. It is a common experience of management trainers that programmes which work with junior managers will not work with more experienced ones; even though their assessed need for the skills and competencies covered in the programme is little different. It will be argued that this different reaction can be traced to different understandings of the nature of managerial activities by these two groups.

The purpose of this chapter is to describe this category of concern, which focuses on managerial assumptions about the relationships between the manager, the organisation and managerial action. I have chosen the term *managerial stance* to label it. The Oxford English Dictionary reports several definitions of stance, which include a standing place for a person to work from, an attitude or policy towards an object and the pitch of a market trader. The use of the word pitch in the last definition refers to place, but its punning link with 'making a sales' pitch suggests the degree to which a stance can be a rhetoricised attempt at making sense of a complicated world. All these meanings imply that managerial stance represents the ways in which managers make a link between understanding their jobs, organisations and environments, and changing them.

A managerial stance therefore is a particular set of assumptions about work and organisations which can be defined in relation to the cultural dimensions developed by Kluckholm and Strodtbeck (1961) and adapted for an organisational context by Schein (1985). These dimensions include beliefs about:

- the nature of human nature, the way people behave at work;
- the nature of reality, and the basis of managerial decision making;
- the nature of human activity, whether managerial activity is reactive or proactive;
- the nature of human relationships, the way people interact in an organisation;
- the relationship between the organisation and its environment.

These dimensions can be used, like co-ordinates on a map, to locate different stances, different ways of understanding the mutual influences between individuals, organisations and their environments.

Schein (1985) points out that such basic assumptions do not change easily or quickly, but they may develop and alter as managers move through their careers. And it will be the argument of this chapter that a manager's stance may develop as the imperatives of their position change. The idea of a developmental sequence of managerial assumptions can be paralleled by Kohlberg's model of ethical reasoning as developed by Snell (1993). It is proposed in this model that managers can move, through various phases and sub-phases of ethical consciousness – from an undeveloped way of deciding what to do in an ethical dilemma (conforming to the preferences of the person who can do the manager most harm) until they reach a stage where resolving ethical difficulties involves much humble, but rigorous, self-questioning. A manager's acquired capacity to use the more sophisticated modes of ethical reasoning does not imply that they will necessarily use it. The more developed ways of thinking do not replace the earlier forms, they are added to them. This model then is based upon a manager's increasing capacity to think in a more complex and ambiguous way; and this approach will be used to explain how managerial stances may develop.

The model, of the development of managerial stances, will be explained in three ways. A fable about the development of a manager will be used to identify the issues involved. This fable is based on many incidents reported to me by managers, or experienced or observed by me in the course of working as a management developer. The development of managerial stances will then be analysed in a more academic style; and a formal conceptual framework will be presented. The argument will then be summarised as a management development 'lecturette'. This will be followed by an epilogue in which some of the implications of my argument for manager development are raised.

A MANAGERIAL FABLE

Chris is a new, and young, manager, just appointed as a Service Supervisor in a service industry company which manages coin operated machines in many kinds of location. Chris is responsible for a small team of four workshop engineers, who install and maintain the machines, and work out of a depot built on an industrial estate. She reports to the Service Manager. Previously an engineer herself, Chris is raw and callow, but enthusiastic and committed. During this phase of her career she goes on some one- and two-day management skill courses, some run in-house and some run by CompetencyTrak, on time management, assertion, managing people and TQM. Chris looks at her job very much from a personal, rather than from an organisational perspective. Gradually she develops a sense of the managerial role from her growing confidence in her ability to handle the engineers in the team. They can be a tricky bunch; but Chris feels they are beginning to have confidence in her. As time passes Chris loses the initial sense of insecurity and begins to formulate, albeit unconsciously, some clear views about being a manager. It's about, she thinks, getting things done through people. Chris tends to be a little uncritical about the wider organisation and tends to assume that she and it are heading in the same direction. The new PURGE programme (Productivity Upgrade Resource thru' Generating Empowerment) has an earnest advocate in Chris who sees it as the organisation putting into effect all the things she has learnt during her management training.

Chris has been promoted now. She has moved to a smaller depot where she is the coordinator in charge of a larger number of service engineers. Chris is very pleased with the promotion, but there has been a price. The sense of being an important member of a small, close knit, team has gone. Chris is now managing teams rather than people in a team. Another change is that Chris has become organisationally self-conscious, aware of other, and competing, groups within the depot. In addition to the service engineers there are also collectors, who collect the cash from the machines. There is not much love lost between the engineers and the collectors. This enmity is reinforced by circumstances. Although both groups visit the same premises the engineers tend to visit in the afternoons and the collectors in the early morning. The collectors have a very routine and organised pattern of visits whilst the engineers can be off anywhere at any time. The collectors are mainly women and the engineers mostly men. There is much backbiting and scapegoating between the two groups. Chris tries hard to stand up for the engineers and sees it as her job to fight their corner for them. Much of her time is now in spent in management meetings with the senior managers in the depot. In her previous role these senior managers had been distant figures and a source of some awe. Chris would never, then, have initiated contacts with them. It would have been 'speak when you are spoken to'. But now, in defence of the engineers, Chris has developed a more equal relationship with them. Chris's political skills have also developed a lot. She can now often bend a meeting to her will without many people noticing how she has manipulated the group. She is particularly good at using the foot in the door ploy This involves getting an apparently small thing accepted by management which necessitates, a short time later, a much bigger allocation of resources and benefits to the engineers. Chris finds that she enjoys organisational politics and is not above setting people up in meetings, although some times the more Machiavellian plans don't work as she expected.

Chris has moved to a larger depot; and she has been promoted to Service Manager with responsibility for all the service engineers, and through the Service Supervisor, the workshop engineers. Perhaps it is because the novelty has worn off, but the fun of playing office politics has diminished. It increasingly looks childish – a return to the 'it's not fair' arguments of the junior school playground. Chris is also beginning to see that if the collectors and the other groups in the depot have caused her aggro in the past it is not always because they are malicious. Rather, it seems to her now, that these problems have grown from the fact that each group has different and pressing demands upon them, which they don't effectively communicate to each other. The problem is not maliciousness but misunderstanding – and a lack of effective systems. Chris has just completed a Managerial Systems and Control course at the local poly (now turned into a university); and she did a couple of interesting options on management science. Chris, as service manager, now feels as much loyalty to the depot as a whole as she does to her engineers. This is partly because she is reporting directly to the Area Manager and is much more concerned with cross-functional issues. A lot of the friction between the different groups in the depot stems from accusations of unfair allocation of workload and of one group causing additional work for another. Chris feels that a proper computerised command and control system which also optimised the flow and allocation of work between groups and individuals would be of great benefit. She is aware that there has been much development in the systems and software available for managing service and maintenance work. She has drafted a few ideas on paper for improving the systems and has presented them to the Area Manager for consideration.

Chris's next promotion is in fact a sideways move, to the job of Business Accounts Manager, in another large depot. The reason for the move is to gain customer and business experience. This change of perspective, away from that of engineering towards a more expressly commercial orientation, has had a major impact on Chris. It has reinforced her belief that everyone in the depot needs to be moving in the same direction by developing a customer-directed approach. She feels that all the groups in the depot need to be brought together, so they can see that they all need to work towards the same goals. She has set up a number of away-day sessions, part funded by the local TEC, to get people to agree a joint vision and mission statement. Given enough time and rational thought, believes Chris, this can be achieved. She no longer sees the depot as, necessarily, an arena for competing factions. She has developed an openness which allows her to empathise with the problems and difficulties of other groups. She is a member of an action learning set comprised of other senior depot managers from across the region. At the end of each meeting they have a 'doghouse' session in which they each admit to their worst mistake since they last met, and review how such errors can be avoided in future. Previously Chris would never have admitted to such foul ups.

Now Chris is Area Manager. She enjoys the job, except for the presence of the Admin. Manager who used to be a member of the action learning set that Chris used to attend. The Admin. Manager, when displeased with the new boss, regales anyone in the depot who will listen, with stories of Chris's past mistakes. Initially this abuse of the trust that was built up in the action learning set made Chris very cynical. But she learnt how to handle the Admin. Manager and doesn't make a big deal of any gossip.

Chris is still committed and enthusiastic about the organisation but is increasingly aware that things don't always work out as you plan or expect. She no longer believes that the solution to conflict within the organisation is bigger (sorry smaller) and better computers; nor does she believe that the existence of a nicely published mission and vision statement actually means that everyone shares the same values and is moving in the same direction. But this ironic awareness does not mean that Chris has become cynical; although this is precisely what has happened to many of her managerial colleagues. She has been doing a MBA course and the problem is that her head is full of too many ideas about how she might develop her organisation. The problem is to avoid bitting and bobbing from one half-implemented initiative to another. All the material she has learnt about organisational culture, processual approaches to organisational behaviour, qualitative research and so on makes it difficult to see the wood for the trees.

Chris has been Area Manager for a number of years now. She feels that she has developed a managerial maturity that is based on her sense of humour and tolerance for ambiguity. She came across an article, during a CD Rom search, by Helson and Wink (1992) whilst doing her MBA dissertation on the role of women in management in the leisure industry. This suggested that women develop greater tolerance of ambiguity as they grow older and the idea intrigued her. Chris continues to work for improvement (whatever that is) but perhaps in a different way. Now Chris believes in proceeding on a ready – fire – aim basis. This means trying small things without too much prior planning, building on them if they work, and modifying or abandoning them if they don't. No big rational masterplans (or metanarratives for anyone with a Gallic cum intellectual cast of mind) any more. When Chris was a management trainee she believed in acronyms like PURGE as many other managers still do; now, if forced, Chris is more likely to come out with an aphorism. As she once told a senior colleague, 'This organisation has a Guns and Roses culture. We have got guns pointed at us. But they have got flowers sticking out of the barrels. Watch it else you get the bullet; but enjoy the sweet flowers'.[*] Aphorisms make you think, acronyms just seek your blind acceptance. Chris accepts both the fragmented nature of the managerial role and the plurality of values within the organisation; and she can get a bit manic/depressive. But nevertheless Chris tries to maintain manners and tolerance when managing the depot's long-term survival. Her attitude is pessimistic wishful thinking.

The fable is not a true story. It is, however, based on a real industry and the reported and observed experiences of managers. Its purpose is to create a face validity for an argument about the ways in which a manager's perception and assumptions about:

- their relationship with the organisation,
- their managerial role, and

[*] This image comes from Tony Watson's ethnographic research in an electronics company (Watson, 1994b).

- the nature of managerial action,

might develop as the manager's role changes.

The argument can be put in a more formal and academic style, and this is what follows.

AN ACADEMIC THESIS

A phenomenology of manager development: the dialectic of managerial stances

An account is given in this paper of how a manager's developing awareness of an organisation, and their impact upon it, can be conceptualised. The model is built around a dialectical framework. According to Pascale (1990, p. 142) it's alright to use the Hegelian dialectic again in organisational analysis. One aspect of the dialectic of managerial stances concerns the developing perception of the relationship between an individual and the organisation they work within. In this process managers create a sense of personal meaning about the organisation, their actions in it and impact upon it. This has its antithesis in another aspect of the dialectic in which the idea of the organisation as a unity is worked out. As in all good dialectics the diversity of responses, of individuals to the organisation, is contradicted by a formal ideal of organisational unity. In brief, this is a dialectic of duty; the manager accepts a duty to work for the organisation. But what is this duty?

> 'The empty form of duty is therefore the first member of a moral triad – the blank identity as usual divorced from all detail.' (Mabbott, 1967, p. 45)

This emptiness is filled by an individual intuitionism that will lead to value pluralism.

> 'This theory is the natural second member of our triad, the plunge into sheer particularity, the field, as ever, of caprice and chaos and unrelated difference.' (ibid.)

In plainer language this represents a tension, in the notion of a managerial duty towards the organisation, between the vagueness of the vision and mission of an organisation, and the varieties of views and values that people within the organisation may have. This contradiction has its synthesis, in the standard dialectic, with the idea of the common good.

> 'Here is a unity of end with a diversity of means, and the reconciliation of form with content.' (ibid., p. 46)

But in civil society, from the analysis of which this argument has been taken, there are many institutions to help define the common good; there is less such help for managers in organisations. Therefore managers have to be aphorists to interpret and apply the organisational common good. A good aphorism doesn't contain easy answers (proverbs do that) neither does it lead to a cynical rejection of all answers (facetious or snide comments do that) but it does cause the reader to think hard for themselves. An aphorism is a prod to lazy thought and platitudes (Gross, 1983, p. viii); and, according to Eco (1987, p. 230): 'Aphorisms are incomplete and therefore require profound participation.' If I can illustrate the contrasts, from my own field of human resource management, people with the proverbial approach to HRM would say 'an empowered organisation is a powerful organisation', people who take the cynical approach would say 'we're into HRM; IPR, TQM, PRP, IIP, the lot'. The aphorist might say 'HRM is the continuation of strategy by other means', which sounds like it might contain an interesting thought; but it is not immediately apparent just what it is.

The manager has to bridge the gap, between the formal unity of an organisation and its empirical diversity, by developing a tolerance of ambiguity and an ability to work hard at creating a sense of meaning. This idea is similar to Reeves' criticism of higher education and the increasing standardisation of teaching and syllabuses. She argues that real (without the rhetorical protection of quotation marks) knowledge cannot be achieved by just 'joining in' with (or, in management jargon, buying into) an idea; it requires a hard search for personally relevant knowledge (Reeves, 1988, p. 14). A manager may also have to go through a hard search for meaning in their organisational life.

There are dialectics within dialectics, and each of the phases listed above has its own internal contradictions which need to be worked out. This process will be described as a sequence; but this is not to suggest that all managers will pass through all these phases in the order presented here. The phenomenology is in a logical and not a chronological order.

The dialectic of the self and the organisation

Managerial consciousness

The first stage in the development of managerial consciousness is one in which the manager is concerned with her or himself. There is an uncritical assumption of unity between the subject and the organisation. The organisation is seen as a misty, if occasionally irritating, context for personal growth. In this stage the manager is, through training, experience and a personal working out of values, developing a practical wisdom for doing the job. For most managers this development centres on their relationship with subordinate staff or with an immediate team of peers. Schon (1983) and Elliot (1991) see the development of such a practical ethic as the essence of professional development. Much manager development and training fits well within this stage of the dialectic because it concentrates on the growth of a manager's personal competency within an unproblematical organisational setting.

Managerial self-consciousness

The first stage, a sort of organisational innocence, is often negated by a growing awareness of plurality and conflict within the organisation. The manager becomes self-conscious; as the easy assumption of organisational unity is contradicted by a growing knowledge of its cultural and micropolitical fragmentation. This can occur when the manager, feeling increasingly confident and competent, starts to act beyond their immediate team or peer group and discovers that their values are not necessarily shared by others. This revelation is often accompanied by a recognition of the informal and covert politics of the organisation. The manager starts to hear gossip and stories about how senior managers really work and draws the conclusion that success means playing organisational politics. During this period of the dialectic the manager takes an aggressive and political stance in defence of the values developed during the first phase. In colloquial terms it means fighting for your corner. Anthony and Herzlinger (1975) illustrate some of the ploys used to fight for a budget in a public sector context. The garbage can theory of organisational decision making (Cohen *et al.*, 1972), with its emphasis on supporting friends and wounding enemies, provides a good description of managerial attitudes in this phase. Gamesplaying, as identified for example by Kakabadse (1982) in his study of social services departments, becomes an important characteristic of the relationship between managers.

These contradictions between uncritical assumptions about the unity of organisations and self-conscious political gamesplaying create their resolution in the dialectic of the unified organisation.

The dialectic of the unified organisation

Managers may come to the conclusion that organisational micropolitics is self-defeating, in at least two ways. Kakabadse identified the first negation in the study of social services departments previously mentioned. He reports that as staff develop ploys to extend their interests the management extend the rules to prevent them playing their little games. A classic Prisoners' Dilemma may develop as minor victories in skirmishes are followed by defeats in the battle. The second negation is that to be good organisational gamesplayers, managers have to be able to put themselves into the minds of their opponents; but by so empathising they begin to see the validity of the other's point of view; and their thirst for victory over them diminishes. The growing awareness of these ironies leads the manager to seek ways of overcoming these organisational conflicts and unifying the organisation.

The rational manager

The unifying project goes through its own dialectical process. In the first aspect the manager uses rationality and scientific methods to try to create organisational unity. Put simply the task of creating unity out of fragmented plurality is seen as possible if we apply enough cold, hard, systematic, rational thought to the situation. The assumption is that if only we use our increasing capabilities, for model building, for data manipulating and for computing, then the need for difficult, value-based decision making (which is at the root of organisational politics) can be transcended. It has been argued within the National Health Service for instance that improved, and IT-based, decision making would abolish all the haggling and decibel management that accompanies resource allocation issues in health care (Boyd, 1979 and Meadows, 1986). In this stage of the dialectic, to use Peters and Waterman's (1982, p. 40) phrase, the looseness of organisational politics is looked down upon from 'analytic ivory towers' and scorned. This approach to management can be well illustrated by the PPBS (planning, budgeting and programming systems) and corporate management approaches to public sector management that were in vogue in the 1970s (Eddison, 1973). These emphasised the importance of identifying the logical connections between an authority's activities and the role of cost-benefit analysis.

But the technocrats' search for better techniques creates its own downfall. The quest for better methods leads to systems that are too complicated to be used or understood. Systems may demand more data and information than it is possible to obtain or assess. As Eco (1985, p. 67) argues:

> *'The modern can go no further because it has produced a metalanguage that speaks of its impossible texts.'*

The story of the Wessex Regional Health Authority and its attempts to create a fully integrated information system may represent the modernist technocrat's nemesis (Cross, 1992).

The cultural manager

This contradiction in the rationalist method leads to a revisiting of the softer aspects of organisational life; a back to basics, neo-traditionalist concern for values, meaning and motivation. The manager's emphasis is no longer on bigger and better systems and computers but on defining clear and simple core values and mission statements. Managers in this phase of the dialectic believe organisational unity can be achieved by empowering everyone within the organisation in pursuit of a commonly agreed vision of the organisation's future. Moral purpose becomes more important to many managers than efficient systems.

But, ironically, the attempt to create a moral organisational consensus emphasises the distances between the official values of the organisation and those of any contra culture that may exist. Managers caught on the horns of this particular dilemma have a number of choices. They can encourage the dissidents to leave; and it is often argued that changing the people is a critical aspect of bringing about a change in organisational culture (Williams *et al.*, 1989). As one chief executive expressed it to me when we were discussing a possible consultancy project:

> *'We do have some cultural conflicts in this organisation; but I have dealt with it, he will have left the organisation within eight weeks.'*

Another option is that managers may use their control of the organisation's communication media to stress the good news and minimise the reporting of dissent. The in-house newsletter, in such a case, becomes characterised by upbeat news bites, telling of successes, rather than by more balanced accounts of organisational debates and arguments.

As a result of the working of these two mechanisms, attempts to build an ethical consensus produce an Olympian view that can lead managers to lose touch with the messy and complex diversity of organisational life and thought. In dialectical terms the absolute, and abstract, vision and mission of an organisation is undermined by its emptiness, its lack of content. So within the dialectic of organisational unity the manager's attempts to develop organisational integration, either by ignoring the abstract and just doing the sums right, or by creating a common sense of purpose, have within them the seeds of their own downfall. A manager's slow realisation of this leads to a synthesis, an approach which can take both the modernist and the neo-traditionalist approach into account whilst being enslaved to neither.

The dialectic of managerial action and ambiguity

The cynical manager

How does a manager react when their tools for structural or cultural change seem not to work? One reaction is to become cynical; and this is the first term in the dialectic of managerial action and ambiguity. The cynic no longer believes in what they are doing, they merely go through the motions. Nothing changes, they feel, and people's motives must always be presumed to be of the worst kind. As Nirad Chaudhuri defined this state of mind: 'cynicism tries to compensate for the lack of moral courage by airing malice.' (Chaudhuri, 1987, p. 128). This stage therefore is of a conceptual void; as there are no ends to seek there can only be managerial busyness – action but no movement.

The aporetic manager

The reaction to cynicism is a state of aporia. This is a stage in which there are so many things that need to be done, so many ends and values to be sought, that it all becomes complicated, and nothing gets done. The formal emptiness of cynicism is replaced by a confusing plethora of projects to be followed. When I talk to HRM people in organisations and find that they are implementing TQM, Investors in People, appraisal, PRP, simplifying salary scales and incremental systems, and moving into competency-based training; the state of aporia (if not at first the word itself) comes to mind. Aporia is a rhetorical figure of speech which, according to one of the illustrative quotations in the Oxford English Dictionary:

> 'Sheweth that (the speaker) doubteth where to begin for the multitude of matters, or what to do or say in some strange and ambiguous thing.'

One characteristic of the aporetic manager is that they suffer from time management problems. Because there are such a multitude of things to do they find it hard to prioritise and so try to cram too many tasks into their working days. Once, when I was running a manager development programme for head teachers in primary schools the course members complained bitterly about how they were overworked. They listed the roles they had to perform – manager, teacher, politician, counsellor and so on – until the roll included citizens' advice work in the wider community. It was hard for them to draw a line between the proper and the improper demands made upon them and so they found themselves short of the time needed to meet all these expectations. As Lyotard questions (Appignanesi, 1989, p. 20):

> 'Are you aware how the lack of time – in general and in particular – is characteristic of postmodern man (quite different in this respect from modern man): because we have, in every situation to challenge time. . . .'

The aporetic manager's dilemma arises from the tension between wanting to do the good thing and being unable to distinguish between the great number of good things that need to be done. The cynic's lack of belief in proper action is replaced by a formless diversity of moral acts.

Other aspects of this stage are similar to the post-modernist sensibility. Porphyrios (Appignanesi, 1989, p. 89–90) in discussing post-modernism and architecture identifies a number of characteristics such as fragmentation of styles, ironic commentary quotation and phantasmagoria. In other words architecture becomes a game in which there are no fixed points or reality or canons of style: but, instead, there is a whole history of architectural themes and motifs to be plundered and assembled according to the individual whim of the client and the estate agent. The aporetic manager may be in a similar condition; the whole panoply of managerial fashion is there to be used but this makes it difficult for the manager to make sense of it all.

The ironic manager

The synthesis of cynicism and aporia is a kind of ironic resourcefulness in which tolerance of ambiguity is related to purposive action. The manager no longer sees the need to give a coherent shape and purpose to their managerial and organisational activities. To use Lyotard's term, there is an 'incredulity towards metanarratives'. In this stage the difficulty of seeing the organisation as a unified whole with simple goals does not prevent the manager undertaking worthwhile enterprises within the organisation. As Rorty argues (1985, p. 168), what is needed:

> 'is a sort of intellectual analogue of civic virtue – tolerance, irony, and a willingness to let spheres of culture flourish without worrying too much about their "common ground", their unification, the intrinsic ideals they suggest or what picture of man they presuppose.'

The manager's view of themselves, in relation to the organisation, is akin to what Watson (1994a) calls soft post-modernism. In this last phase of the phenomenology there is a continuing, but never successful, attempt to reintegrate the managerial subject with the organisational objective; and this is accepted with a sense of irony and a loss of managerial innocence. This ungrounded integration requires some characteristic ways of interpreting organisations and the managerial role.

The first is an acceptance of fragmentation of organisational life. That organisational life is fragmented, formed from brief and disconnected passing episodes, is accepted by those people with a modernist and a post-modernist outlook. The difference is that the modernists believe the pieces can be put back together, whereas the post-modernists think they cannot (Harvey, 1989, p. 251). Some research, by Curley *et al.* (1986), suggests that people reject ambiguity because they feel their colleagues would find it unacceptable. Learning to tolerate ambiguity therefore may be more of a social problem than an intellectual one; and the use of humour and jokes may be one way of bringing about this change in social expectation. The second characteristic is *bricolage*, which means quotation and ironic comment. Managers pick up many bits and pieces of many styles and theories from their management training and other sources. However, the way that they use this theoretical baggage is closer to the technique of the bricoleur than that of the management scientist. For example I have often heard managers refer to the theories of span of control (Filley *et al.*, 1976, Ch. 18) when they are arguing the case for change in organisational structure. Their tone often reflects a pragmatic borrowing rather than a true belief in the concept. Like the bricoleur of anthropology they are creating useful and aesthetically satisfying myths from whatever materials may be available in order that a purpose may be achieved. As Snell (1993, p. 19) puts it, with his tongue in his cheek:

> 'disputes would be solved by outflanking opponents with ever more captivating and enchanting metaphors, and the worst violence would consist of clumsily invoking unpleasant and distasteful metaphors in argument.'

But, it is understood that this activity is not the working out of a grand purpose but an incremental muddling through. As William of Baskerville has it, paraphrasing Wittgenstein, in Eco's medieaval whodunnit:

> 'The order that our mind imagines is like a net, or like a ladder, built to attain something. But afterwards you must throw the ladder away, because you discover that, even if it was useful, it was meaningless.' (Eco, 1983, p. 492)

This brings us to the next characteristic of the manager in this phase of development. They see management decision making as a process of design and not as the process of evaluation of options as suggested by management science. The decision making method of the textbooks assumes the existence of superordinate goals whilst the design approach represents a step by step movement [Peters and Waterman's (1982, p. 119) Ready – fire – aim] which proceeds without a detailed knowledge of the final destination.

A fourth characteristic emerges from this form of decision making; managers may have to present a facade of coherence and pattern which contradicts the more chaotic activities going on behind the facade. Just as buildings may have a facade which is unrelated to the complexity or function of their use, as in the case of the Palladian town house of Georgian England or the 'decorated sheds' of 20th century retail parks, so managers have to present an attractive front to their activities. This is not, in this phase, done cynically. When I was a staff developer I was required by my management to provide performance indicators on such items as the number of people attending courses and their satisfaction with it as measured on a five-point scale. These performance indicators did not bear much relevance to the purposes I thought were important in staff development. I tried as best I could to explain the benefits to management as I saw them, but I also had to accept that the performance indicators did represent a legitimate interest of the people who were funding the service. There is an acceptance in this phase that an organisational activity may have many meanings at several levels to different people.

These characteristics of the final stage of the phenomenology represent a particular stance in relation to the cultural dimensions developed by Kluckholm and Schein and mentioned at the start of this chapter. In summary, human activity is seen as complex and ambiguous; and the nature of reality is viewed as something which responds to a design approach, to decision making, rather than to the formalism of management science. The relationships between people are seen as rhetorical, involving storytelling (Fisher, 1993) and the construction of myths. The relationship between the organisation and its environment is thought of as a complicated one involving the overlapping motives of different stakeholders. The managers of the organisation have to present a variety of facades to meet these various expectations. Human nature, to cope with all this variability, has to be seen as playful, humorous, tolerant and possessing of an ungrounded notion of virtue.

LECTURETTE[*]

Managerial stances and manager development

Managers' senses of their managerial role change and develop with their experience and careers. The way, for example, that new and inexperienced managers make sense of their jobs is not the way of other managers. This suggests that the type of, and approach to, management development used by HRD professionals ought to change to meet the divergent stances of different managers. Put another way, the conclusion that a single type of manager development will not work effectively with all types of managers is not simply conditioned by the fact that some groups of managers are more skilled and competent than others.

Managers' attitudes and reactions to manager development are also related to their managerial stance, which is defined by:

- their assumptions about managerial action; are they in control of things or are things unpredictable and subject to Sod's Law;
- their assumptions about whether decision making is based on hard information and analysis, or on intuition and politics;
- their assumptions about their organisations, whether they see them as united in common endeavour or riven by faction;
- their assumptions about other people in their organisations; if, for example, they are asked by their boss whether they can attend a meeting next Thursday, do they wonder whether a 'yes' will imply that they are not busy enough, and whether a 'no' will be taken as insubordination; or do they just give a plain, and true answer?
- their assumptions about business strategy; do they see it as planning, reaction or PR?

I want to suggest a four-stage model which identifies the stances that a manager may go through during a career. The model is a simplification, but one which may cause you to think about your own managerial stance. The model is summarised in Fig. 2.1, and a more detailed description of the managerial stances is given below.

The developing manager

The key elements of a manager's way of making sense of their job in this phase are:

- a focus on personal development, and only a misty and uncritical awareness of the wider organisation and its environment;
- working on the assumption that the organisation is essentially unified in its common purpose;
- an emphasis on the small team or group of peers with whom the manager works directly;

[*] I have chosen the form and style of a trainers' lecturette, such as can be found in manuals of training material (Jones and Pfeiffer, 1975: 109), to simplify and summarise this chapter's argument.

Managerial stances	Characteristics	% of critical incidents
The developing manager	The development of, and experimentation with, managerial skills	13%
	Organisation of personal time and role	6%
	Confirmation of personal style and values	9%
	Development of stability, coping skills and assertion	14%
	Developing team building skills	13%
		Sub-total 55%
The political manager	Awareness of the informal and covert workings of the organisation	8%
	Acting politically in defence of own section/dept	6%
	Developing relationships with senior managers	6%
		Sub-total 20%
The integrating manager	Developing a perspective beyond one's professional or functional concerns	7%
	Communicating and empathising with other 'cultural' groups	4%
	Building a vision and shared values	2%
		Sub-total 13%
The ambiguous manager	Tolerance of ambiguity and the acceptance of organisational conflict	5%
	Bias to action and ready – fire – aim[1]	5%
		Sub-total 10%

[1] Peters and Waterman *In Search of Excellence* (1982).
The percentages add up to 98, not 100, because of rounding off errors.

Fig. 2.1   The progression of managerial stances

- developing an understanding of what the managerial role is, compared with earlier professional or functional roles, and acquiring the basic managerial competencies;
- developing a personal confidence as a manager and getting a grip on personal priorities and the problems of time management;
- developing notions about proper and improper behaviour in the organisation – constructing an ethical position which moves beyond responding to threats and blandishments.

The political manager

In this, the second phase in the development of managerial stances, the manager becomes aware of the wider organisation, and the cultural and ideological differences it encompasses. Within this context, the manager sees their role as 'fighting for their corner'. This involves:

- getting in on the grapevine and listening to organisational gossip about senior managers; becoming tuned in to the shifting nuances of informal policy;
- developing the devious arts of organisational micropolitics. Making allies, making cases and undermining enemies. Learning the ploys necessary to get you, and your team, the biggest budgets and the highest ratings, and generally to protect them from other, generally malevolent, groups in the organisation;
- spending less time with the immediate work group and more time with senior managers.

The integrating manager

In the next phase of the development of stances it occurs to managers that all the politics and infighting are sub-optimal, as far as the whole organisation is concerned. From this stance the manager becomes concerned to get everybody focused onto a clear and simple organisational vision and mission, which will minimise the conflicts and improve organisational conflicts. This involves:

- viewing the organisation from a corporate perspective and not from a factional one;
- recognising that groups are not necessarily ill-intentioned when they cause problems for each other. They are simply reacting to the pressures upon them, and the difficulties this causes for others are simply unintended consequences of their concern to survive;
- championing techniques for developing common vision, this may include quality circles and other quality initiatives, team building events in the Brecon Beacons or away-days in nice warm hotels.

The ambiguous manager

The ambiguous manager is one who has developed much tolerance for ambiguity; but this does not create cynicism. Rather the ambiguous manager has the moral tenacity to pursue ambitious projects, even though they recognise that the final destination may turn out to be very different to the one intended; and that, when reached, it may prove not to be where they need to be. The key characteristics of this stance are:

- a sense of humour, and a sense of scepticism rather than of cynicism;
- being comfortable with ambiguity, not forever trying to develop policies, computer algorithms, procedures and protocols which will clarify everything. Instead the ambiguous manager relishes ambiguity and the creative freedom it provides;
- developing a design approach to decision making, which uses the manager's intuition and proceeds on a trial and error basis.

The managerial stances and manager development

The argument I want to make is that the standard approaches to manager development, including occupational standards and the National Vocational Qualification, NVQ, structure, are adequate to the needs of the developing managers, but inappropriate to managers with other stances. In 1988 I carried out an evaluation study on a cohort of middle managers who had been on a three-week, in-house, management development programme. All of the participants were interviewed, 6 months to 18 months after they had completed the programme. They were asked to describe critical incidents when they felt the programme had had an impact on how they worked as managers. Thirty-eight participants were interviewed, and this generated 172 critical incidents. Within these incidents, which are stories of organisational life, I identified 374 examples of managerial learning. These examples have been analysed using the stances model, and the resulting frequency analysis is shown in Fig. 2.1.

This analysis shows that most of the managerial learning, arising from this particular programme, fits with the characteristics of the developing manager stance. But a significant minority (20%) of the reported learning impacts can be classified as appropriate to the political manager. The reported learning, which might be classified as typical of the integrating manager or the ambiguous manager, is relatively slight. The sample is too small to be taken as representative of all managers, but the data could be interpreted as meaning:

- that standard management development, which these programmes were, is effective at meeting the development needs of managers with 'development', or 'political' stances;
- that either standard management development is not designed to, and does not, meet the needs of managers with the 'integrating' or 'ambiguous' stance;
- or, that relatively junior middle managers are not receptive to the management development issues appropriate to managers with more sophisticated managerial stances.

Discussion points

1 Does this model have any truth, or face validity, in the light of your own manager development?
2 Does the sequence shown in the model, from developing manager to ambiguous manager, represent healthy growth, or decay?
3 Does this model have any relevance to HRD managers and professionals?
4 How might managers with different stances view the nature and purpose of manager development? Which forms and styles of manager development might be appropriate to each stance?

EPILOGUE

The model presented in the fable, the thesis and the lecturette is not an empirical description of the stages a manager will go through. It is a description of the logical connections and contradictions which bind together various stances managers may take in relation to their roles and their organisations. Most managers, I suspect, will experience some of these tensions and conflicts although not necessarily in the chronological order in which they are presented here. They therefore raise questions about the nature of manager development if not of HRD as a whole.

The first issue is whether the phenomenology represents some teleological development. Is there a sense in which the ironic manager is better than a manager in one of the earlier stages? The fable also implies that there is a relationship between a manager's stance and their career stage. This raises the question of contingency; whether different stances are appropriate to different managerial functions and statuses.

If it is the case that the phenomenology does represents a hierarchical process, it can only be in the sense that the ironic manager has got past the stage of assuming any easy or quick-fix solutions. It is not that the ironic manager has a better answer: it is just that he or she realises, without cynicism, that there is no overriding answer. As Fox writes, the purpose of manager education is:

> 'to provide managers with a new language game . . . management education should neither be a throwback to a golden age, nor a dereliction of value judgements in favour of the illusory neutrality of objective techniques for performance optimisation; it should critically challenge the rules of the management game, thereby encouraging inventiveness and imagination.' (Fox, 1987)

To a manager developer with an academic bent this is a beguiling idea. But it may not be so interesting to hard-nosed HRD directors. There needs to be a debate therefore about whether we should try to help managers work their way through the phenomenology or whether we should stick to the development and assessment of competencies.

It may be that managers should be helped to identify and consider their stances without any presumption that manager development should, or could, help them to a higher form of consciousness. One strong argument for this position is that within any particular organisation, there will be managers with different stances. Helping managers to understand the stances may improve mutual understanding and communication; but it may also lead to glib and inappropriate labelling of people.

A third issue concerns the processes of manager development. If it is thought important to consider stances as part of manager development processes, how can it be done? What training techniques and approaches might be appropriate? A related question is how manager development programmes might be made amenable to people with different stances. A rational manager for example might well be satisfied with a traditionally taught programme on operational research and scientific decision making; but the response of a cynical, or of an ironic manager is likely to be less than enthusiastic. Similarly a cultural stance manager might find completing a NVQ portfolio to be a constraining activity because its focus on tasks would undervalue the importance of selling a vision.

I had also better come clean before I finish. I suspect, but have not of course proved, that managerial stances may be a more important factor in managerial effectiveness (whatever that is) than competency. Possession of competences is important but, by analogy, it is not being able to use a personal computer that matters, it is your attitude and stance towards the machine that affects its contribution to the organisation. Let me illustrate this by a series of questions about your stance towards your desk top or notebook computer. Is it used to increase your personal mastery of the machine? Is it used to show that your machine is better and faster than your colleague's? Is it used to conduct statistical optimisation modelling, or is it used to make sophisticated multi-media presentations of the organisation's vision? Is it cautiously used because you fear it will fail to perform at a critical juncture; or do you have so many software applications that you never get round to using any of them? Or, do you use it in a careful and limited way, keeping an ironic sense of humour about its limitations and not becoming obsessional about its abilities?

References

Anthony, R.N. and Herzlinger, R. (1975) *Management Control in Non-profit Making Organisations*, Homewood Illinois, Richard D. Irwin.

Appignanesi, L. ed. (1989) *Postmodernism: ICA Documents*, London, Free Association Books.

Boyd, K.M. (1979) 'The Ethics of Resource Allocation in Health Care', Edinburgh Medical Group; *Moral Issues in Health Care 2*, Edinburgh, Edinburgh University Press.

Chaudhuri, N. C. (1987) *Thy Hand Great Anarch: India 1921–1952*, London, Chatto and Windus.

Cohen, M.D., March, J.G. and Olsen, J.P. (1972) 'A Garbage Can Model of Decision Making', *Administrative Science Quarterly*, vol. 17, no. 1.

Cross, M. (1992) 'NHS plays the numbers game with patients: Infotech', *The Times*, 11 December.

Curley, S.P., Yates, J.F. and Abrams, A. (1986) 'Psychological sources of ambiguity avoidance', *Organisational Behavior and Human Decision Processes*, vol. 38, no. 2.

Eco, U. (1983) Trans. Weaver, W. *The Name of the Rose*, London, Secker and Warburg.

Eco, U. (1985) Trans. Weaver, W. *Reflections on the Name of the Rose*, London, Secker and Warburg.

Eco, U. (1987) Trans. Weaver, W. *Travels in Hypereality*, London, Picador/Secker and Warburg.

Eddison, T. (1973) *Local Government: Management and Corporate Planning*, Aylesbury, Institute of Local Government Studies and Leonard Hill Books.

Elliot, J. (1991) 'A Model of Professionalism and its Implications for Teacher Education', *British Education Research Journal*, vol. 17, no. 4.

Filley, A. C., House, R.J. and Kerr, S. (1976) *Managerial Process and Organisational Behaviour*, Second edition, Glenview Illinois, Scott Foresman and Co.

Fisher, C.M. (1993) 'The Rhetorics of Appraisal: Story telling and the design of appraisal schemes', a paper presented at the 11th *EGOS Colloquium, The production and diffusion of organisational knowledge*, Paris.

Fox, S. (1987) 'The Casuistry of the Imagination: Post modern management education', a paper presented to the 6th *Conference on Education and Development in Organisations, Centre for Management Learning*, University of Lancaster.

Gross, J. ed. (1983) *The Oxford Book of Aphorisms*, Oxford, Oxford University Press.

Harvey, D. (1989) *The Condition of Postmodernity: An Enquiry into the Origins of Cultural Change*, Oxford, Blackwell.

Helson, R. and Wink, P. (1992) 'Personality change in women from the early 40s to the early 50s', *Psychology and Aging*, vol. 7, no. 1, March.

Jones, J.E. and Pfeiffer, J.W. (1975) *The 1975 Handbook for Group Facilitators*, s.1, University Associates.

Kakabadse, A. (1982) *Culture of the Social Services*, Aldershot, Gower Press.

Kluckholm, F.R. and Strodtbeck, F.L. (1961) *Variations in Value Orientations*, Westport Conn., Greenwood.

Mabbott, J.D. (1967) *The State and the Citizen*, Second edition, London, Hutchinson.

Mansfield, B. (1993) 'Competence based Qualifications: A Response', *Journal of European Industry Training*, vol. 17, no. 3.

Meadows, J. (1986) 'Local Health Service Resource Allocation and Planning', *Public Finance and Accountancy*, 7th November.

Pascale, R. (1990) *Managing on the Edge: How Successful Companies use Conflict to Stay Ahead*, Harmondsworth, Penguin.

Peters, T.J. and Waterman Jnr, R.M. (1982) *In Search of Excellence*, New York, Harper and Row.

Reeves, M. (1988) *The Crisis in Higher Education – Competence, Delight and the Common Good*, Milton Keynes, Society for Research into Higher Education and the Open University Press.

Rorty, R. (1985) 'Habermas and Lyotard on Post Modernity', in Bernstein, R.J. ed., *Habermas and Modernity*, Cambridge, Polity Press.

Schein, E.R. (1985) *Organisational Culture and Leadership*, San Francisco CA, Jossey-Bass.

Schon, D. (1983) *The Reflective Practitioner: How Professionals Think In Action*, New York, Basic Books.

Snell, R. (1993) *Developing Skills for Ethical Management*, London, Chapman and Hall.

Stewart, J. and Hamlin, B. (1992) 'Competence based Qualifications: The Case against Change', *Journal of European Industrial Training*, vol. 16, no. 7.

Watson, T.J. (1994a) *Professing Postmodernism – Soft Postmodernist Thoughts on Education and Management*, Unpublished professorial inaugural lecture, Nottingham Business School, The Nottingham Trent University.

Watson, T.J. (1994b) *In Search of Management: Culture, Chaos and Control in Management*, London, Routledge.

Williams, A., Dobson, P. and Walters, M. (1989) *Changing Culture: New Organisational Approaches*, London, Institute of Personnel Management.

3

Inter-cultural Perspectives on HRD

Valerie Stead and Monica Lee

INTRODUCTION

This chapter is based on two claims by the authors. First, that HRD, as a broad concept which may relate to individuals as well as groupings of people (teams, communities, nations), is a relatively young and predominantly Western concept, which has emerged from management and development thinking shaped by values and events in Western society. Second, by tracing the cyclical and dynamic nature of HRD and by exploring what it means to a nation of people, we can gain some insight into how the nation manages people and the influence HRD might have upon the national future.

ASSUMPTIONS AND LIMITS

The chapter aims to consider these claims by exploring inter-cultural perspectives of Western and Central Eastern Europe through a dual framework of historical socio-economic development and motivational development. The authors recognise that, in attempting to sketch an historical and developmental outline of Western and Central Eastern Europe, only a broad analysis can be reached within the confines of this chapter. The authors intend to take a broad look at Western Europe and Central Eastern Europe, the former Eastern bloc countries, highlighting particular countries where appropriate to illustrate key issues. In focusing on inter-cultural perspectives on HRD, and in an attempt to gain an overarching concept of what HRD means to us today, we recognise that this chapter does not address explicitly the issue of HRD as a progression from training and development, but rather views it as a wider and more holistic concept borrowing from fields of management education, research and training, and organisational and management learning. We also recognise that our perspective of Western European and Central Eastern European developments is essentially Western and as such brings with it limits and implicit assumptions.

Our assumptions fall into three broad areas, which we will explore in turn: first, our understanding of culture, second our understanding of motivation, and third our choice of historical framework.

Culture

Attempting an inter-cultural perspective begs an understanding of culture. In this chapter our particular understanding of the term inter-cultural is based on Hofstede's notion of culture as being 'the collective programming of the mind, which distinguishes the members of one human group from another' (Hofstede, 1980). By taking a brief glimpse through the history of two different sets of nations we will be looking at the effects that such 'programming' might have on the development of HRD and also exploring whether HRD can in fact exist within a certain type of programming.

Motivation

The study of motivation theory is particularly relevant to our mapping of HRD perspectives. Reaching an understanding of the emergence and nature of HRD begs an understanding of what drives us to develop, and the ideas and thinking we will be exploring on our historical journey will have implicit assumptions about motivation (MacGregor, 1960). In recognising that the development of new ideas creates new needs, we are recognising motivation to move from one phase to another.

The study of what brings about this motivation was spearheaded by Abraham Maslow, and was highly influential in the post-war climate, and therefore is one of the key ideas of the era where we start our historical journey. Maslow's research on human motivation theory culminated in the invention of the hierarchy of needs. Maslow maintained that all human beings have a hierarchy of needs and that the satisfaction of one level releases the needs at the next level (Fig. 3.1). Thus once the basic physiological and safety needs had been met they would no longer provide motivation and the higher needs of love, self-esteem and personal fulfilment would be released which in turn become the motivators (Maslow, 1970).

Whilst there has been debate about the details of Maslow's theory of motivation in its use as a universal concept, and in its hierarchical format (Hodgetts and Luthans, 1991; Hofstede, 1991), there is general acceptance of the overall structure. It has formed the basis for a number of studies within organisational settings, most notably those of Herzberg and MacGregor, which will be explored later within the historical framework.

In choosing Maslow's hierarchy of needs to explore the emergence of national, organisational and individual needs within the historical socio-economic development of Western and Central Eastern Europe, we place the start of our journey at the end of the Second World War.

Historical framework

> 'Every few hundred years throughout Western history, a sharp transformation has occurred. In a matter of decades, society altogether rearranges itself – its world view, its basic values, its social and political structures, its arts, its key institutions. Fifty years later a new world exists . . .' (Drucker, 1992)

Within the past 50 years Europe has seen dramatic transformation, and it is against this colourful background that we wish to trace the development of HRD to the current day. This analysis will present an outline of the socio-economic development of Western and

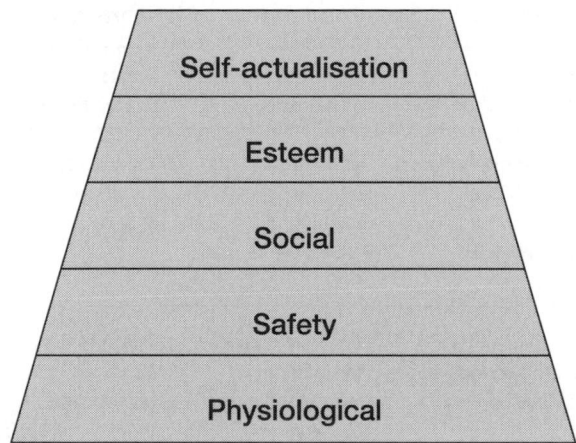

Fig. 3.1   After Maslow's hierarchy of needs

Central Europe focusing on events of the era, ideas of the time, the impact of these ideas on the development of human resources at a national, organisational and individual level and the emergence of new needs. In this way the historical journey will take us from one set of ideas to a creation of needs to a further development of ideas, thus demonstrating the cyclical nature and evolutionary development of HRD.

Our historical framework draws on the model by Pedlar *et al.* in their work *The Learning Company* (1991), which offers a glimpse of the evolution of training and development moving from post-war Britain to the current day. This is based on the argument that as one era presents a need, ideas and solutions are created to meet that need, which create a new approach and perspective (Lessem, 1986; Kinsman, 1990; Pedlar *et al.*, 1991). As the new approach develops, further needs come to light which call for a new perspective, leading to the creation of ideas and solutions in order to develop. It is interesting to note that according to Pedlar *et al.*, this assumption about HRD is in itself a product of its era, mirroring current thinking that learning organisations must evolve, adapt and transform to develop and survive (Argyris and Schon, 1978; Peters and Waterman, 1982; Senge, 1990; Pedlar *et al.*, 1991).

Our analysis of HRD within the historical and motivational frameworks, beginning at the end of the Second World War and taking us up to the current day following the collapse of communist rule in Central Eastern Europe, is outlined in Table 3.1. This schematic table highlights our view of key events within European history and the formation of HRD. The similar historical influences and trends in HRD at the post-war period enable us to begin our analysis by first discussing the historical scene, and second discussing the trends in HRD of both sets of nations together.

Due to the divergence in political, economic and social influences thereafter, our discussion will focus on Western Europe and Central Eastern Europe in turn, by setting the historical scene of each, and then moving on to look at the place of HRD from a motivational perspective for each set of nations. We will then conclude our analysis by considering principles underlying the current nature of HRD and by speculating on its future direction.

Table 3.1   Schematic view of historical influences

Time	HRD West Europe	Events West Europe	Events C. East Europe	HRD C. East Europe
Post-1945	Scientific management. Control through national and organisational hierarchies.	Rebuilding, restabilising, remobilising. Political trend to left.	Central planning structure.	Scientific management. Control through central authority.
1950s – 1960s	Recognition of and research on motivation and development needs.	Economic prosperity then economic crisis. Move to European unity. Civil unrest, concerns about peace and environment.	Death of Stalin. Economic growth and decline. Erection of Berlin Wall. Civil unrest and Soviet crackdown.	Denial of developmental needs. Continued focus on central control.
1970s – mid 1980s	Non-integrated self-development and organisational development strategies.	Economic recession, then stability. High unemployment. Advancing technology. Heavy industry decline, service industry growth. Single European Act.	Economic crisis. Growing lack of confidence in national governments. Gorbachev becomes Soviet leader.	Continued denial and suppression of developmental needs.
mid 1980s – current day	Move towards integrated concept of HRD through TQM and organisation transformation.	Economic growth, then recession. End of Cold War and collapse of communist rule. Transition programmes and aid towards market economies. Move to German reunification. Maastricht Treaty.	Economic crisis. Civil unrest.	Recognition of human rights and developmental needs. Access to and experimentation with Western methodology.

THE POST-WAR YEARS

Western and Central Eastern Europe history

Following the Second World War Western Europe and Central Eastern Europe were in the similar position of having to make the transition from war to peace, and to face the challenge of restabilising and rebuilding social, economic and political structures. At this point in history the national development of human resources in both Western and Central Eastern Europe mirrored these needs and was singular in its aim to rebuild, restabilise and remobilise the workforce. This need called for an approach which would skill up the workforce and regain industrial output quickly. Although governments in

Western and Central Eastern Europe were at different ends of the political spectrum and adhering to different value systems, national needs were at the same basic hierarchical level of securing shelter, safety, food and warmth. At this motivational level, the nations' peoples looked towards clear governmental leadership and responsibility, united in their efforts to gain a better standard of living.

Western Europe stood on the brink of economic collapse following the end of the Second World War in 1945. The defeat of fascism heralded a political trend to the left concerned with restabilisation and the rebuilding of national economies within a democratic framework, following a model of programmes of nationalisation and welfare systems. Although individual countries within Western Europe were primarily occupied with regaining their own stability, the consequences of war also called for strategic planning and policy making at a European level to safeguard economic stability, human rights and future protection of its citizens. To these ends the Charter of the United Nations, chiefly aimed at gaining access for participants in world markets, was drafted and the horrific revelations of the concentration camps led to the European Convention of Human Rights 1950 (Storey, 1993). The iron grip of Stalin's rule in the Soviet Union and in Eastern Europe led to increased tension which developed into the Cold War, encouraging Western Europe to close ranks and thus sowing the seeds of the European Community (Laqueur, 1992).

Central Eastern Europe was in no better shape than the West following the war, and attempts to build a running economy and bring stability brought a period of severe hardship and crisis management (Nikolajew, 1992). The Soviet Union had gained control of all Eastern Europe and the Balkans except Greece, Yugoslavia and Albania and began a gradual programme of political dominance. An initial degree of political independence immediately following the war, with the establishment of all-party coalitions excluding fascist and extreme right wing representation, soon gave way to new coalitions where communists obtained all key positions. This led to the introduction of one-party communist regimes, based on a soviet socialist model adapted from Marxist philosophy with central planning at its core (Nikolajew, 1992). National economies were structured hierarchically under the one-party political systems with the military as a major priority, leading to a focus on heavy industry and machine production with large regional industrial sites often producing one item. National, regional and local policy and planning were steered by commissions and ministries and monitored by the party. Parliaments met infrequently, mainly to rubber stamp policy formulated by the Party and with little debate of major issues.

HRD – Western and Central Eastern Europe

Management thinking at the time emphasised a systematic, ordered and planned approach to training and development which provided a clear way forward. This approach is best characterised by the Weberian premise of control through authority, which reinforced the power base of the national government, and Taylor's scientific concept of management, which was built on the basis that people would be motivated by economic reward and a straightforward rational approach, and that the employers' main concern was low labour cost (Weber, 1943; Taylor, 1947).

Organisations were at the same need level as the nations and their individuals. The war had seen wholesale destruction of major cities, bridges and transport routes. Industry had been geared completely towards the war effort and there was a clear need to rethink organisational strategy in an era of peace. The scientific rational approach enabled this process and brought about organisational structures characterised by central control and lack of individual autonomy. Typical structures resembled Mintzberg's notion of the machine bureaucracy where the focus is a pull towards standardisation and control through formal rules and regulation from a central authority (Mintzberg, 1983). This suited the systematic rationality of scientific management, and also gave credence to what MacGregor saw as the traditional understanding of human nature. Known as Theory X, this concept maintains that the workforce wish to avoid responsibility and need to be firmly controlled and directed by management (MacGregor, 1960). In Western Europe this led to tight top-down management structures with decision making firmly in the hands of directors and chief executives. Efficiency was measured and monitored by time and motion studies, and payment by results systems were established reinforcing the belief that individuals are motivated by financial reward (Huczynski and Buchanan, 1991). In Central Eastern Europe control was further removed and firmly in the hands of the Party, which determined managerial positions, and directed and monitored management decisions.

So immediately post-war, the picture in Western Europe is one of focused national strategy, tight organisational structures and hardworking individuals preoccupied with regaining stability. Central Eastern Europe is similarly focused, but with control remaining clearly at a national level, determining organisational structures and behaviour, and individual advancement and work patterns. Although both sets of nations are united at national, organisational and individual levels in regaining stability, the focus is clearly on the management of human resources rather than development.

THE 1950s–1960s

In both Central Eastern and Western Europe the similar approach to development brought about similar growth. The 1950s saw little unemployment, better housing and healthcare, comprehensive welfare systems and increasing demand for labour. However, the difference in political management of control and authority was to lead the way to change and development in Western Europe, and become a recipe for stagnation and repression in Central Eastern Europe.

Western Europe history

The death of Stalin in 1953 kindled hope in Western Europe that the Cold War may come to an end. As it became clear that this was not so, attempts to establish a more united Europe brought a liaison between West Germany, France, Italy and Benelux in 1958, with de Gaulle refusing entry to Britain. By 1960 Western Europe was enjoying a time of economic prosperity, with the economic boom (Wirtschaftswunder) of West Germany and strong growth in Britain, Italy and France.

However, the 1960s heralded major changes and a questioning of political power structures. By the late 1960s there was major unrest throughout Western Europe.

Britain underwent a series of economic crises and saw the onset of civil unrest in Northern Ireland. In 1968 French student demonstrations led to massive anti-government protest marches in Paris. Student demonstrations were held in West Germany, Italy and Spain and anti-nuclear protests in Britain. Increasing concern about Soviet power, the consequences of the Vietnam War, and the movement of nuclear missiles engendered a mood of dissatisfaction which brought about an upsurge in new parties and movements concerned with peace and the environment, and a move away from the consumer society (Lane and Ersson, 1987). Western Europe was overwhelmed by the pace of change. Perceptions of the world we lived in were challenged by, amongst other things, watching the first steps of man on the moon, by the advancement of technology in the home and at work, by the coming together of a European Community and the possibility of a borderless world (Ohmae, 1992).

Central Eastern Europe history

In Central Eastern Europe the death of Stalin in 1953, and the succession of Khrushchev and later Brezhnev brought about tighter control and a stronger grip on Eastern Europe, leading to an increase in industrial production in the 1950s which gave way to decline in the early 1960s (Laqueur, 1992). The revelations of Stalin's brutality brought a period of discontent to Eastern Europe in the mid 1950s. The Soviet regime was openly questioned in Poland in 1956, leading to a change in government and a purge of intellectuals. Revolution in Hungary was suppressed by a Soviet invasion.

Concerns were heightened in Western Europe by the Soviet development of intercontinental ballistic missiles (ICBMs), and the setting up of rocket bases in Cuba. Further tension arose in 1961 in Berlin when troops erected a wall around the Soviet sector to stem the increasing flow of citizens to West Germany.

In the late 1960s students demonstrating against poor living conditions sparked a series of mass demonstrations and meetings in Czechoslovakia. The Soviet Union invaded with force in 1968 and began a harsh programme of normalisation. The Cold War continued and earlier hopes of liberalisation in Central Eastern Europe had disappeared.

HRD – Western Europe

At a national level in Western Europe the rational and systematic development of human resources had worked well, and provided low unemployment, and skilled workforces who enjoyed the benefits of comprehensive welfare systems. The scientific concept of management expanded in organisations with the development and delineation of functions such as marketing, finance and operations research with a focus on systematic job analysis (Lee, 1995). Britain was typical of this time when the implementation of the Industrial Training Act in 1964 led to systematic training of the workforce in job specific skills, with management ordering and planning this process within functional systems (Pedlar *et al.*, 1991). At a national level the continuation of this human resource strategy seemed appropriate in a time of increasing technology, but organisations and individuals were less happy (Laqueur, 1992). Specific skills development led to highly trained workforces, but also led to a labour force of isolated individuals with little understanding or ability to transfer learning and to work cross-functionally, heightened by the matrix structure of many organisations (Argyris and Schon, 1978).

Dissatisfaction and frustration arose with the scientific approach in the emerging need to find a way to deal with inter-disciplinary problems, to address the problem of transferable skills and to attain a more flexible and less bureaucratic approach to work management. Organisational studies of motivation demonstrated that financial reward was not a motivating factor, and provided an important leap forward in our understanding of HRD.

Herzberg *et al.* (1959) noted, in relating the study of motivation to work, that hierarchies of needs existed within groups and that there were two different ranges of human needs. At one level there was the need to avoid dissatisfaction and concern with the environment such as ensuring good working conditions, appropriate salary and policy and administrative structures, and adequate supervision. At another level there was the need to achieve, gain recognition and personal advancement. Herzberg *et al.* suggest that the latter provides the motivation whereas the former are basic hygiene factors which must be in place before motivation can occur. Following the post-war crisis years the hygiene factors were now in place and organisations as well as individuals were turning their attention to ways in which they could move on from the process of settling and stabilising to further development and achievement. MacGregor (1960) took this further in his attempt to find a way in which business might best gain commitment and harness the potential of the workforce. His Theory Y maintained that the principle of integration should replace direction and control (the basis of Theory X), in that the workforce need the opportunity to achieve through shared responsibility thus gaining personal fulfilment in their work.

MacGregor argued that by satisfying the basic needs of employees through reward and incentives, management could no longer use these methods to exert control. He felt that the time had come for a new approach which would aim to satisfy the self-actualising needs of the workforce: new theory, changed assumptions, more understanding of the nature of human behaviour in organisational settings (MacGregor, 1960).

HRD – Central Eastern Europe

While the West began to experiment with the development of new strategies to meet emerging needs in the face of enormous change, Central Eastern Europe's demands for change were met with firm denial and suppression. The crackdown on individual expression and the demand for individual rights led to greater suppression from central powers and political monitoring of organisations and individuals. Lack of ownership in the rhetoric expounded by the Soviet authority brought about conformity and servility in individuals (Batt, 1990). The sacrifice of individual and organisational development needs to those of a distant all powerful authority led to a period of stagnation. Within this power structure the Western understanding of development as defined in the *Oxford English Dictionary* (1992), as a stage of growth or advancement, is denied meaning, and the very notion of human resource development as cyclical and dynamic responding to emerging needs and creating new strategies to meet these needs, was impossible.

Thus in Western Europe with the satisfaction of security and safety needs, we can see the emerging recognition that human resources have a motivational need to be developed. In Central Eastern Europe, however, with the continued posing of threats to safety and security by an oppressive regime, the recognition of developmental needs is denied and concerns are kept rooted at the basic needs levels, thus effectively blocking the formation of any concept of HRD.

THE 1970s–MID 1980s

Western Europe history

The mood of instability in the 1960s continued into the 1970s. Between 1973 and 1976 Greece, Portugal and Spain had established democratic systems in place of authoritarian regimes. Oil prices increased and the growing pace of technology put severe strain on traditional heavy industry. Economic recession spread in the 1970s and continued into the early 1980s. There was continued social disorder with the rise of terrorism and unrest in West Germany, Italy, Spain and Northern Ireland. Along with the recession and energy crises came a recognition of the consequences of the consumer society and industrial age which manifested itself in ecological concerns typified by the green movement in West Germany and a backlash against NATO's decision to install intermediate nuclear missiles in Western Europe.

The decision to co-ordinate West European foreign policy (D'Avignon report in 1970), brought renewed interest in the move towards European unity, and the fall of de Gaulle brought Britain back into the frame. Economic crisis and dissatisfaction with governments led to calls for greater public autonomy at regional and local level. In Britain, where the recession was particularly severe, the election of Thatcher in 1979 as Prime Minister heralded major changes with the onset of a programme of privatising nationalised industries, reduction in public expenditure and a move towards service rather than heavy industry. Leisure and tourism expanded throughout Western Europe, along with high levels of unemployment.

The mid 1980s brought greater economic stability. In 1986 the Single European Act brought fresh commitment to the European Community, with the aim of establishing a borderless internal market with the free movement of goods, people, and services, and the establishment of a unified monetary system and social legislation by 1992.

Central Eastern Europe history

In Central Eastern European countries, economic decline in the 1970s was followed by economic crisis in the 1980s. Attempts by East Germany and Czechoslovakia to find socialist alternatives to the market economy did not work (Batt, 1991). Increased lending from the West, and in particular from West Germany, did little to ease the crisis although it did help in the release of thousands of political prisoners (Laqueur, 1992). In Poland, strikes at the increase in meat prices met with violence, and by 1976 Poland was bankrupt and facing severe food shortages. Any hopes of change fostered by the birth of Solidarity in 1980 and the spread of strikes all over Poland were suppressed by the introduction of martial law. Hungary, in contrast, seemed prosperous during the 1970s, but lack of confidence in the government brought about economic decline in the 1980s. Opposition to the government in Czechoslovakia remained bitter but suppressed. Support for the manifesto of the opposition, Charter 77, grew despite severe penalties throughout the 1980s.

However, the severe depression of the 1980s brought renewed hope in the succession of Gorbachev as Soviet leader in 1985. For the first time in 40 years true reform seemed likely and hope grew in Western and in Eastern Europe that the period of stagnation was reaching an end.

HRD – Western Europe

The changing needs and shifts in values witnessed throughout the 1960s and 1970s highlighted three broad concerns in the development of human resources in Western Europe. First, at national and organisational levels, economic recession called for new human resource strategies which would bring greater efficiency, increase profit and productivity while retaining a tight control on public spending. With the decline in manufacturing and heavy industry and a growth in service industry there was a national need to pare down the workforce to economise, and provide multi-skilled workers, who could work across functions and fill a variety of roles. Second, there was a need to introduce strategies which would meet the developing needs of organisations in the age of advancing technology. Third, at individual levels, there was a demand for work that brought personal recognition and responsibility, and opportunities for achievement and self-fulfilment.

This clear need for new strategic thinking and the evolved understanding of human motivation in the late 1960s and early 1970s led to a multiplicity of ideas focusing on self-development (Pedlar *et al.*, 1978), action learning (Revans, 1980), organisational development (Handy, 1976; Argyris and Schon, 1978), and quality management (Peters and Waterman, 1982). New thinking led to a more flexible approach to organisational theory and approaches to managing human resources.

Current research maintained that management could not be bound by a set of scientific statements and programmes, and that the true nature of managerial work was fragmentary, characterised by horizontal networking, organisational monitoring and broad decision making rather than pure functional control (Mintzberg, 1973). The notion of 'excellent organisations' seemed to fit the mood and to offer solutions at national, organisational and individual levels, in its exhortation of leaner, flatter organisations, and uncluttered lines of communication. Organisations were encouraged to clarify their value base with mission statements and adopt bottom-up development strategies with a focus on customer needs and care. Peters and Waterman (1982), developed their concept of the excellent company, exhorting organisations to recognise that 'people – not money, machines or minds – as the natural resource may be the key to it all' (p. 39).

Handy (1976) offered new perspectives on understanding organisations, demanding that the advent of computer communication technology called for new integrated structures and questioning ownership in the context of organisations, stating that 'the fruits of success belong in a sense to all the interested parties' (p. 395).

Management education boomed and companies wanted to be a part of this, with a surge in MBA programmes, internal and external management development programmes and a proliferation of outdoor training activities. Individuals were encouraged to explore 'soft' skills, and enhance team working abilities, creative and lateral thinking qualities as expounded by de Bono (1970). Training and development focused on the individual within the organisation, identifying ways in which they could release their own potential in line with organisational goals, and achieve double loop learning by taking action following consultation (Argyris and Schon, 1978).

With the recognition of motivational needs beyond the basic level it is perhaps at this point that we begin to see the emergence of the concept of HRD, in an era where financial reward is no longer enough but needs to be enhanced by personal achievement. However, the notion of human resource development, although gaining influence in wider organisational strategy development, was still focused clearly on the individual and as a product of the time might be aligned to the British Thatcherite years of 'each one for himself'. Although, as we have demonstrated, there was a proliferation of theory and thinking around development at organisational level, something was lacking which led to discontinuity and jagged edges. The hard edge of competition, business survival and achievement of excellence did not seem to fit with the more introspective collaborative, caring ideas expounded by equal opportunity legislation and self-development manuals. On the one hand companies were being encouraged to increase customer liaison and provide personal learning programmes for staff, and on the other hand there was the influx of information technology which threatened to dehumanise the workplace and re-establish systemised bureaucracy.

Organisations became overtaken with concerns on how to manage change, and found themselves juggling the need for long-term strategies with short-term crisis management. Battling at the front line for survival in a constantly changing environment, while attempting to meet developmental needs and environmental concern through strategic planning, called for a change in perspective and a way of managing an environment full of paradox (Davis, 1990; Senge, 1990; Handy, 1994).

The multiplicity of ideas of the 1970s and 1980s had brought about enormous organisational confusion and a piecemeal approach to HRD, with little integration between individual solutions such as self-development and action learning, organisational excellence strategies, and leaner, flatter structures and national development such as privatisation of national industry and services. The underlying survival values of national and organisational strategies encouraged a win–lose mentality which was totally at odds with the win–win values of self-development. Both seemed at odds with the external environment which demanded global vision, expanding networks and environmental awareness. This conflict of values coupled with the speeding pace of change led to a dizzying sense of shock and of not being able to keep up (Toffler, 1970). Although the development of human resources had become a recognised need, the focus remained isolated within different groupings and mainly at an individual level. The time had come to look towards a more integrated approach.

HRD – Central Eastern Europe

The continued suppression and repression in Central Eastern Europe brought about no change in management and development at national governmental and organisational levels, but rather a consolidation of communist rule. As Western Europe looked towards greater strategic integration, Central Eastern Europe was becoming fragmented, and the widening split between will of the government and will of the people was leading to increased frustration. At individual levels, the wish to change and develop, and the increasing frustration at being denied change and development was gathering momentum.

THE MID 1980s–1990s

Western Europe history

Deregulation policies in the main industrial countries and the opening of European borders as a result of the Single European Act (SEA, 1986) had stimulated the economies of Western Europe which from the mid to late 1980s enjoyed a period of economic growth. Although the profitable days of traditional industries such as textiles, iron and steel were still in decline, the service sector continued to bloom. Unemployment remained high and seemed to have become a permanent feature of West European life. Progress in the 1980s towards a unified European Community was slow and troubled by setbacks. The crumbling of the Eastern bloc in 1989–90 and the increased chances of a unified Germany grasped Western Europe's attention, and help in enabling the new Central Eastern Europe to make the transition to a new way of life became a top priority. The collapse of the Soviet empire coincided with economic depression throughout the West. The increased pressure of pumping economic and knowledge aid into Eastern Europe lent greater importance to European unity in terms of trade and security. With the end of the Cold War and the demilitarisation of the Soviet Union the economic, military, political and social map of Europe had shifted with Germany becoming Europe's largest and most powerful member state virtually overnight. The eruption of disorder in Yugoslavia brought further pressure. In 1992 the Maastricht Treaty was drawn up with the main aims of maintaining European unity, internal markets and common foreign and security policy and achieving monetary union within a European system of Central Banks by 1997–9. The forming of the Maastricht Treaty outlined a new Europe and the implications of the changes caused political stirrings and national concerns of lost identity, leading to modifications which recognised individual nation's rights and ways of life. As the economic situation appears to be stabilising the new Europe remains of core concern and importance and as yet faces an unknown future.

Central Eastern Europe history

Gorbachev's succession to Andropov in 1985 and later election to President of the Soviet Union opened the way for radical changes throughout Eastern Europe. His willingness to negotiate with the West, his policy of non-intervention in Eastern Europe and his legislative changes, including the guarantee to protect individual human rights, helped pave the way to the momentous changes in 1989. From the mid 1980s to 1989 East Germany made no attempt at reform and Czechoslovakia continued to live under a harsh rule of suppression. Economic crisis surfaced in Hungary and continued in Poland. Both countries demonstrated little confidence in their governments in spite of efforts to bring in new reforms. This dissatisfaction was to herald the breathtaking events of 1989.

Despite its illegal status, the trade union Solidarity continued to dominate the political scene in Poland, and even formed its own Shadow Cabinet in 1988. The decision to close the Gdansk shipyard due to unprofitability brought increased chaos and talks in Spring 1989 led to the legalisation of Solidarity and an overwhelming victory in Senate elections. By the end of 1989 Poland was the first to have a non-communist government in Eastern Europe, and had negotiated an agreement with the International Monetary Fund, IMF, to move towards a market economy.

Hungary had traditionally demonstrated flexibility in executing Soviet policy and the establishment of a new government in December 1988 led to a reconsideration of policy and party doctrine. However, the continued domination of government by Party members led to further dissatisfaction, and in late 1989 the leadership stepped down and the newly formed anti-communist Democratic Forum, which promised gradual economic and social reform, was elected in 1990.

In Czechoslovakia in November 1989 communist power collapsed following a series of demonstrations sparked by police brutality at a peaceful student rally. The rapid formation of the effective non-communist opposition group, Civic Forum, led to organised mass demonstrations and the threat of a general strike, which forced the resignation of the Politburo. By December the key opposition representative and playwright Vaclav Havel was installed as President of the Republic.

The fall of the GDR from communist rule was equally rapid. Tens of thousands of young skilled people fled with the opening of Hungary's border into Austria in August 1989. This was followed by huge demonstrations and the eventual collapse of the Berlin Wall in November. The opposition party New Forum was legalised and the Politburo resigned. These events were closely followed by the dissolution of the Stasi and an investigation into the corrupt practices of former leaders. In January 1990 the situation was highly unstable. Economic crisis was compounded by total lack of confidence in the government and thousands of people emigrating daily.

The fever of revolution spread with the fall and execution of Rumania's leader Ceausescu and his wife in December 1989. An internal coup took place in Bulgaria in November 1989.

In 1990 the major East European countries began programmes of transition to stabilise economies and move towards a market economy. East Germany began a round of talks with the West culminating in the introduction of a unified German currency in an attempt to stem the labour outflow, and the reunification of Germany was set in train. The initial jubilation at throwing off the chains of suppression has given way to recognition that a hard path lies ahead in the reform of political, economic, social and cultural life before an integrated Europe can emerge (Batt, 1990). The decade of the 1990s now sets the scene for a period of transition and transformation without precedent in history.

HRD – Western Europe

The dismantling of the communist Eastern bloc, the increased dissolution of geographical boundaries, the information and technology boom, the industrial recession, the advent of green consciousness, led to a re-examination of world view and an emerging need to bring about integration. New approaches which combined motivational opportunity with a stable base, and strategies to enable management in a transient world were needed to fit with the new era. As Western and Eastern Europe looked towards the possibility of union, Western management thinking also turned towards creating ideas and strategies which would offer stability and growth, consolidation and development, integration and individual opportunity.

Writers such as Morgan (1986), Senge (1990) and Handy (1994), had begun to voice the need for individual and organisational adaptability and flexibility, questioning traditional thinking, the existence of the traditional workplace and traditional management strategies. In the mid to late 1980s two major strands of thinking emerged – *Total Quality Management*, TQM, and *Organisational Transformation*.

Japan provided inspiration for Total Quality Management where efficiency, quality and individual achievement combined to provide high profit. In his work *Thriving on Chaos* (1987) Peters redefined his notion of excellence by stating boldly, 'There is no such thing as an excellent company' (p. 3) but rather those who were striving for excellence were companies who sought for constant improvement in the face of constant change. Deming argued that quality is to do with co-operation not competition and that management's role was to generate the climate for this (Pickard, 1992). The concept of TQM acknowledged the need for strategic process rather than quick fixes by aiming to respond to the challenges and changes of the external environment through creating systems which would be both profit and needs driven. The dual approach of creating fit lean structures and systems to maximise profit with the establishment of a continuous learning environment would lead to a win–win formula benefiting national, organisational and individual needs levels.

The recognition that we need to develop, adapt and grow with change rather than react to it also gave birth to the idea of organisational transformation and growing interest in the *learning company* concept. Owen's definition of transformation as the shift from one stage of existence to another which is entirely different, is particularly in keeping with the era (Owen, 1987). Senge adds to the idea of organisational transformation by urging us to move away from our perspective of thinking of the world as the creation of 'separate, unrelated forces', towards a view of the integrated whole with its web of interconnections in order to make sense of the world around us (Senge, 1990). Pedlar *et al.* integrate the concept of transformation into their vision of the learning company as a strategy for sustainable development:

> 'A Learning Company is an organisation that facilitates the learning of all its members and continuously transforms itself' (1991, p. 1)

Within this vision they take the view that the members of the learning company include employees and employers, shareholders and customers, suppliers and even competitors, the environment and the community.

If we expand these current ideas to the broader national or European perspective we can see that the concept of transformation gives us a perspective for dealing with the shifting changes in Europe by recognising interconnections and interrelatedness thus giving meaning to the parts, while ideas such as TQM, five systems thinking, the learning company provide strategies to help us manage our world within this understanding. By taking the two essential ingredients of integration and learning from current thinking and relating them to a nation we can see the emergence of HRD as a broad concept which is demonstrated by Fig. 3.2.

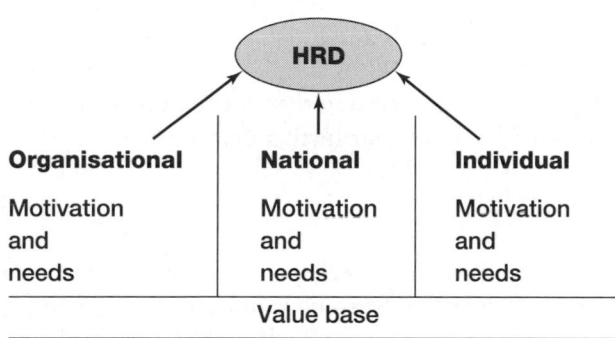

Fig. 3.2   HRD as an integrated concept

Integration

The rigour of integration recognises the interconnections between individual, organisational, community and global, thereby producing a map or framework which enables us to draw in the interconnections of a national perspective. Using Britain as an example in the mid to late 1980s it was still somewhat distant from having 'an educated, trained and flexible labour force' (MSC, 1981). There was little integration in the field of vocational and educational training, and the Government responded with a White Paper 'A New Training Initiative' (MSC, 1981).This document was the forerunner of a national system of vocational education and training (NVQs and GNVQs) aiming to span all professions with the introduction of agreed national standards of competence. It spelled out measures to skill up the workforce into the 1990s targeted at wider opportunities for young people and for adults in acknowledgment that:

> 'The nature of the technological changes now being implemented throughout the world, the emergence of the newly industrialised countries, the redistribution of manufacturing capacity worldwide all mean that we have entered a period of rapid and far-reaching transition.' (MSC, 1981, p. 2).

In theory the mandate to provide 'lifetime' training and development opportunities fits neatly with the idea of transformation. It recognises the organisational concerns of unrealised potential and the need for a strategy encompassing continuous learning through schemes such as Investors in People, and it also acknowledges the need of the individual to achieve and that 'the conscious development of people and organisations have a part to play.' (Lessem, 1986, p. 7).

This is the first British national strategy aimed at meeting the emerging needs of organisations, individuals and the times we live in, and at providing development opportunities across the range of the motivational framework. At a national level this is the integrated approach providing the conceptual map to guide us through this era. This approach is not without problems, and at the time of writing the shape and boundaries of the map are shifting. The introduction of national standards arrived at by a process of functional analysis has raised concern that this approach has more in common with the systematic development exhorted by the principles of scientific management rather than the humanist integrated ideas of today (Burgoyne, 1989, 1990), and that diverse national needs and flexibility may be sacrificed to standardised procedures (Porter and McKibben, 1988). Despite these concerns the formulation of a strategy built on integration is significant in that it attempts to acknowledge needs at a range of levels and it provides a basis for further elaboration.

Learning

The second key element of learning is perhaps better known as *continuous learning*. The qualification acknowledges that learning is not necessarily confined to formal situations but is a continual lifetime process (Pedlar *et al.*, 1991). Continuous learning according to Senge takes on two faces, that of 'survival or adaptive learning' and that of '"generative learning", learning that enhances our capacity to create.' (Senge, 1990, p. 14)

If we hook into our motivational framework we can view the emerging ideas as a way to acknowledge and deal with the existence of various levels of needs in an integrated and interconnected way. The continuing safety and physiological needs or hygiene factors tie into the notion of adaptive learning. At an individual level this might be characterised as learning to cope with new technology, learning to manage in a new role. At an organisational level adaptive learning may take the form of strategies for maintaining market share. At a national level this may include introducing educational measures to skill up the workforce. The higher needs of belonging, social needs, self-actualisation tie into the notion of creative or generative learning. At an individual level this might mean working on an interdisciplinary project team, working through a personal development plan. At an organisational level this might include the development of long-term strategies, or collaboration with a community project. At a national level this might mean providing continual learning opportunities, the collaboration of private enterprise with third world trade projects, consultation with public bodies.

The two key elements of integration and learning emerging from current thinking lead to the overarching concept we have of HRD today. The conceptual map of integration gives us direction and a baseline in a turbulent world, while the evolved notion of learning provides us with flexible processes of management to chart our way through, and enable us to ride the waves of change (Morgan, 1988), giving rise to another concept of our time HRM (Lee, 1995). Within this understanding HRD can be seen to encompass and provide direction for HRM (see also McGoldrick and Stewart, this volume, on the HRM–HRD nexus).

HRD – Central Eastern Europe

In Central Eastern Europe the enormous changes have brought demands for new thinking in the development of human resources. Within our understanding of HRD as a concept which recognises the need and motivation to develop, the denial of human rights and of motivational needs for half a century within Central Eastern Europe places these nations at the beginning of a journey to find an integrated approach appropriate to their developmental needs.

As Eastern Europe takes on the values of a market economy, so must its people learn to work under a new philosophy. This double-order change has implications for all aspects of life from the political to the social and in particular for management and decision making (Sokolowska and Rychard, 1988; Orczyk, 1991; Nikolajew, 1992).

Motivation exists at national, organisational and individual levels to secure basic needs and build structural bases. Although reminiscent of the post-war phase in 1945, the rebuilding, restabilising and remobilising in this era are on the foundation of democratic principles and within a world which is at a different social, political and economic evolutionary point. The demand for recognition of individual human rights, which precipitated a new value system, calls for development strategies to manage difference and address issues of equal opportunity in order to meet the long denied social and ego needs and also the need for self-fulfilment and achievement.

The complexity of emergent needs coupled with the transition and the need to re-adjust to a new world view, poses a new 'problematique' which cannot be managed within traditional models or paradigms (Nikolajew, 1992). The syndrome of future shock (Toffler, 1970), where people have not yet adjusted to the accelerated pace of change and reform and are still using old patterns of behaviour, is evident (Jankowicz and Pettitt, 1993). The difficulty in leaping to a market economy is highlighted by language which is unable to give meaning to the new value system but rather perpetuates the old, therefore denying responsibility and innovation. For example in Polish there exists no word for learning, only the reflexive of the verb 'to teach', i.e. is taught, and the Polish word for manager roughly translates as a blend of commanding, ordering up and ruling (Salaman and Butler, 1990).

Responses to these complex problems have been diverse. Training and development has been named as one of the top immediate and medium-term demands for the next five years (ILO, 1990) with Western organisations and universities gaining funding to provide knowledge and skill-based education and training and business guidance.

The West is learning from experiences with other nations that techniques and strategies do not necessarily travel well, and that ideas developed within one democratic framework may not be appropriate in another, having evolved from a different history and a separate world view (Schnapper, 1980; Ashton, 1984; Easterby-Smith and Snell, 1991). This does not deny the fact that the period of transition requires support and aid from Western Europe in learning to manage within a democratic framework, but rather raises questions about the type of support and aid, and the responsibility of Western Europe in enabling the East European nations to achieve levels of self-sufficiency and independence appropriate to them. These experiences are leading Western Europe to a richer understanding of HRD and, with the threads of Western and Central Eastern

European history intertwining more closely, we are presented with a unique opportunity to reach a clearer understanding of the nature of HRD.

WHAT THIS TELLS US ABOUT HRD

In this concluding section we will reflect on key issues from our analysis and consider future directions of HRD. Following the major transformation brought about by the Second World War, 50 years later we have moved into another such period of transformation. In this chapter we have sought to make sense of the place of HRD within this transformation by taking a broadly hermeneutic stance which argues that our understanding is mainly determined by our history, and largely dependent on our culture and our time (Heidigger, 1962).

From this viewpoint our tour through history demonstrates that HRD, as an overarching concept which recognises national trends, global influences, social values and shifting needs, is a product of our time and of Western thinking which has gained meaning through historical change and transformation. Although its gestation might be traced back to research carried out by Maslow, Herzberg and MacGregor in the theory of motivation it is only in our present era that we begin to recognise HRD as having significant meaning to a nation of people or peoples. In Western Europe we have seen that previous notions of HRD were confined to organisational or individual or national levels and only looking towards particular motivational levels. Our current understanding is that HRD is concerned with integration across the range of individual, organisational and national needs and with learning, in an aim to meet different motivational levels. Figure 3.3 draws our thinking together more clearly to demonstrate the current organic state of HRD and, in conclusion, enables us to make some broad assumptions about its nature and future direction.

Nature of HRD

1 HRD as a holistic concept focuses by necessity on the interplay of global, national, organisational and individual needs.

From our analysis of HRD as cyclical, dynamic and organic, it follows that any form of HRD that only focuses upon any one of the four areas is lacking in depth and ignores key needs and influences from each of the other areas. For example in Central Eastern Europe the narrow focus on national needs within the political, economic and social framework denied the influences and learning from the organisational, individual and global, leading to frustration and stagnation. In Western Europe during the 1970s and early 1980s the separate non-integrated emphases on individual and organisational development brought lack of direction. Our model assumes that for HRD to continue to grow it must feed from and into each of the frameworks, thereby addressing needs holistically.

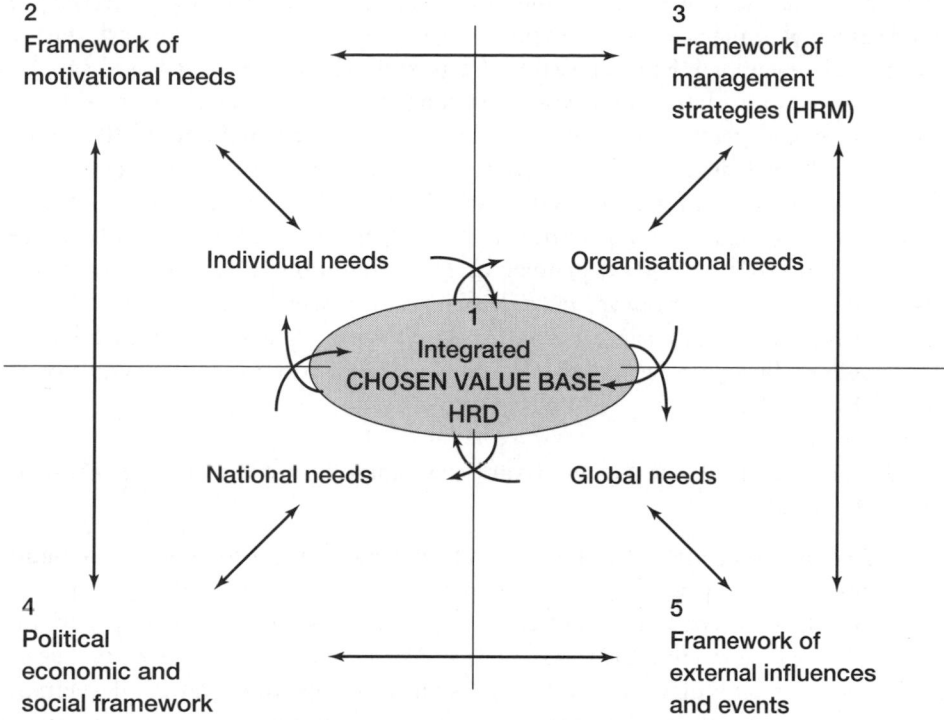

Fig. 3.3   Current nature of HRD

2 HRD can only be developmental if it shifts to accommodate new world views and thus is by nature cyclical and dynamic.

If HRD is to remain relevant and provide a basis for continual learning it must evolve. Experiences in Western and Central Eastern Europe demonstrate that our value systems need to be constantly questioned, re-examined and modified in the light of shifting needs and events in order to maintain a dynamic concept of HRD which is appropriate to current needs and world views. When this does not happen stagnation occurs as is evident in the 1950s to 1980s period in the Eastern bloc countries. As Europe continues to grow and change and as we begin to take on a wider global vision, so our conceptual map of HRD will continue to transform and be redrawn to cope with increasing complexities of needs.

3 Value systems which recognise motivational needs lay the foundations for the growth or hindrance of HRD.

The broad value base in Fig. 3.3 highlights the fact that HRD is organic and can only grow and evolve if certain principles are in place. Our historical journey through Central Eastern Europe has been important in enabling us to reach this conclusion. The imposition of communist rule forced adherence to a value system which denied the existence of human rights and motivational needs, demonstrated by the scourge of intellectuals and the incarceration of human rights thinkers throughout the Eastern bloc.

Within the parameters of such a value system ideas and new ways of thinking are deemed subversive, and attempts to express developmental needs are ignored, thus rendering the existence of HRD impossible. Conversely the demonstrations throughout Western Europe in the late 1960s expressing concern at current values were able to be acknowledged and dealt with within a value system which maintained the right of expression and freedom of speech. The proliferation of research and thinking engendered in this era, and made possible by a system which fostered critical analysis, enabled the further growth and understanding of human resource development to the broad concept it is today. That HRD is clearly dependent on the recognition of changing motivational needs has become evident from the mass demonstrations which heralded the collapse of communist rule in Central Eastern Europe. It is only with a radical change in values that Central Eastern Europe now has the freedom to begin to experiment with possible strategies for HRD.

4   HRD is only sustainable if it gains commitment and ownership from all of those who have a stake in it.

Returning to our motivational frame, and recognising that the collapse of communist rule was precipitated by the will of the people to exercise the right of expression, it is clear that Central Eastern Europe needs a value system and power base in which it can believe and to which it can adhere (Lee, 1995; Rollo *et al.*, 1990.) One of the legacies of the communist rule within Eastern Europe is the awareness that strategic development must be based on values which not only provide opportunities for meeting diverse needs, but which can also gain the commitment of, and be owned by, the nation, its communities, organisations and individuals. Perhaps one of the greatest challenges facing HRD is to facilitate a learning process within Central Eastern Europe which will foster a framework of HRD which truly belongs to and can be owned by its stakeholders. In Western Europe the need for widespread ownership began to emerge in the late 1960s and is only now, within a wider strategic approach to HRD, becoming fully recognised as the key factor in further development, and central to the continued health, wealth and sustainability of organisations and nations (Harrison, 1983; Lee, 1992; Brewster, 1993).

5   HRD cannot be imposed but must evolve from the needs and values of a nation.

In Central Eastern Europe the external and internal influences, the level of evolution and the historical base are different from those of Western Europe which leads to different concerns and needs – and different solutions. The current Western concept of HRD arrived at after a cycle of emerging needs and creative solutions to meet needs is not appropriate elsewhere. Its relevance only has meaning and understanding within the current historical framework of Western Europe. In view of our own learning and from our current understanding of HRD it is perhaps more appropriate to give access to what we have learned adaptively, thus enabling creative and generative learning within a Central Eastern European historical framework.

As within Western history this is something which may take time to evolve as the nations experiment with different ways of managing and developing. However, by taking ownership from the beginning, the emerging concept of HRD will be sustainable and able to continue developing and evolving because it is home grown.

6 HRD encompasses the area of HRM

If HRD is viewed as a strategic integrated map or framework providing direction for emerging needs at national, organisational and individual levels, then HRM can be viewed as a series of possible routes charting a way through. The new concept of HRM in Western Europe builds on the key principle of integration in that it aims to bring together a range of approaches to managing people. In the 1970s and 1980s in Western Europe, management and development strategies were characterised by non-integration and lack of direction. The recent emergence of integrated developmental strategy not only offers direction for HRM but also provides meaning by highlighting the relations and connections within the broader view.

Future directions of HRD

Our discussion on inter-cultural perspectives leads us to conclude that although nations may have similar value and belief systems, the unique historical base of each will determine a different concept of HRD. Although Western Europe may become more politically, economically and socially tied to the new Central Eastern Europe their divergent histories create different contexts of meaning for HRD.

Maslow's research on human motivation recognised that although the routes towards fulfilment of motivational needs may be located in specific cultures, the end destination is more universal (Maslow, 1970). Therefore we are able to consider future directions of HRD although the routes to the end goal may as yet be unknown.

We are already witness to new trends in thinking and new emerging concerns and needs which in turn will call for new solutions and new ways of developing and managing. In Western Europe the concept of HRD has grown and is continuing to grow to embrace all aspects of life and experience. Within the context of our model (Fig. 3.3) the movement towards integration is likely to continue as the consequences of the modern Western world on the environment become clearer. This is bringing with it a growing recognition of the responsibility nations and organisations have to establish and implement strategies of sustainable development to maintain and replenish our planet's resources. The growing awareness of how we interact with our environment and our planet is demanding new ways of making sense, and of how we can continue to develop within such new awareness. These new levels of understanding are also beginning to affect our view of the relationship between national, organisational and individual. Within the 1990s the nature of work appears to be undergoing transformation with more opportunities for project and portfolio work, for part-time and home work. Work is becoming more integrated with home and social, with each offering developmental opportunities for the individual and with organisations recognising the validity of skills and experience gained outside of the traditional workplace. With a change in traditional work practices the boundaries between work and pleasure become blurred and there is an individual move towards seeking work which will enhance the home lifestyle, and leisure which will add to work experience, thus attaining a more holistic life pattern.

The recognition that basic needs must continue to be met (Herzberg *et al.*, 1959), along with opportunities for self-fulfilment and personal growth (MacGregor, 1960), is expanding to include the acknowledgment of a further motivational level concerned with emotional and spiritual needs, and researchers and thinkers are beginning to explore these issues within a holistic framework (Owen, 1987; Kinsman, 1990; Lee, 1995).

In Central Eastern Europe the creation of HRD strategy is likely to be shaped by the adaptive learning of Western Europe which points towards the need for integration and continual learning. Issues which are preoccupying Western Europe will determine to a large extent the priorities of Central Eastern Europe in the period of transition, as they continue to be dependent on funding and aid from the West, and as they begin to move into world markets heavily dominated by the West. Therefore, wide areas of concern in Western Europe, such as the environment and global relations, will to a large extent determine national strategic direction in Central Eastern Europe. Combined with these wider issues, the history of 1989–90 places these nations under pressure to develop strategic plans which will encompass the divergent developmental needs of their citizens if they are to gain confidence and commitment. From this current standpoint it is possible that Central Eastern Europe will move towards an integrated approach to HRD more rapidly than its Western neighbours.

Thus although we view the future of HRD in Western and in Central Eastern Europe moving towards further integration and clearer understanding of the interconnections between individual, organisational, national, global and planetary concerns, the paths that both sets of nations will follow to reach greater integration will remain firmly rooted in their respective historical bases and value systems, and continue to challenge and stimulate the growth of HRD.

References

Argyris, C. and Schon, D. (1978) *Organisational Learning: A Theory of Action Perspective*, New York, Addison-Wesley.

Ashton, D. (1984) 'Cultural Differences: Implications for Management Development', *Management Education and Development*, vol. 15, part 1, pp. 5–13

Batt, J. (1990) 'The Political Context', pp. 6–39, in Rollo, J.M.C. *et al*, (1990) *The New Eastern Europe: Western Responses*, London, Pinter Publishers.

Batt, J. (1991) *East Central Europe from Reform to Transformation*, London, Pinter Publishers.

Brewster, C. (1993) 'The integration of human resource management and corporate strategy: evidence from 14 countries', *The Crafting of Management Research, Proceedings of British Academy of Management Annual Conference*, Milton Keynes.

Burgoyne, J.G. (1989) 'Creating the managerial portfolio', *Management Education and Development*, vol. 20, pp. 56–61.

Burgoyne, J.G. (1990) 'Doubts about Competency', in Devine, M. ed. (1990) *The Photofit Manager in the 1990s*, London, Unwin Hyman.

Davis, J. (1990) *Greening Business*, Oxford, Blackwell.

de Bono, E. (1970) *Lateral Thinking*, Harmondsworth, Penguin.

Drucker, P. (1992) 'The New Society of Organizations', *Harvard Business Review*, vol. 70, no. 5, 95–104.

Easterby-Smith, M. and Snell, R. (1991) 'Peeking through the Bamboo Curtain', in Campbell and Brown eds (1991) *Advances in Chinese Industrial Studies*, vol. 2, JAI Press.

Handy, C. (1976) *Understanding Organisations*, Harmondsworth, Penguin.

Handy, C. (1994) *The Empty Raincoat: Making Sense of the Future*, London, Hutchinson.

Harrison, R. (1983) 'Strategies for a New Age', *Human Resource Management*, Fall, vol. 22, no. 3.

Heidegger, M. (1962) *Being and Time*, New York, Harper and Row.

Herzberg, F., Mausner, B. and Snyderman, B.B. (1959) *The Motivation to Work*, Second edition, New York, Wiley and Sons.

Hodgetts, R.M. and Luthans, F. (1991) *International Management*, Singapore, McGraw-Hill.

Hofstede, G. (1980) *Culture's Consequences: International Differences in Work-related Values*, London, Sage.

Hofstede, G. (1991) *Cultures and Organizations: Intercultural Cooperation and its Importance for Survival: Software of the Mind*, London, McGraw-Hill.

Huczynski, A. and Buchanan, D. (1991) *Organizational Behaviour: An Introductory Text*, Second edition, London, Prentice Hall.

ILO (1990) 'Management consulting in an East-West perspective', *Management Development*, 61, ILO, Geneva.

Jankowicz, D. and Pettitt, S.S. (1993) 'Worlds in Collusion: An analysis of an Eastern European Management Development Initiative', *MEAD*, vol. 24, pp. 93–104.

Kinsman, F. (1990) *Millenium: Towards Tomorrow's Society*, London, Allen and Co.

Lane, J-E. and Ersson, S.O. (1987) *Politics and Society in Western Europe*, London, Sage.

Laqueur, W. (1992) *Europe in Our Time: A History 1945–1992*, New York, Penguin Books.

Lee, M.M. (1992) 'Management education in Central Europe: Problems, practicalities and potential', working paper for Conference *The Role of Higher Education in the Reform Process of Central and Eastern Europe*, Commission of the European Communities, Brussels.

Lee, M.M. (1995) 'Holistic Agency: a multi-level conceptual exploration', under review with *Academy of Management Review*.

Lessem, R. (1986) *Enterprise Development*, Cambridge, Gower.

MacGregor, D. (1960) *The Human Side of Enterprise*, London, McGraw-Hill.

Manpower Services Commission (1981) *A New Training Initiative*, London, Mears Caldwell Hacker.

Maslow, A.H. (1970) *Motivation and Personality*, Second edition, New York, Harper and Row.

Mintzberg, H. (1973) *The Nature of Managerial Work*, Englewood Cliffs, Prentice Hall Inc.

Mintzberg, H. (1983) *Structures in Fives: Designing Effective Organisations*, London, Prentice Hall.

Morgan, G. (1986) *Images of Organization*, London, Sage.

Morgan, G. (1988) *Riding the Waves of Change*, San Francisco CA, Jossey-Bass Inc.

Nikolajew, V. (1992) 'Transitional Economies', *Futures*, September, pp. 635–52.

Ohmae, K. (1992) *The Borderless World: Power and Strategy in the Interlinked Economy*, London, Fontana.

Orczyk, J. (1991) 'System Change and Managerial Values in Poland (1989–1990)', *Preliminary Report for the West-East Management Conference*, Constance, February 1991.

Owen, H. (1987) *Spirit, Transformation and Development in Organisations*, Abbot Publishing.

Oxford Dictionary of Current English (1992), Oxford, Oxford University Press.

Pedlar, M., Burgoyne, J. and Boydell, T. (1978) *A Manager's Guide to Self-Development*, London, McGraw-Hill.

Pedlar, M., Burgoyne, J. and Boydell, T. (1991) *The Learning Company: A Strategy for Sustainable Development*, London, McGraw-Hill.

Peters, T. (1987) *Thriving on Chaos*, New York, Macmillan.

Peters, T.J. and Waterman Jr, R.H. (1982) *In Search of Excellence*, New York, Harper Collins.

Pickard, J. (1992) 'Profile – W. Edwards Deming', *Personnel Management*, June, p. 23.

Porter, L.W. and McKibben, L.E. (1988) *Management Education and Development: Drift or Thrust into the 21st century?*, New York, McGraw-Hill.

Revans, R. (1980) *Action Learning: New Techniques for Management*, London, Blond and Briggs.

Rollo, J.M.C., Batt, J., Granville, B. and Malcolm, N. (1990) *The New Eastern Europe: Western Responses*, London, Pinter Publishers.

Salaman, G. and Butler, J. (1990) 'Why Managers Won't Learn', *Management Education and Development*, vol. 21, part 3, pp. 183–91.

Schnapper, M. (1980) 'A ten-step model for multinational training', in Garratt and Stopford eds (1980) *Breaking Down Barriers*, Hants, Gower.

Senge, P.M. (1990) *The Fifth Discipline*, New York, Doubleday.

Sokolowska, M. and Rychard, A. (1988) 'Alternatives in the Health Area: Poland in Comparative Perspective', in Kohn ed. (1988) *Cross-National Research in Sociology*, London, Sage.

Storey, J. (1993) 'Europe in the global state and market system', in Story, J. ed. (1993) *The New Europe: Politics, Government and Economy since 1945*, pp. 3–61, Insead, Blackwell Publishers.

Taylor, F.W. (1947) *Scientific Management*, New York, Harper and Row.

Toffler, A. (1970) *Future Shock*, London, Pan Books Ltd.

Weber, M. (1943) *The Theory of Social and Economic Organisations*, New York, Free Press.

4

International HRD

Paul Iles

INTRODUCTION

This chapter explores ways in which organisations are using international human resource development (IHRD) strategies to create more strategically coherent, competitive international enterprises, using cases drawn from Asian, US and in particular European organisations. It examines how changes in the international business environment have contributed to the rise in importance of HRM (human resource management) and HRD (human resource development) in particular.

As Iles (1995a) points out, the increasingly global nature of business activities has placed new demands on organisational and managerial performance. International assignments are being increasingly used not only for staffing, control and representational purposes but as vehicles to develop managers' skills and knowledge and as ways of enhancing organisational learning and capabilities. Many managers are involved in managing transnational joint ventures, mergers and acquisitions, and are operating in increasingly diverse environments with multi-cultural teams. Senior managers are often called upon to manage geographically and culturally diverse businesses, balancing the demands of global integration and centralisation with those of local sensitivity and responsiveness. HRD strategies therefore have a key role to play in ensuring that:

- organisational structures and systems enhance global effectiveness, enabling both global integration and local responsiveness;
- organisational cultures are fostered which value diversity and difference whilst creating a sense of unified mission and acting as the 'corporate glue';
- personnel systems attract, place, retain and develop managers with the knowledge, skills and attitudes required to perform effectively in a global business environment.

This chapter proposes a framework for developing international HRD (IHRD) strategies, examining the HRD strategies adopted by a variety of organisations attempting to operate in the international arena. It develops a framework outlining the policy options and choices available in developing appropriate HRD strategies in international enterprise. The chapter begins by examining the importance of international HRD to the globalisation of organisational life, then goes on to explore the distinctiveness of international HRD, before developing a framework for IHRD based on managerial orientations, organisational life-cycle stages and international competencies. The final section explores some models and methods employed in IHRD.

WHY IS INTERNATIONAL HRD IMPORTANT?

There is increasing recognition by companies that people and their skills are perhaps the most important factor of production. Indeed, the importance of people to organisational success is often acknowledged, in rhetoric at least, in company reports and media statements – 'of course our people are our greatest resource' is a ritually repeated phrase, if not a belief much manifested in practice.

The economic rise of Japan and the countries of the Asia–Pacific Rim affirms the key role that human resource development can play. In many cases such countries have had no other resources than the skills of their people and the willingness of their governments to invest heavily in their training and development.

The increasing impact of new information and production technologies also demands new skills and puts a premium on individual and organisational learning. A whole raft of organisational and structural changes, such as trends to delayering, greater devolution of responsibility and the greater use of flexible, multi-skilled self-directed teams in international enterprises also calls for continuous development, new skills, and the development of new competencies in learning to learn – in both individuals and organisations.

The importance of learning in organisations is beginning to be appreciated in strategic management (Pedler *et al.*, 1991). It is now increasingly realised that as product life cycles shorten but skill life cycles lengthen, competition is increasingly based on skills rather than products.

This focus on organisational skills and on *learning* in particular, as a key property of the organisation, is beginning to be recognised in the concepts of 'intellectual property rights' and 'organisational learning'. Indeed, Ray Stata, the CEO of Analog Corporation in the USA has claimed that, certainly for knowledge-based industries, 'the rate at which an organisation learns may become the only sustainable source of competitive advantage, since products and technologies can be very quickly copied and reproduced' (Stata, 1989, p. 63). This puts international HRD and organisational learning at the very heart of corporate strategy. This conception of international strategy and competitive advantage puts people, their skills, and how these are acquired, utilised and managed – in short, international HRD – at the forefront of the development of global capabilities.

THE DISTINCTIVE NATURE OF INTERNATIONAL HRD

Developing people in the domestic context is a relatively well-developed area. How is developing people in an international context different?

One framework that is helpful in considering the distinctive nature of international HRD is provided by Morgan (1986) who presents a model focusing on three dimensions:

- the *three broad HR functions* of procurement, allocation, and utilisation of human resources;
- the *three national or country categories* involved in international HRD: the *host* country where a subsidiary may be located, the *home* country where an international

company is headquartered, and *other* countries that may be the source of labour and finance;

- the *three types of employees* in international enterprise: 1) *HCNs* or local host country nationals; 2) *PCNs* or expatriates/parent country nationals; 3) *TCNs* or third country nationals.

In this model, international HRM is seen as consisting of the interplay among these three dimensions. In general terms international HRM seems to consist of similar functions to domestic HRM: managing human resource planning, staffing, performance evaluation, training and development, reward and compensation, labour and industrial relations, and communications is necessary whether one is operating in Bolton, Bangkok or Baltimore. In this chapter we will focus on HRD, in particular international recruitment and selection, training and career development. However, we will broaden our discussion beyond these traditional functions to also explore the impact of structure and corporate culture on individual and organisational behaviour and learning. As Bartlett and Ghoshal (1989) found in their study of international companies, the major problem these companies faced was not in *devising* appropriate strategies, but in *developing* their capabilities to realise their strategic intent; indeed, 'the main problem was developing and managing the organisational capability to implement the new and more complex global strategies' (p. x). Clearly this puts international HRD in a key position, and also suggests some distinctive features, as 'the management of world-wide operations was the management of complexity, diversity and change' (p. x).

Dowling *et al.*, (1993) suggest that the factors that differentiate *international* HRM from domestic HRM are that:

- *it involves more functions and activities*;
- *it involves a broader perspective* and a global view of issues;
- *it is more involved in employees' lives* including in some cases involving the family in selection and training decisions;
- *it involves a change in emphasis* as international operations mature;
- *it involves more exposure to risk*;
- *it is subject to more external influences* such as the role of the state and supranational institutions and the influence of national and regional *culture*.

The process of globalization requires a radical transformation of the way we think about the role, nature and tools of developing people; international enterprise throws up a series of new challenges for the way people are managed and HRD practices and strategies (see Laurent, 1986). Some of these challenges and responses are illustrated by the Finnish-based company Tampella Power Inc. This example shows how IHRD has come to play a key role in equipping the company with the capabilities required to engage successfully in international enterprise (Saarinen, 1994). As Pucik (1994, p. 4) puts it, 'global human resource management can then provide an organising framework for developing and managing people who are comfortable with the strategic and operational paradoxes embedded in global management and who are capable of harnessing the resultant cultural diversity'.

Tampella Power Inc. is a Finnish-based company engaged in making chemical recovery systems and power boilers for the pulp and paper industry. It was one of the five divisions of the long-established Tampella Corporation until 1991, and is now an independent company. Until the mid 1980s Tampella operated mainly in Finland and the former Soviet Union, but in 1985 it opened a North American subsidiary in Atlanta, USA, and began to strengthen its presence in Central Europe. The company took on large numbers of inexperienced school leavers, managed by a centralised corporate HR function. In 1989 it acquired the US Keeler company to gain access to local manufacturing capacity and a stronger position in the North American market. By 1993 it had production facilities in Finland and the USA, and subsidiaries in Sweden, Canada, the CIS and the Asia-Pacific region. However, there were a number of HR weaknesses – a lack of English language capabilities, a shortage of international managerial expertise, an inappropriate organisational structure, and a failure to respond quickly to recruitment needs for the new challenges posed by international enterprise.

In 1988, the HR function was decentralised with HR departments established for each division in the Tampella Corporation, including the power division. Line managers were encouraged to take more responsibility for HR, but the HR director played a primarily administrative rather than a strategic role in the top management team. The Finnish recession of the early 1990s led to downsizing, the replacement of the CEO, and the acquisition of a 40 per cent interest by the German company L & C Steinmüller G mbh, which offered both security and access to the European Union. Its R and D function was also transferred to the Swedish energy technology company Vattenfall Engineering. The HR function, which was rather distant from the division's business in the 1980s (with no one person having systematic responsibility for HR issues at divisional level and with a primary focus on routine and administrative activities), became a more significant player in corporate strategy after 1988. Major investments were made in upgrading staff competencies at all levels, including language training, computer training, management and leadership training, negotiation skills training, and head-hunting activities to enhance international adaptability (Saarinen, 1994).

DEVELOPING A FRAMEWORK FOR INTERNATIONAL HRD

Perlmutter (1969) has developed a useful approach to international HRM which we can apply to IHRD. He distinguishes between four basic orientations to international enterprise: the ethnocentric, the polycentric, the regiocentric, and the geocentric. An ethnocentric attitude is associated with the view that home country managers' style and practices are superior, whereas a polycentric attitude recognises that national differences and the need for local responsiveness demand the use of local managers and styles in host countries, whilst home country managers and styles remain dominant in headquarters. A regiocentric orientation also recognises the importance of national differences, but perceives these as most important at the regional level (e.g. developing a pan-European HRD strategy). A geocentric orientation takes a global view, drawing managers from all regions and utilising a variety of managerial styles and processes.

Each approach has advantages and disadvantages. In order to maximise local responsiveness, companies often attempt to staff local operations with HCNs rather than with expatriates. Such staff are deemed to know their own cultures, work ethics and markets best (a polycentric strategy). Local subsidiaries may then often operate almost independently, the major controls being financial (e.g. Unilever and Lever Brothers in the USA). However, locals may then find that they are barred from executive positions at headquarters because of their perceived overly-local perspective. Other organisations may take a geocentric orientation; emphasising a global view, they may demand that managers acquire both local and global knowledge and perspectives. The local responsiveness emphasised in the polycentric orientation may push organisations towards decentralised structures, giving maximum autonomy, flexibility, and independence to local enterprises – yet the global perspective of the geocentric orientation may simultaneously call for greater centralisation, co-ordination and integration. Resolving these apparent tensions or dilemmas is a key task for IHRD (Evans *et al.*, 1989).

Stage approaches to international HRD

Another useful framework for understanding the process of engaging in international HRD is presented by Nancy Adler (1991). This approach is based on a 'stage' or 'evolutionary' approach to internationalisation – the idea that firms pass through several phases of organisational development as they internationalise, such as moving from exporting to establishing a sales subsidiary to establishing foreign production to creating an international division. What Adler does is relate these evolutionary stages to HRD policies and emphases. She argues that organisations have typically moved in their international activities though four phases or stages – from purely *domestic* organisations to what she calls *international* (or multi-domestic) organisations, and then from international organisations to *multi-national* organisations. She identifies a fourth, emerging phase of development in international enterprise – the *global* organisation. Each of these phases is characterised by differences in orientation, strategy, technology and product or service. Each phase is also characterised by the increasing importance of international HRD to overall business activities.

The *domestic* organisation is typically characterised by a centralised structure and a focus on functional divisions. The *international* organisation on the other hand typically operates with a more decentralised structure and tends to concentrate its activities in an international division. International affairs are often then isolated from the mainstream of the business, which is seen as primarily domestic in focus. Consequently there may be little interchange or communication between the international division and the rest of the business, whether of ideas, people or practices, and little mutual learning or development.

The *multi-national* organisation attempts to move beyond this by perhaps re-centralising and creating multi-national business lines. As it evolves, it may increasingly enter into global alliances, and decentralise control to a variety of local businesses. Co-ordination may be achieved though a variety of other measures – through the creation and communication of a common, shared mission, through developing a shared sense of purpose and corporate culture, and through using management development practices to create a cadre of corporate resources. Other corporations may seek co-ordination through purely financial controls.

The issue of *culture* assumes increasing importance at each stage of internationalisation. If we draw on the Perlmutter 'managerial orientations' framework, we can see that the domestic organisation typically assumes an 'ethnocentric' perspective to HRD. Cultural sensitivity is of little importance, and the organisation assumes there is only 'one way' (or at least 'one best way') to manage and organise. The international organisation, however, tends to take a more regiocentric perspective, taking Europe or Asia or North America, for example, as the key focus of attention. It may even take a polycentric perspective, and cultural sensitivity therefore becomes of critical importance, especially in dealing with employees of different backgrounds and clients, customers and suppliers of varying cultural backgrounds. It prioritises responsiveness and sensitivity to local labour and product markets – 'many good ways' rather than 'one best way'.

Paradoxically, the *multi-national* organisation in Adler's analysis places somewhat less importance on culture, recognising its importance primarily when dealing with its own employees and managers. Its focus is primarily on 'one least-cost way'. The *global* organisation on the other hand takes a more fully developed geocentric or multi-centric perspective towards its operations. For it, culture becomes of critical importance, whether dealing with employees, executives, customers or suppliers. It takes the view that there are simultaneously 'many good ways' to manage, organise and develop people.

Though such a stage framework carries the risk of determinism, it is possible to extend Adler's analysis to explore the specific HRD implications of different stages of internationalisation (see Figure 4.1).

Organisations at the domestic or export stage only require low level global training, mainly emphasising the local culture of the export target and its consumer values and behaviour, and the interpersonal skills necessary to negotiate, sell and market to that culture. There is a need to carry out some training of host HCNs, mainly in helping them understand home-country products and policies. At the international stage more extensive training is needed, with more emphasis on technology transfer, stress management and local business practices and laws. At the multi-national stage, the emphasis now shifts to two-way technology transfer, corporate values, and international strategy, with more emphasis on the training of HCNs in both technical and cultural issues. The global stage requires more rigorous, extensive training of HCNs and of all employees, including senior executives, in such areas as global operations, global strategy, multiple cultural values, and socialisation into the corporate culture (Black *et al.*, 1992).

So, as an international organisation develops, moving from a domestic/ethnocentric phase through international/ethnocentric and multi-national/polycentric phases to the global/geocentric and transnational/geocentric phases, IHRD becomes increasingly important.

As a company matures, the increasingly complex international environment it is operating in may push it towards global integration, whereas host government pressure and responsiveness to local markets and cultures may push it towards local responsiveness. To address this issue, international companies have sought to go beyond a divisional structure towards other structures, such as mixed, matrix and network structures. Structural change is, however, a very blunt instrument – building attitudes, skills and relations and communicating a shared vision through IHRD may be more effective.

	Domestic/export stage	Multi-domestic/international stage	Multi-national stage	Global/transnational stage
Structural features	Functional divisions	Functional, with international divisions	Multi-national lines of business	Global alliances, heterarchy
	Centralised	Decentralised	Centralised	Co-ordinated, decentralised
Culture				
● Sensitivity	Marginally important	Very important – especially with clients, customers and suppliers	Somewhat important, particularly for employees and managers	Critically important for executives
● Perspective	Ethnocentric	Polycentric, regiocentric	Multi-national, geocentric	Global, multi-centric
● Assumption	'One way'/'one best way'	'Many good ways'	'One least-cost way'	'Many good' ways simultaneously
HRD priorities				
● Degree of rigour required	Low to moderate	Moderate to high	Moderate to high	Moderate to high
● Content emphasis	Interpersonal skills, local culture, consumer values and behaviour	Interpersonal skills, local culture, technology transfer, stress management, local business practices and laws	Interpersonal skills, two-way technology transfer, corporate value transfer, international strategy, stress management, local culture, and business practices	Global corporate operations/ systems, corporate culture transfer, multiple cultural values and business systems, international strategy, and socialisation tactics
● Training and development emphasis	Low to moderate training of host nationals; focus on understanding home-country products and policies	Low to moderate training of host nationals; primary focus is on production/service procedures	Moderate to high training of host nationals in technical areas, product/service systems, and corporate culture	High training of host nationals in global corporate production/efficiency systems, corporate culture, multiple cultural and business systems, and headquarters
● Staffing	International assignments rare; ethnocentric assumptions	Senior managers on international assignments; ethnocentric or regiocentric orientation	Local managers, polycentric staffing	Senior and fast-track managers on multi-cultural assignments, global re-sourcing on geocentric basis

Fig. 4.1 Structure, culture and HRD priorities in the stage approach

(from Adler, 1991, and Black, Gregerson and Mendenhall, 1992)

Forms of organisation

Matrix forms in many international organisations have proved hard to manage due to dual reporting leading to conflict and confusion, a proliferation of channels leading to log-jams, overlapping responsibilities producing a loss of accountability and battles over turf, and barriers of distance, language, time and culture which combine to make it very difficult to resolve conflict. Structural solutions alone seem ineffective, putting IHRD in a key position as, according to Bartlett and Ghoshal (1989), the most successful international organisations are less likely to be searching for an ideal structure and more likely to be developing managerial abilities to operate 'a matrix in the mind'.

As Pucik (1994, p. 3) puts it:

> *'the various dimensions of competitive advantage in global firms have things in common. They are all embedded in organisational systems, processes and cultures and they reflect the capacity of a collective of people to think and act in a fashion that transcends the collective limitations of an ethnocentric framework. To develop and manage a global organisation implies developing and managing people who can think, lead and act from a global perspective, who possess a global mind as well as global skills'.*

This puts a key responsibility on HRD to develop managers with good interpersonal skills and tolerance of ambiguity. By examining the adequacy of organisational structures and processes to manage global operations in a variety of American, European and Japanese companies, Bartlett and Ghoshal (1989) identified fundamental forces pushing companies to *global integration*, *local differentiation*, and *innovative learning*. Whilst European multi-nationals with their strong local presence and responsiveness have tended to maximise responsiveness, Japanese organisations with their global scale efficiencies have focused on global integration. Other organisations like GE, Ericsson or P and G have seemed very good at facilitating innovation. However, the challenge facing international organisations in the future is to *simultaneously* build multiple strategic competencies – 'to compete effectively, a company had to develop global competitiveness, multinational flexibility and world-wide learning capability *simultaneously*' (p. 16). To do this required a new organisational model, the *transnational*, which was able to utilise the advantages of the other organisational forms. (Note that Bartlett and Ghoshal do not use the terms international, multi-national and global in precisely the same way as Adler, making comparisons difficult.)

Bartlett and Ghoshal (1989, p. 61) describe the transnational model as an 'integrated network' in a phrase which 'emphasises the very significant flow of components, products, resources, people, and information that must be managed in the transnational. Beyond the rationalisation of physical facilities, the company must integrate tasks and perspectives; rich and complex communication linkages, work inter-dependencies, and formal and informal systems are the true hallmark of the transnational.'

This discussion has emphasised the value of taking a strategic perspective towards HRD based on the challenges of the international environment and the life-cycle stage of the organisation. The importance of national culture has become increasingly powerful as organisations have developed, requiring us to pay attention to the role of cultural diversity in IHRD. For example, career paths balancing global and local positions, despite possible resistance by both individuals and their line managers, may be useful tools, as may the use of assistant positions and regional HQ positions.

MANAGING THE
MULTI-CULTURAL WORKFORCE

The workforce of all organisations is growing ever more culturally diverse (see also Wilson, this volume). In many countries extensive migration has meant that the workforce often consists of people from a variety of ethnic, racial and cultural backgrounds. Internationalisation has stimulated the exchange and transfer of human resources across borders and across continents. Managing this multi-cultural workforce poses a number of new challenges for HRD. Many organisations, such as British Airways (BA), have sought to incorporate cultural diversity into their products and services in order to meet diverse customer needs and to recruit, retain and motivate a culturally diverse workforce.

BA, for example, has sought to reflect Egyptian culture in its cabin services and products on its London–Cairo routes, offering Arabic music, dates, and Arabic coffee served by a multi-national cabin staff. The reasoning behind this was partly that high quality Egyptian staff would be more likely to be attracted to work for BA, and more likely to be motivated to continue working for them if they saw the airline valuing and incorporating their culture. Equally importantly, Egyptian customers – the predominant group represented in first class – would in turn be more likely to choose BA over a rival carrier that did not offer such culturally appropriate products and services. Unfortunately, at a joint meeting of European and Egyptian BA staff observed recently in Cairo, this strategy, whilst applauded in principle, seemed in practice to have encountered some difficulties. Several of the senior Egyptian managers complained that it was not *Egyptian* culture that was being represented but a somewhat stereotyped 'Middle Eastern/Arab' one – the music was not in fact Egyptian, and Egyptians anyway preferred mint tea to Arabic coffee! This example illustrates the point that the culture being represented may need to be very specific, and that in any case listening to and consulting with actual representatives of the target culture is necessary to avoid 'getting it wrong' and appearing patronising and ill-informed (Iles and Mabey 1994).

Globalisation has also become an imperative for the Whirlpool Corporation based in Benton Harbor, Michigan in the USA with 38,000 employees scattered across the world. In 1988 Whirlpool bought the white goods section of the Dutch giant, Philips, establishing its European headquarters in Italy at Comerio. With seven nationalities reporting just at president level, the cultural mix and the sensitive dynamics necessary just to conduct daily business became enormous. One of the ways the company has attempted to facilitate globalisation has been through training and development to foster a common framework for people to understand Whirlpool and to understand how their jobs, their local country or region impact on the overall Whirlpool Corporation. Cross-functional team-working in such areas as Delivery Teams and Product Business Teams is an established practice in Comerio, whilst Whirlpool managers from many different countries interact in leadership courses such as those run at Ury, just south of Paris. Here a variety of activities, including outdoor activities, are used to create awareness of team dynamics and individual styles of behaviour.

How successful are training approaches, like that adopted by Whirlpool at Ury, in equipping managers to work more effectively with these sorts of issues across cultural and national borders? According to Jaques (1990) this emphasis upon teams and team-building skills is misplaced: 'I doubt that individual insight, personality matching, or even exercises in group dynamics can produce much in the way of organisational change or an overall improvement in leadership effectiveness. The problem is that our managerial hierarchies are so badly designed as to defeat the best efforts of psychologically insightful individuals' (1990, p. 128). Indeed, it is possible that such routes to self-awareness could lead to a masking rather than a valuing of cultural differences. For instance, in the language of DISC two managers – one from Sweden and one from Italy – might assume affinity with each other because they both score highly on the 'dominant' scale; yet we would anticipate that their ways of *expressing* this style would be very different due to the power distance and uncertainty avoidance indices associated with their respective national cultures (Hofstede, 1983). Finally, there is the further cross-cultural complication of importing North American training assumptions, models and facilitators to a European training event (Iles and Mabey, 1994).

HRD IN INTERNATIONAL STRATEGIC ALLIANCES

Many international companies have entered into a variety of strategic partnerships, ranging from mergers and acquisitions, through joint ventures, to a range of other more limited projects such as co-production and out-sourcing. They seem to have heeded the words of Ken Ohmae (1989) that, 'in a complex, uncertain world filled with dangerous opponents, it is best not to go it alone'.

However, though it may be true that 'Globalisation mandates alliances, makes them absolutely essential to strategy' (Ohmae, 1989) there may be a variety of problems that need to be addressed, ranging from a clash of both national and corporate cultures to the fear that such partnerships may in fact be 'Trojan horses', allowing potential competitors easy access to home markets, core competencies and advanced technologies. Many Western companies have been accused of entering into such alliances with Japanese and Korean companies for short-term financial and marketing benefits, given rising costs, difficulties in accessing international markets and the risks of 'going it alone' in developing new products and processes. However, the Far Eastern companies have often approached such alliances with a different orientation (Hamel, 1991). They have often been more oriented to learning over a long time scale, acquiring otherwise unobtainable skills, products and technologies (e.g. Philips and Matsushita over compact discs). Unless both partners weigh up the risks and opportunities and both approach it with 'learning' in mind, the core competencies of one partner may be inadvertently opened up, leaving it hollowed-out and de-skilled, dependent on external partners for supplies, components, technologies, and new designs. Working closely with skilled engineers, scientists and managers leaves many opportunities for learning about converging technologies and future strategies. What we need is a set of IHRD guidelines, so as to maximise the benefits of such strategic alliances and reduce their disadvantages, such as those developed by ICL (Lei and Slocum, 1992):

- treating the collaboration as a personal commitment;
- anticipating that it will take time;
- ensuring mutual trust and respect;
- appreciating the necessity for mutual benefits;
- appreciating the need to tie up tight legal contracts;
- ensuring corporate commitment;
- recognising that both markets and circumstances change;
- ensuring mutual expectations of the nature and time scale of the partnership;
- recognising both partners' interests and independence;
- getting to know one's opposite numbers socially;
- celebrating joint achievements together.

These guidelines of course raise a number of HRD issues, especially around building multi-cultural teams.

Companies may limit the status, number and tenure of people engaged in the venture, minimising opportunities for sustained learning. It is noticeable in this respect that Japanese companies typically assign managers to a venture over its lifetime, whereas Western companies typically use much more time-limited expatriates.

Clearly alliances and partnerships involve more than sharing money, technology and products; they also involve sharing *people* and *HRD practices*. Collaboration is often limited to specific activities, since in other areas the partners remain competitors. Such competitive collaboration raises new HRD issues, even in more limited ventures such as international research consortia (e.g. ESPRIT), R and D partnerships, marketing and distribution agreements and licensing arrangements. Some types of alliance demand more interaction, such as joint ventures. These often demand a collision or blending of national and corporate cultures and styles (e.g. Olivetti and ATT). In addition to teambuilding and two-way communication, such projects may require 'dating' and trust-building on smaller-scale projects like licensing agreements first. For example, Daimler-Benz found difficulty in adjusting its orderly style to Mitsubishi's leaderless group approach. There will need to be attention to issues of job design and attention to issues of recruitment, selection and HR planning, e.g. numbers, skills mix, responsibilities. Who do staff work for – the original partner or the joint venture? Who hires them? How are disagreements handled? If the venture fails, who do its employees work for?

Attention to training and development issues, especially orientation to the venture and attention to issues of corporate and national culture, will also be necessary. There will also need to be attention to *appraisal* issues – whose standards are to be used? Japanese companies often use subjective measures, longer-term goals, team appraisal, and indirect feedback. Attention needs to be given to the purpose of appraisal. In addition, there will need to be a focus on reward issues – will reward systems be linked or brought together? Will rewards reflect the local labour market or the home country? Agreement is necessary to ensure attraction, retention, transfer and consistency, as well as comparability with competitors. IR issues will also need to be considered – differences in systems and relationships with host-country governments will all affect the way employee relations are managed. Finally, HRD will play a role in relation to career issues – especially promotion issues, and whether promotion is blocked to local managers. (Expatriates may be assigned as expert advisors rather than direct bosses, for example.) How potential conflicts of loyalty are to be managed is another issue.

HRD practices and organisational learning

Given that a major reason for entering into strategic alliances of various kinds is to promote learning, a variety of HRD practices may inhibit organisational learning. These include (Pucik, 1988):

- *structural factors*, fragmenting the learning process and diluting responsibility for it;

- *HR planning factors*, operating so that the planning horizon is short-term and static, learning has a low priority and the strategic intent is not communicated;

- *recruitment and selection factors* so that there is insufficient lead-time for recruitment, low quality staff are assigned, and staffing depends on the partner;

- *training and development factors* so that cross-cultural competence may be lacking and the career structure and climate may not be conducive to either learning or its transfer;

- *appraisal and reward factors* so that appraisal is focused on short-term goals, learning is not encouraged, there are few incentives to transfer learning, and rewards are not tied to the global strategy.

Management development may be used to facilitate mergers between organisations from different cultural backgrounds. For example, the major Italian appliance company Zanussi was integrated strategically, operationally and organisationally within the Swedish-based Electrolux group, whilst retaining its distinct identity. It experienced so great a revival in its competitiveness that it moved from making a massive loss in 1983 to a large profit by 1987 (Ghoshal and Haspeslagh, 1990). Difficulties emerged over union opposition to workforce reductions and over the financial structure and ownership of Zanussi. Union leaders were sent from Sweden to Italy and vice versa to reassure the Italians, Zanussi's top management was replaced by Italians experienced in managing Swedish subsidiaries and joint task forces were set up to examine the scope of integration.

The unions agreed to workforce reductions, in part due to their loss of power in Italy in the 1980s, but also because of the open, transparent approach adopted by management, which was felt to be unusual in Italian industrial relations. Production technology was improved, new products were developed and quality was enhanced through a 'total quality' project in which supplier involvement was secured. Team-building sessions with middle management resulted in the generation of mission statements and guiding principles. Specific management development workshops, direct communications with first-line management, front-line manager training programmes and frequent visits by top management to Zanussi facilities were also important features.

THE ROLE OF HRD IN RECRUITING, SELECTING AND DEVELOPING INTERNATIONAL EMPLOYEES

Though some UK-based companies are specifically looking to recruit graduates from other European countries this attitude seems less prevalent than in other European countries. For example, less than 20 per cent of UK companies compared to 45 per cent of French companies were reported to be seeking to recruit in other EU countries in a recent survey (Keenan, 1992). Whereas 60 per cent of the French companies were planning to increase this practice, only 40 per cent of the British had such plans. More French companies emphasised the importance of understanding other European cultures and having work experience abroad. Undertaking part of one's education abroad and being willing to work abroad were also seen as more important by French companies (Sadler, 1994).

If we move from graduate recruitment to the recruitment of more experienced managers, it appears that shortages of such managers are hampering the globalisation efforts of many British and Irish companies in particular (Scullion 1992). The failure to recruit, retain and develop HCNs is of course one factor worsening such a situation. Such firms often appear to lack knowledge of local labour markets, show ignorance of the local education, training and qualifications system, and run into language and cultural problems, and many attempt to export 'domestic' recruitment practices to foreign countries. Similarly, management training and development programmes developed in the parent company may not travel effectively for the development of HCNs. One under-utilised strategy for developing HCNs is through developmental transfers to corporate headquarters in order to expose them to the corporate culture and develop a corporate perspective. A failure to develop and promote such managers of course leaves them open to poaching by competitors. For example, Guinness Nigeria Ltd, a joint venture between Unilever and Guinness, has come to rely increasingly on PCNs in the 1990s after a period of 'Africanising' management in the 1980s, in part due to its failure to develop HRD practices for its HCNs (Hailey, 1994).

For many organisations engaged in international recruitment, selection, development and career-planning activities in the 1980s and 1990s, there are complex sets of issues (Brewster, 1991). There are needs not only to manage local skills and labour shortages but to meet the staffing needs of foreign subsidiaries or joint ventures, to ensure national representation in the host country for political or status reasons, and to control the activities of foreign subsidiaries. HRD involvement is increasingly to use international assignments to develop high potential individuals by giving them experience of a 'bigger' job and to assess and test potential through such assignments, as well as to develop the organisation by encouraging the learning and sharing of new perspectives and the fostering of organisational learning.

Traditionally, many multi-nationals as well as governments and aid agencies have used *career expatriates* to meet staffing needs, ensure national representation and exercise control. This is characteristic of an ethnocentric orientation, low on trust of local expertise and high on control from the home country. However, such a strategy is now less common. Political problems, local resentment and frustration from employees, the need to be more locally responsive, and the expense and decline in the numbers of such career expatriates for a variety of reasons, including dual-career family pressures, have all contributed to other strategies being adopted (Tung 1982, 1988; Scullion 1992).

International management competencies

Though job and technical competence is usually the major criterion in selecting people for international assignments, studies of successful expatriates such as those by Ronen (1989) confirm that a variety of motivational and relational factors contribute to international effectiveness, such as tolerance of ambiguity, interpersonal skills and cultural empathy. It is the case that, however well-developed 'personality' attributes might be, the international manager will only be effective if these are deployed in *behavioural* terms. A review of Danish practice by Gertsen (1990) argues that what she calls 'inter-cultural competence' consists of three dimensions: not only 'affective competence', but also 'behaviour' (or communicative) competence (the ability to communicate effectively both verbally and non-verbally with HCNs) and 'cognitive competence'. By this she is referring to the ability of successful managers to be 'cognitively complex', not using crude stereotypes or narrow categorisations, but dividing up the world in more subtle ways. This capacity seems to echo Ratiu's (1983) research on the ways in which successful international managers use tentative provisional 'private stereotypes' rather than the fixed, inflexible 'public stereotypes' used by the less successful international managers. The Japanese company Matsushita, for example, selects candidates for international assignments against a set of criteria expressed in the acronym SMILE – speciality, managerial ability, international flexibility, language facility, and endeavour.

However, the phrase 'international managers' now refers to a far wider group than just expatriate managers, about which most has been written. We also need to consider the competencies required by senior managers of large multi-national companies, who we might refer to as global managers. As we have seen in our discussion of the transnational organisation earlier, the simultaneous pursuit of global co-ordination, multi-national responsiveness and international learning and adaptation has pushed international organisations further towards collaboration, the sharing of information and the collaborative implementation of strategy through an integrated network where resources, products, information and people flow freely between units. International productive capabilities may be assigned to different national subsidiaries according to their strengths. One example often quoted is the Swedish-Swiss electrical engineering group ABB, which along one dimension is a dispersed global network whilst along another dimension is a collection of national companies serving local markets. The managers running the 50 business areas have both global and local roles. One manager may have global responsibility for one product whilst also having local responsibilities for many projects. This requires senior managers who are not only internationally mobile but who 'in their minds can also travel across boundaries by understanding the international implications of their work' (Barham and Oates 1991; van Houten 1989). HRD will play a key role in facilitating this ability.

For example, Electrolux, a moribund company in the 1960s, lacked significant in-house R and D and had a limited range of products. It embarked on a series of acquisitions of troubled companies in mature markets in the 1970s. Managers were given considerable autonomy in achieving bottom-line results. Decentralisation, cost-consciousness and organisation on a 'country' basis marked the company until it attempted to become a global leader in selected core businesses in volume or niche markets. It embarked on another series of acquisitions in the 1980s (including Zanussi of Italy) to reduce duplication by sourcing on a regional or global basis whilst catering for local tastes within local markets. Instead of centralising or homogenising, Electrolux attempted to leverage diversity by matching national unit competence with responsibility. The Swedish and Finnish units were given the integrated kitchen system business due to Scandinavian flair for modal design, whilst Italy was given the role of compressor design and production. This approach requires managers who can collaborate across boundaries, work across cultures and act more flexibly. A senior manager development programme, EXEC, introduced in 1988, takes high potential younger senior managers with significant international responsibilities and develops general management skills and a common corporate international identity and culture. However, the company felt that deeper international understanding was needed, especially a regional focus on Europe (a regiocentric strategy). Consequently it introduced an International Business Leadership Programme (in conjunction with Ashridge) aimed at top team members of European business units and administered on a regional basis. The programme is structured in a multi-cultural, multi-national, multi-functional way, carries a European face and involves an in-company project (Regan, 1994; Bartlett and Ghoshal, 1992).

International career development and HRD

Most international transfers of human resources and international assignments of whatever kind involve a variety of changes and transitions such as:

- changes of *status*, often to positions of greater power and responsibility;
- changes of *function*, to general management or cross-functional roles from technical or functional roles;
- changes of *division*;
- changes of *boundary*, such as possible exclusions from informal networks due to language or cultural differences when working in another country;
- changes of *corporate culture*, such as when transferring from headquarters to a national subsidiary;
- changes of *national culture*, such as moving from Paris to Dubai.

Some of the HRD implications of the international assignment career cycle are illustrated in Figure 4.2.

Often such changes require considerable *adjustment*. Careful selection and rigorous *training* and *development* may help. However, such considerations are often only taken into account over expatriation. A wider, longer-term career focus is necessary, focusing on other transitions and other kinds of internationalisation issues. Here we will focus on the kinds of cross-border, cross-cultural transitions likely to be made by the international manager, the expatriate, the trouble-shooter, the mobile worker and the technical specialist. The need for rigour, extent and focus of HRD initiatives will of course vary for each group.

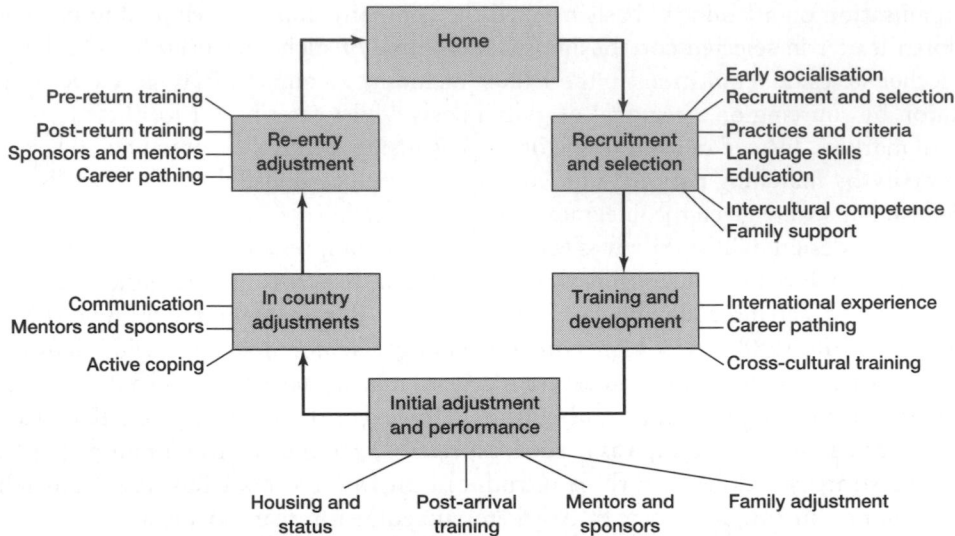

Fig. 4.2 The international assignment career cycle
(adapted from Black, Gregerson and Mendenhall, 1992, and Adler, 1991)

Organisational HRD practices to facilitate international adjustment

Old routines will be disrupted over the course of an international career, leading to uncertainty and confusion. Organisations can take a number of steps to facilitate adjustment to work tasks and roles, HCNs and TCNs and their ways of working, and the general international environment – focusing not just on cultural differences but also on legal, political, regulatory and other differences.

Accurate prior information on work, culture and the general environment may help reduce the 'culture shock' of an international assignment. This applies as much to repatriation as to expatriation. For example, some studies have shown that this can be as confusing and disorienting as expatriation, or even more so, as the organisation's culture, strategic direction and practices may have changed, colleagues may have moved on, and the general political, cultural, economic and social environment altered significantly whilst the expatriate has been away. The expatriate may also have changed significantly in outlook, values and attitudes as the result of an international experience. Among the steps organisations can take here are:

- allowing free choice and self-selection to take place, rather than making an international assignment seem forced or mandatory;
- providing information on the new job, the organisation and its culture;
- giving realistic job previews of the new job and role, perhaps through simulations;
- providing information on the behaviour and expectations of HCNs and TCNs and on the general cultural environment;
- giving pre-departure training, focusing on issues the assignee is likely to encounter, such as likely difficulties in housing, transport and relationships, to ease the shock;

- using appropriate selection criteria;
- providing prior international experience, especially in similar cultures.

To help in *country adjustment*, steps organisations can take include clarifying roles whilst building in some role discretion to enable adaptation to take place and providing social support from supervisor and co-workers, if possible. For example, meeting expatriates on arrival will help signal care and commitment. Providing a 'guide' for the first month or so, such as someone with extensive job and country knowledge, will also help. In addition, avoiding conflicting signals and role ambiguity as much as possible, providing a comprehensive job orientation to speed up learning, and providing relocation assistance and support for partner and children over areas like housing, schools, and shops will also help.

Role conflict and role ambiguity are likely to be greater the more 'novel' the job and the culture are. There may be some tensions and trade-offs between the goal of control and smooth transfer on the one hand, and the goal of testing and development on the other. The latter are more likely to be achieved in high discretion roles in challenging and stretching situations. There may also be tensions between conflicting expectations of the home office and host national superiors, with perhaps conflicting loyalties and commitments. On the one hand expatriates may 'go native', failing to include parent country perspectives into their decision making. Alternatively they may 'leave their hearts at home', failing to identify with the local operation. Pre-departure training may again help, as may the provision of mentors and sponsors to look after the interests of international assignees whilst they are on assignment.

There are a number of steps organisations can take to facilitate *repatriation adjustment*, such as planning for the repatriation career move to assure expatriates of desirable re-assignments on their return and providing mentors and sponsors 'back home' to give information, social support, protection, assistance with desirable repatriation assignments and explanations of strategic and competitive shifts. In addition, providing clear connections between the international assignment and long-term career plans so as to enhance the time, energy and commitment given to international assignments may be useful, as may ensuring that international experience is considered important to the promotion and development of future executives and leaders – apparently less of an issue for Japanese and Northern European companies than American companies. Otherwise there may be problems in persuading managers to take international assignments as these may seem to cut them off from positions of information and power and influence, and make the international assignment seem a bit like being sent to run the power station in Siberia in the days of the old Soviet Empire. Using the international experience and the new skills gained positively on reassignment to develop both individual and organisational learning, allowing long, frequent visits back to the home country and head office as well as telephone, fax and e-mail contacts, and building in greater interdependence between home and host country operations so as to facilitate the grasp of the 'big picture' as well as the local operation – in other words, in the old cliché, helping the assignee both think globally and act locally – are all likely to be effective. Providing post-return training and orientation, including attention to status and housing issues where re-adjustment seems a problem will also be helpful.

For example, whilst expatriates from Marks and Spencer working in the USA after the acquisition of Brooks Brothers reported insufficient support before, during and after expatriation, a lack of mentors and sponsors, a lack of appropriate training and insufficient use of skills and experience on repatriation (Phillips 1992), NEC of Japan make much greater use of HRD, including using expatriate experiences in case studies (Holden, 1994).

It is not of course just the organisation that has the responsibility to ensure that the international assignment is successful. Expatriates or repatriates themselves can do much to help ensure that such transitions are managed effectively. Employees are of course not just passive recipients of corporate assistance. In general, *symptom focused* or palliative coping strategies (such as trying to block out 'culture shock' by drinking, sleeping, dreaming or thinking of the return home and how many days are still left to do) are much less effective than *problem-focused* strategies like asking for information and advice, seeking help, looking for opportunities to interact socially with co-workers, and looking for positive experiences for new learning. For example, trying to become socially integrated, re-appraising the experience positively, and resisting the temptation to withdraw all seem to be more positive ways of coming to terms with confusion, disorientation, and culture shock than blaming one's partner, getting blind drunk, becoming obsessed with home country news, or huddling together with colonies of other ex-pats in a cultural and social ghetto to complain about the locals and their odd, amusing or irritating ways.

However, such career development strategies may run into problems: high potential staff may not wish to relocate if they perceive that their career at home will suffer because of their absence, especially if the organisation does not in practice seem to regard international experience as an essential prerequisite to promotion or career success. This seems less true of Dutch or Scandinavian organisations, for example, than of British or American ones. Potential expatriates may turn down such opportunities for family reasons, such as disruptions to children's education or the reluctance of partners to give up their careers. Some organisations may help in finding jobs for the partner, both within the organisation and with other organisations, but in some countries this may not be possible for legal or cultural reasons.

INTERNATIONAL HRD: TECHNIQUES AND MODELS

Job assignments, visits, 'shadowing' international operations at headquarters, informal briefings and orientation seminars are all likely to be useful in preparing and developing staff for international assignments. However, many Japanese and Scandinavian companies seem to engage in more extensive training for such assignments, and perhaps as a consequence experience fewer failures.

Does cross-cultural training work?

To operate successfully in a global environment it is essential that expatriates are prepared for their assignments. Yet research in the area of work-related cross-cultural interactions have found that such interactions have not always been successful, particularly for American expatriates. On an average, between 20–40 per cent of all American expatriates have returned home early because of their poor performance and/or their inability to adjust to the foreign culture. Nearly half of those who did not return early functioned below their normal level of productivity. The costs of unsuccessful cross-cultural interaction are high. The direct cost of failed expatriate adjustments to organisations in 1985 was estimated to be as high as $150,000 per employee. These costs can run into millions for a typical multi-national organisation that has hundreds of expatriates all over the world (Tung, 1982, 1988).

One means of facilitating effective cross-cultural interactions is cross-cultural training. Various studies have examined if such pre-departure training can help expatriates deal with people from different cultural backgrounds. One argument used in favour of cross-cultural training is that such training allows participants to adjust more rapidly to the foreign culture and thus enables these subjects to be more effective in their new work environment. This process, termed adjustment, enables a person gradually to develop expected behaviours in the new culture. However, in spite of the strong arguments presented for the use of cross-cultural training, only about 30 per cent of US managers sent on expatriate assignments actually receive it. This is because many organisations are still not convinced of the importance of such training. Some believe that a manager who performs well in one place will be effective anywhere. Others believe that there is no conclusive evidence that such programmes are effective. However, the research evidence shows that cross-cultural training does seem to allow participants to adjust more rapidly to a new culture.

According to a review by Black and Mendenhall (1990), cross-cultural training does seem to improve:

● specific cross-cultural skills such as self-confidence and well-being, interpersonal skills, and perceptual/cognitive skills;
● cross-cultural adjustment;
● job performance.

What training methods should we use?

One classification of the various training methods and processes is provided by Ronen (1989). Each method is seen as appropriate for a specific purpose or target.

1 Didactic-information training

Essentially fact oriented training, presented verbally via lectures, handouts, videotapes, and films. It is appropriate for presenting basic information about the host-country environment (area studies), acquainting assignees with company operations, and providing information about the parent country and institutions for assignees who will be required to represent their organisation and society in an informed and credible manner.

2 Inter-cultural experiential workshops

These (cultural assimilators, simulations and role plays) attempt to provide experiential involvement and engage the participant at affective, cognitive and behavioural levels.

The aim is to examine cultural awareness (the impact of one's cultural values on personal attitudes and behaviour), improve specific cultural awareness (target country experiences) and enhance general cultural awareness (general variations in inter-cultural settings).

3 Sensitivity training

This may be useful as a preparatory stage to enable participants to explore underlying values, attributions and personal styles, exploring behaviour in direct confrontations with people. However, the values underlying sensitivity training may not be generally applicable.

4 Field experiences

Preparatory visits, if well prepared, are very useful. Meetings with returned expatriates may also be useful, as may 'mini-cultures' or simulated host country experiences within ethnic communities.

5 Language and communication skills

Fundamental language skills will of course make daily encounters easier and more fulfilling.

When should we use which method?

Facts affecting the choice of method or process include:

- the degree of interaction expected with host-country nationals;
- the degree of cultural similarity between host and home countries;
- the degree of job novelty expected;
- the prior international experience of the assignee.

We need a framework which helps us match the process with the quality we are trying to develop. If we are addressing basic facts and information, then a tightly controlled 'instrumental' process with little learner flexibility is likely to be appropriate. Situation-specific skills are more likely to demand methods which allow greater learner control. Issues of personal development are more likely to be addressable though more 'experiential' methods which permit the highest degree of learned autonomy. The more 'novel' or 'distant' the culture is, the less prior experience the assignee has, the more novel the job is, and the more frequent and important interaction with host country nationals is, then the more 'experiential' methods are likely to be effective.

The issue arises as to when each method is appropriate. Black and Mendenhall (1990) argue that various factors will influence the choice of methods, including: how much interaction with host-country nationals is expected, how novel the job is, how much international experience the assignee has already had, and how culturally similar the host and home countries are. More rigorous training is needed, for example, for naïve assignees taking new jobs requiring extensive interaction in culturally dissimilar countries. Of particular interest here is the concept of 'cultural distance' or 'cultural toughness'. This appears to be similar to the concept of 'psychic distance' often used in research on exporting behaviour and internationalisation. Firms appear to export first to countries which are physically close. This concept and indeed concepts of 'rigour', 'cultural distance' and 'cultural toughness' are intuitively appealing, but rather ill-defined.

It may be possible to measure such differences in terms of scales developed from Hofstede (1980), who finds, for example, the Nordic countries appear to form a cluster distinct from Mediterranean 'Latin' countries, whereas 'Anglo' countries such as the UK and Ireland have more similarity with far-flung countries like Australia and New Zealand than with France or Belgium. 'Germanic' countries like Germany, Switzerland and Austria form yet another distinct cultural cluster.

Matching programmes, targets and types in HRD

In order to address and resolve issues over which training methods should be used when and in which combination, a model has been developed drawing upon the work of Iles (1995), Mabey (1995), Tichy (1995) and Gertsen (1990). The model, which is shown in Figure 4.3, systematically matches types of learning with targets of HRD interventions at different levels of involvement.

The model distinguishes between training which is targeted at basic facts and data, training which is oriented towards situation specific skills, and training which is oriented towards self-development. This model further argues that some methods such as lectures, handouts, area briefings, culture assimilators and case studies may be useful in imparting facts and basic cultural awareness (and to some extent interview and presentation skills) but that other skills and qualities are best developed through modelling, role plays and simulations. 'Deeper' qualities, referred to by Gertsen (1990) as affective and cognitive competence, require less structured methods, such as process workshops, outdoor development exercises and action learning involving multi-cultural teams and sets, job rotations with international assignments, and multi-cultural encounter groups. Issues raised here include whether such methods are necessary to develop such qualities, whether such methods are required more by less experienced international employees, whether such methods are more necessary for working in culturally distant cultures and with teams composed of members of very difficult cultures, and whether such methods are more necessary for sustained rather than limited interaction (e.g. managing inter-cultural teams in a foreign country over a several-year period as compared to a brief trip to a trade fair overseas).

However, much of the attention in IHRD has been given to developing PCN expatriates, rather than TCNs or HCNs. This is likely to become a more important issue in the future. In a survey of 105 European multi-nationals, Derr and Oddou (1993) found that expatriational repatriation was the traditional means of internationalising managers, but that not all companies either prepared their managers sufficiently or took advantage of their expertise on their return. In addition, newer, faster practices for internationalising managers were required. The three most widely used HRD practices were expatriating PCNs, using in-company training seminars, and sending executives on extended, intensive foreign trips. However, the three most important future methods

Type of Learning	Targets of IHRD intervention		
	Individual	*Team*	*Organisation*
Basic data/analytical skills; cognitive competence	Lectures, handouts, videos, cultural assimilators, MBA courses.	Lectures, handouts, case studies, videos.	Lectures, seminars, briefings, presentations, case studies, survey feedback.
Situation–specific skills; behavioural competence	Interview skills training; language training in class; behavioural modelling. Role plays in development centres.	Role plays; team building exercises; interaction process analysis.	Role plays.
Self-development; affective competence	Action learning with multi-cultural set; multi-cultural outdoor development encounter groups. Job rotation, field trips, projects.	Action learning, outdoor development with multi-cultural teams; simulations, projects.	International assignments with debriefing, feedback, sharing of learning.
Organisational development: organisational learning			Action learning with multi-cultural set; team development; learning company initiatives.

Fig. 4.3   Matching programmes, targets and types in IHRD
(adapted from Iles 1995, Mabey 1995, Tichy 1995, Gertsen 1990)

identified were expatriating PCNs, in-company seminars, and, most interestingly, bringing TCNs and HCNs to head office. Other methods cited included expatriating regional nationals to regional offices, using other company personnel in seminars, encouraging international networks, and developing international task forces and project teams. The use of task forces and in company international seminars was also predicted to increase, as was the use of external cross-cultural training for senior managers, often linked to business schools.

Who should be trained?

Given the importance of spouse/partner and family adjustment to the success of international assignments, it seems logical to involve the whole family in cross-cultural training as much as possible.

However, it is not just the long-term expatriate who needs cross-cultural training. Employees involved in brief visits, trade shows and technology transfers may also need training, albeit at a more moderate level, possibly involving more specific task elements. Cross-cultural training is also useful for *repatriation*, for those on *short-term assignments*, and for *succession-planning* purposes. Many high-potential managers may avoid international assignments if they perceive them as not leading to the top. Providing cross-cultural training may help reduce expatriate failure and ensure that future executives do have substantial international experience and training.

Non-work factors

In addition to the 'family' factors already discussed, aspects of the host-country culture also seem to influence ease of adjustment of expatriates to a new culture. For example, cultural distance or cultural novelty – the extent to which the host and home country cultures differ – seems to be a crucial factor, especially in the first few years. In addition, the *previous international experience* of the assignee, particularly in the same country to which the manager is now being assigned, seems to facilitate cross-cultural adjustments.

However, it is not just the *quantity* of the experience but its *quality* that counts, and the approach and orientation of the expatriate towards it.

DEVELOPING GLOBAL MANAGERS AND ORGANISATIONS

Most of our discussion of international HRD has so far focused on developing managers and professionals, developing local managers, and training expatriates. However, we also need to consider the development of senior managers and global leaders, and development of the organisation as a whole.

Most of the methods discussed so far target the individual and use analytical methods like lectures, readings or case studies to develop awareness and cognitive understanding only (e.g. a traditional business school MBA). We have already argued that deeper, more experiential methods are necessary to develop communication skills, problem-solving techniques and 'affective competence'. How can we best develop not individuals but teams and organisations? (See Fig. 4.3.)

For example, GEMS, the world's leading producer in its field, experienced rapid globalisation in the 1980s through European acquisitions and Asian strategic alliances. HRD was used to develop global mind-sets, leadership skills, networking abilities, change agent skills and teams. Its US-based, engineering-dominated culture required transformation for this to be successful. European, Asian and American centres were each given product line responsibilities, and a global leadership development programme was introduced in 1988, using diverse teams working together on common issues and starting at top team level. Common features were team building, future planning, feedback on skills, and action planning. The top 55 people in the company worked on a variety of issues in small multi-cultural teams, coached by a senior manager. Working on 'real' problems in workshops on team and project work and in outdoor development activities, it focused on both hard and soft issues. Project completion required continued networking and the presentation of the projects to a senior 'top team' to enhance dialogue and gain commitment. Other initiatives included secondment, transfers, new programmes, networking and the involvement of other managers in similar programmes (Tichy, 1994).

The features of this initiative are:

- work on both 'hard' issues, e.g. competitiveness, and 'soft' issues, e.g. leadership style, interpersonal skill;
- extensive work outside the classroom;
- work in multi-cultural, multi-functional teams;
- work on 'real' global problems;
- some element of risk, e.g. the outdoor exercise, the career risks involved in the projects and presentations;
- a multi-cultural, multi-lingual training team;
- much use of the methods designated as 'experiential', e.g. outdoor development, multi-cultural action learning, team building.

This particular approach to HRD was based on the work of Tichy (1994). He terms it 'compressed action learning' as it seeks to use shorter cycle-times rather than traditional training in accordance with the need for reduced cycle times in other areas as a consequence of globalisation. It seeks to blend management and organisation development and transfer learning directly to the workplace. Deutsche Aerospace AE (DASA) has used this mode to develop its transnational capabilities, viewing cross-cultural HRD as a core skill, to be developed through a variety of transnational management, team and organisational development programmes. These include recruiting and developing high potentials, exchange programmes, conferences and meetings, and cultural awareness and intercultural skills programmes. Learning is tied to corporate strategy and integrated into ongoing business activities (Sattelberger, 1994).

Following this line of argument, in order to achieve team and organisational development, not just individual development, and in order to achieve fundamental change, not just awareness and cognitive understanding, organisations need to move their HRD efforts further along the path from individually-oriented cognitive methods to corporately-oriented transforming methods using many of the methods described as 'experiential'. For example, one management development initiative using a culturally diverse team assessing community and conservation projects for Operation Raleigh employed a multi-cultural, multi-national (though not obviously multi-lingual) team working on a 'real' project with 'real' consequences for Operation Raleigh. It also involved team building and outdoor development activities as preparation, and the team focused on hard issues (business planning, opportunity assessment) as well as soft issues (leadership, communication, teamwork, cross-cultural skills, etc.). It seemed to have been an important developmental experience for many of the participants personally (Iles, 1995a). However, though the participants were operating in a situation of some risk to themselves, it would appear to be one of only moderate risk – would their careers 'back home' really suffer if they failed? And how much is the sponsoring organisation getting out of this? Ideally, according to Tichy (1994), a team from the same organisation would produce greater transfer of learning to the workplace.

However, it is important to note that national culture is also likely to affect how receptive participants are to different training and development methodologies. For example, sensitivity training and experiential methods with trainers in a facilitating role may work best for participants from cultures comfortable with ambiguity; individual participants from more uncertainty-avoiding cultures may appreciate more direction; those from more collectivist cultures may be uncomfortable with direct, personal feedback; whilst those higher power-distance cultures may expect the trainer to adopt a more expert, prescriptive and distant role, and be uncomfortable in situations where existing status and hierarchy differences appear not to be respected. In short, currently fashionable development models stressing openness, participation, feedback confrontation, egalitarianism and discovery may themselves be culturally restricted and not always culturally appropriate.

CONCLUSIONS

The field of international HRD is relatively immature. This chapter has identified some examples of the key human resource development strategies and tactics employed by organisations attempting to enhance their international and global presence. Supplemented by observations of several case study organisations, we have discovered a variety of HRD initiatives being used to heighten understanding of national diversity, to facilitate operating across international boundaries, to optimise the advantages of employing an increasingly multi-cultural workforce, to create transitions into a more global marketplace and to facilitate transnational strategic alliances.

With regard to organisational learning we have seen some of the commercial synergisms that can be gained from global alliances and joint ventures and acquisitions. However, in each case the organisations concerned had to ensure that their HRD approaches avoided ethnocentric bias. The cases also illustrate some important lessons concerning managing diversity: for example, intercultural experiential workshops and sensitivity training often prove particularly powerful means of creating positive working relationships and customer perceptions.

Inevitably, many questions still remain. For instance, research on 'domestic diversity' (e.g. Walker, 1991; Cox, 1993; Wilson, this volume) demonstrates that valuing minorities helps them achieve better job satisfaction, job involvement, career achievement and lower turnover due to greater value congruence. However, are such findings applicable to internationally diverse organisations? The evidence in this chapter suggests this is the case for attracting and retaining staff, enhancing creativity and problem-solving, and responding to customer needs through developing new products and services, but more work is needed to test such linkages between the HRD approaches and performance outcomes. In particular, future case studies might usefully apply the fruits of the literature on the learning organisation in analysing which HRD interventions most help international enterprises to exploit the learning possibilities available to them.

References

Adler, N.J. (1991) *International Dimensions of Organisational Behaviour*, Boston, MA, Kent Publishers.

Barham, K. and Oates, D. (1991) *Developing the International Manager*, London, Business Books.

Bartlett, C.A. and Ghoshal, S. (1989) *Managing across borders*, London, Hutchinson.

Bartlett, C.A. and Ghoshal, S. (1992) 'What is a global manager?', *Harvard Business Review*, 70 (5), 124–32.

Black, J. and Mendenhall, M. (1990) 'Cross-cultural training effectiveness: a review and theoretical framework for future research', *Academy of Management Review*, 15 (1): 113–36.

Black J.S., Gregerson, H.B. and Mendenhall, M. (1992) *Global Assignment*, San Francisco CA, Jossey Bass.

Brewster, C. (1991) *The Management of expatriates*, London, Kogan Page.

Cox, T. (1993) *Cultural diversity in organisations: theory, research and practice*, San Francisco CA, Berrett Kochler.

Derr, C.B. and Oddou, G. (1993) 'Internationalising Mergers: Speeding up the process', *European Management Journal*, 11(4), pp. 435–42.

Dowling, P.J., Schuler R.S. and Welch D. (1993) *International Dimensions of Human Resource Management*, Belmond, CA, Wadsworth.

Evans, P., Doz, Y. and Laurent, A. (eds) (1989) *Human Resource Management in International Firms*, London, Macmillan.

Gertsen, M.C. (1990) 'Intercultural competence and expatriates', *International Journal of Human Resource Management*, 1 (3): 341–62.

Ghoshal, S. and Haspeslagh, P. (1990) 'The acquisition and integration of Zanussi by Electrolux – a case study', *European Management Journal*, 8, 4, December, pp. 414–33.

Hailey, J. (1994) 'Localising the multinationals: limitations and problems', in S. Segal Horn, *The challenge of international business*, London, Kogan Page.

Hamel, G. (1991) 'Competition for competence and inter-partner learning within international strategic alliances', *Strategic Management Journal*, 12: 83–103.

Hofstede, G. (1980) *Culture's Consequences*, London, Sage.

Hofstede, G. (1983) 'The cultural relativity of organisational practices and theories', *Journal of International Business Studies*, 14, 1: 75–89.

Holden, L. (1994) 'NEC – international HRM with vision' in Torrington, D., *International Human Resource Management*, Hemel Hempstead, Prentice Hall, pp. 122–41.

van Houten, G. (1989) 'The implications of globalism: new management realities at Philips', in Evans, P. *et al.* (eds) *Human Resource Management in International Firms: change, globalization, innovation*, London, Macmillan, pp. 101–112.

Iles, P.A. and Mabey, C. (1994) *Developing global capabilities through management and organisation development strategies*. Paper presented to British Academy of Management Conference, Lancaster University, September 1994.

Iles, P.A. (1995a) 'International HRM', in Mabey, C. and Salaman, G. (eds) *Strategic HRM*, Oxford, Blackwell, p. 366–441.

Iles, P.A. (1995b) 'Learning to work with difference', *Personnel Review*, forthcoming.

Jaques, E. (1990) 'In praise of hierarchy', *Harvard Business Review*, Jan–Feb., 90, 1: 127–33.

Keenan, A.C. (1992) 'Graduate recruitment and the Single European Market', *European Management Journal*, 10, 4, pp. 485–93.

Laurent, A. (1986) 'The cross-cultural puzzle of international human resource management', *Human Resource Management*, 25(1): 91–102.

Lei, D. and Slocum, J.W. (1992) 'Global strategy, competence building and strategic alliances', *California Management Review*, Fall, pp. 81–97.

Morgan, R. U. (1986) 'International Human Resource Management fact or fiction?', *Personal Administration*, 31, 9, 43–7.

Ohmae, K. (1989) 'The global logic of strategic alliances', *Harvard Business Review*, March–April: 143–55.

Pedler, M., Burgoyne, M. and Boydell, T. (1991) *Towards the learning company*, London, Van Nostrand.

Perlmutter, H.V.C. (1969) 'The tortuous evaluation of the multinational corporation', *Columbia Journal of World Business*, Jan–Feb. pp. 9–18.

Philips, N. (1992) *Managing international teams*, London, Financial Times/Pitman Publishing.

Pucik, V. (1988) 'Strategic alliances, organisational learning and competitive advantage', *Human Resource Management*, 27(1): 77–93.

Pucik, V. (1994) 'Introduction' and 'Globalisation and Human Resource Management', in Pucik, V. Tichy, N. and Barrett, C. (eds) *Globalisation Management*, New York, Wiley, pp. 1–11, 61–84.

Rativ, I. (1983) 'Thinking internationally: a comparison of how international executives learn', *International Studies of Management and Organization*, 13, 1–2, pp. 139–50.

Regan, M. (1994) 'Developing the middle manager for globalization: the case of Electrolux', in Kirkbride, P. (ed.) *Human Resource Management in Europe*, London, Routledge.

Ronen, S. (1989) 'Training the international assignee' in I. Goldstein (ed.) *Training and Development*, San Francisco, CA, Jossey-Bass.

Saarinen, J. (1994) *Changing Roles in the Personnel Function: A Case Study of Tampella Power Inc.*, University of Tampere Working Paper Series, No. 48, Finland.

Sadler, P.C. (1994) *Managing Talent*, London, Financial Times/Pitman Publishing.

Sattelberger, T.C. (1994) *Building transnational capabilities*. Paper presented to American Society for Training and Development Conference, Anaheim USA, May 1994.

Scullion, H. (1992) 'Attracting management globetrotters', *Personnel Management*, Jan, pp. 28–34.

Stata, R. (1989) 'Organizational learning: the key to management innovation', *Sloan Management Review*, Spring, pp. 63–74.

Tichy, N.M. (1994) 'Global Development' in Pucik, V., Tichy, N.M. and Barrett, C.K. (eds) *Globalizing Management*, New York, Wiley.

Tung, R.L. (1982) 'Selection and training procedures of UK, European and Japanese multinationals', *California Management Review*, 25(1): 57–71.

Tung, R.L. (1988) 'Career issues in international assignments', *Academy of Management Executive*, 11(3): 241–48.

Walker, B. (1991) 'Valuing differences', in Smith, M.A. and Johnson, S.J. (eds) *Valuing differences in the workplace*, University of Minnesota/American Society for Training and Development. Reprinted in Mabey, C. and Iles, P.A. (1994) *Managing Learning*, Milton Keynes, Open University.

ACTIVITIES FOR SECTION I

1 (a) Construct a rationale for your personal view of Human Resource Development.

(b) Examine this rationale in the light of the arguments presented in the chapters in this section. Explain how those arguments either support or challenge your rationale.

(c) Discuss your results with colleagues. Review your personal position and your rationale in the light of your discussions.

2 (a) Select and describe one *major* or *significant* HRD intervention with which you are currently involved.

(b) Identify and describe the assumptions concerning the nature and purpose of HRD which underpin the intervention.

(c) Discuss the results with colleagues and determine any changes you will make in future designs.

3 (a) Select one chapter from this section which you believe most closely coincides with your own views of HRD.

(b) Prepare a thorough analysis of the strengths and weaknesses of the arguments presented in the chapter.

(c) Present your analysis to colleagues to facilitate debate on the pros and cons of the arguments.

(d) Identify the implications of the results of this activity for your future professional practice.

Section II

HRD STRATEGIES

5

THE STRATEGY–HRD CONNECTION

John Fredericks and Jim Stewart

6

THE PROVISION OF LEARNING SUPPORT FOR NON-EMPLOYEES

John Walton

7

NEW FORMS OF WORK ORGANISATION AND HRD

Michael Kelleher

8

MANAGING DIVERSITY AND HRD

Elisabeth Wilson

9

POWER AND INFLUENCE AND THE HRD FUNCTION

Rita Johnston

5

The Strategy–HRD Connection

John Fredericks and Jim Stewart

INTRODUCTION

This chapter is concerned with the connections and relationships between organisations and HRD. Its primary purpose is to describe and explain a conceptual model devised by the authors to represent how HRD can gain impact at a macro, organisation-wide level and, relatedly, provide a contribution to the continued survival and growth of work organisations.

The previous paragraph suggests an ambitious undertaking. Certainly its achievement will require an examination of several complex concepts which are individually and collectively the subject of widespread study and enquiry, much of which is characterised by disagreement and controversy. It is therefore important to state at the outset that we are not seeking to argue a definitive view of organisations or HRD. What we will describe is acknowledged to be one view of organisations and the role of HRD within them. That view itself can be said to be idiosyncratic since it is based on our individual and joint explorations of the issues and concepts involved. However, those explorations have been and are informed by our wide experience of working as internal and external HRD consultants in varied organisational contexts. The current point we have reached in our thinking is represented by what we refer to as our model of strategic HRD.

The model incorporates a number of key concepts and seeks to highlight and illustrate how they connect and relate. In describing the model, therefore, we have to describe each of the constituent concepts. These descriptions will be necessarily brief since each of the concepts could themselves justify at least a chapter, if not a book, to explore fully the various arguments concerning their meaning. Our descriptions naturally focus on meanings and interpretations of the concepts which fit most closely with our own beliefs and with the relationships represented in our conceptual model. The reader is advised therefore to adopt a critical stance when assessing and evaluating our arguments.

We take it as accepted that the focus of our work, organisation level and wide development, is important and worthwhile. The plethora of publications on related topics such as the learning organisation is an indication of the growing awareness and acceptance of the need to ensure that development and learning have long-term and organisational relevance. Relevance is judged by the benefits and contributions achieved in terms of continuing survival and growth. Our aim though is not to provide an analysis of causal relationships and associated prescriptions for action. Such models do exist (see for example Burke and Litwin, 1989) though we have doubts about both their validity and utility. We are more concerned with offering ideas and provoking thought and reflection as a basis for informing decisions on action.

OBJECTIVES AND STRUCTURE

To elaborate this overall aim, the chapter is intended to achieve the following objectives:

- to describe and discuss a number of key concepts within organisation and management theory;
- to examine critically how these concepts connect and relate with each other to provide an understanding of the processes of organising and managing;
- to provide a framework in the form of a conceptual model for analysing organisational, managerial and HRD practices;
- to examine the implications for and applications of HRD interventions and practice.

The rest of the chapter is structured around six sections to achieve the objectives. The following section is concerned with identifying and briefly discussing the key ideas contained in and underpinning the conceptual model. Given its breadth and ambition, the model itself is the subject of the next three sections. The model is built up over three phases, each of which is explored in a separate section. These sections will also expand on our views and arguments concerning the key ideas and concepts. Implications for and ideas on HRD strategies and practice arising from the model are explored in the penultimate section. The chapter closes with some concluding remarks summarising our argument.

CRITICAL CONCEPTS

There are three sets of key ideas, or critical concepts, which form the basis of our model of strategic HRD. Each of these is discussed separately in this section.

Organisation design

The first set of ideas is to do with the nature of organisations and how to set about designing them. From the work of Taylor onwards there has been a series of analyses and prescriptions for understanding and designing work organisations (Huczynski and Buchanan, 1991).

What is not always recognised or acknowledged in these prescriptions is the assumptions about social reality upon which the prescriptions are based. In other words, prescriptions for organisation design vary not only because of different analyses but also because of different 'paradigms' of what constitutes the social world (Morgan, 1990; Fisher, this volume). The nature of our assumptions about human existence influence our way of seeing the world and our interpretations of our experience. Those assumptions in turn constitute our paradigm.

Our view is that whatever paradigm is adopted the common thread in much organisation and management theory is a concern with organisation *structure*. Prescriptions for organisation design are, almost by definition, prescriptions for structural arrangements. The primary focus of these arrangements is normally the authority relations (Giddens, 1989) governing, at least in a formal or 'official' sense, the way in which individual members and different parts of the organisation relate to one another, and engage with the 'human' (McGregor 1960) and social processes such as objective setting and decision making involved in organising. A key concept within our model then is that of *organisation structure*. We define this to be those organisational arrangements to do with authority relations which, in turn, have the effect of setting limits, or constraining, the actions and behaviour of individual organisation members. In common with Giddens (1989), we also take the view that organisations are maintained by the participation of individuals in those arrangements, and that as individual organisation members, we have to learn 'the way' to participate.

Organisation strategy

The second key concept is that of organisation strategy. In some ways, the concept of organisation strategy can be synonymous with that of organisation structure since it is argued by some writers that the strategic management discourse is such that it acts as a control mechanism and constrains the behaviour of some organisation members to the advantage of others (Knights and Morgan, 1990, 1991). This provides part of a critique of the role and contribution of HR practice in strategic management which would question, largely on ethical grounds, the strategy–HR connection (Thomas and Kovvuri, 1994; see also McGoldrick and Stewart, this volume, for a discussion on the HRM–HRD nexus).

A further problem with the concept of organisation strategy is the wide range of views of its meaning to be found in the management literature. Henry Mintzberg, a writer in the field of strategy, identifies 10 different schools of thought within strategic management, each of which can lay claim to a unique perspective (Mintzberg, 1990).

We do not intend to engage in these debates within this chapter. For the purposes of our argument, and to provide an understanding of our conceptual model, we accept a broad view of strategy. Watson (1994) suggests that strategy is concerned with managing relations with the environment; is related to purposive action; is conditioned to some extent by internal and external constraints and opportunities; is intended to ensure survival; and is characterised by an identifiable pattern within an otherwise ad hoc series of decisions and actions. This latter feature is central to Mintzberg's view of strategy which he describes as 'a pattern in a stream of actions' (1988, p. 14). Our view is that strategy is always 'realised'; that is strategy emerges over time as a 'stream of actions' and interactions within the organisation and across its boundaries.

The second key concept then is *organisation strategy*. We define this to be those organisation decisions and actions which are intended to and/or have an impact on the long-term survival of the organisation within its operating environment.

Management/leadership style

When we speak of 'organisation decisions', the language form implies that an organisation is some kind of independent entity which thinks and acts. This is of course not an accurate view since an organisation does not exist in that sense. Depending on the size, tens, hundreds or thousands of decisions are made within an organisation every day. But these decisions are actually made by human beings, either separately or collectively. Those decisions having strategic impact, or those we label organisation decisions, are *normally* made by top or senior managers. Thus, when we speak of organisation decisions what we really mean is management decisions.

The processes adopted by managers in making their decisions can and do vary. They can decide without reference to or consultation with other organisation members. Conversely, they can adopt participative or democratic processes in decision making which engage the involvement of a wide organisation membership, including non-managerial employees. These varying approaches to decision making lie at the heart of differences in management style.

Management style is essentially concerned with the way in which individual managers conduct themselves in constructing and operating within the formal authority relations referred to earlier. Top managers are normally more concerned with constructing those relationships, while less senior managers are more involved in operating within them. The concept of management style has been the focus of much academic research and enquiry which has led to a plethora of analyses and prescriptions (Huczynski and Buchanan, 1991; Mullins, 1993). Most, if not all, of this research has been conducted from a psychological perspective; that is an assumed relationship between individual characteristics and individual behaviour. So, in simple terms, management style is considered to be a function of the knowledge, skills, beliefs and values of the individual manager. Individual differences in these characteristics find expression in differences in behaviour, including behaviour directed to making managerial decisions. It is those forms of behaviour that are referred to by the term management style.

Our third and final key concept then is that of *management style*. We define this to be actions and behaviour concerned with managerial decision making which is based on the beliefs and values held by individual managers.[*]

There are a number of other concepts contained within our model of strategic HRD. This opening section has been limited to discussing the three we view as most critical to our argument. Each of the other concepts will be considered as we work through the model itself in the following sections.

STRATEGY–STRUCTURE CONNECTION

The first part of our model is concerned with the relationship and connections between organisation structure and organisation strategy. We also introduce here the key role of information flows and the notion of 'actions and behaviour'. The former is considered important since information and information processes are highly significant in decision

---

[*] cf. the idea of management style discussed by McGoldrick and Stewart, this volume.

making. Most if not all theories of organisation and managerial decision making emphasise the significant role of information and information processing (Jennings and Wattam, 1994). This significance is emphasised by the idea of 'bounded rationality' (Simon, 1960) which recognises the physical and psychological limits operating on human beings in our capacity to access and process information. We cannot know everything there is to know about all relevant factors affecting a decision situation, nor can we accurately and thoroughly interpret and analyse everything that we do know (Stewart, 1994). Even if we had the capacity, some things, e.g. future consequences, are by definition unknowable. Thus, what and how information is accessed and processed is highly significant in organisations.

The notion of actions and behaviour represents a view of what organisations actually are. We do not, for the purposes of this analysis, directly apply distinctions between behaviour and action. Watson (1994) defines organisations as 'sets of ongoing human relationships utilising various technologies in which people cooperate to achieve tasks which would otherwise not be possible, either at all or from an equivalent resource base' (p. 32). The important part of this definition lies in the words 'sets of ongoing human relationships'. This implies, or at least suggests, a regular *pattern* of relationships which is constructed by and reflects the actions and behaviour of individuals. Thus, organisations are constituted by regularity and patterning in the actions and behaviour of individual human beings which, to take Watson's definition further, result in co-operation in the achievement of tasks. The extent of that co-operation, and the success or otherwise in achievement of the tasks, of course can and does vary. An important factor influencing success is the amount of co-operation inherent in the pattern of relationships (Watson, 1994) arising from the actions and behaviour of individuals.

The 'regular pattern of relationships' can also be viewed as what we term organisation structure. The authority relations within organisations to some extent condition the actions and behaviour of individual organisation members and thus influence the nature of the regular pattern of relationships. At the same time, however, the actions and behaviour of individuals constitute and create the regular pattern, and thus create organisation structure. This seeming tautology is what Giddens (1984) terms 'structuration'. This term simply means that social systems, whether they be societies or organisations, create structures – i.e. regular patterns of relationships – that can and do constrain individuals but, since it is individual action and behaviour that constitute the regular pattern, i.e. structures, then structures can and do also enable the action of individuals.

The model at this stage then comprises our key concepts of strategy and structure, and additional ideas around information flows and actions/behaviour (see Fig. 5.1). The argued relationships between these concepts are now detailed.

The first connecting line is between strategy and structure. This reflects ongoing debate within the management literature about the relationship between these two concepts. This debate has centred primarily on an assumed dependent relationship between the two factors. Alfred Chandler's classic study is a famous example which argues that structure follows strategy (Chandler, 1962). Our view is that such debate misses the point. We accept the existence of a relationship and connections between strategy and structure. As we suggested earlier, the two concepts can even be seen as synonymous. However, we believe it is more productive to view the concepts as separate but interdependent.

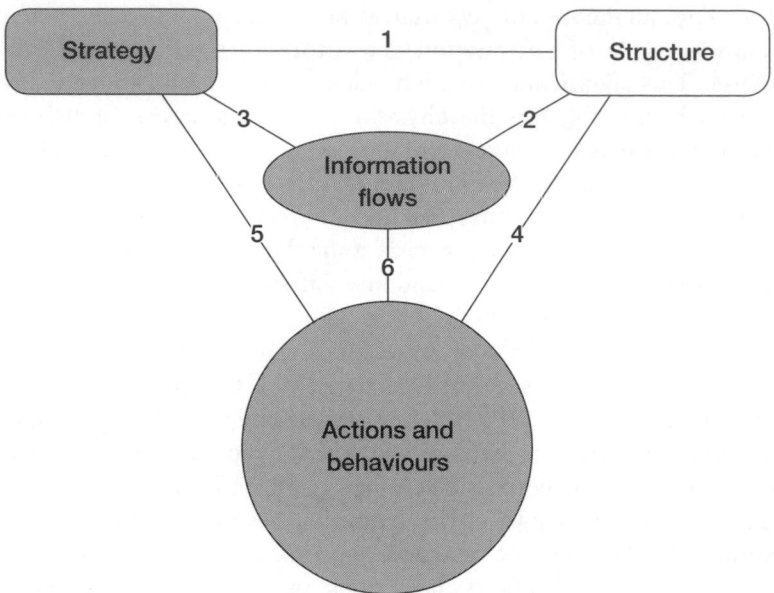

Fig. 5.1   Strategy, structure and organisation behaviour

Strategy is more, or as much, concerned with the external environment and the organisation's relationship with key external agencies, e.g. customers, suppliers, competitors, and the impact each can have on long-term survival. Structure on the other hand is more, or as much, concerned with internal authority relations and the nature of the pattern of regular relationships between organisation members. Thus, we would argue that the concepts are usefully separated.

We do not see a dependent relationship between the two concepts since to do so would suggest a 'causal' connection. Chandler's work suggests that strategy in some way 'causes' structure. We reject this notion on two grounds. First, as both Giddens (1984) and Watson (1994) have pointed out, there is room for individual human agency in organisations. Thus we would argue that managerial thinking and prerogative intervenes in any potential causal relationship. Second, and relatedly, neither strategy nor structure is in any sense 'independent' acting on a 'dependent' variable. Managerial decisions on either are influenced by managers' views and interpretations of the world they find themselves in. Thus, even the operating environment cannot be accepted as an 'objective given'. Managers certainly explore their environment to a greater or lesser extent, but the idea of bounded rationality argues that they cannot truly know the totality of it.

Further, we would agree with the notion of 'enactment' devised by Karl Weick (1979). This would suggest that what managers actually do is to construct their operating environment through defining its reality based on their own selection of significant features. This 'constructed reality' then becomes the basis for managerial decisions on both strategy and structure. These sets of decisions though are not separate and isolated from each other. They are rather interdependent since they are both informed by the same constructed reality and, organisationally, they are as Mintzberg (1988) terms it, the left and right feet of managerial processes.

Connections 2 and 3 in Fig. 5.1 link information flows to both strategy and structure.

The first reflects the fact that information collection, processing and dissemination is essential in operating an organisation structure. Indeed, information sharing is an inherent part of structure since it constitutes an element of the pattern of relationships. The form of the arrangements for information processing will also reflect the nature of that pattern. A simple example would be the extent to which the arrangements allow for and encourage upwards as well as downwards information flow within the formal hierarchy. Another would be the content of those flows. The connection with strategy reflects an assumption that arrangements for information processing will, to a greater or lesser extent, reflect and support *intended* strategy. As we have already argued, it is also the case that information available about the environment will influence the defined reality informing managerial decisions on strategy. Hence, the arrangements for information processing have impact on strategic decisions.

The circle in Fig. 5.1 represents the actions and behaviour of the organisation and its individual members. Our earlier arguments therefore support the fourth connection, that is between the circle and structure. The pattern of actions and behaviour both constitutes and is *influenced* by organisation structure. The one cannot be conceived without the other. Thus, we argue a connection between structure and actions/behaviour. However, an organisation's strategy is also the collective results of actions and behaviour by organisation members. This is what is termed 'realised' or 'emergent' strategy (Quinn *et al.*, 1988), which may or may not be the same as planned or intended strategy. Intended strategy will be intended to, and will in practice, influence the actions and behaviour of individual organisation members. How individual members actually do behave though will constitute the actual, or realised, strategy; that is how the organisation relates to and interacts with external agencies. Thus, we argue a direct relationship also between strategy and the circle representing actions/behaviour.

Our final suggested connection is between information flows and actions/behaviours. We have suggested that organisations 'have' both structures and strategies. What we mean by this is that they have 'intended' ways of patterning internal authority relations (structure) and patterning relationships and interactions with key external agencies (strategy). We have also said though that organisations do not exist, certainly not in the sense that they can have intentions. So what we mean is that *senior managers* make decisions about *their intentions* in relation to structure and strategy. We do not mean to imply that these decisions are totally free or are taken in isolation, but for the purposes of our argument we can assume it to be so. To the extent to which the results of these decisions are known to, understood by and agreed with by organisation members (Stewart, 1991, 1996), they will influence actions and behaviour. However, the level of knowledge and understanding of the results of the decisions, that is the intentions with regard to structure and strategy, will to some extent be affected by information flows within the organisation.

Hence we are arguing, in connection 6, that arrangements for information processing will have an impact on actions/behaviour. This impact, in relation to structure and strategy, will in some ways be mediating since the information systems will affect knowledge and understanding of organisation intentions. However, the impact will also lie outside intended structure and strategy. Arrangements for information processing will affect the nature, form and content of information about their own personal operating environment for each individual organisation member. Since the operation of bounded rationality and enacted environments is not confined to managers, the effect of information flows will be to influence the actions and behaviour of each organisation member. Thus, information flows have both indirect and direct connections with the circle in Fig. 5.1.

Summary

We have at this point in the construction of our model of strategic HRD argued a series of connections between key features or elements of organisations. These are structure, strategy, information flows and actions/behaviour. Before moving on it is important to point out that we are not suggesting simple or unilinear connections between any two of these concepts. An important example of where this applies is the connection between strategy and actions/behaviour. We distinguished between intended and realised strategy and argued that there may well be differences between them. However, by postulating a connection between the two, it is also possible to argue the potential for bringing about consistency between them. If we can *specify* desired or required actions/behaviour to support and enable execution of intended strategy, and if we can then enable or ensure that *actual* action/behaviour matches that specification, then intended and realised strategy will be one and the same. The extent to which those two conditions can be met is in part the focus of the next stage of our model.

MANAGEMENT OR LEADERSHIP STYLE

We now introduce into the model the third critical concept, that of management style. As we argued earlier, this is to do with the beliefs, or paradigms, about the nature of organisations and managing held by individual managers and which influence the processes managers adopt in relation to decision making.

Much of the academic work on management style emphasises differences in relation to focuses on the task or the people being managed. Examples include the famous research carried out by the Ohio State and Michigan Universities in the USA (Huczynski and Buchanan, 1991; Mullins, 1993). These early studies can be characterised by what might be termed an 'either/or' view of management style; that is, managers can *either* have a high concern for the task *or* a high concern for people. Other studies have emphasised the importance of situational variables, for example the work of Fiedler or Reddin (O'Shaughnessy, 1984; Mullins, 1993). More recent work has acknowledged the possibility and argued the requirement for managerial concern for task and people, for example Blake and Mouton, and Hearsy and Blanchard (Stewart, 1991; Mullins, 1993). These studies can be characterised by a 'both' view of management style; that is concern for *both* task and people.

We do not believe that managers either can or do ignore either task or people. In that sense therefore we reject the either/or school of thought. Neither do we believe that managers demonstrating concern for both task and people will be necessarily successful. So we reject also the both school of thought. Finally, we do not believe that it is possible to isolate and analyse all of the complex factors affecting managerial work, and so we reject too situational theories of management style.

We do, however, believe that managers as individual human beings hold varying beliefs and values about themselves, their work, other people in the abstract and particular, and about organisations in the abstract and particular which influence how they approach their work and how they interact with those they manage. The genesis of those beliefs and values is less important than their application. We do therefore wish to apply the basic idea of management style in our exploration of strategic HRD since we believe the notions are useful.

Conformance and enabling

We accept the utility of a distinction between different management concerns, e.g. for task or production and for people or relationships. This distinction we characterise as a continuum, also commonly postulated in traditional management style theory. Our preferred labels for the extremes of the continuum are 'belief in conformance' and 'belief in enabling'. These labels should not though be seen as synonymous with task/production and people/relationships. Our view is that fundamental and deeply rooted managerial paradigms are at work in influencing decisions, actions and behaviour associated with each extreme. The conformance extreme is characterised by a paradigm that values compliance and which reflects an urge to control performance. The enabling extreme characterises a paradigm that values adaptation and development, and which reflects an urge to facilitate performance. Figure 5.2 adds the dimension of management style to our model and the rest of this section proposes some connections with the dimensions already described.

Belief in conformance

Our view is that, broadly, managers adopting a style based on a 'conformance paradigm' will tend to emphasise the importance of structure in their work. This is indicated by the

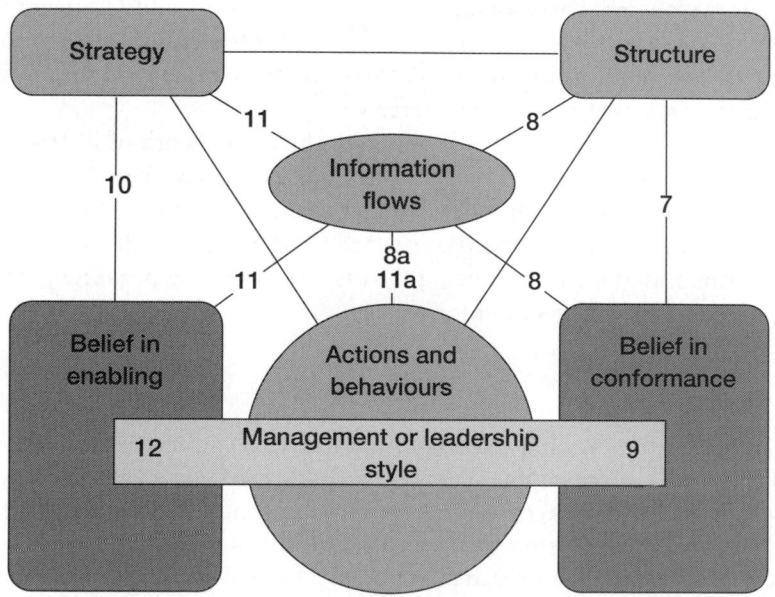

Fig. 5.2   The influence of management style

connecting line number 7 in Fig. 5.2. Managers adopting this stance will view organisation structure as the key co-ordinating mechanism and the most important focus of their work. Thus, top or senior managers with this style will pay most attention to internal authority relations and will seek an appropriate balance between competing internal stakeholders. Organisation power is therefore likely to be based on formal position and status (Johnston, this volume).

Connection 8 suggests that information systems will reflect a control orientation and will be designed to detect and report on variations to planned or prescribed performance. The effects of such systems on actions/behaviour will be to constrain action possibilities by limiting information flows and restricting access to defined and specified information arenas. This is indicated by connecting line 8a.

Management style (connection 9) at lower levels in the organisation, taking the lead set at the top, will tend towards a task orientation and will pay attention to the operation of formal structural relations. Behaviour in the organisation at all levels will tend to be instrumental and, with a lack of clear strategic vision, will be internally biased.

We suggest certain consequences associated with the conformance paradigm. First, strategic success is possible from this paradigm in stable environmental conditions which have a low level of complexity. A related requirement is work processes which are capable of routinisation. This possibility of success also assumes that critical and important activities can be accurately identified and specified, and that appropriate and effective co-ordinating mechanisms can be developed. As part of the latter, target/objective setting and monitoring/review processes need to be defined and operated in ways which pattern behaviour towards market relevant activity. Our second suggestion though is that such a paradigm carries risks. The lack of external focus and environmental reference points can lead to a deficient connection between structure and strategy. The emphasis on structure can further lead to internal processes becoming politicised, with managerial attention becoming centred on status considerations and competition for resources. These factors in turn create the possibility of the organisation becoming misaligned with the environment and internally rigid in the sense of becoming resistant to interventions, from whatever source, which question the status quo or challenge the legitimacy of current structure.

Much of the foregoing analysis is resonant with the classic work of Burns and Stalker (Huczynski and Buchanan, 1991) which suggests a distinction between 'mechanistic' and 'organic' organisation forms. Our view is that the conformance paradigm, with its emphasis on structure, leads to organisations which approximate the mechanistic form detailed by Burns and Stalker. That being the case, the enabling paradigm will be associated with the organic organisation form.

Belief in enabling

Managers adopting the enabling paradigm are likely to emphasise the importance of strategy in their work. Connection 10 in Fig. 5.2 illustrates this view. The stance taken within this paradigm will stress capability and development. Interpersonal processes and skills will be valued above formal structure as a means of achieving co-operation, and organisation members will be expected and/or encouraged to assume responsibility for determination of work processes and achievement of outcomes. The overall organisation and management style is facilitative rather than control orientated.

Information systems indicated in connections 11 and 11a are markedly different within this paradigm. System design is built upon and is responsive to action possibilities. Information flows meet strategic and operational needs and reflect 'client' requirements. This means that information specialists and information systems are viewed as providers of services rather than as agents of control.

Management style (connection 12) throughout the organisation lays emphasis on strategy; that is ensuring the long-term survival of the organisation within its environment. Individual managers across all functions and levels view their role in those terms, rather than as protecting their internal interests (Watson, 1994). Organisation members have responsibility for defining and specifying their responses and work, with reference to a broad strategic framework, or architecture (Hamel and Prahalad, 1994), providing guidance to decisions and action choices. Structure exists as a series of 'envelopes' of concern and outcomes tied into the strategic framework. Individual behaviour is likely to be relationship orientated and directed to reducing ambiguity through seeking clarity, liaison and confirmation of valued outcomes. Managerial activity at lower levels is concerned with supporting those processes.

We would argue different consequences flowing from the enabling paradigm. Our suggestion is that it would be appropriate in an environment characterised by high rates of change, ambiguity and complexity. Organisation products and services are likely to be incapable of standardisation and to require responsive adaptation to market needs and demands. Personal and people based products and services are an example of what we mean here. The key requirements attached to success are the identification of critical outcomes, and development of associated capabilities/abilities within the organisation and its members. The notion of 'core competences' (Prahalad and Hamel 1990) is relevant here.

There are though risks associated with this paradigm. The emphasis on relationships and interpersonal processes may be exclusive of attention to outcomes. High levels of ambiguity within the organisation can be pathological, with activity being directed to reducing uncertainty and anxiety or, perhaps, to exploiting ambiguity to serve individual or sectional ends. A further possible outcome is isolation from the environment through development of a 'special' language and theory, of interest and relevance only to the initiated.

Summary

Within this section then, we have broadly applied the notion of management style to suggest two managerial paradigms, each of which we suggest brings about a stronger focus on and connection with either strategy or structure. In common with established contingency theory applied to both organisations and management style, we have also argued that neither of these paradigms is better or more effective than the other. Rather, our view is that each can be potentially appropriate in particular circumstances, but that both also risk pathology and failure even in their most favoured situation. The final stage in development of our argument and model now requires an examination of our views on action/behaviour and HR practice.

BEHAVIOUR, ACTION AND HR PRACTICE

We argued earlier that organisations are patterns of action on the part of individuals. The participation of individual actors in those structural patterns acts to replicate and maintain 'the organisation'. However, as we also argued with support from Giddens (1984) and Watson (1994), there is scope for human agency, that is individual choice, in the process of replication so that structure both constrains and enables. In more simple terms, individual organisation members have both limits and potentialities in relation to their behaviour and actions arising from their participation in the organisation. More simply still, individuals have discretion within and about the constraints of their organisational role.

We have incorporated this argument into our model which is now presented in complete form in Fig. 5.3. The action/behaviour circle has been re-labelled. What we refer to as *socialised behaviour and actions* are those which are acquired through participation in the organisation *and which* replicate and maintain the structural arrangements. What we label *learnt/learning behaviour and actions* represent those which occur as new behaviours through the exercise of discretion. New behaviours/actions are experimented with or existing behaviours/actions are re-interpreted through new explanations of structure and purpose. Each of these opens up possibilities for change in both structure and strategy.

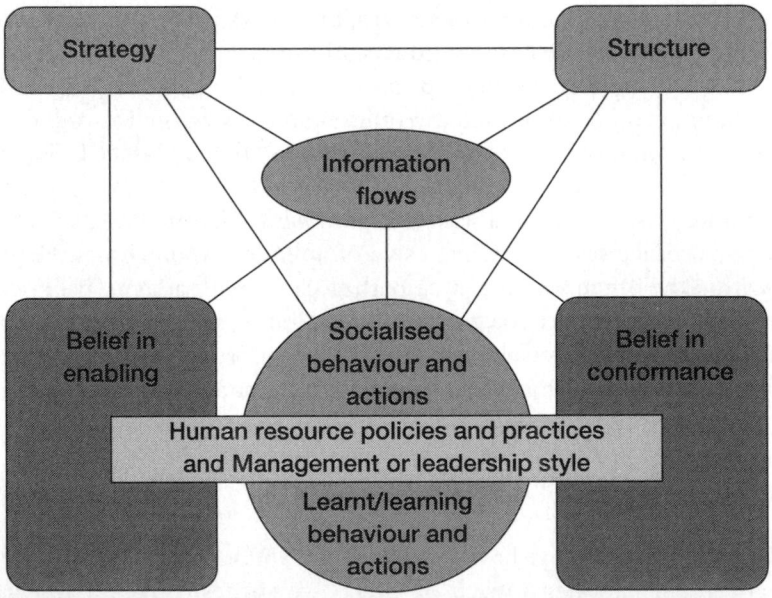

Fig. 5.3   The strategy–HRD connection and strategic HRD

HR practice

Paradoxically, HR practice can and does have effect in both maintaining and changing organisations. Much HR activity is directed to the processes of socialisation which replicate established patterns of behaviour. Indeed, both overtly and covertly, such activity can have the purpose of improving the efficiency of current structure, for example through skill acquisition and enhancement. Conversely, HR interventions can raise the potential for change by focusing on new action possibilities and/or challenging current accounts of how and why the organisation is as it appears to be. In other words, by questioning and challenging the status quo and opening the possibility for learnt/learning behaviours and actions. However, such interventions cannot occur in isolation and therefore have to relate to current patterns of action and explanations of their appropriateness. Practitioners need to be able to act in a way which makes sense to organisation members within *their* established understandings of current patterns.

This analysis of HR practice implies that practitioners in some way 'stand out' from organisation structure. To an extent, we believe this needs to be the case. It is in our view an essential requirement in adopting a proactive stance. Our argument is that HR practice has to be proactive as an essential contribution to organisation survival. Reactive HR practice will be confined to accessing, working within and reinforcing established patterns of behaviour; that is its function and contribution will be limited to socialised and socialising behaviour and actions. It will also be driven by the established managerial paradigm, either conformance or enabling orientated, and will support its continuance. This will, we believe, ignore the organisation's *continuing* ability to maintain alignment with changes in its environment and will risk decay and decline. Proactive HR is concerned with learnt/learning behaviours and actions which in turn are concerned with adaptive change and development.

We will now turn our attention to what we mean by proactive HRD.

IMPLICATIONS FOR HRD PRACTICE

Proactive HRD can be modelled first by contrasting the approach with a reactive stance. Training and development for organisation members traditionally focuses on developing ability to perform an established role. The purpose is to promote conformance; that is skill and efficiency in executing current patterns of behaviour and actions. The desired outcome is that individuals accept a predetermined and specified role, and meet current organisation expectations. This is also often the case where beliefs and values around HRD itself suggest or promote 'enabling' as the purpose. Often, there is no connection between this enabling and strategy. Rather, enabling is fixed into a prevailing conformance paradigm and therefore the result is that individuals are 'enabled' to meet requirements placed upon them by established structural arrangements. In other words, they are socialised into the pattern of actions and behaviour that currently constitute the organisation.

There is some resonance in our argument here with popular notions of organisation culture. The concept of culture itself is subject to much debate and controversy which lies outside the scope of this chapter. However, what we are arguing as a reactive stance to HRD is tied in some ways to ideas of 'official' (Watson, 1994) or 'corporate' (Anthony, 1994) organisation culture. These ideas suggest a distinction between intended, planned or desired culture and actual or lived culture. This distinction is characterised by Peter Anthony as between 'espoused' and 'real' culture (Anthony, 1994). Our suggestion is that reactive HRD develops patterns of behaviour which reflect and promote corporate culture.

113

Becoming proactive

By contrast, a proactive stance within HRD works at and in the connections between strategy and structure, between espoused and real culture, between socialised behaviour and learnt/learning behaviour. It seeks to identify, expose, reflect, question and challenge these boundaries. Becoming proactive though, in our view, first requires some examination of the beliefs and values on which practice is based. We would suggest the following beliefs, or tenets, as promoting the adoption of a proactive stance:

- that strategy is emergent over time and is the result of the collective actions of organisation members;
- that these actions become and are 'patterned' and have explanations attached to them which make sense to those who are part of the pattern;
- that there exist 'pockets' of variations on these patterns in different parts of the organisation which reflect varying sets of 'actions–beliefs' arising from differing professional beliefs, tasks and problems, and group allegiances;
- that patterns of action–belief, working through and influenced by information flows, create structure and that structure creates/maintains action–belief patterns;
- that potential for change is created by dynamic tensions between structure and agency, but that such potential is realised to the extent that consistency between belief–action–structure, and the changed state itself, can be maintained;
- that HRD practitioners need to access and work with parts of the organisation in terms that make sense to and are acceptable to those parts – in other words, ways that reflect established local structures of belief–action;
- that HRD practitioners engender and promote change through participation;
- that, following the two previous tenets, single and organisation wide interventions are unlikely to be successful;
- that the primary role of HRD practice is to *create capability* within the organisation to facilitate change and development in response to environmental transitions. This involves enhancing choices and options in relation to action/behaviours through promoting learning behaviours and actions.

These beliefs set out our view on the stance to be taken in relation to organisations and their management by practitioners seeking to adopt a proactive approach to HRD. The stance will lead to certain elements being present in HRD practice.

The ingredients of proactivity

The first element will be a concern to establish a sense of location and a sense of direction. The first of these, location, is to do with creating an understanding of what might be termed organisation context. This itself has two elements. One is perhaps more analytical and involves application of more or less proceduralised techniques to gain a sense of strategic context. Techniques chosen will focus on both the external environment, for example PEST or Resource Dependency (Watson, 1986) analysis, and on internal capability, for example resource or value chain analysis. The second element is through application of our suggested model. This raises questions such as the following:

- are beliefs orientated to conformance or enabling?

- is there a dominant management style?
- does current HR practice endorse/support that style?
- where is the space between socialised and learnt/learning behaviours?
- how can new actions–beliefs become possible?

This set of activities will provide some sense of location. A sense of direction will emerge from exploring the contradictions apparent in the context. Thus, establishing a sense of location will point to and highlight both potential and preferred directions for change. However, both establishing location and exploring direction require active and productive engagement with organisation members, especially managers. This requirement gives rise to additional elements of proactive practice.

The first of these might be termed active listening. This involves achieving rapport, which in turn means letting go of our own professional pre-suppositions and language, and entering dialogue with parts of the organisation through their language and action–belief systems. Our interpretations of the results of such dialogue has to balance the significance and meaning attached to them by *the parts*, with our understanding of the significance and meaning for the organisation as a whole.

Active listening is reinforced by reflecting back the emerging picture, which in turn will bring to the surface new insights and understandings. This process is one of testing organisational realities. Since rationality is bounded at least by information flows and structured within established action–belief systems current in the usual locus of action of members of the organisation, it is important to test and probe presented or espoused reality rather than merely to accept it.

The two elements of active listening and reflecting back facilitate a process of 'purposeful play', that is guiding thinking and dialogue which allow us to raise questions which, in turn:

- reveal the interplay of sub-structures;
- reveal the dominant local action–beliefs;
- tease out the relationships between structure/task allocation and outcomes, that is, strategic intent;
- provide a 'map' of the organisation which helps to confirm location and a sense of direction.

In summary, these elements of proactive HRD provide consensus on what and where the organisation *is*, and on a possible or potential agenda for action and change. The first of these does not represent the totality of organisation reality, constructed or otherwise, but rather acknowledged and recognised common ground which confirms what binds the organisation together. The second, that is the agenda, emerges from revealed areas of contradiction and tension; that which does or could lead the organisation into dysfunctional activity. However, this does not mean that we advocate the resolution of these contradictions and tensions as 'good management', since this would imply the possibility and promotion of a unitarist view of organisations. Rather, our argument is that it is within the interplay and impact of these tensions and contradictions that the potential for sound and constructive connections between structure and strategy are created. It is through such connections that managers act, or not, in a way that maintains alignment of the organisation with its environment.

Proactive interventions

Having reached a point of constructing a tentative agenda, the question arises of what to do next. Our suggestions constitute further elements in proactive HRD. These elements we term interventions since they are intended to *make different*, even if only at the level of understanding and explanation, current patterns of action and behaviour.

The first of these elements is to utilise all opportunities to create and develop *dialogue*. Our use of this word follows that of Peter Senge who distinguishes between dialogue and discussion (Senge, 1993). The former implies creative exploration of complex issues, in contrast to the latter where the focus is on producing some form of 'best' decision. However, dialogue has a purpose, and our second element is to close dialogue with commitment to action which moves things forward in the agreed direction. This latter implies working with and operating on peoples' understanding of the limitations and opportunities placed on them by structural arrangements.

Our analysis and argument in construction of our model of strategic HRD has emphasised the macro organisation level, and has borrowed heavily from ideas and concepts in sociology. At this point we want to focus on the behaviour of the HRD practitioner in their interactions with others. We consider it axiomatic that individual practitioners model desired behaviour. An explanation of the form and nature of that behaviour requires more psychologically oriented concepts to be applied.

Figure 5.4 represents our argument as it applies to an *individual* member of an organisation. The thick line A to B defines the limits of actions and behaviour prescribed by the formal and informal structural arrangements. However, the individual is a participant in the construction of these limits, and has an idiosyncratic perception of them. Therefore, the range of actual action/behaviour possibilities is different to and, usually, greater than that specified by structure.

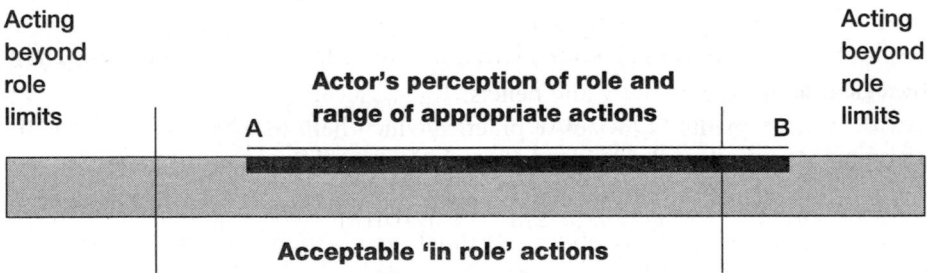

Fig. 5.4   Range of choice of role holders

Figure 5.5 is a representation of an individual's model of self. At the apex, and observable by others, is the range of actions/behaviours the person believes to be appropriate and in which they are willing to engage. This can be expressed as '*I do*'. At the next level, labelled 'capabilities', are those actions/behaviours the person has access to currently. These can be expressed as '*I can/could do*'. Well below the surface and not directly accessible by others lie beliefs. Beliefs become known to others only by information volunteered by the person. They guide reasoning, construction of rationality and actual action/behaviour. As an example, beliefs are where managerial paradigms such as conformance or enabling are located. They find expression in statements such as '*I believe/I believe in*'. The final level, that of identity, is the level of human *being*. It includes the private self-perception which, normally, remains undisclosed and which is revealed in 'accidental' statements such as '*I am*'.

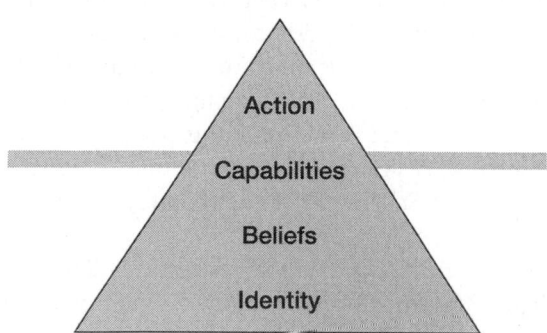

Fig. 5.5   Representation of self

Under normal circumstances, working with individuals in the area of action and capability is straightforward, provided that new behaviours do not confront lower levels of beliefs and values (Stewart, 1991). However, action/behaviour does not always match capability since individuals constrain their behaviour because of beliefs about structural limits. Therefore, it is necessary in HRD practice to facilitate the articulation of such beliefs and to promote the questioning of consistency between capability and action/behaviour. In other words, in order to create change and development in either structure and/or strategy, it is first necessary for the practitioner to enable individuals to surface their personal beliefs about those things, and to examine the degree of match between their actions, capability and beliefs.

There are two elements of proactive practice which help to achieve this. First, interventions are designed and implemented which, whether one-on-one or in group situations, create a safe environment. This requires that individuals feel confident that surfacing capabilities, beliefs and identity will not lead to disconfirmation. Second, and relatedly, practitioners themselves model open behaviours which are inclusive of all levels of the model of self depicted in Fig. 5.5. This is not meant to argue in support of continuous and all pervading self-disclosure. Rather, we are suggesting the need for practitioners to model behaviours of the type Argyris has labelled 'model 2 or model 02' (Argyris and Schon, 1978).

Summary

We have in this section explained the implications for practitioners as we see them arising out of our proposed model of strategic HRD. Our central argument is that the key requirement is for proactive rather than reactive practice. Proactivity in turn requires practitioners to embrace a particular set of beliefs as being central to their work, and implies a particular set of elements, or ingredients, to be applied in HRD practice. The final section offers some concluding remarks to close the chapter.

CONCLUSION

Organisations are complex social systems. Their continued existence is dependent upon individual actors replicating patterns of relationships and on those patterns, and their product in the form of goods and services, remaining relevant and of value to others, e.g. shareholders, customers, governments, in a changing external environment. This dependency creates a tension between maintenance, that is structure which promotes internal consistency, and change, that is strategy which promotes external relevance. This tension is characterised by Edgar Schein (1988) as the need for internal integration and external adaptation.

The relative attention afforded these dynamic processes will to an extent be influenced by managerial paradigms. Commonly held paradigms vary on a continuum between a belief in conformance and a belief in enabling. The operation of these paradigms will tend to favour either structure or strategy as the means of ensuring long-term survival. Both though are necessary for the achievement of that aim.

The actions and behaviours of individuals constitute and realise both structure and strategy. Individual actions and behaviours though are also constrained or limited by structure and strategy, as well as by information systems and flows. Thus individuals are more or less willing actors in their own socialisation, while at the same time having the potential for learning new actions and behaviours outside of perceived or intended structural or strategic limitations.

Our conclusion therefore is that organisations can be usefully conceived as a set of interdependent and connecting relationships which have at their heart the action and behaviour possibilities of individual organisation members. Strategic HRD is concerned with exposing, examining, questioning and challenging the nature and extent of those action possibilities as a contribution to facilitating the continuous development of organisation capability to support long-term survival. This role and contribution requires adoption of proactivity in practice.

We have no simple or quick answers to the questions raised by this conclusion. Our suggested model of strategic HRD provides, we hope, a useful analytical tool. Its application though will produce even more questions which will no doubt be fruitful in provoking further thought and research.

References

Anthony, P. (1994) *Managing Culture*, Buckingham, Open University Press.

Argyris, C. and Schon, D.A. (1978) *Organisational Learning: A Theory of Action Perspective*, London, Addison-Wesley.

Burke, W.W. and Litwin, G.H. (1989) 'A Causal Model of Organisational Performance', *The 1989 Annual: Developing Human Resources*, San Diego CA, University Associates.

Chandler, A. (1962) *Strategy and Structure*, Cambridge MA, MIT Press.

Giddens, A. (1984) *The Constitution of Society: Outline of the Theory of Structuration*, Cambridge, Polity.

Giddens, A. (1989) *Sociology*, Cambridge, Polity.

Hamel, G. and Prahalad, C.K. (1994) *Competing For The Future*, Cambridge MA, Harvard Business School Press.

Huczynski, A. and Buchanan, D. (1991) *Organisational Behaviour*, Second edition, Hemel Hempstead, Prentice Hall.

Jennings, D. and Wattam, S. (1994) *Decision Making; An Integrated Approach*, London, Pitman.

Knights, D. and Morgan, G. (1990) 'The Concept of Strategy in Sociology: A Note of Dissension', *Sociology*, vol. 24, no. 3.

Knights, D. and Morgan, G. (1991) 'Corporate Strategy, Organisations and Subjectivity: A Critique', *Organisation Studies*, vol. 12, no. 2.

McGregor, D.C. (1960) *The Human Side Of Enterprise*, New York, McGraw Hill.

Mintzberg, H. (1988) 'Opening Up the Definition of Strategy', in Quinn *et al.*, *op. cit.*

Mintzberg, H. (1990) 'Strategy Formation: Schools of Thought', in Frederickson, J.W. ed. *Perspectives on Strategic Management*, New York, Harper Row.

Morgan, G. (1990) 'Paradigm Diversity in Organisational Research', in Hassard, J. and Pym, D. eds *The Theory and Philosophy of Organisations*, London, Routledge.

Mullins, L.J. (1993) *Management and Organisational Behaviour*, Third edition, London, Pitman.

O'Shaughnessy, J. (1984) *Patterns Of Business Organisation*, London, George Allen and Unwin.

Prahalad, C.K. and Hamel, G. (1990) 'The Core Competence of the Corporation', *Harvard Business Review*, May–June.

Quinn, J.B., Mintzberg, H. and James, R.B. eds (1988) *The Strategy Process*, Englewood Cliffs, NJ, Prentice Hall.

Schein, E.H. (1988) *Organisation Psychology*, Third edition, Hemel Hempstead, Prentice Hall.

Senge, P. (1993) *The Fifth Discipline: The Art and Practice of the Learning Organisation*, London, Century Business.

Simon, H.A. (1960) *The New Science Of Management Decision*, New York, Harper and Row.

Stewart, J. (1991) *Managing Change through Training and Development*, London, Kogan Page.

Stewart, J. (1994) 'The Psychology Of Decision Making', in Jennings, D. and Wattam, S. (1994), *op. cit.*

Stewart, J. (1996) *Managing Change through Training and Development* (2nd edn), London, Kogan Page.

Thomas, P. and Kovvuri, D. (1994) 'Hanging HRM on the Barbed Hook of Strategy', Paper presented at conference on *Strategic Direction of HRM*, Nottingham Business School, December.

Watson, T.J. (1986) *Management, Organisation and Employment Strategy*, London, Routledge.

Watson, T.J, (1994) *In Search Of Management*, London, Routledge.

Weick, K. (1979) *The Social Psychology of Organising*, Reading MA, Addison-Wesley.

6

The Provision of Learning Support for Non-Employees

John Walton

INTRODUCTION

For a number of years strategic management literature and practice have demonstrated the importance for organisations of operating outside their boundaries and establishing strategic relationships with external stakeholders such as suppliers and distributors. More recently much attention has been given to the growth of strategic alliances and joint ventures. Another trend has been the downsizing of organisations and the out-sourcing of a range of functions which were previously considered to be an integral part of in-house operations. There has also been a move towards sub-contracting of and franchising arrangements for in-house services. Furthermore many voluntary organisations are re-evaluating the use of volunteers for the provision of front-line services.

Thus not only are institutions increasingly relying on and developing relationships with groups operating outside their boundaries but also more and more organisation functions are being conducted by individuals who are not in a conventional employer–employee relationship. The implications of this for HRD practitioners should be far reaching in terms of establishing new market segments for HRD activities and indicating emerging organisational learning needs, but with few exceptions this has not been reflected in mainstream HRD literature and practice. Training managers have traditionally seen their constituents as operating within the organisation they themselves work for. This can be narrowed down even further. Within most organisations the traditional target group for establishing training and development needs and providing learning opportunities has been the employees.

This is reflected in the titles and text of most leading books on the subject. Current examples include Rosemary Harrison's (1994) publication *Employee Development* and Barrington and Reid (1994), *Training Interventions – Managing Employee Development*. In neither of them is the subject of the learning needs of non-employees touched upon.

It is also reflected in the qualification syllabuses of the Institute of Personnel and Development, IPD, the largest professional body operating in the HR arena in the UK. The 1994–95 Professional Education Scheme of the IPD[*], which leads to graduateship and subsequently membership of the Institute, focuses on *Employee* Resourcing; *Employee* Relations; and *Employee* Development as its core syllabuses. Non-employee training and development is nowhere mentioned within the qualification framework.

[*] The IPD is changing its syllabus as of 1996 to reflect the emerging significance of non-employees.

It is also reflected in national initiatives such as Investors in People which provides a set of criteria for organisations to achieve a national standard for effective investment in people which is unashamedly employee-based. Core criteria include:

- an Investor in People makes a public commitment from the top to develop all *employees* to achieve its business objectives;
- an Investor in People regularly reviews the training and development needs of all *employees*;
- an Investor in People takes action to train and develop individuals on recruitment and throughout their *employment*.

No reference is made to the learning needs of non-employees.

This emphasis on employees may have been a valid approach in the past but, with new organisational forms and new approaches to the employer/employee relationship, this way of thinking is rapidly becoming outmoded. One way of addressing this is for training and development managers and others to establish the range of organisation stakeholders who are non-employees and to see the provision of services and programmes for such categories of learner as constituting a significant part of their portfolio.

AIMS AND OBJECTIVES

This chapter is concerned with developing the notion of non-employee learning and providing a framework within which the strategic importance of providing learning opportunities for non-employee stakeholders can be fully understood. By the end of the chapter you should be able to:

- distinguish between different categories of non-employee stakeholder and establish the distinctive contribution that they make to an organisation's operations;
- differentiate between non-employee training, non-employee education and non-employee development as providing different responses to learning needs;
- establish the significance to HRD practitioners and organisational decision makers of strategic initiatives such as out-sourcing;
- establish circumstances under which the provision of learning opportunities for non-employees has been seen to be appropriate.

CONTENT

Non-employees are those individuals or groups who have some relationship with an organisation but are not in an employer–employee relationship. They could be employees of another organisation operating within the boundaries of the 'home' organisation by providing services on a sub-contracting basis. They could be employees working for suppliers of the raw materials on which the organisation depends, or for distributors of organisational products to customers. They could be self-employed or volunteers. They could be members of the general public who in some way or form use, or are affected by, organisational products or services. Thus they could be actual or potential customers, members of environmental pressure groups or even potential members of as yet unformed pressure groups. They could be governors of schools, members of watchdog authorities, prison visitors. The list is potentially endless because of the range of organisations operating in our society.

What constitutes relevant non-employee stakeholders for any given organisation depends upon its particular activities. The learning needs of each group of non-employees identified will depend on the actual and desired relationship with the organisation in question.

In their (1989) publication, *Strategic Human Resource Development*, Rothwell and Kazanas propose an intriguing classification which incorporates non-employees as a potential market for an organisation's HRD activities. They argue that HRD practitioners, operating managers and employees should engage in co-ordinated learning activities to support business and HR plans as the basis of an organisational strategy for HRD. Within such an organisational strategy for HRD they identify the following five functional strategies, each of which may necessitate separately prepared objectives, policies, and activities.

- *Employee training* which they define as consisting of short-term efforts to ensure that individuals have the skills and competences to carry out their existing jobs.
- *Employee education* which they define as an intermediate effort for helping individuals achieve their career objectives, keep abreast of changes in their occupations and gain new insights about themselves. It prepares people for future work.
- *Employee development* which they define as a long-term effort for matching up the collective skills of a work group and the responsibilities assigned to the group by the organisation. Employee development, they feel, makes individuals agents for organisational and group change.
- *Organisation development* which they define as a long-term effort for changing the culture of an organisation or group.
- *Non-employee development* which they define as a long-term effort for improving relations between a 'business', the general public, and external stakeholders.

Their differentiation between employee training, employee education, employee development and organisation development is conventional. The definition of employee development is somewhat unusual – many practitioners in the UK would see the definition of employee education as closer to their understanding of employee development. One might also take issue with the rather narrowly defined parameters within which organisation development is defined. However, what is particularly interesting and ground-breaking about their classification system so far as the HRD literature is concerned is the reference to non-employee development as a planned and significant area for organisation involvement and HRD interventions.

Rothwell and Kazanas develop their position by arguing that HRD has traditionally focused on meeting learning needs within an organisation. They contend that the literature of the HRD field offers surprisingly little advice about identifying the learning needs of external groups. They also argue that any strategic orientation to HRD should emphasise the importance of the external environment and entail a responsibility for scanning the learning needs of groups operating outside the organisation but impacting on it. For example, consumers who do not know how to use a product will not buy it, suppliers who are unaware of an organisation's quality standards may not be complying with them.

Thus the purpose of non-employee development is to enable the organisation to influence its external environment through a planned process of learning so that the skills and knowledge of those outside its boundaries on whom it depends to a greater or lesser extent are enhanced. This in turn will allow the organisation to work more effectively towards achieving its strategic goals. The process of non-employee development can be thought of as enabling organisations, groups and individuals external to the organisation to learn how to interact better with it.

The Rothwell and Kazanas typology as it stands is not complete. Logically if one is talking about employee training, employee education and employee development then there should be non-employee training, non-employee education and non-employee development. Indeed, much of what they describe as non-employee development could more suitably be described as non-employee training or non-employee education. Their classification is also restrictive in that it does not apparently cover the learning needs of non-employees operating within a given organisation, such as sub-contractors or volunteers carrying out a key operational activity.

The following definitions are offered to extend the Rothwell and Kazanas perspective.

- *Non-employee training* can be defined as short-term efforts to ensure that individuals not in an employment relationship with a given organisation, but who are in some way responsible for providing services to it, have the skills necessary to carry out these services.
- *Non-employee education* can be defined as efforts to ensure that individuals who have some current or potential relationship to the organisation are provided with knowledge and understanding about the organisation's products, services and values.

NON-EMPLOYEE STAKEHOLDER ANALYSIS

If training and development managers are going to extend their repertoire to encompass non-employees, including learners operating from outside the organisation, then they need to develop a method for identifying target groups or market segments. One recommended approach is through non-employee stakeholder analysis.

Stakeholders can be defined as the various groupings which have an interest or stake in the organisation. Internal stakeholders are those groups which operate within the boundaries of an organisation, many – but not all – of whom engage in activities which contribute to the development of products or services to external customers. Exceptions will include union representatives and sub-contractors of, for example, the staff canteen, who are providing services to internal customers

External stakeholders are those groupings which operate outside the boundaries of an organisation but who engage in activities which can affect the operation and viability of an organisation. For a typical commercial enterprise they include suppliers, distributors, consumers/end-users and shareholders.

Stakeholder analysis can become quite complicated as one reflects on the range of potential groupings that can impact on a given organisation. Outside of the supplier – distributor – consumer chain of a commercial concern they could include environmental pressure groups, watchdog bodies, local and central government agencies, major debtors and creditors, and so on.

Each organisational type will have its own discrete set of stakeholders. Those for a manufacturing concern will be different to those for a bank, which will be different to those for a local authority, which in turn will be different to those for say, the prison service. Even within an organisation there will be different stakeholder groupings impacting on discrete areas of operation. Thus the stakeholders impacting on a social services directorate of a local authority could be substantially different to those impacting upon an education directorate (see Fig. 6.1).

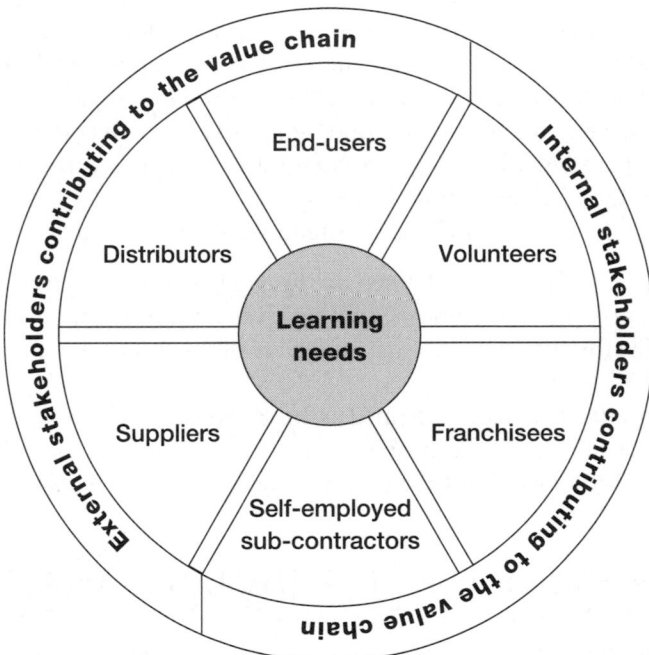

Fig. 6.1   The stakeholder wheel for non-employees

A number of frameworks have been developed for further classifying stakeholders. For example Johnson and Scholes (1993) have developed a stakeholder mapping model based on the two dimensions of degree of interest and degree of power. From an HRD perspective two useful dimensions are: degree of organisational involvement and extent of learning needs (see Fig. 6.2).

The linked typology developed in this chapter is to classify the organisation involvement of non-employee stakeholders in terms of:

● their involvement or otherwise in activities which are part of the organisation's value chain;
● whether they are operating within or outside the boundaries of the organisation;

and to use this categorisation to reflect on learning needs.

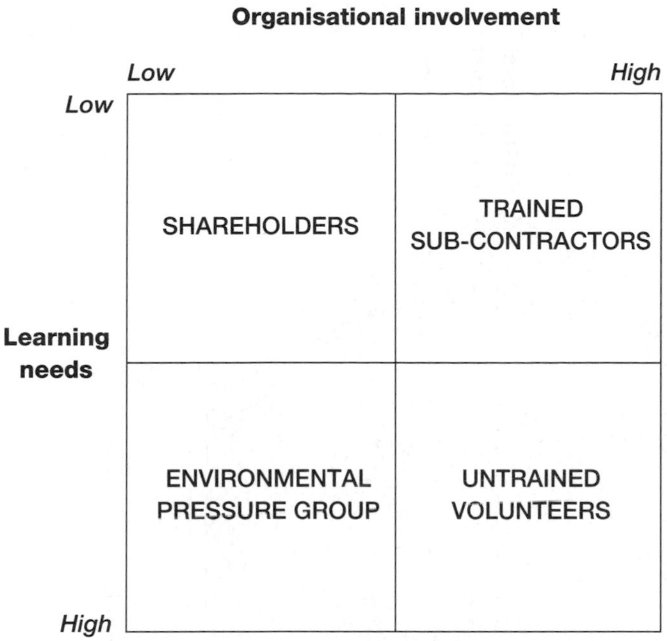

Organisational involvement

	Low	High
Low	SHAREHOLDERS	TRAINED SUB-CONTRACTORS
Learning needs		
High	ENVIRONMENTAL PRESSURE GROUP	UNTRAINED VOLUNTEERS

Fig. 6.2   Non-employee stakeholder matrix

THE VALUE CHAIN AND VERTICAL INTEGRATION

One group of non-employee stakeholders who have in the past been identified as having significant learning needs are those who directly contribute to the *value chain* of an organisation. The notion of value chain is that a sequence of activities needs to be undertaken to translate raw materials and other inputs into a finished product or service that reaches an end-user; and that each one of these should add value to the product. In commercial terms, value is the amount buyers are willing to pay for what a firm provides them with. Within a given value chain Michael Porter (1980) distinguishes between primary and support value activities, each of which are central to the success of an organisation in getting its products or services to its customers.

Primary activities are those leading to the actual provision of a product or service. They entail for a manufacturing concern inbound logistics (receiving, storing, materials handling, etc.); operations (machining, packaging, assembly, etc.); outbound logistics (storing, distribution, etc.); marketing and sales (advertising, promotions, etc.); service (installation, repair, parts supply, etc.). Support activities assist the primary activities through purchasing functions, technology development, human resource management, and an overall infrastructure including planning and finance (see Fig. 6.3).

Porter's definition of value chain can be extended beyond the boundaries of a particular organisation, especially in so far as the primary activities are concerned. This extension becomes particularly helpful when linked to another strategic management term, that of vertical integration. Taking a given organisation's products and services as

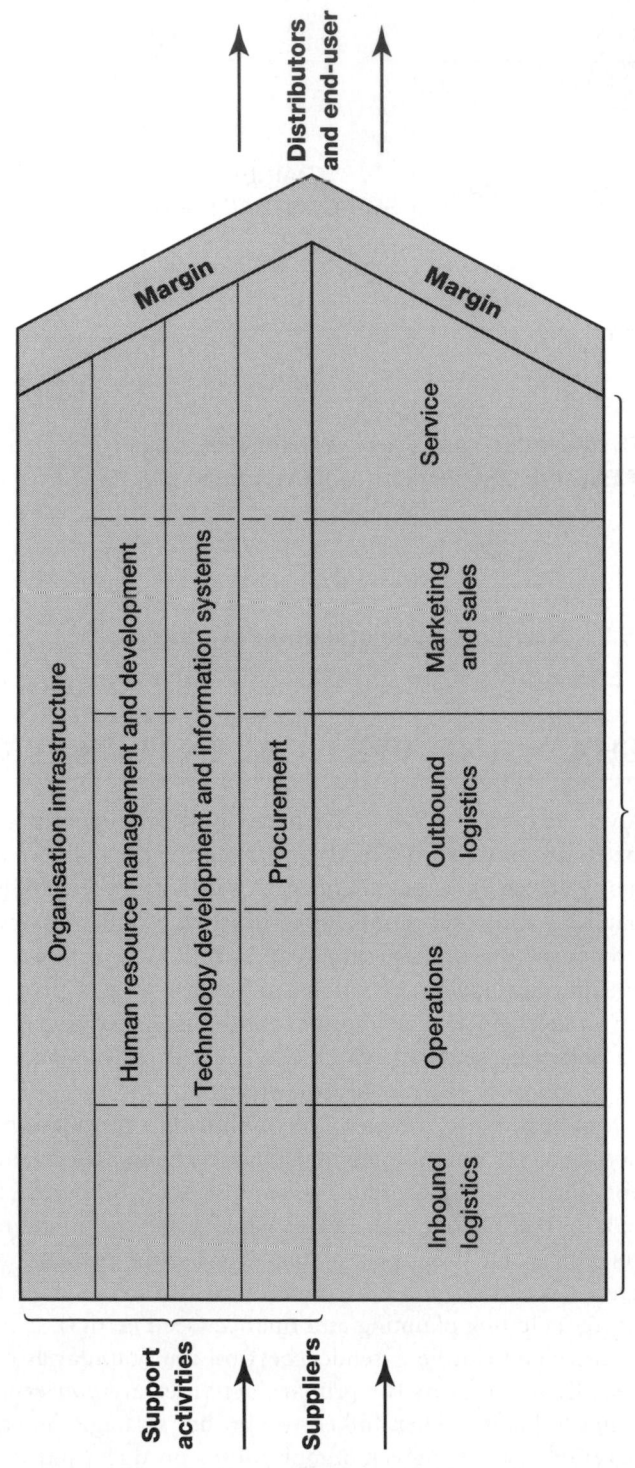

Fig. 6.3   The generic value chain

(based on Porter, M., 1980)

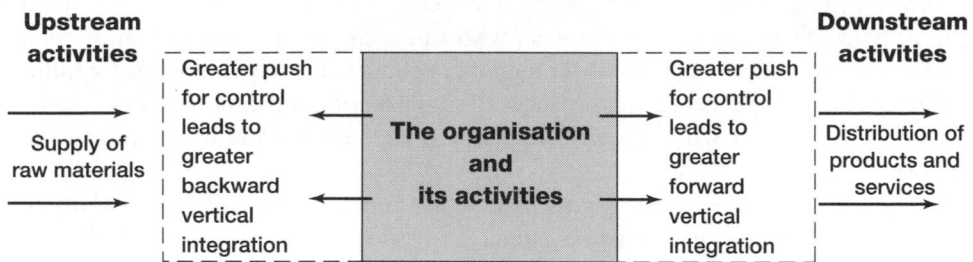

Fig. 6.4   Vertical integration model

the base, one looks at 'upstream' and 'downstream' value chain activities and establishes the degree of existing and desirable backward vertical integration and forward vertical integration respectively (see Fig. 6.4).

Backward vertical integration reflects the extent to which an organisation establishes control over upstream activities, i.e. of the sources of supply of the raw materials for the organisation. Various strategies can be identified including owning the sources of supply, investing heavily as shareholders in supplier organisations, demanding that intending suppliers achieve a quality certification.

Forward vertical integration reflects the degree of control and involvement that a given organisation has over downstream activities, i.e. the channels of distribution whereby a product reaches end-users. Thus some organisations not only operate as manufacturers but also own their retail outlets.

NON-EMPLOYEE STAKEHOLDERS PROVIDING PRIMARY ACTIVITIES WITHIN THE VALUE CHAIN AND OPERATING OUTSIDE THE ORGANISATION BOUNDARIES

Schuler and Macmillan (1985) argue that there are discrete targets or stakeholder groupings for HRD interventions outside the organisation yet which are part of its value chain. For this section a modified version of their classification has been adopted to describe some practical examples of how learning needs are being met.

The supplier as target

Some organisations have adopted as a strategy the establishment of quite stringent controls over their suppliers without actually owning them. They have introduced quality control inspectors to check out the processes being undertaken, and have put restrictions on the extent to which an organisation can supply other competitors. However, organisations are moving away from this type of control model in an endeavour to add value by shifting skills upstream.

As part of its environmental policy, BT has developed a set of environmental procurement standards. These were considered important since minimising the risks at the procurement stage could provide long-term benefits with knock-on effects through the supply chain. BT consider that suppliers who run active environmental improvement programmes are more likely to deliver a quality product. BT have developed a number of different but complementary approaches to supplier communications, all of which are based on a process of working with suppliers to encourage continuous improvement (Tuppen, 1993).

Rosabeth Moss Kanter (1989) argues that, facing imperatives to cut costs and improve quality, leading American companies are creating closer relationships with their suppliers. They are moving away from the old 'adversarial' model which used to dominate purchasing in American corporations. Price was minimised by maintaining a large supplier base with each provider being subject to short-term contracts and frequent rebidding. However such arms-length arrangements do not motivate suppliers to invest in technology to improve quality or manage the complexities of just-in-time inventory. Kanter quotes Digital as a company that has developed partnership arrangements with suppliers which include integrated information systems, regular forums with key suppliers to review business plans, and other activities which are virtually indistinguishable from how a corporation might treat one of its own divisions.

A logical extension of this way of thinking is to introduce HRD initiatives and extend training and development opportunities to suppliers to ensure that organisational standards and requirements are being satisfied. Thus an internal Digital team has organised a training programme for suppliers. Digital has also introduced a 'Vendor Performance Management System' – a performance appraisal system akin to that used for employees – in which suppliers are measured on quality, delivery, price and flexibility.

Cadillac, one of the winners of the 1990 Malcolm Baldrige Quality Awards in the United States, has included over 640 suppliers in its own quality-training programmes (Steeples, 1992). Suppliers are also members of 75 per cent of the 55 product development and improvement teams.

Xerox, a 1989 winner of the Baldrige Award, instituted a supplier certification process in the early 1980s that required suppliers to go through an ordered procedure to analyse their processes. Suppliers that met the requirements were awarded Certified Supplier status. Suppliers were also invited to take part in the *product delivery process*, which allowed them to be significantly involved in product design and manufacturing. Additionally, Xerox began training suppliers in total quality, *statistical process control*, and just-in-time delivery.

A further extension of this way of thinking is to engage in joint ventures between HRD departments to provide a common understanding of issues and problems affecting both organisations. This is moving closer to the Japanese notion of strategic networks or *keiretsu*.

The distributor as target

Many organisations have invested heavily in providing learning support to distributors and dealers. Schuler and Macmillan (1985) refer to Mercedes' strategy of training mechanics in their distributors' garages. This is quite common in the motor/engine manufacturing industry. Perkins Engines as long ago as the 1960s provided training courses at the UK factory in Peterborough for mechanics from dealers' organisations servicing their engines.

Again, a pure vertical integration strategy would entail the 'home' organisation having total responsibility for the process, with the dealer or distributor being in a dependency relationship. However, increasingly organisations are developing partnership arrangements with their distributors similar to those discussed above for suppliers.

In the past Cadillac tended to regard dealers as product distributors. Dealers often didn't see the product until it was introduced to the public. In 1984, Cadillac implemented a *dealer quality improvement process* with its 1600 independent dealers. Dealer suggestions about marketing strategies and current and future products are now encouraged. As part of the initiative, training is provided to support dealers in achieving customer service excellence.

In the insurance and pension industry the 'distributors' of products to individual clients are financial advisers – often non-employees. Such financial advisers are required by law to give best advice. It is clearly important that they have sufficient information on the range of products and benefits individual companies have on offer. Insurance companies are beginning to address the strategic importance of non-employee development for independent financial advisers.

The customer as target

In today's total quality management, TQM, world, quality is seen from the perspective of the customer and organisational cultures are being changed to embrace a focus on customer driven quality and continuous improvement. The provision of learning support for external customers is an obvious aspect of continuous improvement. Customers can facilitate learning processes within the organisation by giving feedback on how their products and services are perceived. It also helps to create barriers to entry to competitors by helping to develop customer loyalty and trust.

According to Madu and Kuei (1993), the traditional approach to TQM has focused on a team approach whereby employees have identified areas for continuous improvement. The emerging *strategic TQM* approach is extending the team approach to incorporate external stakeholder groups in the team decision making process.

The development of TQM as a concept has led to a 'customer comes first' perspective for a number of organisations of which IBM is a good example. For many years IBM adopted a technology driven approach to strategy. Within this overall approach, one way in which it differentiated itself from competitors was by selecting and training programmers for customers, in an era when training in computer programming was not available at schools and colleges. IBM correctly reasoned that without computer programmers there would be no computer sales, so it was important to have as many programmers as possible who were trained on IBM equipment. Other manufacturers followed suit. For example, in the early 1970s I attended a month-long programming course run by Honeywell (now Bull). However, there was no involvement of customers in IBM's processes or operations.

More recently IBM has swung towards a market driven quality, MDQ, model. Launched in 1990 by its Chairman, John Akers, MDQ is grounded on four principles:

> '● *make the customer the final arbiter,*
> ● *understand our markets,*
> ● *commit to leadership in markets we choose to serve, and*
> ● *deliver excellence in execution across our enterprise.'*

IBM Rochester, located in Rochester, Minnesota, is a manufacturer of intermediate computer systems including IBM's flagship midrange business computer, the Application System/400. The quality process at Rochester provides a continuous loop with the customer, from the product-planning process through production and on to delivery. Customers are involved in the development and manufacturing process through methods such as advisory councils, round tables, information systems and prototype trailing. In the case of the AS/400, its basic architecture was the result of customer input. To secure feedback after installation, the company conducts a quarterly marketing and customer satisfaction survey of approximately 2200 AS/400 customers.

Although perhaps not seen as a planned learning programme, this sort of initiative clearly has a major impact in creating an organisational awareness of IBM in its customers, as well as enhancing IBM's own understanding of how its products are perceived. The introduction of planned developmental programmes for customers and their employees is a logical extension.

Other organisations as targets

Rosabeth Moss Kanter (1989) contends that the traditional approach to achieving control through vertical integration is breaking down and that new organisational forms based on strategic alliances are emerging. She suggests that organisations are moving from adversarial to partnership arrangements with both stakeholders and erstwhile competitors on the supplier–distribution chain. She also contends that organisations can become better *PALs* by

● *Pooling resources*
● *Allying to exploit an opportunity*
● *Linking systems in a partnership*

The learning support mechanisms that would allow synergy to develop between strategic partners are both complex and difficult to develop. However, it is clearly significant that if partnerships are to work there should be some approach to shared learning that entails the pooling of HRD resources and the linking of HRD systems.

THE IMPACT OF OUT-SOURCING ON NON-EMPLOYEE LEARNING NEEDS

Carlos Jarillo (1993) argues that vertical integration has been the dominant organisation form of the 20th century. He cites organisations such as Ford, in the early days of its operations, as exemplars of the philosophy that one should establish control over all activities contributing to the value chain of a given product. However, he suggests that this dominant organisational form is beginning to break down in favour of variants of sub-contracting and strategic networks, which essentially constitute an alternative, market-based, organisational form. When an organisation needs an input, why not go to the market and have it delivered by an external party rather than look to internal resources? In other words, proponents of the sub-contracting approach will increasingly seek to out-source activities.

The adoption of this perspective has been indicated for some time by those influenced by the Institute of Manpower Studies, IMS, 'flexible firm' model which distinguishes between core and peripheral activities (Atkinson, 1985 and IMS, 1985). In human resource terms the flexible firm consists of a 'core' group of employees surrounded by peripheral groups of workers who may not be employees. Amongst a number of options for achieving flexibility are so-called distancing strategies which involve the displacement of employment relationships by commercial ones for peripheral workers. Thus only those activities which are core to the organisation's operations are carried out 'in-house'. Others are out-sourced and sub-contracted or franchised out – to non-employees.

Such an approach helps to explain the underpinning philosophy governing the recent trend to contract out and 'market test' central government activities. The UK Government 1993 Next Steps Review (1993) recommended a critical scrutiny (*prior options test*) of any particular government function to assess its status:

- Does the function need to be carried out by government at all or could it be abolished?
- If it does need to be carried out could it be privatised?
- Could it be contracted out to private organisations as a whole?
- Could it be market tested (i.e. unlike contracting out, its allocation to either civil service or private organisations would be decided competitively)?
- Is it sufficiently large to be made into an agency (executive agencies are staffed by government employees but are given autonomy to carry out the executive functions of government within a policy and resources framework set by a government department)?

It also underpins compulsory competitive tendering in the local authority sector. In other words, unless it can be demonstrated that value is added by preserving an activity within the public domain then it is 'out-sourced'.

In strategic terms, out-sourcing creates a major dilemma for senior management. Increasingly it is being argued that what adds value to organisations is the knowledge and skills that individual knowledge workers possess. A product, it is argued, is obsolete the moment it is produced in today's competitive environment; what cannot be replaced and replicated are the distinctive competences that highly qualified staff bring, operating in a culture that can be seen to encourage team learning. Thus the increasing creation of non-employee relationships entails considerable risks unless such distinctive competences can be learned and sustained outside an employment relationship.

NON-EMPLOYEES OPERATING WITHIN THE ORGANISATION WHO ARE CONTRIBUTING TO THE PRIMARY VALUE CHAIN

An obvious example of this category of non-employee are volunteers working for voluntary organisations such as OXFAM or Citizens Advice Bureau who are involved in front-line service delivery. In many ways their learning needs are similar to those of paid employees and many voluntary organisations have well established training and development departments which cater for these needs. Citizens Advice Bureau, for example, has a national training network.

Changes in the employment market have caused a change in the profile of volunteers and their reasons for volunteering, which in turn have caused voluntary organisations to think differently about the volunteers they use. Many of these people are doing voluntary work rather than be unemployed. The changing external environment and increasing competitiveness combined with customer expectations about service delivery are causing voluntary organisations to examine the cost-effectiveness of volunteer involvement and evaluate volunteer achievement. Volunteers themselves are more likely than in the past to see volunteering as a developmental activity and will be attracted to those organisations offering training. There is an increasing likelihood that volunteers will be recruited on the basis of their ability to do a given job and that they will receive training to carry out the work they are doing. The 1991 National Survey of Voluntary Activity in the UK revealed that 11 per cent of people volunteered in order to gain a new skill and that this was more likely with the under 35 age group.

There has been an increasing trend over the last 20 years to use self-employed sub-contractors to carry out core services and functions in lieu of employees. An example of this is in the gas supply industry, where central heating installations are invariably carried out by contractors. The legality of such arrangements was tested as long ago as 1968 in a famous court case involving Readymix Concrete, who used self-employed sub-contractors to drive their lorries. The case against Readymix was that they were trying to escape the contractual obligations of being an employer. The drivers were contractually restricted to only using the lorries on Readymix business; the lorries had the Readymix logo; the drivers wore the Readymix uniform and had to take instructions 'as though they were an employee'. Nevertheless the court held that they could be treated as non-employees on a 'contract for services (self-employed)' as opposed to a 'contract of service (employment)' since they 'owned the instrumentalities of the business' and had to invest their own capital in the leasing of the lorries – even though this was from a Readymix subsidiary!

Public perception of the performance of such front-line individuals is clearly central to the organisation's image and success in the marketplace, and considerable thought and attention should be given to their learning needs.

NON-EMPLOYEES OPERATING WITHIN THE ORGANISATION WHO ARE CONTRIBUTING TO THE SUPPORT VALUE CHAIN

This area is most obviously associated with the use by organisations of external consultants to whom organisations have sub-contracted specialist activities. These typically include:

- the introduction and development of information technology and systems;
- auditing;
- recruitment and selection activities such as development and administration of selection tests;
- design and delivery of management development and other staff development programmes;
- organisation development activities including the introduction of major culture change programmes.

The learning needs of such consultants would depend upon the precise activities in which they were engaged, but could be quite substantial. For example, the development of information systems to meet specific organisational needs can entail considerable consultant time in becoming familiar with existing organisation systems, procedures and practices.

Non-employees in this category also include representatives of organisations to whom in-house services are sub-contracted on a franchise or equivalent basis. Examples include a whole range of office services such as cleaning and catering.

Health and safety legislation requires that employers should ensure that contractors working on any of their sites comply with the law. As an example of this the Scottish Prison Service has special training courses for employees of contractor firms who are working inside prisons, to ensure that they are able to work within prison regimes.

NON-EMPLOYEE LEARNING OUTSIDE THE VALUE CHAIN

In their classification of non-employees, Rothwell and Kazanas (1989) differentiate between external stakeholders, the general public and the family of an employee. Neither the family nor the general public are part of the 'value chain' of the organisation as conventionally defined.

The inclusion of the general public within an HRD framework is an interesting area because of the overlap with public relations, PR. Many organisations invest substantially in PR. Groups are invited to visit factories to see how products are made; major campaigns can be launched to justify an activity or initiative which may impact on a local community. Representatives of organisations will spend vast sums on projecting the organisation image, or in some instances attempting to transform it.

I am not aware of many organisations having established internal links between the training and development function and public relations, nor even whether at strategic level a connection has been made. That is not to say that HRD practitioners should not become players in the PR arena. If we define HRD as being about learning and interventions then clearly HRD practitioners should consider what the relationship with PR should be and perhaps contribute in a more proactive way than heretofore on policy devclopments in this area.

There are a number of instances where the education of specific groups from within the general public can be targeted as part of an organisation's planned learning activities. General practitioners, for example, have been asked by the Government to set up programmes such as clinics for the overweight, screening clinics for cancer (breast and cervical), and awareness groups for young mothers and the elderly.

Much of the provision of learning activities for the general public can best be viewed as examples of non-employee education. This is also the case for another of Rothwell and Kazanas's categories. They include representatives of an employee's family within their framework, arguing that they are silent partners in a 'business'. What happens within affects their well-being and that of the family member employed by the organisation.

Organisations and training and development departments have not really addressed the learning needs of partners and other family members. One exception has been the provision of cross-cultural and language training for families of employees being posted overseas (see Iles, this volume). Barham and Oates (1991) conducted a survey of how organisations prepared their managers for international postings: 42 per cent of respondents included cross-cultural training as one of the 5 most important activities for their organisation; 23 per cent included language training for the family.

THE ORCHESTRATION OF LEARNING PROCESSES FOR NON-EMPLOYEES

The issue now is how to orchestrate appropriate learning processes as part of a coherent strategy for non-employee learning. Rothwell and Kazanas (1989) provide a useful set of guidelines, given below. It is important to recognise that they are postulated on the assumption that most learning activities will be orchestrated from within an organisation that has an established in-house HRD function. They suggest the following steps that HRD practitioners and operating managers should take.

1 Classify external groups by their general interests or concerns.
2 Analyse existing relationships between the organisation and the various groups whose learning needs are to be met.
3 Establish what these relationships should be in the future.
4 Pinpoint discrepancies for both the present and the future between desired and actual learning relationships.
5 Separate HRD from non-HRD solutions.
6 Identify changes in relationships and design HRD activities to meet desired changes.
7 Select instructional content and delivery methods.
8 Follow up over time.

A straw poll of training and development managers responsible for organisational skills development across a range of institutions has indicated that few have analysed the issues. Thus point 6 above becomes a major resource problem with no allocated budget. Accordingly additions to the Rothwell and Kazanas guidelines would be:

- establish what if any percentage of the current resources invested in HRD activities are devoted to non-employee learning and determine whether this is appropriate for future needs;
- develop a negotiating strategy for bidding for additional resources should this prove necessary.

A further recommendation which builds on points 2 and 3 above would be to establish links with HRD departments of organisations with whom one has a significant business relationship in order to consider the options of pooling resources and integrating learning systems.

The final recommended addition is that in-house Training and Development Managers establish the current organisation attitude towards out-sourcing, since this may throw up future target groups. These could well include the training and development function unless HRD practitioners can influence organisation decision makers of the strategic relevance/economic benefit of its remaining in-house or unless (if they are not so already) they themselves become part of the strategic decision making group.

THE LEARNING ARCHITECTS AS NON-EMPLOYEES

What the literature has significantly failed to touch on at all is the impact of out-sourcing the training and development function on organisation activities. The assumption is made that learning processes will be orchestrated by people operating within and employed by the organisation. However, increasingly, many training departments are being out-sourced and are not seen as part of the organisation core services. Similarly many HRD initiatives and training programmes are being developed and delivered by external consultants. In the public sector they are subject to compulsory competitive tendering or market testing. Thus the 'learning architects' themselves are becoming non-employees.

This perhaps is an inevitable consequence of the low status and lack of strategic role that has been afforded to HRD professionals within organisations. However, it is increasingly being argued that knowledge workers help provide the distinctive competences which differentiate one organisation from the other in the perceived satisfaction of customers in the marketplace. It would accordingly seem vital for an orchestration of the learning processes leading to the retention and development of such knowledge workers to be effectively undertaken. With the growth of strategic alliances and networks, it would seem even more essential to have people available within an organisation who have a strategic understanding of learning systems and an ability to apply them.

An alternative, but one that seems to be some way off, would be for out-sourced training and development departments to help develop a strategic network of internal and external stakeholders, of which they themselves are part, and become PALs in the same way as other external contributors. This would be an extension of the idea of 'corporate university' which is being developed by some organisations in the United States such as Motorola.

CONCLUSION

This chapter suggests that non-employees who directly or indirectly impact on an organisation's operations could be usefully classified in terms of:

- those operating outside the organisation who contribute to the primary value chain, e.g. suppliers, dealers, customers;
- those operating outside the organisation who contribute to the support value chain, e.g. out-sourced HRD departments;
- those operating within the organisation who contribute to the primary value chain, e.g. volunteers, self-employed sub-contactors;
- those operating within the organisation who contribute to the support value chain, e.g. consultants, franchisees;
- those operating outside the organisation who do not contribute to the value chain but who have an interest in its activities, e.g. environmental pressure groups, families of employees;
- those operating within the organisation who do not contribute to the value chain but who have an interest in its activities, e.g. union representatives, works convenors.

The schemata in Fig. 6.5 can be used as an enabling framework for classifying the learning needs of non-employee stakeholder groups contributing to the primary value chain.

Non-employees contributing to the primary value chain		HRD strategies to meet learning needs		
Non-employee type e.g.	Learning needs	Training	Education	Development
Suppliers Dealers Consumers Volunteers	High priority Medium priority Low priority			

Fig. 6.5

Similar tables can be developed for non-employee stakeholder groups contributing to the support value chain and also for those stakeholders impacting upon the organisation but operating outside the value chain.

Whatever approach is adopted it is important that those responsible for skills development and learning within the organisation develop a coherent and planned strategy for training, education, development and learning support for these non-employee stakeholders. This clearly becomes more difficult if the learning architects have themselves have been out-sourced; organisational decision makers should reflect on the implications of such a strategic decision for the continuous improvement and development of its human resource.

References

Atkinson, J.S. (1985) 'Flexibility: planning for an uncertain future', *Manpower Policy and Practice*, vol. 1, Summer.

Barham, K. and Oates, D. (1991) *The International Manager*, Economist Books.

Barrington, H. and Reid, M. (1993) *Training Interventions – Managing Employee Development*, London, IPM.

Harrison, R. (1994) *Employee Development*, IPD.

Institute of Manpower Studies (1985) 'New Forms of Work Organisation', *IMS Manpower Commentary*, no. 30, Brighton.

Jarillo, J.C. (1993) *Strategic Networks – Creating the Borderless Organisation*, London, Butterworth Heinemann.

Johnson, G. and Scholes, J. (1993) *Exploring Corporate Strategy*, London, Prentice Hall.

Kanter, R.M. (1989) *When Giants Learn To Dance*, New York, Simon and Schuster.

Madu, C. and Kuei, C. (1993) 'Introducing Strategic Quality Management', *Long Range Planning*, vol. 26, no. 6 (December).

Next Steps Review 1993, HMSO, London, Cm 2430 (1993).

Porter, Michael (1980) *Competitive Advantage*, New York, Free Press.

Rothwell, W. and Kazanas, H.C. (1989) *Strategic Human Resource Development*, London, Prentice Hall.

Schuler, R.S. and Macmillan, I.C. (1985) 'Gaining a Competitive Edge through Human Resources', *Personnel*, April.

Steeples, Marion M. (1992) *The Corporate Guide to the Malcolm Balbrige National Quality Award*, ASQC, Quality Press.

Tuppen, C. (1993) 'An Environmental Policy for British Telecommunications', *Long Range Planning*, vol. 26, no. 5, pp. 24–30.

7

New Forms of
Work Organisation and HRD

Michael Kelleher

INTRODUCTION

After a period of relative remission, the problem of skill shortages may be emerging once again with the latest Employment Department survey showing a rise in the number of reported 'hard-to-fill vacancies' (IFF, 1993). It would appear that as the economy begins to improve, firms will once again begin to recruit and once again face difficulties in filling vacancies, and a return to the situation prior to the current recession.[1]

In this chapter the skill shortage phenomenon is placed in the context of the changing nature of work and skills in British manufacturing industries. Two forms of work reorganisation are identified: horizontal and vertical. The former combines previously distinct tasks of a similar level of skill and responsibility, the latter combines tasks both upwards and downwards in the traditional structure of work and tasks and as such represents a more radical challenge to firms wishing to embark on such as strategy. Horizontal restructuring poses challenges of combining skills associated with new tasks and combining these with existing skill repertoires. As such, the existing vocational training system may provide adequate assistance to firms introducing this form of work reorganisation. The problems associated with the voluntaristic nature of training in Britain are described here and it is argued that firms seeking to introduce vertical restructuring will develop internal strategies for employee development in order to combat deficiencies in the national system of training. Finally, seven case studies describe the training initiatives undertaken by seven different companies.

SKILLS SHORTAGES IN A DECLINING SECTOR

Studies during the late 1980s show that the scale of the problem was significant in all sectors of the economy. Difficulties arose from a shortage of skilled professional people, engineers, nurses, construction workers, craft workers, print workers, computer personnel, secretarial staff, sales staff and those in finance and retailing (Bosworth and

---

[1] I am grateful to the Science and Engineering Research Council for their support during the research upon which this chapter is based.

Dutton, 1990; Financial Times, 1989; Industrial Society, 1988; Virgo, 1987; IRRR, 1988).

A concentration on skill shortages in the manufacturing sector clearly neglects the growing number of reports of shortages in the service sector industries (Bosworth and Dutton, 1990). However, Britain's manufacturing industry is vitally important to the economy both at present and possibly more so in the future and, hence, skill shortages in this sector are particularly significant. As a source of employment, manufacturing has steadily declined during the whole of this century (Massey, 1988).[2] Despite its decline, however, manufacturing remains a vital section of the British economy. According to one source, the engineering industry, which accounts for approximately 50 per cent of manufacturing employment, alone accounts for 11 per cent of gross domestic product, GDP, and 50 per cent of British exports of manufactured goods (EITB, 1989). As a percentage of GDP in Britain, manufacturing accounted for just over 32 per cent in 1960. This had been reduced to under 27 per cent by 1985 (Mayes, 1987).[3] Mayes (1987) argues that the decline in revenue from manufacturing industries has not been compensated for by other sectors of the economy. Lane (1989) adds that the necessary generation of foreign exchange is not only difficult but the subsequent poor balance of payments 'acts as a brake on economy'. The declining contribution made from oil and agricultural industries may increase the importance of manufacturing to the economy in the future (Lane, 1989, p. 12). Thus an examination of skill shortages in manufacturing is justified given its clear importance to the British economy now and in the foreseeable future.

The notion that skill shortages can occur even in sectors experiencing long-term decline needs to be explained. Although craft- and technician-level workers are employed by manufacturers in all sectors, unfortunately figures are not available for occupational profiles of all manufacturing industries as not all of them are covered by the activities of the Engineering Industry Training Board (EITB).[4] The EITB supplies employment figures for those companies who are covered by its activities and in 1978 total employment in engineering stood at 2.93 million. This fell rapidly during the early 1980s to 2.2 million in 1984 and has declined steadily until, in 1988, the total was 1.88 million (EITB, 1989).

In manufacturing there has been an absolute decline in the employment of all but the professional engineers, scientists and technologists. However, managerial staff, technicians and administrative staff have all experienced a relative increase in employment. A relative decrease in employment can be seen at the lower levels. Amongst the craft workers the decrease from 1978 to 1988 is approximately 40 per cent and is probably the result of the massive contraction in craft intensive sectors such as machinery and machine tools that took place during the early 1980s (EITB, 1989). These trends are projected to continue, at least in the medium term (Green, 1990).

[2] In the US, where the employment in the service sector is much larger than in Britain, it has been argued that many service industry jobs rely on their linkages with manufacturing. Similarly, the increasing importance of research and design of high technology goods and services is in order to service the growing demand from within the manufacturing sector for products, such as microprocessors, or production processes, or both. Thus, manufacturing does matter (Cohen and Zysman, 1987).

[3] The precise figures are: 32.1% in 1960 and 22.6% in 1985. A comparison with the US, Japan, Germany, France and Italy shows that only the US manufacturing sector has declined as fast as in Britain (Mayes, 1987, p. 49, Table 1).

[4] The food, drink and tobacco industry is one notable exception.

However, the survey results (IFF: 1991, 1992, 1993) suggest that, despite this decline in employment needs, employers are still reporting a shortage of craft skills. This might be explained by examining the levels of recruitment and training during the same period. The engineering industry relies on trainees as an important source of supply for replacing workers who retire or leave the industry. What is significant about the engineering industry is that not only have companies reduced their recruitment of trainees, but that the reductions have outstripped the decline in employment (EITB, 1989, Table 3, p. 15).

As Green (1990) points out, the annual intake of trainees during the period 1980 to 1983 fell by 55 per cent compared to a 26 per cent reduction in craft employment. During the same period 5500 trainees were made redundant. With the so-called 'demographic time bomb' the number of school leavers is expected to decline until the mid 1990s and only gradually increase thereafter, but will remain below the level of the early 1980s (Training Agency, 1989). The pool of potential trainees is therefore reduced and, according to this scenario, skill shortages at craft- and technician-levels would appear to be a significant factor for the forthcoming future.

TRADITIONAL STRUCTURE OF WORK AND TASKS

The intermediate skills of technicians and craft workers are central to any vertical re-allocation of tasks. Both of these groups of workers could devolve some tasks to lower levels whilst undertaking higher level tasks allocated from higher groups. It is useful to examine what tasks are undertaken at the four levels traditionally found in manufacturing organisations: engineers; technicians; craft workers; operators. For our purposes, tasks are the actions and responsibilities undertaken in any function, and skills are the combination of knowledge and ability possessed by individual workers (Jones and Scott, 1988).

Engineers are positioned at the very top of the technical hierarchy in British manufacturing. There are several different specialisms which have broadly similar responsibilities and routes for access. Although not exclusively so, access to these engineering positions is mainly through obtaining engineering degrees from higher education institutions. After a period of training and practical experience in employment, engineers can become members of the relevant chartered engineering institutes and their position can be enhanced through professional status. Despite the high level of educational qualification, graduate engineers have been reported to be under-utilised in terms of the qualifications they have (Scott *et al.*, 1992). Initially, graduates often tend to be placed in jobs that do not demand the levels of conceptual or innovatory skills that they are supposedly trained for and they are sometimes placed in jobs which are undefined because of the 'novel fields of technology'. However, a high proportion of these jobs appear to be closer to technician-level jobs as the relevant techniques needed become more established. One of the prime causes for this under-utilisation of graduates' skills is the shortage of technicians (Scott *et al.*, 1992). This under-utilisation of graduates suggests that industry could clearly benefit from freeing engineers from the more routine technician level tasks in order to concentrate on higher level responsibilities.

It is difficult to define the exact nature of skills required by technicians. It is possible to identify three levels of technician: *technician engineers* who use the highest levels of skill; *engineering technicians*; and there is a residual category of *other technical staff*, who use the lowest level of skills amongst this group. The technician engineer must possess a broad technical knowledge and good communication skills in order to liaise with other departments and professional engineers. An engineering technician has a narrower knowledge base and applies proven techniques under the supervision of either engineers or technician engineers (Jones and Scott, 1988).[5]

Jones and Scott (1988) point out that technicians are involved in a number of groups of activities, including: design and draughting of equipment or machines and their related drawings; programming, analysis, software engineering and other computer related work; the design of test equipment and procedures, and inspection of equipment and components; the preparation of technical reports, and the interpretation of diagrams and drawings and other aspects of internal communication; liaison with customers involving *inter alia*, the preparation of quotations, contracts and technical specifications; production planning and control, initiating maintenance programmes and other manufacturing related activities; and finally, the measurement/calculations of different materials and related exercises (1988, pp. 18–20).

Forming an intermediate role between the higher level technician skills and the semi-skilled and unskilled operator grades, craft workers play a central role in the manufacturing process. High numbers of workers trained in craft skills are also the key to the new production processes emerging in Germany and play a pivotal role in the flexible specialisation thesis (Kern and Schumann, 1987; Piore and Sabel, 1984). Craft workers perform similar tasks to those of technicians. These include: information and communication, especially diagrammatically and orally; planning jobs by selecting the appropriate equipment; materials, components, operations and their sequence; setting up machines for themselves and others; operating machines and control systems; testing and inspecting finished work (Jones and Scott, 1988, pp. 22–4).

At the bottom of the skills ladder in manufacturing, operators' knowledge and abilities are relatively low given that the tasks they are engaged on tend to be specific to single products or processes and are more highly supervised. These mainly include the performance of individual operations on a specific piece of equipment, such as the assembly of components or the operation of equipment. Both technicians and craft workers exercise four main types of skill: knowledge of materials; knowledge of processes; knowledge of the use of tools and instruments; and the use of mathematical techniques (Jones and Scott, 1988, pp. 20–1). However, the types of skill that they exercise can be distinguished in terms of the degree of theoretical and practical skills required of the job. Ashton *et al.* (1991) suggest that skills can be characterised as routinised, applied, and conceptual. Routinised skills are those that develop from the repetitive performance of similar tasks and are the dominant form of skills amongst operator grades. Applied skills come from the application of theoretical knowledge and its use in a variety of contexts and are the dominant form amongst craft workers. Conceptual skills are problem solving skills involved in higher level technical situations and are predominantly found at technician level and above.

[5] The recently published *Standard Occupational Classification* (EDP/OCPS, 1990) conflates many of the tasks that might distinguish between the levels that Jones and Scott identify. As the former study is based upon more recent research its categories of technicians will be adopted for the purpose of this study. For a critique of certain classifications within the SOC see Kelleher *et al.*, 1993).

WORK REORGANISATION

The companies in the case studies can been distinguished in terms of two forms of task integration: horizontal and vertical (cf. Kelly, 1982). At three of the firms (Case studies 1–3) tasks have been merged horizontally, that is, at the same level of skill in the structure of work. Pressure for these changes has been due to market demands which have ensured that there has been an increased adoption of microprocessor-based equipment in both the product and in the production process. Previously separated craft occupations have been combined into single 'multi-skilled' jobs.

At the four remaining case studies vertical task integration, that is the allocation of tasks to workers in lower occupational grades, has been introduced in varying forms. At one Japanese firm (Case study 7), production operators undertake programming, design modification, costings and quality control checks normally associated with technician-level jobs. This radical departure from traditional British work organisation is the result of the company's decision not to employ technician-level grades in the factory. At another firm involved in the manufacturer of aluminium cans (Case study 5), the 'technician' grades undertake traditional craft-level tasks but, in addition, those workers who are skilled in electrical work also undertake computer diagnostics and programme editing, and operators are involved in craft-level tasks albeit as a member of a small team. Unlike at the Japanese company, separate technician grades undertake tasks normally associated with those grades. This firm adopts the 'technician' title for those employees whose responsibilities include communication, decision making and problem solving. The term applies equally to manual and non-manual employees and, despite its associations with particular types of tasks and skills, represents a departure from the occupational-based classifications used prior to its introduction. Faced with a questionnaire requesting information as to what category of skilled worker they might be suffering shortages of, the use of 'technician' in this unaccustomed manner will lead to misleading data. Similarly, how would the Japanese company categorise shortages of skills it utilises? Its shopfloor workers may be titled 'production operator' but the range of tasks they undertake and the skills they employ are normally associated with craft or technician grades.

At a gear box manufacturing company (Case study 4) vertical task integration has taken on a different form to the previous firms. In this case a number of tasks which had previously been allocated to separate workers have now been consolidated into a single 'process operator' grade. Inspection duties previously allocated to technician-level grades, machine setting tasks previously the domain of craft workers, and a number of materials handling and other labouring tasks have been combined into this new job. At craft-level, although individual occupations have been eliminated, the company has chosen not to amalgamate mechanical and electrical craft jobs, which is in contrast to some of the other firms studied here. If the firm had recognised its situation in terms of skill shortages, how would it have categorised the types of skills it now requires of its operator grades? The combination of technician-level and craft-level tasks with traditional operator-level tasks creates difficulties in classifying the new grade into the traditional group categories.

At the final company (Case study 6) vertical task integration has taken yet another different form. Operators now undertake a large number of minor maintenance tasks which would previously have involved mechanical and electrical craft workers. The monitoring and diagnosis of computerised controls were tasks that did not exist prior to the introduction of microprocessor controlled equipment. Together with these maintenance tasks, they entail higher levels of skill requirements for the operators involved in the production process, and a new grade which is higher than the previous operator grades has been introduced which recognises this situation. On the lines for wrapping the product the operators now have the responsibility for quality control, although this is limited to statistical monitoring of the final product. Quality controls were previously the responsibility of technician-level grades and these appear to be the only such tasks devolved down to operator level. The merging of mechanical and electrical craft tasks into single occupations has allowed the electrically skilled workers to undertake many of the tasks previously allocated to technicians. New grades have been introduced which combine craft-level tasks into single occupations; however, the delegation of technician-level tasks to craft workers has not been formally recognised within the new grading structure. As with the other cases, this company would have difficulties in categorising their new skill requirements in terms of the traditional structure of work in British manufacturing.

These companies may not be representative of their respective industries or product markets but they represent the range of work reorganisation and labour market experiences of a much wider sample of firms contacted during the period between 1989 and 1992. It is just this diversity of labour market and industry perspectives that suggests experiences in these firms might have some resonance for companies in the wider economy. The emergence of these new 'operator' grades, that are not consistent with traditional notions of workers exercising simple routinised skills on highly specified tasks, may be consistent with Kern and Schumann's (1987) arguments about the development of new types of production worker in Germany in the early 1980s. However, Kern and Schumann appear to neglect the changes occurring to the types of skill required by craft workers, or at least fail sufficiently to acknowledge the significant difference between the two groups of workers and associated tasks and skills. The changes have two important features. On the one hand, there is a need to be able to undertake a broader range of tasks that requires an increase in applied skills. On the other hand, in three of the companies, increased conceptual type skills are required in addition to the increase in applied skills.

These changes in skill requirements are not entirely consistent with Piore and Sabel's flexible specialisation thesis (1984). It should be remembered that their arguments concerning the use of highly skilled craft workers was to be able to adapt flexible machinery for flexible batch production. Whilst market needs may be increasing company awareness of quality control issues, as witnessed by the increase in quality related tasks amongst operators, the changes identified here have occurred in firms specialising in small to medium batch engineering and in high volume production techniques. The use of special purpose machines has remained constant yet the skills demanded are the antithesis of the low skills of Fordist production techniques and new polyvalent craft workers are emerging.

VOCATIONAL TRAINING POLICY

The Government is concerned to create high profile strategies for training that provide an impetus towards achieving national targets of attainment. Two key problems with Government policy suggest that skill shortages in the 1990s will create significant difficulties for British industry. First, the Government's persistence with market dominated training policies reinforces, rather than addresses, one of the principal sources of the problem, that is the reluctance of employers to train their employees. According to Cassels (1990), Britain's skill shortages are a result of the continued failure of training and education policies to meet the needs of industry. Much of the literature concentrating on the failure of Britain's education and training policies is critical of the Government's record on training. Secondly, the emphasis on performance related qualifications reduces the need to ensure workers enhance the knowledge base upon which their ability to tackle technological advances will be founded.

Throughout their examination of changing policies during this century Sheldrake and Vickerstaff (1987) argue that shortages of skills are a constant feature of the British economy. Characterised by its voluntaristic nature, the training system appears to have consistently failed to supply sufficient skills to fulfil demand. The long tradition of weak state intervention prior to the 1960s has been documented by Sheldrake and Vickerstaff (1987) who suggest that the present Government's preference for market dominated training principles has a history dating back to the end of the 19th century. However, significant state intervention was introduced during the period between 1960 and 1979 and the corporatist arrangements of this period are in marked contrast to the laissez-faire period since 1979.

As the 1960s dawned it seemed increasingly clear that the voluntarist training system was not meeting national needs. There were not enough skilled workers, the content of apprenticeships was narrow, and outside of the apprenticeship system training tended to be 'conspicuous by its absence' (Sheldrake and Vickerstaff, 1987, p. 31). This view is confirmed by Rainbird (1990) who argues that only a minority of all school leavers received any training at all and that in 1950, for example, the apprenticeship system provided the bulk of training with 33 per cent of boys and eight per cent of girls entering apprenticeships (1990, p. 11).

During the early 1960s a more determined scrutiny of the training system's failure to tackle the perennial problem of skills shortages resulted in a re-examination of training. This resulted in the moves towards greater state intervention in various aspects of training and culminated in the passing of the 1964 Industrial Training Act. This Act legislated for the introduction of Industrial Training Boards (ITB) which would be responsible for improving training within firms under their jurisdiction. The ITBs were organised with an even mix of employers and trade union representatives on their boards, and they were given the power to raise a levy on all firms and to distribute grants to encourage training. This first interventionist approach attempted to create a training system for the benefit of the national economy. One of the first ITBs was the EITB which developed an innovative modular system for training craft apprenticeships and whose record of achievement appears to be excellent (Sheldrake and Vickerstaff, 1987; Rainbird, 1990).

Criticisms of the ITBs were generally from employers and particularly amongst those in small firms. Increases in bureaucracy resulted in complaints from businesses, especially those small firms who paid the levy but did not benefit from grants. The emphasis on 'off the job' training largely neglected the informal 'on the job' training traditionally provided by small firms and the levy system began to be viewed simply as another tax to be paid. The industrial basis of the ITBs meant that the system neglected the rising problem of training and re-deployment of workers from declining industries and also duplicated the training for skills, such as clerical and commercial skills, which are common to many, if not all, industries. The attempts to foster a training system geared towards national skill needs were frustrated by the narrower interests of the ITBs and the employers within those industries (Sheldrake and Vickerstaff, 1987; Ashton *et al.*, 1989; Rainbird, 1990).

These criticisms and increased pressure from employers caused the then Government to review the system in the early 1970s. This review resulted in the passing of the Employment and Training Act in 1973. The adoption of an overtly corporatist strategy was underlined by the introduction of the tripartite Manpower Services Commission (MSC). Under the 1973 Act the powers of ITBs were weakened by replacing the levy-grant with a levy-exemption system. However, the impact of the MSC on the traditional areas of industrial training was lessened due to economic conditions which called for immediate and special measures to counter rising unemployment. The MSC increased its support of training places in industry and developed youth training programmes to help counter the disturbing growth in youth unemployment. It was recognised that no means had been found for ensuring that industry trained with 'an eye to future national needs rather than immediate specific requirements' (Sheldrake and Vickerstaff, 1987, p. 47)

Debates surrounding the collective funding of training and the introduction of training contracts between employers and ITBs floundered on employer opposition. The compromise series of measures that were introduced did not challenge employers' traditional reluctance to train and the increasingly fragile economic position meant that the MSC was forced to consider a larger number of special measures to counter unemployment. These special measures were introduced in an unco-ordinated manner and a large number of temporary programmes were introduced, and this lack of cohesion in training policy was inherited by the Conservative Government in 1979.

The Conservative Government's ideological opposition to corporatism and an adherence to free market economics meant that ITBs were an early target for abolition. State support for ITBs was phased out and the 1981 Employment Act abolished 17 of the 24 ITBs that existed at that time (Rainbird, 1990). However, approximately two-thirds of the ITBs remained in operation until the Government announced the abolition of the remaining boards in 1988. At the time of writing a small number of ITBs still exist, the most notable being the Construction Engineering Training Board. Consistent with the Government's plans to cut public spending the MSC's expenditure was cut by 18 per cent during the first weeks of its term of office. This affected many of the temporary initiatives in place at that time and the number of people completing retraining courses was severely reduced (Ashton *et al.*, 1989).

The MSC continued to introduce new schemes designed to improve the general skill levels of the workforce. Its New Training Initiative was an attempt to introduce a national system of vocational training for all young people entering the labour market as well as alter the apprenticeships schemes' emphasis on time-served qualifications to a standards-based qualification. The Youth Training Scheme, YTS, was a central feature of the initiative and offered young people an alternative to unemployment. Its critics argue that it has remained a training scheme concentrating on low skill jobs and that the problem of adult training and retraining remained unresolved (Ashton *et al.*, 1989).

The Government restricted trade unions' rights to be consulted about specific aspects of training and the TUC eventually voted to withdraw co-operation. This provided the Government with the pretext for incorporating the MSC into the Department of Employment as the Training Agency, which in turn has been disbanded and its work incorporated into the Employment Department. The corporatist experiment in training had been delivered its final, fatal blow. According to Government philosophy, the market would now be able to regulate the supply and demand for skills more efficiently and employers were once again free to develop their own training schemes, or not, as the case may be. Voluntarism returned to dominate the British system of training.

This market-led training philosophy has stimulated a number of criticisms. The notion of returning the onus for training back to employers, with their traditional reluctance to accept their responsibilities in this field, has been viewed with particular scepticism. It is therefore worth considering the macro training policies of recent years and examining their implications for the shortage of skills.

The introduction of the 1981 Information Technology Act established training centres for information technology, ITECs. These were funded through a variety of sources including the Training Agency which used funds available under the YTS and Employment Training, ET, schemes. Unfortunately, recent cuts in funding of these schemes have given rise to rather pessimistic forecasts as to the future of ITECs. The most optimistic note derives directly from the National Association of ITECs who suggest that most ITECs will remain open but that the quality of the training on offer will deteriorate (*Financial Times*, 14.5.90, p. 10). The shortage of information technology skills has been reported by Government departments as well as independent research (Department of Employment, 1984; Connor *et al.*, 1989; IRRR, 1988; *Financial Times*, 1989). The cuts in funding would appear to exacerbate skill shortages in this area.

In parallel to the reduction in central financing of training there has been a shift of emphasis towards local, employer-led determination of training policies characterised by the new Training and Enterprise Councils, TECs. Local firms may have a vested interest in matching skills and competitive manufacturing methods, and might consequently ensure the provision of the requisite skills through TECs. The experience of one of our firms suggests that TECs may not address the needs of manufacturing in areas dominated by other industries and sectors. The existence of a new TEC in the area where one of the firms is located did give rise to some optimism that the company's skill shortages may be addressed in the long term. However, initial indications are that the TEC has identified shortages of information technology, financial and secretarial skills as priorities. In the long term this is not going to help the situation regarding the company's shortage of skills. As the training manager points out 'we are an engineering firm. We are going to have to do something drastic to recruit trainees and hang on to them once we have got them'.

In practice the funding of TECs has been allocated to five key areas: youth training programmes; employment training (unemployed people); enterprise allowance schemes, business growth training, etc; local initiative funding; and administrative costs. The bulk of TECs' budgets will fall almost entirely within the first two of these categories and there is minimal scope for local budget allocations outside of these two areas of training (Peck and Emmerich, 1990). These funding arrangements may well limit the ability of TECs to finance training to surmount skill shortages that already exist amongst local firms.

Thus, the emphasis for tackling the skill shortage problem will be placed upon individual firms. However, if we accept the argument from dualist economic theory (Berger and Piore, 1980) that training is provided by large firms and is concentrated amongst their core workers, this may well mean an increase in firm-specific skills and a decline in the amount of transferable skills that small firms rely on (Phillimore, 1989). In the telematic industry (data processing, electronic mail, electronic data interchange, etc.) there has been a growing tendency to poach staff from any possible source. The shortage of skills in this area is attributed to the collapse of British Telecom's apprentice and technician training programmes. As a result, training policies tend to be linked with a commitment to an internal labour market (Locksley *et al.*, 1990).

Streek (1989) convincingly argues that firms in the advanced industrial countries of the West will encounter difficulties in retaining skilled labour due to the existence of the 'free labour contract'. The right of workers to move to different employers without any obligation to stay with any one employer means that firms who invest in training cannot guarantee a return for that investment. Recruiting workers trained elsewhere reduces overall labour costs despite the existence of higher wage incentives to assist this recruitment. Thus, firms can choose not to train workers and can rely on the skills developed within other companies. Self-evidently, other firms can reach the same conclusion and choose not to train, preferring to poach or recruit skilled labour (Streek, 1989, p. 94). The importance of this argument is underlined by Streek who suggests that this situation creates a chronic shortage of skilled labour. Although firms understand the importance of skills the decision not to train is highly rational (1989). Streek's argument helps explain why British firms in general have failed to provide adequate training for their employees (Cassels, 1990; Senker, 1989) and why, without any regulatory mechanisms imposed upon it, the market will be unable to satisfy demands for skilled labour.

The Training and Enterprise Councils will need to overcome the problems of low priority and firm-specific training in order to provide the required transferable skills. Warner (1986) points out that British firms spend under one per cent (0.15%) of sales turnover on training. In comparison, companies in the US spend up to three per cent (3%) of turnover. Prescribing increasing education and training expenditure as a panacea for the skill shortage problem (CBI, 1989a) neglects the historically poor performance of British industry on training. The TECs' success will depend on the extent to which local employers can exert influence on the larger enterprises in their midst, and the extent to which training can be geared towards the benefits of the economy as a whole. The Government's emphasis on market forces neglects the distinctions between industrialists' attitudes and policies and Britain's chronic shortage of skills. This argument is supported by Cassels who argues that:

> 'The market, where it works or can be made to work, will often deliver the best results. But to enable all parts of the system to work well, a clear sense of direction must be given by the centre, that is by government.' (Cassels, 1990, p. 29)

In contrast to Cassels's argument that the education and training system has failed British industry, Finegold and Soskice (1988) argue that the system corresponds to industries' needs. According to this argument, British industry has largely adopted mass production methods with their concomitant low skills and minimal training requirements. This, the authors argue, is due to the lack of a suitably well educated and trained workforce. Education and training in Britain reinforces the mass production paradigm and prevents industry from responding to new economic needs.

Finegold and Soskice (1988) argue that education and training, and the organisation of work are two components of a low skill/low quality equilibrium. This concept denotes a self-reinforcing network of institutions which also include Britain's industrial relations system, financial markets and state and political structures. The authors argue that policies activated in any one of these elements of the equilibrium will fail as each element needs to be addressed in order to break out of the low skills equilibrium. Thus education and training are inexorably linked to the organisation of work. However, the growing debate that work is being reorganised necessitating higher levels of skill may suggest that a disequilibrium exists, rather than an equilibrium, that is more consistent with the increasing reports of skill shortages in the late 1980s. Finegold and Soskice's thesis relies on skill requirements remaining static and at low levels, is analytically adequate if skills remain static and manufacturers continue to demand workers with low skills. It has been argued here that changes to working practices are creating demands for workers with higher levels of skills at both operator and craft-level, but that the education and training system proves inadequate to meet those demands. This dichotomous position challenges the low skills equilibrium thesis. It is more accurate to define the present situation in Britain as a disequilibrium characterised by a low skills supply and a higher skills demand.

Training for long-term skill needs requires a commitment to long-term investment. If firms are to overcome their traditional resistance to train workers in the required skills then evidence of such long-term investment ought to be available. However, the organisation of the political economy in Britain suggests that such long-term investment has not been forthcoming. Despite the growing adoption of microelectronic equipment and the increase in the number of software applications, this technological investment is not matched by similar investments in skills. British firms would appear to abandon training commitments in times of retrenchment and there is also a tendency to have to 'justify training in terms of short term financial gain' (Campbell and Warner, 1987, p. 97). Thus, training appears to be given a low priority within British industry. This point is confirmed by examining how recruitment and training in engineering skills in British manufacturing has contributed to the shortages in those skills, particularly at craft-level.

British capital has been characterised by the distinct division between the industrial and financial sectors. Financial institutions have not tended to exercise detailed control over industrial matters. They have preferred to keep to short-term loan arrangements and have avoided share holding, long-term loans and involvement in industrial management (Longstreth, 1986). This historic separation of finance and industrial capital has increased the difficulties of industrial capital to invest in training. As Finegold and Soskice (1988) point out, finance capital neglects training in its analysis of performance and, in the absence of industry oriented investment banks, industrial capital has been forced to finance more investment from retained profits that are lower than in other advanced industrial nations. This relationship explains why investment in training is cut during economic downturns and why firms resort to redundancy measures in order to cut costs. Internal financial control systems may also militate against investment in training as short-term profit maximisation to enhance performance related pay discourages long-term investments in training (Keep, 1993). This is particularly problematic in that there are enormous difficulties in determining causality between training and improved productivity and profit. Coupled with the reduction in craft training discussed above, the large numbers of skilled workers made redundant during previous periods of economic recession have compounded the difficulties manufacturing companies now face. As an EITB report argues:

> 'craft workers made redundant by the engineering industry since 1980 have not, apparently, remained available as a readily accessible pool of skilled labour for the industry. Many have found employment in other sectors of the economy or gone into self-employment. Others have retired or otherwise withdrawn from the engineering labour market due to loss of confidence or deterioration of their skills after years of unemployment.' (Mason, 1988, p. 21)

The use of redundancy measures will have a ratchet like effect on skill shortages in manufacturing. As each wave of redundancies reduces the pool of skilled labour and a shortfall continues in the number of trainees recruited, policies implemented during each economic downturn will increase the reports of skill shortages in future upturns in the economy. Thus training investment is characterised by short-term concerns which tend to exacerbate the problem of skill shortages.

The second major concern of this section is whether the new system of vocational qualifications is going to address the changing requirements of firms. The National Vocational Qualification, NVQ, system might meet the needs identified above; however, as yet, information as to the extent of its dissemination within manufacturing industry and how firms are introducing the system is unavailable. Whilst the occupational labour market system prevails, those firms that are reorganising working practices and training internally may successfully tackle their skill shortage problem through new forms of work organisation. The vertical integration of tasks and the accompanying firm-specific skills may not be compatible with a national training system which has been criticised for its low levels of attainment compared to European systems. Where NVQs are being introduced they might not match the levels of skill demanded by vertical task integration. In its early stages the NCVQ system has already been criticised for its rejection of external assessment, and its over reliance on employers to define training needs. This could lead to the introduction of narrow and inflexible qualifications at the expense of the economy's need for people with broader skills (Jarvis and Prais, 1989; Prais, 1991; McCool, 1989, cited in IRS, 1992).

A further problem arises from the emphasis on performance related assessment. It can be argued that the concept of skill has several dimensions including cognitive, motor and social constructions, and is therefore difficult to define. However, in manufacturing it is probably sufficient to argue that skill has three key components: theoretical knowledge, practical performance, and tacit knowledge based upon experience (Grootings *et al.*, 1989; Kusterer, 1978; Libetta, 1989). Whilst the latter is impossible to measure, any alterations to either of the remaining two components seriously affects the complexity of the skill being demanded.

The combination of tasks at existing levels demands increases in the practical element of skills, whereas vertical task integration results in the additional demand for higher levels of theoretical knowledge. With its emphasis on performance rather than theoretical knowledge, the new National Vocational Qualifications will hinder those firms seeking to add to the conceptual-level skills of their craft workers. This may also prove a disastrous policy for the national economy as other European countries retain the theoretical content of their craft training courses (Smithers, 1994). Horizontal task integration would appear to be easily facilitated in the new five level hierarchy of vocational qualifications. However, firms seeking to re-allocate tasks and organise working practices that challenge the existing vertical structure of occupations in Britain will find the existing hierarchy of qualifications is too rigid and will not provide the flexibility required to offer qualifications that recognise the innovate nature of the range of tasks and skills now demanded of their workers. This will reinforce companies' needs to develop their own human resource strategies and to operate outside of the national system. Faced with such a scenario it is therefore important to understand what strategies firms are adopting to meet the needs of their new forms of work reorganisation.

TRAINING FOR OCCUPATIONAL OR INTERNAL LABOUR MARKETS?

The case studies examined here have all undertaken some training and cannot be categorised as being amongst those firms who prefer to poach rather than train skilled workers. In the absence of a central training policy either at government or industry level, firms must develop their own training initiatives in order to tackle the problem of skill shortages. The focus of the following section is whether national or firm-level training arrangements facilitate or obstruct the introduction of work organisation programmes analysed here.

In other countries, such as Germany and Japan, the training systems are regarded as contributing towards the higher levels of skills in those countries (Lane, 1989; Meil, 1992; Sako, 1991). In Germany there is an emphasis on occupational-based training which supplies the external labour markets (Marsden and Ryan, 1991). In Japan, the emphasis is on training for internal labour market needs (Sako, 1991). Critics of the British system complain that macro policies appear piecemeal and fail to steer general training policies in either direction (Marsden and Ryan, 1991). In their comparisons of the training systems in Canada and Hong Kong, Ashton *et al.* (1991) echo that criticism and argue that the lesson Britain needs to learn from comparative studies is that there is an urgent need for some coherent policy. In their comparison of initial training in British and German industry Marsden and Ryan (1991) argue that 'occupational markets encourage the mobility of qualified workers amongst employers and work best with a standardized system of vocational qualifications' (1991, p. 252).

Within an occupational market, workers are trained to levels which are accredited and recognised in the labour market. Marsden and Ryan (1991) acknowledge that the internal labour market provides an alternative option to this occupational market but advocate that Britain adopts the latter approach to training for intermediate level skills such as craft or technician skills. We have already examined the difficulties employers face in terms of the problems associated with the inadequacies of occupational markets to supply firms with sufficient numbers of workers with the requisite skills. In the absence of central control over training policies, the market dominated approach means that research into training for skills must inevitably concentrate on what training firms are providing.

Two alternative strategies appear to be emerging. First, those firms introducing horizontal task integration have concentrated on a mixture of internal and external training. The former is aimed at raising the skill levels of operators and the latter at standardising externally certificated training for multi-skilled craft workers.

CASE STUDY 1: TRUCKS

Training at Trucks, for example, tends to be both internal and external. For instance, current trainees undergo a two-year programme involving single skilled training. This programme is validated externally through the gaining of City and Guilds certificates and internally through a large element of on the job training. At craft-level, apprentices undertake a one-year full-time academic course and complete their training by studying for a further two to three years under the EITB segmented scheme. Once they have satisfactorily completed six segments their skilled status is achieved. Technician trainees also complete the same one-year academic course but then undertake a further two years technical training until reaching NVQ 3 or BTEC national level qualifications. The new dual skilled craft grade is currently undergoing internal training programmes. First, a two-week training course is attended in the cross-trade skill. Second, the employee is required to complete a series of tasks in the new skill and maintain a record of these tasks in a log book. Despite this internal training for the new grade, training clearly tends to be organised within the concept of externally recognised qualifications and the training programme for the Multi-Skilled Tradesmen is to be NCVQ validated.

CASE STUDY 2: MEALS

Training for multi-skilling is more advanced at Meals where all craft workers have now completed their multi-skilled training. This consisted of a 22-week college course in either electrical or mechanical skills followed by a further 22 weeks' training on the shopfloor. On completion of this training programme the craft workers were certificated with a company qualification endorsed by the EITB. Like all other employees craft workers are also being trained in product and people safety issues. Again, these course are organised in conjunction with the local college and involve all aspects of hygiene and health and safety at work. These courses are accredited with externally recognised qualifications. Process operators are being similarly trained in people and product safety. In parallel to this training, internal training is arranged when any new technology is installed. The company believes that it is upgrading the skills of its workforce and that this makes its employees more marketable. However, it has not found that it has lost people after multi-skilling. Those people who have left are small in number and have done so to pursue interests created by the course attended and not through poaching. For instance, a small number of people have left to concentrate on jobs with a predominantly electrical content as opposed to the multi-skilled jobs available at the factory.

CASE STUDY 3: COPIERS

At Copiers there is an Open Learning Centre on the site in the training centre. This is fully equipped with computer terminals and easy to follow, distance learning training programmes. Employees are encouraged to use this facility and according to management shopfloor workers use the centre regularly. However, employees are only allowed to use the centre in their own time and this might account for me not seeing anybody there in any of the four visits to the centre. In fact this is a central criticism from the local trade unions in that they feel that workers should be allowed to train in the centre during their working hours and criticise management intransigence on this matter. Despite this facility the majority of training appears to be externally organised with large numbers of people attending the local technical college. There are currently 119 employees attending courses and of these only eight are apprentices. All of these people are encouraged to continue their vocational education up to BTEC Level 3. However, the company acknowledges that some of the older mechanical workers may not feel able to reach this level. These people are then encouraged to undertake City and Guilds courses in electrical installation. The Training Manager at Copiers believes that it is important to consider the needs of the shopfloor workers in respect to the externally validated courses on offer to the final run and test workers who form the majority of those attending the college. He feels that the ability to show some qualifications outweighs any internal training in the eyes of the shopfloor workers when looking for work with another company. Thus, training in these three firms appears to emphasise externally accredited qualifications which recognise the new range of tasks undertaken by their workforces.

CASE STUDY 4: HIGH GEAR

Amongst the cases introducing vertical task integration only High Gear has taken the external training route towards certificated qualifications. This is due to the limited range of higher level tasks delegated to the operators involved and to the fact that training for these tasks is readily available within the national college-based system. All operators were sent on a three week basic engineering course at the local college during the short closure that followed the 1985 agreement. The course was organised along similar lines and with the same subjects as the EITB modules for mechanical engineering apprentices: lathes, drills, milling machines, maths and theory. All operators were also required to attend a half day SPC course and a further half day appreciation of measurement course. A three day, more advanced, course was also attended in order to increase skills learnt on the three week course. All workers who have successfully completed this training have been awarded company certificates which are endorsed by the Welsh Quality Centre. Ongoing training is being undertaken by many workers and the company is prepared to consider payment of up to half the cost of any local college course that it considers would benefit the company.

In contrast, the three remaining firms have concentrated on training for internal labour markets. In particular, at Containers and Lathes, the concept of continuous learning and the absence of distinct training budgets contribute towards a work environment where skill formation is a central part of the production process and not distinct from it. Supplementary enquiries at Sweets, undertaken more recently, suggest that this firm is also attempting to introduce continuous learning processes.

CASE STUDY 5: CONTAINERS

Training at Containers is almost entirely internally organised. In the early stages of recruitment the company concentrated on the recruitment of supervisors. These then spent approximately two months in the US at the parent company's factory receiving basic training. Further visits to the US and to the company's European plants in Germany and Belgium followed this initial training. Once these employees were grounded in the basic skills required for high speed manufacturing they were used to train newer recruits in-house and they have been trained in instructional skills. These people are responsible for instructing workers using the EITB modular system. There is a well equipped portacabin on site which is used frequently but most of the training is carried out on the production lines. Training to technician level can take between six months and two years depending on the level of new recruits' knowledge. All training is specific to the firm's requirements and there is no accreditation of completed training.

CASE STUDY 6: SWEETS

At Sweets the local skills agency was involved in developing the training packages required to upgrade the skills of craft workers and operators. Each task that has been devolved from craft to operator level was subject to detailed consultation with the craft workers and a modular training programme was devised for each new task. A large number of operators and craft workers have undertaken instructional skills courses and now have the responsibility to train other workers. At a higher level, little formal training in programming skills has been given to the electricians. Although courses were available from manufacturers, these were mostly attended by first line managers. Since taking on increasing programming responsibilities, the craft workers have developed these new skills on the job.

CASE STUDY 7: LATHES

According to Lathes, the technology used at the factory and the level of skills required mean that the type of courses available from external agencies were unsuitable. A limited use of external courses consisted of a small number of operators undertaking first line management skill training at the local technical college. The emphasis is on internal training and the most significant proportion of that is hands-on type training. As at Containers, the skilled craft workers from the initial recruitment phase were all sent to the parent company's factories, this time in Japan, for a period of six to nine weeks. On return to Britain these workers were involved in the installation and commissioning of the plant and the completion of the factory building for approximately 12 months. This latter role was primarily a clerk of the works type function ensuring air conditioning, electrical and water supply and controls were installed satisfactorily. During the second phase of recruitment the initial workforce were made team leaders with responsibility for operations, discipline, overtime and general management functions. However, their prime responsibility was to train the new recruits in the skills required and to promote the company culture. Since that time approximately 60 operators have visited Japan to become versed in the new technology and methods of production. They in turn are then used to train other operators.

These case studies suggest that more radical work reorganisation appears to be facilitated by an emphasis on training for internal labour markets. The widespread adoption of such a strategy may have significant consequences for firms' recruitment difficulties. First, firm-specific definitions of skill requirements and the subsequent internal training to meet their requirements may mean that firms choosing to recruit skilled workers from the external labour market will perhaps experience an even greater shortage of these workers available. Second, the absence of recognised certificates identifying levels of training might create difficulties in understanding recruits' training histories.

CONCLUSIONS

The causes of British skill shortages are extensive and deep rooted within institutions, and traditional responses to the problem do not appear to address its sources. In the absence of central policies that adequately seek to reverse the situation, firms may wish to explore the potential for reorganising working practices in order to overcome their skill shortages. Employers are defining their skill requirements in their own terms and seeking their own ways of utilising the skills they have available to them. By distinguishing between horizontal and vertical reorganisation of tasks it has been possible to examine the extent to which those firms adopting the latter strategy have overcome the constraints imposed by the traditional system of training in Britain.

The three firms adopting horizontal task integration have relied on training that is externally validated and/or college-based for the skills required by the new working practices. Amongst the four firms adopting vertical task integration, three of the companies have concentrated on internally-based training which is an integral feature of work. The extent to which these firms have managed to introduce more innovative work reorganisations appears to be a result of this concentration on internally specific training which is ongoing. In contrast to these firms, High Gear has relied on external training of operators in basic engineering skills and quality control procedures. Thus, there appears to be some evidence, although limited, that firms whose system of training is internally organised for firm-specific skills may be able to reorganise working practices along the more innovative lines investigated here.

Transferability of skills is a central feature of the skill shortage phenomenon. If firms adopted both the vertical integration of tasks and internally specific training programmes, they may be able to overcome their skill shortage problems. However, there is presently no vehicle for recognising qualifications of the new skills involved that could facilitate the transfer of workers between firms in the economy as a whole. NVQs, and the more recently introduced GNVQs, are still in their infancy and need more time to mature and become established in the economy. It will be important to examine the extent to which the new system meets the needs of firms reorganising work, or whether more firms will need to develop their own arrangements for the acquisition of skills.

In the meantime, the continual failure of the vocational training system to meet firms' skill needs and the problems inherent in the emerging performance led qualification structure will force firms wishing to adopt vertical restructuring policies to introduce internal human resource development strategies. Despite the challenges posed by vertical restructuring, this policy may provide a successful strategy given the available alternatives.

References

Ashton, D., Green, F. and Hoskins, M. (1989) 'The Training System of British Capitalism: Changes and Prospects', in Green, F. ed. *The Restructuring of the UK Economy*, Hemel Hempstead, Harvester Wheatsheaf.

Ashton, D.N., Maguire, M.J. and Sung, J. (1991) 'Institutional Structures and Provision of Intermediate Level Skills: Lessons from Canada and Hong Kong', in Ryan, P. ed. *International Comparisons of Vocational Education and Training for Intermediate Skills*, London, Falmer Press.

Berger, S. and Piore, M. (1980) *Dualism and Discontinuity in Industrial Societies*, Cambridge, Cambridge University Press.

Bosworth, D.L. and Dutton, P.A. eds (1990) 'Skill Shortages in the 1990s', *International Journal of Manpower*, vol. 11, no. 2/3.

Campbell, A. and Warner, M. (1987) 'New technology, innovation and training: an empirical study of selected British firms', *New Technology, Work and Employment*, vol. 2, no. 2, Autumn, pp. 86–99.

Cassels, J. (1990) *Britain's Real Skill Shortage: and what to do about it*, London, Policy Studies Institute.

CBI (1989a) *Managing the Skills Gap: Report on Skills Training Survey*, London, Confederation of British Industry.

CBI (1989b) *Towards a skills revolution*, Report of the Vocational Education and Training Task Force, London, Confederation of British Industry.

Cohen, S.S. and Zysman, J. (1987) *Manufacturing Matters: The Myth of the Post-Industrial Economy*, New York, Basic Books.

Connor, H., Buchan, J. and Pearson, R. (1989) *The Changing IT Skills Scene: The IT Manpower Monitor*, IMS Report No. 173.

Department of Employment (1984) *The human factor: the supply side problem*, First report from the Information Technology Skills Shortage Committee.

EITB (1989) *British Engineering: Employment, Training and Education*, EITB Industry Profile, Watford, Engineering Industry Training Board.

Financial Times (1989) 'Warning Over Computer Skills Shortage For 1992', *Financial Times*, 3.1.89.

Finegold, D. and Soskice, D. (1988) 'The Failure of Training in Britain: Analysis and Prescription', *Oxford Review of Economic Policy*, vol. 4, no. 3.

Green, A.E. (1990) 'Craft and Technician Skill Shortages in Engineering', in Bosworth and Dutton eds *op. cit.*

Grootings, P., Jones, B. and Scott, P. (1989) 'Mastering Metals – Problems in analysing and classifying "new" technical jobs in metalworking', *Vocational Training*, vol. 3, pp. 11–20.

IFF (1991) *Skill Needs in Britain*, London, IFF Research Limited.

IFF (1992) *Skill Needs in Britain*, London, IFF Research Limited.

IFF (1993) *Skill Needs in Britain*, London, IFF Research Limited.

IRRR (1988) 'The IT skills crisis – looking for a cure', *Industrial Relations Review and Report*, 2.2.1988, pp. 13–14.

IRS (1992) 'NVQs 3. The controversy: more details', *Industrial Relations Services, Recruitment and Development Report*, no. 26, pp. 15–16.

Industrial Society (1988) 'Bridging the skill shortage', *Industrial Society Magazine*, December, pp. 13–23.

Jarvis, V. and Prais, S. (1989) 'Two nations of shopkeepers: training for retailing in France and Britain', *National Institute of Economic Review*, May.

Jones, B. and Scott, P. (1988) 'Occupational Structure and Vocational Training Provision in The Metalworking Industry in the United Kingdom', a report for CEDEFOP project on the *Comparability of Vocational Training Qualifications in European Community Member States*, unpublished, University of Bath.

Keep, E. (1993) 'Hitting the Targets, Missing the Mark?', paper presented to *Towards the Skills Revolution Conference*, University of Huddersfield, 8–9 July.

Kelleher, M., Scott, P. and Jones, B. (1993) 'Resistant to Change? Some Unexplained Omissions in the 1990 Standard Occupational Classification, *Work, Employment and Society*, vol. 7, no. 3, pp. 437–450.

Kelly, J.E. (1982) *Scientific Management, Job Redesign and Work Performance*, London, Academic Press.

Kern, H. and Schumann, M. (1987) 'Limits of the Division of Labour', *Economic and Industrial Democracy*, vol. 8, no. 2, pp. 151–170.

Kusterer, K. (1978) *Know-how on the job: the important working knowledge of 'unskilled' workers*, Boulder CO, Westview Press.

Lane, C. (1989) *Management and Labour in Europe: The Industrial Enterprise in Germany, Britain and France*, Aldershot, Edward Elgar.

Libetta, L. (1989) *Knowledge on the Job: the importance of working knowledge of unskilled workers*, unpublished PhD dissertation, University of Bath.

Locksley, G., Morgan, K. and Thomas, G. (1990) 'Barriers to growth: skills and training in telematics', *New Technology, Work and Employment*, vol. 5, no. 1, pp. 5–17.

Longstreth, F.H. (1986) *The Dynamics of Disintegration of a Keynesian Political Economy: The British case and its implications*, mimeo, University of Bath.

Marsden, D. and Ryan, P. (1991) 'Initial Training, Labour Market Structure and Public Policy: Intermediate Skills in Britain and German Industry', in Ryan, P. ed. *International Comparisons of Vocational Education and Training for Intermediate Skills*, London, Falmer Press.

Mason, G. (1988) *Occupational Profile: Trends in Employment and Training of Craftsmen and Craftswomen in the Engineering Industry*, Watford, EITB.

Massey, D. (1988) 'What's happening to UK manufacturing?', in Allen, J. and Massey, D. eds *Restructuring Britain: The Economy In Question*, London, Sage.

Mayes, D.G. (1987) 'Does Manufacturing Matter?', *National Institute For Economic Research*, no. 122, pp. 47–58.

Meil P. (1992) 'Stranger in Paradise – An American's Perspective on German Industrial Sociology', in Altmann, N., Koehler, C. and Meil, P. eds *Technology And Work In German Industry*, London, Routledge.

Peck, J. and Emmerich, M. (1990) *Challenging the TECs*, Manchester, Centre for Local Economic Strategies.

Phillimore, A.J. (1989) 'Flexible specialisation, work organisation and skills: approaching the "second industrial divide"', *New Technology, Work and Employment*, vol. 4, no. 2, Autumn, pp. 79–91.

Piore, M. and Sabel, C. (1984) *The Second Industrial Divide: Possibilities for Prosperity*, New York, Basic Books.

Prais, S.J. (1989) 'Qualified Manpower in Engineering: Britain and other industrially advanced countries', *National Institute Economic Review*, no. 127, pp. 76–83.

Prais, S.J. (1991) 'Vocational Qualifications in Britain and Europe: theory and practice', *National Institute Economic Review*, May.

Rainbird, H. (1990) *Training Matters*, Oxford, Blackwell.

Sako, M. (1991) 'Institutional Aspects of Youth Employment and Training Policy: A Comment on Marsden and Ryan', *British Journal of Industrial Relations*, vol. 29, no. 3, pp. 485–90.

Scott, P., Bolton, B., Bramley, A. and Jones, B. (1992) 'The Utilisation and Training of Graduate Engineers and Technicians: The View of Group-level Recruitment and Training Personnel in Case Study Companies', TEST Project, *Working Paper no. 2*, mimeo, University of Bath.

Senker, P. (1989) 'Technical change, work organisation and training: some issues relating to the role of market forces', *New Technology, Work and Employment*, vol. 4, no. 1, Spring, 46–53.

Sheldrake, R. and Vickerstaff, S. (1987) *The History of Industrial Training in Britain*, Aldershot, Gower.

Smithers, A. (1994) *All Our Futures*, London, Channel Four Publications.

Streek, W. (1989) 'Skills and the Limits of Neo-Liberalism: The Enterprise of the Future as a Place of Learning', *Work Employment and Society*, vol. 3, no. 1, pp. 89–104.

Training Agency (1989) *Labour Market and Skill Trends 1990/91 Operational Year*, Sheffield, Training Agency.

Virgo, P. (1987) *The IT Skills Crisis: A Prescription For Action*, Manchester, National Computing Centre.

Warner, M. (1986) 'Technology, Skills and Training in Microelectronics', *Employee Relations*, vol. 8, no. 6, 23–6.

8

Managing Diversity and HRD

Elisabeth Wilson

INTRODUCTION

This chapter re-evaluates the equal opportunities, EO, paradigm by comparing it with the emerging paradigm of managing diversity, MD. After discussing the conceptual differences between these two paradigms, associated HRD strategies and interventions are examined. In particular the chapter argues that there needs to be a shift from HRD strategies focused on entry to the organisation to those supporting promotion and career development. Good practice is addressed through looking at a case study example of an organisation in transition, and by discussing the wider implications for practice. The chapter analyses the strategic HRD implications of the 'managing diversity paradigm' which is becoming more important and more relevant. Further questions for research and practice are suggested.

THE OLD AND NEW PARADIGMS

The difference between the old paradigm of EO and the new paradigm of MD is summarised in Table 8.1, and discussed below. Both paradigms can be related to their historical and social context which is discussed in Iles (1995). I am discussing EO and MD as 'ideal types' to illustrate the paradigmatic shift. In reality, organisations will be more varied and more mixed than the table indicates, and many organisations do not espouse the EO paradigm.

Table 8.1   Equal Opportunities and Managing Diversity compared

The old paradigm Equal Opportunities	The new paradigm Managing Diversity
Externally driven	Internally driven
Operational	Strategic
Diversity perceived as a liability	Diversity perceived as an asset
Group focused	Individual focused
Concerned minimally with process in EO	Concerned with outcomes in EO
Perceive EO costs money	Accept 'business case' for embracing diversity
Supported by narrow positivist knowledge base	Supported by wider pluralistic knowledge base

The driving force for EO is usually external, and varies between a narrow minimalist response to legislative requirements, and a wider concern that people should be treated equally. It starts from a model of the organisation as given and assumes that individuals from diverse and disadvantaged groups should be enabled to fit the existing organisation. This has been described as the 'assimilation' model (Hollister *et al.*, 1993). Managing diversity, on the other hand is internally driven, from a sense of commitment by the organisation and its key players. This distinction between externally and internally driven may at first seem spurious. As a concept MD is more widely used and accepted in North America, particularly the US (see for instance Galagan, 1991; Harisis and Kleiner, 1993; Griffith, 1994) where there has been recognition that the majority of people in the workforce, and indeed the majority of customers, will soon be from traditionally disadvantaged groups, principally women and what are known in the US as (ethnic) minorities. Although a move to accepting diversity in North America is prompted by external demographic changes, once the import of the necessary change is understood and the 'business case' accepted, it has become internalised by individuals and gradually absorbed into the value system of the organisational culture; conceptual changes about the nature of the organisation follow. Equal opportunities by contrast remains an add-on to the value system.

It follows that EO tends to be perceived as an operational issue, perhaps something which is of concern to the personnel department or those who recruit staff, but not as an issue which impinges fundamentally on the organisation. These differences are similar to those discussed by Cockburn (1989) which she characterises as the 'short' and 'long' agenda for EO. Underlying the EO paradigm is the model of the organisation as a rational, even-handed structure, operating fairly and dispensing justice; EO neither changes nor seriously impinges on this model. On the other hand, MD is embraced as a strategic issue, essential for the economic and competitive success of the organisation, and a strategic approach is considered necessary for implementation (Iles *et al.*, 1994). Its values are taken on by top management and become embedded within the organisational culture, and it is translated into policies, plans and accountabilities. Whereas the EO paradigm perceives difference as a liability, the MD paradigm perceives it as an asset (Benest, 1991). Thus the EO paradigm is buttressed by strong but unacknowledged white, male, ethnocentric, ablist, ageist and heterosexist assumptions. Equal opportunities is concerned with helping individuals fit in to the white, male able-bodied norm, and people who are different are seen as problematical. This tendency to compare everything with the male norm has been characterised by Spender (1986), writing about men and women, as 'male' and 'minus male'. With reference to race this would be translated as 'white' and 'non-white'; indeed these terms have been used unproblematically until quite recently. Managing diversity on the other hand embraces differences which are visible such as colour, gender, ethnic origin, dis/ability, and age, and also those which are not immediately visible such as class, sexuality, and work style; these are sometimes referred to as primary and secondary grounds for discrimination. Embracing diversity can go further than these differences; Herriot and Pemberton (1995) point to the different frameworks of knowledge and understanding which people from diverse backgrounds bring to the workplace. Within the MD paradigm people who are in some way different are seen as potentially enriching to the organisation. The belief system of EO is supported by the stereotyping of those perceived as coming from unconventional groups, whereas the belief system of MD is supported by an acceptance of people as individuals and therefore necessarily unique. It could, however, be argued that a shift to MD could lead to a loss of focus on disadvantaged individuals which has been provided by EO.

The EO paradigm tends to focus on a narrow range of groups; many companies limit their concerns to those groups substantially protected by law, which in the UK are women and members of different racial groups, and to a lesser extent people with disabilities, and adopt a group approach to their treatment. This would be respectively positive action in the UK and affirmative action in the US (although these are not legally equivalent). This may be seen as preferential treatment (Galagan, 1991). Opportunity 2000, the UK government-backed initiative to increase the quantity and quality of women's representation in the workforce is often perceived as narrowly directed towards women in management. It is an example of just one such group approach, and has been criticised for its narrow focus. For example the BBC, which is committed to Opportunity 2000, is making progress in appointing more women to managerial posts and has committed itself to a wide ranging charter (Guardian, 1993a) but at the same time was criticised by one of its long standing members of staff, Mark Tully, for the lack of EO for those cleaning staff and commissionaires whose jobs have been contracted out (Guardian, 1993b). Similar criticism could be made of the NHS which is committed to Opportunity 2000 and to a programme of action on ethnic minority staff in the NHS (Equal Opportunities Review, 1994b), at the same time as shedding staff to lower paid jobs via compulsory competitive tendering. A further example of the group approach is a new venture called Race for Opportunity, to promote race as a business issue, which has been launched by Business in the Community (Thatcher, 1995). In contrast to these initiatives, MD does not rely on positive or affirmative action (Kandola and Fullerton, 1994), as it rejects a group approach in favour of developing all individuals. However, it could be questioned as a result of this whether the impact of initiatives may be diluted. Efforts could be spread too widely and thinly.

One of the reasons that diversity may be an easier concept to work with is the multiplicity of groups which may be included in EO policies. This can be seen in Table 8.2.

Table 8.2   List for possible inclusion in Equal Opportunity policy

Women
Ethnic minorities
People with physical disabilities
People with learning disabilities
People with mental health problems
Ex-offenders
Older people
Sexual orientation
Caring responsibilities
Class
People with HIV/AIDS
Political affiliation
Religious affiliation
Employment status
? Regionalism
? Appearance
? Accent

By contrast the MD paradigm looks at individual contributions, and how the organisation can enable and maximise these. To summarise, the EO paradigm is trying to right a wrong for identified groups, whereas the MD paradigm is trying to get it right for everyone. It can be argued that the EO paradigm is a deficit model, whereas the MD paradigm is a model of plenty, even profusion. The counter argument is that the equality focus of EO with its emphasis on rights may be preferable to the developmental focus of MD.

Organisations operating with the EO paradigm translate it into organisational policies which are concerned, often minimally, with process – whether they have acted (or in some cases been seen to have acted) in the right way. Thus they may meet their legal obligations but little more. In contrast, organisations committed to MD are concerned with outcomes, that is with whether policies have worked. They want to know that there has been effective implementation. Equal opportunities organisations tend to perceive organisational practices flowing from their paradigm as a cost, whereas MD organisations accept the 'business case' for embracing diversity and perceive consequent organisational practices as an investment.

Organisations supporting the EO paradigm unthinkingly accept the recruitment of clones. They are insensitive to cultural differences and deny sexuality within organisations. Where they acknowledge the existence of racial and sexual harassment they perceive it as trivial, individually-based conflict. Equal opportunities may exist only if you can meet their exacting requirements (Maddock and Parkin, 1993). Compensation and benefits packages are uniform. By contrast, organisations accepting the MD paradigm accept the moral and business case for recruiting diversely (see Jamieson and O'Mara, 1991), accept the existence of sexuality within organisations (Hearn et al., 1989), and are sensitive to cultural differences. Sexual and racial harassment are acknowledged as caused by the organisational climate, and where they occur are a disciplinary offence. 'Family friendly' or even better 'employee friendly' policies acknowledge employees' caring responsibilities, and there may be a 'cafeteria' of compensation and benefits packages.

The EO paradigm is supported by a narrow positivist knowledge base. As mentioned above the organisation is perceived as a rational, equitable system. Management theory, whether learned on the job or from wider sources, assumes a white male ethnocentric model. Most management theories have been built on this, using restricted samples from which generalisations about the general behaviour of human beings have been extrapolated (Hofstede, 1980). Tanton (1994) states:

'the production of knowledge is always bound up with historically specific regimes of power and, therefore, every society produces its own truths which have a normalizing and regulatory function.' (pp. 22–3)

This social constructionist view is supported by Swan (1994) and Martin (1994) who states that:

'organisational racism and sexism are embedded by management thinking and behaviour, and reinforced by management and organization theory.' (p. 111)

Within the EO paradigm there is a privileging of the received management discourse described by Martin (1994). An example of this in the UK is the Management Charter

Initiative competence model, which has been critiqued for its over-narrow, rationalistic, and gender blind model of management (e.g. Wilson, 1993). Hofstede (1980) has pointed out that differences in national culture may inhibit the application of theories developed within other national cultures, which casts serious doubt on the application of one bank of theories for a diverse population. In contrast, the MD paradigm is supported by a wider, pluralistic knowledge base. It accepts that human beings vary greatly and that cure-all theories are insufficient and misleading. The organisation is more likely to be perceived as a place where emotion and reason co-exist, and where there is a pluralistic alliance of different interest groups. No one discourse is therefore privileged over another (Fine, 1991). Martin (1994) discusses the competing discourses on equality – as objective and as outcome. These are similar to the discourses identified here as EO and as MD.

Just as it accepts a wider knowledge base, so the MD paradigm does not spring from one philosophical root. Some people and organisations are persuaded by the moral arguments, and others increasingly by the business case. Although the business case means MD can much more easily and justifiably be embodied into the corporate aims of the business, resting principally on this foundation makes the MD paradigm vulnerable to a change in perspective, should it be perceived that a diverse workforce does not contribute to the bottom line. Perhaps there is still a case for both moral and business arguments be deployed, as is the case in the Littlewoods group of companies. The MD paradigm recognises that a more diverse workforce may be more creative and more representative of its customers. It should be noted, however, that although the word 'diversity' is widely used within the US literature, the bulk of much discussion centres around the two main groups identified by demographic trends and the subject of enforcement action, women and (ethnic) minorities (Cox, 1994). Cox (1994) warns against the use of the term diversity solely to refer to minority groups, as that will alienate others, and asserts that it should be used to refer to the total workforce. Restricting it to these groups could also lead to the pejoration of the word, which is described in relation to words associated with women (Spender, 1986).

Although the discussion above has presented EO and MD somewhat simplistically as a series of bipolar constructs, the situation in reality is more complex. Many organisations in the UK have barely comprehended the EO paradigm, and few organisations could be said to be operating under the banner of diversity (Dodds, 1995). Jackson *et al.* (1992), based on US experience, offer a useful model of the stages an organisation may go through: first, the exclusionary organisation which is devoted to maintaining existing dominance by one group; second, the club which maintains the dominant group but allows one or two acceptable tokens from minority groups; third, the compliance organisation which seeks to provide access to the organisation without disturbing the status quo, with most minority group members remaining at the bottom; fourth, the affirmative action organisation concerned to tackle racism and sexism, and supporting this with HRD initiatives and changes to promotional practices; fifth, the redefining organisation which is in transit, starting to move towards an acceptance of diversity as a positive benefit in itself; and lastly, the multi-cultural which is the fully diverse organisation and reflects this in its employees, policies, mission and anti-oppressive stance.

Again, we can see that language associations mean this model cannot be translated directly into the UK and EU context. Affirmative action is akin to the EO paradigm, but the different legal basis of US legislation, with provision for class actions and quotas, means that the concepts are not directly comparable. Equal opportunities organisations are probably closer to Jackson *et al.*'s (1992) compliance model. Similarly, 'multi-cultural' has associations in the UK with well meant but limited initiatives within school-based education, now largely discredited; the central criticism of this type of approach to EO as evidenced in the UK was the neglect of issues of power. This criticism could also be levelled at MD, and is the central issue raised by Cockburn (1989) in her description of the 'short' and the 'long' agenda of EO.

WHY CHANGE?

There are several compelling reasons for change. For those persuaded by the moral arguments, the old paradigm of EO has not worked. This is evidenced for example by continuing extensive horizontal and vertical stratification of the workforce by gender (Davidson and Cooper, 1992). A further example is that despite London being now the most cosmopolitan city in the world there are persistently higher rates of unemployment among ethnic minorities: 35% of Bangladeshis, 29.6% of black Africans, and 12.5% of Chinese as compared with 10% among whites (Travis, 1994). So the moral case for EO has not been won.

The enormity of a change of perspective should not be under-estimated. Cockburn (1989) asserts that EO is fundamentally concerned with power. In her study of 'High Street Retail' looking at gender, she identified a number of institutional mechanisms which appeared to serve the reproduction of power in male hands which included: an autonomous approach to the labour market; the way loci of power can shift just as women reach them; and the juxtaposition of male bonding activities with a concomitant hostility to female networking.

Moreover, some of the practices of EO, like women-only management training, had serious deficits as stand-alone policies. Gray (1994) outlines the tensions that women-only training generated: between helping women adapt, and making them responsible for changing gender relations at work, between acceptance by the host organisation and effectiveness, and between creating a supportive environment and recognising differences and competition between women. To this can be added the discontinuity between what can be achieved on such courses and the 'obdurate' organisational climate to which women managers return (Knight and Pritchard, 1994, p. 60). Not only are the chances of change slim, but such programmes unsupported by wider initiatives risk a (white male) majority backlash. Similar arguments can be marshalled against training programmes for ethnic minorities.

A more compelling argument for change is the business case, which has been taken on by large US-based corporations like Digital and Proctor and Gamble (Harisis and Kleiner, 1993). They accept that the potential benefits to the organisation in terms of creativity and better decision making (Maznevski, 1994), and being closer to their customer base far outweigh perceived problems (Griffith, 1994). Lafasto described the reasons Baxter health corporation changed to valuing diversity as including not only a response to demographic pressures, but also the need to maintain competitive edge (Jackson *et al.*, 1992). In contrast, the potential loss of talent to organisations in the UK can be seen from the fact that despite their higher unemployment rates both the black African and Chinese populations have a higher average level of educational attainment than the white population (Travis, 1994). Demographic changes mean that there will be fewer young people entering the workforce, but a higher proportion of these will gain post-18 qualifications, as one third of UK 18-year-olds are now entering higher education. The significant area of growth will be women re-entering the workforce. It is anticipated that women will form 45.3 per cent of the workforce by 2000 (Kandola and Fullerton, 1994).

In the British Institute of Management survey women managers were found to have higher educational qualifications at comparable positions than male managers (Alban-Metcalfe and West, 1991), which begs a question about the waste of female ability amongst those not appointed as managers. The thrust of the business case underpinned Opportunity 2000 and has now been taken up by the Commission for Racial Equality, CRE, in launching in 1995 a new benchmarking standard for employers 'Racial Equality means Business' (MacLachlan, 1995). The EOC is also advocating the business case for sexual equality and family friendly policies (Equal Opportunities Review, 1994c).

In a survey of UK organisations undertaken by Kandola and Fullerton (1994) good business sense was cited as the most common reason for changing to a MD approach, followed by legislation, senior management attitudes and good practice. Developing the potential of individuals, and moral reasons were eighth and twelfth respectively in this list of reasons for change (Kandola and Fullerton, 1994). The CRE's report 'Large Companies and Racial Equality' published in January 1995 found good personnel practice the most compelling reason for change, in order to attract and retain the best people (MacLachlan, 1995). Other reasons in this latter study were to observe the CRE's code of practice and to widen the recruitment pool; and these were followed by other business reasons (MacLachlan, 1995). Dodds (1995) in a qualitative study of 14 large UK companies identified seven as 'diversity' organisations, all of which perceived MD as a strategic business issue.

A further change which must be managed by organisations is the move to what is euphemistically referred to as downsizing or delayering, the shrinking and removal of managerial positions. With the pyramid of higher management no longer there for many, new concepts of success are required built around wider notions of job satisfaction rather than linear progress which depended for its accomplishment on there being others less successful.

The crucial question is whether commitment to MD produces the results promised by the business case. Kandola and Fullerton (1994) evaluate the perceived benefits of MD, dividing these into proven, debatable and indirect. In the first group of proven benefits they include access to talent and enhancing organisational flexibility. They regard as debatable the arguments about promoting team creativity, problem solving and decision making, as well as improving customer service and quality. Lastly they perceive indirect benefits as those which are thought to accrue when both proven and debatable benefits have been achieved. This last group includes more satisfying work environments, improving morale and inter-group relations, greater productivity and competitiveness, and an enhanced public image (Kandola and Fullerton, 1994).

Kandola and Fullerton (1994) propose a 'strategy web' for MD which encompasses organisational vision, top management commitment, audits and assessment of needs, clarity of objectives, clear accountability, effective communication, co-ordination of activity and evaluation. Moving from the strategic to the operational, Jamieson and O'Mara (1991) suggest that there are four tasks to be accomplished to manage diversity successfully: first, attracting and retaining competent employees with a slower growing labour force; second, motivating all employees; third, rewarding employees; and fourth, supporting employees in ways which recognise their individuality. This chapter will next look at how HRD strategies and practices can help in this process.

A SHIFT IN HRD FOCUS

Until recently most organisations concerned to promote EO have concentrated on ensuring entry to the organisation, to enable the demographic spread of the workforce to reflect that of the surrounding population. Thus much HRD effort has focused on training for those involved in recruitment and selection to ensure processes are carried out in line with policy; it is quite common for such training to be compulsory in the UK public sector. Some of this effort has been successful. Achieving entry to organisations is, however, only the first step, and a cursory glance at many organisations reveals a preponderance of disadvantaged groups clustered at the bottom of the organisational hierarchy. For instance in the UK civil service 5.3% of staff were from ethnic minorities in April 1993, which compared favourably with the benchmark of 4.9% in the labour market as a whole (Equal Opportunity Review, 1994a). This appears less favourable when ethnic minority representation at higher levels is examined. Only 2.1% of civil service grade 7 and above are ethnic minority, although representation was reported as increasing (Equal Opportunity Review, 1994a). The same picture may be seen in other organisations and indicates the need for a shift in HRM and HRD programmes to those which encourage progression, and a focus on career development and skills enhancement.

In the flatter organisations of the future, career advancement will not be available for everyone so, paradoxically, a parallel shift in focus is required if the organisation is to continue to utilise the skills of those managers who can no longer be promoted in such organisations. Herriot and Pemberton (1995) point out that many organisations have accepted the structural necessity of a flatter hierarchy, but have then viewed plateaued managers as problematic and less capable, rather than as experienced employees who still have something to offer.

HRD STRATEGIES AND INTERVENTIONS

It is helpful to look at the current range of HRD interventions to promote diversity within the UK. In their survey of both HRM and HRD interventions for MD in 285 organisations, Kandola and Fullerton (1994) found that fair selection training for recruiters was the fourth most frequent intervention, implemented by 74% of organisations, following HRM interventions. However, when ratings for success were requested this training ranked only tenth equal, judged successful by 54% of organisations. Training trainers in EO was considered more successful, by 61% of organisations. Human resource management initiatives were generally ranked as more successful than the HRD interventions examined by this research (Kandola and Fullerton, 1994). What HRD practices are chosen next must depend on the particular context of the organisation.

If it is accepted that EO solutions can no longer be applied to stereotypical disadvantaged groups, but that rather there should be an approach which values all individuals, then this philosophy should also apply to the individual company and there should be a tailor-made approach to MD which answers that organisation's particular needs. Morrison (1992), reporting on a survey of diversity practices, states that there are interventions which work in some organisations but not in others. She advises that any interventions are preceded by research into precisely what the needs of the employees are, and that this should be undertaken by a representative team which includes white males to avoid backlash (Morrison, 1992).

Most interventions will come into one of four groups:

- a general change of values and culture, which reaches out to individual attitudes;
- individual career development for all employees;
- special support which enables disadvantaged groups and individuals but is not targeted solely at them;
- managerial skills for a diverse workforce.

First, a general change of values and culture must start at the meta level, that is, at the higher level at which ideas are conceptualised. This demands a change of discourse, so that HRD interventions are no longer about compensatory or special treatment of disadvantaged groups, but rather about the whole development of all individuals within the organisation. If the organisation is to reap the benefits of its diverse workforce, then it follows that individuals must be developed beyond their current job roles and responsibilities. It must be clearly seen to be led from the top (Bartz *et al.*, 1990; Morrison, 1992; Kandola and Fullerton, 1994, Hammond and Holton, 1991), and may involve some organisational development work. Stand-alone programmes are likely to be insufficient for the degree of change which is required (Griffith, 1994). The Investors in People, IIP, initiative in the UK is a race- and gender-neutral peg upon which organisations could hang a change of strategy; IIP requires employers (among other actions) to formulate, implement and evaluate personal development plans for all employees. In learning to value diversity employees may be offered experiential training, including role play (Jamieson and O'Mara, 1991; Griffith, 1994), so that they can understand others' individuality and cast aside unhelpful stereotyping. There are helpful videos (e.g. Fant, 1980) which help employees understand the experience of difference. This attitudinal training should start in the induction period. Training in communication may have a role in promoting a change in strategy (Kandola and Fullerton, 1994).

Second is the identification and implementation of individual developmental needs and career aspirations (Bartz *et al.*, 1990; Harisis and Kleiner, 1993). For all employees this must start from a training need analysis, coupled with an analysis of current and future skill needs, at the individual, job, team and organisational level. Selection systems and processes should be transparent; when selecting for development or promotion, care should be taken with the use of assessment centre techniques, group exercises, psychometric tests, and appraisal systems (Alimo-Metcalfe, 1994). All of these have potential for bias (see for example, Industrial Relations Review and Report, 1990, for a report on bias in psychometric tests). The UK National Vocational Qualification, NVQ, model of crediting competence for skills developed could be taken on board for assessing potential for promotion and this can include skills developed outside the workplace. Individual help for registered disabled people in the workplace can be given by the Department of Employment, which includes not only the provision of specialised equipment but also training in its use. Career advice to women and associated development placements should take note that some experiences may be valued more than others as preparation for management positions, for instance line experience tends to be valued more than staff (Davidson and Cooper, 1992). It should be noted that women tend to be given less challenging assignments than men (Spencer Stuart, 1993). Formal mentoring programmes are another way of developing individuals, but care needs to be taken both over the allocation of cross-gender mentors and also that such a scheme is not seen as exclusive.

Third, despite what has been stated about an approach which does not privilege one group above another, there will still in some organisations be a need for special support for disadvantaged groups and individuals. Collectively this could take the form of networking or support groups (Harisis and Kleiner, 1993), or special training under the provisions of the Race Relations and Sex Discrimination Acts. Thomas (1990) suggests the 'social consideration' test should be applied to any special intervention: if the policy, programme or principle gives special consideration to one group then he asserts this runs counter to MD. This view is perhaps supported by Kandola and Fullerton's (1994) findings that among the least successful MD initiatives were access training for under-represented groups and providing skills updating for those returning to the workplace, although it should also be noted that these were among the least frequently used interventions. I suggest companies consider Thomas' (1990) test, but do not automatically reject special support measures. One way round this is for companies which perceive a need in a particular group to tailor compensatory training or development to their needs, but make it open to all. An example of this occurred recently in the NHS. As part of its commitment to Opportunity 2000 the NHS wished to encourage more women to take up management posts. During 1993 the NHS Management Executive advertised 'Career development opportunities for nurses, midwives, health visitors and PAMs' (PAMs are the professions supplementary to medicine). Successful applicants were offered bursaries for management training at Masters level. Although administered by the Womens Unit of the NHS, advertisements stressed that applications were welcome from all staff (Guardian 2, 1993). The target professional groups were, however, overwhelmingly women, so it is likely that the majority of beneficiaries would be women.

Last, I turn to managerial skills for a diverse workforce. The potentially beneficial outcomes of a more diverse workforce do not come automatically. Kandola and Fullerton (1994) emphasise that the skills needed for MD are those generally identified as necessary for managing well in any case; MD competence in interpersonal and communication skills is the same as general competence. They therefore suggest that the *managing* rather than the diversity is emphasised (Kandola and Fullerton, 1994). Galagan (1991) suggests that as well as communication, skill development should also involve negotiation. So that they can help develop individuals, managers will need help and support to recognise individual learning styles, and develop coaching and delegating skills.

Running a team successfully can be more challenging for the manager. Whilst more diverse groups can be more creative, they may also be more difficult to manage, may need more time to accomplish tasks and may have more interpersonal conflict (Griffith, 1994). Managers will also need special understanding of the way diversity can complicate decision making and how good decision making in groups might best be fostered (Maznevski, 1994). Herriot and Pemberton (1995) identify that one of the ways in which successful managers obtain and act on information is that they make a point of talking to people who are different from each other, and different from themselves. Looking in particular at diversity within team composition, Herriot and Pemberton (1995) question the validity of Belbin's model of team roles, which was based on simulation exercises, and suggest instead that the personality types established by Myers-Briggs are more helpful in understanding how teams accomplish tasks. They counter the prevailing view that relationships and processes are paramount in group functions, and suggest that successful teams need to question assumptions and manage contextual boundaries successfully, proposing a recipe for successful task accomplishment which depends on acknowledging the assumptions which ride on both visible and less visible differences (Herriot and Pemberton, 1995). They emphasise that just putting together a group of diverse people will not on its own ensure success or creativity (Herriot and Pemberton, 1995). Indeed negative behaviour can be seen, such as the domination of the group by those with formal authority, defensive sub-groups formed by those who perceive themselves as different, and irritation for those used to working in same type teams where decisions were made more quickly (Herriot and Pemberton, 1995). Fine (1991) also reports that decision making can potentially be better, but may also be more fraught with difficulty. One way of countering this is reported by Dodds (1995); he found that two 'high diversity' organisations in his study undertook the training of facilitators for project teams.

CHALLENGES TO TRAINERS

There are two respects in which trainers will have to reconsider learning events, which inevitably overlap: one is concerned with a new range of content, diversity awareness or diversity training; the other reminds us of Marshall McLuhan's dictum 'the medium is the message', in that it is concerned with how to train in a way which in itself acknowledges and enables diversity.

In the US where diversity awareness training is more established, Thomas (1994) outlines some of the common ways in which organisations approach diversity training, first gaining top management commitment and then undertaking a cultural audit, possibly via attitude surveys and focus groups. There are many injunctions about how to run good diversity awareness training. Thomas (1994) warns against presenting diversity as a 'soft' HR issue, when the decision to commit the organisation to this path has been taken on business grounds. He asserts that diversity training in the short term should be about changing behaviour, not attitudes, although the latter may form one of the longer-term aims (Thomas, 1994). Particular problems which may arise from participants include a learned reticence by middle managers, and a general unease by many participants around discussions of sexual orientation (Thomas, 1994). Thomas (1994) considers that women are more likely to open up in mixed group discussions, which may cause men to withdraw. This observation appears to run counter to other research demonstrating the dominance of men in mixed groups (Alimo-Metcalfe, 1993), and cultural perceptions which judge a woman as dominating the conversation when she speaks for half the time (Spender, 1986). Thomas (1994) advises against discussing current affairs, as the discussion can become 'political'. This appears to foster the notion of a divorce between the organisational and political realms, which would be questioned by many feminist theorists. On the other hand, Karp and Sutton (1993) emphasise that there should be a time orientation on the present, rather than spending too much time lamenting the past and fantasising about the future.

Karp and Sutton (1993) identify other common faults in diversity training as: over-emphasis on sensitising the white male manager whilst promulgating a specific series of values; and guilt-driven training combined with an over-sensitiveness to language. They assert that these features add up to a 'deeply flawed approach' (*ibid*. p. 30). Hollister *et al*. (1993) critique existing MD training programmes and conclude that unless the predominant white male managerial culture is prepared to re-examine its values and re-assess and change organisational processes, these programmes will fail. Positive approaches to diversity training include clarity about the objectives and a focused approach avoiding covering too many issues at once (Thomas, 1994).

Williams and Green (1994) offer detailed advice to trainers on how to take cultural diversity into account in designing and delivering training events, and go beyond the visible differences in discussing this. They point out that a mismatch between a learner's culture at work and the culture of the trainer can lead to ineffective learning and transfer and to a longer-term loss of credibility. Ignoring cultural issues may lead to a reinforcement of stereotyping, intolerance within the group, misunderstandings and frustrations, criticism and attacks, and learners and trainers switching off. Williams and Green (1994) look at culture in relation to the national culture and also in relation to organisational cultures and sub-cultures. They advise trainers to assess their own culture and that of learners, and suggest that there are advantages and disadvantages in the two cultures being close or distant from each other. If cultures are close, it is easier for trainers and participants to identify with each other, but easier to collude and more difficult to challenge assumptions; conversely, if cultures are too different it is easier to challenge, but harder to understand and empathise with participants (Williams and Green, 1994).

Building on Hofstede's (1980) work, Williams and Green (1994) look at the dimensions he identified as significant differences between national cultures. They make particularly apposite comments in relation to two of Hofstede's (1980) dimensions, power distance and uncertainty avoidance. Hofstede identified power distance as relating to the inequalities of life, which in an organisational context could be translated into the degree of distance perceived as proper between manager and subordinate, or trainer and participant (Williams and Green, 1994). A learner from a high power distance culture would be more likely to perceive the trainer as an expert, whereas a learner from a low power distance culture would expect a facilitating and enabling approach. They conclude therefore that self-managed learning is only likely to succeed in a low power distance culture. Learners from a high power distance culture may have difficulties with transfer to the workplace, as their managers are less likely to accept new ideas and methods (Williams and Green, 1994).

Hofstede's (1980) second dimension was uncertainty avoidance, the extent to which someone tries to avoid uncertainty. Williams and Green (1994) point out that this has implications for the degree of uncertainty both trainers and learners can tolerate within a training event. Those learners who have a low tolerance for uncertainty may dislike role play; conversely, forward planning of implementation and rehearsing how their behaviour may change on return to the workplace may be particularly helpful to them. Hofstede's third dimension was masculinity/femininity, the degree to which male and female are perceived as very different, or reasonably similar. As with the other dimensions discussed this differs between national cultures. This reminds the trainer that assumptions about male–female differences are predicated on cultural background.

Although there is a strong case for trainers in particular, whether internal or external, to be representative of the diverse workforce (Pemberton, 1992), Karp and Sutton (1993) warn against choosing trainers only from women or ethnic minorities, who thus cannot empathise with white male participants. Members of minority and disadvantaged groups should not be expected to contribute to an 'expert' role in addition to their day-to-day responsibilities. If recruited into mainstream posts, that is their prime responsibility. To expect employees from under-represented groups to undertake special extra tasks in terms of contributing to courses, taking on mentoring, and serving on MD task forces and committees is an abuse of their position by the organisation. The minority or female manager who tries to undertake extra tasks without extra training, payment, and often recognition, is using time and effort which should be directed to their mainstream responsibilities. Lack of suitable expertise is a company, not an individual, problem, and in the HRD field should be tackled by recruiting more trainers or retraining existing trainers and facilitators.

At the micro level, so that trainers model what they want others to achieve, a check should be made on all training materials to eliminate bias and language pejorative to particular groups (Mandell and Kohler-Gray, 1990). Competence models which underlie management development, for instance, should be bias free (Mandell and Kohler-Gray, 1990; Wilson, 1993).

Morrison (1992) suggests that diversity interventions cannot be once and for all. There must be regular evaluation, coupled with further research, and organisations must be prepared to be flexible in their approach to development as in everything else (Morrison, 1992).

HRM SUPPORT

The main thrust of MD is probably via HRM initiatives such as ensuring that recruitment, selection and promotion policies are in place and implemented, and that there is accountability for these processes. For MD to succeed, a strategic approach demands the integration of both HRM and HRD interventions. This section will, however, look at those HRM processes which specifically support HRD.

HRD can be strengthened by HRM policies which include programmes which support training such as creches and flexitime, and can ensure that part-timers, job sharers and shift workers get equal access to training and development opportunities. With increasing emphasis from the EU on the rights of part-time workers, and reference in the Sex

Discrimination Act to training, it may be construed as unlawful not to ensure that part-timers have the same developmental opportunities as full-timers. The organisation can institute policies which recognise the balance between home and work (Jamieson and O'Mara, 1991) and attend to personal needs (Bartz *et al.*, 1990), which will ensure access to training and development by those with family responsibilities.

Managers' accountabilities should include MD targets, and as HRD initiatives encourage them to move towards a more people orientated style of management, reward systems should be adjusted. Task assignment can include consideration of the development possibilities for the individual concerned so that job enrichment and job rotation are purposeful and also available to all, and team work can be encouraged (Jamieson and O'Mara, 1991). The ground rules and standards for success should be opaque and well known (Harisis and Kleiner, 1993). Monitoring and evaluation of HRM and HRD should go hand in hand.

Particular attention should be paid to the effect of the current economic climate on HRD and HRM initiatives. For instance Manchester City Council found that their no redundancy agreement with the Trade Unions worked counter to their EO intentions (Corby, 1992) despite a good record on special leave for carers, job share, positive action training for disadvantaged groups and £200 000 set aside for adaptations and aids for disabled employees. Galagan (1991) found that redundancy programmes could lead to a more homogeneous workforce.

CASE STUDY: BRADFORD COUNCIL

The City of Bradford Metropolitan Council in Yorkshire has a significant ethnic minority population, 15.6% in 1993, principally Asian (City of Bradford, undated). This is a younger and growing population compared with the general population and the largest group are Muslim. It was a response to this which first prompted the Council to develop an EO strategy. Despite changes in political leadership and direction, including the brief establishment of a 'flagship' Conservative administration in the late 1980s, overt commitment to a positive EO policy has persisted and developed, although not always evenly. By 1994, support and commitment from the top appeared in evidence in an Equal Rights councillors sub-committee of the chief committee of the Council, Policy and Resources. This sub-committee was supported by three core groups for race, women and disability, the core groups consisting mostly of operational managers, with link officers in each directorate. There was also a 'champion' for age, but no core group.

It is interesting to note that Bradford moved from talking about EO in the 1980s to *equal rights* in the 1990s, thus emphasising a policy that in theory encompasses everyone, including service recipients. (This can be compared with private sector policies such as Littlewoods 'Dignity at Work' policy which includes bullying as well as sexual and racial harassment.) There is an intention in Bradford that the concept of equal rights should be part of everyone's thinking, and advice is that candidates for Council posts are probed for 'an acceptance of and commitment to the principles of the Council's equal rights policies'. Indeed the Council was starting to refer to MD, for instance in a draft document on 'Managing Equal Rights in Employment' (City of Bradford, 1993). Some managers closely involved with policy development consider that policies will be ineffective unless everyone, including white men, believe they will benefit.

Initial HRD policies in the 1980s concentrated upon the training of those involved in recruitment and selection, with activities such as special access training at entry level for disadvantaged groups. An example of these was the direct recruitment of untrained social workers from ethnic minorities, followed by an orientation programme to social services and guaranteed funding for professional training. These and other HRD activities aimed at entry to Council employment continue, such as pre-employment access projects.

**Table 8.3   Bradford Council: ethnic minority staff
as a proportion of all staff**

(City of Bradford Metropolitan Council, undated)

	Percentage	All staff	Ethnic minority staff
1983	2.1	24 951	514
1993	7.4	24 556	1816

As indicated in Table 8.3, analysis points to a rise in ethnic minority staff from 2.1% in 1983 to 7.4% in 1993, despite a slight overall drop in total staff numbers. Of course this still falls far short of ethnic minority representation in the general population, although comparisons should be tempered by the differential age distribution of the ethnic minority population which has a greater number of members under 35. Whilst initial policies aimed at recruiting ethnic minority staff at entry level have been partially successful, they were poorly represented at higher levels of the organisation, particularly in those areas requiring a professional qualification.

For some years Bradford has exploited the opportunities under the Race Relations Act to provide special positive action training for employees from ethnic minorities, with a positive action budget for the former group of £300 000 in 1994–5. In relation to ethnic minorities the Council provides training opportunities at both professional and technical levels. These include not only a direct entry scheme for Social Services which guarantees training after an initial period of employment, and the training of legal executives and solicitors, but also entry to fields less traditionally sought after by members of ethnic minorities such as environmental health and planning. The Council sees multiple benefits in encouraging professional entry to a wide variety of departments: first it provides employment and hence role models for others to follow; second, it means there is more competition for higher positions which encourages a higher calibre of staff; and third, it increases knowledge within the ethnic minority communities of Council functions and thus makes the services more accessible, particularly important when problems arise in service delivery: town planning is a case in point. The Council tries to ensure that these opportunities go to ethnic minority women as well as ethnic minority men, sensitive to the possibility that racism and sexism may operate in tandem.

As well as the positive action programmes described above, HRD activities include a number of networking and support groups which exist for black workers within individual directorates, in addition to a black workers inter-management group. The term 'black' is used politically, as part of the Bradford discourse, most 'black' workers being of Asian ethnic origin. A 1994 policy recognises transfers and secondment as career development opportunities for disadvantaged groups which can be undertaken as positive action.

Table 8.4   Bradford Council: grading of ethnic minority officers

(City of Bradford Metropolitan Council, undated)

| | Senior officer grade and above | | Below senior officer grade | |
	Number	%	Number	%
1987	204	35.2	375	64.8
1993	322	28.7	801	71.3

Analysis of salary grades of ethnic minority officers shows HRD policies to have some partial success, as shown in Table 8.4. Officers on salary grades of senior officer, SO, and above, the professional and managerial grades, increased in absolute terms from 204 in 1987 to 322 in 1993. However, as a proportion of all ethnic minority officers there was a decrease of officers in the upper grades from 35.2% to 28.7%, whilst those on lower grades increased from 375 to 801, respectively 64.8% to 71.3%. Thus the advancement and promotion of ethnic minority officers had not kept pace with their recruitment.

In relation to women the problem identified was different. There were already large numbers of women in the workforce, the majority on lower officer grades. However, there were a number of women with professional qualifications established within mainstream departments, but their progress to management posts followed patterns familiar in other organisations and described as the 'glass ceiling'. Women-only training under the Sex Discrimination Act therefore concentrated on encouraging women into management, and provided both confidence building and skills-based courses. By 1994 a Women into Management group was also active. Some general HRM policies have HRD implications, such as the assumption that all officer posts are open to job share unless a specific case is made against this. This is likely to open up opportunities for women who may wish to work part-time because of child care responsibilities. Another HRM policy which has HRD implications is the institution of career grade posts in some directorates.

Analysis of salary grades by gender, shown in Table 8.5, demonstrates that in 1993 there were 5047 female officers on lower grades, and 1262 on upper grades, a 80%–20% split. This compares unfavourably with the respective figures for men, 1266 (46.4%) on lower grades and 1458 (53.6%) on upper grades. Whilst the absolute difference at higher levels is not great, women being 46% of higher grade officers, they are heavily weighted towards the lower end of these grades. On lower grades there is a feminisation of the workforce, with women forming 70.9% of all part-time workers (City of Bradford, 1994).

Table 8.5   Bradford Council: all officers by gender in 1993

(City of Bradford Metropolitan Council, 1994)

	Senior officer grade and above		Below senior officer grade	
	Number	%	Number	%
Women	1262	20	5047	80
Men	1458	53.6	1266	46.4

Analysis of the salary profile of ethnic minority officers by gender in 1993 indicates 58 ethnic minority women and 96 ethnic minority men in higher grades of SO 1 and above, and 577 women to 224 men in lower grades, as can be seen in Table 8.6. Thus, as well as the feminisation of the workforce already identified, there is an associated trend towards ethnicisation on lower grades.

Table 8.6   Bradford Council: ethnic minority officers' grade by gender

(City of Bradford Metropolitan Council, undated)

	Senior officer grade and above		Below senior officer grade	
	Number	%	Number	%
Women	58	9	577	91
Men	96	30	224	70

Policies concerning people with disabilities are less developed and their representation on the Council at 1.15% falls short of the legally enforceable 3% quota, although absolute numbers have increased between 1985 and 1994 from 113 to 276 (this latter figure includes those unregistered but self-classified).

To monitor trends the Council instituted a quarterly employment report in 1992, which looks at race, gender and disability within the workforce (e.g. City of Bradford, 1994). The employment profile, together with other indicators such as cases taken to Industrial Tribunal, provides formal, quantitative performance indicators.

There still remain a number of areas where HRD activities could be developed. There is no overall system for selecting employees for training, and no universal appraisal system within the Council, although various of the directorates have personal development planning systems. There are no plans to formulate a policy on mentoring. Part of the reason for this lack of uniformity lies with the decentralisation in 1988 to directorates which have their own training and personnel sections, leaving small residual central functions. The role of the central Strategic Personnel Department is to transmit political expectations, and stipulate minimum standards, not to develop detailed policies.

As a result, general priorities for training and development vary between directorates; for instance, the Housing and Environmental Health Directorate in 1994–5 was concentrating on training front line staff. Social Services on the other hand had a policy of sponsoring 12 first and middle line managers on local Diploma in Management Studies courses, and 3 on the part-time Master of Business Administration at Bradford University. Most directorates were using NVQs as a route to qualification for staff, including the Management Charter Initiative standards, despite misgivings about the gender and race blind content of the latter (which has been discussed in the main body of the chapter).

The evaluation of strategy and practice against outcomes was being extended in 1994–5. The regular review of performance standards for recruitment had already been established, and there were plans to extend a system of peer review by task groups to other areas, including in the HRD area training, secondment, and management development, and in the HRM area redeployment, and general management including grievances, discipline and industrial tribunal cases. One performance indicator which has caused concern is the number of cases which are brought to Industrial Tribunal. Because of this the Council sought help from an external consultant and the subsequent Carr Report: 'Alibis for Inaction' (Carr, 1993) recommended that there should be clearer policies in a number of HRM and HRD areas. The Council is now going through the process of reviewing these policies.

Despite the HRM and HRD strategies described, white able-bodied men are still the majority group in the upper managerial ranks of the Council. In areas where changes have been wrought, for instance the employment of staff with a range of ethnic backgrounds, language skills and gender within the Home Care service, managers acknowledged that taking the next step of developing staff and opening up higher graded posts was more difficult. The organisation had developed expertise at encouraging entry from varied groups, but this had not carried through to enabling individual career development and promotion.

Comment on the case study

Bradford Council is engaged in an ongoing process where incremental steps to improve equal rights are backed by quantitative and qualitative evaluation and HRM and HRD measures. Performance indicators in terms of the demographic composition of the workforce indicate limited success, but much more remains to be done in terms of integrated HRM and HRD policies. It could be argued that this is a matter of time lag; cohort analysis would be instructive.

In terms of the Jackson *et al.* (1992) model Bradford Council appears to be an affirmative action organisation, although attempting at the level of discourse to be a redefining organisation. In relation to the two paradigm model outlined above, the use of 'equal rights' rather than 'equal opportunities' appears to be an attempt to change the discourse to encompass a concept of MD, although this phrase is not used in the forefront of policy discussion. One distinction between EO and MD is between concentration on process and concentration on outcomes. Bradford appears to be more successful at the former. If we take Hawkin's (1994) view that organisational learning does not take place until managerial behaviour at the top is seen to have changed, then the persistence of a white male hierarchy sits uncomfortably with the equality discourse.

Initially EO was accepted for moral reasons, sharpened by a response to the external circumstances of changes in the ethnic composition of the city. Bradford appears to be moving from a moral case to a business case argument, and acknowledges equal rights as a strategic issue, relating to customers as well as staff. However, this seems to lack the urgency found in some private sector organisations. This may relate to its monopoly position as the provider and commissioner of many local services, or may be the outcome of larger political processes. The lack of promotion of individual employees from disadvantaged groups suggests organisational inertia in terms of culture, policy and processes.

RECOMMENDATIONS FOR PRACTICE AND FURTHER RESEARCH

It is striking how much writing has been done in North America, and how little in the UK, particularly in relation to HRD interventions for MD. Cox (1994) suggests that research into MD should proceed on three levels of analysis: individual, group/intergroup, and organisational; to these could be added research at societal level. Cox (1994) contends that wider systemic patterns must be researched to avoid the implication that responsibility for change rests with individuals. This applies to HRD as much as to HRM. There is scope for investigation of the extent to which the 'bottom line' is helped by MD, specifically in the UK and EU context, and in particular which interventions are most helpful in this respect.

In relation to practice the overriding message is that there cannot be prescriptions about how to design and implement HRD interventions which are applicable to every company; indeed prescriptions should be treated with care. All interventions should be preceded by careful audit of precisely what the organisation requires, and followed by evaluation of their success. It would be helpful to have more qualitative case studies of both successful and unsuccessful HRD interventions in this field. Given the crucial interdependence of HRM and HRD interventions, both qualitative and quantitative studies would be helpful to give further insight into how HRD and HRM interventions can support each other.

Acknowledgements

I am grateful to officers of the City of Bradford Metropolitan Council for their assistance with the case study.

References

Alban-Metcalfe, B. and West, M. (1991) 'Women Managers', in Firth-Cozens, J. and West, M. *Women at Work: Psychological and Organizational Perspectives*, Buckingham, Open University Press.

Alimo-Metcalfe, B. (1993) 'Women in Management: Organizational Socialization and Assessment Practices that Prevent Career Advancement', *International Journal of Selection and Assessment*, vol. 1, no. 2, pp. 66–83.

Alimo-Metcalfe, B. (1994) 'Waiting for fish to grow feet: removing organisational barriers to women's entry into leadership positions', in Tanton, Morgan *Women in Management: A Developing Presence*, London, Routledge.

Bartz, D.E., Hillman, L.W., Lehrer, S. and Mayhugh, G. (1990) 'A Model for Managing Workplace Diversity', *Management Education and Development*, vol. 2, no. 5, pp. 321–6.

Benest, F. (1991) 'Marketing Multiethnic Communities', *Public Management*, vol. 75, no. 12, pp. 4–14.

Carr, J. (1993) *Alibis for Inaction*, report on aspects of the City of Bradford Metropolitan Council's procedures for handling complaints of discrimination.

City of Bradford Metropolitan Council (1993) *Managing Equal Rights in Employment: Managers' Guidelines*, consultative draft.

City of Bradford Metropolitan Council (1994) *Bradford's Staffing Profile 1993/4*, *Financial Year 4th Qtr (Wke 27/3/94)*, Chief Executive's Office, Strategic Personnel.

City of Bradford Metropolitan Council (undated) *Did You Know That?*

Cockburn, C. (1989) 'Equal opportunities: the short and long agenda', *Industrial Relations Journal*, vol. 20, no. 3, pp. 213–25.

Corby, S. (1992) 'Equality on a Tight Budget', *Personnel Management Plus*, vol. 3, no. 1, Mar.

Cox, T. (1994) 'A Comment on the Language of Diversity', *Organization*, vol. 1, no. 1, July.

Davidson, M. and Cooper, C. (1992) *Shattering the Glass Ceiling: the Woman Manager*, Paul Chapman.

Dodds, I. (1995) 'Differences can also be strengths', *People Management*, vol. 1, no. 8, 20 Apr., p. 40.

Equal Opportunity Review (1994a) 'Race and the Civil Service: "significant improvement" needed', no. 53, Jan./Feb., pp. 8–9.

Equal Opportunity Review (1994b) 'Programme of action on ethnic minority staff in the NHS', no. 54, Mar./Apr., pp. 25–9.

Equal Opportunity Review (1994c) 'Sex equality makes good business sense, says EOC', no. 58, Nov./Dec., p. 4.

Fant, O.D. (1980) *A Tale of O: on being different*, a training tool for managing diversity (video), Goodmeasure Inc.

Fine, M.G. (1991) 'New Voices in the Workplace: Research Directions in Multicultural Communication', *Journal of Business Communications*, vol. 28, no. 3, pp. 259–75.

Galagan, P.A. (1991) 'Tapping the Power of a Diverse Workforce', *Training and Development Journal*, Mar., pp. 38–44.

Gray, B. (1994) 'Women-only management training – a past and present', in Tanton, Morgan *Women in Management: A Developing Presence*, London, Routledge.

Griffith, V. (1994) 'Management outsiders welcome – US companies are developing workplace diversity', *Financial Times*, 18 Apr., p. 10.

Guardian (1993a) 'Equality charter for BBC news', 24 Mar., p. 5.

Guardian (1993b) 'An ill wind of change on the airwaves', 14 July, p. 6.

Guardian 2 (1993) 'Career development opportunities for nurses, midwives, health visitors and PAMs', advertisement 7 July, p. 13.

Hammond, V. and Holton, V. (1991) *A Balanced Workforce? Achieving cultural change for women: A comparative study*, Ashridge Management Research Group.

Harisis, D.S. and Kleiner, B.H. (1993) 'Managing and Valuing Diversity in the Workplace', *Equal Opportunities International*, vol. 12, no. 4, pp. 6–9.

Hawkins, P. (1994) 'The Changing View of Learning', in Burgoyne, J., Pedlar, M. and Boydell, T. *Towards the Learning Company*, Maidenhead, McGraw-Hill.

Hearn, J., Sheppard, D., Tancred-Sheriff, P. and Burrell, G. (1989) *The Sexuality of Organization*, London, Sage.

Herriot, P. and Pemberton, C. (1995) *Competitive Advantage through Diversity: Organizational Learning from Difference*, London, Sage.

Hofstede, G. (1980) 'Motivation, Leadership and Organization: Do American Theories Apply Abroad?', *Organizational Dynamics*, Summer, pp. 42–63.

Hollister, L., Day, N.E. and Jesaitis, P.T. (1993) 'Diversity Programs: Key to Competitiveness or Just Another Fad?', *Organizational Development Journal*, vol. 11, no. 4, Winter, pp. 49–59.

Iles, Paul (1995) 'Learning to work with difference' *Personnel Review*, vol. 24, no. 6, pp. 44–61.

Iles, P., Auluck, R. and Braich, R. (1994) 'Developing skills and strategies in managing diversity and valuing difference', paper given at conference on *Practical approaches to meeting business needs of the future*, 31 Aug. – 1 Sept.

Industrial Relations Review and Report (1990) 'CRE finds discrimination in psychometric testing', *Recruitment and Development Report 11*, p. 14.

Jackson, B.W., LaFasto, F., Schultz, H.G. and Kelly, D. (1992) 'Diversity', *Human Resource Management*, vol. 31, nos 1 and 2, Spring/Summer, pp. 21–34.

Jamieson, D. and O'Mara, J. (1991) *Managing Workforce 2000: Gaining the Diversity Advantage*, San Francisco CA, Jossey Bass.

Kandola, R. and Fullerton, J. (1994) *Managing the Mosaic*, London, IPD.

Karp, H.B. and Sutton, N. (1993) 'Where Diversity Training Goes wrong', *Training*, July, pp. 30–34.

Knight, J. and Pritchard, S. (1994) 'No we're not colour consultants', in Tanton, Morgan *Women in Management: A Developing Presence*, London, Routledge.

MacLachlan, R. (1995) 'Equality makes good business sense, says CRE', *People Management*, vol. 1, no. 226, Jan., p. 9.

Maddock, S. and Parkin, D. (1993) 'Gender cultures: Women's Choices and Strategies at Work', *Women in Management Review*, vol. 8, no. 2, pp. 3–9.

Mandell, B. and Kohler-Gray, S. (1990) 'Management development that values diversity', *Personnel*, vol. 67, no. 3, pp. 41–7.

Marshall, J. (1994) 'Why women leave senior management jobs', in Tanton, Morgan *Women in Management: A Developing Presence*, London, Routledge.

Martin, L. (1994) 'Power, continuity and change: decoding black and white women managers' experience in local government', in Tanton, Morgan *Women in Management: A Developing Presence*, London, Routledge.

Maznevski, M. (1994) 'Understanding Our Differences: Performance in Decision-Making Groups with Diverse Members', *Human Relations*, vol. 47, no. 5, pp. 531–52.

Mirvis, P.H. (1991) 'Introduction: the New Workforce: The New Workplace', *Human Resource Management*, vol. 30, no. 1, Spring, pp. 1–5.

Morrison, A. (1992) 'Developing Diversity in Organizations', *Business Quarterly*, Summer, pp. 42–8.

Pemberton, C. (1992) 'From Stew to Salad: Men and Women Managers as Contributors to Organizational Diversity', *Industrial and Commercial Training*, vol. 24, no. 4, pp. 12–15.

Spencer Stuart and Associates (1993) *Women in Management – Why so Few at the Top?*, Point of View no. 17, Spencer Stuart and Associates.

Spender, D. (1986) *Man Made Language*, Second edition, London, Routledge.

Swan, E. (1994) 'Managing Emotion', in Tanton, Morgan *Women in Management: A Developing Presence*, London, Routledge.

Tanton, Morgan (1994) 'Developing Women's Presence', in Tanton, Morgan *Women in Management: A Developing Presence*, London, Routledge.

Thatcher, M. (1995) 'Firms prepare campaign to boost racial equality', *People Management*, vol. 1, no. 8, 20 Apr., p. 5.

Thomas, R. (1990) 'From Affirmative Action to Affirming Diversity', *Harvard Business Review*, Mar./Apr., pp. 107–17.

Thomas, V. (1994) 'The Downside of Diversity', *Training and Development*, Jan., pp. 60–62.

Travis, A. (1994) 'London top capital for ethnic mix', *Guardian*, 16 July, p. 12.

Williams, T. and Green, A. (1994) *Dealing with Difference: How Trainers Can Take Account of Cultural Diversity*, Aldershot, Gower.

Wilson, E. (1993) 'The Personal Costs of Managerial Work – Women and Managerial Competences', *Bolton Business School* conference, 28–30 Nov.

9

Power and Influence and the HRD Function

Rita Johnston

INTRODUCTION

In the first chapter of this strategy section, Fredericks and Stewart presented a model which associated strategy with 'enabling' as opposed to 'controlling'. This final chapter of the strategy section is also concerned with enabling, and seeks to promote the concepts of power and influence as forces for empowerment rather than, or at least in addition to, identifying them as elements of coercion or control.

Since the 1980s, trends in human resource development (HRD) have been associated with movements such as empowerment, self-advocacy, and learner centredness, with the HRD specialist seen as a facilitator, resource co-ordinator and mentor. Within this framework, concepts such as power, control, authority and dominance were associated with largely negative concepts such as organisational hierarchies, office politics, and 'jug and mug' training. It is not surprising, therefore, that many researchers (Leduchowicz, 1984; Quick, 1987; King, 1989; Garavan *et al.*, 1993) have noted a reluctance on the part of HRD personnel to identify theirs as power roles:

> *'There is a considerable consensus in the training and development literature that training and development specialists are reluctant to acquire power and use their influencing skills.'* (Garavan *et al.*, 1993)

More recently, however, there has been a shift in definitions of and attitudes towards power. Similarities are now more likely to be drawn with power grids than with symbols of oppression; and this is significant. The old, negative associations of power generally assumed a competitive win/lose situation, the few winners with power dominating the many losers without it. The new interpretations see power as an enabling mechanism, like an electricity grid, open to as many users as wish to take advantage of the system.

Not surprisingly, given this change in perception, HRD specialists have shown more interest in and willingness to espouse power and influence, as evidenced by the proliferation of papers on the subject in contemporary professional journals and recent conference proceedings. How to identify, establish, maintain and enhance organisational power has become an important concern of trainers and human resource developers.

It should be noted, however, that Weber's (1968) classic zero-sum concept of power is also still widely held, see Gill and Johnson (1993), and many would maintain that the shared power concept is naive. It is not the purpose of this chapter to enter that philosophical debate. It is assumed that different groups within an organisation will inevitably be in competition for limited resources or to influence organisational culture and mission, and that all these groups will have some access to power. This pluralist model provides a more actionable base from which to develop an HRD strategy.

AIMS AND OBJECTIVES

This chapter will address these areas of current concern by looking at definitions and taxonomies of power and influence, at both the organisational and the individual levels. It will suggest ways in which HRD professionals might assess the strength and sources of the organisational power of their departments. It will also consider how they might audit the potential of their own individual power and translate this into strategies for influence which are in synch with the organisational culture and value system. With this background HRD specialists, acting as empowered intrapreneurs, may effectively promote human resource development in the interests of their organisation and of the individual employees within it.

The chapter goes beyond these instrumental issues, however, to reflect on the nature of power in relation to the HRD function and the ethical issues surrounding its use. Such theoretical frameworks, combined with individual organisational experience, should encourage the HRD professional to become a reflective practitioner with regard to his or her own power within the organisation.

DEFINITIONS

The Concise Oxford Dictionary defines power as 'the ability to do or act', in accordance with the Latin derivation (potere = to be able), but goes on to give additional definitions including, 'a particular faculty', 'influence or authority', 'vigour, energy', and 'mechanical force'. Influence is defined as 'the effect that one thing or person has on another', and 'moral ascendancy or power'. Handy (1985) has put this succinctly when he says that 'Influence is the process whereby A modifies the attributes or behaviour of B. Power is that which enables him to do it'. Thus the two terms, power and influence, are to some extent interdependent and are generally distinguished by 'power' being used to indicate a force or potential in the abstract, and 'influence' to indicate the application of that power, particularly in a conscious and explicit way. This is the way the terms will be used in this chapter.

The inevitability of giving consideration to power and influence in a text such as this derives from the commonly acknowledged association both of knowledge with power and of organisation with power. It is generally recognised that all education and development implies both knowledge and change based on that knowledge. Change in any field implies movement and, just as in the physical sense, movement implies a moving force or power. As Foucault (1980) has stated:

'Power and knowledge directly imply one another: . . . there is no power relation without the correlative constitution of a field of knowledge, nor any knowledge that does not presuppose and constitute at the same time power relations.'

The necessary association of any organisational behaviour with power was observed by Crozier (1964) and has since been affirmed by Mintzberg (1983), Gill and Johnson (1993) and others.

A recent word association exercise conducted with Masters students, which asked them to quickly write down as many words as possible which they associated with the word 'power' showed that they held, simultaneously, not only positive and negative but even apparently mutually exclusive associations. Polar opposites of 'freedom' and 'controlled', for instance, were common. This is hardly surprising, since power, though neutral in derivation, is such a complex concept. Kaplan (1964) refers to the 'multi-dimensionality of power'. The taxonomies of power given below go some way to explaining how different types of power can produce such different responses.

TAXONOMIES OF ORGANISATIONAL POWER

Different writers have produced different taxonomies. Perhaps the most influential in HRD circles has been the seminal work of French and Raven (1959). They distinguished types of power largely by the effect they had on others. Their five types were identified as follows.

- *Reward* The power to give material (salary, bonus), or non-material (status, title) awards as an incentive to produce the required behaviour or attitudes.
- *Coercive* The power to withhold such rewards as a sanction against undesired behaviour or attitudes.
- *Legitimate* The power associated with formal authority, that of the organisational hierarchy.
- *Expert* The power which flows from specialist knowledge or skill to which others defer. The strength of expert power is in direct negative correlation to the numbers of those holding such expertise.
- *Referent* The power accredited to someone on the grounds of personal wisdom or charisma.

HRD departments with large resources, which can authorise fees for expensive external Masters programmes or exotic conferences, may be relatively well endowed with *reward* and *coercive* power, though this does not necessarily imply that the HRD manager will use those resources in an overtly rewarding or coercive way. It is enough that others recognise that such rewards exist. Garavan *et al.* (1993), in conducting research on training departments in some 50 Irish companies, found that over half of them considered themselves lacking in resource power. It is at least likely that this would be the case for HRD departments generally; reward or coercion would not provide their strongest power bases.

Although HRD specialists clearly have *legitimate* power within their own function or department, many seem strangely loath to exercise it. One reason may be that HRD specialists are less confident in their legitimate power than are managers in other areas of the organisation. This relates to the fact that the HRD function generally operates horizontally within the organisation. The HRD manager can only operate with the collaboration of line managers and individual trainees over whom he or she has no direct vertical control. According to Garavan *et al.*:

> '. . . the ability of specialists to get things done depends more on the number of networks in which they are involved than on their position in the hierarchy.'

Indeed the situation is even more sensitive, as their legitimacy may not be universally acknowledged. Leduchovicz (1984) and Grace and Straub (1991) have suggested that some line managers have a very limited view of the HRD role. Pettigrew (1985) has suggested that some of this antipathy may be mutual, since HRD personnel have traditionally been wary of involving line managers in assessing the HRD needs of their employees, and in the running and evaluation of training and development programmes. Role boundary disputes may also arise, according to Garavan *et al.*, between the personnel department and the training department in organisations where these are separate. There was some suggestion of an element of this in the negotiations preceding the recent merger of the Institute of Personnel Management and the Institute of Training and Development. Hopefully, current moves towards the merger of these functions will help resolve conflicts as to who holds legitimate authority in which areas of work, although, as Handy (1985) has pointed out, legitimate power on its own, as simply a position within the organisation, is no use unless it has resources and unless it is seen to be backed by senior management. Unfortunately, according to Garavan *et al.*, there is evidence that little has changed since the Manpower Services Commission report (Coopers and Lybrand, 1985) found general apathy amongst managers with regard to the training and development function.

There could be another reason, however, for the reluctance of some HRD specialists to exercise legitimate power. Arguably, they may have been seduced by their own professional rhetoric of participation, involvement, empowerment, facilitation, and democratisation, and thus become reluctant to demonstrate overt legitimate power. The appropriateness of this stance is at least debatable.

Power is perceptual; if others believe that someone has it, then they do have it. The reverse is also true; whatever the organisational chart may say, if others do not acknowledge someone's power then they have none. This is the situation of the 'lame duck' president. The exercise of legitimate power can be an important signal to others. As Garavan *et al.* have pointed out:

> '. . . the exercise of authority is expected and desired in an organisational setting. Thus the exercise of authority may actually serve to enhance the amount of authority subsequently possessed by the function. The transformation of power into hierarchical authority is very important because once transformed it is not resisted and the function no longer depends on the resources or determinants which may have produced it in the first instance.'

Perhaps surprisingly, it is not unknown for those who reject legitimate power to espouse *referent* power. This is not something that most trainers and developers would recognise in themselves, but they would immediately recognise it in others. A good indicator of referent power is volunteerism. Whenever people volunteer to help with a project or to be associated with a workshop for little or no obvious reward, then there is a chance that referent power is at work. Referent power may be accorded to someone on the grounds of their wisdom and reliability, in the Civil Service such a person may be known as 'a safe pair of hands'. Alternatively, it may be given to someone who is inspirational, or a guru. Of all French and Raven's types of power this is the most volatile and potentially dangerous. It is the power exercised by Bob Geldof to produce Band Aid, and by Jonathan Porritt to promote green issues, but it is also the power of the tyrant, the racist and the bigot throughout the ages. Handy (1985) sounds a further note of caution with regard to referent power. Although it is generally seen as the most personal of powers, he maintains that it is, in fact, closely linked with position power, and cites as evidence the number of ex-sports stars and ex-politicians whose charisma clearly diminished when they were no longer in their national teams or in office.

For professionals, the exercise of *expert* power is fundamental. Of all power sources this is probably the one which is most acceptable, both to the person exercising it and to the person receiving its influence. What is more, it is the one power source the strength of which is entirely within the professional's own hands. He or she can augment expertise by becoming as highly qualified as possible within their profession. Until 1988 the highest taught qualification in training and development was a post-graduate diploma. When in that year the University of Sheffield inaugurated the first Masters degree in this area, it was inundated by applications. Since then Masters degrees in the field of HRD have become widely available in different institutions and through different modes of delivery. This indication of market demand is evidence of the desire of HRD personnel to accrue the maximum expert or specialist power.

The professional institutes (particularly the now amalgamated Institute of Personnel and Development, formerly the Institutes of Personnel Management and of Training and Development) recognise the importance of this power source to their members. It is for this reason that they have required evidence of continuing professional development (CPD) as a condition of continuing membership. This is increasingly necessary, since the general diffusion of knowledge inevitably means that the specialist information of yesterday becomes the common knowledge of tomorrow. (The diffusion of computer literacy is an instance of this.) Keeping up with new knowledge therefore becomes an imperative for the professional who wishes to stay an expert.

There are charlatans in all professions, claiming expert powers, and because this power is so critical for professionals it is essential that these claims be subject to scrutiny. Allied to the HRD function are a number of what may be regarded as fringe practices; some would regard graphology, and some psychometric testing to be in this category. The expert power of all is threatened if that of some can be demonstrated to be fraudulent, and for this reason some professional institutes, such as the British Psychological Association, offer assessment and registration of tested practices.

The taxonomy of power produced by French and Raven is not the only one of relevance for the HRD specialist. Kaplan's (1964) groupings confirmed their taxonomy, with his four bases: *carrot and stick*, *personal identification*, *legitimacy* and *expertness*. Garavan *et al.* (1993) have added a further three sources:

- *Associative* Deriving from the support of a strong mentor or sponsor, in a position both to supply information and advice, and to promote one's career.
- *Assigned* The power that comes from making oneself indispensable to someone senior, by taking on tasks which they dislike and would otherwise have to do.
- *Political* Becoming politically involved in groups (committees or unions) which have access to information and are involved with decision making.

The classic work by Etzioni (1961) only differentiated between three types, but these were based on the types of organisation or institution in which they were most generally exercised, and so offers another framework within which to consider organisational power. His three types were:

- *Coercive* Mainly associated with physical force, as used by such institutions as the armed services, prisons and police forces
- *Remunerative* The material or resource distribution generally employed in the workplace to stimulate or reward productivity
- *Normative* Operating to produce and manipulate conformity in such organisations as religious or political groups.

One would not normally expect to encounter *coercive* physical power outside the organisations specified by Etzioni, however, it could be argued that the power of dismissal is essentially a physical one, removing an employee from the workplace. At the other end of the industrial spectrum, a rail strike which prevents others from getting to work could be construed as exerting physical power, or at least coercive power with a physical effect, over them. As more and more HRD personnel are becoming involved with early retirement and outplacement activities, and as some get involved as parties to management/union negotiations, it may be argued that they come into contact with the exercise of physical power. It could be helpful, therefore, to consider that one of the reasons why so many find this type of work seriously stressful and depressing, is that they are being involved with a type of power which is alien to their whole professional value system.

Etzioni's *remunerative* or resource power has obvious similarities with French and Raven's reward and coercive types. It has always been the power most widespread within organisations. The growth of the large public sector bureaucracies in the inter- and post-war years tended to modify the more blatant exercise of this power as more rewards were statutory and role or grade linked, and sanctions were subject to employment law and union/management agreements. The rise of the enterprise culture and market economics in the most recent decade has, however, led to a strengthening of this power base. Evidence of its increased strength is the growth, despite much research against it, of rewards and sanctions, as manifested in individually negotiated salaries and perks packages, performance related pay and salary linked appraisal schemes. All of these generally involve the HRD function to some extent and it is important that those involved recognise that this is a power exercise and not just a piece of administrative or staff development work, otherwise they may be at a loss to understand and deal with the strong feelings and emotions which frequently surround such exercises.

As with the coercive power, some HRD personnel might assume that Etzioni's *normative* power is confined to the organisations or groups which he identifies. Sociologists and social psychologists would argue, however, that this force is at work within all organisations. Induction programmes generally have among their specific objectives to introduce new employees to the organisational culture. Organisational culture is largely an all-pervasive normative force to which mission statements, company slogans and even such endeavours as team building exercises and mentoring systems all contribute. Again, it is useful if the HRD worker recognises the power implications in these functions. Indeed it could be argued that the entire growth of the HRM movement is related to the increasing use of normative or persuasive power by organisations.

COMPARISONS AND IMPLICATIONS

One major distinction can be made between, on the one hand, those sorts of power which flow from the *organisation* [reward, coercive, legitimate (French and Raven), carrot and stick and legitimacy (Kaplan), and physical and coercive, material and resource, normative (Etzioni)], and those types which stem from the *individual* on the other [expert and referent (French and Raven), personal identification and expertness, (Kaplan), and associative, assigned, political (Gavaran *et al.*)]. Because they are linked to the organisation, the first group may be regarded as 'fixed' power, whilst the latter types may be categorised as 'free' power.

Organisations tend to have different attitudes towards these different sources of power. Fixed power is generally underwritten and supported as a stabilising force in the organisation, preserving the status quo of the organisational chart. The empowerment movement, often masquerading as individual power, is based on an interpretation of subsidiarity, where power to make decisions is pushed as far as possible down the *organisational* chart. It is both a dissemination of organisational power and a confirmation of its legitimacy.

Organisational attitudes towards free power are generally more ambivalent, however. Expert power is portable power and could be lost to the company if the individual holding it left. A maverick employee could use referent power as a disruptive force within the organisation. Associative power is generally mistrusted by peers, whether the sponsor is internal or external to the company. Organisations often both reward and attempt to restrict or control specialist and charismatic power. The computer expert or financial specialist may be highly paid and deferred to in specialist decision making, but it is not unusual to find that their offices are physically distanced from other central functions and that their influence is negligible outside their own confined area of expertise. All uniforms, even uniform company car fleets, can be seen as manifestations of organisational attempts to limit the effects of free power.

HRD departments, with their general stress on individual needs and flexible responses, can be seen, particularly in highly bureaucratic organisations, as posing a threat to the organisational balance between fixed and free power, and as such may be suspect or distrusted. In such cases, the need for a sensitive influencing strategy is obvious.

INFLUENCING

Identifying the nature of one's power base is a first step towards determining a strategy for exercising organisational influence. Handy (1985) and others have noted that different sources of power underlie different methods of influencing, and the wider and stronger one's power base, the more influencing strategies are available. A person's influencing style is, however, a more complex matter than just a cerebral assessment of the probable effectiveness of the options available however. Tendencies towards one style or another will have developed over a long time in reaction to various pressures. Early conditioning is perhaps the most obvious. A childhood dominated by rewards and punishments will set in train tendencies different from those of a child persuaded by argument. There are also basic personality traits, such as a tendency towards authoritarianism or a strong need to be liked, which exert an effect. Role models, experience of particular work cultures, and more transitory factors such as stress levels and general feelings of self-esteem have an additional impact.

Kaplan (1964) has associated different personality types with different preferences in influencing styles. According to him there is a clear link with value systems in general, and he suggests three basic approaches.

- *Subjective* A person with this approach tends to elevate the affective above the cognitive. The emphasis is on feelings – 'How does this affect me, how will it affect them? – and a power base relying on rewards and identification is likely to be chosen.
- *Absolutist* People with this type of personality have firm convictions as to what is the right approach, and will consider every other approach to be wrong. They will use a coercive power base or, more subtly, will use legitimacy to propound an ideology. This leads to the influencing style of the 'conviction' politician.
- *Relativist* Unlike the subjective approach, the relativist has a strong sense of objective reality, but believes that the 'right' approach is always contextual. The relativist tends to rely on expertise to persuade others of the full situational implications.

Personality type, early conditioning, general life experience and organisational experience will all, then, produce a tendency to prefer to influence from a particular power base. Before exerting that preference in an organisational setting, however, it is useful to take an inventory of what is possible.

The persuasive power of *reward and sanction* is only available to someone with a strong reward and coercive power base. Even given such a base, it is a style of influencing which would only be appropriate within an organisation with a strong power culture, operating in a market economy where staff could easily be replaced since such a forceful method of persuasion, used insensitively, could lead employees to leave. As we noted earlier, however, it is often unnecessary to use this power in order to influence, because the knowledge on the part of others that this power is there will inevitably affect the dynamics of any negotiating situation.

A strong legitimate power base provides the bedrock for an influencing style based on invoking *rules and procedures*. This is the favoured style of most large bureaucracies, because once a precedent has been established, then the need for separate decision making on every isolated instance is done away with. It is also a favoured method with influencers and influenced alike because it depersonalises the situation. A is not exerting power over B, A is simply informing B of the regulations which apply in all cases of the kind. Too heavy a reliance on this style of influencing, however, may indicate a personality that is reluctant to deal directly with the conflicts that inevitably and often legitimately, arise in organisational life.

Another generally acceptable style of influencing is that of *logical persuasion*, associated with a high expert power base. It is most acceptable in organisations with people or task cultures and matrix management structures, but it does rely ultimately on the credibility of the person exercising the style. At its least acceptable, or with a person of low credibility, it may be dismissed as 'blinding with science'. Whilst all of the styles of influence can be effectively employed horizontally, or when relating to those lower on the organisational chart, this is generally accepted as the most effective style of influencing when communicating upwards with top management. One way to diminish credibility with regard to expert power is, unfortunately, often adopted to try and enhance it – that is the use of professional jargon.

The last style of influencing, often described as *common vision*, relies on firing the imagination, enthusing and energising others towards perhaps non-specific or abstract goals such as mission statements. Clearly this is a style easier to adopt by people who have, or believe themselves to have, a high level of referent power. It is a forceful, personal style that is valued in task cultures particularly in times of organisational change. However, the high stress it places on loyalty and commitment can lead to 'groupthink' and become oppressive. If things are going wrong it can produce an equal and opposite reaction of hostility. People deliberately adopting this style often seek to enhance it by image management, at both ends of the spectrum, either by 'power dressing' or by adopting an ultra casual style.

Many apparently small factors can have an effect on how one is perceived by others in the organisation and thus on one's referent power. How an office is arranged and personalised, and even the use of language in memos and meetings can enhance or erode a personal power base. Ryan (1989) has raised a caveat about this environmental manipulation:

> '*In education or training . . . the "impression management" approach could create a preference for sophistication of presentation over soundness of the content of learning materials. Keeping the customers happy may become more important than substantively facilitating their learning.*'

Personal power can also atrophy by personal neglect. Argyle (1987) has researched the depressing and debilitating effects of isolation; Josefowitz (1985) has identified such organisational behaviours as mistrust, making excuses, cultivating dependency, and blaming others, as essentially depowering behaviours.

A method of influencing which is often not recognised as such is one which is related to Etzioni's normative power. This is what Lukes (1974) has called 'the third dimension of power', and Fox (1990) has described as a post-modern conditioning, and identified as a characteristic of strategic human resource management. It may be initiated, as has been suggested, through induction, and may be carried on through team building and mission affirming events. Its effect is to establish a 'taken for granted' situation, or as Fox (1990) has termed it a 'cultural centre'. Such organisational designer culture, as opposed to that which develops organically, can be extremely powerful and Gill and Johnson (1993) have cautioned:

> '*By signifying what is normal and routine, hegemony is a subtle and insidious form of power.*'

particularly since,

> 'This power is so masked that its beneficiaries may themselves be unaware of their role in its application and perpetuation.'

A similar caution against the 'symbolic interaction', whereby an organisationally constructed 'reality' is first created and then colluded with, has also been given by Ryan (1989).

No style is better than any other except in a particular context. The context must take account of the influencer's power base and personal tendency as well as the organisational culture. Success also depends on the degree to which the person being persuaded acknowledges both that power base and the organisational culture. Handy (1985) illustrates the importance of contextuality with an example taken from family, not organisational, life. He notes (without value judgement) that professional parents frequently seem to produce unruly offspring. His explanation for this is that there is a mismatch of context and influencing style. Professionals have a strong power base of expertise and tend therefore to adopt an influencing style of logical persuasion. The optional styles, of using rewards and sanctions or adopting parental legitimate power, are rejected because they would be inappropriate at work. Within the family situation, however, their professional expertise has no relevance, and logical persuasion is not notably effective on the average two-year-old. Chaos reigns.

Much research, including that of Pettigrew *et al.* (1982) confirms the belief that influence is most effectively exerted by training and development personnel when there is synchronisation between their personal influencing style, their power base within the organisation, and the general culture and value system of the company. Pettigrew's research also found that such harmony was most usually found where the HRD specialist interpreted the training and development role as one of proactive organisational change consultant, rather than as simply a passive provider of services. In order to bring about that situation it is necessary to consider the power position of the HRD unit or department within the organisation.

ASSESSING THE INFLUENCE OF THE HRD FUNCTION WITHIN THE ORGANISATION

Although at the start of this chapter an image of power as a non-zero/sum concept was advocated, it is generally apparent that distribution of power is uneven within organisations. To return to the metaphor of the electric power circuit, a house may be totally wired up to the National Grid and in theory anyone may access that power at any point in the house without disadvantaging another user. In terms of 'fixed' power, however, some areas (such as the kitchen) will usually have more power access points than other areas (such as the bathroom). The same is true within organisations. Depending on the type of company, different sections – it may be marketing in one company, production in another – will have greater access to power than other departments. Their 'power points' may be manifest in such things as seats on important committees, direct access to the MD on a regular basis, access to budgets. It is essential that the HRD specialist has an accurate grasp of the power of that function as perceived by the rest of the organisation. A number of writers have suggested criteria against which this may be assessed. Kanter (1977) identified:

- *Centrality* Is the section centrally located? Is resourcing centrally organised? Is the section organically integrated with the whole? Is it mainstream?
- *Criticality* Are the issues of HRD critical to the organisation's mission and strategic plan?
- *Relevance* Are the areas of work the department is involved in seen to be politically popular at the current time?
- *Visibility* Is the department featured in the house magazine? Are the personnel instantly recognised in the organisation?
- *Flexibility* Is the function able to respond quickly to organisational changes? How much of its work is pilot or experimental as opposed to routine?
- *Opportunity* Do staff's job contents change and develop?
- *Autonomy* Does the department have a degree of freedom to set its own priorities and take initiatives? Can it authorise budgets?

Kanter also notes some negative criteria which mitigate against the power of a department. These are:

- *Numbers* Is it seen as a minority interest operating on the lowest possible numbers?
- *Stereotyping* Does the section have a negative or fringe image in the company?
- *Tokenism* Does the department exist largely due to some external (e.g. government/union/EC) pressure rather than internal organisational commitment?

Interestingly, Kanter found that those individuals who were operating within high power jobs were actually less authoritarian in their behaviour and delegated more than those working in low power jobs. They also demonstrated higher morale and were more energetic and enthusiastic about their work. This confirms the empirical work of Pelz (1952) who found a close correlation between the levels of power and influence of supervisors and the morale and productivity of their staff.

Other writers on organisations have produced different sets of criteria by which the organisational strength of a section or department may be assessed. Salanicik and Pfeffer (1977) proposed five critical considerations or 'strategic contingencies'.

- *Dependency* The degree to which other departments need or want the services of the group or section.
- *Financial resource* The size and flexibility of the departmental budget.
- *Centrality* The salience of the department to the central function to the organisation.
- *Substitutability* The degree to which others within the organisation could perform the department's function, or the ease with which outside services could be brought in to provide it.
- *Capacity to cope with uncertainty* In a changing business environment power accrues to those departments who can help the organisation to adapt most quickly and efficiently.

Batstone *et al.* (1978) produced four very similar influencing factors.

- The extent to which a group or section has skills which are in scarce supply and are non-substitutable by others in the organisation.
- The degree to which they are crucial to the key process of the organisation.
- The ease with which they could disrupt the organisation's functioning.
- The extent to which the group can create or cope with uncertainty.

Capacity to cope with uncertainty, centrality, criticality of output, and substitutability were the criteria also identified by Hickson *et al.* (1971). In general, as Gill and Johnson (1993) have maintained:

> 'The more central a segment is, the more uncertainty it can cope with, and the less substitutable it is, then the more power it will have.'

Taking these factors as guidelines could pose problems for the HRD specialist, however, since what is being advocated is, in effect, the creation and maintenance of an intra-organisational dependency. Given the empowerment ethic of the HRD culture, such a recommendation could produce cognitive dissonance or an internal conflict of ideals. More acceptable may be the concept of reciprocity, the cultivation – by networking – of mutual interdependence, particularly with line managers.

From a consideration of all these factors it should be possible for the HRD manager to calculate the potential organisational power of his or her department. Where this power is high, a range of influencing strategies is available to the HRD specialist. Where organisational power is found to be low, according to Handy (1985), then a smaller number of influencing strategies is available, and these are generally ones with a lower likelihood of success. However, an audit of power based on such an analysis can also be used to provide the base for a planned policy of empowerment for the department. Increasing such elements as relevance, flexibility, visibility, and the ability to cope with uncertainty, which are within the department's own control, would be an obvious example.

EXERCISING POWER

Garavan *et al.* (1993), using Daft's (1992) framework, suggest a composite strategy which involves producing a comprehensive policy, with clear goals, based on corporate objectives, culture and philosophy, which has the explicit approval of top management. They recommend that the policy needs to be supported by highly developed communications, networking and internal consultancy skills and to be carried out by personnel who are acknowledged to have high professional credibility.

Having conducted an audit of personal and departmental power, and having given consideration to preferences of personal style, the HRD specialist needs to consider the implementation of his or her influencing strategy. The politician Tony Benn has, in numerous speeches, recited the five questions he maintains the public needs to have answered by anyone in a position of power.

- What power have you got?
- From whom did you get it?
- In whose interests do you exercise it?

- To whom are you accountable?
- How can we get rid of you?

They are useful questions to ask of anyone, HRD specialists included. This chapter has provided pointers to answering Benn's first question by examining the various taxonomies which distinguish the types of power that one might have, and in considering organisational salience it has looked at ways to estimate the strength of that power. To answer the second question it is necessary to distinguish between the fixed powers which stem from occupying a role in the organisation and those free powers which accrue to the professional as an individual because he or she has built up skills in an expert area and developed or been blessed with those interpersonal skills which combine to produce charisma.

The last question relates to the second. Organisational power can be withdrawn by the organisation, ultimately by dismissal, but there is no way that anyone can get rid of someone else's personal power. This is why these power sources are so valuable and indeed, as Peters (1994) is continually maintaining, they are the only ones which can give any degree of career, if not job, security.

Benn's two middle questions impinge on matters of professional ethics, and the two questions are almost inevitably linked. To exercise power against the interests of those to whom one is accountable is rare, and is usually, as in the case of whistle blowers, justified in terms of a wider accountability to the public or the environment. For HRD professionals, the question 'To whom are you accountable?' is a complex one. Is the prime accountability to the company, whatever its value system? What degree of accountability should be shown towards individuals who pass through the department's courses or guidance procedures? Where do the interests of the economy as a whole come into the picture? What if the sets of interests are in conflict? The answers are of supreme importance, as they will determine in whose interests power is exercised.

A test case might be the acceptance of the NVQ system of assessing and accrediting the workforce. The system has been promulgated as a learner centred one, where individuals have their own portfolios which may be changed or added to in accordance with their own career development needs, thereby encouraging lifelong learning. The fact that the qualifications will be flexible and cross-credited should also mean that individuals can exercise personal preferences in choice of providers – even more learner centred. Tobias (1993) has identified ways, however, in which this accreditation system may be less learner centred than at first seems apparent, and indeed may operate more in the interests of other stakeholders. He suggests that it might give rise to 'credentialism' – the notion that people can only be skilled if they have a qualification. This may result in a disproportional effort being put into providing *evidence* of a skill, as opposed to that devoted to *developing* it. It may also inhibit their developing more general non-accredited education or interests. Arguably, the accumulation of units, chosen individually, with individually chosen providers, progressed at a personally decided pace, may not only lead to a fragmentation of learning, but also, by isolating one learner from another, to the deprivation of the support of peers in a learning community. He also suggests that in setting up a system based on continually identifying 'learning needs', there is a danger of turning skills into products and the learner into a driven consumer. Ultimately, the result of continuous pressure for ongoing professional development may not be empowering but rather depowering, as people are left with a permanent feeling of inadequacy.

At the same time as he questions its learner centredness, Tobias suggests that such an industry led and validated qualifications framework could increase the power of employers by producing a system whereby units of qualification become requirements for job security or progression.

The cross-accreditation and recognition of qualifications, allied to consumer choice, is also in tune with the prevailing economic/political ethos of the market economy, and serves the interests of that constituency. Providers must compete for customers, and since probability of success may be a significant criterion for choice, there must be the possibility, at least, that a higher overall level of qualification may be achieved at the expense of a lower standard of assessment.

This example is not given with the intention of criticising the NVQ system as a legitimate and useful tool of HRD. It is simply illustrative of the complexity of answering the questions 'In whose interests do you exercise it?' (power) and 'To whom are you accountable?' once it has been accepted that all organisational behaviour has a power dimension.

CONCLUSIONS

The following chapters, in the final section of this book, deal with practice. They explore issues of implementation and realisation of the perspectives and strategies outlined in the preceding chapters. What this chapter has set out to demonstrate is that power and influence, whilst being both perceptual and strategic concepts, cannot exist except in practice. Even 'potential' or 'latent' power is already existing in practice to the extent that it is acknowledged by others as a possibility and thus has consequences in the minds or behaviour of those who perceive it.

The issues of power and influence in practice are wide ranging. The accurate audit of one's own power as a HRD specialist, of the influence of one's HRD department, and of the pervasive influence of HRD ideology within a workplace culture, is an essential prerequisite for effective operation. A knowledge of types of power, both personal and organisational, and a strategy for consolidating and augmenting influence is virtually imperative if the HRD department is to survive, particularly with the growth of management multi-skilling and flatter organisational hierarchies. An understanding of and commitment to the development of influencing skills is an almost required CPD accomplishment of the HRD professional.

Finally, there is an ethical dimension to any use of power. Business ethics is a growth industry. The professional Institute of Personnel and Development has its own code of ethics incumbent upon its members. Whilst ethics in HRD clearly applies to many issues other than just the exercise of power, there can never be any situation involving the use of power which does *not* present an ethical issue. Traditionally it has been assumed that the exercise of legitimate power is, by definition, ethical, but that is to take the view that organisational authority is beyond question. This chapter should have provided evidence that power and influence are concepts which should be subject to analysis and debate, both theoretically and pragmatically in the organisational context.

References

Argyle, M. (1987) *The Psychology of Happiness*, London, Methuen.

Batstone, E. *et al.* (1978) *The Social Organisation of Strikes*, Oxford, Blackwell.

Coopers and Lybrand Associates (1985) *A Challenge to Complacency: Changing Attitudes to Training*, Sheffield, Manpower Services Commission.

Crozier, M. (1964) *The Bureaucratic Phenomenon*, Chicago, University of Chicago Press.

Daft, R.C. (1992) *Organisation Theory and Design*, Fourth edition, West Publications.

Etzioni, A. (1961) 'A Comparative Analysis of Complex Organisations', in Matteson, M.J. and Ivancevich, J.M. eds (1989) *Management and Organisational Behaviour*, Illinois, BP Irwin.

Foucault, M. (1980) *Power/Knowledge*, Brighton, Harvester Press.

Fox, S. (1990) 'Strategic HRM: Postmodern Conditioning for the Corporate Culture', *Management Education and Development*, vol. 21, part 3, Autumn.

French, J.R.P. and Raven, B.H. (1959) 'The Social Bases of Power', in Cartwright, D. ed. (1959) *Studies in Social Power*, Ann Arbor, University of Michigan Press.

Garavan, T.N., Barnicle, B. and Harriet, N. (1993) 'The Training and Development Function: Its Search for Power and Influence in Organizations', *Journal of European Industrial Training*, vol. 17, no. 7, pp. 22–32.

Gill, J. and Johnson, P. (1993) *Management Control and Organizational Behaviour*, London, Paul Chapman.

Grace, P. and Straub, C. (1991) 'Managers as Training Assets', *Journal of Training and Development*, June, pp. 49–54.

Handy, C.B. (1985) *Understanding Organisations*, Harmondsworth, Penguin.

Hickson, D.J., Hinings, C.R., Lee, C.A., Schneck, R.E. and Pennings, J.M. (1971) 'A strategic contingencies theory of intraorganisational power', *Administrative Science Quarterly*, vol. 16, pp. 216–29.

Josefowitz, N. (1985) *Paths to Power*, Columbus.

Kahn, R.L. and Boulding, E. (1964) *Power and Conflict in Organisations*, London, Tavistock Publications.

Kanter, R.M. (1977) 'Power Failure in Management Circuits', *Harvard Business Review*, July–August.

Kaplan, A. (1964) 'Power in Perspective', in Kahn, R.L. and Boulding, E. eds (1964) *Power and Conflict in Organisations*, London, Tavistock Publications.

King, W. (1989) 'Advisory Power and Predicament in Organisational Training', *Journal of European Industrial Training*, vol. 13, no. 3. pp. 19–31.

Leduchowicz, T. (1984) *A Guide to Trainer Effectiveness*, Sheffield, Manpower Services Commission.

Lukes, S. (1974) *Power: A Radical View*, London, Macmillan.

Mintzberg, H. (1983) *Power in and Around Organizations*, Englewood Cliffs NJ, Prentice Hall.

Pelz, D.C. (1952) 'Influence: A key to effective leadership in the first-line supervisor', *Personnel*, no. 29, pp. 3–11.

Peters, Tom. (1994 Columns 'On Excellence', weekly, *The Independent on Sunday*.

Pettigrew, H.M. (1985) *The Awakening Giant – Continuity and Change in ICI*, Oxford, Basil Blackwell.

Pettigrew, H.M., Jones, G.R. and Reason, P.W. (1982) *Training and Development Roles in their Organisational Setting*, Sheffield, Manpower Services Commission.

Pfeffer, J. (1981) *Power in Organisations*, Marshfield MA, Pitman.

Quick, T.C. (1987) 'Building Your Own Power Base', *Journal of Training and Development*, June, pp. 16–22.

Ryan, M. (1989) 'Political Behaviour and Management Development', *Management Education and Development*, vol. 20, part 3, Autumn.

Salanicik, G.R. and Pfeffer, J. (1977) 'Who Gets Power and How They Hold Onto It – A Strategic Contingency Model of Power', *Organisational Dynamics*, Winter Issue.

Tobias, R. (1993) *The Politics of Meeting Learner Needs*, paper presented to the annual conference of the Aotearoa/New Zealand Association for Community and Continuing Education, August 27–30, Christchurch, NZ.

Weber, M. (1968) *Economy and Society*, New York, Bedminster Press.

ACTIVITIES FOR SECTION II

1 (a) Describe your view of strategy.

(b) Consider how your view is reflected in the chapters in this section of the book.

(c) Discuss the results with colleagues. Attempt to reach a consensus on what can constitute strategy.

2 (a) Formulate a design for a HRD intervention which could be considered to have strategic impact.

(b) Consider how the arguments presented in this section can be used to justify your design.

(c) Present your design and supporting arguments to colleagues.

(d) Review the results of this activity and their implications for the design of future HRD interventions.

3 (a) Prepare a strategic analysis of your organisation.

(b) Critically evaluate the role and contribution of current HRD interventions in supporting the strategic needs of your organisation.

(c) Consider how the ideas and arguments presented in this section can be used to inform development of HRD to support organisation strategy.

(d) Prepare and present to colleagues a revised HRD strategy.

Section III

HRD PRACTICE

10

THE TRAINER AS CHANGE AGENT:
ISSUES FOR PRACTICE

Bob Hamlin and Goronwy Davies

11

INFLUENCE, COMMUNICATION AND
NEURO-LINGUISTIC PROGRAMMING IN PRACTICE

Ursula Lyon

12

ACTION LEARNING AS A CROSS-CULTURAL TOOL

Monica Lee

13

THE ROLE OF THE ACTION LEARNING SET

Sue Williams

14

RESEARCH METHODS AND HRD

Goronwy Davies

10

The Trainer as Change Agent: Issues for Practice

Bob Hamlin and Goronwy Davies

INTRODUCTION

One of the problems facing the human resource developer in the 1990s is the different focus given to the challenge of managing people at work, where organisations are having to deal with uncertain futures, are striving to survive in turbulent and harshly competitive markets or working environments, and are having to develop survival strategies which take account of these factors. Morgan (1988) suggests the need for managers to create semi-permanent order out of turbulence and Handy (1989) indicates that the major problem for managers in the future will be dealing with what he calls discontinuity in organisational environments. The result of this analysis has led to the advocacy of different forms of organisation (Peters, 1988; Drucker, 1988; Handy, 1990 amongst others) which has led to the development of a strategic managerial emphasis within organisations. This emphasis, adopted by strategic thinking managers, has shifted progressively from that of stressing values of efficiency to one where efficiency, quality, flexibility and innovativeness as managerial value imperatives are now part of the everyday experience of people at work. Employees, as a collective at work, are being exhorted to become more efficient, more quality oriented, more flexible and more innovative – in order to keep costs down and to ensure organisational survival. They are being forced or encouraged to change the way they work, and to accept different ways of being organised and managed in order to gain competitive advantage.

Clearly, within these transformations of working practice, of organisation and managerial thinking, there are implications for the role of the trainer. In the past there has been much practical confusion about the role of the trainer and of the training department. Often the function has been located and subordinated within a more amorphous personnel department, or has found itself separated and peripheral to the mainstream activities of the business. As such this functional subordination or separation has frequently affected the way that the deliverer of training has been involved in the development of the organisation. At best, the trainer may have been involved in dealing with human resource issues and policies, with training being delivered within that involvement or, at worst, the trainer will have mechanistically delivered training within some policy vacuum – where training has been seen by the organisation as an end, not as a means of realising part of a coherent organisational strategy. In the 1990s this quasi debate about the relative role, value and importance of the training function as opposed to the more generalised, policy-driven personnel function, has been overtaken by the recognition of the need to develop human resource strategies that meet organisational objectives for competitive advantage and survival.

Organisations appear to be in a state of permanent change, are being strategically driven and therefore need human resource specialists who can think strategically about the organisation. Within this different orientation, the training role and function is changing so that the trainer needs to develop a different set of expectations concerning new and different roles. Phillips and Shaw (1989) refer to trainer roles being in transition from training to consulting. They have identified three distinctively different development paths for trainers, namely that of the training consultant, the learning consultant and the organisation change consultant respectively. Particularly in the latter role the human resource specialist needs to develop expertise in scanning the environment, in thinking strategically about the implications of organisational strategy for 'the human resource', in contributing fully at a senior level in the development of organisational strategy or at least influencing it, and in devising and implementing strategies for change – and organising and delivering training effectively within this context. The trainer must understand what is required to become an effective agent of change and successful human resource development manager. This chapter aims to make clear to trainers that decisions concerning the effective management of change in this evolving organisational role necessarily involve an understanding of theoretical complexity implicit in the different stages of a change process. However, we do not develop this analysis naively because we are aware of the academic debate concerning the development, effectiveness and value orientation of the term *human resource management*, and what it means theoretically and practically. We share some of the misgivings concerning the definition of the term and what the implications of the term are for management myth making, and who benefits from strategies based on the value orientation of 'human resource management' as practised. (For a more comprehensive map of this debate see Blyton and Turnbull, 1992.) However, as the role of the trainer is in transition for the reasons briefly identified above, in what follows we restrict ourselves to questions that need to be answered theoretically and practically by a trainer who is embarking on a strategically defined organisational change initiative; we then go on to discuss what this process could mean for the trainer acting in the role of change agent. The chapter is developed to answer questions which reflect decisions that need to be taken in relation to the effective management of change. These are:

- how can I make sense of my organisation?
- how can I devise an appropriate strategy for change?
- how can I implement the strategy?
- how can I evaluate the effectiveness of the implementation strategy?
- how does this challenge my role as a change agent?

ORGANISATIONAL ANALYSIS

How can I make sense of my organisation?

Organisational analysis, or making sense of the organisation, involves a greater depth of understanding on the part of the trainer as change agent than has traditionally been required when carrying out conventional training needs analyses. This is because structure, function and their relationship to the core activity of the organisation need to be analysed in depth before developing appropriate strategies for change. Crucially, such analysis develops a set of spectacles through which the change agent will 'look at' the organisation. However, the way in which organisations are looked at will affect the way in which change agents should act to initiate and manage change subsequently.

Historically, the academic analysis of organisations has been influenced by the way that social scientists, psychologists, biologists, information theorists and anthropologists have applied theoretical explanations within those disciplines. In attempting to understand organisations the field of study has moved from an original industrial–business focus to a wider application embracing both private, public and voluntary sector organisations. We are aware that the line between the private, the public and the voluntary sector has become increasingly blurred as we have moved ever closer toward the new millennium. However, the distinction serves our purpose within this context. The theory which is apparently designed to inform organisational analysis has developed into the field of organisational behaviour, and as such is theoretically diverse. When analysed it is eclectic in its application to the world of the organisation of work. The main problem that confronts the trainer as change agent is that sometimes there is a conflict between the implicit theories of the individual based on a personal evaluation of the experience of a particular role within an organisation, and the different requirement needed to develop analytical, strategic thinking which, by its nature, is more abstract and therefore difficult to apply.

In what follows we give very brief descriptions of the main assumptions behind various theoretical perspectives, and state how these provide a focus for the study of organisations; we then state what the change advocated by the theory would imply. (In order to develop the appropriate depth of understanding that we believe is essential, it is important that readers develop their own depth of insight by making use of the references at the end of the chapter, particularly Mullins, 1993.)

'Structural Functionalism' perspective

Organisation A set of structures within which people are directed to function.

Analysis Analyses both the formal and informal structures of the organisation and focuses on conflict, particularly between managers and workers.

Change Change the structures and hence the functions in order to reduce conflict within the organisation.

'Human Relationship' perspective

Organisation   A network of patterned relationships, where the pattern is determined by the organisation.

Analysis   Analyses the needs and motives of individuals in order to understand the conflict between organisational goals and individual needs.

Change   Facilitate change so that organisational structures and functions more readily meet the needs of the individual.

'Psychodynamic' perspective

Organisation   A psychodynamic defence against anxiety.

Analysis   Analyses the individual's projections, rationalisations, dependence and counter dependence behaviours.

Change   Facilitate the individual to realise the implications of defensive behaviour and then implement the implications of these realisations for behaviour in relation to different structures and functions within the organisation.

'Systems Theory' perspective

Organisation   A hard system of variables (within and across functions) interacting with soft variables (people) within the organisation.

Analysis   Analyses the organisational systems, understanding that any part of the system analysed will be affected by the other parts – systematically.

Change Change parts of the system, understanding that this change will have systematic effects on the other parts of the organisation making up the whole.

'Contingency Theory' perspective

Organisation   A set of systems and sub-systems which are dependent on the particular contingencies of the environment of the system or sub-system.

Analysis   Analyses the organisational systems of management and understands how these systematic features of the organisation are contingent upon the nature of organisational tasks and the organisational environment.

Change   Change the contingencies within the system in order to develop the most appropriate structure and management system.

'Action Frame of Reference' perspective

Organisation   A network of actively constructed meanings.

Analysis   Analyses the interactions within organisations to establish the meaning of the interactions from the participants' point of view, in order to understand the rules which govern organisational behaviour.

Change   Change the rules which govern behaviour in order to change and transform the meaning of the organisation for the individual.

'Cultures, Ethnographic and Metaphorical' perspectives

Organisation   Interpreted as a constructed, distinctive symbolic culture.

Analysis   Interpret the symbolic significance of the actively negotiated, shared symbols and meanings within the organisation by understanding the emerging pattern of inter-actions and meanings from the participants' point of view.

Change   Change the meaning of the symbols within the culture of the organisation.

Newer perspectives

Newer perspectives have developed which tend to be more classificatory in their analysis, where distinctions are drawn between what is extant now and what should be in the future. For instance, there is a view that much of what is identified above is mechanistic in terms of the analytical approach to be adopted, and this is contrasted with an organic approach to understanding features of organisations. As an example, Buchanan and Boddy (1992) differentiate between 'crisp' rules of authority as features of mechanistic organisations, whereas 'fuzzy' rules are associated with organic structures (see Burns and Stalker, 1966, for a fuller account of this mechanistic/organic distinction). Another distinction which is being drawn by academics is that between the modern, mechanistic organisation, and a post-modern critique which develops ideas concerning the post-modern organisation (see Hassard and Parker, 1993, for a fuller understanding of this debate). These analyses tend to be academic in nature but others locate their analysis within what has been a developing managerial perspective.

Stacey (1992) applies *chaos theory* when he advocates a discontinuous form of strategic intervention in order to change organisations faced with an unpredictable world; Peters and Waterman (1982) argue that organisations need to develop a form of attribute analysis in order to achieve excellence; Kanter (1989) indicates the need for the development of the post-entrepreneurial organisation and Handy (1989) suggests that new knowledge-based structures must evolve within organisations of the future. Currently, there is also much discussion of the *learning organisation*. (See Pedler *et al.*, 1991; Swieringa and Weirdsma, 1992; and Semler, 1993, who provides a good analysis of the stages within a process of democratisation of organisations in Brazil.)

In using different approaches for understanding, changing and developing organisations, Hallworth (1994) argues the case for combining the best of the *hard* systems perspectives (e.g. through organisational structures and systems etc.) with the best of the *soft* systems perspectives (e.g. through motivation, HR, team development, etc.) and draws attention to the concept of *re-engineering learning processes*. This approach focuses on those key processes that are interlinked dynamically and which have significant influence over any organisational development, namely *business strategy*, *organisational culture* and *organisation learning*. In his view these are the three major determinants of successful organisational change.

The difficulty that the trainer as change agent has is in deciding on an appropriate form of analysis – for example, whether to locate the analysis in theoretical terms as applied in the different academic frames identified above, or whether she/he wishes to adopt a more grounded approach which is eclectic, rooted in experience and which has direct functional consequences in terms of strategies for the change to be adopted. Our view is that an analysis of the organisation must take place as the important first step. We believe this understanding acts as the groundstone for the development of an appropriate strategy for change, and also for the successful implementation of the change within the organisation subsequently.

However, we are aware that there may be significant control issues for the trainer as change agent and we acknowledge that there are different consequences for action depending on whether or not the trainer is involved in the change process from the beginning. In the next section we discuss the different strategies that are available for implementation.

STRATEGIES FOR CHANGE

How can I devise an appropriate strategy for change?
Currently strategic management is undergoing a re-examination in terms of its assumptions and implications (see Stacey, 1992). However, there have been different perspectives which can be distinguished. Johnson (1987) suggests the process can be distinguished in terms of whether the approach used reflects a rationalist, adaptive or interpretative view. A rationalistic view of strategic management is seen as the outcome of a sequential, planned search for an optimal solution to defined problems, with implementation following on from the decisions made about such problems; an adaptive view of strategic management is one which is incremental and evolves as an additive pattern; and an interpretative view is one in which strategy is seen as the product of individual or collective sense making.

Our position is that any devised plan for action used as a strategy must include reference to time, to process and to context, and that change agents must be strategically rational. However, having devised some plan for action we also, with Buchanan and Boddy (1992), understand that rational strategies have to account for the fact that change is chaotic because of continuous changing agendas, and because of discontinuous management activities and unexpected events occurring within organisations which affect the change strategies adopted.

As a result, if the organisation as devised and experienced by people at work reflected an ideal, it would be easier to be prescriptive about what would be necessary in order to plan appropriate strategies for change. However, as organisations have different objectives and do not constitute an ideal type, this means that strategies for change themselves need to be analysed and characterised in order for them to be used appropriately by change agents operating in different circumstances or organisations. Having understood and developed an appropriate framework for the analysis of the organisation so that the particular organisational context can be understood, we believe that the change agent then needs to reflect about the possibilities for appropriate change. What proves possible will be dependent on the following parameters (Buchanan and Boddy, 1992) which indicate there are different consequences for change depending on whether:

1 the change is incremental over time and will involve a change to the organisation that will affect the core objectives of the organisation;
2 the change is incremental over time and will involve a change to the organisation that is peripheral to the objectives of the organisation;
3 the change is a radical, major change over time and will involve a change to the organisation that will affect the core objectives of the organisation;
4 the change is a radical, major change over time and will involve a change to the organisation that is peripheral to the objectives of the organisation.

Also, the change agent will need to consider the extent to which the change will involve a participative or forced evolution of the organisation, and whether the transformation involved would be charismatic or dictatorial in terms of the authority, power and leadership characteristics to be shown by management involved in the changes advocated (Dunphy and Stace, 1988).

We believe that as well as the need to analyse the organisation in some depth, there is also a strategic need to characterise the type of organisational change that has been determined. There will be clear implications for the change agent in terms of the way a particular strategy can be specifically implemented within the organisation, and adopted more generally for organisational life. The implementation of strategy within the organisation will be bounded by the considerations we have developed here. For instance, both private and public sector organisations are currently considering or applying managerial, off-the-shelf strategies for change to meet quality and efficiency objectives. BS5750 has been adopted by a large number of organisations as a first step towards introducing total quality management, TQM; similarly in manufacturing certain organisations have attempted to develop Kaizen strategies to change working practices and increase the quality and competitiveness of products. As part of this change in managerial thinking, the present Government, through the Training and Enterprise Councils in England and Wales and Local Enterprise Companies in Scotland, is sponsoring an Investors in People strategy for organisational change which has clear implications for the human resource development function. Further, and more recently, organisations are developing strategies for change which focus on re-engineering the business process. Business process re-engineering, BPR, focuses on organisational processes rather than organisational functions, and is designed to cut costs by identifying process features which need consideration for change within the way the organisation is structured. CSC Index (1994), a leading re-engineering consultancy, claim that 69 per cent of US and 75 per cent of European organisations have at least one ongoing re-engineering project.

As change agents, trainers need to be aware that research tells us that various quality and process strategies for change, such as those identified above, may not always produce the expected benefits. Kearney(1994) suggests this is the case with TQM strategies, and Hamel and Prahalad (1994) report the same for BPR initiatives. Clearly, there are problems concerning the implementation of particular change strategies, where all those mentioned above have human resource management and development implications.

Bearing this in mind, we will now consider problems concerning the implementation of strategies for change.

STRATEGY IMPLEMENTATION

How can I implement the strategy for change?

As we have said in the previous section there appears to be some concern expressed in the literature about the relative failure of the implementation of particular change strategies adopted in different kinds of organisations. (For examples see Anthony, 1994.) We believe that an appropriate depth of organisational analysis and knowledge of the particular characteristics of the change strategy to be adopted, as determined through the skills and abilities of the change agent, are crucial in ensuring the relative success of implementation. The other issue is a practical one. In the past, it was common within managerial practice to pick a change strategy 'off the shelf' and then to implement the strategy by formula. We believe there is a need to develop a managerial stance which acknowledges that the discontinuities of organisational life are continuous, that the change advocated will be likely to increase the discontinuities, and that the change process needs to be constant and continuing in terms of the care and attention given to its implementation over long periods of time. Organisational change cannot be a 'quick fix' in order to ensure survival.

Advocates of the implementation process have developed a recipe formula for implementation which has unfortunate connotations. However, within the recipe there may be some useful ideas which could be of value to the change agent . . . but it depends on the change and organisational context within which the trainer as the change agent is implementing strategy.

Early developments in the field of change implementation and organisation development rest on the work of Lewin (1958) who suggested a three-stage model for successful change. The first stage involves unfreezing the attitudes and behaviours being expressed currently within the organisation; a second stage involves changing these attitudes and behaviours in the desired direction; followed by a third stage of refreezing these changed attitudes and behaviours so that the desired behaviours will be maintained permanently.

This model has more recently been refined by Johnson (1990) so that implementation strategy represents a series of symbolic acts to be utilised by the change agent as shown in Table 10.1. These models infer that organisations are not in a state of flux initially, which is how they are experienced, and they implicitly assume that the change process is discrete rather than continuous. They also assume that people within organisations can be taken out of refrigerators, changed and then put back to be frozen permanently. We believe that this way of thinking has a limited value; this is because it does not reflect the contextualisation of the change process within an organisational framework, where the change agent has to show other skills and abilities to ensure the success of the implementation of the change both inside and outside the refrigerator.

Harrison (1994) also draws attention to the need for change agents to move beyond the traditional organisation development model. As he points out, this model has been based on a very narrow view of organisational effectiveness and the training and small

Table 10.1

Change agent acts	Change agent behaviour
Unfreezing	Challenge current ways of doing things, close down parts of the organisation, move people around
Flux	Foster conflict and dissent through open argument
Information building	Set up task forces, use consultant reports, commission special reports
Experimentation	Devise management development training programmes, signal change with new product displays, services and other departures from the previous way of doing things
Refreezing	Send signals of irreversible and permanent change, through celebrations and new key appointments

group interventions favoured by OD practitioners have often failed to grapple with the realities of organisational politics and culture. For these reasons he argues that traditional OD techniques appear not to work well in organisations that emphasise status and authority differences, or in countries that do not share the values underlying organisation development. Furthermore, even where they have been appropriate, traditional OD interventions have usually yielded only minor, incremental improvements in organisational effectiveness, as opposed to the radical transformations required to recover from crisis and decline (Dunphy and Stace, 1988).

As we have stated earlier, we believe that the change agent must acknowledge the relative importance of the change within the overall objectives of the organisation, and how much the change to be adopted will be disruptive of previously valued behaviour. Therefore, the change agent must develop skills of leadership, of communication sideways, upward and downward depending on the organisational structure, and of organisational 'nous' in order to manage the process in terms of the power and politics of the organisation. Therefore, as well as developing role skills of the kind identified here the trainer, when involved in the role of change agent, must constantly analyse and monitor the politics of the situation in order to develop political strategies which enable the change to take place with political support within the organisation. We believe that if these contextual issues are identified and managed one set of managerial barriers to change will have been removed, more or less.

Other problems confront the change agent at this stage of implementation which can be defined in terms of the more commonly reported barriers to change. The barriers to change commonly recited are well known to human resource specialists and revolve around individual, group and organisational problems. (See Carnall, 1990, for a comprehensive list of individual and group 'blocks' to change.) Further, Carnall (1991) identifies reasons for the failure of the implementation stage of the process by indicating organisational features which need to be considered by the change agent. The most commonly cited reasons for failure are:

'Implementation took more time than originally allocated; major problems surfaced during implementation which had not been identified beforehand; Co-ordination of implementation activities was not effective enough; Competing

activities and crises distracted management from implementing the change deci-sion; The capabilities of the employees involved were not sufficient; Training and instruction given to lower level employees was inadequate; Uncontrollable fac-tors in the external environment had an adverse impact on implementation.'
(Carnall, 1991)

From this it can be seen that the trainer has to think strategically about strategy implementation within the context of how the organisation has been defined, and of how the strategy for change can be classified. He/she also has to act practically to implement the strategy within the power and political context of the organisation, bearing in mind the particular barriers to change which will occur within a specific organisational setting. We believe the whole process of implementation must be man-aged effectively all of the time – with the change agent 'performing' across all of the different levels of the organisation in order to facilitate the change process at the indi-vidual, group and organisational level. However, before failure is contemplated spuriously, the change agent needs to know how to evaluate the effectiveness of the change implemented.

EVALUATION OF CHANGE EFFECTIVENESS

How can I evaluate the effectiveness of the implementation strategy?
In the previous section we identified reported reasons for the failure of change imple-mentation strategies in 93 organisations (Carnall, 1991). We made no comment about the fact that the reasons developed could have reflected an estimate in the minds of man-agers concerning the effectiveness of the change strategies adopted, rather than having resulted from an ongoing evaluation which clearly identified the causes of failure. The area of evaluation is a problem in terms of the processes of change management because there is a paucity of studies indicating whether commonly accepted recipes for action actually work – in some, or in all organisations. Therefore, we make the plea to change agents that they should build ongoing evaluation into all of the change processes which they control or help to facilitate.

We believe that if trainers are going to take on the mantle of change agent, they must be placed in a position of being able to contribute to the process of strategic decision making concerned with planning organisational effectiveness for the future. This is a dif-ferent way of saying that those involved in the formulation of mission statements and in business planning for effectiveness should include those who will have to bear the con-sequences of such decisions. As it is now broadly recognised that one of the major consequences of such visionary planning is related to changes in human resource man-agement practices, the need to involve trainers and other HRM specialists in the process of planning strategic change appears to us to be self-evident. With involvement at this early stage, influential human resource managers will help derive objectives which can act as criteria for deciding on the effectiveness or otherwise of the strategy for change, or changes implied within such strategic activity.

The use and value of a 'deep' analysis of the organisation as advocated in this chap-ter will enable the trainer acting as a change agent to derive a series of effectiveness/

ineffectiveness statements concerning the organisation. This will enable the change agent to monitor the effect of the change strategy envisioned in discussions of organisational strategy, because in the process of business planning the organisational analysis made will act to enable appropriate criteria to be tested out against reality, once the change is in process. We believe the change agent must adopt the stance of evaluation at the beginning of the planning process. Carnall (1990) suggests that change effectiveness can be assessed if, as part of the change process, appropriate questions are asked concerning people, finance, marketing, operations, and business development . . . over time, in order to monitor and evaluate appropriately.

Otherwise the problem of the evaluation of strategies for change needs to be recognised as one of the most under reported issues in the British management literature. This may be because the problem is seen as a research issue. However, the implication for trainers operating as change agents is that they have a need to address the problem of developing the appropriate evaluative and research skills required to address the validity of claims that could be made in relation to the success or otherwise of a change strategy. (The reader should be aware that Chapter 14 covers research skills later.)

THE ROLE OF THE CHANGE AGENT

How does this view of the processes of change challenge my role as change agent?
Clearly what has been said in the previous sections will have direct implications for the changing role of the trainer and manager of the training function. We believe that there are different expectations developing for those who function within the field of human resource development and human resource management. What has become clear over the past 10 years is that the role of the trainer is having to change in order to meet the increasing demand for HRD professionals who have specialist knowledge and expertise within the disciplines of organisational behaviour and organisational development as well as training and development. This changing role has clear implications for the development of new sets of skills and abilities in the area of change management. Buchanan and Boddy (1992) and Carnall (1990) more fully identify the competencies necessary in order to develop expertise as a change agent, and we believe that their emphasis on role expectations as expressed will be helpful to the trainer, particularly in the context of coping with change.

Any change usually creates anxiety and stress because of associated uncertainties. In the case of the changing role expectations as briefly identified here, we believe that it is important for trainers to develop a support network in order to cope with the stress that can be created by the differing pressures associated with the change agent role. Carnall (1991) is helpful in identifying a process which accounts for different performance variations over time, and also a psychological process which the change agent will be involved with and will need to account for during the implementation stage of the change. He suggests that individuals and groups in the organisation will experience differential effects on performance because of the change process. New systems, procedures, processes and ways of behaving will have to be learned which will take time and will reflect a learning curve effect. When these new behaviours are being learned there will also be a progress effect in that modifications will have to be developed to deal with 'snags' as they arise within the change process. Finally, he suggests that significant organisational change will have differential effects on the self-esteem of different individuals in the organisation as they become affected by the implications of the change.

The change agent must be aware of these implications in terms of the significance for behaviour of direct change processes and also of an associated psychological process. Carnall describes these processes in relation to stages, the first being a denial of the need to change, successively followed by stages of a defence of the old ways of doing things, a discarding of these old behaviours by the majority before adaptation to the new changes, followed by a stage of internalisation of the change behaviours. Change agents need to understand these elements within the change process, as well as how to take care of themselves in order to deal successfully with the implications of change strategies and the high stress levels associated with the role. So, take care!

ILLUSTRATIVE CASE STUDY 1

Background to the case

The company in question is a producer of raw materials used in the manufacture of high technology products and is located in the North of England. The business was originally a family run private company but in 1986 was purchased by a UK multi-national plc and positioned into one of its major divisions. At the time of takeover the company, which had a history of stable employment, comprised two discrete businesses operating on the same site with on-site directors in direct control.

Following the change of ownership this all changed, with each of the two businesses being subsequently managed by a local management team reporting to divisional managers based elsewhere, and who also had world-wide responsibilities. Financial control was now double-headed with a dual reporting relationship both to the Divisional Headquarters and to the Head Office plc in London. In 1992 the division was restructured into a vertically integrated organisation which manufactured everything from raw materials through to finished products, in a closed chain of geographically remote but organisationally connected companies. Non-core businesses were either sold off or closed down.

This meant the company featured in this case no longer marketed its materials to external customers, but instead sold them into the division's internal customer chain. Furthermore, during the seven years from the time of the takeover the overall numbers employed had been cut back by about 60 per cent. As a result there was much suspicion, cynicism and antagonism towards the 'new outsider' managers who were blamed for the pain caused by the contraction of the labour force.

In mid 1993 a new CEO was appointed who was charged with the task of merging the two businesses whilst at the same time increasing profitability. His business agenda was to concentrate the business onto core activities, to reduce costs, combine sales and to rationalise the administration and technical support functions. The challenge facing the organisation as defined by the CEO was how to:

- fully integrate the two businesses and remove the pre-existing rivalries;
- establish an effective organisational structure;
- eliminate disparity in pay and conditions between the two businesses;
- improve quality and the level of customer service;
- improve productivity;
- reduce lost time accident rates;
- remove the traditional inflexible working practices;
- overcome the suspicion and cynicism of the workforce;
- rebuild confidence and teamwork;
- develop an environment where everyone became involved and took responsibility for their own learning.

This provided the context and focus for a major organisational change initiative.

The organisational analysis

As part of the change agenda the CEO decided there was a need to adopt a research approach for some of the issues. Therefore, with the help of an external training consultant, he compared the three main options for conducting business research, namely 'pure' research, consultancy and action research respectively. (See Gill and Johnson, 1991, for a detailed comparison.) 'Pure' research was rejected as it would not meet the necessary requirement to contribute immediately and directly to the development of the organisation. Consultancy was dismissed because the company was now wary of anything that might look like prescription or was overtly interventionist. In the event an action research approach was chosen and the research project was split into three separate project groups which focused upon Management and Organisation Development issues, Pay and Conditions, and Health and Safety respectively.

It was decided that each project group would comprise a team of internal managers and key staff led by a senior executive who would be supported by one or more external consultants acting as change agents/facilitators. The latter comprised a professional trainer from an industry related training organisation plus three academics who were experts in their respective specialist fields.

The theoretical perspectives utilised for underpinning the research activities of these three groups, and for providing the necessary diagnostic focus for the respective studies, were drawn mainly from the literature on *structural functionalism*, *systems theory* and on *cultures*. A perspective that was deployed across all three projects was one that could be described by the notion of the *learning organisation*.

Strategies for change

The Management and Organisation Development Project Group, which was seen as the key group for triggering and effecting change within the organisation, was charged with a two-fold task: first, to create a vision and set targets for what the business had to achieve; and second, to identify and put into practice the most appropriate managerial philosophy and approach for achieving the targets. The requirement was to define the company mission, its values and the way forward; to identify clearly the problems and causes affecting the organisation's ability to achieve its corporate objectives; to develop a management action plan for personal and organisation development; and to formulate specific plans of action for initiating the required organisational change.

The change strategy adopted was to mount a series of management conferences that were held off site, the outcomes of which were linked through individual action plans and regular reporting of progress at the monthly on-site executive meetings. In addition the external facilitators actively worked with managers, helping them to address their respective personal development plans as well as the various group dynamic issues that had arisen. Furthermore it was decided to classify the organisational culture in an attempt to develop a framework by which to both plan and monitor the changes taking place. Additionally an analysis was also made of the existing overt and covert power structures, and of the impact of the use and interplay of power within the organisation.

The methods used included, for example, communication audits, attitude surveys, managerial and team role analyses and leadership style diagnostic instruments.

One important conclusion arising from the organisational diagnosis was that the managerial style deemed most appropriate was the 9.9 style on the Blake and Mouton Managerial Grid (1988). Consequently training and development strategies were implemented to move all of the managers at all levels of the organisation towards this style of management.

The Pay and Conditions Project Group, which comprised a range of employees drawn from all disciplines and all levels of the organisation, was tasked to develop a new pay structure covering all non-managerial employees of the company. It had to be equitable, skills-based and acceptable both to the organisation and to the trade unions and workforce.

A three stage strategy was adopted: first, an analysis of the emerging organisational context including the issues of culture and commitment; second, the design of the pay system; and third, the planning and execution of training and assessment strategies to ensure smooth implementation.

The main strategy adopted by the Health and Safety Project Group, which comprised a small multi-functional team of managers drawn from all departments, was first to have themselves trained in the skills of training by the external facilitator attached to the group. Then through the process of action learning they developed a learner-centred health and safety training programme which was designed specifically to encourage all employees to take more responsibility for their own and others' safety. This programme was facilitated by the project group with each team member contributing their own specialist knowledge and expertise.

Evaluation of change effectiveness

At the outset of the change programme it was anticipated that the company would move significantly towards becoming a learning organisation, and that evidence of this shift would indicate how successful the change strategies had been.

Hence, besides the regular monitoring of progress against specific change objectives set by the different project groups, a separate evaluation was carried out at the end of the action research project to assess the extent to which the characteristics of a learning organisation had become obvious. The particular models used for this purpose included the five-phase model of Jones and Hendry (1992) and the cyclic model of Garratt (1990), plus benchmarking against key performance measures for world class manufacturing organisations as published by Anderson Consulting (1993).

In the case of this particular company most of the change objectives were actually achieved. Furthermore it was concluded that the process of building into the everyday life of the company the components that make up a learning organisation, had in fact been a significant factor in bringing about successful and beneficial organisational change.

Case references

Anderson Consulting (1993) *The Lean Enterprise Benchmarking Project.*
Blake, R. and Mouton, J.S. (1988) *The Managerial Grid III – The Key to Leadership and Excellence*, London, Gulf.

Garratt, B. (1990) *Creating a Learning Organisation*, Fitzwilliam.
Gill, J. and Johnson, P. (1991) *Research Methods for Managers*, London, Paul Chapman.
Jones, A.M. and Hendry, C. (1982) *The Learning Organisation*, HRD Partnership.

ILLUSTRATIVE CASE STUDY 2

Background to the case

This case describes the contributions of a training manager and her team of trainers acting in the role of change agent at the time of a major organisational change when two directly managed hospital units within a District Health Authority were merged to become eventually an NHS Trust Hospital. One of the two hospitals had a 'centralist' type of organisational structure supporting a certain amount of devolved authority at the point of service delivery. However, the culture and management style tended towards a top down 'hands-on' approach. In contrast the other hospital had a management style compatible with a totally devolved structure and a 'hands-off' culture. Clearly, for the merger to succeed the two hospitals had to become fully integrated which meant a new style and culture had to be developed.

The organisational analysis

Some time prior to the merger actually being initiated the training manager of one of the hospitals was asked by the newly designated CEO for the new Trust Hospital to carry out an OD audit of both hospital units. Its purpose was to identify all of the OD issues that needed to be addressed in order to ensure the effective implementation of a new organisational structure and style. The CEO intended to introduce new management arrangements which incorporated a fully devolved managerial style with decision making and the managing of resources taking place at the lowest level of the organisation. The audit involved carrying out strategic and organisational capability analyses in order to understand better the potential capabilities of the new Trust Hospital required for meeting fully the immediate needs of the different markets it served, for continuous improvement and for longer-term organisational survival.

The analysis focused on such key elements as the strategies required to meet the marketing needs, the leadership required to drive these strategies and the linkage of these to the new culture, structures and processes of the hospital. Aligning the strategy with the culture was perceived as key to the successful implementation of the organisational change and therefore early consideration was given to this issue. Effective communication was also considered to be extremely important for keeping all staff and managers informed of specific actions and issues along the way. Hence the major effort was focused on facilitating both 'culture' and 'communications' audits which were carried out at the same time.

Strategies for change

The training manager plus her team of trainers worked on various organisational development interventions and actions throughout the change programme, providing personal and organisational development support on an internal consultancy basis. Many of the interventions were delivered as 'project managed' assignments with emphasis being given to evaluation and feedback which often triggered further OD interventions and projects. Much of the OD effort was concerned with understanding the data that had been gathered and the conditions surrounding it; a strong emphasis was placed on problem solving rather than on an attempted enforcement of anticipated required behaviours. Throughout the change programme the major concern was with managing and planning changes in beliefs, values, behaviours and culture within the organisation. To this end the role of the trainers acting as internal consultants/change agents was very much focused on working alongside individuals and teams, facilitating and advocating in order to enable staff to find 'their own way' through their problems, helping them address their personal development needs, and supporting the shift towards a more empowered style of management. Invariably the major emphasis of the OD effort was on diagnosis rather than jumping quickly to 'solutions' and 'outcomes'. In many instances effort was concentrated on tracing a specific process back through the organisation to its primary focus. This often led to the process being 're-engineered', with the original task and objectives taking on another meaning and becoming far more effective and efficient. On occasions outside consultants as opposed to the internal trainers were used in order to obtain independent and objective viewpoints.

Project management was used extensively throughout the period of change with many projects delegated to individuals or small teams of staff drawn from various departments throughout the Trust Hospital. Training in project management was provided and project managers appointed for each team. All projects were linked to the business plan via a 'business project implementation plan' which outlined all of the various change programmes and projects. These were co-ordinated by the training manager.

A number of specific and major OD interventions were facilitated by the training team including team building and a senior manager review, as follows.

- *Team building*   For this the trainer in question devised a framework whereby facilitative support was offered to the various clinician management teams, most of which had been newly formed. This involved in the first instance assessing the type of event that would best meet the requirements of the particular team. Each event was then tailor-made for each purpose incorporating the features of fact finding and analysis, negotiating the contract with the clients, pre-workshop diagnosis and proposals, implementation, further facilitation and follow up events as necessary, with evaluation throughout and upon completion. Upon request similar team-building support was also made available to other teams throughout the Trust.
- *Senior manager review*   A review was carried out by the trainer leading this OD intervention in order to clarify the role and purpose of the clinical unit managers. This review concentrated on: clarifying the key relationships of the clinical unit managers with the staff inside their respective units, with those in other units, and also with the corporate directorates; demystifying the many mixed perceptions surrounding their

role; and making recommendations relating to the problems that had surfaced and on the future role of these managers.

Evaluation of change effectiveness

In the case described the training manager applied a range of change management models to the evaluation of the planned and unplanned events which had made the change process both effective and ineffective, and also to an evaluation of how successful the change had been. In particular the works of Beckhard and Harris (1987), Buchanan and McCalman (1989) and Goss *et al.* (1993) were drawn upon both for planning, facilitating and evaluating the various OD interventions.

Case references

Beckhard, R. and Harris, R.T. (1987) *Organisational Transitions Managing Complex Change*, New York, Addison-Wesley.

Buchanan, D. and McCalman, J. (1992) 'Perceptual Transition Management', in McCalman, J. and Paton, R. (1992) *Change Management*, London, Paul Chapman.

Goss, T., Pascale, R. and Athos, A. (1993) 'Management of Change USA', *Harvard Business Review*, Nov/Dec, pp. 97–108.

ILLUSTRATIVE CASE STUDY 3

Background to the case

This case is concerned with a national voluntary organisation which is a registered company and charity totally dependant on external funding. Its national headquarters is based in the South of England and there are regional units located throughout the UK. The subject of the case focuses on one area of management performance, namely the effectiveness of the senior management team's meetings.

The key person who acted as the change agent in this case, and who facilitated the change process was the Training Officer. She was one of eight managers of mixed gender and race who comprised the senior management team which had been fairly newly formed. Soon after its formation all of the senior managers had begun expressing their concerns in one way or another about the effectiveness of their team meetings. These included such issues as the need for clarification of the role and responsibilities of the team itself, a questioning of the procedures and ground rules, the perceived differences of managerial philosophy amongst the team members and the behaviours exhibited in the meetings. Clearly the senior management team had a crucial role to play in influencing the direction and operational health of the organisation nationally; of paramount importance was the need for this team to be healthy and effective and this was fully recognised by all. Hence it was agreed that the Training Officer should develop a framework of organisational analysis to enable members of the team, both individually and collectively, to undertake some form of self-examination and to find ways to improve their team effectiveness.

The organisational analysis

Following a search of the literature the Training Officer concluded that qualitative methods would be more appropriate bearing in mind the interpersonal nature of many of the concerns and issues that had been raised. She was encouraged by the fact that such methods would mirror the culture of the organisation which was one of consultation. Within the qualitative approach she chose an *action research* orientation linked to a framework of *co-operative enquiry*, a methodology which asks participants what the focus of analysis should be and the questions they would like to ask and have answered. This approach was considered to be particularly in tune with the organisation's culture of valuing partnerships and empowerment. Furthermore, it was thought the co-operative enquiry approach would give cultural explanations of human behaviour including gender and race issues.

Reference to the work of Checkland (1981), who had implemented an action research programme deploying the methodology of co-operative enquiry for the purpose of developing a soft systems theory and for exploring ways in which systems ideas could be used in tackling soft, ill-structured problems, reinforced the view that these approaches would be the most pertinent ones to use.

Strategies for change

The initial strategy formulated for bringing about the required change comprised five key stages that were to be implemented over a 12 month period, as follows:

Stage 1   Gaining acceptance of the action research project
Stage 2   Action research – phase 1
Stage 3   Evaluation of phase 1
Stage 4   Action research – phase 2
Stage 5   Overall evaluation

Considerable time and effort was expended both in formal and informal settings to secure the support of the whole of the senior management team, to allay individual fears and to clarify any misunderstandings. The first phase of action research using the co-operative enquiry approach involved conducting individual and group diagnostic analyses, mainly via the regular senior management meetings, supported by the minutes. The latter offered an opportunity to look for patterns, to note differences between what had been revealed in private and in the public arena, and to note differences or common concerns across race and gender. A whole range of issues surfaced and were successfully addressed during the change process. However, in response to the frustration at not resolving certain 'team-working' issues, the Training Officer was to run a workshop on effective meetings for the team. Its objectives were to identify the key requirements for running more effective senior management team meetings, to identify the roles taken in their meetings and the consequent helpful/less helpful behaviours, and to agree a method of taking forward agreed working formats into future meetings. A range of structured exercises and self-diagnostic questionnaires was used to help facilitate the workshop which offered a springboard for analysis. A wide range of valuable outcomes resulted in terms of changes in behaviour which subsequently led to noticeable improvements in the effectiveness of the meetings. However, whilst the workshop had been helpful and useful it was anticipated it could not address a number of fundamental issues. Hence a second phase of action research was initiated comprising several one-day training events to address, for example, the issue of interpersonal awareness and various concerns relating to race issues that had arisen within the team. External facilitators were engaged to run these events.

Evaluation of change effectiveness

The Training Officer initiated a range of evaluation activities at various stages of the change process. For example, immediate verbal feedback was obtained from co-subjects whilst participating in the various workshop sessions. They were also required to complete end of workshop evaluation forms. Further evaluation was then initiated six months after completion of the co-operative enquiry and of the subsequent training interventions.

The main conclusion arising out of the evaluation process was that individually all of the senior managers had learned something from the OD interventions. Some, but not all, had been able to put that learning into practice. However, overall behavioural changes required from everyone to bring about the most desired improvement in team effectiveness were seemingly taking a long time. Nevertheless the general consensus was that the interventions had helped the team move towards achieving professional maturity. On reflection it was considered that a team working event leading to a better understanding of people's positions on race, gender, management style and philosophy would have been more helpful earlier on in the team's life.

Resulting from a further reading of the literature the Training Officer concluded that an explanation as to why the most desired behavioural changes were taking an inordinate amount of time could perhaps be more fully understood by the effects of the 'punctuated equilibrium paradigm' as explored by Gersick (1991). In his exploration he refers to the highly durable underlying order or 'deep structure' within organisations which persist and limit change during periods of organisational stability or equilibrium. It was concluded that perhaps a change in the 'deep structure' was also called for in this case – a need that required to be diagnosed using other perspectives of organisational analysis.

Case references

Checkland, P.B. (1981) *Systems Thinking & Systems Practice*, London, Wiley.

Gersick, C. (Jan. 1991) 'Revolutionary Change Theories: a multilevel exploration of the Punctuated Equilibrium Paradigm', *Academy of Management Review*, vol. 16, no. 1, pp. 10–36.

References

Anthony, P. (1994) *Managing Culture*, Milton Keynes, Open University Press.

Blyton, P. and Turnbull, P.(1992) *Reassessing Human Resource Management*, London, Sage.

Buchanan, D. and Boddy, D. (1992) *The Expertise of the Change Agent*, London, Prentice Hall.

Burns, T. and Stalker, G. (1966) *The Management of Innovation*, London, Tavistock.

Carnall, C. (1990) *Managing Change in Organisations*, London, Prentice Hall.

Carnall, C. (1991) *Managing Change*, London, Routledge.

C.S.C. Index (1994) *The State of Re-engineering*, CSC Consultancy.

Drucker, P. (1988) 'The Coming of the New Organisation,' *Harvard Business Review*, Feb., pp. 43–53.

Dunphy, D. and Stace, D. (1988) 'Transformational and Coercive Strategies for Planned Organisational Change', *Organisation Studies*, vol. 9, no. 3, pp. 317–34.

Hallworth, M. (1994) 'Re-engineering Learning Processes', *Training and Development*, October, pp. 36–37.

Hamel, G. and Prahalad, C. (1994) *Competing for the Future*, Boston MA, Harvard Business Press.

Handy, C. (1989) *The Age of Unreason*, London, Random Century.

Handy, C. (1990) *Inside Organisations*, London, BBC Books.

Harrision, M.I. (1994) *Diagnosing Organisations. Methods, Models and Processes*, London, Sage.

Hassard, J. and Parker, C. eds (1993) *Postmodernism and Organisations*, London, Sage.

Johnson, G. (1987) *Strategic Change and the Management Process*, Oxford, Blackwell.

Johnson, G. (1990) 'Managing Strategic Change: The Role of Symbolic Action', *British Journal of Management*, vol. 1, pp. 183–200.

Kanter, R.M. (1989) *When Giants Learn to Dance*, New York, Simon and Schuster.

Kearney, P. (1994) 'Business Process Re-engineering', *Training and Development*, March, pp. 14–17.

Lewin, C. (1958) 'Group Decision and Social Change', in Maccoby, E., Newcomb, T. and Hartley, E. eds (1958) *Readings in Social Psychology*, London, Holt, Rhinehart, Winston.

Morgan, G. (1988) 'Emerging Waves and Challenges: The Need for New Competencies and Mindsets', in Henry, J. ed. (1988) *Creative Management*, London, Sage.

Mullins, L. (1993) *Management and Organisational Behaviour*, Third edition, London, Pitman.

Pedler, M., Burgoyne, J. and Boydell, T. (1991) *The Learning Company*, London, McGraw-Hill.

Peters, T. (1988) 'Restoring American Competitiveness: Looking for New Models of Organisations', *The Academy of Management Executive*.

Peters, T. and Waterman, R. (1982) *In Search of Excellence*, New York, Harper Row.

Phillips, K. and Shaw, P. (1989) *A Consultancy Approach for Trainers*, Aldershot, Gower.

Semler, R. (1993) *Maverick*, London, Century.

Swieringa, J. and Weirdsma, A. (1992) *Becoming a Learning Organisation, Beyond the Learning Curve*, New York, Addison-Wesley.

11

Influence, Communication and Neuro-linguistic Programming in Practice

Ursula Lyon

INTRODUCTION

Human resource development can be defined as encouraging people to develop and grow from dependency to independency and then to interdependency. Thus the HRD specialist needs a wide range of resources and skills to enable and encourage others on their journeys.

Nearing the 21st century, any book on HRD needs to include some mention of the very latest technology which enables people to develop their potential and become more resourceful in their life. Neuro-linguistic programming, NLP, the study of subjective experience and the study of excellence or a way of looking at human learning, is just such a technology.

My intention in this chapter is to identify how some of these processes work and how an HRD specialist can operate, allow and encourage development to take place. One way is by giving examples of how people have used NLP with themselves or others and the benefits they or the organisation has gained. To do this I carried out some original research. My objective was to collect information from non-HRD people regarding NLP practice and to discover which NLP techniques are used most often and how they have been of value to the individual and the organisation.

WORKING WITH NLP

Having attended, organised and tutored on NLP courses I have been curious as to how, where, when, and with whom participants use the various skills/strategies in their workplace and how, specifically, these have been of benefit. The people I chose had not less than six days NLP training and were working in occupations outside the HRD area, thus providing information on how people are able to use NLP in their everyday life. I wrote, asking them to identify which particular NLP skills or techniques they used most often; and whether they used it for themselves or with a colleague(s) within the organisation. I also asked for a brief description of how they had used the technique, what happened and with hindsight how it had been of benefit to either themselves, their colleague(s) or the organisation.

More than 30 people responded and I thank them for their contribution. I have included some of their replies where they related to the specific skills I have described below. Some gave specific examples of using a particular pattern and others gave examples which encompassed several. All those who responded indicated that they had integrated the patterns and that their communication, self-awareness, and confidence had improved. (I have changed the names of the contributors to protect their privacy.)

THE DEVELOPMENT OF NLP

NLP was researched and developed in the early 1970s by *John Grinder and Richard Bandler*, who were lecturers at the University of Santa Cruz; John was a linguist, Richard a mathematician, a seemingly unlikely partnership. Initially, the common ground was an interest in Gestalt, and this developed with the question, 'What is it that makes the difference between somebody who is merely competent at any given skill and somebody who excels at the same skill?' The focus was on what can be done *now* to turn the competent person's performance into one of excellence, rather than on what made the difference in the past. Their research included observation and study of excellent communicators, such as Milton Ericson and Virginia Satir.

Their initial research, which is documented in *The Structure of Magic I and II*, explored the structure of language – surface and deep structure – and identified 'Milton' or vague language patterns in which there are deletions, distortions, and generalisations and identified a form of questioning – the 'meta model' – as a way of gathering the specific information which had been deleted.

ELEMENTS OF NLP

There are four basic elements of NLP.

1 Having a goal or outcome – knowing what you want in specific terms.
2 Having the *behavioural flexibility* to attain your outcome – 'If what you are doing isn't working do something else'.
3 Having the *sensory acuity* to notice the effect of your behaviour on others – noting what works and what doesn't.
4 *Self-maintenance* – having the ability to stay resourceful and on target.

Later they observed the use of the representational systems in language and eye movements. These observations led them to note that there were four elements:

- *techniques/skills* or *external behaviour*
- *thinking processes/strategies* or *internal computation* – [what, and the way in which they think]
- *internal state* – [what and how they feel]
- *attitudes/beliefs/values*

They developed strategies to elicit *Models of Excellent Behaviour* which may be applied in business, sport, therapy, education, the arts, theatre and so on. They noticed attitudes, which seemed to enhance communication and named these *presuppositions* – thoughts which are useful to presuppose when aiming for excellence. Some major examples of presuppositions in NLP are:

- 'The meaning of the communication is the response which you get'
- 'There is no failure only feedback'
- 'The map is not the territory'
- 'The mind and the body are part of the same cybernetic system'
- 'If it is possible for someone in the world, it's possible for anyone'

To test a presupposition, act as if it were true and notice the results that you get. There will be exceptions to all these presuppositions, and they are a useful basis for communication. If you are interested in these areas then NLP has a lot to offer the individual and the organisation.

I have chosen to give a brief description of the basic NLP techniques of:

- Rapport
- Anchoring
- Language – meta model
- Representational systems
- Well-formed outcomes
- Perceptual positions

and then give examples as to how these people applied it.

Rapport

Rapport is defined as responsiveness or a process of contacting or being with another person or people that is buildable. This foundation skill in communication is emphasised and highlighted by calibration and sensory acuity skills. Even richer and more varied ways of establishing and maintaining rapport at different levels have been developed. In her book *Influencing with Integrity* Genie Z. Laborde (1984, p. 27) says:

> 'Without rapport, you will not get what you want – not money, not promotions, not friends. You may not even be able to get a letter typed correctly, unless you do it yourself. Rapport is like money; it increases in importance when you do not have it and when you do have it, a lot of opportunities occur.'

People have different ways of experiencing rapport. It may be a level of comfort or a sense of shared understanding. Bandler and Grinder (1975) recognised different levels of rapport, shown in Table 11.1.

Table 11.1

Surface	Deeper Level
Physiology	Thinking processes
Voice	Knowledge
Language	Experience
Behaviour	Attitudes
	Beliefs/values

Rapport can be built by matching:

- Body Posture/Facial Expressions/Hand Gestures/Weight shifts/Breathing/Movement of feet/Eye movement
- Vocal and Verbal mirroring/Tempo of speech/Auditory tone/Predicates

Here are two examples of how people practised rapport.

RUTH'S STORY

Ruth worked in a large department store. She was a particularly good sales assistant, in that she easily established rapport with the customers no matter who they were. She seemed to have many different ways of getting them to feel at ease and buy. In fact, she was often sought out by customers even if they had to wait for her to be available. However, Ruth felt most uncomfortable and lacked confidence when talking to her manager. She would become tongue tied and stand looking at her feet. Often giving the impression that she was not interested. This concerned her, especially as she wanted to offer suggestions regarding the display.

Having learned about ways of establishing rapport, and that both parties have that responsibility, Ruth realised that she had never really attempted to establish rapport with her manager. In fact, she had expected her manager to establish contact. She decided that she would practice building rapport with her manager.

The first time, although only a brief interaction, she matched body position and moved alongside him, rather than opposite, and she noticed that he listened more attentively to what she said. She also observed that in that position she felt better and gave him eye contact. On the next occasion, Ruth decided to make a suggestion about the display, having prepared what she wanted to say. She decided that this time she would add to her previous experience and match voice tone and pace. This time the manager spent more time with her, listened to her suggestion, and after discussing it with her agreed to test it out.

BARBARA'S STORY

Barbara, a manager of a commercial department in a large organisation, had difficulty in many situations with a colleague with whom she was supposed to work closely. Often their communications resulted in conflict and bad feeling which created hassle for them and others. It also wasted a lot of time sorting out the mis-communications. Barbara sensed and had also been told that her colleague saw Barbara as a threat.

Following the rapport training, Barbara decided to do her best to establish rapport with her colleague at their next meeting. As they would be sitting at a table, she decided to sit beside her colleague and match some of the upper body posture and voice tone.

Later Barbara said, 'It wasn't a perfect meeting but it was an improvement. At times

I found it difficult to carry out my intention, and I did consciously match throughout. My colleague and I managed to speak to each other on a more adult basis and it did make a difference. Next time I will do my best to build on this small breakthrough.'

Robert Dilts (1989), a student of Grinder and Bandler, noticed that people's eyes moved in connection with their thoughts (see Fig. 11.1). His research showed that when people were thinking in visual terms (pictures) their eyes went up; when in auditory terms their eyes moved on a level with their ears; when in kinaesthetic terms (including smell and taste) their eyes went down and to one side; and when they were having an internal dialogue their eyes went down and to the other side. One side is for recall or memory and the other side is for constructing or future. The side may depend on whether you are right handed or left handed.

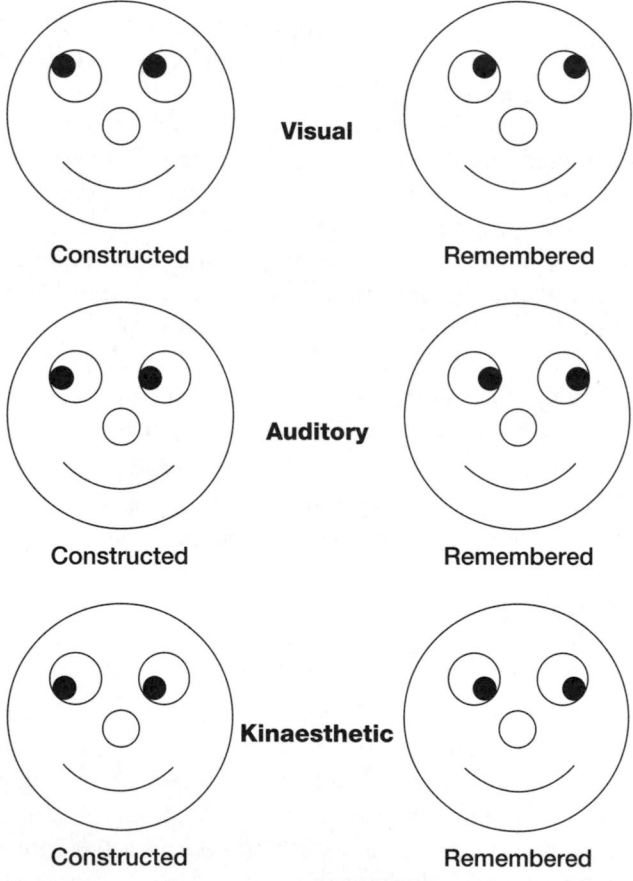

Fig. 11.1   Accessing cues

Note: Some people do not conform to the general pattern described above. When in doubt, 'check it out'. Although it may be untypical, each person has systematic eye movements when accessing different representational systems.

The words we use also indicate how we are thinking – if we are thinking in pictures we will use visual words; if in auditory or kinaesthetic terms likewise our words will match that sense (see Table 11.2).

Table 11.2

Visual	Auditory	Kinaesthetic
See	Hear	Feel
Clear	Listen	Hold
Look	Tune in/out	Get a grip
Paint a picture	Overtones	Tap into

By watching a person's eye movements and listening to their language we can match their representational system and even more skilfully establish rapport.

Here are some examples of how this was used.

ADRIAN'S STORY

Adrian works in the Careers Service, interviewing long-term unemployed. During his NLP training he felt he increased his ways of establishing rapport. He particularly recalls an interview with a new client. Somehow, Adrian felt that he was not establishing rapport. He tested various ways of matching the client and it did not seem to make much difference. His internal dialogue suggested using what he had learned and focusing on the language. Adrian's primary representational system is visual, then kinaesthetic and lastly auditory.

So he concentrated on his client's words, doing his best to identify which representational system he was using. Shortly he heard – 'listened' and 'sounds like' and 'tone'; Adrian identified that his client was chiefly auditory. For a few moments Adrian did his best to think of at least one auditory word. Visual and kinaesthetic words came to mind quickly but auditory ones eluded him. Then he had a flash of inspiration and said, 'That rings bells for me too.' Instantly the client looked at him, half smiled and seemed to relax visibly. The interview took a turn for the better after that simple intervention. Adrian said, 'It was literally like a light being switched on – amazing. I now really pay attention to language, particularly when interviewing difficult or reluctant clients.'

JAMES' STORY

James, a project engineer and team leader, decided to change his weekly team meeting by establishing rapport with each person as they came into the room. At the beginning of the meeting he wrote the agenda item on a flip chart, thus focusing the group visually; any action or decision was also written up on the chart.

Afterwards James said, 'I had never thought to spend time establishing rapport before. Actually I did it as an experiment and I could not believe the difference it made to the atmosphere of the meeting. It was more good humoured. I decided to use the flip chart to add a visual aspect. Often we are reading our own notes and sometimes actions have been confused and chaotic. Having the items and decisions displayed really kept the group focused and clear about the decisions. The other benefit really surprised me – the meeting was actually much shorter than usual!'

Anchoring

Anchoring is another core skill, one which we often use without awareness, and is thus of even more value when used with precision and care. Anchoring is the process by which an event or symbol is linked to a reaction. A phobia is an extreme example of an anchor.

The reaction maybe useful or not. (A difficult situation may trigger determination or despair for you.) It may be conscious or unconscious. (You may know why depression descends on you as you walk through a certain door, or just feel it.) It may be relevant or irrelevant. (It may be that this person is a problem, or it may be that unconsciously they remind you of someone you did not get on with years ago.)

You can link an anchor to a tone of voice, a position, a symbol, a person, a movement or anything else. Simply elicit or create the response you want and link it by sight, sound or feeling to the trigger you have decided upon.

An *anchor* is a learnt response and can be changed. The difficulty is that many anchors have been learnt at a subconscious level and will have to be changed at that level. It is not necessary to remember when and how you learned that response in order to change it. It is only necessary to understand how it is triggered. You can learn to recognise the triggers which you respond to, and then get rid of the anchored response if it is not useful.

It is useful to identify anchors and change those which do not serve us, or those people around us, particularly well. It is very useful to anchor positive resources in ourselves. Anchoring and collapsing anchors are basic to NLP patterns.

There are four steps to the anchoring process:

- have the person or yourself recall a vivid experience using all representational systems;
- provide a specific stimulus at the peak (see Fig. 11.2);
- change the person's state;
- test the anchor.

There are four components to anchoring:

- the timing of the anchor;
- the intensity of the anchor;
- the purity or uniqueness of the anchor;
- the accuracy of duplicating the anchor.

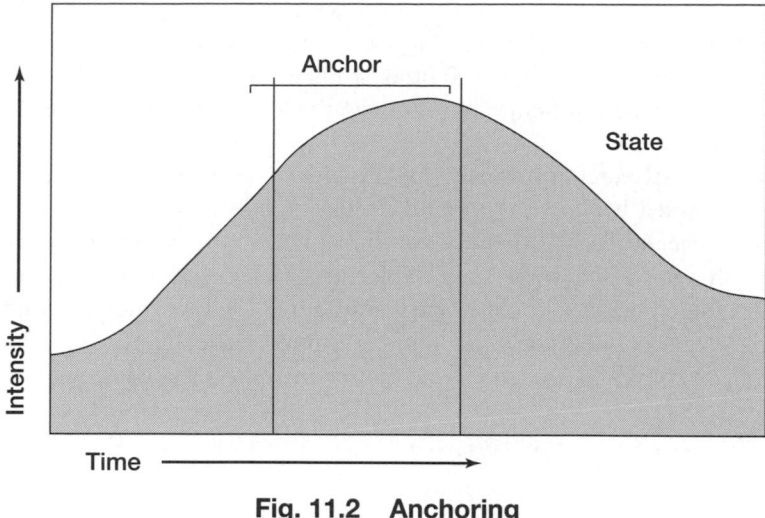

Fig. 11.2 Anchoring

Here are some examples of how people have used anchoring to feel more confident.

SHARON'S STORY

Sharon, an administrative officer in a pharmaceutical firm, was going for an interview for promotion to a higher grade when she learned the anchoring pattern – Circle of Excellence. Her experience of internal interviews was negative; she often seemed not to hear the questions, felt tongue tied and then panicked. Her supervisor at work supported her application, and had told her she could do the work but she would need to interview well, as the other people due to be interviewed were all highly qualified for the post.

This seemed an opportunity not to be missed. So, in the practice session with the help of her partner, she decided to anchor confidence, clarity of thought and speech. At the end of the pattern she future paced the interview. In the intervening days Sharon did some mental rehearsal, and just prior to the interview she re-accessed her circle and the resources of confidence and clarity of thought and speech.

The interview went well, she remained calm and confident. When asked a question which was vague or unclear she checked what exactly they wanted. She surprised herself. At the end of the interview she felt that she had given of her best and was pleased with her performance. Sharon was not successful in gaining promotion on that occasion; however, she had positive feedback on her interview.

TINA'S STORY

Tina is an under-graduate student who is reading Business Studies. Prior to coming to university she had been in a school which had a small sixth form; consequently she was used to working in small groups with close supervision. Coming to university was a big cultural change in many ways, but the biggest problem for Tina was in the lecture theatre. Here she was with more than 100 other students, and she found that her attention wandered. She really had difficulty in following the lecture and did not feel able to ask for clarification.

Tina decided to self-anchor curiosity and attentiveness. Her experience was that the attentiveness enabled her to really attend to what the lecturer said and she began to screen out the other students – she thought this a success and continued to use it whenever she felt she was losing interest in the lecture. Her experience with curiosity was mixed in that sometimes she would be curious about her fellow students which was distracting. She experimented with this and fine tuned curiosity to the subject or the lecturer's style of delivery. Later she found that attentiveness served her better in the lecture theatre.

Outcomes

An *outcome* is the result that you want, defined in terms of:

1 the way you would like to see things;
2 the way you want to feel;
3 what you will hear when you have your outcome.

Most business people are aware of *goal setting* and *management by objectives*; however, goals and objectives are in a broader category than outcomes. Outcomes are goals which have been clarified and finely honed by using the following steps.

1 Decide what you want in *specific terms*.
2 State it in *positive terms*: e.g.
   I want to be confident when making a presentation;
   I want to be successful as a parent.
   Note that to 'stop doing X' is more of a goal than an outcome.
   Going for what you do not want is a booby trap.
3 Now ask:
   ● what will I see when I get my outcome?
   ● what will I hear?
   ● what will I feel?
   Imagine at least *four* things for each of the above. Write down your answers.
   Now you have specific criteria to check against the evidence, when you have achieved your outcome.

Well-formed outcomes are a series of questions which focus attention on what is wanted, so that it is clearly defined in specific terms.

1 What do you want? Is the outcome: stated in the positive (what you want, not what you don't want); initiated and controlled by you?
2 *Where*, *when*, and *with whom* do you want it? (*context*)
3 What will having this outcome get for you? (*meta outcome*)

4   How will you know when you have got it? (*Evidence procedure*) Is the evidence described in sensory-based terms? (See, hear, feel, smell, taste)

5   What stops you from having your outcome now?

6   What are the positive and negative consequences of getting your outcome? (*Ecology check*)

7   What resources do you already have? What resources do you need to get your outcome? (Information, attitude, internal state, training, money, help or support from others)

8   Is the first step to achieving your outcome specific and achievable?

9   Is there more than one way to get your outcome?

10   What time frame is involved?

11   Imagine stepping into the future and having your outcome fully. Look back and determine what steps were required to achieve the outcome now that you have it.

Here I include an example which encompasses other patterns as well.

JOHN'S STORY

John, a part-time tutor for an independent business college, was asked at short notice to take over a course which was in trouble. Everyone from the Director to the Technician warned him that there was much ill will and bad feelings within the group. Some of them were actually threatening to demand a refund of their fees. In all fairness, the group had, in fact, had four or five tutors over the last 18 months. Each tutor had widely different styles, experience and abilities.

When John first met the group they looked and sounded extremely angry. There were negative 'vibes' and defensive/aggressive body language. John did his best to establish rapport. Then he encouraged the group to state what their present position was, and what they already had in the way of skill in that particular subject. Although he had to listen to some rude and emotive comments, the atmosphere in the room began to change and became less angry.

John then moved the group forward to agree the outcomes they wanted, and what resources and skills they needed to achieve those outcomes. The more the group defined specifically what they wanted, and what they did not want, the more positive became the feelings and attitudes of the group. By the time they summarised all the well-formed outcomes and time scales which they had discussed and agreed, the vibes were good, the energy level was buzzing and the group were positive, enthusiastic, motivated and cohesive.

HANNAH'S STORY

Hannah, a Student Service Officer for a major national bank, used to have difficulty setting goals for herself or even being clear about what she wanted. This applied to most aspects of her life. Often she found herself experiencing tremendous internal dialogue when deciding what she wanted. This caused her a great deal of stress.

By using well-formed outcomes, as a process, she has found that she is now clearer about what she wants as she is able to focus more easily and thus put things into perspective. This proved especially helpful when she was preparing for her annual appraisal as she was clear about how she would like to develop her role within the job. Having this clarity she felt more confident about the interview. The appraisal went well and her manager complimented her on the thoroughness and preparation which he felt had helped the interview.

Hannah said, 'Now I use well-formed outcomes when interviewing students who want overdrafts. This really helps me, having a structure enables me to be objective and my experience is that the students become more realistic.'

Meta model

Effective information gathering is the key to effective interventions, whether in therapy, business, or day to day living. When you gather information, you draw on your own personal history in making an internal representation of what the other person says in order to understand it. As you do that there is a strong tendency to delete or distort information and add details which were not mentioned by the other person and are not in the other person's internal representation.

The *meta model* is a set of questions which allow you to gather information which specifies someone's experience, in order to get a full representation of that experience. It is one of the essential tools which separate a good NLP practitioner from a sloppy one. When clients, business partners, employees, students, etc. communicate with you, or offer you a difficulty to solve, knowing what questions to ask makes all the difference. Many people do not know what questions to ask, and they end up solving the wrong 'problems'. They *think* they understand, and begin to solve something they do not know about. Often they do more harm than good. For example, management may say, 'We need to produce more.' So the supervisor speeds up the assembly line, causing more defects. The manager may have meant more quality or he may have meant different kinds of products. Often you can have 'meaningful' conversations and arguments without knowing what the other person is talking about. The meta model is a way not to do that. When you gather information you use the questions: 'what? which? who? when? where? how?' Notice that 'why?' is not used in the meta model because it does not ask for specific detail. The answer to 'why?' is usually 'because . . .' and a historical or theoretical explanation.

The meta model was the beginning of NLP – a great deal of NLP has been developed by using it. NLP strategies were created by exploring the question 'how?'

To use the meta model effectively it is essential to have good rapport and sensory acuity as sometimes the questions could be thought invasive. So they need to be softened either by the tonality of the questioner or by using a soft front end, for example, 'I'm really interested in your painting, so, how specifically do you get that effect?', as opposed to 'How specifically do you get that effect?' In general other skills are crucial to using the meta model successfully and this is emphasised in the examples which follow.

MICHELLE'S STORY

Michelle, is a solicitor who works in a city centre advice centre, she said, 'Having recently qualified from Law School, where I had concentrated on Law and little else, I realised very soon after taking up by appointment that I needed some help in interviewing and communicating effectively with all kinds of people. Surprisingly, these skills had not been taught on my particular course. I enrolled for an NLP Practitioner course on a friend's recommendation.

I have found that I use the meta model questions mostly. It really helps me to be clear as to what the client really wants to know and thus saves me time. Although I have found to my cost that it can't be successful without really having rapport.

One day I was very busy and I suppose a bit tense and I was, to my mind, being super efficient, and using the meta questions with a rather anxious client. Instead of gathering the facts easily the client seemed to withdraw into herself and I went on asking questions in a routine way and getting nowhere. It was awful and I didn't improve . . . Finally I ran out of time and suggested that she come back for another appointment. She was visibly relieved when I suggested this.

Later a colleague asked about the case and in telling him I realised that I had not bothered to establish rapport. It was a salutary lesson. One that has stood me in good stead – first have rapport and recognise when you have not!

I often use well-formed outcomes with clients and when I am preparing cases and I have found that this helps focus my attention on what I want to achieve in any negotiation.'

HARRY'S STORY

Harry, an accountant in a large international business, found the meta model of especial value for himself when preparing the end of year report and presentation. By asking himself meta questions he really became precise and clear about the details that might be questioned. In previous years he had always been nervous about this presentation so he took the opportunity to practise any NLP skill that seemed suitable. He used well-formed outcomes to help him structure the presentation; and considered how and where to establish and maintain rapport and use the representational systems both in the report and his presentation. The final preparation was to anchor the positive resources of calmness, a sense of well being, and humour.

'It went like a dream,' said Harry, 'I handled all the questions, including a difficult one from the chairman, without getting the slightest bit ruffled. I'm not really sure which particular skill helped most – I think it was a combination of them all and of course preparation.'

Perceptual positions

It is considered that people learn in different ways (see Lee, M., this volume); some learn by changing *perceptual position*:

1 by being present and experiencing the here and now;
2 by stepping into the other person's shoes;
3 by observing and listening to others.

The ability to look at a subject from different perspectives can add greatly to the amount of information we have on the subject, and can help us in making better choices and decisions (see also Fisher, C., this volume). As well as seeing things from different perspectives it is also of value to hear and feel things from those perspectives. Thus taking on the different perceptions enables us to:

- consider things from your point of view – 1st or *self* position;
- consider things from the point of view of the other person – take on their position see, hear and feel the world from that position – 2nd or *other* position;
- consider things from the neutral, uninvolved observer who is outside the situation – 3rd or *observer* position.

This flexibility in perception is invaluable in negotiation and I include examples of how some have used it.

PENNY'S STORY

Penny is the Head of Administration in a college of further education. She was preparing for staff development and appraisal interviews of her staff and as part of her preparation she took on the different perceptual positions. This enabled her to re-consider the seating arrangements – sometimes changing it for the different people. She realised the importance of varying her way of establishing rapport and her use of language thus taking account of the different individuals. So having practised, she made some notes and mentally rehearsed, thus adding a further dimension to her preparation.

Later, having completed the interviews, her observation was that each interview had been a rewarding learning experience. In some the atmosphere compared to previous times was more constructive and positive, while in others some really were able to 'open up'. Penny said, 'I know that people are different and previously I thought that I had taken that into account, but to be honest I think I kept to the same pattern – mine! This was a real challenge for me. I really had to think and actually that made the interviews far more interesting for me as well as a better experience for the staff.'

MARTIN'S STORY

Martin is a sales representative. Over the years he has worked in many industries and organisations. Martin said, 'I really came to the NLP training because my wife was interested and it seemed something worth doing together. I didn't really think it had much to teach me about communication – I have done so much sales training. How wrong I was! Each technique seemed to have relevance for me – rapport, representational systems, language – I gained so much. When we did perceptual positions I practised by using one of my awkward customers as an example. On stepping into second position, looking at Martin, hearing him, I really experienced what that felt like. It was not pleasant . . . In observer position I gathered even more information and some ideas as to how to change things. Later in self position I reviewed what I had learned and then rehearsed the changes in my head.

Later in the week I did meet with this customer, quite unexpectedly so I didn't have time to rehearse or think about what I would or would not do. I don't know exactly how or what I did but I do know that there was a big difference in that meeting. It was much more genial and I was given an order without having to really try – amazing!

Some of my colleagues have commented that I seem to be less pushy – so maybe that is the difference. I have suggested to the Sales Training Manager that they include the perceptual position exercise in the sales training.'

Other examples were offered by the respondents regarding other patterns not covered in this work. Many of the 'sub-modality' processes offered in *Using Your Brain for a Change* by Richard Bandler and in *Change Your Mind and Keep the Change* and *Heart of the Mind* by Steve and Connirae Andreas were mentioned as significant in their development. The *motivation* and *decision making strategies* were mentioned by several people as making a big difference to their lives. Others had used the *responding to criticism* strategy to very good effect in their work and private lives. I will leave Alice, a secondary teacher, to have the final comment.

ALICE'S STORY

'How do you know when you have communicated effectively? That was one of the questions posed early in the training. I had never really thought about this before – well not in detail. Identifying this with one person was interesting in that it changed so very much depending on the person I selected. This is probably obvious but it did both surprise and delight me.

However, considering how I knew I had communicated effectively with a group was not easy. In fact, this caused me a great deal of thought and soul searching. This was so close to home – in that I questioned my effectiveness as a teacher. So I set out to do my best to apply NLP in the classroom and with the students. At first this was consciously and it felt strange but gradually I felt easier testing out new things.

It really is difficult to separate one skill from another because now they are so interlinked. When I am planning lessons I use well-formed outcomes, perceptual positions, consider language and representational systems and which presuppositions would be useful to have for myself and the students. I also think about how I will establish rapport and create a learning environment. This appears onerous and at first I suppose it was but now, after two years, I do it more or less automatically and it doesn't take too much time.

You asked about the benefits – on reflection I am aware that I enjoy it more and what I have noticed is that I appreciate the students and their differences. Before I wanted the students to match my map of the world; now, by respecting their map, I learn so much more.'

According to the respondents some of the things which created the biggest paradigm shifts were seemingly small insignificant incidents, comments, behaviours that others may have found difficult to recall. And yet, that comment, gesture, story was a real gem and had a significance for them at that moment and became a turning point in their life – the bit that made the difference.

There are three books which, for me, have made a difference; they seem to dovetail theories, skills and practice in HRD: *The Four Fold Way* (Angeles Arrien Ph.D.), *Influence – The Psychology of Persuasion* (Robert Cialdini Ph.D.), *The Seven Habits of Highly Effective People* (Stephen Covey). They offer models of balance and suggestions to achieve equilibrium. Briefly, Arrien's research suggests that there are four archetypes to draw on which create balance within ourselves and the environment. She refers to these as the *Warrior*, the *Healer*, the *Visionary* and the *Teacher*:

- the Warrior shows up and chooses to be present;
- the Healer pays attention to what has heart and meaning;
- the Visionary tells the truth without blame or judgement;
- the Teacher is open to outcome, rather than attached to outcome.

She outlines the leadership skills and the shadow aspects of each of these archetypes. Using her descriptions I have summarised these in Fig. 11.3. Learning and being aware of these archetypes will enable us to maintain balance within and offer it to others in our environment.

Influence and communication skills are of paramount importance in enabling personal growth. In his book, *The Seven Habits Of Effective People*, Stephen R. Covey emphasises the importance of personal change, growth and development in all areas of our life. Covey invites us to begin by developing ourselves – working from the inside out. He asks us to consider how we are centred and influenced – thus raising awareness of how we function. He offers *The Pro-Active Model* (Covey, 1992, p. 71) stating that we have the ability to choose our response. The freedom to choose is fed by self-awareness, imagination, conscience, and independent will. He also offers a model to help check our centredness regarding *security*, *guidance*, *power*, and *wisdom*. I have developed his ideas and drawn up Fig. 11.4, which illustrates this model more fully.

The core to development is 'self' – keeping yourself balanced and flexible; knowing yourself, your strengths, your areas for development and your strategies for learning/handling different situations; people; skills and change, and being very much aware of the processes which support that development for the individual and the organisation.

The Warrior's way	
Leadership skills: • To honour and respect • To align words with actions • To respect limits and boundaries • To be responsible and disciplined • To demonstrate the right use of power	*Shadow aspects:* • Rebellion • Authority issues • Patterns of invisibility: hiding or holding back; working behind the scenes; riding the coat tails of powerful people

The Visionary's way	
Ways that maintain integrity: • Truth telling without blame or judgement • Freedom from patterns of denial and indulgence • Alignment of words and actions • Honouring self in equal proportion to others	*Shadow aspects:* • Self denial • Need for love • Need for approval and acceptance • Need to keep the peace • Need to maintain balance • Need for harmony at all costs

The Teacher's way	
Aspects of wisdom: • Clarity/objectivity • Discernment/detachment *The spirit of detachment* • Whoever is present are the right people • Whenever it begins is the right time • Whatever happens is the only thing that could happen • When it's over it's over	*Shadow aspects:* • Fear of losing status • Judgement – being attached to outcome • Fear of not knowing • Fear of losing control

The Healer's way	
The four chambered heart: • Full hearted • Open hearted • Clear hearted • Strong hearted – have the courage to be all of who we are in life – ability to stand by one's heart or core To acknowledge what we appreciate about ourself – strengths/ contributions/love – given and received	*Shadow aspects:* • Being half hearted – doing something we don't want to • Closed hearted – being defensive and protecting oneself • Doubting/ambivalent/indifferent • Lacking the courage to be authentic or say what is true • Neediness and withdrawal • Being a martyr and being addicted to negative life patterns

Fig. 11.3

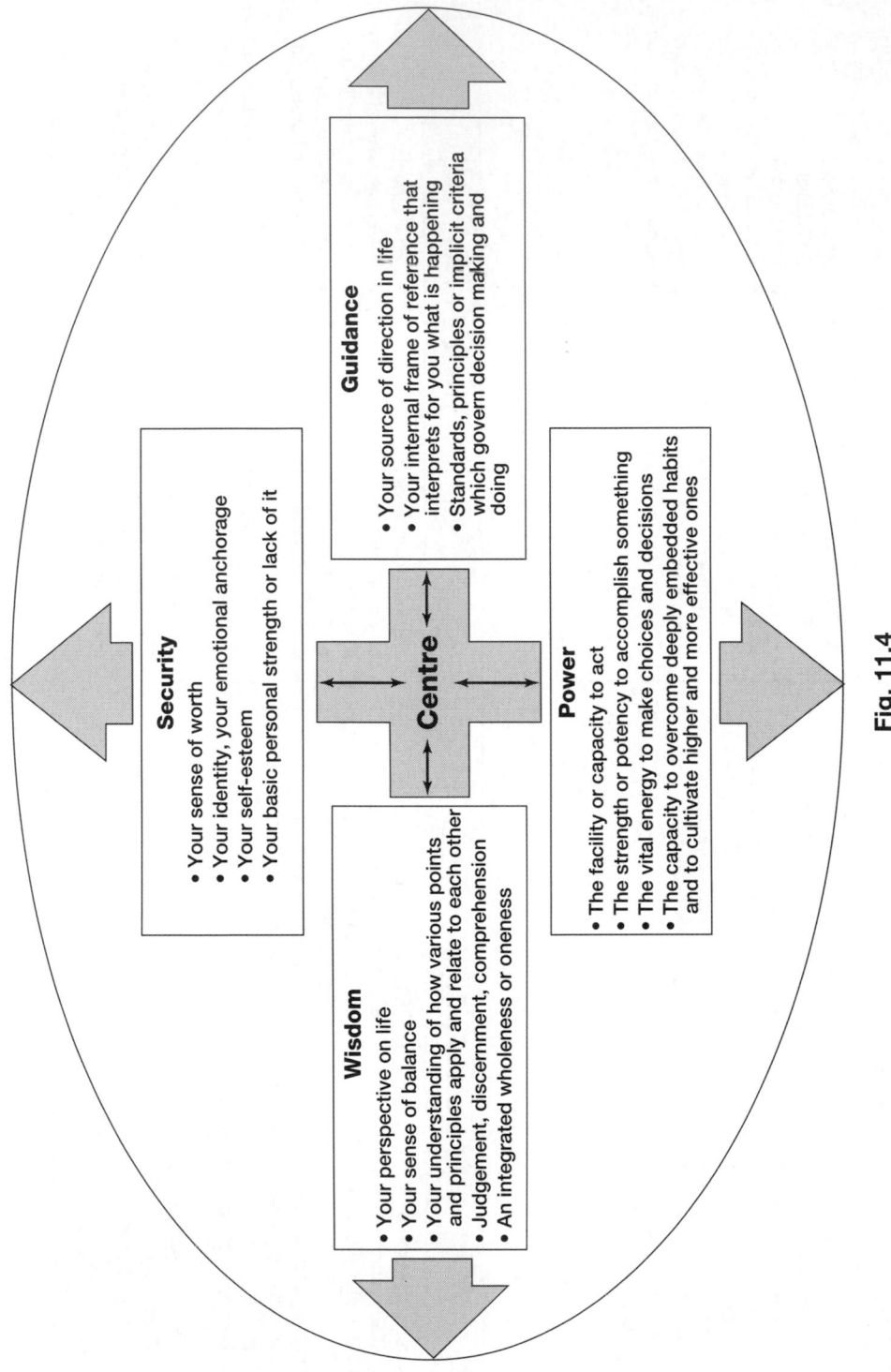

Fig. 11.4

It is important to identify initially how the specialist is aware of his/her own skills and qualities, and which ones they use appropriately with different people throughout the organisation. This requires that the specialist is able to observe objectively where the different skills are used and effectively support and encourage development.

With these in mind, Cialdini (1993) covers a wide range of influencing skills/techniques which people use intuitively or consciously. His argument is that you need to be aware of these techniques – the ones you use and those which others use. Awareness is 90 per cent of the solution – if you are aware, you have the choice as to whether to use that particular skill or not. Suggestions and advice are also offered as to how to recognise and resist the skill. This is of value in HRD and worthy of study.

A factor to bear in mind is the image, symbol, model which we personally hold and act out in our daily life. Frequently, this is recognised and observed by others. This symbol guides us and focuses us consciously and unconsciously. Being aware of this is vital, if we want to be congruent and aligned to our purpose.

One excellent way of communicating our purpose is by metaphor. In HRM – and management in general – many metaphors and much of the language has a military theme: e.g. captain of industry, winning the sale, strategies/skirmishes, tactics/troopsfeed, water, pay, etc., win/lose, aim/target/fire, bite the bullet/trench warfare, sniping, and so on.

METAPHORS FOR HRD

And so for HRD, I offer metaphors which focus on growth, development, empowerment, acceptance and flexibility.

The sports coach

An excellent coach knows the players, their strengths, the situations in which they excel, and the areas where they need help and encouragement. The coach must recognise the stage of their development both as a player and a team member, in order that the team plays well and operates interdependently, thus being more effective and efficient. The coach needs to know the game, and the rules of the game, to offer clarity and, if necessary, discipline; to recognise potential and offer visionary leadership.

The objective of the team is not only to win, but to play well and to provide entertainment and education for their supporters. To do that they require another team to play against in order to demonstrate their skill and their flexibility; and also to learn from others, thus increasing and developing even more skills. If this is done well, a learning environment has been created.

The repertory director

A second metaphor can be that of the director of a repertory company. Here also is the coaching and development of the younger, less experienced – identifying their skills, building on them, enabling them to grow in confidence and test out new skills and styles which may be required later. Also establishing the importance of all roles within the company – supporting roles are vital to the play – so interdependence is more important than just one person playing the 'star role'.

Good directors have the ability to get alongside both the experienced and inexperienced actors, recognising where they are powerful and where they need to develop, then seeking out opportunities to enable that development. All the company is included – the performers, the stagehand, the backstage management – all are part of the play. The director needs to consider the entertainment, enjoyment and education of the audience because the audience responds to the performers, the performers responds to the audience – a circle – which drives which? (See Peter Anthony's *Managing Culture – Management as Acting*, pp. 67–72.) The director considers how the directing can achieve the maximum benefit for all involved.

The gardener

A third metaphor I offer is that of the gardener. The expert gardener knows the potential for each plant – what it can achieve in height, spread, fruit or flower. Knowing the kind of soil it prefers, where to position it where it will be best displayed and in contrast to what – thus displaying the whole garden to advantage. The gardener also notices when a plant is not thriving and either gives extra assistance in the form of nourishment or moves it.

The above are useful metaphors or symbols for the HRD specialist. It is of value to consider your own, for within those metaphors there are styles of communication, styles of operation, ways of influencing, and ways of offering support. As we enable ourselves – working from the inside out – we set a model for others to grow and develop. We need to be aware of our attitudes and behaviour, whether we are balanced, and know what it is we do which helps or hinders that process of growth and development within ourselves. We also need to be aware how we enable the people in the organisation to 'be', to flower, and grow from dependence to independence and eventually interdependence, recognising their value and contribution as a team member and thus re-aligning the whole organisation. Some people suggest that this is demonstrated in total quality management in that we are all moving towards the same objective and vision/mission.

CONCLUSIONS

Some of the treasures I have gathered are not just from books but from observing and listening to, and modelling excellent trainers. It is customary to acknowledge authors of books and I include a list of books for reference and further reading. Here I want to acknowledge and thank the many people who have encouraged and inspired me in my own journey of growth and development. One such person is Lara Ewing an international NLP trainer who introduced me to the following story.

Many, many years ago, we lived in tribes of hunters and gatherers. Archaeologists have conducted research as to how these people made their living and they discovered that it was largely through hunting but when they analysed the actual contents of the diet they discovered that the vast majority of the nutrients that the human being survived on was contributed by the gatherers.

Ursula Le Guin, in her book *Dancing on the Edge of the World*, includes an article that she calls 'The Carrier Bag Story of Fiction'. In this she talks about what actually sustains and nurtures and supports the development of the human race, and she considers the story and how it influences and guides where we place our attention. Having established that the human race survived through gathering with perhaps only 15 per cent of the diet actually contributed by the hunters, Le Guin goes on to say in her article that it is very difficult to make a story out of gathering. If you talk about how Ug and Oom and Boo gathered first one wild oat and then another and another and then as they came around the bushes they discovered a huge crop . . . Somehow it does not quite have the same excitement compared with how Omla and Bula stalked the enormous mammoth. How, with very simple tools and their cunning and planning they overcame the mammoth as Omla thrust his spear into the mammoth and the blood spurted out drenching Omla and then the mammoth fell and crushed Bula. . . .

This is a story! It has a hero, and because it has action, drama and a hero we in the human race have elevated the dramatic story to a high place in our attention. In our culture, stories direct our attention and where we place it, but Le Guin says that if we look back at what has sustained us as a culture, the first tool, the first support that humans probably had was the lowly carrier bag – for you can hold many more wild oats in a carrier bag than in your two hands. She speculates about what this says about a culture that has elevated the knife and its legacy into stories where we place our attention. In fact our survival has been sustained by the carrier bag and its descendants, other kinds of containers – the home, the organisation or the community.

Human resource development abounds in 'gatherers' – busy collecting information, skills, knowledge and stories which they use to sustain, support and develop both themselves and others. I hope these gatherings have added to your carrier bag.

References

Andreas, S. and C. (1987) *Change Your Mind and Keep the Change*, Utah, Real People Press.

Andreas, S. and C. (1989) *Heart of the Mind*, Utah, Real People Press.

Anthony, P. (1993) *Managing Culture*, Buckingham, Open University Press.

Arrien, A. (1993) *The Four Fold Way*, San Francisco, Harper.

Bandler, R. and Grinder, J. (1975) and (1976) *The Structure of Magic I & II*, Palo Alto, CA, Science of Behaviour Books Inc.

Bandler, R. (1985) *Using Your Brain for a Change*, Utah, Real People Press.

Bandler, R. and Grinder, J. (1979) *Frogs into Princes*, Utah, Real People Press.

Bandler, R. and Grinder, J. (1981) *Transformations*, Utah, Real People Press.

Bandler, R. and Grinder, J. (1982) *Reframing*, Utah, Real People Press.

Bretto, C. (1988) *A Framework for Excellence*, CA, Capitola.

Cialdini, R.B. (1993) *Influence – The Psychology of Persuasion*, New York, Quill William Morrow.

Covey, S.R. (1992) *The Seven Habits of Highly Effective People*, New York, Simon and Schuster.

Dilts, R. (1989) *NLP in Training Groups*, Ben Lomond CA, Dynamic Learning.

Dilts, R. (1990) *The Parable of the Porpoise*, Ben Lomond CA, Dynamic Learning.

Dilts, R. with Bonnissone, G. (1993) *Skills of the Future*, CA, Meta Publications.

Laborde, G.Z. (1984) *Influencing with Integrity*, CA, Syntony.

Laborde, G.Z. (1988) *Fine Tune Your Brain*, CA, Syntony.

Le Guin, U. (1992) *Dancing on the Edge of The World*, London, Paladin.

Lloyd, L. (1990) *Classroom Magic*, Oregon, Metamorphous Press.

12

Action Learning as a Cross-Cultural Tool

Monica Lee

INTRODUCTION

In this chapter I will argue that *action learning* feeds into strategic HRD through the enabling and promotion of individual, group and organisational learning. In order to do this I will draw upon two main lines of evidence, namely notions of holistic learning and of the co-regulation of social development. Through these I will move to an examination of the role of experience in learning, presenting action learning as a holistic learning method which is flexible and transferable across cultures given that it is, by definition, grounded in the specific political and cultural contexts in which it is applied. Finally I will draw upon evidence gained from experiences of action learning in Western and Central Europe to examine some of the problems and benefits of implementation within a cross-cultural environment. In doing this I range across a variety of what are more normally seen as traditional and disparate disciplines. Therefore, in the following analysis I have provided a plethora of references, both to contextualise the (at times controversial) ideas presented here, and to provide leads for those who wish to explore areas that I have skimmed over.

LEARNING AND DEVELOPMENT

Gross (1987) argues that when discussing learning the lay person tends to emphasise *what* has been learned, whilst educationalists and psychologists focus on the *process* of learning. As a society we have valued the attainment of progressively 'higher' qualifications, and have used these as criteria for judgement about what has been learnt, and, following from this, the form and level of work the person might be suitable for (Lee, 1994a). However, the increasing emphasis upon experience and competence evident in recent research (i.e. Cannon, 1994; Taylor, 1994; Raelin and Schermerhorn, 1994), is forcing a review of our educational paradigms. We are presented with a wide range of models and accounts of learning and development, with, at times, scant attention to the processes that underlie these.

Whilst the notion of fundamental processes that underlie the behavioural and social sciences is debatable, I follow Barklow *et al.* (1992) in working from the assumption that such processes exist, that all such sciences look (at some level) at the variation or uniformity in practices, preferences, or modes of reasoning across cultures, and thus, that the causal core of the field is the study of the mechanisms that allow humans to absorb, generate, modify and transmit culture. Part of the challenge in this chapter, therefore, is to synthesise the plethora of information about learning, development, culture, and educational practice in a way that winds these disparate strands into a coherent account of the way in which action learning (as an educational practice) influences strategic HRD (as planned cultural change) through learning and development. In order to do this I first have to address what I mean by the *process* of learning and development.

Schools of thought about the processes of learning have approached learning from different directions. Thus, if I take the liberty of reducing detailed descriptions of major bodies of knowledge and research to a few short paragraphs, the most prominent of these can be characterised as shown in Fig. 12.1.

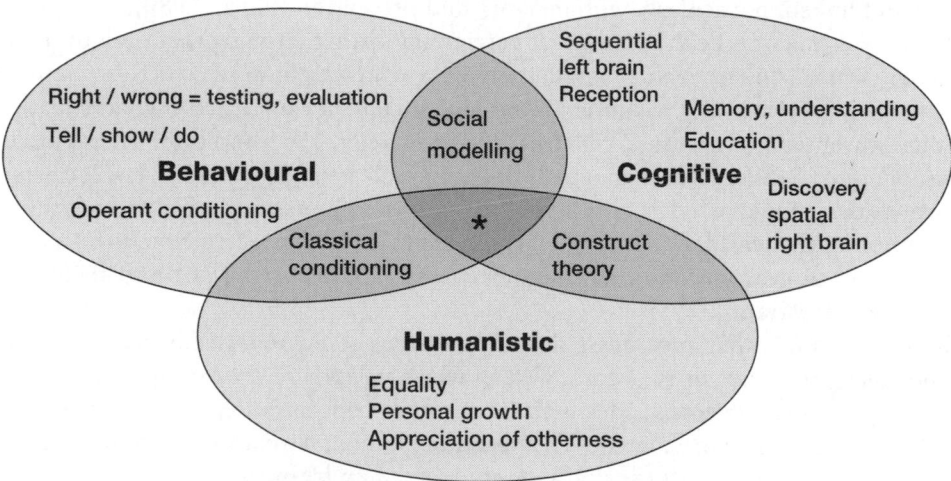

Fig. 12.1   Aspects of learning

Behaviourists might argue that 'learning can be defined as a relatively permanent change in behaviour due to past experience' (Coon, 1983). In other words, learning is directly linked to a behavioural outcome – e.g. learning to drive – which has been achieved, normally, by a series of linked steps associated with reward for appropriate behaviour at each stage. In this example the reward might be extreme pleasure at finally being able to change gear without accompanying crunching noises.

It is worth, at this stage, making a distinction between conscious, subconscious and unconscious learning. These three categories can be seen as stages of accessibility or awareness. The learner is now probably fully aware (and conscious) that he or she can shift gears whereas previously they had been unable to. He or she also has subconscious learning (for example, about the relationship between engine noise and the need to shift) that is accessible upon introspection, and thus is able to be made conscious. Regardless of the depth of introspection, however, there is some learning that remains inaccessible – in this case at the physical level of nerve impulses and cognitive-motor co-ordination. The making conscious of 'unconscious' learning (by explaining the physical stages and strategies that are undertaken in order to shift gear) can result in an apparent de-skilling.

Cognitivists, on the other hand, would point to the need to examine potential behaviour. The learner might know much that is not translated immediately into action. The learner might not even be aware that they know it. To extend the above example, the learner driver might have improved their gear shifting by learning more about how the gear box operates from reading a manual, or even from a forgotten conversation with a friend about the problems he or she encountered when in a similar position, thus experiencing the situation second-hand and possibly without being consciously aware of it (*social learning theory* and *observational learning* – see, for example, Bandura, 1977).

Cognitivists would also point to our ability to transfer our learning from one situation to another; the way in which we build 'maps' of understanding of the relationships between events and concepts; and the way in which learning might appear to be cumulative and linked, particularly with memory and perception (Howe 1980).

Humanists might take the concept of perception further, arguing that each of us creates our own version of 'reality' based upon the way in which we structure (or map) our individual perceptions and memories of our unique suite of experiences and anticipations of the future (see, for example, *construct theory* – Kelly, 1955 and more recent discussions of cultural differences in mapped concepts, such as Jankowicz, 1994a). 'Learning' is seen as the gaining of a deeper insight into our view of ourselves as located within our perception of the world. For example, whilst going through the frustrations of furthering the skill of gear changing, our learner might gain deeper insight into their usual reactions to frustration.

In more common parlance, these three approaches could be styled as learning based in the *hands*, the *head*, or the *heart*. We can see this clearly in the example of a normal university lecture. Students and lecturer are normally concentrating upon learning at the *head* level – the academic content. They are all colluding with a variety of behavioural norms at the *hands* level (those that new students often learn at school and that sometimes cause problems when dealing with 'experienced managers' who refuse to collude with the traditional educational norms) such as when to question and how to take notes. There is also learning at the *heart* level – perhaps an increasing dislike of sitting still and being talked down to.

Learning is therefore not restricted to what is being taught – we make sense of our experiences holistically (combining the 'learning' from head, hands and heart), and our perception of our history and anticipation of the future will influence our current learning (Lee, 1994b). Some of the key points to take from this are that if there are 40 people experiencing the same educational process, each will approach it from different directions and 'learn' different things from it; that whilst we often focus upon the product of learning as the learning itself, learning can, and often does, occur below the level of conscious awareness, such that the educational process is, in part, the making conscious of that which we already 'know'; and that 'experience' will play a part in any learning, regardless of whether it is acknowledged within the educational process.

This discussion of individual learning outlines a holistic overview – but one that is inherently static and cumulative. When we incorporate the role of experience into our accounts of learning we have, also, to accommodate our understanding of the underlying processes.

Upon introspection, most of us would argue that our learning is essentially dynamic and developmental – in other words, it is a process we go through – and from that we change and develop. In the examples above we can see that the road sense we acquired when learning to ride a bike becomes modified and extended as we become more aware of the limits of the car's ability to brake; an understanding of the car's gear box helps us when constructing a model with our children; a deeper awareness of how we behave when frustrated helps us develop more useful strategies for coping with our frustration. In Fig. 12.1, cumulative learning could be characterised by increasing the size of the circles, whilst developmental learning would necessitate the inclusion of a third axis. In moving along that axis the way in which we characterise the world and the relationship between what we know we have learnt and what we might make of it, changes.

Some authors, such as Bateson (1973), argue that there exists a hierarchy of learning, in which one level provides the context for the level below. Writers such as Klein (1989) and Burgoyne and Hodgson (1983) speculate that levels of learning are not unique, rather that higher levels emerge from the gradual erosion of those below. Fiol and Lyles (1985) review a variety of theories about levels of learning and conclude that there are two principal levels. The lower level is characterised by repetition of past behaviours, whilst the higher level entails the development of complex rules and associations in order to facilitate new actions. This can be seen in the light of Bartunek and Moch's (1987) description of second and third order change, in which second order change attempts are designed to phase in particular frameworks in which events are understood (schemata) and phase out others, whereas third order change attempts aim to help organisation members develop the capacity to identify and change their own schemata as they see fit. They argue that the two approaches present change agents with different roles and ethical dilemmas. In second order change the agent would advocate a particular interpretation of events, whilst in third order change the agent would help the organisation members develop the ability to determine for themselves when second order change is required and then help them implement it. Similar notions of shift can be seen in double/triple loop learning (Garratt, 1987; Hawkins, 1991) and the Rogerian approach, in which a facilitator helps others to help themselves (Rogers, 1951, 1959). Within this view both the manager and the management educator become change agents working with a holistic text (Mangham, 1990) from a broadly based background and polymath approach (Moore, 1990). Concepts such as holistic learning (and thus the roles of experience and subconscious processes in learning) and the interactive emergence of something novel in development are also mirrored in views of social development, and, as will be argued below, in the development of 'culture'.

DEVELOPMENT AND CULTURE

Fogel (1993) builds a strong case for social development as a process of creative interaction, a process that starts at birth and by which we become acculturated, and through which 'individuals dynamically alter their actions with respect to the ongoing and anticipated actions of their partners' (p. 34). Thus 'culture' is co-regulated by the participants, and the underlying processes of this are the same whether we are talking of family and friendship groupings, temporary 'micro-cultures', organisational or national culture

(Lee, 1994c). An essential element to this notion of co-regulated culture is that individuals negotiate a form of communication and meaning specific and new to the group (Smith, 1992) and relatively un-accessible or un-describable to those who were not part of the process (Lee, 1994c). Thus culture and relationships are seen to exist within mutually constructed conventions or frames of reference, which can be mutually dissolved by participants through ratification (Duncan, 1991, p. 345; Moreland and Levine, 1989). This is not, however, to imply that these processes are conscious, or easily accessible to conscious control. As Fogel argues, 'communication, self and culture are just different ways of talking about relationships, different points of view on the same phenomenon' (1993, p. 24). The importance of self can be seen as a culturally specific phenomenon. Pascale (1978) states that 'The western notion of mastery is closely linked with deep-seated assumptions about the self. . . . In contrast, the Eastern frame of reference views pragmatically appropriate limitations of the ego as a virtue.' Co-regulation is more in tune with Eastern concepts of interdependence (Cushman, 1991) in that the individual's experience of self-hood is seen to be a reflection of continual social interactions in the course of life (Scheibe, 1986, p. 131). Fogel (1993, p. 157) argues that although:

> 'the multiple dialogical self does not preclude a sense of self-cohesion or a sense of harmony between different aspects of one's social or private life . . . The experience of cohesion probably occurs when each of the relationships in which one engages are informationally consonant with each other, mutually supportive and similarly creative. A self in which one voice and one relationship dominates all others is not cohesive: it is rigidified and exclusionary, it is one that experiences disjunction between each of its real and imagined relationships. Developmental change, therefore, is the process of elaboration, dissolving, comparing and consolidating dialogical self-frames.'

Co-regulation negates the notion of control to the extent that behaviour and goals are not planned in advance but emerge creatively out of social discourse. Moreover, Fogel (1993, p. 114) implies that the need for control of self or another leads to relationships that are 'marked by rigidity and sameness, by a motivation to avoid creativity around particular themes, by a sense of obligation without pleasure'. This split between consensual and rigid relationships is similar to Marshall's (1984, p. 218) two states of union-seeking communion and independence-seeking agency, and Rogers' (1959) concepts of unconditional and conditional regard. For each writer, in the first case individuals are prized for their intrinsic value as human beings, whilst in the latter case acceptance is conditional upon meeting the evaluative criteria of others.

Figure 12.2 shows that if we apply this notion of co-regulated development to educational provision the participants in each educational micro-culture collude to focus upon particular aspects of learning. Taking a simplistic approach for the sake of illustration, the 'head' environment will carry with it group norms about received wisdom, the value of qualifications – and thus the power vested in those who have achieved them and those who can give them – the importance of cogent argument and the relative lack of importance of applicability and individual difference. The archetypal 'problem' student would be someone who was insufficiently intelligent to master the required concepts. The 'hands' environment would focus upon activity, functionalism, and the importance of the end result, thus the norms would be about open contribution where appropriate, identifying competence, and filling the 'training gap' to achieve appropriate levels of competence. Here, the archetypal problem trainee would be someone who was unable to demonstrate the required competence. In the 'heart' environment the focus would be upon difference, equality, and the inappropriateness of received wisdom (in so far as it epitomises a particular view of reality) or of identifiable and assessable 'competencies' (in so far as they epitomise a 'right' way of doing things). In this case, the problem participant would be unwilling to explore and share their affective and attitudinal aspects.

In reality and regardless of the rhetoric, any situation has an impact upon the 'whole' person. Thus no learning environment is as simplistic as is presented here, and bearing in mind the co-regulation of the educational micro-culture, the 'problem-person' is more likely to be driven by the perceived need to challenge the educational norms as implicitly agreed to and colluded with by the rest of the community. These notions do, however, provide some framework for understanding the different approaches taken by the academic community, organisations and individuals as stakeholders in the educational process. They also provide a framework for understanding national differences in approach to learning and development (Easterby-Smith and Lee, 1992). For example, as documented elsewhere in this book (Stead and Lee) and by Jankowicz (1994a) educational provision in Central Europe has traditionally involved an ex-cathedra approach. As will be discussed later, this generates both problems and potential when non-Central European nationals attempt to work cross-culturally using alternative methodologies, such as action learning.

EXPERIENCE, MANAGEMENT AND ACTION LEARNING

The above sections have both pointed to the way in which the 'whole person' (including self-hood and experience) learns and develops. An essential premise to the arguments that will be presented in this section is that effective 'management', HRD, and the creation and strategic change of organisational culture also, by necessity, involve that 'whole person'.

Management is becoming both more complex and more generalist (Dobson and Stewart, 1990). This notion of increasing complexity, tied to that of the interdependent nature of organisations situated in a universe that is itself an integrated self-organising system (Jantsch, 1980) is a fundamental part of the holistic, systematic co-evolutionary view propounded in recent publications (Davis, 1990; Lessem, 1990, 1991; Lievegood, 1991; Norgaard, 1988; Senge, 1990). It is intrinsic to the notion of the learning organisation (Pedlar et al., 1991) and is developed in areas of research such as soft-system methodology (Checkland, 1981). This view of management is also linked to the ability to adapt and change in response to the changing environment, to the concept of learning as a new form of labour and knowledge as a resource (Drucker, 1993), and to the erosion of distinctions between managers and managed, with organisations structured around human beings and the relationships between them (Zuboff, 1989).

This approach entails a shift in the way in which organisations and the nature of management are viewed, and has implications for the managerial role (Clegg, 1990; Dobson

	Head	Hands	Heart	Holistic
Focus	Accretion of conventional wisdom	Demonstration of skilled practice	Exploration of affective aspects of self and in relation to others	Integration of all aspects of self, and of self with surroundings
Catch-phrase	Rigorous thought	Functionalism	Authenticity	Managing boundaries
Arena	Development of conceptual ability, understanding and memory	Transmission of craft and skills through practice and feedback	Deepening sense of self through the making conscious of emotions, attitudes and value bases	Perception of self as complex, balancing dark and light sides of inner self, skills and conceptual ability
Roots of power	Expertise and knowledge, as recognised by external criteria	Proven ability to achieve practical goals	Personal power based upon self-belief and direction	Empowerment by reflective and ethical management of own and others' agendas
Implicit norms of micro-culture	Defer to experts, the transmission and passive reception of knowledge. Searching for the 'correct' answer	Defer to experts, the measurement of performance against accepted practice, acknowledged 'right way' of doing things	Multiple realities, irrelevance of expertise and external evaluatitive criteria, though others' perceptions of self provide an important mirror	Multiple realities, expertise given due value, seeking equitable balance between interests of self and others
Common approach	Generally the product of academe as stakeholder. Progressive levels of theoretically-based qualifications Academe and traditional education	Generally the product of the organisation as stakeholder. Competency-based achievement against progressively harder 'craft' standards	Generally the product of the individual as stakeholder. Facilitated non-evaluative exploration of affective self, normally through sharing with others	Generally the product of multiple stakeholders. Interdisciplinary, broad-based collaborative provision meeting individual and self-defined needs
Common methods	Ex-cathedra = lectures, tutorials, exams and tests of knowledge, sometimes of understanding	Apprenticeship, guided practice, mentoring, 'tell-show-do', 'Systematic approach to training'	Encounter groups, outdoor development, self-development groups, confrontation and support	Experiential learning, action learning, Life-long/open learning. Multi-cultural – managing diversity

Fig. 12.2   Correlates to archetypal views of learning

et al., 1992; Dumain, 1990). A series of writers have pointed to the fragmented nature of managerial work (i.e. Mintzberg, 1973) and have suggested that no one managerial style is uniquely successful (Knotter, 1982), but that economic advantage will come to those who are best able to spot opportunities, to learn rapidly, and to create appropriate commitment amongst colleagues (Freedman, 1992; Handy, 1985; Kanter, 1982). Apparent roles vary with managerial level, form of organisation, culture and research methodology (Smith and Peterson, 1988). A continuing role for managers, however, is in monitoring and influencing culture and managing meaning, in so far as organisations are systems of wholly or partly shared meanings (Mangham, 1990; Pfeffer, 1981; Pondy 1978; Schein, 1985). The manager is a manipulator of organisational symbols (Johnson, 1990), who can inspire and influence others by managing the communicative climate through process skills, whilst maintaining a core of ethicality and strong self-concept (Adler, 1974; Snell, 1988, 1993). This concept of the managerial role is one of creating a business environment in which people can flourish spiritually and emotionally, by nourishing creative tension generated by a balance between a focus on human resources and personal well being on one hand and a clear, hard, management on the other (Pascale, 1990), and involves the 'knowledge and acceptance of a wider repertoire of ways of being' (Kinsman, 1990). The manager is expected to be leader, mediator and linchpin (Graen *et al.*, 1978; Likert, 1961; Pelz, 1951; Stryker and Statham, 1985), and to be engaged in lateral and hierarchical transformational transactions as an 'equal' collaborative colleague (Kahn *et al.*, 1964; Sayles, 1964), by which:

> *'one or more persons engage with others in such a way that leaders and followers raise one another to higher levels of motivation and morality . . . a process of mutual exchange where the function of leaders and followers is fused.'* (Burns, 1978, p. 20)

Superior–inferior relationships are eliminated (Samovar and Porter, 1976), subordinates become colleagues and espoused equals, and the ex-leader's power (and perceived high performance) is more firmly located in personal ability to manage the processes of the interactions than in position or expertise (Martinko and Gardner, 1984, 1987).

Several writers have queried the applicability of the 'Utopia' described above. Ferlie and Bennett (1992) found that, in practice, change agents need to have status or access to other sources of power to be effective. Role conflict is the normal lot of the manager (Stewart, 1976, 1982; Roethlisberger, 1945), and can lead to polarisation, particularly in times of rapid change (Bass, 1965; Smith *et al.*, 1969), and developmental organisational structures carry high personal cost (Lee, 1994c). However, as a growing number of researchers from a variety of disciplines point to the central and strategic role that the development of the 'human' aspects of the organisation plays in the creation and maintenance of organisational health and longevity, corporate decision making and national wealth (Ashforth and Humphrey, 1993; Brewster, 1993; Lee, 1991; McKiernan and Morris, 1993; Papadakis, 1993; Smith and Peterson, 1988), there is an increasing focus upon process, symbolic management and 'people' skills as an important attribute of effective management (Buchanan, 1991; Kobrin, 1984; Taylor, 1994; Cannon, 1994). A glance at the advertising literature for short-cycle post-experience courses emphasises the current trend towards 're-educating' managerial people skills as a method of effecting change in managerial attributes, and thus (it is assumed) aiding planned organisational change. Implicit within this view is the need for managers to accept responsibility for the ways in which they choose to act, and that it is this element of conscious choice of behaviours that aids managers in implementing their intentions (Whittington, 1990). This is supported by Marshall and Stewart's (1981a, b) finding that the majority of their middle management respondents saw their behaviour as largely fixed by external constraints. A positive view of self-hood appears to be a useful attribute for the developmental manager to possess and to create in others. It is correlated with an increased ability to relate to others (Hewitt and Kraft, 1973; Reddy, 1973; Rosenberg, 1965); a decrease in ethnic prejudice (Rubin, 1967a, b), minority groups (Rogers, 1951) and polarisation (Bowers, 1963); reduced levels of anxiety (Coopersmith, 1967; Ausubel and Robinson, 1969); high performance (Robertson and Sadri, 1993); and increased ethicality (Kohlberg, 1973; Maclagan and Snell, 1992).

More generally, Campbell and Dunnette (1968) found that self-development aided by focused groups (such as T groups) correlated with long-term behavioural change associated with an increase in self-insight, self-acceptance, self attitudes and attitudes to others. Of particular relevance are the findings that the traditional approach to relating to others (one of evaluation, competition, restriction in establishing warm personal relationships, routine activities, power-based monologue and a focus upon the right answer) is correlated with low self-esteem, whereas a participatory approach (defined as active, other-centred, creating divergent thinking, and generating time for others to talk) are related to high self-concept (Burns, 1976), and that failure in change of approach (even though desired by the individual) may be due to the effects of a negative self-concept (Barker Lunn, 1970). However, even self-concept appears to be socially regulated. Fey (1954) found that prototypic 'well-adjusted' people with high self-other acceptance are perceived not to 'need' friendships, their psychological robustness is resented, and they become isolated by those with lower self-acceptance who are able to meet each other's feelings of being needed. The withdrawal of friendship, however, is likely to lead to a lessening of self-acceptance, which in turn can be rewarded by increased friendship. It is possible that this mechanism is partly co-regulatory, and thus level of self-acceptance becomes one of the 'norms' of the micro-culture. If such social support is not provided, however, the individual increases the distance between themselves and others in order to protect their self-concept, thereby preserving psychological security by creating an out-group that can be classed by the individual as both alien and of lower social standing (Burns, 1984).

It would appear, therefore, that managerial development, in so far as it contributes to the long-term health of the organisation, needs to include nebular attributes (such as ethicality and the acceptance of diversity) and attitudinal factors (such as proactivity, responsibility, awareness of self and others, conscious choice and strategic thinking) as well as the more normally accepted aspects of knowledge and skill. As was noted above, these attributes cannot be 'transferred' to the manager in a directive manner. The form of educational provision adopted must be in tune with the educational norms implicit in holistic learning, thereby respecting the individual's past and current experience and facilitating the understanding of the range of viewpoints implicit within co-regulated micro-cultures, whilst simultaneously supporting the learning of knowledge and skills. It also, and perhaps most importantly, cannot be divorced from the work arena (Seely Brown and Duguid, 1991). At a meta-level, all members of the organisation co-regulate its structure and norms (even if by passivity), thus the surfacing of assumptions between members is part of the organisational learning process (Argyris and Schon, 1978; Senge, 1990), as well as part of an individual's learning.

In theory, the construction of a uni-focused, multi-disciplinary product, such as integrated competency-based provision with measurable outcomes might best meet the widely differing needs of the stakeholders (Binsted, 1988; Constable and McCormick, 1987; Handy *et al.*, 1987; Powers, 1983). In practice (as evidenced by Smithers, 1993), it is hard to reconcile the underlying value systems of the different stakeholders. The elements that appear most threatening to providers of higher education are those linked to access (the extent to which skills-based experience is seen as both necessary and sufficient for access), assessment (raising issues of how to accredit prior experience for entrance, and how to assess development on experientially-based provision) and provision (in which potential providers are assessed for their suitability and accredited as providers under a system that is separate and potentially inimicable to that of higher education). A positive view would encourage the belief that, with flexibility and communication, these problems are surmountable; however, there are other issues that are less easily resolved. Deeper concern focuses upon the drive for standardisation which is seen to reduce diversity at a time when flexible structures are needed to facilitate the meeting of changing needs and shifts of national policy (Porter and McKibbin, 1988), and doubt about generalisability of skills (Thorpe, 1990). The nature of the assessment processes, which threatens the ideal of holism and does not reflect the variable nature of the managerial role (Burgoyne, 1989, 1990), also gives concern, as do the cultural and political ramifications of choice of membership of a 'standardising body' (Nespor, 1988). The focus upon measurable outcomes (the assessment of being able to DO) forces standardisation, and thus presents a dilemma to those who wish to move from central planning towards provision that allows more individual freedom, whether it be focused upon opportunistic or sustainable development.

An alternative way of meeting these challenges, and in keeping with the wider view of 'competency' (Lee, 1995a), and in defence of individuality, is to work across the different approaches, leading to a multi-focused product. Morgan (1993) noted that co-operation between proponents of different approaches is rare, and the supremacy of one view over another is more a product of internal politics between academic departments than of disinterested debate. However, evidence from the UK (Swan *et al.*, 1993) and from Western and Central European nations (Lee, 1993; Ryder and Easterby-Smith, 1992) indicates that programmes designed to bring together those who would normally have little contact with each other (crossing discipline and institutional barriers) are successful in helping participants acknowledge, understand and build upon this diversity by locating their own approach and adopting what they see as 'good practice' in other approaches. Such programmes provide breathing space for such debate, but in doing so they challenge participants to become interdisciplinary (Mudroch, 1992), question whether the business school environment is the most appropriate setting for managers to learn in, and challenge the assumed expertise of the management teacher. They are complex and politically sensitive. They bridge the stakeholders and thus need to be established within the macro-structure, but in so far as they question and challenge, they cannot easily be institutionalised.

Such multi-focused programmes, however, only facilitate holistic learning in so far as the educational methodology enables participants to balance knowledge, experience and self-development. Programmes that focus upon curricula tend to be static, revolving around a conventional core whose relevance to management practice can be questioned (Asher, 1984). An alternative is to focus upon experience, following Honey and Mumford's (1989) view that any 'experience' is an opportunity for learning. One of the best known models of experiential learning is that of Kolb (1974, 1984) (see Fig. 12.3). Kolb suggests that the process of holistic learning is cyclical, and whilst the 'cycle' can be entered at any point, it is most usually approached from that of an experience. In order to learn from that experience we need to be able to reflect upon it (in other words, make conscious that which might have been subconscious – answering the question 'what happened?'), conceptualise it (why did it happen?), and then plan future action in the light of the hypotheses that have been generated (what will I do differently? the same? and how?). The continuation of the cycle is generated by the testing of the hypotheses by further experience.

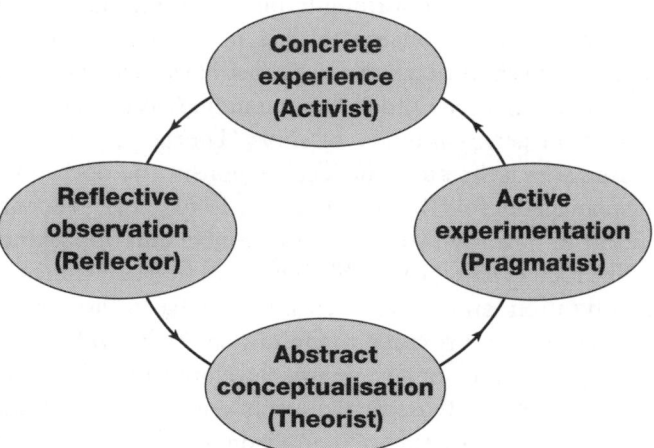

Fig. 12.3 Kolb's learning cycle

There has been some criticism of the model. Burgoyne (1992) argues that in bringing out some important aspects of the learning process it obscures others, dealing less clearly with the emotional aspects of learning, and in not making explicit the potential difference between effective and ineffective learning – if people only 'see what they want or expect to see' in the experience they are substantially blocked from effective learning. These points are partially addressed by placing emphasis in the interpretation of the model upon: holistic learning, as opposed to, for example, the direct transference of knowledge; some process, either internal or externally facilitated, that enables critical observation and evaluation of the experience, such that the learner is able to distance themselves from it rather than 'replay' it; and the ability to translate the experience into potentially actionable, and realistically testable, future experience. Development might be built into the model by seeing the cycle as a spiral. A further extension of the model is to suggest that each of us has a preferred learning style which correlates directly with one of the stations on the model (given in brackets in Fig. 12.3) such that we may tend to use some part of the cycle at the expense of the others (Kolb, 1976).

Kolb's model implies that for the learning opportunity to be translated into an effective learning experience, activists and pragmatists might need to be encouraged and supported in reflection and conceptualisation, whilst reflectors and theorists might need similar support in relating the potential learning to active and practical outcomes. It also calls into question the degree to which much of current educational provision recognises the different learning preferences of both students and educators, and the extent to which it is designed to utilise prior experience in a way that maximises effective learning (Beckwith, 1991).

Action learning is an educational approach that bears many similarities to Kolb's cycle, and, in so far as it is described theoretically, offers the potential of facilitating experientially-based individual learning in a holistic and creative manner. Initially championed by Revans (1980) it has developed into an increasingly popular methodological choice in the West, both within 'traditional' management programmes and in the organisational setting (Raelin and Schermerhorn, 1994). It is generally group-based, and can be seen as a way by which the (normally) facilitated group helps individuals to review their experiences by non-evaluative exploration of the issues, as presented by the individual, leading to: deeper reflection about the learning inherent in these experiences; the creation and incorporation of a wider understanding of the import of this learning in relation to others' experiences, theories and models; and the building of possible future ways of working, and evaluating and modifying these approaches (Lee, 1995b). Successful action learning is rooted in a belief that we can do something about our situation – a positive approach to life – and is based upon trust and confidentiality (McGill and Beaty, 1992).

In that action learning focuses upon the making sense of experience in a strategic and holistic way and normally leads to actionable outcomes, it appears to be an excellent methodological choice for educational provision that purports to support individual, organisational and cross-cultural learning and development. Theoretically, action learning is politically and socially unbiased; thus the membership of the action learning set defines both the task and the process by which it might be achieved, and in doing so co-regulates the processes of the group within their own socio-political context. Thus a Central European action learning group could theoretically be very different from one functioning in the West, whilst still meeting the criteria of action focused holistic learning. The final section of this chapter will explore some of the implications of the practice (as opposed to theory) of action learning within a cross-cultural arena.

THE PRACTICE OF ACTION LEARNING

Implicit in the concept of societal co-regulation discussed above is the idea that education, in itself, is a form of social engineering, therefore the attitudes underlying educational provision will be transmitted, even if the providers attempt to avoid attitudinal issues. As a methodology, action learning is firmly located within a particular set of value-based assumptions. It assumes the value of:

- equality of voice
- interdisciplinarity
- open and frank discussion
- helping and working with others
- assimilating others' perspectives
- active engagement of all participants
- a proactive stance to self and learning
- minimising the power of external 'experts'
- the ability to appreciate and work with diversity
- a relatively high level of trust and confidentiality
- working with experience and action in the learning process

This is not intended to be an exhaustive list, rather, it is presented to illustrate the complexity of the issue. There are, of course, individual differences in each of these. Much of the complexity and challenge of working with and in action learning sets revolves around the creation of a micro-culture in which there is some agreement about the implicit norms (often made explicit in the form of learning contracts) that are specific to the group and acceptable to all members of the set. This is a dynamic process, and, as such, one with no 'resolution'. As the implicit norms become voiced they also become reified. In other words, 'trust', for example, becomes voiced as an important value; however, the very voicing of it leads to it being objectified, used as a catch-word. Each individual assumes that they know exactly what the others mean by it, and deeper discussion and analysis of its multiple meanings for each individual is hampered. Multiple and changing meanings of trust (in that it is a value and thus, to a certain extent, subconscious) remain within the group as an issue that permeates other issues, yet become harder to discuss, because the naming of 'trust' has given false legitimacy to the conscious 'presenting face'.

These challenges are accentuated by increased diversity in the value base of the group. In other words, I am arguing that the issues and complexity are the same regardless of whether the group contains people from one nation, or from many, but the more multicultural the group the more these issues are seen as problematic. Attempts to explore deeper, co-regulated 'holistic' meaning of the word 'trust' in a uni-cultural group might prove to be difficult; in a multi-cultural group in which part of the group has experienced the ambiguous and negative overtones associated with the concept, the differing values associated with the word can hamper understanding and learning. Examples of this can be found in Lee (1995c), in which I illustrate some of the difficulties of using action learning within the Central European context – one in which people's beliefs about trust and freedom of choice had been eroded over many years of 'domination'. It is not within the remit of this chapter to explore this example in detail, but it is raised here to demonstrate that whilst these tensions are inherent in all forms of educational provision, provision that accentuates the focus upon individual difference will, by its very nature, be more challenging as the differences increase.

In addition, and as illustrated in Fig. 12.2, different forms of educational provision carry with them different understandings and values about the educational process. As noted above, any form of educational provision is also a form of social engineering. This presents little problem if the form of provision and the societal norms match. Conversely, the greater the mis-match the greater the challenge experienced by recipients and providers. Perhaps what typifies the West most, within the realms of management education, is the wide diversity of views, approaches, and understandings of the implications of both management and education (Snell and James, 1994). When, for example, this assumption of the value of diversity, implicit in action learning, is laid upon the educational processes of those who do not value this, and instead wish to be told the right answer, then a central tenet of the interaction is being challenged. This is particularly obvious when attempting to use action learning within the Polish education system which traditionally adopted an ex-cathedra approach (Jankowicz, 1994b, c; Jankowicz and Pettitt, 1993; Lee, 1995c), but can also be found in the West. Evaluation of a similar programme in the UK showed that some of those new to management education feel that: there 'should be' a single and clear definition of what management 'is'; a unitary body of knowledge that 'should' be taught; a 'best' method of delivery; and that the tutor, as expert, should be able to deliver these accurately and without hesitation (Swan *et al.*, 1993).

Furthermore, the product of action learning is *action* – the need to work towards an implementable goal. Whilst it is generally accepted that the role of the action learning set adopts the Rogerian (1959) approach – that true development is fostered by helping individuals to help themselves – this leaves open the question of how much flexibility individuals have in taking action within their own culture, whilst under the implicit constraints and expectations placed upon them by a methodology and other participants who are coming from a different culture. For example, in the Central European programme discussed above participants were teachers of management in institutions of higher education, and were encouraged to review their choice of methodology and the design of their curricula. However, Central European educational systems are not geared to alternative forms of methodology, thus adoption of these requires strategic and structural change in the organisation, as well as changes in course design and provision. Many of these were outside the participants' sphere of influence, and their potential inability to create the changes they wished led, in some cases, to severe frustration.

A further problem with action learning as an educational methodology is inextricably linked to its holistic nature. This is the problem of assessment. Knowledge and skill are relatively easy for an outsider to assess in so far as they have measurable outcomes, but how can another person sufficiently understand an individual's self-development in order to assess it in a way that is congruent with both the individual's own understanding and externally imposed criteria? Anything other than self-assessment is alien to the philosophy of action learning. However, as noted above, the subconscious elements in learning mean that the individual can only 'know' what they have learnt retrospectively. Similarly, whilst learning can be seen as a widening of the circles in Fig. 12.1, and development as a change in the circles, much development is painful, in so far as it forces deconstruction followed by reconstruction of the individual's world-view. This process might well take some time, thus the results of attempts to assess such change will co-vary with time. Attempts to assess holistic learning and development, therefore, are fraught with problems associated with who is the most appropriate assessor, and when is the 'best' time to assess.

Some action learning programmes attempt to recognise this by providing a range of forms of assessment, such as log-books, and self- or group assessment. Other assessed programmes follow more traditional models, whilst adopting a non-assessed 'action learning' component. Such flexibility in design and forms of assessment facilitates a compromise between the need to meet externally defined criteria whilst promoting individual development; however, assessment poses a second form of challenge to action learning – that of power differentials. Theoretically, each participant is responsible for their own issue and takes equal responsibility for the group. This breaks down with the introduction of externally imposed criteria for assessment. Those who pose the criteria and manage the assessment are, *de facto*, in a position of superior power. Power related implicit norms within the action learning set become complex and particularly fluid as each participant (individually and collectively) works through the gamut of emotions, such as tension, elation, submission and rebellion, associated with being 'judged' and doing the 'judging'.

I have presented a series of problems associated with adopting an action learning approach in a cross-cultural environment. I wish to draw this chapter to a close by indicating why I feel that, despite these problems, it is an essential tool in cross-cultural provision. Tensions and challenges that present a problem to action learning are rooted in the underlying processes that influence human existence – such as learning, development and societal co-regulation. They are a fundamental facet of our existence and aspects of these processes, such as empowerment, power-difference and diversity, are an integral part of our lives – regardless of colour or creed. In respecting this, 'learning' within an action learning framework has meta-level applicability to whatever and whoever we are.

Action learning is a method that, in theory, is designed to promote holistic and experiential learning. Similar claims can be made of any form of provision that purports to synthesise knowledge and experience, whether it be Beckhardian organisation development interventions (Beckhard, 1967; McMillen *et al.*, 1994), or the broad sweep of approaches which attempt to create a community of enquiry in the classroom rather than providing an exposition (Novak, 1990; Forray and Mir, 1994). However, action learning also lends itself as a methodology which specifically allows/requires an explicit investigation of conflicting micro- and macro- cultural norms, both as they are perceived to exist, and as they are dynamically co-regulated. Thus, action learning is an approach through which the individual is able to re-analyse their role in the creation and development of the processes they are part of, and in doing so is encouraged to confront their own ideas, unsurfaced assumptions, biases and fears (Argyris, 1990), thereby addressing the development of themselves and others from an ethical standpoint. This notion is similar to Lane and DiStefano's (1992, p. 394) commitment in relativism 'in which a person understands the relativistic nature of the world, but makes a commitment to a set of values, beliefs, and a way of behaving within this expanded world view'. Thus the extent to which we, as providers and 'recipients', wish to work with the challenges of action learning must depend, in part, upon our own commitment to the vision of a relativistic multi-cultural world.

Action learning is a methodology of strategic change. Central to this chapter is the notion that long-term and stable change cannot be imposed, but must be whole-heartedly championed by those it affects. All participants in action learning are presented with fundamental decisions (often implicit) about the form of future they wish to create through the enactment of the attributes they influence (Lee, 1995a). This process is complex, challenging and problematic, but there are no easy ways of being a holistic change agent.

References

Adler, P.S. (1974) 'Beyond Cultural Identity: Reflections on Cultural and Multicultural Man', *Topics in Culture Learning*, vol. 2, Honolulu, East-West Culture Learning Institute.

Argyris, C. (1990) *Overcoming Organisational Defences*, Boston Mass, Allyn and Bacon.

Argyris, C. and Schön D.A. (1978) *Organizational Learning: A Theory of Action Perspective*, Reading Mass, Addison-Wesley.

Asher, K. (1984) *Master of Business: The MBA and British Industry*, Harbridge House Europe.

Ashforth, B.E. and Humphrey, R.H. (1993) 'Emotional labour in service roles: The influence of identity', *Academy of Management Review*, vol. 18, pp. 88–115.

Ausubel, D.P. and Robinson, F.G. (1969) *School Learning*, New York, Holt.

Bandura, A. (1977) *Social Learning Theory*, Englewood Cliffs NJ, Prentice Hall.

Barker Lunn, J.C. (1970) *Streaming in the Primary School*, NFER, Slough.

Barklow, J.H., Cosmides, L. and Tooby, J. (eds) (1992) *The Adapted Mind: Evolutionary Psychology and the Generation of Culture*, New York, Oxford University Press.

Bartunek, J.M. and Moch, M.K. (1987) 'First-order, second-order, and third-order change and organization development interventions: A cognitive approach', *Journal of Applied Behavioural Science*, vol. 23, pp. 483–500.

Bass, B.M. (1965) *Organisational Psychology*, Boston Mass, Allyn and Bacon.

Bateson, G. (1973) *Steps to an Ecology of the Mind*, London, Palladin.

Beckhard, R. (1967) 'Optimising Team-building Effects', *Journal of Contemporary Business*, vol. 1, pp. 23–32.

Beckwith, J. (1991) 'Approaches to Learning, their context and relationship to assessment performance', *Higher Education*, vol. 22, pp. 17–30.

Binsted, D. (1988) 'The development of interpersonal competencies', *Training Officer*, vol. 24, no. 11, pp. 338–42.

Bowers, D.G. (1963) 'Self-esteem and the Diffusion of Leadership Style', *Journal of Applied Psychology*, vol. 47, pp. 135–40.

Brewster, C. (1993) 'The integration of human resource management and corporate strategy: evidence from 14 countries', in *The Crafting of Management Research*, Proceedings of British Academy of Management Annual Conference, Milton Keynes.

Buchanan, D.A. (1991) 'Vulnerability and agenda: Context and process in project management', *British Journal of Management*, vol. 2, pp. 121–32.

Burgoyne, J.G. (1989) 'Creating the managerial portfolio: Building on competency approaches to management development', *Management Education and Development*, vol. 20, pp. 56–61.

Burgoyne, J.G. (1990) 'Doubts about Competency', in Devine, M. ed. *The Photofit Manager in the 1990s*, pp. 20–27, London, Unwin Hyman.

Burgoyne, J.G. (1992) 'Frameworks for understanding individual and collective professional development', *Education and Child Psychology*, vol. 9, no. 2, pp. 45–52.

Burgoyne, J.G. and Hodgson, V.E. (1983) 'Natural Learning and Managerial Action: A Phenomological Study in the Field Setting', *Journal of Management Studies*, vol. 20, no. 1, pp. 387–99.

Burns, J.M. (1978) *Leadership*, New York, Harper and Row.

Burns, R.B. (1976) 'Self and teaching approaches', *Durham Research Review*, vol. 36, pp. 1079–85.

Burns, R.B. (1984) *The Self Concept: in Theory, Measurement, Development and Behaviour*, New York, Longman.

Campbell, J.P. and Dunnette, M.D. (1968) 'Effectiveness Of T. Group Experiences In Managerial Training And Development', *Psychology Bulletin*, vol. 70, pp. 73–104.

Cannon, T. (1994) Working Party Report: Developments since Handy and Constable. Management Development to the Millennium Research, *The Institute of Management*, Northants.

Checkland, P. (1981) *Systems Thinking, Systems Practice*, London, Wiley.

Clegg, S.R. (1990) *Modern Organisations: Organisation Studies in the Postmodern World*, London, Sage.

Constable, J. and McCormick, R. (1987) *The Making of British Managers*, London, British Institute of Management and Federation of British Industry.

Coon, D, (1983) *Introduction to Psychology – Exploration and Application*, West Publishing Company.

Coopersmith, S. (1967) *The Antecedents of Self Esteem*, San Francisco CA, Freeman.

Cushman, P. (1991) 'Ideology obscured: political uses of self in Daniel Stern's infant', *American Psychologist*, vol. 46, pp. 206–19.

Davis, J. (1990) *Greening Business*, Oxford, Blackwell.

Dobson, S., Borucki, C.C. and Byosiere, P. (1992) 'Changes in the role of middle management: A European view', paper presented at *Third International Personnel and Human Resource Management Conference*, Ashridge.

Dobson, S. and Stewart, R. (1990) 'What *is* happening to middle management?', *British Journal Of Management*, vol. 1, pp. 3–16.

Drucker, P. (1993) *Post-Capitalist Society*, New York, Harper Business.

Dumain, B. (1990) 'Creating a New Company Culture', *Fortune*, vol. 15, pp. 55–8.

Duncan, S. (1991) 'Convention and conflict in the child's interraction with others', *Developmental Review*, vol. 11, pp. 337–67.

Easterby-Smith, M. and Lee, M. (1992) *United Kingdom management education in the '90's: policies and priorities*. Unpublished report commissioned by Institute for Public Policy Research. Available from Lancaster University, UK.

Ferlie, E. and Bennett, C. (1992) 'Patterns Of Strategic Change In Health Care: District Health Authorities Respond To Aids', *British Journal Of Management*, vol. 3, pp. 21–37.

Fey, W.F. (1954) 'The Acceptance Of Self And Others And Its Relation To Therapy Readiness', *Journal Of Clinical Psychology*, 10, pp. 266–9.

Fiol, C.M. and Lyles, M.A. (1985) 'Organizational Learning', *Academy of Management Review*, vol. 10, no. 4, pp. 803–13.

Fogel, A. (1993) *Developing through Relationships: Origins of Communication, Self and Culture*, Hemel Hempstead, Harvester Wheatsheaf.

Forray, J.M. and Mir, A.H. (1994) 'Envisioning a New Paradigm: Synthesis in Management Education', *Management Learning*, vol. 25, no. 2, pp. 201–14.

Freedman, D. (1992) 'Is management still a science?', *Harvard Business Review*, November, pp. 26–38.

Garratt, B. (1987) *The Learning Organisation*, London, Fontana.

Graen, G.B., Cashman, J.F, Ginsgurgh, S. and Schiemann, W. (1978) 'Effects Of Linking-Pin Quality Upon The Quality Of Working Life Of Lower Participants: A Longitudinal Investigation Of The Managerial Under Structure', *Administrative Science Quarterly*, vol. 22, pp. 491–504.

Gross, R. (1987) *Psychology: the Science of Mind and Behaviour*, London, Arnold

Handy, C. (1985) *Understanding Organisations*, Harmondsworth, Penguin.

Handy, C., Gow, I., Gordon, C., Randlesome, C. and Moloney, M. (1987) *The Making of Managers*, London, National Economic Development Office.

Hawkins, P. (1991) 'The spiritual dimension of the learning organisation', *Management Education And Development*, vol. 22, pp. 172–87.

Hewitt, J. and Kraft, M. (1973) 'Effects Of An Encounter Group Experience On Self Perception And Interpersonal Relations', *Journal Of Consulting Clinical Psychology*, vol. 40, p. 162.

Honey, P. and Mumford, A. (1989) *The Manual of Learning Opportunities*, Maidenhead, Berks, Peter Honey.

Howe, M. (1980) *The Psychology of Human Learning*, London, Harper and Row.

Jankowicz, A.D. (1994a) 'Parcels from Abroad: the Transfer of Meaning to Eastern Europe', *Journal of European Business Education*, (in Press)

Jankowicz, A.D. (1994b) 'The New Journey to Jerusalem: Mission and Meaning in the Managerial Crusade to Eastern Europe', *Organisation Studies*, vol. 15, no. 4, (in Press)

Jankowicz, A.D. (1994c) 'The Construction and Construing of Teaching Microcultures in Eastern Europe', in Kalekin-Fishman, D. and Walker, B. eds *The Construction of Group Realities: Culture and Society in the Light of Personal Construct Theory*, New York, Krieger.

Jankowicz, D. and Pettitt, S. (1993) 'Worlds in collusion: An analysis of an Eastern European management development initiative', *Management Education and Development*, vol. 24, pp. 93–104.

Jantsch, E. (1980) *The Self Organising Universe*, Oxford, Pergamon.

Johnson, G. (1990) 'Managing strategic change; The role of symbolic action', *British Journal of Management*, vol. 1, pp. 183–200.

Kahn, R.L., Wolfe, D.M., Quinn, R.P., Snoek, J.D. and Rosenthal, R.A. (1964) *Organisational Stress: Studies In Role Conflict And Ambiguity*, Wiley, New York.

Kanter, R. (1982) 'The Middle Manager As Innovator', *Harvard Business Review*, pp. 95–105.

Kelly, G. (1955) *A Theory of Personality: The Psychology of Personal Constructs*, New York, Norton.

Kinsman, J. (1990) *Millenium: Towards Tomorrow's Society*, London, Allen and Co.

Klein, J.I. (1989) 'Parenthic Learning in Organizations: Toward the Unlearning of the Unlearning Model', *Journal of Management Studies*, vol. 26, no. 3, pp. 291–308.

Knotter, J. (1982) *The General Managers*, New York, McGraw-Hill.

Kobrin, S. (1984) 'International Expertise In American Business Or How To Learn To Play With The Kids On The Street', Institute For International Education, cited in Lane and Distefano, *op. cit.*

Kohlberg, L. (1973) 'Continuities In Childhood And Adult Moral Development Revisited', in Baltes, P.B. and Schaie, K.W. eds *Life-Span Developmental Psychology: Personality And Socialisation*, New York, Academic Press.

Kolb, D. (1974) 'On management and the learning process', in Kolb, D.A., Rubin, I.M. and McIntyre, J.M. eds *Organisational Psychology*, Second edition, Prentice Hall.

Kolb, D. (1976) *Learning Style Inventory: Technical Manual*, Boston Mass, Mcber.

Kolb, D. (1984) *Experiential Learning*, Eaglewood Cliffs, NJ, Prentice Hall.

Lane, H. and DiStefano, J. (1992) *International Management Behaviour*, Second edition, Boston Mass, PWS-KENT Publishing Company.

Lee, M.M. (1991) 'Spirituality in organisations: Empowerment and purpose', *Management Education and Development*, vol. 22, pp. 221–6.

Lee, M.M. (1993) *Central European Management Teacher Development Programme: Final report*, JEP-0183-89-93, Brussels.

Lee, M.M. (1994a) 'Empowerment: Management Education, Power and Organisations', in Boydell, T., Pedlar, M. and Burgoyne, J. eds *The Learning Company Conference Book 3*, in press.

Lee, M.M. (1994b) 'Clothing and collusion', *Proceedings of the SCOS Conference*, Calgary.

Lee, M.M. (1994c) 'The isolated manager: Walking the boundaries of the micro-culture', *Proceedings of the British Academy of Management Conference*, Lancaster.

Lee, M.M. (1995a) 'Competence and the new manager' in Lee, M.M., Letiche, K., Crawshaw, R. and Thomas, M. (eds) *Management Education in the New Europe: boundaries and complexity*, London, Routledge (forthcoming).

Lee, M.M. (1995b) 'Holistic Agency: A multilevel conceptual experience exploration', *Academy of Management Review*, paper submitted for publication.

Lee, M. M. (1995c) 'Working with freedom of choice in Central Europe', *Management Learning*: 26, pp. 215–30.

Lessem, R. (1990) *Developmental Management*, Oxford, Blackwell.

Lessem, R. (1991) *Total Quality Learning*, Oxford, Blackwell.

Lievegood, B. (1991) *Managing the Developing Organisation*, Oxford, Blackwell.

Likert, R. (1961) *New Patterns Of Management*, New York, McGraw-Hill.

Maclagan, P. and Snell, R. (1992) 'Some implications for management development of research into managers' moral dilemmas', *British Journal of Management*, vol. 3, pp. 157–68.

Mangham, I. (1990) 'Managing as a performing art', *British Journal of Management*, vol. 1, pp. 105–15.

Marshall, J. (1984) *Women Managers: Travellers in a Male World*, Chichester, John Wiley and Sons.

Marshall, J. and Stewart, R. (1981a) 'Managers' Job Perceptions: Part 1 – Their Overall Frameworks And Working Strategies', *Journal Of Management Studies*, vol. 18, pp. 177–89.

Marshall, J. and Stewart, R. (1981b) 'Managers' Job Perceptions: Part 2 – Opportunities For And Attitudes To Choice', *Journal Of Management Studies*, vol. 18, pp. 263–75.

Martinko, M.J. and Gardner, W.L. (1984) 'The Observation Of High-Performing Educational Managers: Methodological Issues And Managerial Implications', in Hunt, J.G, Hosking, C.A., Schriesheim, C.A. and Stewart, R. eds *Leaders And Managers*, pp. 142–62, New York, Pergamon Press.

Martinko, M. J. and Gardner, W. L. (1987) 'The Leader/Member Attribution Process', *Academy Of Management Review*, vol. 12, pp. 235–49.

McGill, I. and Beaty, L. (1992) *Action Learning: A Practitioners Guide*, London, Kogan Page.

McKiernan, P. and Morris, C. (1993) 'Strategic Planning and Financial Performance in UK SMEs: Does Formality Matter?', in *The Crafting of Management Research*, *Proceedings of British Academy of Management Annual Conference*, Milton Keynes.

McMillen, M.C., Boyatzis, R.E. and Swartz, L. (1994) 'Contextual Integration of Knowledge, Experience and Action Learning for Management Education', *Management Learning*, vol. 25, no. 2, pp. 215–29.

Mintzberg, H. (1973) *The Nature of Managerial Work*, London, Harper and Row.

Moore, P.G. (1990) 'Where does the ownership of a decision lie?', *British Journal of Management*, vol. 1, pp. 35–44.

Moreland, R.L. and Levine, J.M. (1989) 'Newcomers and Oldtimers in small groups', in Paulus, P. ed. *Psychology of Group Influence*, Second edition, pp. 143–86. Hillsdale NJ, Erlbaum.

Morgan, G. (1993) 'The challenges of management research', *The Crafting of Management Research*, *Proceedings of British Academy of Management Conference*, pp. 497–8, Milton Keynes.

Mudroch, V. (1992) 'The future of interdisciplinarity: The case of Swiss universities', *Studies in Higher Education*, vol. 17, pp. 43–54.

Nespor, J. (1988) 'Theoretical observations on applied behavioural science', *Journal of Applied Behavioural Science*, vol. 24, pp. 277–95.

Norgaard, R. (1988) 'Sustainable Development: A Co-evolutionary View', *Futures*, vol. 20, no. 6, pp. 606–20.

Novak, J.M. (1990) 'Advancing Constructive Education', in Neimeyer, G.J. and Neimeyer, R.A. eds *Advances in Personal Construct Psychology*, London, JAI Press.

Papadakis, V. (1993) 'The contribution of formal planning systems to strategic investment systems', *The Crafting of Management Research*, *Proceedings of British Academy of Management Annual Conference*, pp. 51–70, Milton Keynes.

Pascale R.T. (1978) 'Zen and the art of management', *Harvard Business Review*, March–April

Pascale, R. (1990) *Managing on the Edge*, London, Penguin.

Pedlar, M., Burgoyne, J. and Boydell, T. (1991) *The Learning Company: a Strategy for Sustainable Growth*, London: McGraw Hill.

Pelz, D.C. (1951) 'Leadership Within A Hierarchical Organisation', *Journal Of Social Issues*, vol. 7, pp. 49–55.

Pfeffer, J. (1981) 'Management As Symbolic Action: The Creation And Maintenance Of Organisational Paradigms', in Cummings, L.L. and Staw, B.M. eds *Research In Organisational Behaviour*, vol. 3, pp. 1–52, Greenwich CT, JAL.

Pondy, L.R., (1978) 'Leadership Is A Language Game', in McCall Jr., M.W. and Lombardo, M.N. eds *Leadership: Where Else Can We Go?*, Durham NC, Duke University Press.

Porter, L.W. and McKibben, L.E. (1988) *Management Education and Development: Drift or Thrust into the 21st Century?*, New York, McGraw Hill

Powers, E.A. (1983) 'The AMA management competency programmes: A developmental process', *Exchange*, vol. 8, no. 2, pp. 16–20.

Raelin, J.A. and Schermerhorn, J. Jr (1994) 'A New Paradigm for Advanced Management Education', *Management Learning*, vol. 25, no. 2, pp. 195–200.

Reddy, W.B, (1973) 'The Impact Of Sensitivity Training On Self Actualisation', *Small Group Behaviour*, vol. 4, pp. 407–13.

Revans, R. (1980) *Action Learning: New Techniques for Action Learning*, London, Blond and Briggs.

Robertson, I.T. and Sadri, G. (1993) 'Managerial self-efficacy and managerial performance', *British Journal of Management*, vol. 4, pp. 37–45.

Roethlisberger, F.J. (1945) 'The Industrial Foreman: Master And Victim Of Double-Talk', *Harvard Business Review*, vol. 23, pp. 283–94.

Rogers, C.R. (1951) *Client Centred Therapy*, Boston Mass, Houghton Mifflin.

Rogers, C.R. (1959) 'A theory of therapy, personality, and interpersonal relationships as developed in the client-centred framework', in Koch, S. ed. *Psychology: a Study of a Science*, vol. 3, New York, McGraw-Hill.

Rosenberg, M. (1965) *Society And The Adolescent Self Image*, Princetown, Princetown University Press.

Rubin, I. (1967a) 'Increased Self Acceptance', *Journal Of Personal Social Psychology*, vol. 5, pp. 233–8.

Rubin, I. (1967b) 'The Reduction Of Prejudice Through Laboratory Training', *Journal Of Applied Behavioural Science*, vol. 3, pp. 29–50.

Ryder, J. and Easterby-Smith, M. (1992) 'Working together in Europe: The case of the European Management Teacher Programme', *Journal of European Industrial Training*, vol. 12, no. 2, pp. 12–16.

Samovar, L.A. and Porter, R.E. (1976) *Intercultural Communications: A Reader*, Belmont CA, Wadsworth Publishing Company.

Sayles, L.R. (1964) *Managerial Behaviour*, New York, McGraw Hill.

Scheibe, K.E. (1986) 'Self Narratives And Adventure', in Sarbin, T.R. ed. *Narrative Psychology: The Storied Nature Of Human Conduct*, pp. 129–51, New York, Praeger.

Seely Brown, J. and Duguid, P. (1991) 'Organizational Learning and Communities of Practice: Toward a Unified View of Working, Learning and Innovation', *Organization Science*, vol. 2, no. 1, pp. 40–57.

Schein, E.H. (1985) *Organisational Culture and Leadership: A Dynamic View*, San Francisco CA, Jossey-Bass.

Senge, P. (1990) *The Fifth Discipline*, New York, Doubleday.

Smith, P.B. (1992) 'Organisational behaviour and national cultures', *British Journal of Management*, vol. 3, pp. 39–51.

Smith, P.B. and Peterson, M.F. (1988) *Leadership, Organisations and Culture*, London, Sage.

Smith, P.B., Moscow, D., Cooper, C.L. and Berger, M. (1969) 'Relationships Between Managers And Their Work Associates', *Administrative Science Quarterly*, vol. 14, pp. 338–45.

Smithers, A. (1993) *All our Futures – Britain's Education Revolution*, Centre for Education and Employment Research, University of Manchester.

Snell, R. (1988) 'The ethics of consultancy in education', in Gray, H.L. ed. *Management Consultancy in Schools*, Eastbourne, Cassell.

Snell, R. (1993) *Developing Skills for Ethical Management*, London, Chapman Hall.

Snell, R. and James, K. (1994) 'Beyond the Tangible in Management Education and Development', *Management Learning*, vol. 25, no. 2, pp. 319–40.

Stewart, R. (1976) *Managers and their Jobs*, London, Macmillan.

Stewart, R. (1982) *Choices For The Manager*, London, McGraw-Hill.

Stryker, S. and Statham, A. (1985) 'Symbolic Interaction And Role Theory,' in Lindzey, G. and Aronson, E. eds *Handbook Of Social Psychology*, vol. 1, Third edition, pp. 311–78, New York, Random House.

Swan, J., Aspin, T., Holloway, J., Lee, M.M. and Perica, L. (1993) 'The future of management education and development: An evaluation of the ESRC Management Teacher Fellowship Scheme in the UK', *The Crafting of Management Research, Proceedings of British Academy of Management Annual Conference*, pp. 231–2, Milton Keynes.

Taylor, F.J.W. (1994) 'Working Party Report: The Way Ahead 1994–2001', *Management Development to the Millennium Research*, The Institute of Management, Northants.

Thorpe, R. (1990) 'An alternative theory of management education', *European Journal of Industrial Training*, vol. 14, pp. 3–15.

Whittington, R. (1990) 'Social structures and resistance to strategic change: British manufacturers in the 1980s', *British Journal of Management*, vol. 1, pp. 201–13.

Zuboff, S. (1989) *In the Age of the Smart Machine*, Oxford, Heinemann.

13

The Role of the
Action Learning Set

Sue Williams

INTRODUCTION

The International Foundation for Action Learning (IFAL) was set up in 1977. It exists to identify and encourage a network of enthusiasts who support the work of action learning world wide. The originator and a major proponent of action learning, Reg Revans, began his work in 1946. Yet of a class of some 25 students on an HRD (MSc in Human Resource Development) course there were but half a dozen or so who had direct experience or knew something about action learning sets other than through the reading of the course literature. This perhaps indicates the rather specialist place action learning sets have held in organisations' management development programmes so far. This picture may change in the coming years as the move towards using action learning sets in a variety of postgraduate, post-experience courses seems to be gathering pace. What are the issues or philosophies that underlie such moves? Is there something about what happens in an action learning set that appears to support and help would-be HRD specialists and managers to absorb or manage current trends and changes in organisational analysis, in management education and in individuals' developmental and learning needs? It is these issues that are the focus for this chapter, setting the scene for an analysis of the students' perspectives of participating in an action learning set from which some lessons for tutors and staff alike may be drawn.

CHANGES IN ORGANISATIONS

Within the literature on organisations, there can be seen to be developing a series of dichotomies, or 'dilemmas of organisation' (Carnall, 1990) and it is within this two sided coin that HRD people have to function, how can this be squared or, more to the point, how can HRD people operate under such circumstances, resolving or juggling successfully these dilemmas at the point in which they are working for the organisation?

In writing *The Human Side of Enterprise* McGregor (1960) clearly identified two management philosophies: that of Theory X – the mechanistic view of organisations that does not value people, seeing them as units of production leading to an authoritarian style of management; and Theory Y – which values all members of the organisation and leads to a more participative style. In the research that led to Cox and Cooper's (1988) work on the anatomy of managerial success they were 'fascinated and appalled' by management students' underlying assumption that managers have 'a right to manage . . . the right to order about another part (of the community) who then do as they are told'. Their research supported by others suggested that high flyers, i.e. the chief executive officers (CEOs) and managing directors (MDs) of their study saw themselves as very person oriented, as team leaders and as having a Theory Y philosophy. Cox and Cooper (1988) go on to comment, however, that this was based on self-perception, i.e. their 'espoused theory', rather than 'theory in use'. Their interviews also indicated that such MDs placed great value on rationality and coolness and on maintaining a distance from employees and a degree of paternalism which does not sit easily with their espoused value of team working. Part of the role of action learning sets can perhaps be to help set members to identify their own and others' management philosophy – not just espoused philosophy but philosophy in use. A similar dichotomy is seen in the works of those authors that discuss the concepts of modernist or Fordist models of organisations and the post-modernist model e.g. Clegg (1990). He describes modernist organisations as those that can be likened to Weber's bureaucracies with mechanistic structures of control, 'a fully rationalised base of divided and deskilled labour' and forming the basis of two complementary principles: that of the assembly line, a linear flow of changes and processes applied to the raw materials; and that of fixed and limited job tasks over which the workforce had no control. The intellectual work of design, conception and communication is differentiated from the processes to produce the product. Clegg argues that such rigid structures and organisations have been breaking up since the Second World War but particularly during the 1980s and that such Fordist style organisations will be increasingly found only in less developed areas of the world economy. Table 13.1 gives a list of some of the comparators that have been identified by, for example: Clegg, 1990; Brown, 1992; Torrington and Weightman, 1994.

Table 13.1

Modernist	Post-modernist
Rigid structure/organisation	Flexible organic structure
Mass production/a lot of the same	Niche markets/one-offs/options
Control	Craft tradition, co-operation
Restrained by technology	Technological choices
User defined	
Demarcated/deskilled/specialist jobs	Multi-skilled/interwoven
All company employees	Subcontracting
Networking	
Few sites/plants, common procedures	Global/many relatively independent sites
Strong corporate culture	Personal career paths & development
Mistrust of leadership	Trust in leadership
Disempowerment	Empowerment

Overlying these comparators and influencing the exact nature of these differences and developments is the political philosophy of the country in which the company is to be found: for example whether the post-modernist organisation maintains strong links with trade unions as in Sweden where membership is approximately 90 per cent; or whether its links are less strong and more variable as in the US where union membership is low (approx. 17 per cent, Clegg 1990); or in the UK with less than 50 per cent membership of the workforce. Alternatively the influence for change may come from external factors such as legislation or from pressure or choice in accepting for example employee representation at board level as in the current EC debate. To illustrate the differences between a modernist and post-modernist organisation Clegg (1990) used Blunt's (1989) seven organisational imperatives or perennial problems that organisations have to address, these being:

1 articulating mission, goals, strategies and main functions;
2 arranging functional alignments;
3 identifying mechanisms of co-ordination and control;
4 constituting accountability and role relationships;
5 institutionalising planning and communication;
6 relating rewards and performance;
7 achieving effective leadership.

Taking the last two as examples a modernist organisation rewards individual performance, a post-modernist collective performance; a modernist organisation leads from an attitude of mistrust and a post-modernist from values based on trust. A question then for HRD specialists is how are they able to track and support an organisation through such changes, how can they identify, describe, prepare people for different ways of working without being able to explore these ideas and concepts for themselves?

Brown (1992) questions whether such changes are widespread and significant enough yet to form 'a second industrial divide'. Brown (1992) goes on to suggest that in Britain there are few signs of management being able or willing to make the necessary investments in equipment and training to produce this post-modernist ideal. In looking at the political environment it could be said that elements of UK government policy for some public sector organisations are seen as contrary to many aspects of the post-modernist view.

Moran *et al.* (1993) continue the theme of the new work culture describing the 'duties of the new work culture leadership' and stating that the workplace must value the 'diversity of its personnel and their varied talents'. The management of diversity is becoming a common theme in the latest management textbooks. One of the features of this type of organisation will be many 'intense temporary relationships with colleagues'. Such a scenario requires individuals to gain the maximum understanding and appreciation of others in a relatively short space of time. No longer can a job for life provide the occupants with much time to get to know each others' foibles and ways of working. The skills acquired in the intensity of action learning sets may provide individuals with more flexibility and more ability in managing diverse peoples effectively and appropriately.

Let us return to Brown's (1992) point that the development of post-modernist organisations is limited. This is perhaps not surprising if one considers the work of Ritzer (1993) which clearly sets out to demonstrate how the modernist style of organisation which many might associate only with major manufacturing processes, assembly lines, etc. has come to dominate our high streets and retail industry. Ritzer(1993) uses

MacDonalds as the example but notes many other chains which work in the same highly controlled manner, with mass production, and clearly defined skills and tasks. These dominate our consumer habits, particularly in fast food service. What they offer to the consumer he suggests is something we find irresistible and therefore we collude with and enable the perpetuation of this highly successful organisational model for our convenience. Ritzer (1993) highlights four basic reasons why this style of organisation is successful and therefore why modernism is likely to stay.

1 It offers efficiency to the consumer, i.e. the optimum method for getting from one point to another. In MacDonalds' case it is the optimum method of getting from hungry to not hungry and, since we are a highly mobile society with both parents often working, fast food is an attractive option.
2 The service is quantified and calculated in terms of what you get and how long it takes to achieve the not hungry state.
3 Predictability – what we eat one day is the same at any other time and any other place.
4 It controls its operations which links back to predictability. It does this particularly through the substitution of non-human for human technology. 'The humans who work in fast food services are trained to do a very limited number of things in precisely the way they are told to do them'. Ritzer (1993) in attempting to answer the question: 'is such a situation advantageous or not and what are the costs and risks of such a demonstration that Fordism and modernism is alive and very well?' suggests that we clearly have not changed from one era to another but have a mixture of organisational types. Although it must be noted that very recently MacDonalds have indicated some relaxation in their tight control over task definitions – a move forward?

Contrast this with the discussion by Lessem (1993) on the development of more craft-based, communal learning communities more typical of post-modernist organisations not only identified in the work of such authors as Piore and Sabel (1984), Badaracco (1991) but also based on his own experiences within an organisation following on from an attempt to put in place a computerised sales information system. This 'opened a Pandora's box' in the desire of individuals at all levels to comment, to debate, to suggest ideas concerning the system and the way the company operated. It is within this setting that HRD specialists have to operate, to cope for themselves and to help others to manage effectively too. How then are HRD specialists able to work at their most effective, to implement a change programme if deemed necessary, act as consultants, become change agents, try to push the organisation towards a learning community within what may be very prescribed and controlled limits? Clearly organisations are not independent from the people that work in them although Hosking and Morley (1991) argue that much of organisational behaviour literature is couched in such separatist terms. Individuals need the help of others to construct their sense of self and sense of social order to add value to their lives (i.e. they are 'intelligent social actors) for which, if one accepts Vaill's (1989) description of managing today as 'the organisational world of permanent white water', the need is ever greater. Vaill (1989) continues by arguing that the 'modern leader is required to be able to reflect and philosophise to a degree that . . . astonishes the down to earth, no-nonsense . . . men and women who traditionally held these jobs'. His fear is that 'we don't realise it for the most part and even those who do realise it have not yet cracked the problem of how we are going to foster the development of such individuals'. It is for him an unlearning process but for many such a process is also paradoxical in that if you are an expert, a specialist, you know and understand your area of work but many of the problems for organisations lie in communicating that knowledge, wisdom, insight, judgement, sensibility to others, in conveying what something really means to you or to your part of the organisation. Vaill (1989) sums up these perplexities in a poem, part of which is reproduced here.

THE LAYMAN'S LAMENT

You understand something and I don't.
You understand that I don't understand, but
You don't understand what it is that I don't understand. I understand that I
  don't understand, but
I don't understand what it is I don't understand.
Not only do you not understand what it is I don't understand,
You don't understand how you came to understand What it is that you
  understand . . .

My understanding doesn't feel simple rather,
It feels chaotic and confused . . .

You and I have a problem
If I am to come to understand what you understand and if you are to come to
  understand what I don't understand.

To gain understanding, to resolve the problem, to manage the paradoxes requires reflection on processes, it requires discussion. It requires many managers to change their model of management or espoused theory and theory in use. As Vaill (1989) comments 'this is easy to say until it is realised how . . . the North American managerial mentality is geared for crisp technical communication . . . structured agendas . . . keeping it on track . . . with action steps' – a common occurrence in many other Western or Western style organisations too. Although Thurley (1989) suggests that the European management tradition is less prescriptive, there are similarities and a desire to mirror US success. Indications from feedback from HRD course members suggest that elements of the action learning set operation, the skills, the space, the trust engendered can provide a helpful environment for some of these paradoxes to be worked through and addressed, although it can never provide the total answer to aspects that reflect society's own dilemmas. Action learning sets may be viewed as a possible way forward not only in the exchange of techniques but also in the development of less prescriptive views, more awareness of variation.

PHILOSOPHICAL AND EDUCATIONAL ISSUES

Underlying the concept of organisations becoming learning communities as discussed by Lessem (1993), Garratt (1987) are some philosophical and educational issues for those involved in some way in imbuing individuals, teams, etc. with these ideas. Lessem (1993) for example finds that for him the underlying philosophy is one of humanism, the tenets of which are 'a society in which most individuals are devoted to a collective well-being will attain greater happiness, and make more progress than one in which private self interest and advancement are the prime motivation' Lessem (1993). For Senge (1991) the development of a learning organisation is based on a systemic approach of not 'seeing ourselves as separate from the world' . . . but . . . 'being connected to the world, from seeing our problems as caused by someone or something "out there" to seeing how our actions create the problems we experience' (Lessem, 1993, p. 112). If managers focus only on themselves and their own work or tasks they do not see or realise how their actions extend beyond their world and affect others. Senge aligns himself in some ways with what he identifies as part of an existential philosophy by suggesting that the challenge to be faced is to create new relationships based on reason and choice. Senge suggests that 'Heidegger and Sartre, I am told, have recognised this task by calling it a project, which is their term for the goal-directed actions that shape and give meaning to an individual's life' (Lessem, 1993, p. 113). Action learning has the potential to provide a forum for individuals to look beyond their own tasks, to unite with others in defining their actions and the impact or connections of such actions on others. It could have the potential to be able to help in addressing Senge's (1991) ideas concerning the problems of learning underlying his development of the systemic view of learning, i.e. the laws of his fifth discipline. For example he suggests that organisations are concerned with specific events rather than longer-term patterns and causes of change, that people are working too fast to see slow gradual processes that are going on. Therefore managers, in particular, should be learning from experience. But, since they do not always directly experience the consequences of their major decisions and then frequently only if their decisions have immediate, noticeable ill-favoured consequences, this learning from experience occurs only infrequently and reflection does not become an ingrained habit. Organisations are made up of teams but often such teams' energies are spent maintaining their own position and power rather than looking at the overall picture. These dilemmas have to be balanced to provide the basis for a learning and changing community which understands something of where it is heading and how. So teams should develop the reflective habit too.

Human resource development programmes generally have as an objective the development of people, both the organisation's employees and themselves, and the course must reflect that in its learning processes. Action learning sets could emulate Senge's (1991) team learning which he maintains has three critical dimensions: the need for insights on complex issues, the need for innovative, co-ordinated action, and the role and impact of team members on other teams. This is addressed through the development of skills of discussion and dialogue. Lessem (1993) describes these two as:

> 'in dialogue there is the free and creative exploration of complex and subtle issues, a deep listening to one another and suspension of one's own views. By contrast, in discussion, different views are presented and defended and there is a search for the best view to support decisions . . .'

Teams or sets can learn to move easily between these two modes and avoid being involved in defensive behaviours.

Echoes of the need for this more holistic approach to the ways we view the world, our realities, can be found in the literature of the philosophy of science and knowledge. In particular Feyerabend (1978) criticises those who try to create distinctions that might destroy science. 'The idea that science can and should be run according to fixed and universal rules is both unrealistic and pernicious. It is unrealistic for it takes too simple a view of the talents of man and of the circumstances which encourage or cause development. And it is pernicious, for the attempt to enforce the rules is bound to increase our professional qualifications at the expense of our humanity.' He argues that modern society treats science with exaggerated esteem, 'even human relations are dealt with in a scientific manner . . . almost all scientific subjects are compulsory subjects at school.' Scientific method assumes that new ideas or problems precede action, investigation, formulation refutation – but that is not the way small children develop; they have a much more anarchistic approach, playing with and combining ideas and processes. Feyerabend (1978) sees no reason why such processes should stop on becoming an adult. The creation of an idea or thing and full understanding of that phenomenon are 'very often parts of one and the same indivisible process' (p. 26).

This argument is often to be found echoed in discussions concerning the impact of the researcher on the research process and the subject matter being studied; for example asking people to talk about their experiences in relation to a particular series of events such as going to school. The type of questions posed, the person you are perceived to be by the subject, the version of those events the subject happens to hold at the time of interview are all issues which can 'interfere' with the objectivity of the story being recalled. Therefore Feyerabend (1978) argues controversially for the introduction of a more anarchistic approach to scientific methods in order to achieve progress. The process of sharing that can occur within a learning set, the space that they can give from the everyday setting, creates opportunities for a more child-like, anarchistic exploration of the various realities of the issues presented for discussion.

This is reflected in work concerning knowledge or human understanding. The former can be divided into two aspects, strong and weak knowledge. Strong knowledge is described as the predictable facts: it is about being competent, in control; there is order and correctness and rightness in the way things occur. It is, for education, the meat of most subjects taught: it is the method to arrive at the correct answer; the steps; the models; who has conducted what research that illustrates best method or practice; how you should or should not approach a particular task; what facts or techniques are needed to complete a particular operation; etc. On the other hand there is weak knowledge or thinking something that is private, very particular to an individual: it is tentative, ad hoc, volatile, hard to pin down; it is a knowing depending on circumstances and people involved; it is a thinking that may or may not be right or appropriate; it is our own theory that is untested or only partly tested; it may be something that you might pin down now or enlightenment may strike much later and often in a different context; it is the 'stuff' that is very hard for the 'expert' to impart, particularly to a larger audience. The intimacy created within a learning set may be able to tease out and identify more clearly aspects of this 'weak' knowledge. Lessem's (1993, p. 209) comment is that for organisations 'a natural place to begin, as a pragmatist, is with action learning sets, preferably and gradually spread throughout the organisation'.

In keeping with this 'softer' knowledge acquisition, action learning sets are an illustration of a method of accessing some of that knowledge. In the ongoing debate about what education and management education in particular is attempting to achieve, what is taught and how, e.g. Davies and Williams (1993), Pedlar *et al.* (1989), Mintzberg in Spender (1989), Bolton (1994) and Freedman *et al.* (1982), there surfaces the debate about pedagogical or androgogical approaches to teaching, whether the tutor operates a dependent learner culture and is generally directive in style or whether a tutor considers an independent learner culture more appropriate. Then there are various stages in between. Underlying these approaches is a view about how adults learn, whether they learn in a way that is different from children and should therefore be provided with different learning opportunities and whether adult educators have a responsibility to develop learning independence in adults. Gibbs and Jenkins (1992) on a more pragmatic level indicate the need to make strategic teaching choices between a system which highly controls and structures the student experience and an education system which relies on learner independence in the face of increasing numbers of students on post-graduate programmes. The work of Knowles (1975, 1990), Brookfield (1985) and Rogers (1983) supports the argument that adults do learn very differently from children, that adults bring motivations, goals, expectations, experiences and a differing biological make-up to the learning situation, so that the teaching techniques should reflect that. Knowles identifies adults as self-directed learners (SDL), adapted later by Hammond and Collins (1991) as critical SDL defined as 'a process in which learners take the initiative, with support and collaboration of others, for increasing self and social awareness: critically analysing and reflecting on their situations:'. Heron (1988) considers that 'the objective of the process of the emergence of an educated person . . . someone who is a self determining person . . . who can set his own objectives, devise a rational programme to attain them . . .'. Tennant (1988) suggests, however, that SDL being a foundation concept, its precise definition is open to many interpretations, that Knowles's assumptions are not articles of faith but are located as described by Brookfield (1985a) within three distinct schools of thought:

> 'to the banner of self directed learning can be rallied those philosophers who advocate the development in students of powers of critical insight, independent thought and reflective analysis, . . . humanistically inclined adult educators can also claim philosophical kinship with the idea since it appears to be but an educational interpretation of the notion of self actualisation'. (Knowles falls into this tradition.) 'Finally critical theorists of adult education such as Friere and Mezirow can also lay claim to the concept as . . . it should be concerned to bring into the learner's critical consciousness those assumptions beliefs and values uncritically assimilated and internalised during childhood and adolescence.'

For Hammond and Collins (1991) the immediate goal of SDL is to help learners take control of their learning. 'Its ultimate goal is to empower learners to use their learning to improve the conditions under which they and those around them live and work'. Although Hammond and Collins (1991) are describing the outcomes from a series of projects attempting to design a course to help rural health worker educators in South Africa there are many similarities in what they were trying to achieve, i.e. the empowerment of local people to change their conditions with the aim of a human resource development course which is trying to encourage students to become change agents in their own organisations, to involve their own workplace people in learning to learn, develop and reflect on the way they wish to modify or cope with their conditions at work. The use of action learning sets where fellow-learners 'individually engaged in projects but regularly trading information, advice and ideas' (Lessem, 1993) is one of a number of approaches available to adult educators to enable self-directed learning to take place. It can provide the support and expectation that Knowles (1990) sees as a necessary adjunct to enable a learner to achieve a higher level of intellectual performance; it may also provide the space in which the learners can define for themselves how the hard or soft knowledge could be acquired according to their own preferences or learning styles. It is a reflection of Rogers' views on teaching and learning:

> 'Teaching for me is a relatively unimportant and vastly overrated activity . . . but if there is one truth about modern man it is that he lives in a environment which is continually changing and therefore the aim of education must be the facilitation of learning.' (Knowles, 1990)

Action learning sets also illustrate the principles of experiential models of learning and are in themselves an example of learning from experience. For Revans (1980) such learning sets were very much about taking actions, being practical, pooling members' own expertise and gaining from others' knowledge. They worked because they dealt with the realities of the work situation. The realities of the work situation, for those engaged in developing others in their organisations as with those on an HRD programme, require making an effort to understand the processes that are being enacted in their own sets. As Brookfield (1993) explains from his own experiences as an educator 'I don't espouse one way of working and then behave in a way which contradicts my avowed beliefs'. The way he models behaviour he feels is 'directly connected to learner's willingness to behave in the same way'. For HRD students if they wish to use experiential methods of learning in their own roles in the workplace this comment suggests a need to work through similar processes themselves. Kolb and Fry's (1975) explanation is one of the earliest and representative of a number of models indicating the circular nature of the various processes that are thought to occur in an experiential learning mode. (See Fig. 13.1.) A

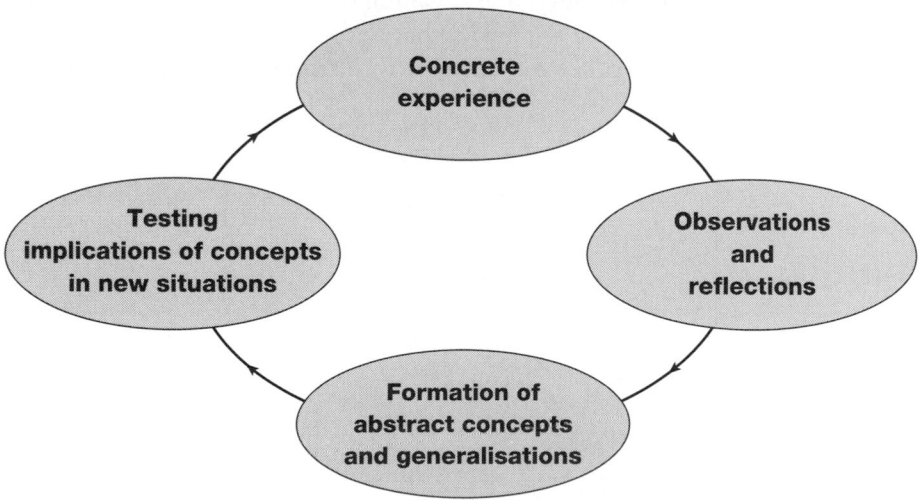

Fig. 13.1 Learning circle
(Kolb, Fry, 1975)

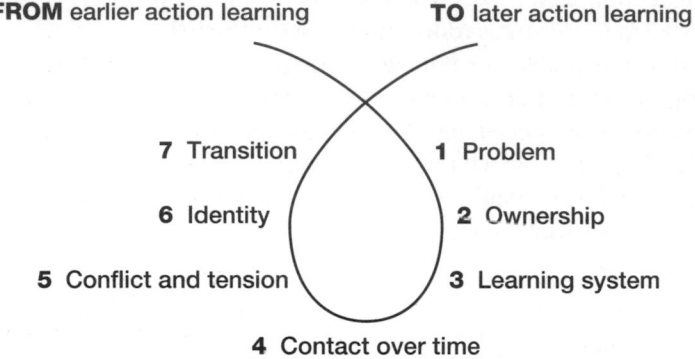

FROM earlier action learning   **TO** later action learning

7 Transition   **1** Problem

6 Identity   **2** Ownership

5 Conflict and tension   **3** Learning system

4 Contact over time

Fig. 13.2   Pedlar's spiral (1991)

number of students through their learning journals and portfolios identified their learning experiences in this way.

Another student made use of Pedlar's (1991) spiral (see Fig. 13.2) to describe what was happening and how to make appropriate links between the different facets of development. Alternatively Postle (1993), whose main work focus is currently in the psychotherapy counselling field, found Heron's multi-modal learning model particularly helpful in moving away from what he described as the 'key element of our white western mindset . . . the overvaluation of the practical and conceptual modes of learning'. Heron's initial model (1990) indicated four modes of learning, each dependent on each other and arranged in a hierarchy, as in Fig. 13.3.

The top of the hierarchy is the *practical*, learning by doing, competent practice of skills, conceptual concerns, the analysis, logic, debate about the subject, learning about it; the *imaginal* allows the person to visualise, extemporise on alternatives, on the future, what might be or could have been; and lastly the *affective* mode offers the capacity to learn at an emotional level, the sensation of the experience in question, e.g. what did it feel like to say no to a request? Other authors have engaged in the task of identifying more clearly the processes inherent in learning from experience and in

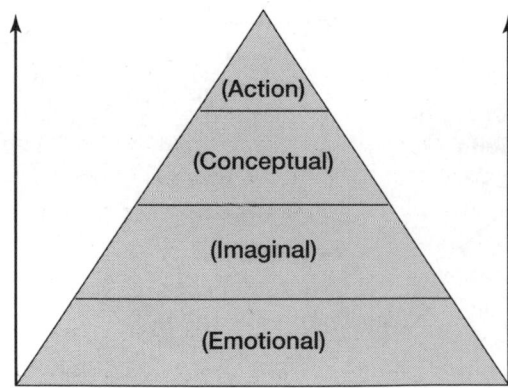

Fig. 13.3   Heron's model (1990)

talking about or reporting such experiences. Boud *et al.* (1993) suggest that learning from experience has to be actively engaged in order to reap the benefits. They quote Costas Criticos (1993) that 'experience has to be arrested, examined, analysed, considered and negated to shift it to knowledge'. The experiences do not have to be recent for learning to occur so that learning sets have the opportunity to explore, 'to recapture, notice and re-evaluate' past examples of their work and lives to illuminate the current issue and develop knowledge. Such reflection can of course be an individual activity but engaging in the process with others can change the meanings drawn from the experience. The recounting of commonalties and differences can shed light on the individual's unique history and highlight differing interpretations of events. The unique history also influences the individual's construction of those experiences and the recounting of them. For Brew (1993) this can lead to an unlearning through experience, i.e. 'unlearning is like unravelling the whole and knitting it all up again'. For Brew (1993) this meant trying to break the rules of a traditional view of scientific enquiry, the rules of objectivity, of separation or detachment of the researcher from the researched. For those engaged in acting as a change agent in their own organisation the separation and the detachment will be hard to do; learning sets may provide that avenue for detachment. In all of these aspects it is more valuable in this context that the reflection and the recounting or discourse should be something that is directed, focused, disciplined and to some extent systematic in order to draw out the knowledge and develop an individual's theories about the particular world that is under scrutiny. However, in this analysis of experience as Usher (1993) warns us 'experience . . . always says less than it wishes to say there is always more that can be read into it. Its meaning is never exhausted, it never reaches a destination of total clarity and understanding.' Progress in exploring how others cope in an HRD role, balance that role with the many others they hold and what has influenced their choices along the way will always be incomplete and progress will be variable. The discussion so far has tried to provide a background and a series of frameworks in which action learning sets on HRD programmes can be set and the nature of the relationships between the individual, the programme, and organisational development can be understood. So what have been the experiences of the students who have taken part in action learning sets on an HRD course?

ACTION LEARNING SETS: THE STUDENT EXPERIENCE

This section of the chapter examines student experiences to see what if anything can be learnt from them. Is there any indication of Heron's modes of learning (action, conceptual, imaging) and above all any indication of the emotional cost or benefit, the positive or negative influences affecting those participating in the action learning sets. Do they indicate any acquisition for example of soft knowledge, or any greater awareness of the type of organisation they are working in, or the demands being made of them, or the impact of their actions on others.

These are the reflections of a sample of students from two courses The 'data' have been gathered from three main sources: an end of course student questionnaire used to provide feedback to one institution's course committee; the feedback from a more specific questionnaire designed to gain reactions to the action learning set aspect of the course which covered courses in different institutions (Appendix 1); and finally comments made by the students as part of their learning journals. The first source provided from the tutor's viewpoint a rather comfortable statement to the effect that 'these have, in the main, been of great benefit and have provided sound learning opportunities and additional support for individual students.' Barriers of travel and work commitments and the need to maximise the time when on the one-day sessions were noted.

The second questionnaire specifically looking at the action learning sets was set around the themes of the strengths and weaknesses of this mode of learning, the benefits and disadvantages and any advice students had to offer travellers who were to follow in their footsteps. The strengths and weaknesses section began with a series of descriptors which was followed by the students' own responses and perceptions of the experience. For a small number of respondents the 'prescribed' descriptors proved difficult. With many questionnaires there is often a problem of interpretation. What does the author mean by this or that statement? How shall I answer this or that point? What does this scale of 1–5 imply in terms of strength of feeling? What does low or high mean? The descriptors themselves were actually drawn from other students' own efforts to assess the value of action learning sets for themselves – an effort to try and define in words the experiences they had gone through – and the author appreciates their willingness to share their efforts at evaluation. There was no set meaning for the descriptors used; students could put their own views on them in their own words, particularly as they had space to elaborate on the them within the strengths and weaknesses section or could use their own descriptors. Commitment, motivation, supportiveness, group participation, hard working and contribution level all scored consistently 4/5 on the scale, i.e. were words closely associated with the process. Honesty scored mainly between 3 and 5, a broader range of responses.

Two thoughts spring to mind here. One is an issue for the facilitators as to how far they should encourage honesty and openness; and the second is for the students as to how ready, willing and able are some students to use the process honestly or whether they recognise the need to do so – or perhaps they do not feel sufficiently skilled to be constructive on all occasions, particularly if the group is getting along well, having a good time, etc. As one student commented later, the process should above all be fun but yet another felt that the group missed opportunities to be more open and honest. Task achievement gained most of its score at 3 and 4. Bearing in mind the possible range of tasks any group might set themselves, not only the achievement of the assignment tasks but personal developmental agendas too, this could then be seen as an encouraging sign of the value students gained from this method. Organisation again gained a mix of 3 and 5. Other descriptors added to the list were challenge, expertise, empathy, conflict, fun, clarity of purpose/process.

Of those that replied only one student, the same one, gave a rating of 1 to commitment, task achievement and contribution level. This relates to their comment on disadvantages, indicating that the set of which they were a member had a number of members who openly disagreed with the concept and attended unwillingly. There are implications here for the management of the experience by both the tutors/facilitators and the group members.

We return for the moment to the comments made by the respondents in relation to their perception of the strengths of this method of exploring their experiences, making some sense of them and acting upon them. Some of the statements listed were repeats or similarities to the descriptors used. Using Heron's (1990) model of modes of learning the phrases used indicate a perception of moving through all modes though there is no indication of the depth of these moves. For example statements such as 'method of control: personal achievement of tasks between attendance on modules', 'useful network,' 'using our own skill and expertise', 'members adapt the process to suit their needs', 'verbal communication skills', 'practical and immediate application of learning', 'sharing of problems' all suggest an action mode (learning by doing, competent practice of skills, learning about subjects, debating the issues). The conceptual mode comes across in such statements as 'new angle on things', 'alternate views', 'operate across most of the cognitive/experiential learning levels', 'assist the individual to arrive at their own solution', 'dynamic – using live material in a dynamic human context'. Imaging comes across in comments such as 'like minds (common visions) to bounce ideas off', 'several minds working together can be better than one', 'spontaneous mutual firing off of ideas'. Finally to the emotional or affective mode, which comes across in comments such as 'support from fellow sufferers', 'enriched self perception', 'excellent rapport within the group'; the word supportive appeared frequently in a number of the comments made as did the idea of the sets being a source of help.

The weaknesses of the experience for some were couched in terms of the practicalities of managing the groups alongside other commitments, for example difficulties in taking time off, geographical constraints on meetings, need for more meetings, different work pressures. Some comments demonstrated the dilemma of balancing the need to acquire and debate the theoretical concepts presented and complete the assessments correctly with the wish to tackle work or personal/social development issues. For one person this led to the feeling that there was a lack of commitment from others 'who prefer to work in academic isolation'.

For another it meant a group that focused on completion of next assignment rather than what they perceived to be 'real issues'. For yet another this led to a lack of openness and honesty, a sense of competition. The disadvantage of a link to a formal course was reiterated when discussing benefits in the workplace and again when the course expected set members to complete peer assessment, which was seen to mitigate against an honest and open approach. Comments also focused on the role or lack of it of the facilitators and set management: 'no access to skilled facilitator may have been a disadvantage', 'lack of adequate facilitation and ground rules in the early stages', 'limited knowledge of process at outset'. The facilitation issue is an important one in managing the group as improvements may have an impact on the perceived lack by one respondent of the unwillingness of members to 'be overtly critical of each other (constructively of course)'. Another felt that there was 'no real feedback' from another The random selection and numbers of set members was for some also a weakness which highlighted differing abilities and levels of commitment within the groups. In discussing the benefits to the students' organisation the comments fell into three categories: whether or not they would introduce them into their organisations (one had already introduced them to the senior managers and would be moving down through the organisation); the benefit to the individual and by implication, therefore, to the organisation (for example 'got affirmation of my own strengths and skills', 'personal growth (positive)'; and finally, one comment suggesting that insufficient time and space had been given to discussing the organisational issues of actually implementing such a method of development into an organisation (whether this was seen as a task for the tutors or for the learning set was not indicated).

The discussions around the question of disadvantages or adverse effects were again centred around the individual and their experience of the process rather than a wider organisational view. For some there were no disadvantages but a number were concerned about groups becoming 'entrenched', 'the blind leading the blind'. Others expressed concern about missing out on wider exchanges with the rest of the course members – whether they were becoming too insular within their sets. The initial contract was highlighted in that set members needed to be honest about what they might be looking for from a group: to be 'with like minded people', 'for support or to be challenged?' This latter statement suggests a view that the two aspects cannot go together which is not the view held by all students as indicated by other comments elsewhere.

From their experiences the respondents provided some advice for future courses. Their review reflects on the whole the issues iterated in the other questions, for example the careful selection of set members, ensuring a good facilitator is to hand until the group is ready to operate alone, being clear on objectives, needs, outcomes and ground rules, reading around the subject to help to make maximum use of the time, having regular reviews, being committed and honest. One piece of advice suggests an experience that was too restrictive in its coverage, that the group stuck to course related issues when one member wanted to look at wider, real work problems. There is again evidence of differing approaches as to how the meetings should be run, some advise structure in the meetings, others allowing the meeting to flow by perhaps having themes but 'play with the process and go down the leafy lanes of discussion, its amazing what comes out'.

What of the comments made by individual students through their own very individual pieces of work in the research learning journals? Did any of their comments illustrate Seneca's statement quoted by Bacon (1597) 'that the good things which belong to prosperity are to be wished; but the good things that belong to adversity are to be admired' or, as Bacon phrases it, 'if miracles be the command over nature they appear most in adversity.' For one group the process of working in the learning set was felt to be a sufficiently personal one that a written evaluation with specific details of development was not for public consumption, a more massaged compilation of views was the result. However, an indication perhaps of Heron's emotional mode of learning is suggested by the phrase: 'The quest to know oneself is a life long journey and we tried to act out our lives through the action learning set in 8 to 9 meetings'. Other examples from other commentaries support the idea that set working can create conditions for the gaining of soft knowledge, of emotional modes of learning and of real reflection. For example on developing listening skills: 'the set members . . . indicated that it was not an issue of listening or not but rather . . . of interrupting . . . this reinforced comments . . . although the set members were decidedly more forthright'; 'My confidence was dented and I was very angry, however I reflected . . . the period of reflection was valuable . . . a steep learning curve.' Others too resorted to more philosophical readings – the sayings of Lao Tzu a Chinese sage, for example, or models of the processes that might be happening such as Pedlar's (1991) learning spiral – as a way of trying to express the personal changes and reflections thrown up by the action set process.

Other modes of learning were apparent in such statements as the 'ALS was of most benefit to me in . . . resolving organisational problems, interpretation of the rules and rigours of academia', 'explore new theories and approaches', 'crystallise ideas', 'the impact of this process hasn't ended with me. It has impacted on my team at work who have modified practice as a direct result of what I have taken back from the ALS'. Taking the experience from the learning set and into the workplace is echoed by another comment: 'I have been successful in influencing/helping a number of other staff who were encountering similar internal conflicts'. They have been seen to enable the development of a range of interpersonal skills. It appears that the learning set has provided for many the encouragement and support in difficult times to enable some to take a more scientific, detached view of their organisations and their specific workplaces. For Brew (1993) the experience of conducting research led her to acknowledge that there were 'a number of issues which I did not want to think about, which I did not want to acknowledge'. She feared them. A hint of such dilemmas is perhaps apparent in the remark 'even in writing this journal I'm censoring some thoughts and feelings'. A need for rules or at least guidance is seen in comments about what should or should not be discussed in the sets; for example, what did the course tutors want? This raises the issue for reflection by the various course teams as to how the action learning set component is introduced to course members and with what level of initial and ongoing support. There is evidence within the reflections that there is a need initially at least for the course tutors to set out more clearly the list of expectations, the ground rules, the learning contract that the sets themselves spend time establishing in their first meetings. For some participants the language of experiential learning, of reflection, of review and feedback, of managing the process aspects of the meetings is not innate just because they work in the training, education and development fields. The expertise and the confidence needs to be acquired; however, the programme is a relatively short period in their lives and that confidence could do with being acquired quickly. For some the urgency of the tasks and quantity of hard knowledge requiring to be completed or learnt focused the mind well, hence the advice 'be honest in what you're looking for and what you can offer (it's 15 months of your life)'. But for others more specific measures to establish the appropriate atmosphere, language and artifice could be needed whether this uses the experience of those within the group or comes from outside the course participants. Another dilemma was whether tutors should be more prescriptive or encourage boundary breaking! Although there are examples of sets that operate without a facilitator from the beginning, for the majority of these participants the role of a competent facilitator was initially crucial and an essential early component of a longer-term positive outcome. Despite these issues the feedback suggests that action learning sets can help students to focus in a way that enables them to balance the very eclectic managerial and organisational world in which they work, learning sets enable choices and personal assessments to be made as a result of shared reasoned consideration and meditation and in, for many, a pleasurable setting.

References

Badaracco, J. (1991) *The Knowledge Link*, Harvard, Harvard Business School.

Bacon, F. (1597) 'Of Adversity Essay V', in Hawkins, M. (1992) *Francis Bacon Essays*, London, Everyman.

Blunt, P. (1989) 'Strategies for Human Resource Development in the Third World', opening address to the International Human Resource Development Conference, University of Manchester 25–28 June.

Bolton, A. (1994) 'Reshaping Business School Provision', *Training & Development Journal*, Oct., pp. 13–14.

Boud, D., Cohen, R., Walker, D. (eds) (1993) *Using Experience for Learning*, Buckingham/Bristol, SHRE/Open University.

Brew, A. (1993) 'Unlearning Through Experience', in Boud, Cohen and Walker (eds) *op cit*.

Brookfield, S. (ed.) (1985) *Self-Directed Learning: from theory to practice*, San Francisco, Jossey-Bass.

Brookfield, S. (1985a) 'Self-Directed Learning: A critical review of research', in Brookfield, S. (1985) *op. cit.*

Brookfield, S. (1993) 'Through the Lens of Learning: How the visceral experience of learning reframes teaching', Chapter 1 in Boud, D. *et al*. (1993) *op. cit.*

Brown, R. (1992) *Understanding Theoretical Perspectives in Industrial Sociology*, London, Routledge.

Carnall, C., (1990) *Managing Change in Organizations*, Hemel Hempstead, Prentice Hall.

Clegg, S.R. (1990) 'Modernist and Postmodernist Organization', Chapter 11 in Salaman (ed.) *op. cit.*

Cooper, C. (ed.) (1975) *Theories of Group Processes*, London, J. Wiley.

Cox, C., Cooper, C. (1988) *High Flyers: An Anatomy of Managerial Success*, Oxford, Blackwell.

Criticos, C. (1993) 'Experiential Learning and Social Transformation for a Post-apartheid Learning Future', Chapter 11 in Boud, D. *et al*. (1993) *op. cit.*

Davies, G., Williams, S. (1993) 'Management Development in Higher Education: The Theory-Practice and Outcomes', Conference paper, CORE, June 1993.

Feyerabend, P. (1978) *Against Method*, London, Verso.

Freedman, R., Cooper, C., Stumpf, S. (eds) (1982) *Management Education Issues in Theory, Research and Practice*, London, Wiley and Sons.

Garratt, B. (1987) *The Learning Organisation*, London, Fontana/Collins.

Gibbs, G. and Jenkins, A. eds (1992) in McGill and Beatty (eds) *op. cit.*

Hammond, M., Collins, R. (1991) *Self-Directed Learning: Critical Practice*, London, Kogan Page.

Heron, J. (1988) 'Assessment Revisited' in Boud, D. (ed.) (1988) *Development Student Autonomy in Learning*, Second edition, London, Kogan Page.

Heron, J. (1990) *Helping the client*, London, Sage.

Hosking, D-M., Morley, I. (1991) *A Social Psychology of Organizing: People, Processes and Contexts*, Hemel Hempstead, Harvester Wheatsheaf.

Knowles, M. (1975) *Self-Directed Learning*, New York Association Press.

Knowles, M. (1990) *The Adult learner: A Neglected Species*, Fourth edition, Houston, Gulf Publishing Co.

Kolb, D. and Fry, R. (1975) 'Towards an applied theory of experiential learning' in Cooper, C. (ed.) (1975) *op. cit.*

Lessem, R. (1993) *Business as a Learning Community*, London, McGraw Hill.

McGill I., Beatty L. (1992) *Action Learning: A Practitioners Guide*, London, Kogan Page.

McGregor, D. (1960) *The human side of enterprise*, New York, McGraw-Hill.

Mintzberg, H. (1989) in Spender *op. cit.*

Moran, R., Harris, P. and Stripp, W. (1993) *Developing the Global Organisation: Strategies for Human Resource Professionals*, Houston, Gulf Publishing Co.

Pedlar, M. (1991) *Action Learning in Practice*, Second edition, Aldershot, Gower

Pedlar, M., Boydell, T., Burgoyne, J. (1989) 'Towards the Learning Company', in *Management Education and Development*, vol. 20, part 1, pp. 1–8.

Poire, M. and Sabel, C. (1984) *The Second Industrial Divide*, New York, Basic Books.

Postle, D. (1993) 'Putting the Heart back into Learning', in Boud, Cohen and Walker eds *op. cit.*

Revans, R. (1980) *Action Learning: New Techniques for Action Learning*, London, Blond and Briggs.

Ritzer, G. (1993) *The MacDonaldization of Society*, Newbury Park CA, Pine-Forge Press.

Rogers, C. (1983) *Freedom to learn for the 1980s*, Columbus, Merrill.

Salaman, G. ed. (1992) *Human Resource Strategies*, London, Sage/Open University.

Seneca in Bacon, F. (1597) 'Of Adversity', in Hawkins (ed.) (1992) *Francis Bacon Essays*, London, Everyman

Senge, P. (1991) *The Fifth Discipline*, Random Century.

Spender, J.C. (1989) 'Meeting Mintzberg: Thinking Again about Management Education', *European Management Journal*, vol. 7, no. 3, p. 254–66.

Tennant, M. (1988) *Psychology and Adult Learning*, London, Routledge.

Thurley, K., Wirdenuis, H. (1989) *Towards European Management*, London, Pitman.

Torrington, D., Weightman, J. (1994) *Effective Management People and Organisation*, Second edition, Hemel Hempstead, Prentice Hall.

Usher, R. (1993) 'Experiential learning or learning from experience: Does it make a difference?', Chapter 12 in Boud, D. *et al.* (1993) *op. cit.*

Vaill, P. (1989) *Managing as a Performing Art: New Ideas for a World of Chaotic Change*, San Francisco CA, Jossey-Bass.

Appendix

Evaluation of Action Learning Sets

Action Learning Sets has a number of aims amongst which are to encourage members to take ownership of identified problems so that the process of self-development can take place. As part of this process it is hoped that an atmosphere of openness, genuineness and trust is generated. The following questionnaire asks you to evaluate that process and identify your perception of the effectiveness of the work you did within the set.

1. Using a scale 1–5 (1 = low, 3 = average, 5 = high) tick as appropriate for all the following words. Please add any words or phrases that come to your mind that best describe the process you went through and mark accordingly in the spaces provided or add extra

Statement	1	2	3	4	5
Commitment					
Motivation					
Honesty					
Hard working					
Supportiveness					
Task achievement					
Group participation					
Contribution level					
Organisation					

2. Please identify your personal perception of the strengths of the learning sets.

Strengths	
1	
2	
3	

3. Please identify your personal perceptions of the weaknesses of your learning set

Weakness	
1	
2	
3	

4. What is your perception of the benefits of your action learning set experiences to your workplace(s)

_____

_____

_____

_____

_____

_____

5. What is your perception of the disadvantages or adverse effects of learning sets?

_____

_____

_____

_____

_____

_____

6. What advice would you give to a set that was just beginning?

_____

_____

_____

_____

_____

_____

14

Research Methods and HRD

Goronwy Davies

INTRODUCTION: HUMAN RESOURCE DEVELOPMENT – THE CHANGING ROLE

The human resource management role is beginning to change as organisations attempt to develop strategies for survival when faced by turbulent, unpredictable, economic conditions and markets. Without reiterating what Davies and Hamlin (1995, in this volume) have suggested is a response to perceptions strategic managers have to such change, it appears there are several implications which need to be considered. One of these implications is that organisations seeking to survive such conditions are changing, where the changes advocated have a direct bearing on HRM practices. Organisations are having to expand the role of the HRD specialist. This evolving role carries with it a demanding set of expectations where the specialist has to show the ability to think strategically, to have expertise in change management and to take on the role of change agent more generally within the organisation. University programmes are being offered at the post-graduate level to develop the expertise needed in the area of change management. As part of these programmes there is a requirement for the HRD specialist to develop research skills for two main reasons. On the one hand, there is a need when performing in the role of change agent to evaluate the effectiveness of the change strategy adopted in the organisation. As has been pointed out by Davies and Hamlin (1995) elsewhere in this book, there is a paucity of evaluative studies of the effectiveness of change strategies adopted in different organisational contexts. So it is important that change specialists are equipped with the appropriate skills of evaluation to make sense of a complex process, in a very practical way. On the other hand, there is normally a formal university programme requirement for research to be conducted to meet academic criteria at the post-graduate level. Currently, HRD specialists are being expected to develop the appropriate level of analysis and evaluation of academic models of change and change management. They are expected to research a change process within an organisation, at the appropriate academic level. Within a limited time, the HRD specialist taking an academic programme of study will constantly be moving between theory and practice, and action and reflection. At some point in the programme the student will need to record and make sense of this process by applying a research method. This chapter is designed to inform that choice of method when HRD specialists are being asked to perform in the role of change agent by their organisations and to develop research methods to meet academic requirements. Implicit in what follows, however, are distinctions which need to be made between the expectations that organisational sponsors may have for a management report of an organisational intervention as opposed to the academic expectations for an academic dissertation, reporting the same phenomena. The management report serves as a summary of action taken including some descriptive estimate of what has been achieved, to inform management thinking. The academic dissertation analyses and evaluates in depth to inform strategic management thinking about the effectiveness of the organisation. Also, the latter will meet the academic requirements the HRD specialist will have to satisfy on a particular post-graduate programme of study. I am suggesting that research and evaluation of the type that is required of the HRD specialist may be significantly different to the type of activity the trainer would traditionally have been involved in in the past.

ACADEMIC DEPTH FOR RESEARCH AND EVALUATION

To make these distinctions clearer, we need to recognise there is a difference between approaches to research and evaluation as developed in the social sciences and the need for descriptive, functional 'data' that estimate the effects of a training intervention within an organisation. One approach attempts to analyse and understand the factors behind the effectiveness of an intervention whereas the second describes the effects of an organisational intervention, more loosely. I believe that HRD specialists need to know which type of interventions made within different organisations work and why.

Managers and HRD specialists, particularly HRD specialists, are encouraged to use and develop different means of analysis and explanation from those used in the social sciences. However, where the recommendation on lower level programmes of study in the past may have been 'to suck it and see' in evaluating whether some recipe worked in practice, the requirements of a post-graduate programme need to be recognised as being different. On such programmes, the HRD specialist must adopt an analytical and evaluative stance to be able to state what a probable outcome for an organisational intervention would be. The organisational change literature is littered with guidance, recipes, some reports of the implications of research and a great deal of exhortation from the sidelines.

I believe it is necessary to make distinctions between evaluation and estimation on the one hand and descriptive as opposed to analytic research on the other, for example see Fig. 14.1. Within this framework it is important to recognise that 'data' serve different purposes. When describing some phenomenon using data, the data is summarised and this summary provides the basis for an estimation of the phenomenon and the likely associated effects. The estimation involves making a judgement of likely outcomes based on data sets that have not been designed to allow predictive inferences to be made. A trainer can give out a feedback proforma after a training intervention, the data can be collected and summarised and an estimate can be made of the effects of the training intervention. From a weak description of the effects of the training intervention, use is made of a description of data, summarised to make an estimate for future action. On the other hand, in terms say of the same training intervention, data would be collected from multiple organisational sources. The data could then be analysed and interpreted and relatively objective statements could be derived about the training event, but in the context

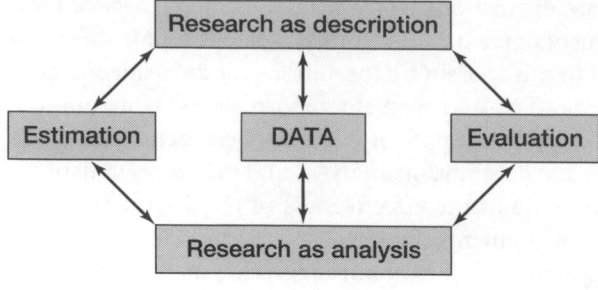

Fig. 14.1

of both an analysis of organisational effectiveness and organisational strategies for change. That is, relatively well informed inferences can be made because the data has been manipulated in some way. The conclusions reached would identify the multiple causes of the success or otherwise of the intervention within that context. I am suggesting that descriptive research seeks to answer 'what' questions, whereas analytic research seeks to answer 'what and why' questions. Both types of questions are appropriate to ask, but analytic research implies both are necessary to prescribe future action. Descriptive research cannot be prescriptive in the same sense.

RESEARCH SKILLS: WHAT SKILLS ARE NECESSARY?

In order for the HRD specialist to understand what is necessary to meet the requirements for doing research, prospective researchers need to audit the skills that they have at the beginning of the research process. Easterby-Smith *et al.* (1991) have developed a checklist identifying the important qualities of researchers. They locate researcher qualities within a framework of knowledge, skills and personal qualities. The prospective researcher is asked to estimate the extent to which they have the following.

- Knowledge
  - awareness of different assumptions about the world;
  - awareness of the methods of collecting data;
  - awareness of different research designs;
  - knowledge of the immediate subject of study;
  - knowledge of related subjects/disciplines;
  - knowledge of key networks and contacts in one's chosen research area.

- Skills
  - ability to plan, organise and manage one's own time;
  - ability to search libraries and other sources;
  - ability to gain support and co-operation from others;
  - ability to argue and structure a case in writing;
  - ability to defend and argue views orally;
  - ability to learn from experience.

● **Personal qualities**
  - awareness of own strengths, weaknesses and values;
  - clarity of thought;
  - sensitivity to events and feelings;
  - emotional resilience;
  - flexibility;
  - creativity.

Clearly, this framework has direct application to the HRD specialist researcher. The skills and personal qualities identified are those that are associated with the competencies of the successful change agent (Buchanan and Boddy, 1992), whereas the knowledge qualities refer to what would normally be associated with a post-graduate degree in HRD. As such, the rest of the chapter will examine in more detail the first three knowledge qualities suggested by Easterby-Smith, Thorpe and Lowe.

WAYS OF THINKING ABOUT RESEARCH PARADIGMS

The word paradigm has had a long history in the sociology of knowledge, since Kuhn (1972) invented the term to explain revolutionary changes in scientific knowledge. The term was not accepted universally and engendered an academic debate concerning how the term was defined and whether it has any usefulness as an explanatory device. (For those interested in the debate, refer to Lakatos and Musgrave, 1970.) I believe the term is still helpful because if it is defined in a particular way it can help to illuminate thinking about the assumptions we make, when we become involved in any action – in this case research.

Davies (1986) defines paradigms as a way of seeing (an activity) which then leads to a particular way of doing (the activity). He further suggests that the way of seeing is affected by what we selectively choose to see and that what we choose to see reflects the psychological assumptions we make about the activity. He further suggests that these psychological assumptions reflect our values, that is, what we believe is right or wrong about the actions we take. He also indicates that the actions people take, in this case research, need to be understood in the social context or culture within which the action takes place. Our ways of seeing a particular organisational problem will affect the way we approach the doing of research within this particular social and cultural system. The whole activity can be interpreted as being paradigmatically based and revealing of our values and assumptions. Davies concludes this analysis of the paradigmatic basis for explaining action by suggesting the researcher and the research can be interpreted as having a symbolic function within a particular social and cultural context. Diagrammatically, this can be represented as in Fig. 14.2. Therefore, it appears that when HRD specialists are at the point of choosing which research to do, they should be aware of the values and assumptions behind the research topic chosen, as well as what research methods are to be used. Research, particularly management or organisational change research, is value loaded; that is, it is paradigmatically based and researchers must be aware of the assumptions they make when they are researching on, or with, other people.

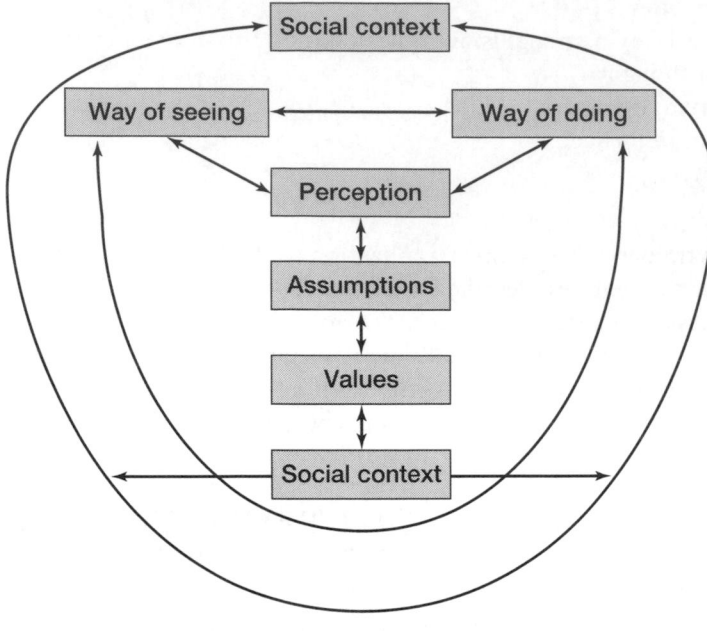

Fig. 14.2

Research methods which stress measurement, for example questionnaires, reflect a particular form of reality. This reality, which is one-dimensional, assumes researcher knowledge as the source for understanding that form of reality. Within the method, there is value placed on statistical interpretations and explanations in developing theory to explain such reality. I call this predominant paradigm research (Davies, 1986) and contrast this with alternate forms of doing research, which Reason and Rowan (1981) call a 'new' paradigm. This different paradigm stresses the research relationship with other people as the method for attaining knowledge with others, thus acknowledging that there are multiple forms of reality which people experience personally, socially and in organisations. Within this paradigm, the assumption is made that knowledge is shared, is open to negotiation and evolves through the research process. Researchers place a value on open methods of collaboration to negotiate research interpretations of grounded experience and theory.

My view now is that it may be enough for researchers to know within which paradigm they choose to do research. I also recognise that organisational life reflects the values and assumptions of both paradigms briefly discussed here, particularly if power and control are seen to be paradigmatically based within organisations, as they are in research. Therefore, we may need to use multi-paradigmatic methods of research to reflect the multi-paradigmatic values and assumptions that people within organisations experience directly. Bearing this in mind, I will now discuss more practically the range of methods available to the researcher who is just beginning.

APPROACHES TO PLANNING RESEARCH AND EVALUATION

The first problem that the HRD researcher is faced with is one of defining the topic for investigation and then identifying what is necessary to complete the research process. We need to be aware that what I have said about paradigms in this chapter has direct implications for the process of planning and implementing the research. Herbert (1990) suggests that planning involves different stages the research student passes through in time. The important idea contained in this approach is that if the researcher can plan ahead they will be prepared for each eventuality as it arises. This is good 'common sense', if the researcher is going to superimpose this framework on the research process. Herbert suggests there are nine important stages to move through, which are:

1 identify the problem;
2 formulate the research questions or hypotheses;
3 decide on the research strategy;
4 choose the research design;
5 plan how to collect the data;
6 collect data;
7 analyse and interpret data;
8 conclude based on what has been found out through the data in relation to the original research problem identified;
9 write up.

See Herbert (1990) for more detail.

This approach implies a clear identification of hypotheses or research questions at the beginning of the research or evaluation. This view can be contrasted with one that recognises research as a process whose structure is looser and can be described in terms of questions that need to be answered as the research progresses. They are:

● what problems am I faced with, and whom do they affect within the organisation?
● how can I negotiate a forum for identifying appropriate questions to be researched?
● what methods should we use?
● what will be the basis for negotiating appropriate sets of multiple data?
● how and who will be responsible for the collection and interpretation of the data?
● how and when will we negotiate the meaning of the data assembled?
● how will we make sense of the meaning of the data to develop theory reflective of our experience?
● do I need to consider validity issues?
● how will I write about the processes of the research to analyse, explain and report on appropriate theory?
● how can the literature help me in the research process?

Whichever way the research process is organised there will be consequences in terms of particular methods that can be used. What I suggest above is a simplification of the assumptions made about methods of planning research. By categorising planning in this way I have clarified issues involved in different types of research. However, the problem of what researchers ultimately choose as a research strategy may be a function of paradigmatic values they espouse. The choice will be a reflection of the kind of person they are and the particular styles of thinking they habitually use. Perhaps, researchers are the paradigm of the research strategy they develop.

Pheysey (1993) indicates that distinctions can be drawn between a number of different research styles. They are:

1 The abstract thinker who believes that research data collected cannot be understood without reference to theory. Theory is made up of tightly defined concepts from which detailed propositions can be derived and tested.
2 The experimentalist who is interested in acquiring data from which to make inferences about the effects of the manipulation of experimental variables to understand the cause, causes or relationships between data.

Both these types of researcher are found to use models of research derived from the natural sciences, and are detached and method centred. Other researchers tend to be problem centred and involved with the processes of the research. They are:

3 The intuitive synthesiser who believes total objectivity is impossible and blends inductive and deductive methods of enquiry according to their intuitive understanding of the conceptual links within the data gathered.
4 Qualitative researchers argue that objectivity is impossible and that the researcher must include their own assumptions within the research process. These researchers believe that perceptions, interpretations and feelings deeply affect the objectivity of any research and have devised different methods to account for this recognition.

Rather than discuss the implications of this typology, I will distinguish more simply between open and closed methods of enquiry. Closed methods are those used by the abstract thinker and experimentalist and open methods are those used by qualitative researchers. Intuitive synthesisers may wish to use both. Therefore, in the next section, I contrast closed with open methods of enquiry. Closed methods apply to the researcher who wishes to answer theory driven research questions and wishes to use what are quantitative research techniques of measurement to reach research conclusions. Open methods apply to the researcher who wishes to answer experientially, or practically driven, negotiated questions by using a range of qualitative methods. Open methods take into account the assumptions and interpretations others make when they build their own implicit theories about the world. New researchers can choose to work using both methods, but they need to be aware of the implications of both approaches for the development of appropriate research strategies, methods and conclusions about the research questions posed. They also need to be aware that the different methods chosen provide different answers to problems concerning the explanation of organisational contexts.

METHODS OF RESEARCH AND EVALUATION

Post-graduate students may have particular problems in choosing an appropriate research strategy because of the practical consequences of the roles they are asked to perform on some masters degrees. Some programmes ask that students take on the role of change agent and require that they evaluate and research the change processes implied in taking on such a role. Therefore, the student must be aware of the extent to which the research strategy illuminates the role, the change strategy and the need for research and evaluation within the time span of the programme of study being followed. So, if for some students there is a need to adopt this utilitarian view of research, I will discuss:

- experimental and quasi experimental approaches;
- quantitative methods of data collection;
- closed and open qualitative approaches;
- action research.

Experimental and quasi experimental approaches

Experimental design

Experimental designs tend to follow strict guidelines and are based on experimental methods which emanate from experimental psychology. Experimentalists formulate a research problem by identifying variables that can be quantified in different ways, and then they separate out these variables into an independent variable or variables and dependent variables. For instance, the research problem may be one where the researcher is interested in whether different managers performing in different functions across an organisation use different management styles. Therefore, the independent variable would be the different management functions and the dependent variable would be the questionnaire response made by the managers. The independent variable represents a decision that the experimenter makes about what needs to be controlled within the research problem, whereas the dependent variable is always that which is measured.

Having defined the problem in terms of the variables that are important within the research, the researcher then needs to formulate a hypothesis which must state a relationship between the independent and dependent variable. In our example, our hypothesis would be that we expect there to be no significant difference in the management style [the dependent variable (the questionnaire)] used by managers performing in the different functions of the organisation (the independent variable). Hypotheses are stated in the null form so that they can be tested by applying statistics that indicate whether there is a probable, significant difference between, in this case, the management styles used across functions in the organisation. The method is developed in this way because of the need for falsification procedures in science.

After formulating hypotheses, and specifying the population of managers to be sampled, the researcher measures the dependent variable, collects the data, applies appropriate statistics to test the hypothesis and then interprets the results with theory. For more information on this approach see Robson (1990).

The HRD researcher should note that this way of approaching research is reflected in the guidelines for planning a research project identified above (Herbert, 1990). The method is rigorous but in my terms it is closed and relatively weak for research on organisational processes. The approach has difficulty in defining the multi-variable nature of organisational processes, where the causes of the effects being researched may be confounded by intervening variables that have not been measured. However, there has been a development of the experimental method for application to field studies. Instead of passively manipulating data, an experimenter can create some form of organisational intervention and then measure the effects caused by the intervention. These methods are called quasi experimental designs.

Quasi experimental designs

We shall discuss this way of approaching research by referring to a hypothetical research strategy that seeks to establish the effects of a particular change intervention in an organisation. One approach that could be used would be where the researcher selects a group for testing such effects, administers a questionnaire before the change implementation and then tests the same group using the same questionnaire after the change has taken place. For example: this can be characterised using the following diagram.

Select group . . . Group A

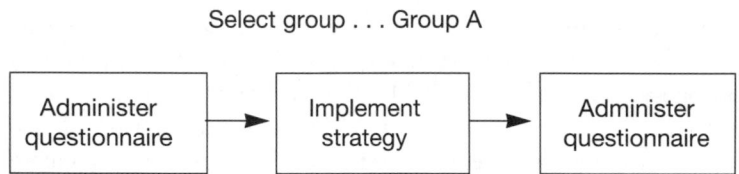

This simple design for evaluating and researching the effects of such an intervention does not, however, account for certain problems that would affect the validity of the design. Campbell and Stanley (1966) suggest that the design does not account for problems concerning internal and external validity. By internal validity, they mean the extent to which the change recorded in the questionnaire used can be explained or affected by factors internal to the procedure. For instance, they suggest that the change which may have been recorded could be due to maturation of the experimental group through time; a lack of validity of the questionnaire used; a test–retest effect; selection bias of group A; or experimental mortality.

By external validity, Campbell and Stanley suggest that the design limits the extent to which we can generalise from the test group (Group A) to other groups in the organisation. This may have been because of a bias in the selection of Group A that interacted with the change intervention. For example, Group A may have been made up of volunteers who wanted the change to take place. Another form of bias may have been an interaction between the content of the questionnaire and the subsequent change intervention. The questionnaire may have sensitised subjects to the intervention. They also identify another source of bias as multiple treatment effects, where subjects respond to the second questionnaire having been sensitised to its content by having already completed the first. This last source of bias is particularly applicable if the researcher is involved in a repeated measures strategy over time. Campbell and Stanley stress that there is a need to develop more experimental sophistication to control for these bias effects and increase the validity of the research design. They go on to identify 21 different research designs that account for the sources of bias reported here. I will briefly discuss the three that have the greatest utility for the HRD researcher so that the validity of the generalisations a change agent may wish to make can be increased.

In what follows, a simple code is used that makes the diagrams self-explanatory. The example that is being used is the same as the one discussed above.

E: Experimental group, which is the group chosen to undergo the experimental treatment.

C: Control group, which is the group with whom comparisons are made after the experimental treatment.

R: Groups where subjects have been allocated at *random* from an organisation.

M: Groups where the subjects making up the group have been *matched* on some criteria important to the research problem, in our example subjects could be matched in terms of age, sex, experience, level of skill, and management grade.

T: Test by administration of an appropriate questionnaire.

X: The experimental treatment, in this case the organisational change intervention.

Design One

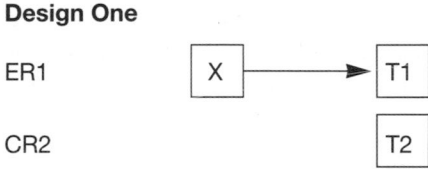

ER1   X → T1

CR2   T2

In this design, testing is carried out on both groups after the change intervention has been carried out with ER1 only, and then comparisons are made with the questionnaire responses made by the E and C groups. If there are significant differences we would be able to conclude that this was caused by the change intervention.

Design Two

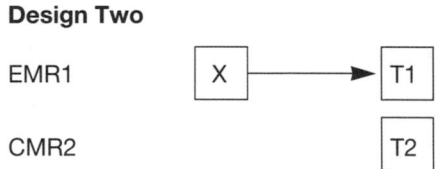

EMR1   X → T1

CMR2   T2

Testing and comparisons between groups are carried out under the same conditions as with design 1. In this design subjects are matched and then randomly assigned to the experimental and control groups.

Design Three

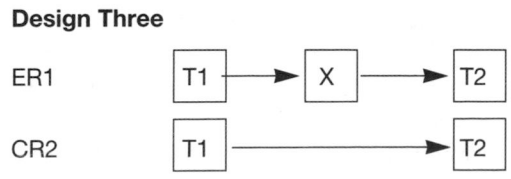

ER1   T1 → X → T2

CR2   T1 → T2

In this design, subjects are randomly assigned to the experimental and control groups. Both groups are tested before and after the intervention is carried out with the experimental group. Comparisons can then be made between the two tests completed by both groups before and after the intervention.

Quantitative methods of data collection

In management research there has been a heavy reliance on survey methods, of both the descriptive and analytic, inferential types. The survey method relies heavily on questionnaire design and development and the selection of appropriate samples to survey. I will not be discussing how to structure and develop questionnaires except to say that one of the basic requirements of a questionnaire is that the questions asked should reflect the variability of the phenomena that the questionnaire is designed to describe. Questionnaires should be consistent in the way they discriminate between individuals and different groups of individuals, that is, designed to meet reliability criteria. They should also meet criteria relating to content, face, concurrent and construct validity as identified in detail by Oppenheim (1966) and as briefly described later in the chapter.

The other problem associated with survey designs is the need to define a sampling strategy. Decisions need to be made as to whether the sample to be chosen is to be stratified or random to meet the criterion of representativeness. Representativeness is important because if this criterion is met, generalisations can be developed to support the original research questions asked. Also, researchers would need to ask questions as to whether the data collection should consist of one shot or multiple shots of the sample under investigation. If the data collection is multiple in form then attention would need to be paid to the validity issues I referred to earlier. Surveys have a place in the researching of organisational change because functional surveys of the kind Carnall (1990) advocates could act as a base line from which to measure the effects of the change strategy being adopted within a particular organisational context. This approach would allow for a form of evaluation of the effectiveness of the change, where greater depth could be achieved if the survey data was supplemented by an analysis of a range of qualitatively based sets of data.

Closed and open qualitative approaches

The range of qualitative methodologies that have been used in the social sciences reflects a debate within sociology, social psychology and even experimental psychology concerning the validity and scientific value of experimental and survey methods. In these academic subjects there is a tension between how experimenters as researchers structure the world through academic theory as opposed to how people structure, make sense and act in relation to their own experience. Therefore, qualitative methodologies have been devised to try and understand the other person's experience from their point of view, rather than blindly apply academic theory. Hence, qualitative methodologies are used to understand meaning. Gill and Johnson (1991) suggest that these methodologies are interpretative and designed to represent the reality of the other person or persons involved in a research process. However, it is also important to recognise that some qualitative techniques can be applied in order for them to be analysed statistically, hence my earlier distinction between closed and open methods of research. Therefore, in this section I will briefly and selectively discuss closed methods of qualitative research and then discuss more open methods.

Closed methods

By closed methods of research, as I suggest earlier, I mean those methods that rely on the theory of the researcher, or somebody else's theory, to frame the questions that can be asked of others involved in the research. The other criterion I use is the extent to which the method is internally organised to be able to produce data suitable for statistical analysis. These are:

Closed interviews

Closed interviews are those where the researcher develops a closed list of questions that are derived directly from a research hypothesis of the kind I identify in earlier sections. The format of the interview is entirely determined by the researcher and the subject of the research is required normally to answer closed questions. This approach can be directly contrasted with open interviews but both imply knowledge on the part of the interviewer in terms of understanding social interaction and interviewer bias. Both also require the interviewer to obtain trust and create a situation which puts the interviewee at ease. This type of interview can produce data that can be scored and analysed in the same way as questionnaire data can.

Repertory grid technique

Kelly (1957) suggests that man when involved in behaving and relating to a personal world acts very much in the way that scientists claim they do. He suggests that our perceptions of the world are affected by how we bring personal cognitive structures – constructs to bear when perceiving and behaving in relation to others – to groups and to organisations. He further suggests that our construct system acts as a series of hypotheses about the social world that we constantly test out through different forms of interaction. I believe we tend to act inductively and we constantly need to attempt to falsify our personal hypotheses, otherwise we would not develop – our construct system would not expand, deepen and change. How individual construct systems are changed as a result of an involvement in an organisational change process could be tested out, by applying the repertory grid technique initially developed by Kelly.

Participant observation

Participant observation can be theory driven and closed in the sense that the researcher involved in the participation is observing behaviour from a particular perspective. This kind of activity is sometimes associated with research conducted by those who wish to engage with others and then interpret the engagement in terms of theory. Theories that have been applied in this way are phenomenology, psychodynamic perspectives or certain humanistic orientations. The point of the technique is that although it is relatively closed in my terms, the research engagement is interpreted from a strict theoretical perspective. As an example, researchers who are interested in psychodynamic explanations of organisational change phenomena may wish to adopt this approach (see De Board, 1976).

Open methods

In what follows it is important to recognise that total openness as a research stance has some theoretical explanation and justification. Openness in my terms involves the emphasis and value placed on the other person/s involved in the research. We need to be aware that open data generated in this way need further interpretation by the researcher who can apply a particular framework, or orientation of the kind I discuss later.

Open interviews

Open interviews can be conducted where the role of the interviewer is to collaborate with the other person to establish the perceptions, feelings and interpretations of the other about the research topic. This means that openness by the interviewer must be constrained in relation to a previously negotiated agenda that is research related. This type of interview would need to be recorded, with permission, so that transcripts can be prepared for further data analysis.

Group interviews

These follow the same pattern as indicated for open interviews. They must be recorded by the interviewer for the analysis of data concerning the group process to be distinguished from the data that applies more directly to the research problem. However, depending on the research stance taken by the researcher, decisions need to be made about the relative value and importance of both sets of data. This is because what is interpreted as group process issues may be reflective of the group processes of the organisation being researched.

Workshops

Workshops can be developed where groups are invited to participate in exploring issues that are central to a particular research process. So for example, persons affected by change within an organisation could be invited to a workshop to explore what the change meant to them. They would discuss the issues, write reports of what had happened to them and identify what this process meant. A development of this would be to organise workshops where the persons invited would be asked to recount stories of themselves as they experienced the change, to draw themselves undergoing the change process and then to identify what this experience meant to them. By using this method, collaborators are creating and interpreting data entirely within their own frames of reference. The researcher's role would be to facilitate the process of the workshop with the minimum of interference in the process.

Participant observation

This is a form of activity that persons are constantly involved with when they participate in organisational life. In order for the participant in a role, say of change agent, to make explicit what they implicitly act out daily and in order for the activity to qualify as research, participants need to record what they observe, explicitly. (See Diary and journal methods below.)

Non-participant observation

This involves a form of research activity where the researcher 'actively' adopts a strategy of observing but from an atheoretical point of view. This atheoretical form of observation has been labelled by phenomenologists as 'bracketing off'. This is where the observer chooses to suspend the beliefs, attitudes and feelings which interfere and cloud our perceptions and interpretations of what we observe. When stated in this way the method of 'bracketing off' appears to be easy; however, the purity of observation implied indicates the need for a form of processual training commonly associated with the Zen masters! However, this does not negate the need for the observer to check out observations that are being made in terms of their contextual validity. Ask another person in the organisation!

Critical incident technique

Participants involved in research looking at change strategies could be encouraged to record individual, group, or organisational incidents that have affected them in a negative or positive way. As a result, the researcher is being sent data that is based on the interpretations others are making of the processes of change being directly experienced (Davies, 1986). HRD researchers, however, should be aware of the use that has been made of this technique in management research and should consult Easterby-Smith *et al.* (1991).

Diary and journal methods

HRD specialists researching change processes need seriously to consider keeping a journal or a diary to record different aspects of the process. The journal can also be used as another source of data when trying to make sense of the role of the change agent in the context of what has happened through the implementation of the change strategy. Also, researchers can negotiate agreements with key persons within the organisation to keep diaries or journals at different times during the change process. Again this is a way of negotiating with collaborators to produce self-generated data within the framework of the ongoing research. Clearly, researchers should establish what is possible when establishing commitments to this form of data collection by collaborators.

Action research

Gill and Johnson (1991) suggest that this form of research is *the* one that makes a difference within organisational settings. This is because it can be used as a planned intervention which if researched can contribute to existing forms of knowledge. Action research strategies can also help to resolve some of the practical concerns of people facing a problematic situation. The approach when used is problem centred and Gill (1986) identifies different stages in the process that I have adapted in relation to organisational change. My adaptation assumes that the HRD specialist is acting as an internal change agent within the organisation:

- *Entry:* Researcher or other members of the organisation present the problem of how to change the organisation. The group identify mutually agreed goals.
- *Contracting:* The group identify what the expectations and function of the group are to be in relation to the changes being suggested for the organisation thereby negotiating a psychological contract.
- *Diagnosis:* Joint diagnosis of the organisation by group members in terms of what is agreed is important, so that an agreed set of concepts are mutually applied.
- *Action:* Having gained feedback which may have created dissonance through the diagnosis, joint action plans can be negotiated and agreed and action taken.
- *Evaluation:* Review of the effects of action undertaken leading to a new diagnosis being developed for action to be taken again. Generalisations concerning the effectiveness of action taken may emerge.
- *Withdrawal:* Formal evaluation of the change intervention may cease with the original group being self-supporting.

My own interpretation of action research involves seeing the process in circular forms. In this case, the researcher is involved in taking action to monitor, evaluate and research a change intervention as shown in Fig. 14.3.

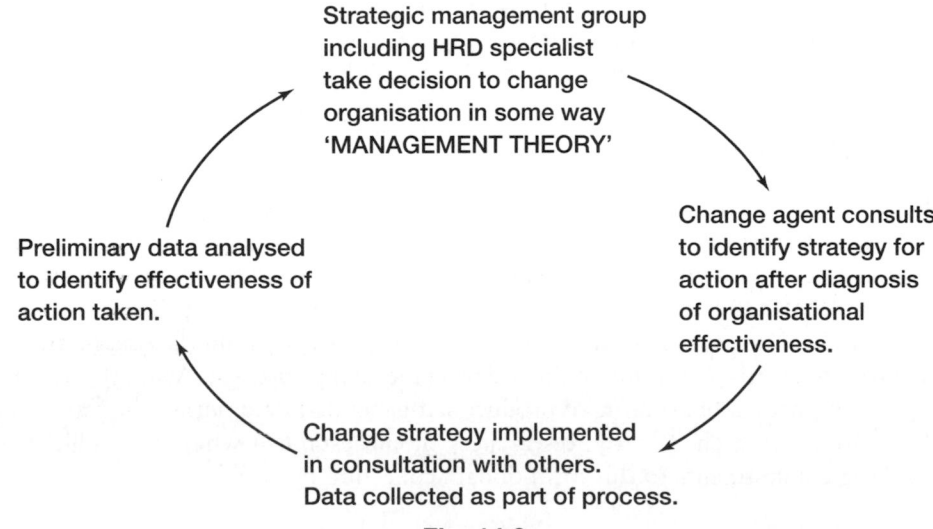

Fig. 14.3

Whichever form of research is adopted, both act as guidelines to doing action research without specifying the nature and type of data to be collected and analysed. My own view is that either quantitative or qualitative data can be collected, depending on researcher characteristics, the limitations on time and organisational constraints. In terms of the circular form I describe above, if the researcher was to conceive of this as being the first of a series of cycles of research, in the first cycle, the data collected could be quantitative and purely functional. In subsequent cycles, the researcher could move into a more qualitative mode to deepen levels of understanding and enrich theory. However, as one of the assumptions behind action research is that it reflects an inductive form of acquiring research knowledge, the researcher would need to consider the issues of reliability and validity that I discuss in a later section.

DATA ANALYSIS

Quantitative data analysis presents few problems for those who as part of their education, training, or workplace experience have developed the skills of applying inferential statistics to reach conclusions about research problems. Sophistication and confidence are two prime assets in the application of statistics to multiple sets of data that represent organisational processes. This chapter is not designed to teach statistics but I would refer the reader to Robson (1990) and Guilford and Fruchter (1973) for an appreciation of the possibilities for statistical analysis of data derived as part of a research strategy.

Qualitative methods, on the other hand, appear to be relatively simple to apply. However, all of these methods present the researcher with the problem of making sense of the data. Data analysis of qualitatively-based data poses particular problems for the HRD specialist. I believe it is not sufficient to merely report what other people said or did without framing the analysis within some deliberately applied perspective. The perspective applied will help in the later development of theory, where theory helps to explain in depth. Researchers who apply what I term open methodologies to research organisational problems do so within what could be regarded as a 'research stance'. By a research stance, I mean that the researcher applies a qualitative method or methods, understanding that there is a particular way of analysing the data that will follow. Qualitative methods are used within a philosophy of where the data analysis will lead to and what the basic assumptions and values of the research are. I give four examples in what follows.

Content analysis

This is an application of a method of counting key words, phrases or statements that refer to the topic under investigation and occur within interview protocols, diaries, and journals. The approach is systematic and allows for an estimate of the frequency with which concepts are referred to in a data set.

Discourse analysis

Discourse analysis is a technique developed within social psychology to analyse spoken forms of interaction and can therefore be readily applied to analysing written and tape recorded reports of the kind I identify above. Potter and Wetherell (1987) develop a full account of the methodology and provide interesting insights into how the technique can be applied. The assumptions behind the technique are that language functions to construct versions of meaning, reality and action. This occurs because of the way that language varies within the different situations in which it is presented. Potter and Wetherell have a concern to understand meaning which they believe is constructed and co-constructed by the way we as humans use different repertoires, acts and talk. Therefore, the task in the analysis is to code the discourse of the research with categories and patterns of meaning that reveal the connection between what we say and what we do. Discourse analysis has great possibilities for the HRD specialist because the deeper levels of the meaning of change strategies and the role of the change agent would become explicit, if so analysed.

Cognitive mapping

This technique can be used either individually or with groups of people within organisations. The approach is a modified form of the repertory grid. Participants are asked to identify a range of problems and issues concerning the research problem. These issues and problems can then be interrogated by a computer to produce a map of the ideas, concepts and issues of the individual or the group as they relate to the research problem. A less sophisticated form of the technique is to ask participants to identify issues and for a partner to record what the evolving map may look like. This can be checked for appropriate interpretation by the interaction being tape recorded and fed back to the participant for commentary and expansion. In this way the full complexity of the cognitive map can be explored. Cognitive mapping is a means of accessing the cognitively complex models individuals develop and as such could be used to understand the effects of a change strategy being experienced within an organisation.

Grounded theory

Grounded theory was first developed by Glaser and Strauss (1967) where they suggest that the important theory to consider is that which informs everyday action. As a result, they suggest that theory should be built up from this grounded experience by using the type of open qualitative methods I describe earlier. They suggest that the data thus generated in the research should be interrogated to establish appropriate research specific themes which they argue act as first order explanatory concepts. They then suggest that by reviewing the themes as first order concepts, and linking them, second order theory can be developed. In this way grounded theory can be built upward to provide explanatory power for the research topic at an appropriate depth.

Ethnography

Ethnographers enter the field of research seeking to understand the significance of the language, ritual and other symbols of the organisation by interpreting the organisation as culture. Ethnographers have used the full range of qualitative methods I discuss earlier, but they have used the data to establish the extent to which the symbols of the culture reveal the beliefs, values and attitudes of the participants in that culture. HRD specialists could use this approach to understand the organisational context within which change strategies are being implemented. Clearly, what I say here is a parody of the vast literature available on the subject, and I would suggest that readers refer to Pheysey (1993) for one exposition of how ethnography can be applied to understand culture and organisational development.

We need to be clear that these approaches all favour an inductive approach to resolving research issues and because there is a need for research to meet certain academic criteria of validity, it is important that I discuss this in the next section.

VALIDITY AND RELIABILITY

Validity and reliability criteria appear to be absolute, and therefore appear to be absolutely irrefutable when applied to quantitative methodologies. The researcher developing questionnaires should attempt to meet these criteria as far as possible. However, they should also be aware that some commonly used tests of personality developed by psychologists may not meet these criteria absolutely. Briefly, I will outline the questions that the researcher should be able to answer to meet the reliability and validity criteria for questionnaires and therefore also for closed qualitative methodologies, if they are to be used. They are for reliability:

- how consistent is this test in discriminating amongst a population?
- will the test provide similar results if administered in a month's time?

and for validity:

- does the test cover the range of possible questions that could be asked about the topic? (content validity)
- does the test look as if it is testing what it claims to be testing? (face validity)
- does the test give similar results to other tests measuring the same phenomena? (concurrent validity)
- does the test adequately measure the research concept behind the test? (construct validity)
- does the test adequately predict behaviour? (predictive validity)

For qualitative methodology the criteria that are applied to establish rigour are of a different order and value. Reliability issues are currently being questioned because they imply a form of consistency that is not reflected in the research activity itself, which has been characterised as being messy and inconsistent over time (Davies 1986). However, one reliability criterion that should be applied is to ask to what extent the conclusions reached within the research avail themselves of alternative explanations.

Validity issues revolve around whether the engagement of the researcher with the collaborators of the research is genuine. Genuineness in this sense refers to a form of psychological validity concerning the quality of the relationship between the researcher and others in the research. A different criterion used refers to the form of contextual validity developed within the research process as a whole. The wise qualitative researcher should build validity checks into the procedures of the research. The checks will allow for a form of psychological validity to be claimed. Researchers need to claim validity within the research relationships by referring to how different relationships produced similar interpretations from different collaborators at different times in the research process. Contextual validity can be claimed in two ways. First, it could be claimed that the procedures were carried out in different contexts and yielded similar forms of interpretation by collaborators in the research. Second, a form of triangulation (Gill and Johnson, 1991) can be used, where it can be claimed that different collaborators interpreted similar research phenomena when different methods were used in the same context. Rigour is defined in the application of these methodologies by the extent to which the researcher can claim relative objectivity whilst illuminating subjective experience. Judgements about the rigour of the research are normally made at that time within the research process when the research is written up and presented to a different, relatively sophisticated research audience.

CONCLUDING COMMENTS – WRITING THE RESEARCH REPORT FOR DIFFERENT AUDIENCES

In an earlier section of the chapter I make distinctions between estimation and evaluation, and research as description as opposed to research as analysis. In this section I wish to discuss the implications of these distinctions for the writing of reports for different audiences. I believe that post-graduate HRD students sometimes confuse the issue by believing that the report written to satisfy internal organisational sponsors will also satisfy the requirements of academic external examiners. The difference between the two forms of report is that normally the management report will require clear description of what was done, before an estimate is made in management terms about what the description would mean for future action. The academic report, however, will require clear description, analysis, synthesis and evaluation of process and academic concepts derived from the research. In what follows, I seek to clarify the issue for the postgraduate student caught within the difficult process of writing to meet different sets of expectations.

The management report

Internal organisational sponsors of students expect a report that indicates what the objectives of the change strategy were, what the change agent did, what was achieved by the change agent in relation to the organisational objectives and what recommendations there are for future action. My experience of this form of report writing is that if the report is longer than four pages and does not contain an explicit executive summary, the report will not be read! Senior managers and executives claim they do not have the time to read pages of academic argument and they also claim that what they want is a series of bullet points that summarise activity, with recommendations made which point to future activity. Perhaps this form of thinking is appropriate in organisations that are action oriented; however, it does increase the frustration experienced by a change agent who has to consider the needs of the sponsoring organisation and has to meet other academic requirements reporting the same activity.

The point I wish to make is that the description and estimation involved in writing the management report to meet the expectations of senior managers and executives is not appropriate for meeting academic requirements – because these reports fail to meet academic criteria. The post-graduate student would be better advised to write the academic report first, and then translate this into the appropriate form of management writing to meet the expectations of others within the sponsoring organisation.

The quantitative academic research report

If the research has been cast within a quantitative paradigm, the format advised is as rigid as the research design implies and should adhere to the following pattern.

Introduction

The research problem would need to be located within an academic literature search relevant to the practical organisational problem to be researched. The introduction should, through a process of analysis, lead logically to the formulation of the research problem as expressed in the appropriate hypotheses or research questions. Lead the reader from the theory found in the literature search to the practical change problem and so derive the hypothesis or research questions through the quality of the analysis made.

Method

This section should be a clear description of what the research procedures and strategy were. Information would need to be included about the subjects used, how they were categorised, which tests were used and when they were administered. Also, a description of the statistical tests should be included in this section. Provide enough description so that I could replicate your research if I wanted to.

Results

The results consisting of summary data and the results of the statistical manipulation of the data should be described in this section. Main findings should be listed towards the end of the section. This section is descriptive of what the researcher did so that the procedures could be followed by another researcher wanting to replicate the research.

Conclusion

The conclusion should discuss what the researcher found out in terms of the original hypothesis stated in the introduction and what this means for the development of theory and practice as analysed in the introduction. In this section the skills of academic evaluation and synthesis should be shown. The conclusion should reflect what the implications of the findings of the research were in relation to what was identified as appropriate theory in the introduction.

The report of academic research using mixed methods

This report should use the pattern identified above. Due attention should be given to describing the qualitative methodology in the methods section and the data gathered must be adequately summarised in the results section. Also, in the concluding section the researcher would need to discuss how the qualitative and quantitative data were combined to resolve the research questions posed in the introduction.

The qualitative academic research report

This poses a particular problem for those researchers who wish to produce a report on research which reflects the process and processes of the research as a whole. The difficulty in this form of write-up is that the report needs to be clear about methodological descriptions and how the researcher established valid research findings. My own view is that it is possible to write an academic report reflecting the research process. The writer would need to describe, analyse and evaluate to answer the following questions:

- why was there a need for the research?
- what was done in the research?
- what does the above mean for informing theory and organisational practice?
- how does the research, if conducted through cycles, account for reliability and validity issues?

This type of report needs to state at the outset how it is internally organised. The researcher must then present clear summaries in the main body of the work. These will act as signposts to help the reader disentangle the meaning of the research presented in such a way.

FINAL REMARKS

Research is one of the ways we have of satisfying our curiosity about the world. I hope I have dealt with the post-graduate student's curiosity about the possibility of successfully completing different forms of research. I also hope I have helped the reader to cope with their anxiety concerning planning, executing and writing about their research. As an academic, I wait with unbounded joy . . .

References

Buchanan, D. and Boddy, D. (1992) *The Expertise of the Change Agent*, Hemel Hempstead, Prentice Hall.

Campbell, D. and Stanley, J. (1966) *Experimental and Quasi Experimental Designs for Research*, Rand McNally.

Carnall, C. (1990) *Managing Change in Organisations*, Hemel Hempstead, Prentice Hall.

Davies, G. (1986) Student Intentions and Institutional Experience: An Evaluation of different Psychological Explanations of Student Behaviour, *Unpub. Ph.D. thesis*, University of Bath.

De Board, R. (1976) *The Psychoanalysis of Organisations*, London, Tavistock.

Easterby-Smith, M., Thorpe, R. and Lowe, A. (1991) *Management Research: An Introduction*, London, Sage.

Gill, J. (1986) 'Research as Action: An Experiment in Utilising the Social Sciences', in Heller, F. ed. (1986) *The Use and Abuse of Social Sciences*, London, Sage.

Gill, J. and Johnson, P. (1991) *Research Methods for Managers*, London, Paul Chapman.

Glaser, B. and Strauss, A. (1967) *The Discovery of Grounded Theory*, Berlin, Aldine.

Guilford, J. and Fruchter, B. (1973) *Fundamental Statistics in Psychology and Education*, Fifth edition, Maidenhead, McGraw-Hill.

Herbert, M. (1990) *Planning a Research Project*, London, Cassel.

Kelly, G. (1957) *The Psychology of Personal Constructs*, vol. 1 and 2, London, Norton.

Kuhn, T. (1972) *The Structure of Scientific Revolutions*, Second edition, University of Chicago Press.

Lakatos, I. and Musgrave, A. eds (1970) *Criticism and the Growth of Knowledge*, Cambridge University Press.

Oppenheim, A. (1966) *Questionnaire Design and Attitude Measurement*, Oxford, Heinemann.

Pheysey, D. (1993) *Organisational Cultures: Types and Transformations*, London, Routledge.

Potter, J. and Wetherell, M. (1987) *Discourse and Social Psychology, Beyond Attitudes and Behaviour*, London, Sage.

Reason, P. and Rowan, J. (1981) *Human Inquiry: A Source Book of New Paradigm Research*, London, Wiley.

Robson, C. (1990) *Experimental Design and Statistics in Psychology, An Introduction*, Harmondsworth, Penguin.

ACTIVITIES FOR SECTION III

1 (a) Using the approaches and methods described in this section, produce a critical evaluation of your current practice.

 (b) Present the results to colleagues to facilitate discussion and debate.

 (c) Formulate an action plan for implementing changes in your current practice.

2 (a) Select one chapter from this section.

 (b) Prepare a thorough analysis of the strengths and weaknesses of the arguments presented in the chapter.

 (c) Present your analysis to colleagues to facilitate debate on the pros and cons of the argument.

3 (a) Select a current problem or opportunity facing your organisation.

 (b) Consider how an HRD intervention could or would be relevant to the situation.

 (c) Produce a proposal for an HRD intervention which incorporates an approach or method discussed in this section.

 (d) Formulate and present to colleagues an implementation plan for applying your intervention.

Editors' Conclusion: The Future of HRD?

Jim Stewart and Jim McGoldrick

This short chapter concludes the book. It has the following three purposes:

- to offer some summarising remarks;
- to speculate on factors influencing the future of HRD;
- to suggest a brief agenda for future research and practice.

We suggest that achieving those purposes is as far as a book on HRD can go at the moment. We lack the knowledge and understanding, let alone the confidence, to offer universal prescriptions. Indeed, having come this far, it will be obvious to the reader that we as editors would not have included the chapters we have if we believed simple solutions were possible. We do not, completely at least, discount the possibility of a definitive analysis of the nature and meaning of HRD, and of its contribution to organisation success. Such an analysis is though not yet available and is unlikely to be so for the foreseeable future. Which really brings us to addressing our first purpose.

MESSAGES FROM THE BOOK

Our first concluding comment is that there is no definitive view of what constitutes HRD. This statement is a simple recognition of the fact that the preceding chapters are not based on a consistent definition of HRD. However, this does not mean that there exists a total lack of agreement among the authors. We suggest that the views of HRD implicit in the various contributions reflect a welcome degree of coherence. This coherence is evidenced in a number of common arguments which occur explicitly in some chapters and implicitly throughout the book.

The first of these arguments is that HRD is implicit in issues of organising and managing. Organising and managing do not simply set a context for HRD. Rather, questions about organising and managing cannot be resolved without reference to HRD. Related to this is the argument that perspectives on organising and managing inform and influence perspectives on HRD. While it may be the case that views on HRD vary, it is also the case that these views are consistent with, and are capable of legitimation by, established perspectives on the nature of organisations and the purpose of managing.

A further common argument is that perspectives on HRD inform both strategy and practice. A key factor therefore influencing decisions on strategy and practice is the view that is taken on what constitutes HRD. Relatedly, there is a strong message from the book that strategy informs practice, and vice versa. The former could be said to have the status of conventional wisdom in management theory. However, the latter is perhaps a less common argument which nevertheless provides coherence to this book. An additional argument emerging from the contributions is that HRD methods reflect both perspectives and strategy. Thus, methods cannot be seen as abstract or objective and value-free tools and techniques. The argument is that design and application of HRD methods is central to a construction of what constitutes HRD and the role it can play in achieving organisation success.

This discussion allows us to offer a final argument. We have organised the book around three areas of content: perspectives, strategies and practice. This could be taken to mean that we view these as being separate. However, we actually view the headings more as a convenient categorisation than a representation of reality. Our view is that practitioners adopt perspectives, perhaps unconsciously, which influence their practice which, in turn, affects strategic direction. We could make the arguments in reverse; that is that practitioners, perhaps unconsciously, adopt strategies which influence their practice which, in turn, affects their perspectives. We would argue therefore that distinctions between perspectives, strategy and practice, though useful, are abstract and artificial. Thus, a message from the book is that HRD needs to be analysed holistically rather than as unrelated components.

THE FUTURE OF HRD

This brings us to our first speculation on the future of HRD. We believe it is likely to develop organically, rather than mechanistically. It is not likely to make great progress, either as a subject of academic enquiry or as an area of professional practice, if it is addressed as a set of discrete activities. This is not to say that elements of HRD cannot be isolated for in-depth analysis. The chapters by Johnston, Lyon, and Williams among others in the book are examples of where this can be beneficial. The point is that such analyses are enhanced when set in a wider context such as this book attempts to provide.

The book as whole also allows us to argue that HRD and, therefore, by extension, its future, cannot be divorced from the future of organisations and the changing nature of work. The chapters by Iles, Kelleher and Walton suggest some of the directions in which these are moving. The chapters by Lee and Wilson highlight key issues arising from these changes for organising and managing. Thus, the future of HRD lies in both facilitating and adapting to the changing nature of work, and perhaps, non-work, organisations.

One of the commonly held conventions regarding factors affecting the future of organisations is that of the condition of continuous and rapid change. Charles Handy is one of the leading writers on the implications of that condition for the future of work. In his recent analysis, Handy argues the importance of what he calls 'the three senses'; a sense of continuity, a sense of connection and a sense of direction; for balancing the potentially harmful consequences of change both to organisations and to individuals (Handy, 1994). We would suggest that satisfying and building on these senses is the natural terrain of HRD. Thus, HRD in the future will be concerned with devising and applying processes which enable the three senses to be developed. The chapters mentioned in the previous paragraph, perhaps, especially those by Iles, Lee and Walton, already suggest some possibilities. We would argue that the issues highlighted in those chapters will become of increasing importance to HRD.

A further speculation concerns connecting HRD and the concept of the learning organisation. It is possible to argue that the concepts can be connected by simply assuming that the purpose of HRD is to create, or contribute to the creation of, a learning organisation. We doubt though that matters are that simple. However, even if they were, the argument would rest on two further assumptions. Firstly, that agreement exists on what constitutes a learning organisation, and secondly that the concept can be operationalised so that positive and certain actions can be taken to facilitate its creation. Unfortunately, neither of these assumption is valid.

While the concept has been the subject of much research and writing in both the UK and USA (see for example Pedlar *et al.*, 1991; Senge, 1993), there is in our view enough disparity to conclude that the concept remains insufficiently developed. However, we believe the concept to be important in its own right, and to be significant to further progress in the development of HRD. Therefore, we would argue that a future concern for HRD will be incorporation of theory and research around the concept of the learning organisation (see also Stewart, 1996).

A similar argument applies to the notions of competence and competence-based HRD. This concept is, currently at least, the subject of much confusion arising, in part, from national policies on vocational qualifications. Confusion surrounds definitions and meanings in particular, paradoxically because of very specific and precise definitions applied in NVQs, and because of the arguments and debates concerning the appropriateness and efficacy of applying the concept at the heart of national policy. However, we are confident that the notion of competence will be a key factor in the future direction of HRD. The concept has not been directly addressed in this book, in the sense of specific chapters, for reasons similar to those that apply to the idea of the learning organisation. It is though difficult to imagine a future for the theory and practice of HRD which does not include some incorporation, at a serious and conceptual level, of the notion of competence.

A final factor affecting the future of HRD is perhaps that concerning its connections with and relationships to HRM. Our joint chapter at the beginning of the book begins to address this question. However, we do not claim the final word on the matter. The HRD/HRM nexus is an issue which will we believe concern both academics and practitioners alike for the foreseeable future. The recent creation of the IPD to replace the former ITD and IPM is more likely in our judgement to stimulate than to depress interest in the issue. Thus, we suggest HRD will in the future develop a clearer and more articulated notion of its relationship with HRM.

IMPLICATIONS FOR RESEARCH AND PRACTICE

This brief survey of potential future developments within HRD allows us now to express our views on a way forward. We believe there are a number of issues which both academics and practitioners will need to pay attention to in the immediate and short-term future. These are naturally those issues we have identified in the previous section. They are suggested as a research agenda for academics and as key future developments for practitioners. In summary, we would argue that the following are particularly important:

- HRD in and for new organisations forms;
- HRD and new ways of working;
- HRD as a means of facilitating and providing a sense of continuity, connection and direction;
- HRD and 'the learning organisation';
- The HRD/HRM nexus.

These issues though should not be seen in isolation, or as constituting separate agendas. We reiterate our earlier point that HRD is holistic and that development of theory and practice needs to be within a coherent context. As Graham Salaman argues, managing learning is central to the task of organising and it cannot be achieved as a separate and discrete activity (Salaman, 1995). Since HRD itself is central to the task of managing learning, it too cannot be achieved by separation and reductionism.

SUMMARY

We believe this book represents an important contribution to our proposed agenda. It does not deal directly with all of the issues, nor does it provide definitive answers to those questions it does address. We intend and hope though that it has and does provoke thought and action. The interplay of both will, in the end, provide the basis for progress in the development of HRD as professional practice and academic discipline.

References

Handy, C. (1994) *The Empty Raincoat*, London, Hutchinson.
Pedlar, M., Burgoyne, J. and Boydell, T. (1991) *The Learning Company: A Strategy for Sustainable Development*, Maidenhead, McGraw-Hill.
Salaman, G. (1995) *Managing*, Buckingham, Open University.
Senge, P. (1993) *The Fifth Discipline*, London, Century Business.
Stewart, J. (1996) *Managing Change through Training and Development* (2nd edn), London, Kogan Page.

ACTIVITIES FOR CONCLUSION

1 (a) Identify the main themes and arguments of the book.

   (b) Produce an analysis of the implications of these themes for your organisation.

   (c) Present the results of your analysis to colleagues.

2 (a) Produce your own analysis of the future of HRD.

   (b) Compare and contrast your analysis with that provided in the concluding chapter.

   (c) Present the results to colleagues. Attempt to reach a consensus on the key challenges facing the future development of HRD.

3 (a) Review your definition of HRD from Activity 1 in the introductory chapter.

   (b) Revise your definition in the light of your understanding of the key themes of the book.

   (c) Identify the implications of your revised definition for your future professional practice.

   (d) Formulate a development and action plan to take forward desired changes in your professional practice.

   (e) Discuss and refine your plan with a colleague.

INDEX

ABB Group 84
action research 293–5
active listening 115
Adler, N.J. 15, 75, 76, 78
Adler, P.S. 247
affirmative action 160, 162–3
Akers, J. 128
Alban-Metcalfe, B. 164
Alimo-Metcalfe, B. 166, 169
Analog Corporation 72
Andreas, S. and C. 233
Anthony, P.D. 12, 13, 113, 206, 237
Anthony, R.N. 35
Appignanesi, L. 37, 38
Argyle, M. 188
Argyris, C. 49, 54, 56, 57, 117, 249, 254
Armstrong, M. 14
Arrien, A. 234
Asher, K. 250
Ashforth, B.E. 247
Ashton, D. 63, 141, 145, 146, 150
Atkinson, J.S. 131
ATT 81
Ausubel, D.P. 248

Bacon, F. 274
Badaracco, J. 264
Bandler, R. 221, 222, 224, 233
Bandura, A. 242
Barham, K. 84, 134
Barker Lunn, J.C. 248
Barklow, J.H. 240
Barrington, H. 120
Bartlett 73, 78, 85
Bartunek, J.M. 243
Bartz, D.E. 166, 171
Bass, B.M. 247
Bateson, G. 243
Batstone, E. 190–1
Batt, J. 54, 55, 59
Baxter Health Corporation 163
BBC 160
Beardwell, I. 10
Beaty, L. 251
Beaumont, P.B. 10, 12
Beckhard, R. 216, 254
Beckwith, J. 251
behaviour patterns 112
Benest, F. 159
Benn, Tony 191–2
Bennett, C. 247
Berger, S. 147

Binsted, D. 249
Black, J.S. 76, 89, 90
Blake, R. 108, 213
Blanchard, K. 108
Blunt, P. 263
Blyton, P. 12, 200
Boddy, D. 203, 204, 205, 209, 283
Bolton, A. 268
Bosworth, D.L. 138–8
Boud, D. 271
Bowers, D.G. 248
Boyd, K.M. 35
Bradford Council case study 171–6
Bratton, J. 10
Brazil 203
Brew, A. 271, 275
Brewster, C. 66, 83, 247
British Airways (BA) 79
Brookfield, S. 268, 269
Brown, A. 18, 19, 262, 263
Bryman, A. 15, 16
BT 127–8, 147
Buchanan, D. 52, 102, 104, 108, 110, 203, 204, 205, 209, 216, 247, 283
Burgoyne, J.G. 62, 243, 249, 250
Burke, W.W. 102
Burns, J.M. 247
Burns, R.B. 248
Burns, T. 110, 203
business ethics 193
business process re-engineering (BPR) 203–4, 205
Butler, J. 63

Cadillac 128, 129
Campbell, A. 148
Campbell, D. 288–9
Campbell, J.P. 248
Cannon, T. 241, 247
career development 85
of women 167
Carnall, C. 207, 208, 209, 261, 290
Carr, J. 175
Carter, P. 12
Cassels, J. 144, 147–8
Central Eastern Europe
history
1940s 50–1
1950s–1960s 50, 53
1970s–mid 1980s 50, 55–6
mid 1980s–1990s 50, 58–9

HRD
1940s 50, 51–2
1950s–1960s 50, 54–5
1970s–mid 1980s 50, 58
mid 1980s–1990s 50, 63–4
Chandler, A. 105, 106
change
agents 209–10
effectiveness of 208–9, 213, 216, 218
in organisations 261–5
strategies 204–6, 212–13, 215–16, 217–18
implementation 206–8
chaos theory 203
Chaudhuri, N.C. 37
Checkland, P. 217, 245
Cialdini, R. 234, 237
Citizens Advice Bureau 132
Clegg, S.R. 245–6, 262, 263
Cockburn, C. 159, 163
cognitive mapping 296
Cohen, M.D. 35
Collin, A. 24
Collins, R. 268
Commission for Racial Equality (CRE) 164
commitment 20–3
emotional involvement 21–2
employee involvement 22–3
Common Vision 188
communication skills 234–8
metaphors 237–8
competitive advantage 11
compliance 20
conformance 109–11
Connor, H. 146
consciousness, managerial 34
Constable, J. 249
Construction Engineering Training Board 145
Coon, D. 241
Cooper, C. 22, 163, 167, 262
Coopersmith, S. 248
Corby, S. 171
Covey, S.R. 234
Cox, C. 262
Cox, T. 95, 162, 176
craft workers 139, 140–1, 143
Criticos, C. 271
Crozier, M. 182
culture 17–20
and development 243–5

and HRM/HRD 18–20
inter-cultural perspectives 47, 48, 162
and leadership 16–17
and managing diversity (MD) training 168–70
Curley, S.P. 38
Cushman, P. 244
customers 129–30
Czechoslovakia 53, 55, 56, 59

Daft, R.C. 191
Daimler-Benz 81
data analysis 295–7
Davidson, M. 163, 167
Davies, G. 268, 280, 283, 284, 293, 297
D'Avignon report 55
Davis, J. 57, 245
De Board, R. 292
de Bono, E. 57
Deal, T. 18, 19
Derr, C.B. 92
Deutsche Aerospace AE 94
development
    and culture 243–5
    and learning 240–3
Digital 128, 163
Dilts, R. 224
DiStefano, J. 254
distributors 120, 128–9
Dobson, S. 245–7
Dodds, I. 162, 164, 168
Dowling, P.J. 73
downsizing 17, 22
Drucker, P. 48, 199, 245
Duguid, P. 249
Dumain, B. 247
Duncan, S. 244
Dunnette, M.D. 248
Dunphy, D. 205, 207
Dutton, P.A. 139

Easterby-Smith, M. 63, 245, 249, 282, 283, 293
Eco, U. 34, 36, 39
Eddison, T. 36
education 122, 123
Electrolux 82, 84–5
Elias, N. 18
Elliot, J. 34
Emmerich, M. 147
emotional involvement 21–2
employees
    craft workers 139, 140–1, 143
    development 122
    education 122
    international roles 80
    involvement 22–3
    part-time workers 170
    personal development plans 166
    technicians 140–1
    voluntary workers 132
    and working practices 199
Employment Act (1981) 145
Employment Training Act (1973) 145
Employment Training (ET) 146
empowerment 12, 16, 23–4, 186
enablement 109–11

engineering industry 139, 140
Engineering Industry Training Board (EITB) 139, 144
equal opportunities (EO) 158–63
    reasons for change 163–5
Ericson, M. 221
Ersson, S.O. 53
ethics, business 193
ethnic minorities 159, 162, 163, 165
ethnograhy 296–7
Etzioni, A. 20, 21, 185, 186, 188
Europe, see Central Eastern Europe; Western Europe
European Community 51, 53, 55
Evans, P. 75
Ewing, L. 238

Fant, O.D. 166
fascism 51
Ferlie, E. 247
Fey, W.F. 248
Feyerabend, P. 267
Fiedler, F.E. 108
Filley, A.C. 38
Fine, M.G. 162, 168
Finegold, D. 148
Fineman, S. 16, 21
Fisher, C. 232
Fisher, M. 39, 102
Flam, H. 21
Fogel, A. 243, 244
Ford Motor Company 130
Forray, J.M. 254
Foucault, M. 181–2
Fox, S. 44, 188
Fredericks, J. 10, 180
Freedman, D. 247
Freedman, R. 268
French, J.R.P. 182, 184, 185, 186
Fruchter, B. 295
Fry, R. 269
Fullerton, J. 160, 164–5, 166, 167

Gabriel, Y. 16
Galagan, P.A. 159, 160, 167, 171
Garavan, T.N. 180, 182, 183, 184, 186, 191
Gardner, W.L. 247
Garratt, B. 213, 243, 265
Gaulle, Charles de 52
GEMS 93–4
General National Vocational Qualification (GNVQ) 61, 155
Germany 59
Gersick, C. 218
Gertsen, M.C. 84, 92
Ghoshal, S. 73, 78, 82, 85
Gibbs, G. 268
Giddens, A. 17, 18, 103, 105, 106, 112
Gill, J. 181, 182, 188, 191, 212, 290, 293, 294, 298
Glaser, B. 296
Gold, J. 10
Gorbachev, M. 56, 58
Goss, D. 10
Goss, T. 216
Grace, P. 183

Graen, G.B. 247
Gray, B. 163
Green, A.E. 139, 140, 169, 170
Griffith, V. 159, 163, 166, 168
Grinder, J. 221, 222, 224
Grootings, P. 149
Gross, J. 34
Gross, R. 240
grounded theory 296
groups, see teams
Guest, R.H. 12
Guilford, J. 295

Hailey, J. 83
Hallworth, M. 203
Hamel, G. 11, 80, 111, 205
Hamlin, Bob 28, 280
Hammond, M. 268
Hammond, V. 166
Handy, C. 56–7, 60, 181, 183, 184, 186, 189, 191, 199, 203, 247, 249, 304
Harisis, D.S. 159, 163, 166, 167, 171
Harris, R.T. 216
Harrison, R. 66, 120
Harvey, D. 38
Haspeslagh 82
Hassard, J. 12, 203
Hawkins, P. 176, 243
Hearn, J. 161
Hearsy 108
Heidegger, M. 64, 266
Helson, R. 32
Hendry, C. 10, 213
Herbert, M. 285, 288
Heron, J. 268, 270, 273, 274
Herriot, P. 159, 165, 168
Herzberg, F. 48, 54, 64, 67
Herzlinger, R. 35
Hewitt, J. 248
Hickson, D.J. 191
hierarchy of needs 48, 49
Hodgetts, R.M. 48
Hodgson, V.E. 243
Hofstede, G. 48, 80, 91, 161, 162, 169, 170
Holden, L. 10, 88
Hollister, L. 159, 169
Holton, V. 166
Honey, P. 250
Honeywell 129
Hosking, D.M. 264
Houten, G. Van 84
Howe, M. 242
HRD
    future direction 67–8, 303–5
    and HRM 9–10, 24–5
    meaning and nature of 12–13, 64–7
    see also international HRD; proactive HRD
HRM
    and HRD 9–10, 24–5
    meaning and nature of 10–12
Huczynski, A. 52, 102, 104, 108, 110
Humphrey, R.H. 247
Hungary 56, 59
Hunt, J.W. 18

IBM 129–30
ICI 81
IIP (Investors in People) 61, 121, 166
Iles, P.A. 71, 79, 80, 92, 94, 159, 304
induction programmes 186
Industrial Training Act 53, 144
Industrial Training Boards (ITBs) 144–5
influencing 186–9, 234–7
information flows 106–7, 109, 111
Information Technology Act (1981) 146
Institute of Manpower Studies (IMS) 131
Institute of Personnel and Development
    (IPD) 120, 184, 193
integration 61–2
International Foundation for Action
    Learning (IFAL) 261
international HRD
    forms of organisation 78
    framework 74–8
    importance 71–2
    nature 72–4
    organisational practices 86–8
    stage approach 75–7
    strategic alliances 80–2
    techniques and models 88–93
interviews in research 292
Investors in People (IIP) 61, 121, 166

Jackson, B.W. 162, 163, 175
Jackson, N. 12
James, K. 253
Jamieson, D. 161, 165, 166, 171
Jankowicz, D. 63, 242, 245, 253
Jantsch, E. 245
Jaques, E. 79
Jarillo, J.C. 130
Jarvis, V. 149
Jenkins, A. 268
Jennings, D. 104
Johnson, G. 11, 124, 204, 206, 247
Johnson, P. 181, 182, 188, 191, 212,
    290, 293, 298
Johnston, R. 110
Jones, A.M. 213
Jones, B. 140, 141
Josefowitz, N. 188

Kahn, R.L. 247
Kakabadse, A. 35
Kandola, R. 160, 164–5, 166, 167
Kanter, R. 128, 130, 190, 203, 247
Kaplan, A. 182, 184, 186, 187
Karp, H.B. 169, 170
Kazanas, H.C. 13, 122, 123, 133, 134,
    135
Kearney, P. 205
Keenan, A.C. 83
Keenoy, T. 12
Keep, E. 149
Kelleher, M. 304
Kelly, G. 242, 291
Kelly, J.E. 142
Kennedy, A. 18, 19
Kern, H. 141, 143
King, W. 180
Kinsman, F. 49, 68
Kinsman, J. 247

Klein, J.I. 243
Kleiner, B.H. 159, 163, 166, 167, 171
Kluckhohn, C. 17
Kluckholm, F.R. 29, 39
Knight, J. 163
Knights, D. 103
Knotter, J. 247
Knowles, M. 268, 269
Kobrin, S. 247
Kohlberg, L. 248
Kohler-Gray, S. 170
Kolb, D. 251, 252, 269
Kovvuri, D. 103
Kraft, M. 248
Kuei, C. 129
Kuhn, T. 283
Kusterer, K. 149

Laborde, G.Z. 222
Lafasto, F. 163
Lakatos, I. 283
Land Rover 24
Lane, C. 139, 150
Lane, H. 254
Lane, J.E. 53
Laqueur, W. 51, 53, 55
Lashley, C. 12, 23
Laurent, A. 73
Le Guin, U. 239
leadership 14–17
    and culture 16–17
    style 104, 108–11
learning 62, 82, 203
    action learning 245–51, 269–75
    practice of 251–5
    and development 240–3
    non-employee 130–1, 133–6
    processes 241
    self-directed learners (SDLs) 268
    see also training
Leduchowicz, T. 180, 183
Lee, M.M. 53, 62, 66, 68, 232, 240, 242,
    244, 245, 247, 249, 250, 252,
    253, 304
Lei 81
Lessem, R. 49, 61, 245, 264, 265, 266,
    267, 269
Lever Brothers 75
Levine, J.N. 244
Lewin, C. 206
Libetta, L. 149
Lievegood, B. 245
Likert, R. 247
Littlewoods 162
Litwin, G.H. 102
Local Enterprise Companies 205
Locksley, G. 147
Longstreth, F.H. 148
Lorenzi, P. 15, 17
Lowe, A. 283
Lukes, S. 188
Luthans, F. 48
Lyotard, Jean-François 37

Maastricht Treaty 58
Mabbott, J.D. 33
Mabey, C. 79, 80, 92

McCalman, J. 216
McCool 149
McCormick, R. 249
MacDonalds 264
McGill, I. 251
McGoldrick, J. 12, 13, 23, 103
McGregor, D. 48, 52, 54, 64, 67, 103,
    261
McHugh, D. 17, 18, 19
McKibben, L.E. 62, 249
McKiernan, P. 247
McKinlay, A. 12
MacLachlan, R. 164
Maclagen, P. 248
McLagen, R.A. 13
Macmillan, I.C. 127, 128
McMillen, M.C. 254
Maddock, S. 161
Madu, C. 129
management
    and action learning 245–51
    competencies 84–5
    of multicultural workforces 79–80
    style 104, 108–11
    women in 32, 160, 163, 164
Management Charter Initiative 161–2
manager development 28–9, 33–4, 40–3,
    44
managerial consciousness 34
managerial self-consciousness 34–5
managerial stances 28–9, 33–4, 40–3,
    44–5
managers
    ambiguous 41, 42–3
    aporetic 37–8
    cultural 36–7
    cynical 37
    developing 40–2
    global 93–5
    integrating 41, 42
    ironic 38–40
    political 41, 42
    rational 35–6
managing diversity (MD) 158–63
    awareness training 168–70
    HRD strategies and interventions
        165–8, 170–1
Manchester City Council 171
Mandell, B. 170
Mangham, I. 243, 247
Manpower Services Commission (MSC)
    145–6, 183
Mansfield, B. 28
manufacturing in Britain 139
Marchington, M. 12, 21, 22, 23
market driven quality (MDQ) 129–30
Marks & Spencer 87–8
Marsden, D. 150
Marshall, J. 244, 248
Martin, L. 20, 21, 161, 162
Martinko, M.J. 247
Maslow, A.H. 48, 64, 67
Mason, G. 149
Massey, D. 139
Matsushita 80, 84
Mayes, D.G. 139
Maznevski, M. 163, 168

Meadows, J. 35
Megginson, D. 12
Meil, P. 150
Mendenhall, M. 89, 90
Mercedes 128
metaphors 237–8
Miller, P. 11
Mintzberg, H. 52, 56, 103, 106, 182, 247, 268
Mir, A.H. 254
Mitsubishi 81
Moch, M.K. 243
Moore, P.G. 243
Moran, R. 263
Moreland, R.L. 244
Morgan, G. 60, 62, 102, 103, 199, 249
Morgan, R.U. 72
Morley, I. 264
Morris, C. 247
Morrison, A. 166, 170
motivation 63
motivation theory 48
Mouton, J.S. 108, 213
Mudroch, V. 249
Mullins, L.J. 15, 104, 108, 201
Mumford, A. 250
Musgrave, A. 283

National Health Service (NHS) 35
National Vocational Qualifications (NVQs) 43, 44, 61, 149, 155, 167, 192, 193
NEC 88
needs, hierarchy of 48, 49
Nespor, J. 249
neuro-linguistic programming (NLP) 220–39
    anchoring 226–8
    development 221
    elements 221–2
    eye movements 224–6
    meta model 230–1
    outcomes 228–30
    perceptual positions 232–4
    rapport 222–6
    working with 220–1
New Leadership 15, 16, 17
Next Steps Review 131
NHS 160, 167
Nicholls, J. 20, 21
Nikolajew, V. 51, 63
non-employee development 121–3, 134–6
    and out-sourcing 130–1
    and value chains 132–4
Noon, M. 12
Norgaard, R. 245
Novak, J.M. 254
NVQs see National Vocational Qualifications

Oates, D. 84, 134
OD, see organisation development
Oddou, G. 92
Ohmae, K. 53, 80
Olivetti 81
O'Mara, J. 161, 165, 166, 171
Oppenheim, A. 290

Orczyk, J. 63
organisation design 102–3
organisation development (OD) 13, 20, 122, 215–16, 218
organisation strategy 103, 104–8
organisation structure 103, 104–8
organisational analysis 201–4, 212, 214, 217
organisational learning 62, 82, 203
Organisational Transformation 60
organisations
    HRD relationship 101–2
    as learning communities 265–71
    modernist 262, 263
    post-modernist 262, 263–4
O'Shaughnessy, J. 108
Ott, J.S. 15
out-sourcing 130–1
Owen, H. 60, 68
OXFAM 132

Papadakis, V. 247
Parker, C. 203
Parker, M. 12
Parkin, D. 161
Parsons, T. 18
part-time workers 170
Pascale, R. 33, 244, 247
Peck, J. 147
Pedlar, M. 49, 53, 56, 62, 72, 203, 245, 268, 270, 274, 305
Pelz, D.C. 190, 247
Pemberton, C. 159, 165, 168, 170
performance 11
Perkins Engines 128–9
Perlmutter, H.V.C. 74
Peters, T.J. 16, 35, 39, 49, 56, 192, 199, 203
Peterson, M.F. 247
Pettigrew, H.M. 183, 189
Pettitt, S.S. 63, 253
Pfeffer, J. 190, 247
Pheysey, D. 286, 297
Philips, N. 79, 80, 88
Phillimore, A.J. 147
Phillips, K. 200
Pickard, J. 60
Piore, M. 141, 143, 147, 263, 264
Poland 53, 55–6, 59, 63
Pondy, L.R. 247
Poole, M. 11
Porritt, Jonathan 184
Porter, L.W. 11, 62, 249
Porter, M. 125
Porter, R.E. 247
positive action 160
Postle, D. 270
Potter, J. 295–6
power
    and compliance 20
    definition 181–2
    departmental 189–91
    and emotional involvement 21
    ethical dimension 193
    exercising 191–3
    organisational attitudes to 186
    perception of 180–1

sources of 186–9
types of 182–6
Powers, E.A. 249
Prahalad, C.K. 11, 111, 205
Prais, S. 149
Pritchard, S. 163
proactive HRD 112–17
    interventions 116–17
Proctor and Gamble 163
public sector management 35–6
Pucik, V. 73, 78, 82

Quick, T.C. 180
Quinn, J.B. 107

Race for Opportunity 160
Race Relations Act 167
racial harassment 161
Raelin, J.A. 240, 251
Rainbird, H. 144, 145
Ratiu, I. 84
Raven, B.H. 182, 184, 185, 186
re-engineering 203–4, 205
Readymix Concrete 132
Reason, P. 284
recruitment 83–4, 140
    and managing diversity (MD) 170–1
Reddin 108
Reddy, W.B. 248
redundancy measures 149
Reeves, M. 34
Regan, M. 85
repertory grid technique 291
research
    approaches 281–2, 285–6
    closed methods 291–2
    data analysis 295–7
    experimental design 287–8
    interviews 292
    issues 305–6
    open methods 292–5
    paradigms 283–4
    qualitative approach 290–1
    quantitative methods 290
    quasi experimental designs 288–90
    reporting results 298–300
    skills needed 282–3
    validity and reliability 297–8
Revans, R. 56, 251, 269
Richardson, R.J. 15
Ritzer, G. 263–4
Robertson, A.J. 22
Robertson, I.T. 248
Robinson, F.G. 248
Robson, C. 287, 295
Roethlisberger, F.J. 247
Rogers, C.R. 243, 244, 248, 268, 269
Rollo, J.H.C. 63, 66
Ronen, S. 84, 89
Rorty, R. 38
Rosenberg, M. 248
Rothwell, W. 13, 122, 123, 133, 134, 135
Rowan, J. 284
Rubin, I. 248
Rumania 59
Ryan, M. 188, 189

Ryan, P. 150
Rychard, A. 63
Ryder, J. 249

Saarinen, J. 73, 74
Sabel, C. 141, 143, 263, 264
Sadler, P.C. 83
Sadri, G. 248
Sako, M. 150
Salaman, G. 12, 17, 63, 306
Salanicik, J.R. 190
Samovar, L.A. 247
Sartre, Jean-Paul 266
Satir, V. 221
Sattelberger, T.C. 94
Sayles, L.R. 247
Scheibe, K.E. 244
Schein, E. 29, 39, 118, 247
Schermerhorn, J. 240, 251
Schnapper, M. 63
Scholes, K. 11, 124
Schon, D. 34, 49, 54, 56, 57, 117, 249
Schuler, R.S. 127, 128
Schumann, M. 141, 143
Scott, P. 140, 141
Scottish Prison Service 133
Scullion, H. 83, 84
Seely Brown, J. 249
self-consciousness, managerial 34–5
Semler, R. 203
Senge, P.M. 49, 57, 60, 62, 116, 245, 249, 266, 305
Senker, P. 147
Sex Discrimination Act 167, 170–1
sexual harassment 161
Shafritz, J.M. 15
Shaw, P. 200
Sheldrake, R. 144, 145
Simon, H.A. 105
Sims, D. 17, 21
Sims, H.P. 15, 17
Single European Act 55, 58
Sisson, K. 10, 14
skills shortages 138–40, 144, 154–5
Slocum, J.W. 81
Smith, P.B. 244, 247
Smithers, A. 150, 249
Snell, R. 29, 39, 63, 247, 248, 253
Sokolowska, M. 63
Soskice, D. 148
Soviet Union 51, 53, 58
Spencer Stuart and Associates 167
Spender, D. 159, 162, 169
Spender, J.C. 268
Stace, D. 205, 207
Stacey, R.D. 19, 203, 204
stakeholders 123–5
Stalker, G. 110, 203
Stanley, J. 288–9
Starkey, K. 12
Stata, R. 72
Statham, A. 247
Stead, V. 245
Steeples, M.M. 128

Stewart, J.D. 10, 13, 22, 28, 103, 105, 107, 108, 117, 180
Stewart, R. 245, 247, 248
Storey, J. 10, 12, 51
strategic alliances 80–2, 130
strategic relationships 120
strategy 10, 14
  for change 204–6, 212–13, 215–16, 217–18
    implementation 206–8
  organisation strategy 103, 104–8
Straub, C. 183
Strauss, A. 296
Streek, W. 147
Strodtbeck, F.L. 29
Stryker, S. 247
Suhadolnik, D. 13
suppliers 120, 127–8
Sutton, N. 169, 170
Swan, D. 161
Swan, J. 249, 253
Swieringa, J. 203

Tampella Power Inc. 73–4
Tanton, M. 161
Taylor, F.W. 51, 102, 240, 247
teams 167–8, 215, 266
technicians 140–1
telematic industry 147
Tennant, M. 268
Thatcher, M. 160
Thatcher, Margaret 55
Thayer, S.K. 15
Theory X 52, 54, 261
Theory Y 54, 261–2
Thomas, P. 103
Thomas, R. 167
Thomas, V. 168, 169
Thompson, P. 17, 18, 19
Thorpe, R. 249, 283
Thurley, K. 265
Tichy, N.M. 92, 94
Tobias, R. 192, 193
Toffler, A. 57, 63
Torrington, D. 262
TQM (Total Quality Management) 20, 60, 61, 129, 205
training
  cross-cultural 88–9
  functional strategies 122–3
  for internal/external markets 150–4
  in managing diversity (MD) 168–70
  methods 89–93
  perception of 200
  spending on 147
  vocational training policy 144–50
  see also learning
Training and Enterprise Councils (TECs) 146–7, 205
transformational leadership 15, 16
Travis, A. 163, 164
Tully, M. 160
Tung, R.L. 84, 89
Tuppen, C. 128

Turnbull, P. 12, 200

Unilever 75
United Nations 51
Usher, R. 271

Vaill, P. 264, 265
value chains 125–7, 132–4
vertical integration 125–7, 130
Vickerstaff, S. 144, 145
Virgo, P. 139
vocational training policy 144–50
voluntary workers 132

Walker, B. 95
Walton, J. 20–1, 304
Warner, M. 147, 148
Waterman, R.M. 16, 35, 39, 49, 56, 203
Watson, T.J. 17, 18, 20, 23, 38, 103, 105, 106, 111, 112, 113, 114
Wattam, S. 104
Weber, Max 51, 102, 180–1
Weick, K. 106
Weightman, J. 262
Weirdsma, A. 203
Wessex Regional Health Authority 36
West, M. 164
Western Europe
  history
    1940s 50–1
    1950s–1960s 50, 52–3
    1970s–mid 1980s 50, 55
    mid 1980s–1990s 50, 58
  HRD
    1940s 50, 51–2
    1950s–1960s 50, 53–4
    1970s–mid 1980s 50, 56–7
    mid 1980s–1990s 50, 60–2
Wetherell, M. 295–6
Whirlpool Corporation 79
Whittington, R. 248
Whyte, L.A. 17
Williams, A. 36
Williams, S. 268
Williams, T. 169, 170
Wilson, E. 162, 170, 304
Wink, P. 32
Wittgenstein, Ludwig 39
women
  career development 167
  in management 32, 160, 163, 164
work reorganisation 142
work structure 140–1
workforces 79–80
  see also employees
Workplace Industrial Relations Survey 12
workshops 292–3

Xerox 128

Youth Training Scheme (YTS) 146

Zanussi 82, 85
Zuboff, S. 245